PICTURE WRITING FROM ANCIENT SOUTHERN MEXICO
Mixtec Place Signs and Maps

UNIVERSITY OF OKLAHOMA PRESS : NORMAN

PICTURE WRITING FROM ANCIENT SOUTHERN MEXICO

Mixtec Place Signs and Maps

by Mary Elizabeth Smith

Library of Congress Cataloging in Publication Data
Smith, Mary Elizabeth, 1932–
    Picture writing from ancient southern Mexico.
    (The Civilization of the American Indian series, 124)
    Bibliography: p.
    1. Mixtec ~~Indians~~—Writing. I. Title.
II. Series.   Language
F1219.S58   ~~970.3~~   72–869
ISBN 0–8061–1029–5

Picture Writing from Ancient Southern Mexico: Mixtec Place Signs and Maps is Volume 124 in *The Civilization of the American Indian Series*.

To

ALFONSO CASO

with admiration and gratitude

PREFACE

This book is concerned primarily with one aspect of a group of pictorial manuscripts from the Mixtec-speaking region of southern Mexico: the signs that represent names of places, usually called "place signs." One of the most important and influential manuscript painting traditions of pre-Conquest Mexico developed in the Mixtec-speaking region. From this region has survived the only group of history manuscripts produced before the Spanish conquest of Mexico, a group of manuscripts which were painted on screenfolds of animal hide and which set forth historical and genealogical events by means of picture-writing rather than by writing in alphabetic script. Moreover, after the Spanish conquest of Mexico, the Mixtec pre-Conquest drawing and painting traditions did not immediately die out but continued in sixteenth-century genealogical manuscripts and community maps.

The early Colonial manuscripts show increasing acculturation—that is, intrusions of European style and iconography—and by the end of the sixteenth century the pre-Conquest style of painting had, for the most part, disappeared. These early Colonial manuscripts often provide invaluable clues to the interpretation of the pre-Conquest histories, because the post-Conquest manuscripts are often annotated with writing in European script or can be related to written documents which help to explain the pre-Conquest pictorial motifs—including the place signs.

In the past two decades our understanding of the content of the Mixtec historical-genealogical manuscripts has advanced rapidly, primarily because of Dr. Alfonso Caso's monumental studies of their genealogical content and his detailed sign-by-sign descriptions of several of the major manuscripts. It is now possible to analyze some of the specific problems connected with the Mixtec histories, and the interpretation of the pictorial signs that represent place names is one of the major problems yet to be solved. The aim of this book is to summarize what is known at the present time about Mixtec place signs and to suggest methods that may prove productive for the identification of place signs.

The general content of the book is divided into two sections: the first section (Chapters II through V) includes a general discussion of the Mixtec histories and their place signs, and the remainder of the book (Chapters VI through X) is concerned with early Colonial Mixtec maps and includes a detailed analysis of three maps from one section of the Mixtec-speaking region. The purpose of the first part of the book is to characterize the pre-Conquest historical manuscripts and to define the general and specific problems of identifying the place signs in these manuscripts. The second part demonstrates that early Colonial maps are one key to place-sign identification because (1) they present place signs in a cartographic context where these signs can be more easily identified, and (2) it is often possible to relate the pictorial maps to written land documents which help to explain the general content and the specific place signs of the maps.

In Chapters II and III the style and pictorial conventions of the pre-Conquest Mixtec historical manuscripts will be considered, because an understanding of them is necessary to the interpretation of the early Colonial maps. Chapter IV discusses the composition of Mixtec place names and signs, and Chapter V is devoted to an analysis of the place signs that have thus far been interpreted.

In the second section, Chapter VI characterizes the part of the Mixtec-speaking region that is bordered on the south by the Pacific Ocean, because the three early Colonial maps to be considered in detail are from this Coastal region. Chapter VII is concerned with two versions of a map of the community lands of Santa María Zacatepec, and Chapter VIII with a map of the community lands of San Pedro Jicayán. These three maps are what are usually termed *lienzos*—that is, they are drawn or painted on cotton cloth. All three show one town surrounded by the place signs of the names of that town's boundaries. In Chapter IX the Lienzo of Jicayán is compared with three other Colonial Mixtec maps of one town and its boundaries; these three maps, in common with the Jicayán lienzo, are annotated with glosses in the Mixtec language. A general discussion of the stylistic and iconographic characteristics of Colonial Mixtec maps is included in Chapter X.

Only manuscripts which are essentially historical, genealogical or cartographic will be considered in this book. The important ritual manuscripts of the "Borgia Group," which may be Mixtec or Mixtec-related are excluded because the place signs in them are provisionally assumed to represent mythological rather than actual places.

The first draft of this book was prepared under the direction of Professor George Kubler of the Department of the History of Art at Yale University. Professor Kubler first suggested the topic and also suggested that at least a rudimentary knowledge of the Mixtec language was necessary for the analysis of the place signs. He very generously loaned me photographs and his personal files on Mexican pictorial manuscripts, but above all, he was generous with his time and patience, and offered many perceptive comments and continuing encouragement.

To Dr. Alfonso Caso, I owe a special debt of gratitude. Dr. Caso's advice and assistance have been invaluable, and his pioneering studies of the Mixtec historical-genealogical manuscripts are the foundation on which this book is based. He very graciously read and commented extensively on an early draft of this book and later lent me his own unpublished paper on the first Lienzo of Zacatepec.

Conversations and correspondence with Dr. John B. Glass, Professor Floyd G. Lounsbury of Yale University, Mr. Ross Parmenter, Professor Donald Robertson of Tulane University, Professor Ronald Spores of Vanderbilt University, and Mrs. Nancy Troike of the University of Texas have also been stimulating and helpful. That the 1893 copies of the two Lienzos of Zacatepec were in the municipal archive of Santa María Zacatepec I first learned from Dr. Glass when he was in Mexico in 1963–64, conducting research for his catalog of the pictorial manuscript collection of the Museo Nacional of Mexico. Dr. Howard F. Cline, Director of the Hispanic Foundation of the Library of Congress, has kindly sent me the Working Papers of studies to be published in the four ethnohistory volumes of the *Handbook of Middle American Indians* and has provided much useful information on Mexican pictorial manuscripts.

Also productive of ideas were the "brainstorming" sessions of the informal conference on Mixtec history manuscripts organized by Professor John Paddock and held at the Instituto de Estudios Oaxaqueños in Mitla in the summer of 1969. The participants in this conference, in addition to Professor Paddock, were Ross Parmenter, Emily Rabin, Donald and Martha Robertson, William B. Taylor, and Cecil R. Welte. Mrs. Rabin is in the process of classifying and recording on punched cards all the pictorial motifs in the Mixtec history manuscripts—a file that will be invaluable to future studies of the manuscripts.

Many rewarding hours were spent in the Archivo General de la Nación in Mexico City, and I wish to thank Dr. Ignacio Rubio Mañé and Sr. Miguel Saldaña for making available the resources of this rich archive. Professors Wigberto Jiménez Moreno and Barbro Dahlgren of the Centro de Investigaciones Históricas placed at my disposal this center's fine collection of microfilmed documents. Both of these scholars made many helpful suggestions, as did Professor Evangelina Arana Osnaya and Ing. Jorge L. Tamayo. Sr. Francisco Javier Carreño Avedaño aided me in locating several pertinent documents in the Archivo General del Departamento Agrario in Mexico City. Ing. Juan Mas Sinta, Director of the Dirección de Geografía, Meteorología e Hidrología, permitted me to consult this institution's large collection of maps. Miss Helen Ashdown of the Mexico City center of the Summer Institute of Linguistics made available to me vocabulary lists and other material on the Mixtec language. Miss Marjorie LeDoux of the Latin American Library of Tulane University and Miss Nettie Lee Benson of the University of Texas Latin American Library allowed me to consult their excellent collections when I was able to make brief trips to New Orleans and Austin. I am also most appreciative of the patience and co-operation of Mr. R. Martin Ruoss, the Special Collections librarian at the University of New Mexico.

The late Dr. Eusebio Dávalos Hurtado, former director of the Instituto Nacional de Antropología e Historia, arranged to have ultra-violet photographs taken of Codex Colombino which were indispensable in the transcription of this manuscript's Mixtec glosses. These special photographs were made by Professor Arturo Romano, former director of the Instituto's Department of Physical Anthropology.

The citizens of Tututepec, Jicayán, Santa María Zacatepec, and other towns in the Mixtec-speaking region of the Coast of Oaxaca provided a great deal of data on place names. In the spring of 1963, the officials of Jicayán permitted me to photograph the Lienzo of Jicayán. In 1964, the officials of Santa María Zacatepec allowed me to photograph the 1893 copies of the two Lienzos of Zacatepec.

Many friends and colleagues provided both assistance and encouragement throughout the preparation of this book, but special thanks are due to Miss Helen Chillman and Professor Douglas R. George. The line drawings that illustrate the book were made by Mrs. Louise H. Ivers, and the maps were drawn by Richard De Sanchez. Some of the photographic illustrations were prepared by Jim Kraft and Steven Shearer. I was assisted in the chores of proofreading by Miss Nancy Lindas.

Continuing fellowship aid from the Graduate School and the Council on Latin American Studies of Yale University has been indispensable in preparing and completing this book. Grants from the Doherty Foundation and the Pan American Union enabled me to do research and field work in Mexico from August 1962 to August 1964.

Unless otherwise indicated, the translations given of all Spanish and Mixtec texts and glosses are my own. The sources of the Mixtec language and the symbols used in this study to represent the sounds of this language are discussed on page 8.

For the sake of convenience and in order to avoid repetitious citations, the present location and the most accessible reproductions of most of the published pictorial manuscripts mentioned in this book are listed in Part II of the Bibliography.

MARY ELIZABETH SMITH

June, 1970
Albuquerque, New Mexico

CONTENTS

CHARTS AND DRAWINGS

MAPS

ILLUSTRATIONS

PICTURE WRITING FROM ANCIENT SOUTHERN MEXICO
Mixtec Place Signs and Maps

ABBREVIATIONS

AGN   Archivo General de la Nación, Mexico City.

BSMGE   *Boletín de la Sociedad Mexicana de Geografía y Estadística.*

Caso, *Bodley*   Alfonso Caso, *Interpretation of the Codex Bodley 2858*, Mexico, 1960.

Caso, *Colombino*   Alfonso Caso, *Interpretación del Códice Colombino/Interpretation of the Codex Colombina,* Mexico, 1966.

Caso, *Selden*   Alfonso Caso, *Interpretación del Códice Selden 3135 (A.2)/Interpretation of the Codex Selden 3135 (A.2),* Mexico, 1964.

HMAI   *Handbook of Middle American Indians*

ICA   *Proceedings of the International Congress of Americanists.*

INAH   Instituto Nacional de Antropología e Historia, Mexico.

JSA   *Journal de la Société des Américanistes de Paris.*

Peñafiel, *LZ*   Antonio Peñafiel, *Códice Mixteco. Lienzo de Zacatepec*, Mexico, 1900.

PNE   Francisco del Paso y Troncoso, ed., *Papeles de Nueva España*, 2a. série (Geografía y Estadística), 7 vols., Madrid, 1905–1906.

RMEA   *Revista mexicana de estudios antropológicos.*

RMEH   *Revista mexicana de estudios históricos.*

Smith, *Colombino*   Mary Elizabeth Smith, *Las glosas del Códice Colombino/The Glosses of Codex Colombino*, Mexico, 1966.

I

INTRODUCTION

At the time of the Spanish conquest of Mexico in the early sixteenth century, the dynastic histories of many native cities and communities were being recorded in pictographic writing. These pictorial histories often present local and contradictory versions of the same story, and their historical narrative is sometimes obscured by mythology; but they provide an invaluable record of some of the hereditary rulers in central and southern Mexico in the "post-Classic" period, which began about A.D. 750 and ended with the Spanish conquest.

The region of Mexico that is best known through pictographic historical documents is the Nahuatl-speaking region in and around the Valley of Mexico. From this region a substantial corpus of pictorial documents which deal with dynastic history has survived, as well as a great wealth of accounts of pre-Conquest history that were written down in Spanish, Latin, or Nahuatl in the early Colonial period.[1]

But all of the known pictorial histories from the Valley of Mexico were drawn or painted after the Spanish conquest. The only extant historial manuscripts painted *prior* to the arrival of the European conquerors are a group of eight animal-hide screenfolds from the Mixtec-speaking region of southern Mexico. On these screenfolds, often called "codices," anonymous scribes recorded in a pictographic fashion the genealogies and achievements of numerous Mixtec rulers. These painted manuscripts contain chronological accounts of the births, marriages, conquests, and deaths of families who reigned over some of the principal towns of the Mixtec-speaking region.

This region, usually called the "Mixteca," comprises the western third of the present-day state of Oaxaca and extends into the eastern section of the state of Guerrero and the southern part of the state of Puebla (Map 1).[2] Antonio de los Reyes, a Dominican friar who wrote an important sixteenth-century grammar of the Mixtec language, divided the Mixteca into three sections: Alta, Baja, and Costa.[3] The approximate extent of these three sections is shown in Map 2. The Alta is the mountainous region west of the state capital of Oaxaca and includes the former districts of Coixtlahuaca, Teposcolula, Nochixtlán, Tlaxiaco, and the western half of Sola de Vega. The Baja is the lowland section north of the Alta, consisting of the former districts of Huajuapan, Silacayoapan, and Juxtlahuaca in the state of Oaxaca, as well as a substantial portion of southern Puebla and northeastern Guerrero. The Costa designates the section bordered on the south by the Pacific Ocean and is comprised of the former districts of Putla, Jamiltepec, and the western half of Juquila in the state of Oaxaca, as well as part of the southeastern corner of Guerrero. Some writers refer to this coastal area as the "Baja," because it is a lowland region; but in this study the term "Baja" indicates the northern Mixteca as described above, and the Costa is called "the Coastal region" or merely "the Coast."

The small group of pre-Conquest historical manuscripts from the Mixteca is extremely important for the information they provide on Mixtec dynastic history from the late seventh century to the middle of the sixteenth century.[4] In addition, the type of pictographic writing employed in the early Colonial manuscripts from the Nahuatl-speaking region around the Valley of Mexico was probably derived from the Mixtec system of writing at some time before the Spanish Conquest, and thus the pre-Conquest Mixtec manuscripts may be considered as possible prototypes of the lost pre-Conquest manuscripts of the Valley of Mexico.[5]

---

[1] The basic study of the various types of manuscript paintings known from the Valley of Mexico is: Donald Robertson, *Mexican Manuscript Painting of the Early Colonial Period: The Metropolitan Schools* (New Haven, 1959). An excellent and comprehensive survey of pictorial manuscripts of all types and from all regions of Middle America has been prepared by John B. Glass and will appear in volume 14 of the *Handbook of Middle American Indians* (hereafter referred to as *HMAI*). Included with this survey will be a census of the over 400 known pictorial manuscripts, compiled by Glass, Donald Robertson, and H. B. Nicholson. Each census entry will contain a brief description of the manuscript and a discussion of the bibliography pertaining to it. Volumes 12 through 15 of the *HMAI*, under the editorship of Howard F. Cline, will be devoted to Middle American ethnohistory, and the essays in these volumes will deal with the written as well as the pictorial sources of native history.

[2] A general study of all aspects of pre-Conquest Mixtec culture is: Barbro Dahlgren de Jordan, *La mixteca: su cultura e historia prehispánicas* (Mexico, 1954). The history and social organization of the Mixteca Alta region have been examined by Ronald Spores, *The Mixtec Kings and Their People* (Norman, 1967). A sociological-geographical study of the present-day Mixtec-speaking region is: M. T. de la Peña, "Problemas sociales y económicos de las Mixtecas," *Memorias del Instituto Nacional Indigenista*, Vol. II, Núm. 1 (Mexico, 1950).

[3] The edition of the Reyes grammar, *Arte en lengua mixteca*, used in this study is that published in *Actes de la Société Philologique*, Vol. XVIII, 1888 (Paris, 1890), hereafter cited as Reyes, "Arte en lengua mixteca."

[4] Alfonso Caso has summarized some of the important aspects of these manuscripts in "The Historical Value of the Mixtec Codices," *Boletín de estudios oaxaqueños*, No. 16 (1960), 1–7.

[5] Robertson, *Mexican Manuscript Painting*, 9–14.

MAP I.   Location of the Mixteca in southern Mexico

The pre-Conquest Mixtec manuscripts as well as the Colonial Nahuatl manuscripts use a similar set of pictorial conventions, but the iconography of the later Nahuatl manuscripts is better understood because many of these manuscripts are accompanied by explanatory written texts. By way of contrast, no known pre-Conquest Mixtec manuscript is accompanied by a text in a European language. Thus an understanding of Nahuatl manuscripts is useful in the interpretation of their Mixtec counterparts. For example, specific pictorial motifs, such as birds or plants, can be identified in Mixtec manuscripts by comparison with Nahuatl pictorial documents which have texts that provide the names of the motifs.

But the interpretation of Mixtec manuscripts in terms of later Nahuatl manuscripts is often unsatisfactory, and it is certainly an inadequate approach to the Mixtec pictorial histories. For the pictures in these histories are not merely paintings but also a form of writing, and they should be related to the language which the writing expresses. It is therefore necessary to determine Mixtec rather than Nahuatl names for the persons, places, deities, and motifs that are represented in the pre-Conquest historical manuscripts. Instead of attempting to relate the

Mixtec manuscripts to later manuscripts that reflect the Nahuatl language, it is preferable, I believe, to try to relate them to early Colonial manuscripts from the Mixtec-speaking region itself.[6]

In the Mixteca, the pre-Conquest traditions of style and iconography persisted well into the Colonial period, and in relatively isolated regions of western Oaxaca, native pictorial conventions were still utilized in the last decade of the sixteenth century.[7] Mixtec manuscripts of the early Colonial period do not exhibit a completely new and imported style of manuscript illustration but are a continuation of the pre-Conquest tradition, with European modes of representation becoming increasingly apparent until finally the native style and conventions are completely supplanted. Thus many of the early Colonial pictorial

[6] The merit of using early Colonial manuscripts as a key to the pre-Conquest pictorial histories has been amply demonstrated by Alfonso Caso, who identified the pre-Conquest dynasties of the two Mixteca Alta towns of Tilantongo and Teozacoalco in his perceptive study of a 1580 map of Teozacoalco. ("El Mapa de Teozacoalco," *Cuadernos Americanos*, Año VIII, No. 5 [1949], 145–81.)

[7] As, for example, in three pictorial manuscripts from the Mixteca Alta: a 1590 land-grant map from the Coixtlahuaca region (Fig. 46), a 1595 land-grant map from Cuquila (Fig. 133), and a 1597 genealogy from Tlazultepec (Fig. 30).

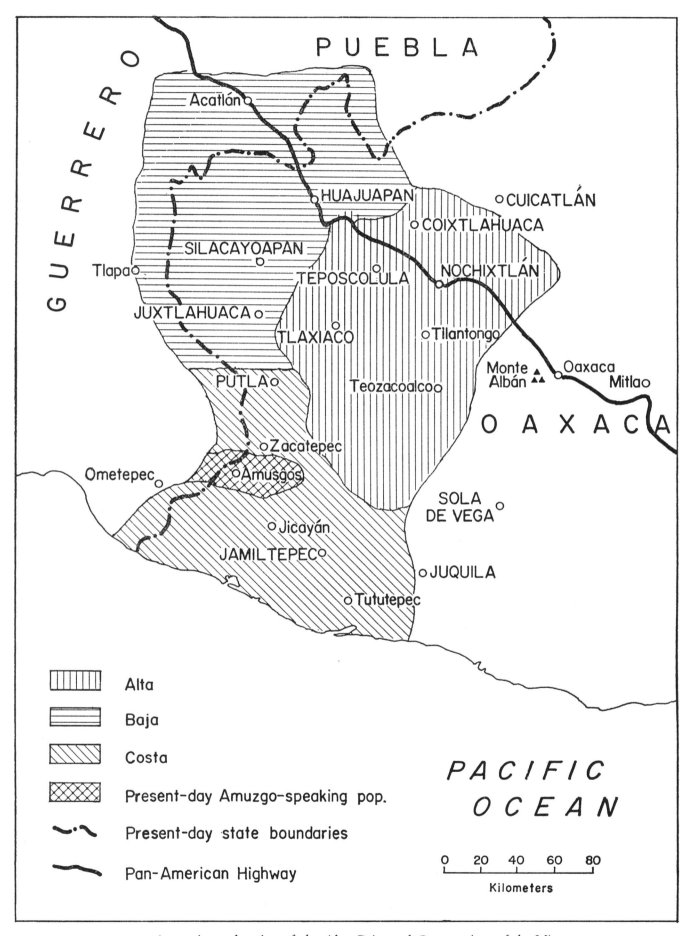

MAP 2. Approximate location of the Alta, Baja, and Costa regions of the Mixteca

manuscripts cannot be interpreted without an understanding of pre-Conquest style and iconography. And conversely, the Colonial manuscripts are often indispensable to the understanding of their pre-Conquest predecessors, either because the later pictorial manuscripts are accompanied by written texts or because their pictographic content is presented in a context where it can be more readily identified.

COLONIAL SOURCES OF MIXTEC HISTORY

Somewhat ironically, the Mixtec-speaking region, with its unique corpus of pre-Conquest historical manuscripts, is very little known in the published accounts of the Colonial period. In contrast to the Valley of Mexico region, whose history and customs were the subject of many Colonial accounts, the history of the Mixteca and the customs of its people at the time of the Spanish conquest are known principally through a few seventeenth-century sources and through the 1579–82 *Relaciones Geográficas*.

The most important Colonial writer on the Mixteca was the Dominican friar Francisco de Burgoa, whose two works, *Palestra historial* and *Geográfica descripción*, were written in the 1660's.[8] The literary style of Burgoa's books is extremely diffuse and gongoristic, and both works deal primarily with the early Colonial activities of the Dominican Order in Oaxaca. But they also contain invaluable, if sometimes scanty, information on pre-Conquest history and customs, principally in the Mixteca Alta and the Valley of Oaxaca, where the Dominican friars had large monastic establishments.

Another Dominican friar, Gregorio García, includes a brief account of the mythological origins of the Mixtec people in his *Origen de los indios de el Nuevo Mundo e Indias Occidentales*, first published in Madrid in 1607.[9] This account was drawn from a pictorial manuscript which was in the Dominican monastery of Cuilapan, but which is now lost.[10]

A short section on the Mixteca is also included in Antonio de Herrera's *Historia general de los hechos de los castellanos en las islas y tierra firme del Mar Océano*, which was first published in Madrid in 1601.[11] Herrera was the court historiographer of Philip II, and his *Historia general* draws on many other works, both published and unpublished, but the sources of his chapters on Oaxaca are unknown.

By far the best source on western Oaxaca in the early Colonial period is the group of *Relaciones Geográficas* written from 1579 to 1582. The *Relaciones* are replies to a questionnaire sent out by Philip II in 1577 to ascertain more precisely the character of towns and lands in the New World.[12] The questionnaire consisted of fifty inquiries seeking information on geography, population, and actual and potential economic resources. Question 10 requested that a map of the town be included with the reply.[13] Questions 38–50 were to be answered only by those towns which were ports or maritime communities, and Question 42 of this section requested a map or chart of the coastal region. Of greatest value to those interested in the pre-Conquest period are Questions 11 through 15, which were directed to towns with a large Indian population. This section of the questionnaire requests information on the native language spoken in the town, including the name of the town in this language, and asks for a description of pre-Conquest government, ceremonial customs, and methods of warfare.

From the Bishopric of Oaxaca, thirty-four texts of replies and twenty-one maps have survived.[14] Not every town in the Mixteca is covered by an extant *Relación*, nor are the replies of the known *Relaciones* uniform in length or in informative content, but they are nonetheless an indispensable source of information on the Mixtec-speaking region in the early Colonial period.

An earlier survey of the towns of Colonial Mexico, the *Suma de Visitas* compiled about 1547–50, is also a useful source of data on the Mixteca because it includes many towns for which there are no extant *Relaciones* of the 1579–82 period.[15] However, the descriptions of towns in

---

[8] *Palestra historial* was first published in Mexico in 1670; *Geográfica descripción* in Mexico in 1674. The two works were reprinted in 1934 as *Publicaciones del Archivo General de la Nación*, XXIV (*Palestra historial*), XXV (Vol. I of *Geográfica descripción*), and XXVI (Vol. II of *Geográfica descripción*). All references to Burgoa in this study are to the 1934 editions. Burgoa was born in Oaxaca about 1600, served as *provincial* of the Dominican Order in Oaxaca, and later as vicar of the parish church in nearby Zaachila. He died in Zaachila in 1681.

[9] Libro V, cap. iv, "Del origen de los indios mixtecos." The edition consulted was the second edition (Madrid, 1729), in which this chapter appears on pp. 327–29.

[10] According to García, this manuscript was "composed" by the vicar of the monastery of Cuilapan in the Valley of Oaxaca. ("[El vicario] . . . tenia un Libro de Mano, que el havia compuesto, i escrito con sus Figuras, como los Indios de aquel reino Mixteco las tenian en sus Libros, o Pergaminos arrollados, con la declaracion de lo que significaban las Figuras en que contaban su Origen, la Creacion del Mundo, i Diluvio General. El qual libro procurè, con todas veras, comprar; mas como era trabajo, i obra de este Religioso, gustaba de tenerlo en su poder, i no menos preciarlo, i echarlo de casa.") Unsuccessful in his effort to purchase the manuscript, García received permission to make a transcription of the mythological-origin legend. The account of this legend is quoted in Alfonso Caso, *Interpretación del Códice Gómez de Orozco* (Mexico, 1954), 12–13.

[11] Década tercera, cap. xii–xiv. Consulted in the edition issued by the Academia de Historia and annotated by Angel González Palencia (17 vols., Madrid, 1935–1957), where the section on the Mixteca appears in Vol. VI (Madrid, 1947), 317–28.

[12] The basic study and survey of the texts of the *Relaciones Geográficas* is: Howard F. Cline, "The *Relaciones Geográficas* of the Spanish Indies, 1577–1586," *Hispanic American Historical Review*, Vol. XLIV (1964), 341–74. An essay by Cline on the *Relación* texts will also appear in Vol. 12 of the *HMAI*.

[13] An essay by Donald Robertson on the *Relación Geográfica* maps ("The Pinturas [Mapas] of the *Relaciones Geográficas*, with a Catalog") will appear in Vol. 12 of the *HMAI*. Robertson has also discussed these maps in *Mexican Manuscript Painting*, 186–89 *et passim*, and in "The *Relaciones Geográficas* of Mexico," *ICA* XXXIII, Vol. II (San José de Costa Rica, 1959), 540–47.

[14] Cline, "The *Relaciones Geográficas*," summary chart V. Many of the *Relaciones* from Oaxaca are published in: Francisco del Paso y Troncoso, ed., *Papeles de Nueva España*, 2a. sér. (hereafter referred to as *PNE*), Vols. IV and V (Madrid, 1905); and in *Revista mexicana de estudios históricos* (hereafter referred to as *RMEH*), Vols. I and II (Mexico, 1927–28)). Detailed studies of a single *Relación* map from the Mixteca include: Alfonso Caso, "El Mapa de Teozacoalco," *Cuadernos Americanos*, Año VIII, No. 5 (1949), 145–81; and Joyce Waddell DeBlois, "An Interpretation of the Map and Relación of Texupa in Oaxaca, Mexico, and an Analysis of the Style of Map" (unpublished M.A. thesis, Tulane University, 1963).

[15] The *Suma de Visitas* is published in: Francisco del Paso y Troncoso, ed., *PNE* I (Madrid, 1905). A comprehensive study of the data on popu-

the *Suma de Visitas* are usually very short—averaging about four or five sentences—and deal primarily with population and tribute.

For the most part, information on the Mixteca in the early Colonial period must be sought in what Ronald Spores has called "informal texts"—that is, written texts such as legal documents whose principal purpose was not to describe or explain native culture or pictorial manuscripts. There is in legal documents and other "informal texts" a great deal of pitchblende and very few grams of radium, but they often do contain valuable, if fragmentary, data. Spores has summarized the situation admirably:

> The writers of sixteenth-century documents were not trained ethnologists, and they could not foresee the interests of twentieth-century anthropologists [or historians]. Consequently there are limitations to the use of such records, particularly in the study of social and community organization. Unfortunately there are no treatises on the Mixtecs that are comparable to those of Sahagún for the Aztecs and Landa for the Mayans. Available documents often record hints and suggestions on many aspects of Mixtec life, but it is sometimes difficult to find sufficient material to complete the picture of a particular cultural element. Despite these limitations, unpublished archival material contains more specific cultural data than one might suspect. For the anthropologist the major obstacle to the use of this documentation is the laborious process of gleaning information that was considered useful to Spanish administrators from a mass of verbiage and legal formulary and converting it to pertinent ethnographic data. This task calls for considerable patience, but the effort will pay substantial dividends.[16]

COLONIAL AND MODERN SOURCES ON THE MIXTEC LANGUAGE

The Mixtec language is crucial to this book because the manuscripts to be discussed are pictographic expressions of this language. The Mixtec language is here used as a tool, as a means to an end, and will not be discussed as a language or from a linguist's point of view. Published studies on the language from both the Colonial and modern period are utilized as sources of vocabulary, and these are supplemented by my own field work in the Coastal region of the Mixteca.

The two most important Colonial sources on the Mixtec language are a grammar and a Spanish-Mixtec dictionary, both written by Dominican friars and both published in Mexico City in 1593. The author of the grammar, *Arte en lengua mixteca*, is Fray Antonio de los Reyes, who was vicar of the Dominican monastery of Teposcolula in the Mixteca Alta when the grammar was published.[17] The dictionary, *Vocabulario en lengua mixteca*, was compiled by Fray Francisco de Alvarado, who was vicar of the monastery at Tamazulapan in the Mixteca Alta in the last decade of the sixteenth century.[18]

The Mixtec language as it is recorded in Reyes and Alvarado is not a phonetic transcription in the twentieth-century sense. Mixtec is a tone language with high, middle, and low tones, and also glottal stops and nasalized vowels. Because none of these features occurs in the Spanish language, they are usually omitted in the Colonial transcriptions of Mixtec. The one exception is the glottal stop which occurs between two vowels, which is very consistently written as *h*. For example, the Mixtec word for "mouth," *yu'u*, which has a glottal stop between the two *u*'s, appears in the Reyes grammar and the Alvarado dictionary as *yuhu*.

However, the lack of any indication of tone in the sixteenth-century vocabularies has a compensating advantage. Once the Mixtec vocabulary of the Alvarado dictionary is analyzed and divided into groups of words which are the same except for variations in tone and nasalization—that is, homonymous—it is possible to see the entire range of meanings of a word, or the entire complex of meanings which varies with tone and nasalization. "Tone puns," in which a word pronounced with one tonal pattern implies the word made up of the same sounds but pronounced with a different tonal pattern, are very common in Mixtec.[19] And as will be seen in the discussion of the Mixtec history manuscripts in Chapters III through V, these manuscripts use pictorial "tone puns," in which the pictorial sign of a word implies another unillustrated word that has a different meaning but is homonymous with the word depicted except for differences in tone. For example, in the dialect of San Miguel el Grande, Oaxaca, the Mixtec word *cá'nu* (with a high tone on the first syllable) means "large," and the word *ca'nù* (with a low tone on the last syllable) means "to break." Because it is easier to depict the action of breaking than it is to illustrate the concept "large," a pictorial sign in which something is being broken often implies that the adjective "large" should be applied to the motif in question.[20]

Another great advantage of the Reyes grammar and the Alvarado dictionary is that they deal with essentially the same dialect of the Mixteca Alta. Thus the combined data in both works provide an extremely large sample of vocabulary in one dialect which can be used for comparison with vocabulary from other dialects.

In the twentieth century, the Mixtec language has been studied in detail by Kenneth L. Pike, Robert Longacre, Cornelia Mak, Anne Dyk, and many others associated with the Summer Institute of Linguistics, and by Evangelina

---

lation in the *Suma de Visitas* is: Woodrow Borah and S. F. Cook, *The Population of Central Mexico in 1548: An Analysis of the Suma de visitas de pueblos* (Berkeley and Los Angeles, 1960; Ibero-Americana, 43).

[16] *The Mixtec Kings and Their People*, 187.

[17] See note 3, above.

[18] The edition of the Alvarado dictionary consulted is the facsimile edition published in 1962 by the Instituto Nacional Indigenista and the Instituto Nacional de Antropología e Historia (INAH), with an introductory study by Wigberto Jiménez Moreno.

[19] The term "tone puns" to describe words which are homonymous except for tone was originated by Kenneth L. Pike ("Tone Puns in Mixteco," *International Journal of American Linguistics*, Vol. XI [1945], 129–39). Pike estimates that in Mixtec: "Possibly fifty per cent of the vocabulary is homonymous in this way." (*Ibid.*, 130.)

[20] The principal source of Mixtec vocabulary from San Miguel el Grande is a dictionary prepared by Anne Dyk and Betty Stoudt, cited in note 23, below. Alfonso Caso was the first to note the use of pictorial tone puns in the Mixtec history manuscripts (*Interpretation of the Codex Bodley 2858* [Mexico, 1960], 16–17.)

Arana Osnaya of the Escuela Nacional de Antropología in Mexico City.[21] Two extremely useful Mixtec dictionaries have been published recently, one based on the Mixtec vocabulary in the sixteenth-century dictionary of Fray Francisco de Alvarado, and the other the result of twentieth-century field work by the Summer Institute of Linguistics in the town of San Miguel el Grande in the Mixteca Alta. In the first of these, Evangelina Arana and Mauricio Swadesh have in effect converted the Alvarado dictionary, which is Spanish into Mixtec, into a Mixtec into Spanish dictionary by compiling the basic Mixtec words of the sixteenth-century dictionary and listing all of the possible meanings of these words.[22] The second dictionary, compiled by Anne Dyk and Betty Stoudt for the dialect of San Miguel el Grande, contains a quantity of vocabulary, both Mixtec into Spanish and Spanish into Mixtec.[23] The

latter dictionary supersedes for the most part an earlier multilithed vocabulary with a similar format compiled by Miss Dyk.[24] Also particularly helpful is Anne Dyk's *Mixteco Texts*, a collection of folk tales in the dialect of San Miguel el Grande.[25] Each of the stories is accompanied by a word-for-word translation into English, with a Mixtec-English vocabulary appearing at the end of the volume.

When vocabulary from *Mixteco Texts*, the Dyk-Stoudt dictionary, or other contemporary sources is quoted in this book, an acute accent (´) over a vowel indicates high tone, a grave accent (`) indicates low tone, and no accent indicates middle tone. An *n* following a vowel or preceding a consonant signifies nasalization, and a glottal stop is written with an apostrophe ('). The symbol *i* (an *i* with a circumflex) represents a high central unrounded vowel not present in Spanish or English. The remaining vowels and consonants have essentially the same sounds as equivalent letters in the Spanish alphabet.

---

[21] A bibliography of twentieth-century studies of the Mixtec language is included in Jiménez Moreno's introduction to the 1962 edition of the Alvarado dictionary, pp. 103–105. Studies of Mixtec by linguists associated with the Summer Institute of Linguistics are also listed in *Twenty-fifth Anniversary Bibliography of the Summer Institute of Linguistics* (Glendale, California, 1960), 32–34.

[22] *Los elementos del mixteco antiguo* (Mexico, 1965).

[23] *Vocabulario mixteco de San Miguel el Grande* (Mexico, 1965; Instituto Lingüístico de Verano, Vocabularios Indígenas, 12).

[24] *Vocabulario de la lengua mixteca de San Miguel el Grande, Oaxaca* (Mexico, 1951).

[25] Norman, Oklahoma, 1959 (Summer Institute of Linguistics, Linguistics Series, 3).

II

THE MIXTEC HISTORICAL MANUSCRIPTS AND THEIR STYLES

Eight examples survive of Mixtec genealogical-historical manuscript painted in a pre-Conquest style: Codex Nuttall (British Museum),[1] Codices Bodley and Selden (Bodleian Library, Oxford),[2] the reverse of Codex Vienna (National-bibliothek, Vienna),[3] Codex Colombino (Museo Nacional de Antropología, Mexico City),[4] Codices Becker I and II (Museum für Völkerkunde, Vienna),[5] and Codex Sánchez Solís (Egerton 2895, British Museum).[6]

[1] The standard edition of this manuscript is: Zelia Nuttall, *Codex Nuttall, Facsimile of an ancient Mexican codex belonging to Lord Zouche of Harynworth, England* (Cambridge, Mass., 1902). This reproduction is a drawing rather than a photographic facsimile. Some of the errors in the reproduction are noted by Cottie A. Burland, "Some errata in the published edition of Codex Nuttall," *Boletín del Centro de Investigaciones Antropológicas de México*, Vol. II–1 (1957), 11–13; and by Alfonso Caso, *Interpretación del Códice Colombino* (Mexico, 1966), 15, 115.

[2] Codices Bodley and Selden have been published in photographic facsimiles with detailed commentaries by Alfonso Caso: *Interpretation of the Codex Bodley 2858* (Mexico, 1960) (hereafter referred to as "Caso, *Bodley*"); and *Interpretacion del Códice Selden 3135 (A.2)/Interpretation of the Codex Selden 3135 (A.2)* (Mexico, 1964) (hereafter referred to as "Caso, *Selden*"). The text accompanying Codex Bodley was issued in two separate editions, Spanish and English; all references in this study are to the English edition. The text accompanying Codex Selden is a one-volume bilingual edition (Spanish, pp. 11–54; English, pp. 61–100). Codex Selden is sometimes designated as "Codex Selden II" to distinguish it from a post-Conquest Mixtec manuscript from the Selden collection which is sometimes called "Codex Selden I" or the "Selden Roll." Black-and-white photographs of the latter manuscript, as well as one detail in color, appear in Cottie A. Burland and Gerdt Kutscher, *The Selden Roll* (Berlin, 1955). Throughout this study whenever I refer to "Codex Selden" or merely "Selden," I am referring to the screenfold, Selden 3135 (A.2), alias "Selden II."

[3] The most recent reproduction of Codex Vienna is Otto Adelhofer, *Codex Vindobonensis Mexicanus I* (Graz, Austria, 1963). This edition is a reprinting of the excellent color plates of an earlier edition of the manuscript, Walter Lehmann and Ottokar Smital, *Codex Vindobonensis Mexicanus I, Faksimile-ausgabe der mexikanischen Bilderhandschrift der Nationalbibliothek in Wien*, Vienna, 1929. Both the 1929 and 1963 editions include short discussions of the codex and its history. Alfonso Caso, "Explicación del reverso del Codex Vindobonensis," *Memoria de el Colegio Nacional*, Vol. V–5 (1950), 9–46, includes black-and-white photographs of the reverse, or historical section, as well as a commentary on its content. The basic study of the obverse, or ritual section, is Karl A. Nowotny, "Erläuterungen zum Codex Vindobonensis (Vorderseite)," *Archiv für Völkerkunde*, Vol. III (1948), 156–200.

[4] A photographic color reproduction of Codex Colombino was published by the Sociedad Mexicana de Antropología (Mexico, 1966) with two commentaries in both Spanish and English: Alfonso Caso, *Interpretación del Códice Colombino/Interpretation of the Codex Colombino* (hereafter referred to as "Caso, *Colombino*"), and Mary Elizabeth Smith, *Las glosas del Códice Colombino/The Glosses of Codex Colombino* (hereafter referred to as "Smith, *Colombino*").

[5] Karl A. Nowotny, *Codices Becker I/II* (Graz, Austria, 1961), reproduces both manuscripts in color photographic facsimiles, with a short commentary on the contents of the two codices. An unpublished one-page

Up to the beginning of the present century the content of this group of manuscripts was considered to be ritual and calendrical. In 1902 Zelia Nuttall was the first person to suggest that the story told in Codex Nuttall was historical.[7] In 1912 James Cooper Clark summarized the biographical data found in the manuscripts on an important personage whose name is 8-Deer "Tiger Claw."[8] Portions of 8-Deer's life are illustrated in all the manuscripts mentioned above with the exception of Codices Sánchez Solís and Becker II; and the entirety of Codex Colombino and the reverse of Codex Nuttall, as well as part of Becker I, are devoted to 8-Deer's conquests and activities.

In 1926 Richard C. E. Long outlined the genealogical material on the front of Codex Nuttall;[9] and in 1935 Herbert J. Spinden definitively isolated this group of manuscripts as being "devoted primarily to genealogies, sequences in political events, and other truly historical matters, fixed in both time and place."[10] However, the exact time and place were not yet known. It was still a matter of conjecture as to how the dates given in the manuscripts correlated with Christian calendar years, and the provenience of these manuscripts was described vaguely as "southern Mexico."

The major breakthrough in the study of the historical manuscripts came in 1949, with the publication of Alfonso Caso's brilliant essay on the post-Conquest Map of Teozacoalco, which accompanied the 1580 *Relación Geográfica* of that town.[11] The Teozacoalco map contains not only a cartographic representation of the town, but also depicts a long series of married couples who represent the rulers of Teozacoalco and Tilantongo in the Mixteca Alta. By

fragment in the Museum für Völkerkunde, Hamburg, is thought to be a section of Codex Becker II.

[6] Cottie A. Burland, *Codex Egerton 2895* (Graz, Austria, 1965) contains a photographic facsimile and a brief description of this manuscript.

[7] *Codex Nuttall* commentary, 20 ff.

[8] *The Story of "Eight Deer" in Codex Colombino* (London, 1912).

[9] "The Zouche Codex," *Journal of the Royal Anthropological Institute of Great Britain and Ireland*, Vol. LVI (1926), 239–58.

[10] "Indian Manuscripts of Southern Mexico," *Annual Report of the Smithsonian Institution, 1933* (Washington, 1935), 429.

[11] "El Mapa de Teozacoalco." Caso's study includes a color photograph of a nineteenth-century copy of the Teozacoalco map which is in the Mapoteca of the Dirección de Geografía, Meteorología e Hidrología in Mexico City (Colección Orozco y Berra, No. 1186), as well as several black-and-white details of the copy. The original of the Map of Teozacoalco is in the Latin American Library of the University of Texas (García Icazbalceta Collection, No. 1770). It is published in Fernando Benítez, *Los indios de México* (Mexico, 1967), following p. 320.

comparing the lineages of the Teozacoalco map with analogous passages in the pre-Conquest historical manuscripts, Caso was able to establish a correlation between the Mixtec dates depicted in the manuscripts and Christian calendar years. As a result of this correlation, Caso reconstructed the dynastic history of the two important towns of Tilantongo and Teozacoalco. The lineages of Tilantongo date from 855 through the Spanish conquest; those of Teozacoalco seem to begin in the eleventh century.

According to the story told in the Map of Teozacoalco and the pre-Conquest manuscripts, Teozacoalco was controlled by Tilantongo by means of interdynastic marriages. In addition, we now know that the important personage named 8-Deer, who appears in all but two of the historical codices, was the second ruler of the second dynasty of Tilantongo and that he lived from 1011 to 1063. Caso's study of the Map of Teozacoalco truly "opened the door" for subsequent studies of the Mixtec histories: his own detailed descriptions of their content and his forthcoming biographical dictionary of all the persons who appear in these manuscripts, and also the studies by other scholars of individual manuscripts or of specific iconographic problems connected with them.

MIXTEC MANUSCRIPT STYLE

All eight manuscripts are painted in a pre-Conquest style, although not all were painted before the arrival of the Spanish conquerors. For example, the latest date in Codex Selden is 1556,[12] which indicates that the manuscript was finished after the mid-sixteenth century.

It has been argued that Codices Becker II and Sánchez Solís should be considered "post-Conquest" because they have a format that is different from the traditional pre-Conquest historical-genealogical manuscript.[13] Usually, as in Codices Nuttall, Vienna, Bodley, Selden, Colombino, and Becker I, the sequence of reading is arranged in a meander or boustrophedon pattern indicated by red guidelines (as shown in Fig. 1), and the pictorial motifs are distributed more or less evenly on a page. In Becker II and Sánchez Solís the meander pattern is not utilized. Both of these manuscripts have a format that divides the page into two registers, with the principal genealogy appearing in the lower register and subsidiary genealogical information in the upper register. This two-register format is explicit in Becker II: the upper and lower sections of the page are divided by a horizontal red line similar to the guidelines used for meander patterns. In Sánchez Solís the two-register format is implicit: no horizontal line divides

the upper and lower sections of a page, but as in Becker II the relationships between the lower-register figures and those in the upper register are indicated by connecting vertical lines and footprints.

It is difficult to ascertain whether the double-register format is a post-Conquest phenomenon or whether it was a variant form of depicting genealogical material that was developed before the arrival of the Spaniards. However, both Becker II and Sánchez Solís, the two manuscripts that use the double register, are otherwise typically pre-Conquest manuscripts in that they are screenfolds of animal hide and show no evidence of intrusive European style and iconography. Moreover, in the early Colonial period, the usual way in which genealogies were arranged was not in a double-register format, but in long vertical rows of marriage pairs, as for example in the 1580 Map of Teozacoalco (Figs. 25, 132). Each couple in the vertical row represents a generation of rulers, with the couple at the bottom of the row being the earliest generation. It is not known precisely when the vertical-row format of presenting genealogical information was first used in Mixtec manuscript painting, but this format is now known only in post-Conquest manuscripts.

Perhaps the subsidiary genealogical information presented in the upper register of Sánchez Solís and Becker II functions in somewhat the same manner as the "footnote" band at the beginning of the Bodley reverse. Pages 40–34 of Codex Bodley are divided into four horizontal sections; the lower three sections contain a pictorial text arranged in the traditional meander patterns, and the top band, which is separated from the remainder of the manuscript by a continuous red line, contains what Alfonso Caso calls "explanatory notes," which supplement the story told in the three registers below.[14] The double-register format of Becker II and Sánchez Solís may be a variant of this combination of meander pattern with a discrete upper register that contains "footnotes."

It is impossible to establish a definite date, such as 1530 or 1550, as the dividing line between the "pre-Conquest" and "post-Conquest" periods, because Mixtec pre-Conquest style persisted long after the arrival of the Spaniards in western Oaxaca. To separate Codex Selden from the pre-Conquest group because its dated narrative stretches beyond the mid-sixteenth century, or to designate Codices Becker II and Sánchez Solís as post-Conquest because their format is not of the traditional meander pattern, would emphasize differences that are relatively unimportant and ignore very real similarities that are shared by the eight manuscripts listed above.

Donald Robertson has suggested: "A guiding principle might be that any undated manuscript with no sign of acculturation in either artistic style or content can be called 'Native Style,' while those with sure evidences of Spanish contact can be called 'Early Colonial.' "[15] Using this definition, all eight manuscripts may be considered

---

[12] Caso, *Selden*, 13, 61.

[13] John B. Glass, in a preliminary draft (April 26, 1965) of the "Western Oaxaca" section of his survey of pictorial manuscripts (to be published in *HMAI*, Vol. 14) states that the group of western Oaxaca manuscripts includes "perhaps five pre-Conquest examples." On further inquiry he specified the five examples to be Becker I, Colombino, Bodley, Nuttall, and Vienna. He indicated that he felt Sánchez Solís and Becker II should not be considered pre-Conquest because they lack the scattered-attribute pattern and the typical pattern of guidelines found in the five manuscripts cited as pre-Conquest. He considered Codex Selden as post-Conquest because of its post-1550 date. (Letter of July 10, 1965, and later conversation.)

[14] Caso, *Bodley*, 51.

[15] "Review of *Codices Becker I/II*," *American Antiquity*, Vol. XXVII-2 (1962), 254.

as painted in the "native" or "pre-Conquest" style. In addition, all are animal-hide screenfolds, sized with a white clay base, and all contain figures painted in color.

With the exception of the differences in format seen in Becker II and Sánchez Solís, all eight manuscripts exhibit the essential features of Mixtec pre-Conquest style as delineated by Robertson.[16] That is, Mixtec painting style is characterized by flat areas of color enclosed and separated by a black "frame line." It is conceptual rather than perceptual, and very little or no attempt is made to represent an illusion of three-dimensional space. It is an art of convention: as in Egyptian painting, the human body is represented as a compendium of separable parts. Usually these parts are the same as those of Egyptian painting—profile legs, front-facing torso, and a profile head—although a few figures in Mixtec manuscripts are represented with front-facing heads, and some of the seated figures are shown with front-facing crossed legs. Most of the persons who appear in the genealogical manuscripts are of the ruling class, but no inkling of portraiture occurs, as it does in Mochica ceramics of pre-Conquest Peru. In Mixtec manuscripts persons are identified by their names, not by their physical features.

Nor do Mixtec figures express much emotion. At times, the teeth of a figure are bared when he goes into battle, and occasionally captives or those who are sacrificed are shown as shedding a conventionalized tear (Figs. 15b, 16). For the most part, expression is conveyed through a few stereotypes of posture and gesture. The torso of a figure whose captor holds him by the hair is bent abruptly forward (Fig. 15b), and the captive's flexed arms suggest tension, while his outstretched fingers convey his helplessness. Similarly, the lifelessness of a sacrificial victim (Fig. 17) is shown not only by his closed eyes, but also by his arms which hang inertly from his body, and by his legs which dangle weakly under the weight of the person who performs the sacrifice.

SUB-STYLES OF THE HISTORICAL MANUSCRIPTS

The eight historical-genealogical manuscripts may be divided on the basis of their styles into four sub-groups:
1. Nuttall-Vienna
2. Colombino-Becker I
3. Bodley-Selden-Becker II
4. Sánchez Solís

The very brief consideration of these sub-styles that follows is intended only to present a cursory characterization of the four groups, a characterization based principally on color and the representation of the human figure. It cannot be denied that each of the eight manuscripts has its own distinctive stylistic characteristics, or, as is the case for Vienna and Nuttall, two distinctive styles, one on the obverse and one on the reverse. In addition, more than one drawing or painting style may be evident within one

side of a single manuscript.[17] The short discussion below does not attempt to be an intensive analysis of all the stylistic elements of the eight Mixtec histories, but a summary of some of the general similarities that are shared by several manuscripts and that seem to be significant.

Utilizing the information presented in the Mixtec glosses written on Colombino-Becker I and Sánchez Solís, I shall suggest a hypothetical provenience for these two groups—or rather, their probable location in the early Colonial period when the glosses were added.

Nuttall-Vienna

The front of Codex Nuttall (pages 1–41) contains a series of parallel genealogies, and the information given extends to about the mid-fourteenth century.[18] The back of Nuttall (pages 42–84) presents a detailed biography of part of the life of 8-Deer, from the first marriage of his father in 992 to 8-Deer's sacrifice in 1050 of two individuals who had sacrificed his half-brother. The Vienna obverse (pages 52–1) contains essentially ritual or mythological rather than historical data. The back of this manuscript (pages I–XIII) sets forth genealogies that terminate by the year 1357.[19]

The obverses of both Nuttall and Vienna are the most colorful and elaborate of all the Mixtec screenfolds, and they resemble each other in figural style and draftsmanship. The color scheme of the front of Vienna, however, is closer to that of the Nuttall reverse. For example, the Vienna obverse and the Nuttall reverse lack the light-green and lemon-yellow colors seen throughout the front of Nuttall. The light green is the color of all the hill-signs on the front of Nuttall; on the back of Nuttall and the front of Vienna, hills are brown or ochre. On the front of Nuttall lemon yellow is used for human flesh; a more golden yellow or ochre is used for human flesh on the back of Nuttall and the front of Vienna. Common to both sides of Nuttall and Vienna is a more frequent use of the color purple than is seen in any other history manuscript with the possible exception of Codex Bodley.[20] A color that

---

[16] *Mexican Manuscript Painting*, Ch. 1, "Mixtec Pre-Conquest Manuscript Style," 12–24. In this discussion of Mixtec painting style, Robertson focuses on Codex Nuttall as a representative Mixtec manuscript.

[17] Nancy P. Troike, in "A Study of Some Stylistic Elements in the Codex Colombino-Becker," to be published in *ICA* XXXVIII (Stuttgart, 1970), has identified three different styles of handling human figures in Codices Colombino and Becker I, which are thought by many to be sections of the same manuscript. Mrs. Troike has spent considerable time in Europe making a careful analysis of the Mixtec histories at first hand, and her forthcoming studies should add greatly to our knowledge of the stylistic characteristics and physical make-up of these manuscripts.

[18] Caso, "El Maa de Teozacoalco," *Cuadernos Americanos*, Año VIII, No. 5 (1949), 177. Elsewhere (*Colombino*, 46; 144), Caso suggests that the front of Nuttall was completed about 1330.

[19] Caso, "Explicación del reverso del Codex Vindobonensis," *Memoria de el Colegio Nacional*, Vol. V–5 (1950), 44.

[20] In Nuttall, purple is used in the costumes of both men and women, and occasionally as the body color of men. In Vienna, however, purple may appear in the decorative details of men's costumes, but it is used as the color of large areas of textiles only in the costumes of women. On the front of Vienna, purple is used principally for female costumes in the beginning of the manuscript, but in the last twenty pages purple appears as part of other motifs, such as buildings and place signs. To my knowledge, a chemical analysis has not been made of the purple color used in Vienna and Nuttall. It is possible that this color is the purple shellfish dye that is still made in the Coastal region of the Mixteca, as described in Peter Gerhard, "Emperors' Dye of the Mixtecs," *Natural History*, Vol. LXXIII (1964), 26–31.

sometimes resembles purple—and sometimes resembles a dark blue or blueish grey—is seen throughout Bodley; and a brownish-purple is occasionally used for the flesh of figures in Sánchez Solís (as, for example, in the male figure in the upper-left corner of page 21). But the purple in both Bodley and Sánchez Solís is neither as saturated nor as prevalent as it is in both Vienna and Nuttall. Purple does not appear at all in Codices Selden, Colombino, Becker I and II.

Another characteristic that the front of Vienna shares with both sides of Nuttall is the use of vertical guidelines that divide the screenfold pages into three or four vertical rectangles, as shown in Fig. 1. The vertical pattern of guidelines is not seen in any of the other extant Mixtec screenfolds. On the back of Vienna the narrative is arranged in a horizontal meander pattern that is different from the horizontal patterns used in Bodley, Selden, Colombino, and Becker I. As can be seen in Fig. 1, the guidelines on the back of Vienna are what might be called a reversing "T" pattern, with the vertical section of the "T" placed along the fold of the manuscript and with an upside-down "T" alternating with a right-side-up "T." In some respects this "T" pattern seems to be a variation on the vertical guideline pattern, for the upright section of the "T" is reminiscent of the vertical guidelines in Nuttall and on the front of Vienna.

The style on the back of Vienna is very different from that on the front of the manuscript; and the Vienna reverse almost seems to be the "poor stepchild" of Mixtec history painting, principally because of its draftsmanship, which is more slovenly than that of any other known example of pre-Conquest Mixtec painting. A distinctive iconographic trait of the Vienna reverse is the face paint worn by most of the women. This consists of two red horizontal lines across the face at eye level, at times with geometric designs below the lines, and a thick red outline around the mouth, rather like badly smeared lipstick. This pattern of face paint is also worn by female figures on two pages (6 and 7) near the beginning of Nuttall, but it is not found in any other manuscript of the historical-genealogical group.

The back of Nuttall exhibits a slightly different style from that of the Nuttall front, but the contrast is not as great as that between the Vienna front and back. As was noted above, the colors used on the back of Nuttall are different from those on the front. In addition, the figures on the back are larger and not as tightly packed into the two-dimensional space of the page as they are on the front.

Nancy Troike has recently made the important discovery that the back of Nuttall—that is, the section of the manuscript devoted to the biography of 8-Deer—was painted before the front of the manuscript. She has perceptively observed that in the places in Nuttall where there are small holes in the manuscript, paint from the front of the manuscript has seeped through to the back and appears on top of the paint on the back.[21]

Codices Vienna and Nuttall are thought by some to be the two manuscripts which Hernán Cortés sent, along with the famous "Moctezuma treasure," to Charles V in 1519.[22] If this were the case, it is not known where or how Cortés obtained the two manuscripts. But whether Vienna and Nuttall were sent to Europe by Cortés or arrived there in some other manner, they are believed to have left Mexico soon after the Spanish conquest, and thus it may now be difficult to determine their provenience in the New World.[23]

Colombino-Becker I

Codex Colombino deals in detail with part of the life of the eleventh-century ruler 8-Deer, and Becker I relates other portions of 8-Deer's life as well as part of the story of another important Mixtec ruler named 4-Wind "Fire Serpent."[24] Many scholars believe that Colombino and Becker I are actually sections of the same manuscript, and if this is true, the group of eight historical manuscripts would be reduced to seven.[25]

Alfonso Caso has presented very convincing arguments that the two manuscripts were originally one.[26] He has made a careful correlation of the stories told in Colombino and Becker I and the parallel narrative of 8-Deer's life presented on the back of Nuttall, and he has demonstrated that at no point is there any overlap between the story told in Colombino and that told in Becker I. His study includes a reconstruction of how the two manuscripts may have originally fitted together, and he suggests that many of the slight differences between Colombino and Becker I may be accounted for by changes in style within Colombino itself.[27]

[21] "The Provenience of the Mixtec Codices Nuttall and Colombino-Becker," a paper presented at the sixty-eighth Annual Meeting of the American Anthropological Association, held in New Orleans, November 20–23, 1969.

[22] Nuttall, *Codex Nuttall* commentary, 9–11; Adelhofer, *Codex Vindobonensis* commentary, 9–10. In the list of the treasure that Cortés sent to the Spanish king along with his First Letter, the manuscripts are merely described as "two books such as the Indians have" (*dos libros delos que tienen los yndios*).

[23] There is a short Latin text on Vienna to the effect that it belonged to King Manuel I of Portugal, who died on December 13, 1521—which indicates that the codex was in Europe by this date. Mrs. Nancy Troike is now investigating the history of Nuttall in Europe. At present, the earliest record of Nuttall is that it was in the Dominican Monastery of San Marco in Florence in 1859 (British Museum, *Catalogue of additions to the manuscripts, 1916–1920* [London, 1933], 141–43).

[24] The biographical data on 4-Wind that appear in all the historical manuscripts have been assembled by Alfonso Caso in: "La vida y aventuras de 4. Viento 'Serpiente de Fuego,'" *Miscelánea de estudios dedicados al Dr. Fernando Ortiz* (Havana, 1955), 291–98.

[25] Eduard Seler, "Die Columbus-Festschriften der Königl. Bibliothek in Berlin und die mexikanischen Regierung," *Gesammelte Abhandlungen* . . . , Vol. I (Berlin, 1902), 155; Walter Lehmann, "Les peintures mixteco-zapotèques et quelques documents apparentés," *JSA*, n.s. Vol. II (1905), 260; Alfonso Caso, *Colombino*, 14–17; 114–117 *et passim*.

[26] Caso, *ibid*.

[27] For example, the pattern of red guidelines at the beginning of Colombino is different from the pattern of Becker I. In Colombino four pages are read as a unit (as can be seen in the guideline pattern labeled "Colombino" in Fig. 1); in Becker I, two pages form a unit (as seen in the guideline pattern labeled "Colombino-Becker I, Variant Form" in Fig. 1). Caso points out that the four-page unit of guidelines ceases on page XIX of Colombino and does not reappear in the remainder of the manuscript, and he observes that page XXIV of Colombino utilizes the Becker I pattern of guidelines. A similar type of change that Caso has not noted is the use of the color green in Colombino-Becker I. As Henri

Nancy Troike, who also believes that the two codices are the same manuscript, has described in detail the physical make-up of both Colombino and Becker I, and she has analyzed the sequence of guideline patterns in the extant pages of the two manuscripts to demonstrate several ways in which the two originally might have fitted together and the problems involved in determining where the two manuscripts might have been joined.[28] She has further identified three sub-styles of representing human figures in Colombino and Becker I: the first of these sub-styles is evident on pages III–X of Colombino, the second on pages XI–XV and XVII–XIX of Colombino, and the third throughout the entirety of Becker I.[29]

The biography of 8-Deer as it appears in Colombino and on pages 1–14 of Becker I is similar to that narrated on the back of Codex Nuttall.[30] Also, Nancy Troike has demonstrated that the preparation of the animal hide is the same in Colombino, Becker I, and Nuttall, because (1) the height and width of the individual pages of all three codices is the same, and (2) the holes in the animal hide in these three manuscripts are mended with cord, a method of mending that is unique and not seen in the other Mixtec historical screenfolds, which are mended by means of a small leather patch that is glued over the hole.[31]

Notwithstanding the similarities in hide preparation and in iconography shared by Colombino, Becker I, and Nuttall, the painting style seen in Colombino and Becker I is very different from the Nuttall-Vienna style. First, the colors of Colombino-Becker I are less saturated than those of Nuttall-Vienna. Second, the costumes worn by the individuals in Colombino-Becker I are more standardized and less elaborate than the costumes of Nuttall and Vienna; and in Colombino-Becker I, much less emphasis is given to complex patterns of face paint and to helmets with animal heads.

One of the distinctive features of Colombino-Becker I is the way in which the toes of the human foot are depicted in about thirty-three of the total of forty extant pages of the manuscript. The majority of toes in both Colombino and Becker I are shown somewhat in the same manner as teeth. They appear as a white border at the end or bottom of the foot, and this border is divided into a row of small, neat white squares, each of which represents one toe (as in Fig. 6c).[32] In Codex Nuttall, on the front of Vienna, and on about seven pages of Colombino (III–X), toes are usually indicated by a series of parallel lines extending upward from the base of the foot (as in Figs. 5b, 15b). Sometimes the first toe is left white or unpainted to depict the toenail of the big toe. In figures where one toe of each foot is left unpainted, the figure appears to have two right or two left feet, depending on which direction he is facing. On the back of Vienna, the representation of toes appears to be a synthesis of the toe style of Colombino-Becker and that seen in Nuttall and on the front of Vienna. The toes of most of the figures on the back of Vienna are represented by the white border divided into cubes which is common to Colombino-Becker I, but the lines that divide these cubes are extended upward into the flesh-colored area of the foot, as in Nuttall and in the Vienna obverse.

In addition to the stylistic features shared by Colombino and Becker I, both manuscripts were annotated during the Colonial period with glosses in the Mixtec language. Codex Colombino contains many Mixtec glosses, and they may have been written on the Codex in 1541, a date which appears on the last page (XXIV) of the manuscript. The glosses have nothing to do with the biography of 8-Deer presented in the painted narrative of Colombino, but refer almost exclusively to Mixtec names of boundaries of towns in the Coastal region of the Mixteca—towns which were subject to, or within the sphere of influence of, Tututepec, the capital of the Coast. In 1717 Codex Colombino was presented as evidence in court by the native ruler of Tututepec. Thus this manuscript is known to have been in the possession of the ruling family of Tututepec at least as early as 1717.[33] As we shall see in the discussion below, Colombino probably belonged to Tututepec's rulers as early as 1541.

Codex Becker I has a few glosses that are still visible, and there are indications that glosses originally written in many sections of the manuscript have been scraped off or erased. Although I have not had an opportunity to study the Becker glosses in the original manuscript or in ultraviolet photographs, my impression is that several of these glosses also refer to towns in the Coastal region. On page 12 of Becker I, below the large building on the right side of the page, is the gloss: *aniñe yuta atu*. *Aniñe* is the Mixtec word for "palace," and *yuta atu* is the Mixtec name for the *Río de la Arena*, one of the principal rivers on

---

Saussure first pointed out in a short commentary accompanying a color lithographic edition of Becker I (*Le Manuscrit du Cacique* [Geneva, 1892], 6), the color green is rare in Becker I: it appears only twice, on page 4, once in a feather headdress and once in the leaves of a cattail plant inside a temple in the lower-left corner. In contrast, at the beginning of Colombino green appears very frequently, especially as the color of hill signs. At about page XIX of Colombino the color green begins to disappear, and the common color of hill signs becomes brown or ochre—the same color used for hill signs in Becker I.

[28] "Observations on Some Material Aspects of the Codex Colombino," to be published in *Tlalocan*, Vol. VI–3; "Observations on the Physical Form of the Codex Becker I," to be published in *Archiv für Völkerkunde*, Vol. XXIII; "The Structure of the Codex Colombino-Becker," to be published in *Anales del INAH*, época 7, Vol. 2, No. 50.

[29] "A Study of Some Stylistic Elements in the Codex Colombino-Becker," to be published in *ICA* XXXVIII (Stuttgart, 1970). Mrs. Troike is presently preparing a book-length manuscript on Colombino-Becker I.

[30] Caso (*Colombino*, chart II *et passim*) has correlated the parallel scenes in Nuttall and Colombino-Becker I. Some of these scenes are also discussed and illustrated in James Cooper Clark, *The Story of "Eight Deer" in Codex Colombino*.

[31] "The Provenience of the Mixtec Codices Nuttall and Colombino-Becker," a paper presented at the sixty-eighth Annual Meeting of the American Anthropological Association, held in New Orleans, November 20–23, 1969.

[32] The two types of toes seen in Colombino-Becker I and the distribution of each type is discussed in Troike, "A Study of Some Stylistic Elements in the Codex Colombino-Becker."

[33] A more detailed discussion of the Colombino glosses appears in: Mary Elizabeth Smith, "The Codex Colombino: A Document of the South Coast of Oaxaca," *Tlalocan*, Vol. IV–3 (1963), 276–88; and in Smith, *Colombino*. Both studies contain the 1717 description of Colombino, from AGN-Vínculos 272–10, fol. 42/v–43/v.

the Coast. On page 5 of Becker I, written across the roof of a building in the center of the bottom line, is what appears to be *doyo yuhu*, the sixteenth-century Mixtec name of Pinotepa de Don Luis, a town on the Coast that was a subject of Tututepec at the time of the Spanish conquest.

If Colombino and Becker I were originally sections of the same manuscript, they were separated at least before 1717, because the description of Colombino on the occasion of its presentation in a law court in that year matches the present pagination of the manuscript. In 1717 Colombino was described as consisting of twenty-four sections or pages; the date 1541 was said to appear on the last page; and the Mixtec names of the boundaries of two Coastal towns, Juchatengo and Ixtapa, were written on the first two pages. The same description applies to Colombino today.

The first notice that we have of Codex Becker I is that it, too, was presented as evidence in a law court, in Puebla in 1852. Unfortunately we do not know where the Spanish documents are which originally accompanied Codex Becker I, or the location of the documents concerning the 1852 lawsuit.[34] Henri Saussure reported that, according to tradition, Becker I told the story of a Mixtec ruler named *Sar-Ho*, who was married to a woman named *Con-Huyo* and who was the ruler of a town named *Tindú*, or "the ball."[35] A town named Tindú is located southwest of the town of Huajuapan de León in northern Oaxaca. According to Martínez Gracida, the original Mixtec name of this town was *yucu ita*, or "hill of the flowers" (*yucu* = "hill"; *ita* = "flowers").[36] Whether this Tindú is the same Tindú referred to in the tradition or whether the native who brought Codex Becker I into Puebla was from Tindú or the Huajuapan region of northern Oaxaca is not known.

What may have happened is that Codex Colombino was annotated twice—the first time when it and Becker I were still the same manuscript, and a second time after it and Becker I were separated. After the separation many of the glosses on the section which is now Becker I were very carefully scraped off, for throughout this manuscript there are many faint vestiges of glosses which are scarcely visible and no longer legible. Similarly, many of the extensively erased portions of Colombino (for example, pages II–2 and XVIII–52 and 53) contain scarcely visible traces of writing.[37] Thus the glosses that are visible today, which

list the boundaries of Coastal towns, may represent a *second* glossing of Colombino.

It is my opinion that this hypothetical second layer of glosses was added to the manuscript after its separation from Becker I. On the first and the last pages of Colombino as we know it today is a *rúbrica*, a type of mark or flourish often added to a person's signature on Spanish documents. Because this *rúbrica* appears on the first and last pages, it seems to signal the beginning and end of the presently visible annotations. On page I it appears at the left of a place sign in the center of line 4; on page XXIV it appears at the left of the large place sign in the upper-right corner of the page. What seems to be the same *rúbrica* is also written on the first and last pages of Becker I.[38] It is likely that these *rúbricas* were placed on Colombino and Becker I after the two sections of the manuscript were separated, and it is possible that they were written on the two sections by an official at some time when these sections were presented as evidence in court cases.

In addition to the *rúbrica* on the last page (XXIV) of Colombino, on the base of the large place sign on this page on the base of the large place sign on page XXIV is a two-line gloss which appears to me a "sign-off" statement common in legal documents. The second line of this gloss consists of the word *cuiya* (the Mixtec word for "year") and the date 1541. Unfortunately, the first line of this gloss is so faint that it is difficult to read, let alone translate. In the tradition of legal documents it may say something to the effect that this document—i.e., the glosses —is sworn to and signed on a certain day in 1541. On the other hand, it might also indicate that these glosses were faithfully copied from another document dated 1541. I am inclined to believe that the 1541 date, which is the only visible date on either Colombino or Becker I, is the date when the second glosses were written on Colombino.

This hypothesis appears to be confirmed by the content of three short glosses on Colombino which contain the name of Don Pedro de Alvarado, the native ruler of Tututepec from 1522 to about the mid-sixteenth century. From Colonial documents dealing with the native rulers of Tututepec, it is known that Don Pedro had died by 1554, but the exact date of his death has not been ascertained. It seems likely that Don Pedro was either alive in 1541, or that he died in 1541 and the glosses on Colombino represent a clarification of his land holdings at the time of his death. The first of the three glosses in which the name of Don Pedro appears is on Colombino V–17, across the roof of the place sign of Tututepec (Fig. 49a): *s pᵒ yucu dzaa aniñe don pᵒ de aluarado*, or "San Pedro Tututepec, the palace of Don Pedro de Alvarado." This implies that

[34] The Archivo de Justicia in Puebla is a possible repository for these documents, but unfortunately this archive has not been catalogued nor have its contents been placed in any order so that they may be readily consulted.

[35] *Le Manuscrit du Cacique,* 5–6.

[36] *Colección de "Cuadros Sinópticos" . . . del Estado . . . de Oaxaca* (Oaxaca, 1883), n.p.

[37] Page II of Colombino was much erased at least as early as 1717. When the manuscript was brought into court in that year, the court interpreter translated the boundary names on pages I and II from Mixtec into Spanish. He translates fourteen of the boundary names on page II, and then adds that although other names of boundaries occur, he cannot read them because they have been erased ("aunque dio otros puestos de linderos por estar borradas las letras de las figuras que lo manifiestan no he podido venir de su significacion"). (AGN-Vínculos 272–10, fol. 43/v).

[38] The *rúbricas* on the first and last pages of Becker I are not visible in the photographic facsimile of this codex (Nowotny, *Codices Becker I/II*); hence my earlier assertion that there were no *rúbricas* on Becker I (Smith, *Colombino,* 68; 165). However, the presence of these *rúbricas* was noted by Saussure (*Le manuscrit du cacique,* 7), and the *rúbrica* on the first page is illustrated in the lithographic copy of Becker I that accompanies Saussure's text. According to Nancy Troike (personal communication), both *rúbricas* on Becker I are visible under ultra-violet light.

Don Pedro was the native ruler of Tututepec at the time the gloss was written. The second gloss is on Colombino XI–34 at the right of the large ballcourt:

yaa chito ndaa
aniñe chi toniñe
dⁿ pº de alvarado,

which I have translated as "here is taken care of (or protected) the palace of the sovereign Don Pedro de Alvarado."[39] My interpretation of this sentence is that the lands of Don Pedro are protected in that their boundaries are set forth in the glosses written on Codex Colombino.

Throughout the Colonial period, once a land dispute was settled, the two or more parties involved in the dispute participated in an *amparo de posesión* (literally, "a protection or sanction of possession"), which usually entailed a visit to the boundaries or sites of land under dispute in order to verify the agreement reached by the litigants. Because most of the glosses on Colombino set forth boundaries of lands belonging to Tututepec, I believe that "protection" is used on page XI of the Codex to refer to the confirmation of Don Pedro's land holdings on the Coast.

The third gloss also appears on page XI of Colombino, a two-line text above the ballcourt which ends with the two words "don pedro" (*don pº*). Again, as in the case of the two-line text on page XXIV, this gloss is very difficult to read. However, these three references in the Colombino glosses to the person who ruled Tututepec from 1522 to no later than 1554 would indicate that the 1541 on page XXIV is the date when the second, or visible, set of glosses was added to the manuscript.

A further indication that when these glosses were added Colombino was paginated in the same manner as it is today is the placement of the boundary names of the Coastal town of Santa Elena Comaltepec on pages XV *and* XVI. As several scholars have pointed out, the present page XVI of Colombino is out of place and does not belong between pages XV and XVII.[40] Exactly where page XVI of Colombino originally fitted into the Colombino-Becker narrative sequence is uncertain. Alfonso Caso has suggested that its proper place may be after the end of the sixteen extant pages of Becker I.[41] Thus it is probable that when the second set of glosses was added to Colombino, page XVI was where it is today, following page XV, because it does not seem likely that the annotator would have put the beginning of the boundaries of Comaltepec on page XV and then continued writing these boundary names on a page much later in the manuscript, or even on an unattached page. In all other instances in Colombino where the boundaries of one town occupy two pages, they are always consecutive: the boundaries of Santiago Jocotepec on pages III and IV, those of Tututepec on pages V and VI, and those of San Pedro Jicayán on pages XIII and XIV.

It would seem, then, that at some time between the Spanish conquest of Tututepec in 1522 and the second annotation of Colombino in 1541, Colombino-Becker I as one manuscript was annotated with a first set of glosses —most of which have been scraped off both sections of the manuscript. By 1541 the two manuscripts were separated, and Colombino became paginated in the same way as it is today—in twenty-four sections or pages, with the out-of-order page XVI inserted between pages XV and XVII. In 1541 a second set of glosses—those which are still partially legible today—was added to Colombino, and this set of glosses lists the boundary names of lands belonging to the sixteenth-century native ruler of Tututepec, Don Pedro de Alvarado.

It is possible that some of the glosses still visible on Colombino, particularly those on the rooftops of buildings, may be part of the first annotation of the manuscript. A careful comparison of the handwriting of the glosses in both Colombino and Becker I should be made, but such a comparison is outside of the scope of this book. My principal reason for discussing the Colombino-Becker I glosses at such length is that the glosses indicate the probable location of the two manuscripts at the time of the Spanish conquest: the Coastal region of the Mixteca.

Of course, merely that Colombino-Becker I belonged to the native rulers of the Coastal capital of Tututepec in 1541 is no sure indication that the manuscript was painted on the Coast. The dynastic relationships of native Mixtec rulers are complex and entangled, and it is possible that the native rulers of Tututepec may have acquired the Codex by marriage with a person from another region of the Mixteca or by inheritance from another dynastic line which left no direct heirs. Although, as I have suggested elsewhere,[42] I believe that Colombino tells the story of 8-Deer's life from a Coastal point of view, the rulers of the Coast may have imported an artist to paint the manuscript. In other words, I do not believe that Colombino-Becker I can as yet be considered to form the nucleus of a "Coastal style." We still have no clear idea of when the manuscript was painted or where the painting was actually done.

However, if and when it is possible to determine the early-sixteenth-century location of other historical-genealogical manuscripts, it may also be possible to determine whether the differences in style observable in the four groups outlined here are differences of time, or differences of region, or both. Determining the provenience of Codices Nuttall and Vienna may be difficult, for both manuscripts seem to have left the Mixteca very soon after the Spanish conquest. But we may be able to learn more about the provenience of the remaining historical-genealogical manuscripts if, as in the case of Codex Colombino, written texts that originally accompanied the painted manuscripts can be located.

Bodley-Selden-Becker II

The primary concern of these three manuscripts is the depiction of dynastic genealogies. Codex Bodley is painted

---

[39] Smith, *Colombino*, 62–63; 159.
[40] Clark, *The Story of "Eight Deer" in Codex Colombino*, 4; Caso, *Colombino*, 16–17, 45, 116–17, 143.
[41] Caso, *ibid.*

[42] Smith, *Colombino*, 69–73; 166–70.

on both sides: the front (pages 1–20) contains a chronological account of several dynasties from the time of their mythological origin in 692 up to about 1520, the eve of the Spanish conquest of Oaxaca, and the back (pages 40–21) contains several short accounts of the dynastic histories of other towns.

Codex Selden presents the genealogy of the rulers of one town whose identity is not known, but whose place sign is usually described as "Belching Mountain." The story of these rulers begins with their mythological origins in the late eighth century and terminates in the mid-sixteenth century. This story appears on the front (pages 1–20) of Selden; sections of the back show evidence of a palimpsest, now covered with white sizing and no longer legible.[43] As can be seen in Fig. 1, Codex Selden is unique among the extant historical screenfolds in that the sections of the screenfold are read vertically, from down to up, rather than horizontally.

Becker II is a fragment which consists of four screenfold sections containing a series of married couples from a town which is not named in the four pages. Nor do these pages contain a date. Becker II is arranged in a two-register format, with the principal genealogy painted in full color in the lower register; the upper register contains subsidiary genealogical information outlined in black but not filled in with color.[44]

Each of these three manuscripts utilizes a different color scheme. The colors of Codex Bodley are dark and muddy, and the paint, particularly the red and black, seems to have a tendency to flake. Codex Selden's predominant colors are brown, ochre, and a particularly bright, pungent red. The colors used in Becker II are light in hue, but most of the colors, especially the blue, seem more saturated than the colors of Colombino-Becker I.

The principal reason for grouping these three manuscripts is their great similarity in the representation of the human figure. As in the case of the Vienna-Nuttall and Colombino-Becker I style groups, one of the most distinctive features of this group is the manner in which human toes are depicted. Characteristic of the Bodley-Selden-Becker II group is what may be called the "one-toed foot." The toes of the majority of figures in the three manuscripts are shown as a single white circle at the end of the foot, thus suggesting the idea of a profile foot where only one toe is visible (as in Figs. 6a, 7c).

Another feature which distinguishes Selden and Bodley (especially the front of Bodley) from Nuttall-Vienna and Colombino-Becker I is that the pictorial narrative in Bod-

ley and Selden is rigidly confined by the relentless pattern of the red guidelines. In Nuttall, Vienna, and Colombino-Becker I, the guidelines may be shifted or omitted to leave space for a "big scene" of an important event (as in Colombino XI, Becker I-10, and Nuttall 80), and at times they are completely absent so that the painted scene may occupy an entire page (Colombino XXII and XXIII, Becker I-12, and Nuttall 75). Another device used in Nuttall, Colombino-Becker I, and on the front of Vienna to emphasize a scene is to place it in the corner of the page where the shorter guideline opens up more space for a larger scene (as in Colombino V and XIII, Becker I-7, 9, and 15, and Nuttall 52, 69, and 70).

The "big scene" is not utilized in Selden and Bodley, except on the first two pages of Selden and in a few instances on the back of Bodley, such as pages 22–21 where the guideline that separates the two top registers is omitted, allowing the artist to paint a scene that is two registers high. In the case of Codex Bodley, it is obvious that the guidelines were painted in before the pictorial narrative, because on both the front and back, the pages that follow the end of the painted story are covered with white sizing and divided by guidelines.

For the most part, the human figures, place signs, and scenes of Bodley and Selden are of a uniform size, and the narrative moves briskly along without even the larger scenes to punctuate the corners where the guidelines are shortened to indicate a shift in the direction of reading. In Bodley and Selden, emphasis is given in terms of length only, rather than by making a scene larger in both height and width. For example, one of the important moments in the biography of 8-Deer is the occasion when this hero delivers a prisoner of war and then receives a nose ornament which signifies that he is a *tecuhtli*, or "great lord." In Codex Bodley 9-II, the size and importance of this scene is suggested by the length of the place sign that indicates where the events took place (Fig. 61). The base of the place sign consists of a frieze with geometric decorations that extends across two-thirds of the line and is divided by a throne; on the right side of the throne the prisoner of war is brought in and received, and on the left side, 8-Deer receives the nose ornament. By way of contrast, the same nose-piercing scene in Codex Colombino is placed in the upper-left corner of page XIII (Fig. 55), and the guideline that divides the top and middle registers of this page is shortened to leave room for the large rectangular scene. In Colombino this important event and place are emphasized not only by the great length of the base of the place sign, but also by the height of the large temple, which extends from the center of the middle register to the upper border of the top register.

Concerning the date of the Bodley-Selden-Becker II group, I believe that it is reasonable to assume that the style seen in these three manuscripts was one of the prevailing Mixtec painting styles at the time of the Spanish conquest. In the first place, the events narrated in two of the manuscripts of this group extend into the sixteenth century. The last couple shown on the front of Bodley

---

[43] Philip Dark and Joyce Plesters, "The Palimpsests of Codex Selden: Recent attempts to reveal the covered pictographs," *ICA* XXXIII, Vol. II (San José de Costa Rica, 1959), 530–39; Caso, *Selden*, 14–18, 62–66.

[44] Donald Robertson (*American Antiquity*, XXVII, 254) suggests that the figures of the upper register were painted later than those in the lower register, because their line is coarser and the human forms are different. I believe that the upper and lower registers are in the same style and probably executed at the same time. The reason the line in the drawing of the upper register looks "coarser" is because it is not "bolstered" from within by flat areas of color as is the line in the lower register. But both the line and human figures in the two registers are the same.

were the rulers of Tilantongo at the time of the Spanish conquest, and the latest date in Codex Selden is 1556. In the second place, the figural style of these three manuscripts is also the predominant style of such early Colonial Mixtec manuscripts as the Lienzo of Yolotepec (Fig. 67),[45] the Lienzo of Philadelphia,[46] and the Genealogy of Tlazultepec (Fig. 30).[47]

The Lienzo of Yolotepec, now in the Museum of Natural History in New York, was removed from the local archive of the town of Santiago Amoltepec in southern Oaxaca in 1889.[48] Alfonso Caso suggests that it may have been drawn in the first half of the sixteenth century, because the only distinctly European motif in the lienzo is a church near the center of the manuscript.[49] Otherwise, the style of the lienzo is very close to that of Bodley-Selden-Becker II.

The Lienzo of Philadelphia, now in the University of Pennsylvania Museum, is also conservative in style and is also considered to have been executed in the first half of the sixteenth century. The only obviously European motif in this lienzo is a type of arrow used to represent the day-sign Reed; this arrow is illustrated on the left side *(a)* of Drawing 1, below. The non-native Reed sign shows the feathers at the butt of the arrow as triangular appendages marked with horizontal lines that indicate the feather's barbs. This typically European method of representing an arrow occurs in none of the pre-Conquest manuscripts; and in the Lienzo of Philadelphia, this type of arrow appears side by side with the usual native style of arrow, which is illustrated on the right side *(b)* of Drawing 1.

DRAWING 1: "Reed" Signs in the Lienzo of Philadelphia
a, European-influenced sign; *b*, Native sign

Alfonso Caso has suggested that this lienzo is from the Coixtlahuaca-Tlaxiaco-Texupan region of the Mixteca Alta.[50] Ross Parmenter has attempted to pinpoint its provenience more precisely and has presented the convincing hypothesis that the lienzo is from the region south of

Tlaxiaco. As Parmenter has observed, the major place sign in the Lienzo of Philadelphia and also one of its dates are found in the Lienzo Córdova-Castellanos, which is said to be from San Esteban Atlatlahuca, a town about 15 miles south of Tlaxiaco.[51]

The Genealogy of Tlazultepec (Fig. 30), in the Archivo General de la Nación in Mexico City, was drawn in 1597 for the specific purpose of demonstrating one litigant's claim to the *cacicazgo* or native rulership of the town of Tlazultepec in the Mixteca Alta.[52] The Tlazultepec Genealogy is an important document because it demonstrates that—at least in one section of the Mixteca—the figural style of Bodley-Selden-Becker II persisted until the end of the sixteenth century. By 1597 this figural style had lost the taut frame line that is so characteristic of pre-Conquest style, but the human figures of the Tlazultepec manuscript retain all the essential features of this native substyle, including the one-toed foot.

Thus we see that the Bodley-Selden-Becker II style must have been one of the prevailing Mixtec styles at the time of the Spanish conquest and that it persisted in at least one region of the Mixteca Alta until the end of the sixteenth century. It may not have been the only Mixtec style contemporary with the arrival of the Spaniards, and its distribution in the Mixteca cannot as yet be charted with any accuracy. When it is possible to determine the provenience of the three major examples of this style—Codices Bodley, Selden, and Becker II—we may be able to link this style with a specific region of western Oaxaca.

Sánchez Solís

Codex Sánchez Solís is a genealogical manuscript painted on both sides of the screenfold, with pages 1–17 on one side and pages 18–32 on the other. Page 2 presents a mythological-origin scene; pages 3 and 4 contain a procession of eight persons bearing royal insignia;[53] and pages 5–30

45 Alfonso Caso, "El Lienzo de Yolotepec," *Memoria de el Colegio Nacional*, Vol. XIII-4 (1958), 41–55, includes black-and-white photographs of the lienzo and a commentary on its content.

46 Alfonso Caso, "El Lienzo de Filadelfia," *Homenaje a Fernando Márquez-Miranda* (Madrid-Seville, 1964), 135–44, includes a black-and-white photograph of the lienzo, as does Ross Parmenter, "Break-Through on the 'Lienzo of Filadelfia,'" *Expedition*, Vol. VIII-2 (1966), 14–22. Both studies discuss the iconography of the lienzo.

47 Ronald Spores, "The Genealogy of Tlazultepec: A Sixteenth Century Mixtec Manuscript," *Southwestern Journal of Anthropology*, Vol. XX-1 (1964), 15–31, includes a drawing of the manuscript, as well as an analysis of the Genealogy.

48 Caso, "Lienzo de Yolotepec," *Memoria de el Colegio Nacional*, Vol. XIII-4 (1958), 41. Amoltepec is located 97°30' W. and 16°36' N. The "Yolotepec" referred to in the lienzo's title is probably Santa María Yolotepec, 97°30' W. and 16°51' N.

49 *Ibid.*, 41–42.

50 "El Lienzo de Filadelfia," *Homenaje a Fernando Márquez-Miranda* (Madrid-Seville, 1964), 139.

51 "Break-Through on the 'Lienzo of Filadelfia,'" *Expedition*, VIII-2 (1966), 21. The present location of the original of the Lienzo Córdova-Castellanos is unknown. According to Antonio Peñafiel, who calls the manuscript "Codex Javier Córdova," it belonged in 1905 to Córdova, the *jefe político* of Cholula, who had obtained it in the town of San Esteban Atlatlahuca, located 17°5' N., 97°10' W. Two copies of the lienzo have been published, one by Peñafiel (*Ciudades coloniales y capitales de la República Mexicana*, vol. V: *Las cinco ciudades coloniales de Puebla* [Mexico, 1914], Plates 24–32) which includes a drawing of the entire lienzo, as well as details of each of the place signs. In the text accompanying these plates (*ibid.*, 31–34), Peñafiel describes the contents of the lienzo and translates the Nahuatl glosses that set forth the names of the thirty place signs which are arranged around its border. Peñafiel's description was also published in an earlier article ("El códice mixteco precortesiano Javier Córdova y un antiguo plano de San Andrés Cholula," *Revista Histórica Mexicana*, Vol. I [1907], 75–80) which lacks the drawings of the lienzo. A second copy was published by William Gates as *Codex Abraham Castellanos*, Maya Society Publication No. 5 (Baltimore, 1931). The Gates copy was a redrawing of photographs of a tracing made by Nicolás León; the León tracing is now in the Garrett Collection at Princeton University. The background of the Gates publication is discussed in: Ross Parmenter, "The Identification of Lienzo A: A Tracing in the Latin American Library of Tulane University," Tulane University, Middle American Research Institute, *Philological and Documentary Studies*, Vol. II-5 (1970).

52 Tlazultepec is present-day San Agustín Tlacotepec, located 17°12' N. and 97°28' W. The genealogy is bound with the documents concerning the litigation in AGN, Ramo de Tierras, 59–2.

53 The ceremony known as "offering of the royal insignia" was first identified by Alfonso Caso, "El Mapa de Teozacoalco," *Cuadernos Americanos*, Año VIII, No. 5 (1949), 160, 162.

each contain a seated royal couple.[54] Sánchez Solís utilizes a two-register format rather than arranging its scenes in a traditional meander pattern. The royal couple occupies the lower two-thirds of the page, and on the pages which contain subsidiary genealogical information (6, 10, 15–17, 20–21, and 26–31), these data are placed in the upper third of the page, and the human figures are about half the size of the principal couple below.

Although many features of Sánchez Solís may be related to manuscripts in the other three style groups, its figural style is distinctive, and for this reason I am inclined to place the manuscript in a class by itself. The human figures of the principal rulers in Sánchez Solís are unusually large and boldly delineated. Most of the female figures and some of the male figures wear prominent necklaces attached around the neck with wide straps (Fig. 6f). These necklaces consist of the pictorial signs which represent the personal names of individuals. The depiction of personal names as a necklace is not common in the other historical manuscripts, but it is very typical of Sánchez Solís.[55]

All of the seated female figures except one on page 30 of the Codex are shown in a kneeling position, with their legs tucked underneath their torsos (as in Fig. 6f). This pose is also assumed by some of the female figures on the front of Nuttall and on both sides of Codex Vienna, but in the latter manuscripts it is not predominant and alternates with the traditional Mixtec seated posture, in which the female figure sits with her legs placed in front of her (as in Fig. 6a). The kneeling pose of seated women so prevalent in Sánchez Solís is also typical of the post-Conquest style in the Valley of Mexico; in fact, it is sometimes designated as the "Aztec woman pose."[56]

The method of representing the human foot and toes in Sánchez Solís is most similar to that seen on the back of Vienna. That is, the toes are shown as a row of small white squares, and the lines separating the squares extend upward into the flesh-colored section of the foot (Fig. 6f). However, the feet of some of the barefoot figures on the Vienna reverse contain a small projecting knob to indicate the spur of the heel, whereas the heels of barefoot figures in Sánchez Solís are smooth and rounded.

With one exception in Sánchez Solís (on page 15 of the Codex), when the women's skirts are not left blank but painted, they are decorated with a red pattern of criss-crossed lines with interspersed dots. This type of pattern is also seen on the skirts of 21 of the 69 female figures on the Vienna reverse, as well as in the blouses of two other women.

The hills that appear in connection with place signs in Sánchez Solís (as in Fig. 38) have a similar kind of criss-cross pattern in black, although the patterning of the hills is bolder, the lines are wavy rather than straight, and they enclose a small circle instead of a dot. This "hill" pattern is also used in two plots of earth on the front of Vienna (pages 13 and 20) and in five place signs in Codex Selden (pages 1–I, 2–II, 4–II, 6–III, 16–II). Again, as was the case of the "kneeling" female pose, this criss-cross patterning of the hills is a feature that is found occasionally in other manuscripts, but is a distinctive trait of Sánchez Solís. And again, this manner of hill-patterning seems to be more characteristic of several post-Conquest manuscripts from the Valley of Mexico, particularly Codex Xolotl, a cartographic document from Texcoco. Codex Xolotl consists of ten maps of the region within and around the Valley of Mexico at different periods of time, and the hills of the many place signs in this Codex all have a criss-cross pattern similar to that in Sánchez Solís.[57]

Although Codex Sánchez Solís is essentially Mixtec in style, it exhibits in greater quantity than the other Mixtec historical manuscripts details which are common to Valley of Mexico manuscripts of the early Colonial period. This suggests that Sánchez Solís is from a Mixtec region that was transitional between the Mixteca and the Valley of Mexico. This hypothesis is, I believe, confirmed by an interpretation of some of the glosses on Sánchez Solís that refer to place signs. The manuscript was annotated with Mixtec glosses, apparently by several different hands, at an unknown date (or dates) in the Colonial period. A translation of the glosses that accompany two of the place signs which appear most frequently in Sánchez Solís indicates that the Codex may be from the Mixteca Baja region in northern Oaxaca and southern Puebla. The place sign of Acatlán in southern Puebla appears four times (pages 16, 20, 23 and 24), or more frequently than any other place sign. The place sign of San Pedro and San Pablo Tequixtepec, located in one of the northernmost sections of Oaxaca, northeast of Huajuapan, appears twice (pages 22 and 25).[58] It is thus reasonable to assume that at least the section in which these signs appear—pages 16 through 25—deals with genealogies of the Mixteca Baja, the important Mixtec region which links the remainder of the Mixteca with central Puebla, Tlaxcala, and the Valley of Mexico. According to the *Relación Geográfica* of Acatlán written in 1581, the native rulers of this town were said to have descended from royal lineages of the Valley of Mexico, and at the time of the Spanish conquest. Moctezuma was considered to be the supreme ruler of this region.[59]

A further analysis of the Sánchez Solís place signs and their accompanying glosses will probably substantiate a Mixteca Baja provenience for this manuscript. At the present time, both the style of Sánchez Solís and the prominence it gives to the place signs of two towns in the south-

---

[54] A royal couple also undoubtedly appeared on page 31, but the two figures have been completely scraped off.

[55] The various conventions of representing personal names are discussed below, pp. 27–29.

[56] Donald Robertson, "Los manuscritos religiosos mixtecos," *ICA* XXXV, Vol. I (Mexico, 1964), 430; Caso, *Bodley*, 14.

[57] Charles E. Dibble's commentary on Codex Xolotl (*Códice Xolotl*, Mexico, 1951) includes black-and-white photographs of the Codex, which is extremely important for its genealogical as well as its cartographic content.

[58] The place signs of Acatlán and Tequixtepec are discussed in more detail below, pp. 61, 76–77.

[59] *PNE* V, 59.

ern Puebla-northern Oaxaca region seem to indicate that this manuscript is from the Mixteca Baja.[60]

DATING

Two scholars have offered hypotheses as to the possible dates of execution of the historical manuscripts. George Kubler has divided the manuscripts into two groups, a pre-1350 group which includes Nuttall, Colombino-Becker I, and the front of Vienna, and a post-1350 group which includes Bodley, Selden, and the back of Vienna. Although the last year-date that occurs on the back of Vienna is 1357, he guesses that the differences in style between the front and back of Vienna represent "widely separated historical stages," and that "the reverse of the Vienna manuscript may be regarded as a late recension of early subject matter."[61]

Alfonso Caso believes that Colombino-Becker I is earlier than any of the other Mixtec manuscripts and may have been painted in the thirteenth century. The front of Vienna may also be very early, but the reverse cannot be earlier than 1357. Nuttall was painted about 1330, Bodley in 1520, and Selden in 1556.[62]

Kubler's and Caso's conclusions on the chronology of this group of manuscripts are rather similar, because both are based on the *terminus ad quem* of the latest date or event that occurs in the painted narrative of the manu-

scripts. In the case of strictly genealogical manuscripts (such as Bodley, Selden, and the front of Nuttall), this method of dating seems feasible, because it is likely that the native ruler who commissioned the manuscript would be seeking a pictorial record that culminated in his generation or that of his children. However, in the case of Colombino-Becker I, which is devoted to the biography of an eleventh-century hero, it is always possible that this manuscript was a much later copy of an earlier manuscript or was merely telling a story that was centuries old at the time the manuscript was painted. But these eventualities are difficult to determine now, and at the moment we must use the latest date represented in the manuscript and its style characteristics as guides to the approximate date of its execution.

Neither Kubler nor Caso includes Becker II or Sánchez Solís in his discussion of dating. Both manuscripts would undoubtedly be placed in Kubler's post-1350 group, and I would tend to place them in a 1450–1550 category, because both are related stylistically to manuscripts of a known sixteenth-century date. As we have seen, Becker II is closest in style to Bodley and Selden, both of which were painted in the sixteenth century, and Sánchez Solís shares several characteristics with early Colonial manuscripts from the Valley of Mexico. I would, in addition, agree with Kubler that the Vienna reverse should be in the post-1350 group, and perhaps at least a century later than its latest date of 1357, not only because of its unsure draftsmanship and the contrast between its style and that of the Vienna obverse, but also because of the features it shares with Sánchez Solís: the representation of the toes of the human foot, the prevalence of criss-cross patterns in the women's skirts, and the consistent representation of numeral dots as concentric circles.

---

[60] My hypotheses concerning the provenience of Sánchez Solís were first set forth in: "Codex Sánchez Solís: A Manuscript from the Mixteca Baja?" presented at the XXXVII Congress of Americanists, Mar del Plata, Argentina, September 9, 1966. This paper will appear in a forthcoming number of *Oaxaca Notes*, published by the Instituto de Estudios Oaxaqueños under the editorship of John Paddock.

[61] Kubler, *The Art and Architecture of Ancient America* (Baltimore, 1962), 100–102.

[62] These hypotheses on dates appear in Caso, *Colombino*, 46, 144.

III

THE PICTORIAL CONVENTIONS OF THE MIXTEC HISTORIES

Because of the studies of Alfonso Caso, Herbert J. Spinden, and other scholars, the pictorial conventions in the historical manuscripts are now fairly clear. Once these pictorial conventions are understood, it is possible to "read" the Mixtec historical manuscripts in much the same manner as it is possible for someone who is completely familiar with the everyday traditions of Western civilization to "read" contemporary comic strips and cartoons.

For example, a throne-room incident depicted in a cartoon from *Punch* (Fig. 2) is very effectively related by the use of costumes and gestures. The roles of all three characters in the cartoon can be easily identified by anyone who knows the traditional iconography of European royalty. The person who wears a crown and a robe decorated with ermine and who sits ensconced in a large chair with an elaborately carved crest is obviously a king. The slim figure in pied costume and a cap hung with tassels or bells is the court jester, whose principal duty is to amuse the king. The bulky figure wearing a large black hood and carrying an ax is the palace executioner. The story is told in a sequence of six pictures, principally by means of gestures. In the second scene the jester raises one finger to his mouth to express his doubt and apprehension. In the fourth scene the king places a finger on his cheek which indicates he is thinking. In the fifth scene one leg and one arm are raised to illustrate that he is convulsed with laughter.

Many of the pictorial conventions of the cartoon from *Punch* would be unintelligible to someone from a culture completely alien to our own. So, too, the story told in the Mixtec historical manuscripts is often difficult to understand until we know the meaning of their pictorial conventions. What the Mixtec manuscripts have in common with the *Punch* cartoon is their mode of story-telling. The story is conveyed entirely through a sequence of pictures, without the use of a written alphabetic language.

But both the intent and content of Mixtec manuscripts are very different from the intent and content of comic strips and cartoons. The Mixtec histories were not intended to amuse or to relate pleasant anecdotes about the capriciousness of kings in general; they were intended to record the genealogies of named rulers from specific towns. Unlike cartoons, which are a mass-produced form of pictorial communication, available and understandable to all newspaper and magazine readers. Mixtec manuscript

painting was an art of the ruling class. The pictorial histories were painted by and for the ruling families, to describe events participated in only by persons of rank. In addition, the art of pictographic writing utilized in these manuscripts was practiced by a very few painters and was understood by a few specially trained persons who had memorized the stories and had been taught the pictorial conventions used to depict them.

According to Padre Burgoa, the painted manuscripts were executed by the sons of noble families who were chosen to be priests and were taught from childhood the art of pictographic writing and the stories and legends to be painted. Burgoa also states that the historical manuscripts were explained by Indians who were learned in the stories of the lineages and their achievements, and he mentions that the painted screenfolds were placed around the rooms of nobility as decoration.[1]

In intent as well as content, the Mixtec pictorial histories are closer to the late-eleventh-century Bayeux Tapestry (Fig. 3) than to twentieth-century cartoons or comic strips. The Tapestry is a narrow strip of cloth over 230 feet long on which is embroidered a detailed narrative of the events leading up to the invasion of England in 1066 by William the Conqueror and the battle of Hastings, in which King Harold of England is killed.[2] The Bayeux Tapestry, in common with the Mixtec historical manuscripts, is a linear pictorial narrative of important events participated in by ruling families. In addition, the Tapestry is one of the principal extant descriptions of the events it portrays. It was embroidered in the last three decades of the eleventh century—that is, not more than a generation later than the battle it depicts.

Very few reliable written accounts of the Norman Conquest have survived, and the Tapestry is thus one of the basic sources of information on this important event. Similarly, the oral traditions on which the Mixtec pictorial manuscripts were based have survived only in a few fragmentary legends, and the manuscripts themselves are

---

[1] Burgoa, *Palestra historial*, 210; *Geográfica descripción*, I, 288.

[2] The basic monograph on the Bayeux Tapestry, and the one on which this discussion is based, is Sir Frank Stenton *et al.*, *The Bayeux Tapestry: A Comprehensive Survey*, 2nd ed. (London, 1965), which contains over a hundred black-and-white photographic details of the Tapestry, as well as thirteen details in color. The Tapestry is now in the former Bishop's Palace in Bayeux, France. It measures 230′ 10¾″ in total length and 19¾″ in height.

the most important documents on Mixtec history of the pre-Conquest period. A local point of view is evidenced in the story of the Norman Conquest told by the Tapestry, and a regional viewpoint may also be noted in the Mixtec histories, as for example in Codex Colombino, which appears to present a Coastal version of the life of the eleventh-century ruler 8-Deer. In the case of the Tapestry, the point of view is that of Normandy, and the prominence given to the Norman town of Bayeux and to its bishop suggests that the work may have been commissioned by this bishop. Because of this regional point of view, several of the scenes in the Tapestry cannot now be interpreted, since they represent local details of the story that are not related in the other sources on the Norman invasion.[3]

Unlike Mixtec manuscripts in which the pictorial narrative follows a meander pattern set forth by red guidelines, the narrative of the Tapestry occupies the large central band of the horizontal strip of cloth and proceeds left to right on a straight line. At the top and bottom are narrow decorative borders, which contain animals and birds that illustrate popular fables, genre scenes such as hunting and bearbaiting, and footnotes to the battle scenes. The scenes represented in the large central register are often separated by vertical accents such as stylized trees (Fig. 3b) or buildings (Fig. 3a). In several instances the central band is divided into two registers, as for example in the final scene of the Tapestry (Fig. 3b), in which a thick line suggesting the outline of a hill separates a group of fleeing Englishmen from the scene below, which shows horsemen with whips apparently pursuing a man who is entangled in vines. The fate of the Englishmen who did not escape is depicted in the lower border, which contains decapitated bodies and a truncated figure whose arm has been chopped off.

The pictorial narrative of the Bayeux Tapestry is supplemented by Latin glosses which are embroidered along the top of the central register. These glosses merely relate the skeletal outline of the story and name the principal persons and places depicted. It is the series of pictorial scenes which relates the story in detail, and in common with Mixtec manuscripts, this story is conveyed in part through pictorial conventions. In the Tapestry, for example, Englishmen are distinguished from Normans by their hairdress. The hair of the Englishmen is usually long, and the back of the neck is unshaven, while the hair of the Normans is usually very short in back. In addition, many of the Englishmen are shown with moustaches, whereas the Normans are always clean-shaven. Towns are represented in an iconic manner by one building or complex of buildings with no attempt to present a landscape view of the entire town or its site.[4] For example, the town

of Dol on the Norman Coast (Fig. 3a) is depicted as a stylized castle which rests on a mound whose interior is decorated with red and green scallops and a pair of heraldic birds.

One major difference between the Tapestry and Mixtec manuscripts is that the Tapestry includes many persons who are not named and who function as foot soldiers, cavalry troops, and royal attendants, in contrast to the Mixtec manuscripts, in which virtually every person is accompanied by a name and is either a nobleman or an important priest. In the Mixtec histories there are no genre figures, no spear holders, no bystanders. When a conquest is illustrated in the Mixtec manuscripts, only the figure of the ruler who effects the conquest is shown, as in Fig. 51a, which depicts 8-Deer's conquest of the town of Acatepec. Occasionally a ruler may be accompanied by one or two other nobles who function as allies, but he is never shown with a contingent of soldiers. The event is merely recorded, showing the conquering ruler, the sign of the town conquered, and sometimes the ruler of the conquered town as a prisoner. The Mixtec histories do not portray the action or vicissitudes of an actual battle, as the Tapestry does with its rows of charging Norman invaders and falling English defenders. In contrast to the continuous, overlapping, cinematographic battle scenes in the Tapestry, the Mixtec portrayal of conquest is more analogous to a still photograph of one important person at one instant in time.

But the major factor which differentiates Mixtec manuscripts from both the Bayeux Tapestry and cartoons is that the Mixtec histories utilize a partial system of logographic writing. That is, many of the configurations in Mixtec manuscripts are not merely pictures, but logograms—signs which represent one or more words in the Mixtec language.[5] The names of persons and places which appear in the Latin glosses of the Bayeux Tapestry, and which might appear in placards or in speech balloons in cartoons and comic strips, are represented by pictorial signs in the Mixtec manuscripts.

The purpose of the discussion which follows is to examine how the pictorial conventions of the Mixtec histories tell their stories and to determine, where possible, what relationship exists between these conventions and the Mix-

---

[3] For example, one scene that cannot be interpreted shows an unidentified clergyman reaching for a woman named Aelfgyva (*ibid.*, 10; plate 19). The accompanying Latin gloss says "Where a clerical and Aelfgyva" (*ubi unus clericus et Aelfgyva*), but neither of these persons figures in the other accounts of the Norman Conquest.

[4] The schematic trees and buildings in the Tapestry were offensive to the nineteenth-century sensibilities of the English landscape painter John

Constable, and he compared them derogatorily to Mexican painting. In a series of lectures on landscape delivered in 1833, Constable cites as a prime example of unrefined landscape in medieval art, "the Bayeux tapestry, which is indeed little better than a Mexican performance." (C. R. Leslie, *Memoirs of the Life of John Constable, R.A.* [London, 1937], 376.) The "Mexican performances" seen by Constable were probably the color drawings of Mexican manuscripts in volume I of Lord Kingsborough's *Antiquities of Mexico*, which was published in London in 1831 and which includes two of the pre-Conquest Mixtec histories: Codices Bodley and Selden.

[5] The best general discussion of logograms, their position in the development of writing systems and their use in various languages, is in: I. J. Gelb, *A Study of Writing*, rev. ed. (Chicago, 1963), 65ff., 99–107 *et passim*. Gelb also discusses logograms in some detail in "Review of Marcel Cohen, *La grande invention de l'écriture et son évolution*," *Language*, Vol. XXXVIII–2 (1962), 207–11. Some scholars of the history of writing use the term "ideogram" rather than "logogram" to describe this type of pictorial sign, but the latter term seems to me to be better, because it clearly denotes that the pictorial signs are based on words.

tec language. As we shall see, some of the configurations, such as those that represent birth and death, appear to have no relationship to the Mixtec language but are pictorial conventions only. Others, such as calendrical names and dates, are logograms, but can be understood as pictorial signs without reference to the language. Still others such as the signs of place names, often called "place signs," are logograms which cannot be understood until their specific pictorial motifs are associated with specific words in the Mixtec language. The difficulties involved in interpreting the place signs in the Mixtec histories will be discussed in detail in Chapters IV and V.

DATES

In common with other historical-genealogical records, the Mixtec manuscripts set forth dates of important events. Both years and days are represented by a standard vocabulary of pictorial signs.

Years

The presence of a year date in the Mixtec histories is indicated by an interlaced "A-O" sign, accompanied by one of the four day-signs which function as "year bearers" and by a numerical coefficient (Fig. 4). In Mixtec manuscripts, as in those of the Valley of Mexico, the four year-bearer signs are House, Rabbit, Reed, and Flint, and these four signs combine with thirteen numerals, from one to thirteen, in a fifty-two-year cycle. Thus any given Mixtec date may occur once every fifty-two years. For example, 1970 is a Nine-Rabbit year in the Mixtec calendar, but so were 1918, 1866, 1814, and so on, at fifty-two-year intervals.

Wigberto Jiménez Moreno was the first person to correlate the Mixtec calendar with Christian chronology,[6] and Alfonso Caso has correlated the dates in the Mixtec historical codices with Christian calendar years.[7] This correlation was extremely important because it demonstrated that the story told in the group of historical manuscripts under discussion covers almost 900 years, from 692, the first legible date in Codex Bodley, to 1556, the latest date in Codex Selden. Most of the earlier studies of this group of manuscripts considered the events recorded to have taken place in the fifteenth century, and utilized the Aztec correlation of year dates with Christian chronology.[8] The latter

correlation differs from the Mixtec correlation by 12 years. For example, the year 1519 is a One-Reed year in the Aztec calendar and a Thirteen-Reed year in the Mixtec calendar.

As can be seen in Fig. 4, the A-O year sign as it is represented in the Mixtec pictorial documents has several variant forms.[9] The "O" may be either an oval or a rectangle, and the apex of the "A" may be flat or have a rounded point. As Alfonso Caso has observed, these forms are used interchangeably within the same manuscript, and the variations appear to have no significance.[10]

The year-bearer signs may appear at the top of the A-O sign, or within the center of the sign itself.[11] The base of the A-O configuration is often filled in and enclosed by a fringe-like border. An eye, in one case explicitly shown to be the eye of an owl (Fig. 4b), may appear on the projecting "O" form, and this eye is sometimes surmounted by a tuft of feathers. If the year sign has a trapezoidal appendage above the "O," as it does in Codex Colombino (Fig. 4f), then the eye-feathers motifs are placed on this trapezoidal frame.[12] Although the A-O year sign and its variants appear in sculpture from many regions of Middle America,[13] the appearance of this sign in pictorial manuscripts seems to be restricted to documents from the Mixtec and Mixtec-related regions of southern Mexico.[14]

What the A-O year sign may represent is a sun-ray sign bound by a rope. The "A" section of the sign resembles in its general shape the Mixtec-Aztec sun-ray motif, and the "O" that is interlaced with the "A" may symbolize a rope that binds the sun ray.[15] This hypothesis seems to be con-

---

[6] "Signos cronográficos del códice y calendario mixteco," in Wigberto Jiménez Moreno and Salvador Mateos Higuera, *Códice de Yanhuitlán* (Mexico, 1940), 69–76.

[7] "El Mapa de Teozacoalco," *Cuadernos Americanos*, Año VIII, No. 5 (1949), *passim*; "Base para la sincronología mixteca y cristiana," *Memoria de el Colegio Nacional*, Vol. VI–6 (1951), 49–66; "El calendario mixteco," *Historia mexicana*, Vol. V–20 (1956), 481–97. Caso's *Bodley* and *Selden* also contain lists of the dates that appear in these codices and the correlation of these dates with Christian calendar years. The "Base para la sincronología" study is accompanied by a table which gives the Mixtec equivalents of Christian years from 2 B.C. to A.D. 2026. Unless otherwise specified, all date correlations made in this study will be based on this table.

[8] As, for example, Nuttall, *Codex Nuttall* commentary; Clark, *Story of "Eight Deer"*; Spinden, "Indian Manuscripts of Southern Mexico," *Annual Report of the Smithsonian Institution, 1933* (Washington, 1935). Richard C. E. Long ("The Zouche Codex," *Journal of the Royal Anthropological Institute of Great Britain and Ireland*, Vol. LVI [1926], 242) postulated that the events on the front of Nuttall begin "about the end

of the tenth century" or perhaps earlier, but did not attempt to correlate specific dates in Nuttall with Christian calendar years.

[9] Other examples and further discussion of the year sign in Mixtec manuscripts appear in: Caso, "Calendario mixteco," *Historia mexicana*, Vol. V–20 (1956), 491, 493, and *Bodley*, 15–16; and Rafael García Granados, "Observaciones sobre los códices pre-hispánicos de México y reparo que estas sugieren acerca de su clasificación," *El México Antiguo*, Vol. V, 1–2 (1940), 43–44.

[10] Caso, *Bodley*, 15.

[11] As García Granados ("Observaciones sobre los códices . . ." *El México Antiguo*, Vol. V, 1–2 [1940], 43–44) observes, the latter convention appears only in Codices Nuttall and Vienna.

[12] In the historical manuscripts, the year sign with an attached trapezoidal form appears only in Codex Colombino (García Granados, "Observaciones sobre los códices . . ." *El México Antiguo*, Vol. V, 1–2 [1940], 43–44). In Codex Borgia, a ritual manuscript of undetermined provenience, the year sign appears once, on page 52, with the trapezoidal form taking the place of the interlaced "O."

[13] José García Payón, "El símbolo del año en el México antiguo," *El México Antiguo*, Vol. IV, 7–8 (1939), 241–53.

[14] The A-O year sign appears in two non-Mixtec manuscripts that supposedly come from the Cuicatec-speaking region of northeastern Oaxaca: Codex Porfirio Díaz and Codex Fernández Leal. (The former is illustrated in Alfredo Chavero, *Antigüedades mexicanas*, Vol. II [Mexico, 1892]; the latter in John Barr Tompkins, "Codex Fernández Leal," *The Pacific Art Review*, II [1942], 39–59.) Both of these manuscripts use year-bearer signs that are different from the Mixtec-Aztec year-bearers; instead of House, Rabbit, Reed and Flint, they use Wind, Deer, Grass and Movement. An unpublished "Map of Ecatepec and Huiziltepec," supposedly from southern Puebla, also utilizes the A-O year sign. This map is now in the Charles Ratton collection in Paris.

[15] The use of a rope motif in year signs throughout Middle America is discussed by Alfonso Caso, "Calendario y escritura en Xochicalco," *RMEA*, Vol. XVIII (1962), 49–79; and by H. B. Nicholson, "The Significance of the 'Looped Cord' Year Symbol in Pre-Hispanic Mexico: An Hypothesis," *Estudios de Cultura Nahuatl*, Vol. VI (1966), 135–48.

firmed by one of the boundary signs in the 1771 Map of Xoxocotlán (Fig. 162), in which the A–O sign is described as a rope. Within the hill at the left side of the group of hills at the top of this map is an A–O year sign, and the Nahuatl gloss that accompanies this sign is *mecatepeque* or "rope hill," while the accompanying Mixtec gloss is *yucu yoho* or "hill of the rope."

Days

The days in Mixtec codices are expressed by a combination of twenty day-signs (illustrated in Chart 1) and thirteen numerals, one through thirteen. It has not yet been possible to correlate the days in Mixtec manuscripts with specific days in the Christian calendar.

The day signs in Mixtec and Valley of Mexico manuscripts are represented in the same manner,[16] and both the signs and their numerical coefficients have counterparts in the Mixtec and Nahuatl languages (listed in Charts 1 and 2). In Nahuatl, the everyday vocabulary of the language is used to designate calendrical signs. For example, the word *ce* for "one" and *acatl* for "reed" are combined as *ce acatl* to indicate the day or year One-Reed. In the Mixtec language, however, a special set of words is used for the calendrical signs, whether day-signs or year-bearers, and for the numbers that are affixed to these signs. The day or year One-Reed in Mixtec is not *ee ndoo* (*ee* = "one" and *ndoo* = "reed" in the normal Mixtec vocabulary), but *ca huiyo*.

The special Mixtec vocabulary for calendrical signs and their accompanying numerals has been compiled from Mixtec glosses written on post-Conquest pictorial documents and from the texts of the *Relaciones Geográficas* from the Mixtec-speaking region of Oaxaca. In 1928 Alfonso Caso assembled the Mixtec calendrical vocabulary from the *Relaciones Geográficas*.[17] In 1940 Jiménez Moreno included the Mixtec glosses from Codex Sierra that refer to year signs and their numerals in his study on the correlation of the Mixtec calendar.[18] Barbro Dahlgren published a more complete list of the calendrical vocabulary in 1954, adding the information given in the glosses of the Lienzo of Natívitas.[19] In 1956 Alfonso Caso presented still further data on this special vocabulary; he utilized the sources mentioned above, plus the glosses on the Map of Xochitepec and Map No. 36.[20]

For the sake of simplicity, and at the risk of oversimplification, in Chart 1 of the day signs I have reduced the variations of calendrical vocabulary listed by Dahlgren and Caso to one version per day sign, with the exception of the day sign House, for which two very different versions appear within one manuscript, the Lienzo of Natívitas. In this chart I have attempted to place the words of the special calendrical vocabulary in the same dialect as that of the Alvarado Mixtec dictionary in order to compare the calendrical vocabulary with the normal words in the Mixtec language for the day-sign motifs.

In a few cases the day-sign names are similar to the normal vocabulary words: *tuta* and *nduta* for "water" suggest mere differences in dialect, and *chi* for the day-sign Wind may be an abbreviated form of *tachi*, the standard word for "wind." Also, one of the words for "deer" in some dialects of Mixtec is *sacuaa*, which is very close to the *cuaa* which means "deer" in the calendrical language.[21] But most of the names for day-signs are very different from the normal vocabulary, and the special vocabulary may, as Dahlgren has suggested, represent an archaic form of Mixtec.[22] For example, the names of two day-signs—*mahu(a)* for Death and *mau*, one of the words for House—begin with *m*, one of the least common phonemes in present-day Mixtec. In addition, *huaco*, the day-name Flower, is a word that occurs very infrequently in Mixtec and may be a loan word. To my knowledge, the only two occurrences of *huaco* in the normal Mixtec

---

[16] A comparison of the variations in representing the twenty day signs in the pictorial manuscripts is presented in Rafael García Granados, "Estudio comparativo de los signos cronográficos en los códices prehispánicos de Méjico," *ICA* XXVII, Vol. I (Mexico, 1942), 419–69.

[17] *Las estelas zapotecas* (Mexico, 1928), 69–73. The *Relaciones Geográficas* from which Caso compiled his list are published in *PNE* IV and V, and *RMEH* I and II.

[18] *Códice de Yanhuitlán*, 70, 75–note 16. Codex Sierra is published in: Nicolás León, *Códice Sierra* (Mexico, 1933). The manuscript is in the Academia de Bellas Artes in Puebla.

[19] *La mixteca*, 366–70. The Lienzo of Natívitas, a cartographic-genealogical document in the municipal archive of Santa María Natívitas (located 17°40′ N., 97°40′ W.), is unpublished. It belongs to the "Coixtlahuaca Group of Manuscripts" discussed in Appendix C.

[20] "Calendario mixteco," *Historia mexicana*, Vol. V–20 (1956), chart in front of p. 489. The Map of Xochitepec, in the National Museum in Copenhagen, is illustrated and discussed in Alfonso Caso, "El Mapa de Xochitepec," *ICA* XXXII (Copenhagen, 1958), 458–66. The glosses on

Map No. 36 (Fig. 21) are discussed in Appendix E of this book. These glosses were first transcribed by Vladamiro Rosado Ojeda, "Estudio del códice mixteco post-cortesiano Núm. 36," *Anales del INAH*, Vol. I (1945), 147–55.

[21] *Sacuaa* is given as the Mixtec word for "deer" in an unpublished vocabulary from the Mixteca Baja region of southern Puebla compiled by Josep Mariano Tupeus ("Vocabulario, doctrina y oraciones," on microfilm at Yale University Library); in an unpublished vocabulary from the eastern Guerrero region of the Mixteca Baja which is part of a manuscript by Fray Miguel de Villavicencio ("Arte, Prontuario, Vocabulario y Confesionario de la lengua mixteca," nineteenth-century copy by Francisco del Paso y Troncoso, Museo Nacional de Antropología, Archivo Histórico, Colección Antigua, no. 3–60 bis); and in a gloss accompanying a place sign with a deer in the 1686 Map of Xoxocotlán, a town in the Valley of Oaxaca (AGN-Tierras, 129–4). But *sacuaa* seems to be a less common word for "deer" than *idzu* or *isu*.

Concerning the unpublished manuscripts cited above: Josep Mariano Tupeus was a priest who lived in the city of Puebla, and he began compiling his manuscript in 1800. His "Vocabulario, doctrina y oraciones" consists of 148 pages and is comprised of the following sections: a Spanish-Mixtec vocabulary (pp. 3–84), instruction in the Christian faith (*doctrina*) in Mixtec (pp. 85–94), a section of the Gospel of St. John (*Evangelio*) in Mixtec (pp. 95–110), a procedure for conducting confessions (*confesionario*) in Spanish and Mixtec (pp. 111–20), and a group of prayers (*oraciones*) in Mixtec (pp. 121–48).

Fray Miguel de Villavicencio was associated with the Dominican monastery at Chila in southern Puebla in the seventeenth century. The nineteenth-century copy of his manuscript consists of ninety-four folios and contains the following sections: Spanish-Mixtec vocabulary (fol. 1–45/v, 59/v–60/v), a manual for administering the Sacraments in Spanish and Mixtec (fol. 46–55/v), instruction in the Christian faith (*doctrina*) in Mixtec (fol. 57–59/v), and a procedure for conducting confessions (*confesionario*) in Spanish and Mixtec (fol. 61–94/v). The original of the Villavicencio manuscript is reported to be in the Palafox Library in Puebla, in the "Gramáticas y Diccionarios" section, casilla no. 212.

The four known maps of the town of Xoxocotlán are discussed in Appendix F.

[22] *La mixteca*, 367.

CHART 1: The Twenty Day Signs

	Day Sign	Nahuatl	—————— Mixtec ——————	
			Normal Vocabulary (Alvarado Dictionary)	Special Day-Sign Vocabulary
ALLIGATOR		cipactli	coo yechi	quevui
WIND		ehecatl	tachi	chi
HOUSE	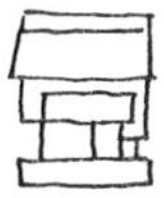	calli	huahi	cuau; mau
LIZARD		cuetzpallin	(ti)yechi	q(ue)
SERPENT		coatl	coo	yo
DEATH		miquiztli	ndeye, sihi	mahu(a)
DEER		mazatl	idzu, sacuaa	cuaa
RABBIT		tochtli	idzo	sayu
WATER		atl	nduta	tuta*
DOG		itzcuintli	ina	hua

*From glosses on Codex Sánchez Solís, pp. 15, 27.

CHART I. *(cont.)*

| | Day Sign | Nahuatl | — — — — — — — Mixtec — — — — — — — | |
			Normal Vocabulary (*Alvarado Dictionary*)	Special Day-Sign Vocabulary
MONKEY		ozomatli	codzo	ñuu
GRASS		malinalli	yucu	cuañe
REED		acatl	ndoo	huiyo
TIGER		ocelotl	cuiñe	huidzu
EAGLE		cuautli	yaha	sa
VULTURE		cozcaquautli	(ti)sii*	cuii
MOVEMENT		ollin	tnaa, nehe†	qhi
FLINT		tecpatl	yuchi	cusi
RAIN		quiauitl	dzavui	co
FLOWER		xochitl	ita	huaco

*From Anne Dyk, *Mixteco Texts* (*tíjìì* in the dialect of San Miguel el Grande, Oaxaca).
†"Earthquake" (*temblar la tierra*).

CHART 2: The Thirteen Numerals

	Nahuatl	Normal Vocabulary (Alvarado Dictionary)	Special Vocabulary (Lienzo of Natívitas)
1	ce	ee	ca, co
2	ome	vvui	ca, co, cu
3	yei	uni	co
4	naui	qmi, cumi	qui
5	macuilli	hoho	q
6	chicuace	iño	ñu
7	chicome	usa	sa
8	chicuei	una	na
9	chicunaui	ee	q
10	matlactli	usi	si
11	matlactli once	usi ee	si i
12	matlactli omome	usi vvui	ca
13	matlactli omei	usi uni	si

vocabulary are *tehuaco*, which means "guacamaya" or "macaw" (*te-* is an animal prefix), and the word for the *guaco* plant, given in Cornelia Mak's study of Mixtec medicinal plants as *yucù vácó* (*yucù* is a plant or shrub, and *vaco* is the equivalent of the *huaco* of the Alvarado dictionary dialect).[23] Both of these occurrences of *huaco* appear to be loan words, possibly but not necessarily from Nahuatl.[24]

The special Mixtec vocabulary for numeral prefixes of calendrical signs is presented in column 4 of Chart 2. Again, for the sake of comparison and simplicity, one word-list is used, that compiled from the glosses of the Lienzo of Natívitas, as transcribed by Alfonso Caso.[25] The Natívitas glosses include the words for all thirteen numerals, and the dialect is close to that of Alvarado's dictionary (column 3 of Chart 2).

In the case of seven of the thirteen numeral names, the calendrical form appears to be an abbreviation of the normal form:

[23] Mak, "Mixtec medical beliefs and practices," *América Indígena*, Vol. XIX–2 (1959), 147. *Guaco* is the popular name used to designate a number of plants of the genus *Mikania*.

[24] F. J. Santamaría's *Diccionario de mexicanismos* states that *guacamaya* comes from the Haitian *hucamaya*, but also states that on the Pacific coast of Mexico the word *guaco* may refer to the "pájaro vaquero" (*Herpetotheres cochinans*, L.), a large, falcon-like bird. It might be

profitable to compare the twenty Mixtec day-sign names with the same words in other languages of Middle America to ascertain possible connections and perhaps even a possible origin for the Mixtec calendrical system, but this type of comparison is outside the scope of this book.

[25] "Calendario mixteco," *Historia mexicana*, Vol. V–20 (1956).

4 – qmi	– q
6 – iño	– ñu
7 – usa	– sa
8 – una	– na
10 – usi	– si
11 – usi ee	– si i
13 – usi uni	– si

In the other six cases, the relationship between the two forms of numerals is less clear.

As can be seen in Chart 2, *ca* in the calendrical numerals may mean either 1, 2, or 12, and *si* may mean 10, 11, or 13. In spoken Mixtec these syllables were probably differentiated by tone, for Mixtec is a tone language with high, mid, and low tones which permits three possibilities for one syllable.[56]

In the pictorial manuscripts the numerals that accompany both the year and day signs are represented by multicolored contiguous dots which resemble circular beads on a string. Each dot represents a unit of one. When the numeral coefficient is higher than three, the rows of dots are sometimes divided into groups of two, three, four, or five, and a black line connects the subdivided groups of dots (Fig. 4 *a, d, f, g*). In Codex Sánchez Solís and on the back of Codex Vienna the numeral dots are always represented as concentric circles (Fig. 6 *e, f*); in the other historical manuscripts, the numerals 1 and, occasionally, 2 are represented with concentric circles (Fig. 5*b*).

The "dot" system of representing numerals is utilized in almost all the surviving manuscripts painted outside the Maya area in the post-Classic and early Colonial periods. In the earlier Classic period, the "bar and dot" system was the common method of numeration in the Maya area and at Teotihuacán in the Valley of Mexico and Monte Albán in Oaxaca. In the bar and dot system, a unit of five is expressed by a bar and a unit of one by a dot. The number 13, for example, is written with two bars and three dots, rather than with thirteen dots, as it is with the dot system. The origin of the less economical dot system and the reasons for its adoption in post-Classic manuscripts are unknown.[27]

Although, as we have seen, both the day signs and their numerical coefficients can be denoted in both the Mixtec and Nahuatl languages, the reading of calendrical signs is not dependent on language. For example, a day or year Two-Flint may be called *ome tecpatl* in Nahuatl and *ca cusi* in Mixtec, but in pictorial manuscripts from both Mixtec-speaking Oaxaca and Nahuatl-speaking Valley of Mexico the day or year Two-Flint is represented by an oval flint blade and two dots. These simple logographic day-signs function somewhat in the manner of the more complex and abstract Chinese logograms. The calendrical signs are immediately intelligible to speakers of widely different languages, such as Nahuatl and Mixtec, just as Chinese writing is an understandable means of communication for two persons who speak different and mutually unintelligible dialects of the Chinese language.

NAMES OF PERSONS

One of the purposes of the Mixtec historical manuscripts is the depiction of kinship ties between members of the ruling class, and each individual of this class is carefully identified and labeled with two types of names. The first of these is usually called a "calendrical name," and the second is referred to as a "personal name" or "nickname."

Calendrical Names

The calendrical name is the day on which a person was born. If such a system existed in our society, George Washington would be known as "22nd of February" and Abraham Lincoln as "12th of February." Calendrical names are represented in exactly the same manner as the day dates discussed immediately above—that is, the twenty day-signs combine with thirteen numerals. The special Mixtec vocabulary for day signs and numeral coefficients described above and listed in Charts 1 and 2 is also utilized for calendrical names. For example, the calendrical name of the hero 8-Deer in Mixtec would be *na cuaa*.

Personal Names or Nicknames

In addition to a calendrical name that is synonymous with his birthdate, each person of rank has a second name, usually called a "personal name" or "nickname." According to Herrera,[28] this name was given to a child at the age of seven by a priest, but how it was determined which personal name was to be ascribed to an individual is not known.

In the historical manuscripts the personal name may appear close to the figure of the person to whom it refers (Fig. 6*d*), or be attached to the figure by a black connecting line (Fig. 5*a*), or be held in the hand of the individual (Fig. 5*b*). Sometimes the representation of this name forms part of the person's costume (Fig. 6*a*), or is worn as a headdress (Fig. 5*c*), a helmet (Fig. 6*b*), or a necklace (Fig. 6*f*).

The conventions of depicting a personal name of an individual may vary from one manuscript to another. For example, a personage whose calendrical name is 5-Rain and whose personal name is "Smoking Mountain" is shown in Codex Nuttall wearing a smoking mountain as a helmet (Fig. 6*b*). In Colombino-Becker I the smoking mountain motif appears next to the figure of 5-Rain and is attached to him by means of a black line (Fig. 6*c*).

The personal names in the Mixtec historical manuscripts have not been examined in any detail as a system of nomenclature. A few personal names are associated exclusively with men, such as the "ballcourt" motif, which is the typical H-shaped plan of a Middle American ballcourt (Fig. 5*c*). One motif that occurs only in the names of

---

[26] Kenneth L. Pike discusses in detail the tonal system of the Mixtec dialect of San Miguel el Grande, Oaxaca, in *Tone Languages* (Ann Arbor, 1948), *passim*.

[27] Caso (*Selden*, 29; 76) suggests that four black bars that appear in connection with an offering in Selden 3–I are numeral bars. Similar bars appear in connection with offerings in three ritual manuscripts of the Borgia Group: Codices Cospi, Fejérváry-Mayer, and Laud. However, bar numerals are never used in the Mixtec and Borgia-Group manuscripts to accompany a day sign.

[28] *Historia general*, VI, 321.

women is the *quechquemitl*, a female garment worn by many of the women in the Mixtec pictorial histories (Fig. 6a). The *quechquemitl* is a square of cloth that is worn over the head with one diagonal of the square on the shoulders so that two corners of the square form a triangle in front and back. But most of the motifs that appear in personal names—tigers, eagles, jewels, and so on—are associated with both male and female personages.

In Codex Selden we have one notable instance of a change in an individual's personal name, apparently because of an important victory in battle. The story of a female ruler whose calendrical name is 6-Monkey is told in detail on pages 6–8 of Codex Selden, because she was the ruler of "Belching Mountain," the town with which Selden is primarily concerned.[29] At the time of her birth early in the second decade of the eleventh century, 6-Monkey's personal name is shown to be "Serpent Quechquemitl," a name which she wears until 1038, when a series of significant events occurs. In this year she visits two other rulers who insult her (Selden 7–III), and by way of retribution, 6-Monkey personally conquers the towns of these two lords, and they are sacrificed (Selden 8, I–II). Immediately after their sacrifice is a scene in which a priest sprinkles 6-Monkey with pine branches, and she is shown wearing a new personal name, "Warband Quechquemitl" (Selden 8–III). Her former personal name, "Serpent Quechquemitl," appears beside her, attached to her figure by a black line (Fig. 6a). Because the new element in 6-Monkey's second personal name is the band of chevrons that signifies war and because she receives this name immediately following the sacrifice of her two prisoners of war, it is assumed that she is awarded the second name because of her prowess in battle. In 6-Monkey's appearances in other manuscripts, such as Nuttall 44b, Becker I–10 and 11, and Bodley 36–34, she is shown with only the "Warband Quechquemitl" personal name, even though in both Nuttall and Bodley she appears in connection with events of a pre-1038 date. To my knowledge, the amendment of 6-Monkey's personal name is unique in the historical manuscripts and undoubtedly represents an exceptional case rather than a prevailing practice.

It is possible that certain personal names may be connected with, or at least preferred by, specific dynasties of rulers. For example, the ballcourt motif appears often in the personal names of male rulers of the early dynasties represented in Codex Selden,[30] although the "Ballcourt" name is connected with individuals from different towns.

Later in the same manuscript, the small figure which Alfonso Caso calls "Xolotl" (Fig. 5a) occurs in the personal names of twelve women,[31] two of whom are related as mother and daughter and two as grandmother-granddaughter. Two pairs of sisters-in-law are also included in this group of twelve. A very careful study of the personal names in the historical manuscripts should be made, to ascertain whether these names relate in any way to specific lineages or to the Mixtec kinship system as a whole.

The personal names undoubtedly function as logograms—that is, one pictorial sign represents one or more words in the Mixtec language. But very little of the Mixtec personal-name vocabulary has been uncovered, and for the most part, the personal names are described in terms of their pictorial motifs—"Eagle Ballcourt," for example—rather than in terms of the Mixtec language. Often the motifs are related to Nahuatl words that apply to similar pictorial motifs in the Valley of Mexico manuscripts, such as the "Xolotl" figure mentioned above, or the personal name of the ruler 5-Alligator, usually described as "Tlaloc-Sun" or "Tlachitonatiuh" (Fig. 7a).

The two manuscripts which may give us some insight into the relationship of pictorial personal names to their counterparts in the Mixtec language are Codex Sánchez Solís and the post-Conquest Codex Muro.[32] Virtually all the figures in these two documents are accompanied by Mixtec glosses which set forth the person's entire name, the personal name as well as the calendrical name. Although many of the glosses of Sánchez Solís are now extremely faint, and the glosses of Codex Muro are sometimes difficult to read because they are written over the pictures, the texts of both manuscripts deserve a careful study because they contain Mixtec vocabulary that is now lost and present this vocabulary in conjunction with its pictorial counterpart.

A legible and easily translatable example of a gloss that

---

[29] The biography of 6-Monkey as it appears in Codex Selden is described by Spinden, "Indian Manuscripts of Southern Mexico," *Annual Report of the Smithsonian Institution, 1933* (Washington, 1935), 434–37, and Caso, *Selden*, 32–37; 79–84.

[30] Male individuals in Codex Selden whose personal name includes the ballcourt motif are:

I–I	11-Water "Smoking Ballcourt"
I–II, 2–II	4-Eagle "White Ballcourt"
5–I	5-Flower "Warband Ballcourt"
5–II	3-Rain "Ballcourt with Lines" (also in Bodley 2–IV)
5–III	1-Lizard "Ballcourt"
5–IV	1-Reed "Observatory-Eye Ballcourt"
8–IV, 9–II	1-Alligator "Eagle Ballcourt"

[31] Female individuals in Codex Selden whose personal name includes the "Xolotl" motif are:

10–I	7-Grass	"Xolotl Jewel"
10–I	10-Water	"Red Xolotl Jewel"
13–III	3-Rabbit	"Xolotl Emerging from Cobweb" (grandmother of 8-Flower below)
13–IV	8-Flower	"Xolotl Emerging from Jewel" (granddaughter of 3-Rabbit above)
14–II	9-Wind	"Xolotl Emerging from Jewel-Flint Quechquemitl"
14–IV, 15–II	5-Water	"Xolotl Emerging from Jewel" (daughter of 10-Water below and sister-in-law of 5-House below)
14–IV	10-Water	"Xolotl Emerging from Feather Mat" (mother of 5-Water above)
15–II	5-House	"Xolotl Emerging from Jewel" (sister-in-law of 5-Water above)
18–I	13-Death	"Xolotl Emerging from Feather Mat" (sister-in-law of 8-Reed below)
18–II	8-Reed	"Xolotl Emerging from Jewel" (sister-in-law of 13-Death above)
18–II, 18–III	2-Movement	"Xolotl Emerging from Butterfly"
19–IV	10?-Death	"Xolotl Emerging from Feather Mat"

[32] Codex Muro, originally from the town of San Pedro Cántaros, located east of Nochixtlán in the Mixteca Alta (at approximately 17°32′ N., 97°10′ W.), is now in the Museo Nacional de Antropología in Mexico City (No. 35-68). Only one of its eleven pages has been published (page 2; in John B. Glass, *Catálogo de la Colección de Códices* [Mexico, 1964], plate 71).

deals with the name of a person is found on page 23 of Codex Sánchez Solís (Fig. 6e). Above the male figure on this page is the gloss:

[y]ya gn mao çahui yuchi

or "the lord 5-House 'Tlaloc Flint.'" Yya means "lord" or "a person of the ruling class." The phrase gn mao is the Mixtec equivalent of this personage's calendrical name "5-House"; the pictorial equivalent of this name is attached to the figure's foot by a thin black line. Çahui (dzavui in the Alvarado dictionary) is the Mixtec equivalent of the rain deity known in Nahuatl as Tlaloc and in Zapotec as Cosijo. Alvarado's dictionary gives dzavui as meaning both "rain" and "idol," and the Mixtec-speaking people call themselves ñuu dzavui, or "the people of the rain deity." In Sánchez Solís the personal name çahui is indicated pictorially by a rain-deity mask with typical attributes such as a circular eye represented as a star, a curvilinear mouth with fangs, and a conical hat with tassels. The last word of the Mixtec gloss, yuchi, means "knife," and this second half of 5-House's personal name is depicted by a flint blade superimposed on his cape.

MARRIAGE AND CONFERENCE

The basic convention for marriage is the confrontation of a male and a female figure, both in seated positions (Fig. 7 a, c). Male and female figures can be distinguished by their costume and hairdress. The men usually wear a long gown with tassels that is known in Nahuatl as a xicolli (Figs. 5c, 6c) or merely a loincloth (Fig. 6b); the women wear a skirt and a loose overblouse (Figs. 5 a, b, 6f).[33] Although both men and women are sometimes shown with long, straight hair, many of the female figures wear their hair braided with multicolored ribbons (Figs. 5a, 6a, f), clearly distinguishing them from the male figures. Because the calendrical names and many motifs of personal names may be used for either men or women, the botanical symbols ♂ for male and ♀ for female are placed before names of persons in most of the studies of the historical manuscripts.[34]

According to Herrera, a Mixtec man and woman could not marry if their calendrical names had the same numerical coefficient, such as ♀ 4-Flower and ♂ 4-Tiger, because the numerical coefficient of the man's calendrical name had to be higher than that of the woman's.[35] But this prohibition is not borne out in the Mixtec pictorial histories. In many instances, the numeral of a woman's calendrical name is higher than that of her husband's, as for example the wife of 8-Deer named 13-Serpent (Fig. 7b); and in a few instances, such as the marriage of ♂ 3-Death "Gray Eagle" and ♀ 3-Serpent "Garland of Cocoa Flowers" (Fig. 7c), the numerical coefficients of the two names are the same.

In Nuttall, Becker I, and on the back of Vienna, one or both of the marriage pair may be seated on a low throne or on a small platform covered with a tiger skin (Fig. 7a). In Bodley, Selden, and Becker II the couple is seated on a woven straw mat called a petate (Fig. 7c) or on a place sign (Fig. 7o). On the front of Nuttall the couple sometimes shares an undecorated platform, and in several sections of this manuscript (pages 17, 23–26, and 41 of the obverse) the pair is seated before the entrance of a building (Fig. 7b), presumably their "palace" or official residence in the town which they rule. Occasionally, as in Fig. 7b, the bride may offer to the bridegroom an earthenware vessel containing chocolate or pulque, an alcoholic beverage made from the maguey cactus.

In two instances, marriage is represented by bathing scenes. In Selden 7–I, the marriage of ♂ 11-Wind "Bloody Tiger" and ♀ 6-Monkey "Serpent Quechquemitl" is depicted by the nude figures of the bridegroom and bride swimming in a river (Fig. 7d). In an elaborate wedding scene on page 19 of Nuttall, the nude figures of ♂ 13-Wind "Smoking Eye" and ♀ 3-Flint "Feathered Serpent" are shown being rinsed with water poured by two women. In both bathing scenes, the male figures appear with their personal names, but the personal names of the females are omitted.

When a man and woman are seated together on a petate or place sign and they face the same direction rather than each other (Fig. 41), they are considered to be already married. This type of scene does not represent an actual marriage ceremony, but is used to depict parents of a bride or groom in an adjacent marriage scene, or a couple who receives a visitor, such as the scene in Bodley 9–III in which ♂ 1-Death "Serpent Sun" and ♀ 11-Serpent "Flower-Feathers" receive a visit from 8-Deer (Fig. 68e). In Codex Bodley the personal and calendrical names of a married couple sometimes appear alone above a place sign, with the human figures omitted (Fig. 8–left). This

---

[33] The local variations in both costume and costume terminology in the Mixteca are discussed in Dahlgren, La mixteca, 105–22.

[34] In the case of calendrical names, although the pictorial signs for these names are the same whether they are attached to a male or female personage, the Mixtec language contains a complex set of prefixes denoting male or female. As described in Ch. IV (pp. 17–20) of the Reyes sixteenth-century Mixtec grammar, the male-female prefixes used as terms of reference vary with the sex of the speaker. When men talk of women, a prefix do is used, and Reyes gives two examples that utilize the special calendrical vocabulary: docochi [♀ 3? Wind] and dosi huiyu [♀ 10, 11, or 13 Reed], and two examples with Christian names: do Maria and do Juana. When women talk of men, the prefix dzu is used; for example, dzu Pedro. When men talk of other men, the prefix used is ye, from tai yee, the word for "man"; for example, yecochi [♂ 3? Wind] and ye Pedro.

But these prefixes are undoubtedly used by the common people and not by the nobility, because a special set of prefixes and suffixes utilizing the terms yya and ya is reserved for the ruling class. This special vocabulary for nobility is listed in Ch. XXI (pp. 74–81) of the Reyes grammar and has been studied by Evangelina Arana Osnaya ("El idioma de los señores de Tepozcolula," Anales del INAH, Vol. XIII [1961], 217–30.) In the glosses of Sánchez Solís which set forth the complete names of persons (as in Fig. 6 e–f of this study), the names of both males and females are always prefixed with yya, signifying that the person is a member of the nobility. The names of most (but not all) of the women also include the word cii between the initial yya and the calendrical name. The meaning of cii is uncertain, but it is probably a dialectical variation of sihi (si'i) meaning "woman" which omits the glottal stop between the two vowels.

[35] Historia general, VI, 320: "Cuanto a los casamientos, los Papas y los religiosos conocían los impedimentos, y era defecto esencial tener un mismo nombre en el número, porque si ella se llamaba Cuatro Rosas, y él Cuatro Leones, no se podían casar, porque era necesario que sobrepujase el número de él al de ella . . . ."

abbreviated form of notation is used only to designate the parents of an individual and his or her town of origin. It is never used for marriage scenes.

When two persons of either sex sit or stand facing each other, they may also be having a conference. Conference scenes are distinguished from marriage scenes not only because the two conferees may both be of the same sex, but also because they are usually not united by a place sign. Often one of the individuals will be seated on a temple platform or place sign, indicating that the other person or persons in the scene are visiting him.

Some of these "conference" scenes are of the nature of religious pilgrimages, in which the personage being visited is a priest or "deity impersonator"—an individual who has the calendrical name and attributes of a deity. The deity impersonators can be identified as such by their appearance on the front of Codex Vienna, which is populated by non-historical deity figures and mythological personages, or by their appearance in the historical manuscripts over a period of time that is longer than a normal lifetime. For example, one of the most famous impersonators of a death deity, ♀ 9-Grass "Skull," who is associated with an unidentified place described as "Skull Temple," appears six times on the Vienna obverse (33c, 28d, 25b, 24b, 23a, 15b). In addition, she appears in the historical manuscripts in both a ninth-century and an eleventh-century context. According to Codices Bodley (4–III and 34–35, I) and Nuttall (20b), ♀ 9-Grass was instrumental in defeating a group of warriors known as the "Stone Men," one of the significant events in late-ninth-century Mixtec history.[36] In the eleventh century she was frequently consulted by the two important rulers, 8-Deer and 4-Wind, and she appears to have been the protectress of the princess 6-Monkey "Warband Quechquemitl."[37] An important impersonator of a solar deity is ♂ 1-Death, who was also consulted by 8-Deer and 4-Wind at a temple in a place described as "Hill of the Sun."[38]

A conference between two or more personages may indicate a political alliance. In one scene on the back of Nuttall (80 c–d), immediately following a scene that shows 8-Deer and a person named ♂ 4-Tiger engaging each other in personal combat, the two men meet and sacrifice a bird. The post-battle meeting is undoubtedly a peace conference, and 8-Deer holds up two fingers to indicate that this is the second time they have conferred.[39]

The first alliance is illustrated in an earlier passage (52 b–c) of Nuttall.

The largest conference in the historical manuscripts is represented on pages 54–68 of Nuttall, where 8-Deer and his half-brother 12-Movement "Bloody Tiger" receive a group of 112 nobles and deity impersonators, all of whom are presumed to be allies or subjects of the two half-brothers. This same scene appears in Colombino XV–47 and XVII–48, but in Colombino the number of conferees is reduced to twelve or thirteen.

Because one of the main purposes of the historical manuscripts is to set forth the genealogies of ruling persons, marriage is one of the events most frequently represented in these manuscripts. We shall examine now what relationship may exist between the pictorial conventions for marriage discussed above and the idioms of the Mixtec language that refer to marriage between persons of nobility.

Alvarado's sixteenth-century dictionary gives two Mixtec phrases for the marriage of a nobleman (*cassarse el señor*): *tnaha ndaha ya* and *cuvui huico yya*. The first means that the nobility join hands; *tnaha* = "to join" (*juntarse*); *ndaha* = "hands" (and also "tribute"); and *ya* is the suffix that denotes nobility. The second phrase means that there is a royal celebration; *cuvui* = "to be, be able, happen"; *huico* = "celebration, feast day"; and *yya* again denotes the ruling class.

Reyes, in the section of his sixteenth-century grammar which lists the special vocabulary pertaining to nobility, gives four phrases for the marriage of a nobleman.[40] Two of these are very similar to the two from the Alvarado dictionary, discussed above. The first, *cuvui huico yuvui ya*, is the same as Alvarado's *cuvui huico yya*, except for the addition of the word *yuvui*, meaning "petate." The phrase in Reyes probably should be translated as "there is a royal celebration of the petate," and as we have seen (Fig. 7c), a royal bride and groom are often shown seated on a petate in the pictorial manuscripts. Another definition in Reyes, *tnaha ndáya ya*, is the equivalent of Alvarado's *tnaha ndaha ya* ("the nobility join hands"), except that Reyes has used the nobility vocabulary for the word "hand" (*ndáya ya* = "the hand of a nobleman") instead of the normal word for "hand" (*ndaha*).

A third phrase in Reyes, *ndoo siña ya*, means "to sanctify the empire"; *ndoo* = "to sanctify, purify, wash"; *siña ya* = "empire." I believe that the implication here is that because the marriage occurs between two persons of royal blood, the children of this marriage, who will inherit the domain of their parents, will also be of royal (i.e., pure) blood. The occurrence in this phrase of the verb *ndoo*, which also means "to wash or cleanse" may explain the two marriage scenes in Selden 7–I and Nuttall 19, in which the bride and groom are shown bathing together.

Reyes says that another phrase for royal marriage, *nisiñe saha ya*, also means "the nobleman began to drink pulque." In an earlier section of his list, Reyes gives as the definition for "the nobleman drinks wine or pulque," *sai*

[36] Caso, *Bodley*, 76.

[37] Colombino III–10 and Nuttall 44 (a–b) show ♂ 8-Deer and ♀ 6-Monkey making an offering to ♀ 9-Grass in the year Six-Reed (1031). Bodley 9–IV presents an analogous scene taking place in the same year, but here the offering is made by 8-Deer only. In Selden 7–IV, ♀ 6-Monkey confers with ♀ 9-Grass immediately after she has been insulted by two noblemen and receives the weapons with which she subsequently defeats her detractors; this occurs in the year Thirteen-Rabbit (1038). In Selden 6–IV and Bodley 35–II, ♀ 6-Monkey and her prospective husband ♂ 11-Wind "Bloody Tiger" make an offering to ♀ 9-Grass in the year Five-Reed (1043). In Bodley 33–V, ♂ 4-Wind (the son of ♀ 6-Monkey and ♂ 11-Wind) confers with ♀ 9-Grass in the year Eleven-House (1049); and in Bodley 32–V, 4-Wind presents an offering to her in the year Three-Reed (1067).

[38] Alfonso Caso, "El dios I. Muerte," *Mitteilungen aus dem Museum für Völkerkunde und Vorgeschichte*, Hamburg, Vol. XXV (1959), 40–43.

[39] Clark, *Story of "Eight Deer,"* 24.

[40] "Arte en lengua mixteca," 76.

saha ya ndedzi. Sai means "to buy, receive, take or drink"; *saha*, according to Reyes, means a vessel from which a nobleman drinks (*vaso, en que esta la beuida del señor*); *ya* denotes nobility; *ndedzi* means "pulque." Thus the phrase *sai saha ya ndedzi* literally means "the nobleman drinks a royal vessel of pulque." The phrase *nisiñe saha ya*, listed under the group of royal marriage terms, perhaps should be translated "a royal vessel was placed [before the nobleman]." *Ni* is a past-tense prefix; *siñe* means "to be put or placed"; *saha* is "royal vessel"; *ya* denotes nobility. This idiom of the language is also reflected in some of the marriage scenes in the pictorial manuscripts, in which the bride offers an earthenware vessel of pulque or chocolate to her husband (Fig. 7*b*). But offering of pulque are not restricted to marriage scenes; they may also be made to deity impersonators, as in Bodley 32–V where the ruler ♂ 4-Wind "Fire Serpent" presents an offering of pulque to the deity impersonator ♀ 9-Grass "Skull."

The phrase *nisiñe saha ya* may have still another meaning, "the nobleman made footprints," for *siñe saha* means "footprints" (*rastro de pisada*). This idiom of the language is also utilized as a pictorial idiom in Codices Bodley, Selden, Becker II and Sánchez Solís, as well as in the large wedding scene in Nuttall 19, where the figure of either the bride or groom is connected with his or her town of origin by a series of footprints (Fig. 8). As Spores has observed, the residence practice of the Mixtec ruling class was ambilocal; that is, a newly married couple could reside in the town of the groom's family or in the town of the bride's family.[41] The example in Fig. 8 shows the latter case. The groom, ♂ 4-Alligator "Serpent-Burning Copal," has journeyed from his birthplace to his bride's town. This journey is illustrated by two footprints leading from the place sign of his town of birth and the personal and calendrical names of his parents to the place sign of his wife's town, where he and his wife ♀ 13-Flower "Jade Quetzal" appear as a marriage couple.

It is possible that a jar of chocolate held in a woman's hand represents the woman's dowry. According to Reyes, the word for "royal dowry" (*arras, entre señores, de casamiento*) is *ynodzehua. Dzehua* means "chocolate" or "cocoa." The precise meaning of *yno* or *ino* in this context is not clear. This word usually means "tobacco" or "henbane" (*Hyoscyamus niger*), and *tnu ino* is a juniper tree (*tnu* being a prefix used for trees, from *yutnu*, meaning "wood"). Perhaps this word also refers to the blossoms of the cocoa plant, for in several instances (e.g., Nuttall 5c), these blossoms are represented as sprouting from the bowl of chocolate.

Thus we see that several of the pictorial motifs that are sometimes associated with the representation of marriage in the historical manuscripts also appear in various idioms of the Mixtec language that are to describe dynastic marriage. But such motifs as the petate (*yuvui*), the royal vessel (*saha*) containing either pulque or chocolate, and the footprints (*siñe saha*) linking one of the marriage pair with his or her town of origin do not invariably appear

in connection with a marriage scene. The essential convention for marriage—a male and female figure who sit facing each other—is strictly a pictorial convention and has no corollary in the Mixtec language. The similar convention for conference is also a pictorial convention which, in common with the convention for marriage, depends on the placement of human figures in relationship to each other and has no direct connection with an idiom in the Mixtec language.

BIRTH AND AGE

The birth of an individual is always indicated by his appearance immediately or soon after the marriage of his parents. In Nuttall and the back of Vienna a marriage scene is usually followed by the figures of the children born of that marriage, often accompanied by the year signs indicating the dates of their birth. For example, on Nuttall 26 and 42, immediately after the marriage scene of ♂ 5-Alligator "Tlaloc Sun" and ♀ 9-Eagle "Garland of Cocoa Flowers," are the figures of their three children in the order in which they were born: ♂ 12-Movement "Bloody Tiger," ♂ 3-Water "Heron," and ♀ 6-Lizard "Jade Ornament." Only the year of the birthdate of the firstborn 12-Movement is given: Seven-House (993). Then, in both Nuttall 26 and 42, there follows a female figure, ♀ 11-Water "Blue Bird," who may be thought to be a second daughter of ♂ 5-Alligator and ♀ 9-Eagle. But because this woman sits in front of a building in Nuttall 26 and on a platform covered with tiger hide in Nuttall 42, we know that she is the second wife of ♂ 5-Alligator. The figure of ♀ 11-Water is accompanied by the date of her marriage to ♂ 5-Alligator—the day Six-Deer in the year Ten House (1009)—and next in the pictorial sequence are the figures of the children of this marriage: ♂ 8-Deer "Tiger Claw" accompanied by the date Twelve-Reed (1011), ♂ 9-Flower "Copal Ball with Arrow" accompanied by the date Three-Reed (1015), and ♀ 9-Monkey "Quetzal-Jewel" accompanied by the date Thirteen-Flint (1012). We know the relationships of the nine individuals in this sequence because of their placement in a pictorial context that expresses these relationships: ♂ 5-Alligator and his two wives appear in a marriage context and are thus known to be the parents of the unmarried persons who are listed immediately after the marriage scenes.

In Codices Bodley and Selden the pictorial convention for birth is more explicit. In these two manuscripts birth is indicated by attaching to a figure a small red band which Spinden first identified as an umbilical cord (Fig. 9 *a, b*).[42] In Selden the band is always red and has a wavy outline; in Bodley the contour is smooth, and although the band is usually red, it is sometimes brown, gray or black. Often the umbilical cord unites the figure with the year sign of his birth (Fig. 9*b*). Occasionally the umbilical cord connects the individual with his mother, as in Bodley 6–I and in the only two representations of the umbilical cord in Nuttall, on pages 16 and 27 (Fig. 9 *c, d*). In many

---

[41] *The Mixtec Kings and Their People*, 11.

[42] "Indian Manuscripts of Southern Mexico," *Annual Report of the Smithsonian Institution, 1933* (Washington, 1935), 432.

instances, the umbilical cord terminates in a small circle (Fig. 9*a*), which undoubtedly represents the afterbirth. In the two examples in Nuttall illustrated in Fig. 9 *c, d*, both of which show an actual parturition, a red circle indicating the afterbirth appears between the woman's legs.

These two birth scenes in Nuttall are among the rare instances in which the person being born is presented as a child—that is, smaller in size than his mother and unclothed. As Spinden has observed, most individuals are represented at birth as adult-size personages and as entirely clothed with their complete regalia, including their personal names.[43] Nor do historical personages show evidence of age or decrepitude. Both men and women are shown as "elderly" by representing them with a mouth that contains only one tooth or a small cavity of toothless gum (Fig. 10); but this "toothless" convention is used for priests and mythological personages rather than for the ruling nobility.[44]

The conventions for birth discussed above appear to be pictorial conventions only and have no direct relationship to the Mixtec language. For example, the use of the umbilical cord (*siti coho* in Mixtec) to indicate birth is a pictorial symbol and does not occur as an idiom to describe birth in the language. The "toothless" motif used to depict old age also seems to be a pictorial convention with no relation to any of the Mixtec terms for elderliness.

ROAD AND WARPATH

A series of human footprints or a band containing footprints signifies a road, and one frequently represented variation of the road motif is a band that contains a chevron pattern instead of footprints and indicates a "road to war" or "warpath."

Roads

Roads have essentially two meanings in the Mixtec historical manuscripts. First, they are used in connection with figures "going to" some place, as in the journey of 8-Deer to visit ♂ 1-Death "Serpent-Sun" and ♀ 11-Serpent "Flower-Feathers" (Fig. 68*e*). Second, in Codices Bodley, Selden, Becker II, and Sánchez Solís the road appears in a "coming from" sense, because in these manuscripts footprints are used to connect one person of a marriage pair with his town of origin and the figures or names of his parents. As we have seen in an example from Codex Bodley (Fig. 8), the two footprints indicate that ♂ 4-Alligator "Serpent-Burning Copal" comes from the town of Tilantongo, whose place sign is a frieze containing black-and-white stepped frets,[45] and also that he comes from, in a biological and genealogical sense, his parents ♂ 8-Deer "Tiger Claw" and ♀ 13-Serpent "Flowered Serpent." Of course, the "going to" and "coming from" senses are not truly separable, for ♂ 4-Alligator not only comes from his parents and his town of birth, he also

goes to the town of his wife ♀ 13-Flower "Jade Quetzal." However, in the type of carefully delineated dynastic genealogies represented in these manuscripts, we can be sure that no one goes to be married until his prospective mate is completely sure of where he "comes from." Indeed, the principal purpose of a manuscript such as Codex Bodley is to demonstrate where the Mixtec native rulers came from, beginning with their mythological origins in the late seventh century.

A band containing footprints is a logogram of the Mixtec word for "road" (*ichi* or *yaya*), as we see in a place sign from the post-Conquest Map No. 36 (Fig. 11), which consists of a hill that encloses a road and which is accompanied by the gloss *yucu ichin*. (*Yucu* = "hill"; *ichi* = "road," and the final *n* probably indicates that the second *i* is nasalized.) In the pre-Conquest historical manuscripts, however, the road is not used in a modern cartographic sense to indicate a definite route from one location to another. It is used in the associative sense of "journey," whether to a specific place or from a specified origin.

In one notable instance, the band of footprints is used in connection with what might be termed an "escape" or "taking refuge" scene. In the eventful biography of ♀ 6-Monkey as it is related in Codex Selden, this princess is shown as diving into a rectangular patch of earth (Fig. 13*a*). Only the lower section of 6-Monkey's body is depicted as protruding from a cavity in this piece of earth, and appended to her feet is an L-shaped band of footprints. I believe that this scene indicates that 6-Monkey hides or takes temporary refuge from those who are attempting to usurp her throne at the town known as "Belching Mountain."[46] In all likelihood, the convention of a figure diving into the earth to indicate this person's escape or temporary refuge is a purely pictorial convention, with no relationship to words or idioms in the Mixtec language. The L-shaped road has the suggestion of a circuitous journey because of the angle or "bend" in the road; and the combination of this road with a human figure descending into the earth portrays an almost universal idea of escape, flight, or temporary refuge—an idea which is expressed

---

[43] *Ibid.*, 433.

[44] In Selden 5–IV, the ruler 8-Deer appears as "toothless," but only because he also wears the facial paint of a priest.

[45] The place sign of Tilantongo is discussed in more detail below, pp. 55, 5̶7̶.

[46] My interpretation of the scene in Selden 6–III as an "escape" differs from the interpretations of this scene proposed by Alfonso Caso and Herbert J. Spinden. Caso (*Selden*, 34; 61) postulates that 6-Monkey goes into the earth, possibly a cave, "as a magical trial." Spinden ("Indian Manuscripts of Southern Mexico," *Annual Report of the Smithsonian Institution, 1933* [Washington, 1935], 435) conjectures that 6-Monkey is going to her death at a future date has been prophesied in the preceding scene by the two priests ♂ 10-Lizard and ♂ 6-Vulture. But it is my feeling that 6-Monkey's descent into the earth has political rather than religious motives. In the scenes just preceding this descent, it would seem that all is not well at "Belching Mountain," the town ruled by 6-Monkey.

The problems at this town begin before 6-Monkey's birth, when her three brothers are shown as prisoners of war (Selden 5–IV, 6–I) and thus undoubtedly awaiting sacrifice. Following this scene, 6-Monkey is born (Selden 6–I), and at her birth she is seen conferring with the elderly priest, ♂ 10-Lizard, who appears to function as her mentor throughout her life as it is related in Codex Selden.

In the next line (Selden 6–II), 6-Monkey's father, 10-Eagle "Stone Tiger," is shown defending "Belching Mountain" against an attacking warrior. 10-Eagle has the warrior by the hair, indicating that his defense was successful at this time; but he does not appear again in Codex Selden,

in a similar fashion in the English idioms "head for the hills" and "go underground."

Nor does the L-shaped band of footprints always appear in an escape scene. In Bodley 33, III–II (Fig. 13b), ♀ 6-Monkey's son, ♂ 4-Wind "Fire Serpent," is shown as diving into a sign that consists of tall flames resting on a front-facing mouth of the rain deity, Tlaloc, and Alfonso Caso has identified this as an escape scene on the basis of its context.[47] The context of the series of events that occur before and after an individual dives into the earth is the principal means of determining whether or not the descent into the earth represents an escape, because persons who are sacrificed are also occasionally shown as descending into a crevice or a pictorial sign (as in Fig. 14d). The distinguishing features of an escape scene seem to be: a conflict of some type, followed by a person's diving into the earth, and his later re-emergence. If the person re-emerges, an "escape" has been effected.

Warpaths

When the road along which a figure travels contains a pattern of red, white, and black chevrons (Fig. 51), the individual is known to be going to war, and this road with chevrons is often called a "warpath."[48] At times the chevrons are not red, black, and white, but black and white,[49] or red and white,[50] or multicolored.[51] The person who travels the warpath is always shown as armed with a spear or other weapon, and a battle of conquest is usually represented at the end of the warpath.

The chevron pattern probably represents the Mixtec word *yecu*, which means "enemy." In Codex Sánchez Solís a place sign that occurs twice and whose principal element is a band with warpath chevrons (Fig. 12) is accompanied by the gloss *yoco ño yco*.[52] In the dialect of the place-sign glosses on this manuscript the *u* of the Alvarado dictionary becomes *o*, and thus this gloss in the dialect of Alvarado would be *yucu ñu ycu*. *Yucu* means "hill," and *ñu[u]* means "place where something exists." Neither *ycu* nor *yco* makes any sense as a word in the Mixtec language, and I believe that *yco* is the annotator's transcription of the Mixtec word *yecu*. The word *yecu* alone means "enemy," and *yecu tnañu* means "war." (*Tnañu* alone means "battle" [*pelea*].) In addition, one of the Mixtec phrases which Alvarado gives for a person waging a war campaign (*hueste de gente de armas*) is *tay caca yecu*—literally, "a man who walks [to] the enemy." (*Tay* = "man"; *caca* = "to walk"; *yecu* = "enemy.") Therefore, in the pictorial manuscripts, when a person walks along a road containing the chevron pattern, he is on a road that leads to the enemy—or in other words, he is going to war.

CONQUEST

Conquest is depicted by an arrow inserted in the place sign of the conquered town (Fig. 51). This pictorial convention has a definite analog in one of the idioms for "conquest" in the Mixtec language. The first definition given in Alvarado's dictionary for the verb "to conquer" (*conquistar*) is *chihi nduvua ñuhu ñaha*, which means "to put an arrow into the lands of another person." (*Chihi* = "to put, place"; *nduvua* = "arrow"; *ñuhu* = "land"; *ñaha* = "another" or "another person.") The same idiom, shortened to *chihi nduvua ñuhu*, is also given by Alvarado as one of the definitions of the verb "to give battle" (*combatir*).

Occasionally small red flames are appended to the place sign of the town being conquered (Figs. 51a, 52b), indicating that the place in question was burned at the time of the conquest. This convention, too, is reflected in one of the definitions in the Alvarado dictionary for the verb "to combat," which is *sami ñuu*, "to burn the town." (*Sami* = "to burn"; *ñuu* = "town.")

At times, when a town is captured, the conquering ruler is shown holding the ruler of the subjugated town by his hair (Figs. 15b, 51a), and prisoners of war usually carry a long rectangular banner (Figs. 15a, right, 61, right). Prisoners may also be shown as bound, by ropes around

and it is possible that he was killed in a subsequent attack on "Belching Mountain," because the Mixtec histories rarely depict the defeats of the important rulers or dynastic lines shown in a manuscript.

On the following line (Selden 6–III), in the scene immediately preceding the "escape" scene, 6-Monkey confers with two elderly priests, ♂ 10-Lizard and ♂ 6-Vulture. The latter are shown emitting two speech scrolls, perhaps advising 6-Monkey that she should take refuge until the troubled times at "Belching Mountain" are over. A line of footprints leads from the figure of 6-Monkey as she is shown seated at the conference with two priests into the patch of earth where she is shown "escaping" (Fig. 13a).

In the scene that immediately follows the escape scene, footprints lead from the patch of earth to the now-upright figure of 6-Monkey. The temporary crisis is now apparently over; and 6-Monkey's first activity after this re-appearance is a conference with the important death deity impersonator, ♀ 9-Grass of "Skull Temple," a conference which is also attended by 6-Monkey's future husband, 11-Wind "Bloody Tiger."

The appearance of the two priests just before 6-Monkey's disappearance into the earth and her conference with a death deity impersonator immediately after this disappearance might support the hypothesis that her descent into the earth is of a religious nature—either a trial, as Caso has suggested, or a pilgrimage. But considering the political and dynastic vicissitudes that occur in the lines of Codex Selden just prior to the disappearance—that is, the sacrifice of 6-Monkey's three brothers and the attack on "Belching Mountain"—it seems to me more likely that her disappearance relates to the temporary "escape" of political refuge.

[47] *Bodley*, 61. Immediately preceding 4-Wind's escape, a personage named ♂ 4-Tiger holds 4-Wind by the wrists, suggesting the capture or attempted capture of 4-Wind, and undoubtedly giving 4-Wind sufficient cause to seek refuge. In the scene immediately following 4-Wind's escape (Bodley 33–II), the solar deity impersonator, ♂ 1-Death, holds 4-Wind and his former adversary 4-Tiger by the wrists—a scene which Caso (*ibid.*) has interpreted as a reconciliation between 4-Wind and 4-Tiger.

[48] This convention was first identified by Alfonso Caso, "Explicación del reverso del Codex Vindobonensis," *Memoria de el Colegio Nacional*, Vol. V–5 (1950), 14.

[49] For example, in Nuttall 10a and 67b, and in Selden 8–III, 11–III, 12–II, 15–IV, 16–III.

[50] For example, in Nuttall 44b and 76b.

[51] For example, in Nuttall 32a and in Selden 5–I, 8–III.

[52] In the gloss accompanying the place sign on page 31 of Sánchez Solís (Fig. 12b), the phrase *noho qui biyo* is added to the name of the place sign. *Noho* is the equivalent of Alvarado's *nuhu* and here probably means something like "home town," because Alvarado gives *nuhu* as one of the Mixtec words for "to go to one's own town" (*ir a pueblo propio*). *Qui biyo* (*qui huiyu* in the Alvarado dialect) is the calendrical name 4-Reed, and thus the entire gloss indicates that the place *yucu ñu ycu* is the home town of a person named 4-Reed. The figure of 4-Reed may well have originally been painted in front of the place sign on page 31, in the section that is now completely erased.

their necks (Fig. 51a) or by sections of rope tied around their arms as in the series of 14 prisoners in Nuttall 76–77. The hair-holding, banner, and rope motifs all appear to be pictorial conventions for representing prisoners, because the Mixtec words for hair (idzi), flag or banner (huayu), and rope (yoho) do not appear in any of the idioms of the Mixtec language that refer to prisoners of war.

DEATH AND SACRIFICE

Dead persons are usually represented with closed eyes and in either a prone or seated position (Fig. 14 a, b), or as mummy bundles (Fig. 14c). In one unusual group sacrifice scene in Bodley 36–35, I, the death of thirteen of the sixteen individuals who were sacrificed is shown by the victims' descent into the earth, which is depicted as a semicircle with a crevice-like opening (Fig. 14d).[53] All of these variant representations of death appear to be strictly pictorial conventions.

The death of the majority of personages in the historical manuscripts is not represented at all; they merely fulfill their role as parent, husband or wife, or in-law, and then do not re-appear in the historical narrative. And with very few exceptions, when a ruler is shown as dead, the depiction of his death either coincides with or immediately follows his sacrifice.[54]

The sacrifice is usually performed by opening the victim's chest with a flint blade and extracting his heart (Figs. 15a, left, and 17). Two notable exceptions to the traditional practice of sacrifice by removal of the heart are represented in a passage of Codex Nuttall which shows the ritual sacrifice of two brothers (Fig. 16). Both brothers wear the costume of the deity known in Nahuatl as Xipe-Totec: red-and-white headdresses with a sharp point that resembles a flint blade, and red-and-white sashes which are suspended from their shoulders or from the waistband. One of the brothers is put to death by gladiatorial sacrifice, a ritual in which the victim is tied to a circular stone and given dummy weapons to defend himself against adversaries armed with real weapons (Fig. 16a). The other brother is killed by arrow sacrifice, in which the victim is tied to a wooden scaffolding and executed by arrows flung from a throwing-board (Fig. 16b).[55]

Undoubtedly the Mixtec language contained vocabulary to describe ritual immolation, whether effected by extraction of the heart, by gladiatorial combat, or by arrows. But this vocabulary seems to have been lost, and these immolations are known principally through written descriptions of them in post-Conquest manuscripts from the Valley of Mexico such as the Florentine Codex and Codex Magliabecchiano.[56]

SPEECH SCROLLS

Human speech is represented by small volutes, usually called "speech scrolls," which are shown being emitted from a person's mouth (Fig. 18). Speech scrolls seem to be a purely pictorial convention and are found at least as early as the Classic period in several regions of Mexico, as for example in the wall paintings at Teotihuacán in the Valley of Mexico and on stelae and in wall paintings from Monte Albán in the Valley of Oaxaca.

In several instances in the Mixtec historical manuscripts, flint blades or stones are attached to speech scrolls, indicating harsh or "cutting" words.[57] We know, for example, in Selden 7–III that ♀ 6-Monkey is insulted when she visits the two lords ♂ 6-Lizard "Hair-Bent Hill" and ♂ 2-Alligator "Hair-Cacaxtli" because the speech scrolls emerging from the mouths of these two men are accompanied by flint blades (Fig. 52a). In Bodley 9–II (Fig. 61), when 8-Deer presents a prisoner of war to ♂ 4-Tiger, his speech scrolls contain the pictorial symbol of a stone, indicating stern or "stony" speech. These variants of the speech scroll also appear to be pictorial conventions only, with no counterparts in the Mixtec language.

SUMMARY

As noted above, many of the conventions used to impart information in the Mixtec histories are purely pictorial conventions that do not appear to express specific words or idioms of the Mixtec language. The pictorial conventions include:

1. The representation of marriage as a confrontation between a male and a female personage
2. The representation of a conference as a confrontation of two or more persons of either sex
3. The representation of birth as a human figure attached to an umbilical cord that often has a circle to indicate the afterbirth
4. The representation of elderly persons as having one tooth to indicate that they are "toothless"
5. The representation of dead persons as mummy bundles or with closed eyes
6. The representation of human sacrifice
7. The representation of prisoners as persons who are

[53] Caso, Bodley, 57. As noted above under "Road and Warpath," the pictorial convention of persons diving into the earth, used to represent the death of sacrificial victims in Bodley 36–35, I, is similar to the pictorial convention for "escape." Variant accounts of the group sacrifice scene on the back of Bodley also appear on the Bodley obverse (3–4, III) and in Nuttall 20; in these analogous scenes, the number of sacrificial victims is fewer than that shown in Bodley 36–35, I, and they are all represented as mummy bundles or as persons with closed eyes.

[54] One exception to the general rule that the representation of death in the Mixtec histories is closely associated with sacrifice is the death of 8-Deer's father, 5-Alligator "Tlaloc-Sun," who appears as a mummy bundle in Bodley 8–V and Vienna VII–1, with no indication that he met death by sacrifice. Also unusual are the final four pages (17–20) of Codex Selden, in which eight rulers are shown as mummy bundles and do not appear to have been sacrificed.

[55] This scene is also depicted on page 10 of Codex Becker I. As Alfonso Caso (Colombino, 40; 138) has pointed out, in Becker I the roles of the two brothers are reversed: ♂ 10-Dog "Copal-Eagle" dies by arrow sacrifice and ♂ 6-House "Strand of Flint Blades" by gladiatorial combat.

[56] Especially Book II of the Florentine Codex which deals with ritual and ceremony, Arthur J. O. Anderson and Charles E. Dibble, ed. and trans., Florentine Codex, General History of the Things of New Spain, by Fray Bernardino de Sahagún, Book 2, The Ceremonies (Santa Fe, 1951); and Codex Magliabecchiano XIII.3 (Rome, 1904), fol. 29/v–30, 65/v–66, 69/v–70.

[57] Spinden, "Indian Manuscripts of Southern Mexico," Annual Report of the Smithsonian Institution, 1933 (Washington, 1935), 435.

held by the hair, carrying long rectangular banners, or tied with rope

8. The representation of human speech as a volute emitted from the mouth.

Some of the elaborations on the basic pictorial convention for marriage appear to be based on idioms in the Mixtec language that refer to royal marriage. These are:

1. The representation of a marriage pair on a petate or straw mat, which appears to reflect the Mixtec idiom for royal marriage, "to have a royal festival of the petate"

2. The representation of a marriage pair with a vessel containing pulque or chocolate, which refers to a Mixtec idiom for royal marriage, "a royal vessel was placed before the nobleman," or, a vessel of chocolate may represent the dowry of the bride

3. The representation of footprints connecting one of the marriage pair to his birthplace refers to an idiom for royal marriage that can be translated as "the nobleman made footprints."

Several of the motifs utilized in the Mixtec histories are logograms of specific Mixtec words. A band with foot-prints depicts the word for "road" (*ichi*), and a "warpath" or band with chevrons represents the word for "enemy" (*yecu*). The depiction of conquest as an arrow in a place sign expresses one of the idioms in the Mixtec language for the verb "to conquer," which is "to place an arrow in the lands of another." The appearance of flames on the sign of a conquered town also represents one of the Mixtec idioms for "to give battle," which is "to burn the town."

Dates and names of persons, whether calendrical or personal names, are also logograms of words in the Mixtec language. But both dates and names are usually described in terms of their pictorial motifs rather than in terms of the Mixtec words which these motifs represent. For example, the name of the person in Fig. 6e can be described as 5-House "Tlaloc-Flint" by the observation and description of the five dots attached to the day-sign House and the attributes which the figure wears: a flint-blade necklace and a mask of the rain deity known as Tlaloc in Nahuatl. This type of description can be made without reference to the accompanying Mixtec gloss, which tells us that this figure is the nobleman 5-House "Rain Deity-Flint."

IV

THE MIXTEC PLACE SIGN

At the present time, the identification of the place signs in the historical manuscripts is one of the principal problems awaiting solution. Because of our understanding of the pictorial conventions discussed in Chapter III, we now have a general idea of what events took place and who participated in them, but we have very little idea of where the participants lived or where the events occurred. At least several hundred place names are depicted in the historical codices; only about twenty place signs have been identified.

The decipherment of the place signs in the Mixtec codices not only would add to our knowledge of the manuscripts themselves, but also would give us a better idea of the geographical extent of the Mixtec territory in the post-Classic period. For example, Codex Colombino and the back of Codex Nuttall contain over a hundred pictorial signs of places shown as conquered by the eleventh-century ruler 8-Deer, plus about seventy-five place signs that represent ceremonial sites visited by this hero or towns which were his allies or subjects. If the names of these places could be ascertained, we could gain a clearer picture of the domain of the Mixtec-speaking people in the eleventh century.

In addition, it is likely that the place signs that are emphasized in any one historical manuscript are those that were important to the lineage of rulers who commissioned the manuscript. Undoubtedly, once it is possible to identify the most prominent and most frequently represented place signs in a manuscript, it may also be possible to gain some idea of the provenience of the manuscript, because the places depicted by the signs given the most space in a manuscript were probably the towns most closely connected with the dynastic line for which the manuscript was painted. For example, Codex Selden is devoted to the genealogies and achievements of one town whose place sign is described as "Belching Mountain." It is assumed that Selden was painted for the rulers of this place. Thus, if the "Belching Mountain" sign were identified, we would know more exactly the origin of this manuscript.

Mixtec place signs are logograms, pictorial representations of a place name in which the pictorial units are the equivalent of one or more words. One of the principal problems, then, is to determine what Mixtec words are depicted by the signs.

Unfortunately, we have no large collection of Mixtec

pictorial signs accompanied by glosses of their names written in European script, such as Codex Mendoza and other early Colonial manuscripts provide for place signs that reflect the Nahuatl language.[1] None of the eight pre-Conquest Mixtec histories is accompanied by a text in a European language, and only three of the eight have annotations in Mixtec written in European script. In the case of two of the three, Codices Colombino and Becker I, the annotations in Mixtec are only occasionally related to the pictorial story told in the codices. Instead, these glosses deal with sixteenth-century boundaries of towns in the Coastal region of the Mixteca.[2] It is regrettable that the glosses of these two manuscripts do not appear to describe the pictures they accompany, because Colombino contains between 115 and 120 place signs, and Becker I about 40 place signs. In addition, both manuscripts depict in detail the eleventh-century conquests and alliances of 8-Deer and set forth a narrative that has analogies in other Mixtec histories which lack glosses, principally the back of Codex Nuttall. The glosses on the third annotated manuscript, Codex Sánchez Solís, appear to deal specifically with the story told in the painted codex, and almost all of the thirty different place signs in this manuscript are accompanied by a Mixtec place name written in European script. But as yet only a few of these place-sign glosses have been interpreted.[3]

The remaining five Mixtec histories are now in European repositories and are accompanied by no extensive texts which would help identify the place names depicted in the manuscripts. Of these five, Codices Nuttall, Bodley, and Selden contain the greatest number of place signs. As

---

[1] Codex Mendoza contains 541 different place signs, accompanied by their Nahuatl names written in European script. An excellent color reproduction of this manuscript, along with a detailed commentary on its contents, is in: James Cooper Clark, ed. and trans., *Codex Mendoza: The Mexican Manuscript known as the Collection of Mendoza and Preserved in the Bodleian Library*, 3 vols. (London, 1938). Studies of Nahuatl place signs based on the collection of signs in Codex Mendoza include: Antonio Peñafiel, *Nombres geográficos de México* (Mexico, 1885); Robert H. Barlow and Byron McAfee, *Diccionario de elementos fonéticos en escritura jeroglífica: Códice Mendocino* (Mexico, 1949); and Karl Anton Nowotny, "Die Hieroglyphen des Codex Mendoza: Der Bau einer mittelamerikanischen Wortschrift," *Mitteilungen aus dem Museum für Völkerkunde, Hamburg*, Vol. XXV (1959), 97–113.

[2] Concerning these glosses, see Smith, *Colombino*; and the discussion above, pp. 14–15.

[3] Concerning the place signs in Sánchez Solís that have been identified, see below, pp. 61–62, 76–77, 150–51.

indicated above, the back of Codex Nuttall has over 175 signs of places connected with the biography of 8-Deer; in addition, at least 60 place signs are shown on the front of Nuttall. Codex Bodley, the most detailed and lengthy of the Mixtec histories, contains approximately 115 different place signs; and Codex Selden has between 65 and 70 place signs in addition to the unidentified "Belching Mountain" which is the home town of the principal ruling line shown in the manuscript. Codex Becker II and the back of Codex Vienna contain fewer place signs. The extant published pages of Becker II do not include the place sign of the principal ruling line described by this manuscript, although legible signs of about ten subsidiary places are shown. The Vienna reverse contains only about a dozen place signs, and the genealogies of this sketchy manuscript have been reconstructed by Alfonso Caso by comparison with other Mixtec histories, principally Codices Bodley and Nuttall.[4] Thus, because there are so few written texts that identify Mixtec place signs with the Mixtec words which the signs represent, the identification of place signs has progressed slowly.

Another complicating factor in the identification of Mixtec place signs is that since the time of the Spanish conquest and continuing to the present day, many towns in the Mixteca are known officially by names in the Nahuatl language, rather than by their original Mixtec names. The Mixtec name of a town is often still known and used in conversations in regions of Oaxaca where Mixtec is still spoken; but this name is rarely used on maps and in other official documents.

Some of the "official" Nahuatl names have the same meaning as the Mixtec name of the town. For example, the Nahuatl name of Tututepec in the Coastal region of Oaxaca means "bird hill" (*tototl* = "bird"; *tepetl* = "hill"); and this town's Mixtec name, *yucu dzaa*, means "hill of the bird" (*yucu* = "hill"; *dzaa* = "bird"). But in the case of many of the towns in the Mixteca, the Nahuatl and Mixtec names of a town have very different meanings. For example, the Nahuatl name of Acatlán in the Mixteca Baja means "place of the reeds," whereas this town's Mixtec name, *yucu yusi*, means "hill of the turquoise jewel." Because the place signs in the historical manuscripts are assumed to be logographic renderings of *Mixtec* place names, it is necessary to delve beneath the contemporary stratum of Nahuatl toponymy to determine the original Mixtec names.[5]

SOURCES OF MIXTEC PLACE NAMES

The sources of Mixtec place names are numerous. The most important sixteenth-century source of town names is a list published at the end of the 1593 Mixtec grammar of Fray Antonio de los Reyes. The Reyes list contains the Mixtec names of 146 towns: 40 in the Mixteca Alta; 30 in the Mixteca Baja; 10 in the Coastal region; 6 in the "Teutila," the region surrounding Cuicatlán in northeastern Oaxaca;; 13 in the Zapotec-speaking region of central Oaxaca; and 47 in the Nahuatl-speaking area of the Valley of Mexico and the present-day States of Puebla and Morelos. Seventy-seven of the names in the Reyes list are analyzed by Wigberto Jiménez Moreno in his introductory section to the 1962 facsimile edition of Fray Francisco de Alvarado's Mixtec dictionary.[6]

Another sixteenth-century source of Mixtec place names is the group of *Relaciones Geográficas* from the Mixtec-speaking section of Oaxaca. The *Relaciones Geográficas* often list the Mixtec names of the major towns and their dependencies and usually give a Spanish translation of the Mixtec place name.[7]

A valuable nineteenth-century compendium that includes many Mixtec place names is the *Cuadros sinópticos* compiled by the Oaxacan scholar Manuel Martínez Gracida.[8] The *Cuadros sinópticos* contains a large quantity of geographical information on every town in the State of Oaxaca, and it often gives the Mixtec names not only of towns, but also of hills, rivers, lakes, caves, and the like. An abbreviated list containing only the towns, haciendas, and ranches of Oaxaca, with their native names and etymologies, was published by Martínez Gracida in the *Boletín de la Sociedad Mexicana de Geografía y Estadística* of 1888.[9] In 1955 José María Bradomín issued a similar listing of towns and ranches in Oaxaca, including a critique of a number of the etymological analyses made by Martínez Gracida in *Cuadros sinópticos*, particularly those of Nahuatl names.[10]

Several studies contain Mixtec place names for specific regions within the Mixteca. Included in a seventeenth-century Spanish-Mixtec vocabulary by Fray Miguel de Villavicencio are the Mixtec names of towns in eastern Guerrero,[11] and the Mixtec-German vocabulary published by Leonhard Schultze-Jena in 1938 also gives Mixtec town names from this same region.[12] Lists of Mixtec names of towns in the Coastal region of the Mixteca are found in Antonio Peñafiel's commentary on the Lienzo of Zaca-

[4] "Explicación del reverso del Codex Vindobonensis," *Memoria de el Colegio Nacional*, Vol. V–5 (1950), *passim*.

[5] Similar problems in the Tarascan-speaking region of Michoacán in western Mexico are discussed in: Donald D. Brand, "Place-Name Problems in Mexico as Illustrated by Necotlán," *Papers of the Michigan Academy of Science, Arts and Letters*, Vol. XXXIV (1948), 241–52.

[6] *Vocabulario en lengua mixteca*, 87–98. Because the Reyes list is the principal early-Colonial source of Mixtec place names, it is reproduced in its entirety in Appendix A–1 of this book.

[7] As, for example, the *Relaciones Geográficas* of Teozacoalco (*RMEH* I, 174), Tilantongo (*PNE* IV, 70–71), and Cuilapan (*Tlalocan*, Vol. II–1, 22–26).

[8] *Colección de "Cuadros sinópticos" de los pueblos, haciendas y ranchos del Estado libre y soberano de Oaxaca* (Oaxaca, 1883). This volume is arranged by ex-districts of Oaxaca, with the towns, haciendas, and ranches of each district in alphabetical order; unfortunately it has no page numbers.

[9] "Catálogo etimológico de los nombres de los pueblos, haciendas y ranchos del Estado de Oaxaca," *BSMGE*, 4a época, Vol. I, 5–6 (1888), 285–438 (hereafter referred to as "*BSMGE* 1888").

[10] Bradomín, *Toponimia de Oaxaca (crítica etimológica)* (Mexico, 1955).

[11] "Arte, Prontuario, Vocabulario y Confesionario de la lengua mixteca," fol. 59/v–60/v of the nineteenth-century copy by Francisco del Paso y Troncoso in the Archivo Histórico del Museo Nacional de Antropología, Mexico City (Colección Antigua, 3–60 bis). The place names in the Villavicencio manuscript are listed in Appendix A–2 of this study.

[12] *Indiana, III: Bei den azteken, mixteken und tlapaneken der Sierra Madre del Sur von Mexiko* (Jena, 1938), 88–110.

tepec,[13] and in Martínez Gracida's unpublished study of the native rulers of Tututepec.[14] Ronald Spores has compiled Mixtec names of many of the lands belonging to Yanhuitlán in his study of the social organization of the Mixteca Alta.[15]

Two productive sources of Mixtec place names that have yet to be completely explored are land documents of the Colonial period and the present-day inhabitants of the Mixtec-speaking region. In the post-Conquest period, a great deal of litigation was carried on concerning land ownership and rights, and the documents relating to these disputes often contain Mixtec names of boundaries and other sites. A particularly rich archival source is the Ramo de Tierras of the Archivo General de la Nación in Mexico City, which contains 3,702 volumes of land documents, including many from the Mixteca.[16] Finally, one of the best methods to find out Mixtec names of places is to go to the Mixteca and ask. There are still about 200,000 speakers of Mixtec in western Oaxaca, and many of them are well informed on the place names of towns, rivers, and hills in the immediate vicinity of the town where they live.

COMPOSITION OF MIXTEC PLACE NAMES

In common with many indigenous place names in Mexico, Mixtec place names usually consist of two parts: a geographical substantive and a qualifying element. For example, in the Mixtec name of Tututepec, *yucu dzaa*, the initial word *yucu* ("hill") is the geographical substantive, and the second word *dzaa* ("bird") is the qualifying element.

In the discussion that follows, comparisons will be made between Mixtec place names and the more extensively studied Nahuatl place names, to show how place names in the two languages are similar and how they are dissimilar. As can be seen in the Tututepec example, the Mixtec and Nahuatl languages differ in the syntax of forming place-name compounds. In the Nahuatl name "tututepec," the first section—*tutu* from *tototl* ("bird")—is the qualifying element, followed by the geographical substantive *tepec*, a combination of *tepetl* ("hill") and the locative suffix *-c* (usually translated as "in"). Thus in Nahuatl place names the qualifying element usually precedes the geographical substantive, whereas in Mixtec place names the qualifying element follows the geographical substantive.

In both Mixtec and Nahuatl place names, the qualifying elements are many in number, and they may refer to colors, sizes, deities, numerals or calendrical signs, animals, plants, household objects, weapons, and so on.[17] The geographical substantives are few in number, and they are always a landscape feature, either natural or manmade.

GEOGRAPHICAL SUBSTANTIVES USED IN MIXTEC TOWN NAMES

The most common geographical substantives used in the Mixtec names of towns are: *ñuu* ("town, place where something exists"), *yucu* ("hill"), *yodzo* ("plain" or "valley"), and *yuta* ("river"). In Chart 3 these four substantives are listed in the column at the left, with their meanings as geographical substantives given in the second column. In the third column are the non-geographical meanings of the word itself or of other Mixtec words with which it is homonymous except for variations in tone. The English definitions of the words in the second and third columns are followed by the word's definition in Spanish as given in the sixteenth-century Alvarado dictionary. The fourth column of the chart shows the pictorial sign usually used to represent each of the Mixtec substantives. In the two columns at the right are the Nahuatl equivalents of these substantives and the pictorial sign of the Nahuatl substantive as it appears in manuscripts from the Nahuatl-speaking region.

Ñuu ("town, place where something exists")
This geographical substantive is usually represented in Mixtec manuscripts by a long rectangular frieze decorated with multicolored geometric patterns, frequently arranged in a stepped-pyramidal design. This type of frieze does not occur in signs which reflect the Nahuatl language. In fact, Nahuatl place signs do not include a pictorial element that represents the Nahuatl word for "town," which is *altepetl*, a combination of *atl* ("water") and *tepetl* ("hill"). The closest Nahuatl equivalents to the Mixtec word *ñuu*, when the latter word is translated as "place where something exists," are a group of locative suffixes, which are listed below with an example of how each is used in a place-name combination.[18]

-co, -c	"in, within"
Example:	*tlachco* "in the [place where there is a] ballcourt"
	tlach from *tlachtli* = "ballcourt"
	-co = "in"
-can, -ca	"place where something exists, in"
Example:	*cacalomacan* "place where crows are hunted"
	cacalo from *cacalotl* = "crow"
	ma = "to hunt, capture"
	-can = "place"

[13] *Códice Mixteco. Lienzo de Zacatepec* (Mexico, 1900), 3. (Hereafter referred to as "Peñafiel, *LZ*.") The list of Coastal place names given by Peñafiel was compiled by Cristóbal Palacios, *jefe político* of the District of Jamiltepec.

[14] Manuel Martínez Gracida, "Reseña histórica del antiguo reino de Tututepec" (1907), pp. 200–202 of the Van de Velde copy and pp. 314–19 of the Castañeda Guzmán copy. The various copies of the Martínez Gracida manuscript are discussed in Appendix D.

[15] *The Mixtec Kings and Their People*, 158–59, 165–67 *et passim*.

[16] About 3,000 volumes of Ramo de Tierras have been described in short notes in the *Boletín del Archivo General de la Nación*. These brief descriptions, arranged in numerical order by volume, begin in Vol. II, No. 3 (1931) of the *Boletín* and are continuing to appear in that publication.

[17] A brief survey of the subject matter of the qualifying elements in Mexican place names, with the greatest emphasis on Nahuatl names, is: Joseph Raymond, "The Indian Mind in Mexican Toponyms," *América Indígena*, Vol. XII-3 (1952), 205–13. The qualifying elements of the Nahuatl place names in Codex Mendoza have been catalogued by Barlow and McAfee, and by Nowotny, in the studies cited in note 1 of this chapter.

[18] One of the most detailed discussions of Nahuatl locative suffixes is found in: José Ignacio Dávila Garibi, *Toponimias nahuas*, Instituto Panamericano de Geografía e Historia, Publication 63 (Mexico, 1942), 19–63.

	CHART 3: Mixtec Words Most Frequently Used as Geographical Substantives in Town Names				
Word	Meaning as Geographical Substantive	Mixtec Homonyms	Pictorial Sign	Nahuatl Equivalent	Nahuatl Pictorial Sign
ÑUU	town (pueblo) town site (lugar por pueblo) city (ciudad) place where something exists (estança donde esta algo)	night (noche) dark, darkness (oscura cosa, tinieblas) drum (atabal) craw of a bird (buche de las aves)		-co, -c -can, -ca -tla, -la -tlan, -lan -yan, -ya	-tlan is sometimes illustrated as teeth: The others are not illustrated
YUCU	hill (cerro, monte)	shrub, grass (arbusto, hierba) desert (desierto) undomesticated, wild		-tepec	
YODZO (variants: yoso, yodo; so-)	field (campo) flat land (tierra llana) valley (valle) plain (vega)	flat stone for grinding corn (metate) above, on top of (arriba, encima de) bird's gizzard (molleja de ave)		-ixtlahuacan	
YUTA (variants: yucha; ta, te-)	river (río)	tender or immature thing (tierna cosa, cosa no madura)		-apan	

-tla, -la   "where an abundance of something exists"
Example: cilla "where there is an abundance of small seashells"
     cil from cilin = "small seashells"
     -la = "where there is an abundance of"

-tlan, -lan   "place where something exists; near, close to, within, below"
Example: tuchtlan "rabbit place"
     tuch from tochtli = "rabbit"
     -tlan = "place"

-yan, -ya   "place where some action occurs"
Example: ixicayan "place where [water] oozes"
     ixica = "to ooze"
     -yan = "place where the action occurs"

With the exception of tlan, the Nahuatl locative suffixes are rarely represented in place signs by pictorial elements which correspond to their respective sounds. Tlan is sometimes—but by no means always—represented by two or three teeth, for tlan is an abbreviated form of tlantli which means "teeth." An example of a Nahuatl sign utilizing the "teeth" element may be seen in the sign of Yanhuitlán, as illustrated in Fig. 43a, where the rectangular motif (a sign for yancuic or "new") is placed above two teeth (-tlan).

In contrast to Nahuatl place names, which have the complex set of locative suffixes listed above to indicate "place where something exists," most Mixtec place names utilize the unabbreviated word ñuu. As indicated above, ñuu is usually represented by a frieze with geometric patterns, a pictorial sign that is absent in Nahuatl logographic writing.

Yucu ("hill")

The sign for the Mixtec word yucu or "hill" is essentially a conventionalized "picture" of a hill. It is usually a green or brown bell-shaped form on a base that consists of a narrow red or blue band, below which there is often a yellow scalloped border. At times, the lower corners of the hill sign curl inward, forming volutes on either side. Often the outline of the hill shape is broken by small curvilinear or rectilinear projections which indicate the roughness or "bumpiness" of the hill.

The hill sign has several variant shapes. For example, one side of the hill may be extended in a manner that suggests a slope (as in Figs. 48, 79, 81), and at times this extended slope functions as a platform for human figures (as in Figs. 51a and 70). In addition, the shape of the hill in signs representing the same place name may vary from one manuscript to another, as can be seen in comparing four different signs for Tututepec in three different codices (Fig. 49) or two different signs for Acatepec in two codices (Fig. 51).

The Nahuatl pictorial sign for "hill" is basically the same as its Mixtec counterpart. However, it does not represent one single word-unit as the Mixtec sign represents the word *yucu*. Rather, it usually represents *tepec*, a combination of the word *tepetl* ("hill") and the locative suffix -*c*, meaning "in." Thus the Nahuatl place name "comaltepec" literally means "in the hill of the *comal*, or clay griddle," and the sign for this place name, illustrated in Fig. 78, consists of a round yellow disk representing a *comal* placed within the hill sign. As noted above under the discussion of *ñuu*, the locative suffix -*c* is not illustrated by a pictorial sign.

Use of the Ñuu and Yucu Signs

Frequently, there seems to be some ambivalence about the use of the hill sign (representing *yucu*) and the frieze with geometric patterns (representing *ñuu* or "town"). At times, the two pictorial signs are used interchangeably. A sign with a rib cage appears once in both Codices Nuttall and Colombino, and because the two signs are shown in the same context, they are known to be the same sign. In Nuttall, the rib cage is shown in connection with a hill sign (Fig. 20*a*); in Colombino, the rib cage is shown with a frieze (Fig. 20*b*). Thus it is difficult to determine whether the place name represented by this sign has as its geographical substantive *yucu* or *ñuu*.

In other place signs, both the hill sign and the frieze with geometric designs appear together. For example, Fig. 19 illustrates two signs with a Venus-staff motif, one from Nuttall and one from Colombino, and again these two signs are known to represent the same name because they appear in a similar context in the two manuscripts. In the sign in Colombino, the Venus-staff appears in connection with a frieze and a building, whereas the comparable sign in Nuttall shows the Venus-staff with a frieze and a hill. In this instance, it would seem that the geographical substantive of the Venus-staff sign is *ñuu* or "town," because the frieze is the common geographical feature shared by the two examples of the sign.[19]

The insertion of a hill sign where no word for hill occurs in the place name is also seen in a number of Nahuatl place signs. In Nowotny's analysis of the 541 different place signs in Codex Mendoza, the hill motif is part of the place signs of 41 towns whose names do not include the geographical substantive *tepec*.[20] In the case of Codex Mendoza, it is possible to note, if not completely explain, the discrepancies between a place name and the sign for

the name, because all of the pictorial signs in this manuscript are accompanied by a gloss written in script which sets forth the town's name. In the case of Mixtec place signs, we have no comparable manuscript showing a large number of signs accompanied by glosses or explanatory texts. Thus it is often difficult to ascertain precisely the general rules of place-sign composition—especially the general rule that each pictorial element of a place sign represents a specific word in the Mixtec language.

In other Mixtec place signs in which the frieze and hill signs appear together, it is possible that the function of the frieze is to indicate that the place sign represents the geographical unit of a town (*ñuu*). Many people in the Mixtec-speaking region today, when asked the Mixtec name of a town, preface this name with the word *ñuu*, even if *ñuu* is not part of the name itself. For example, the Mixtec name of the Coastal town of San Juan Colorado is *yoqua'a*, or "the red rope." (*Yo* is a shortened form of *yo'o*, meaning "rope"; *qua'a* means "red.") Many Mixtec speakers, when asked the Mixtec name of San Juan Colorado, reply "*ñuu yoqua'a*," which they translate as "the town of San Juan Colorado." The same use of *ñuu* as an initial word meaning "town" appears in Anne Dyk's 1951 Mixtec vocabulary, in which a number of Mixtec town names are listed under the entry *ñuu*. Included in this list are several names to which *ñuu* is merely added as an initial word, such as *ñuu yucu ndaa* for the Mixtec name of Teposcolula in the Mixteca Alta. The Mixtec name of this town is usually given as *yucu ndaa*, meaning "hill of the maguey cactus" according to Reyes, who lived in Teposcolula.[21] Thus in cases where a frieze (*ñuu*) occurs with a hill sign (*yucu*), it is possible that the frieze is a logogram of the optional prefix *ñuu* and may indicate that the sign in question represents a town unit.

It would seem, then, that the appearance of the frieze with geometric patterns or the hill sign does not always guarantee that the words they represent—*ñuu* in the case of the frieze and *yucu* in the case of the hill—are part of the place names depicted by the signs in which the frieze or hill appears. At times, the two motifs are used interchangeably; in other instances, they appear together in the same place sign. Thus, both the frieze and hill signs seem to have an almost emblematic character and often signify a populated place in general or even "place sign in general," in addition to their usual function as logograms depicting the specific words *ñuu* and *yucu*.

Yodzo ("plain, valley")

In Mixtec manuscripts, the pictorial sign for the geographical substantive *yodzo*, meaning "plain" or "valley," is a rectangular mat composed of multicolored feathers bound together by vertical bands. (Examples of this motif in a place-sign context are illustrated in Figs. 40, 42, 47, and 55 of this book.) The word *yodzo* also means "large feather" in Mixtec, and thus a tone pun is involved in the

---

[19] A place sign with a Venus-staff and a frieze only appears also in Bodley 6–IV, in a context that is different from that of the Venus-staff signs in Colombino and Nuttall. The latter signs appear in connection with the conquests of 8-Deer in the year 1033, whereas the sign in Bodley is a town ruled by a nobleman named 10-Reed around the middle of the tenth century. However, the sign in Bodley may well represent the same place name as the similar signs in Nuttall and Colombino.

[20] "Die Hieroglyphen des Codex Mendoza," *Mitteilungen aus dem Museum für Völkerkunde, Hamburg,* Vol. XXV (1959), 98–103, 110–11.

[21] "Arte en lengua mixteca," 7: "yucundaa, *de yucu q.d. sierra y daa que significa nequen; por Tepuzculula la sierra de nequen . . . .*" Other meanings of the word *ndaa* are listed below, note 34, Chapter V.

feathers utilized in this sign, or what I. J. Gelb terms a logogram of "phonetic transfer," in which the pictorial sign of feathers (*yodzo*) informs the reader that the sign represents the word "plain" (*yodzo*).[22] The shape of the sign—a rectangle that is longer than it is high and lacking the projections indicating "bumpiness" that occur in the hill sign—reinforces in a pictorial fashion the idea of the flatness of plains or valleys.

The Nahuatl sign for the suffix -*ixtlahuacan*, meaning "plain, valley," has the same long rectangular shape as the Mixtec sign for *yodzo*. However, the interior of the *ixtlahuacan* sign is not comprised of feathers, but of squares representing tilled fields. Often the field motif that represents *ixtlahuacan* is accompanied by a pair of inverted eyes, as in the Nahuatl sign for Coixtlahuaca (Fig. 43*b*), where the eyes are placed above the serpent (*coatl*), which is the qualifying element of *coaixtlahuaca* or "serpent plain."[23]

Yuta ("river")

The sign for the geographical substantive *yuta* or "river" is usually shown as a conventionalized cross-section of a river—that is, an area of blue or green enclosed on two sides and at the bottom by a wide trough-like border. The shape of the entire sign may be rectangular with right angles at the lower corners of the border (as in Figs. 7*d* and 39*a*), or it may be U-shaped with rounded corners at the base (as in Fig. 68 *a*, *c*). The ground of the border is usually green or brown, suggesting the earth of a river bed, and the border is divided into sections by red or yellow stripes. In addition, the border may be elaborated by several thin bands of decoration placed either inside or outside the main trough-like form. One of the most common of these is a narrow white band divided into small squares. This band usually encircles the inside border of the trough, as in Figs. 7*d* and 68*a*.

The water within the border is sometimes represented as an undecorated area of blue or green; at other times, the interior of the river also has horizontal black lines, with straight and wavy lines alternating, to indicate the ripples of the water (as in Fig. 68 *a*, *b*). The top border of the river sign may be completely flat (as in Fig. 68*b*); it may include a narrow white band whose top edge is comprised of a series of curlicues that indicate ripples or foam (as in Fig. 7*d*); or the top of the river may consist of a series of small projections that terminate in a circle or seashell to represent the flowing or splashing quality of water (as in Fig. 68*a*). Occasionally, one side of the trough-like border is omitted, and the projections that represent spouts of water extend beyond the base of the river sign (as in the sign on the right border of Fig. 96).

The closest Nahuatl equivalent of the Mixtec word *yuta* is the suffix -*apan*. *Apan* literally means "on the water" (*a*- from *atl* or "water" plus -*pan*, "above, on") and not "river," which is *atoyatl* in Nahuatl. *Atoyatl*, in common with *altepetl*, the Nahuatl word for "town" or "populated place," never appears in a place name as a geographical substantive. Thus the "water" referred to in the *apan* compound may be any body of water, such as an arroyo, river, lake, or lagoon. This is in contrast to the Mixtec substantive *yuta*, which specifically means "river."

Yuta, in common with the Nahuatl *apan*, is the most prevalent geographical substantive referring to water that occurs in names of towns. In addition, the pictorial sign for *apan* is very similar to the pictorial sign for *yuta*. *Apan* as a pictorial sign represents the Nahuatl word *apantli*, or "irrigation canal or ditch"; and the *apan* sign, in common with the *yuta* sign, is an area of blue enclosed by a trough-like border on two sides and the bottom. Furthermore, the flat blue area in the *apan* sign usually has black horizontal lines indicating ripples as well as projections with circles and shells at the top of the water—two features that occur in many of the Mixtec signs for *yuta*.

General Differences Between Mixtec and Nahuatl Names of Towns

A number of basic differences exist between the syntax of place names in the Mixtec and Nahuatl languages. As was seen in the above discussion of geographical substantives found in the names of towns, Mixtec and Nahuatl differ notably in that Mixtec place names are composed of a geographical substantive followed by the qualifying element, whereas in Nahuatl, the qualifying element precedes a locative suffix (such as -*c*) or a geographical substantive compound with a locative suffix (such as *tepec*, from *tepetl* plus -*c*). Further, the locative element, which is a common feature of Nahuatl place names, is almost completely absent in Mixtec place names. For the most part, simple nouns, such as the geographical substantives *ñuu*, *yucu*, *yodzo*, and *yuta*, are utilized in Mixtec place names, and not locative elements which can be translated as the prepositions "in," "near," and so forth.

The principal exception to this generalization is the Mixtec prefix *a*-, which means "at" or "in" and which is represented in place signs as a human jaw with a mouth. Two examples of signs which illustrate Mixtec place names with the prefix *a*- may be seen in two signs from the post-Conquest Codex of Yanhuitlán; both signs represent names of towns in the Valley of Yanhuitlán in the Mixteca Alta.[24] One sign, consisting of a mouth and a

---

[22] Gelb, *A Study of Writing*, 102ff. The tone pun involving the two meanings of *yodzo* was first noted by Caso (*Bodley*, 17–18).

[23] The phonetic meaning of the eye motif has been interpreted in several ways by different scholars. James Cooper Clark (*Codex Mendoza*, analysis of sign no. 510, fol. 43/r) analyzes *ixtlahuacan* as follows: *ixtlapal* = inverted, ideograph for *istlauatl* = a plain; *can* = place. According to this translation, the *inverted* position of the eyes is the element that is phonetically significant.

Peñafiel (*Nombres geográficos de México*, 76–77) suggests that the etymology of *ixtlahuacan* is *ix* from *ixtli* ("eyes"), plus *tla* from *tlalli* ("earth"), plus *hua*, a possessive word used with the locative suffix -*can* ("place"). He further postulates that the eyes present the additional idea that a plain or valley is a "place where one has a view."

It is also possible that the eye motif is used to distinguish the sign for *ixtlahuacan* from the sign for the Nahuatl word *milpa*, or "field," which is also represented by a long rectangle of tilled earth. In the case of the *ixtlahuacan* sign, the eye motif would serve as an indicator that lets the reader know that the initial syllable of the word depicted is *ix* rather than *mil*.

[24] The largest section of the Codex of Yanhuitlán (11 folios, plus some fragments) is in the Academia de Bellas Artes, Puebla, and this sec-

nopal cactus (Fig. 24a), represents Nochixtlán, a town about ten miles southeast of Yanhuitlán (17°32′ N., 97°21′ W.). The Mixtec name of Nochixtlán is *atoco*, "in the place of the cochineal." *Toco* means "cochineal," a red dye made from worms which live in the nopal cactus, and this word is represented by the cactus in the sign. The locative prefix *a-* is represented by the human jaw from which the cactus emerges. A second sign from the Codex of Yanhuitlán consists of an arrow placed within the jaw motif (Fig. 24b) and represents the town of Anduvua, present-day San Andrés Andúa, located about five miles southwest of Yanhuitlán and formerly a subject of Yanhuitlán. *Nduvua* means "arrow" in Mixtec; the *a-* prefix is represented by a human jaw which contains the arrow; and the frieze and hill which form a base for the jaw do not illustrate any portion of the name *Anduvua*.

But the use of the locative prefix *a-* rather than using the substantive *ñuu* which can mean "place where something exists" is comparatively rare in Mixtec place names. Furthermore, the *a-* seems to be very much a local feature, for it is found principally in place names in and around the Valley of Yanhuitlán. It is not known why the human jaw with an open mouth represents the prefix *a-*. The Mixtec word for "mouth," *yuhu*, may also mean "at the edge of, bordering," but the word *yuhu* appears to have little relationship with the prefix *a-*. It is possible that *a-* may be an abbreviation of the Mixtec word *dzaa*, which means "chin"; however, this interpretation would explain only the pictorial element of the human chin, and would not explain why the prefix *a-* means "in" or "at."

Another characteristic of Nahuatl place names which distinguishes them from their Mixtec counterparts is that the words which form Nahuatl place names are usually abbreviated. For example, in the Nahuatl name *tecamachalco*, which means "place of the stone jawbone" and whose sign is illustrated in Fig. 77, the element *te* is a shortened form of *tetl* ("stone"), *camachal* is an abbreviation of *camachalli* ("jawbone"), and *co* is a locative suffix meaning "in" or "place."

In Mixtec place names, abbreviated forms are much less common. The qualifying element of a Mixtec place name contains only those abbreviations which are utilized in the Mixtec language as a whole. The two most frequent of these are the prefix *tnu-* which designates trees and shrubs and which is derived from the word *yutnu* or "wood," and the prefix *te-* (usually written phonetically as *ti-*) which is used to designate animals and some fruit-bearing plants and is an abbreviation of *quete* or *quití* ("animal"). Thus in the Reyes list of Mixtec town names, the name of the Mixteca Baja town of Acatepec is given as *yucu tnuyoo*, which has the same meaning as the town's

Nahuatl name, "hill of reeds," for *yucu* is "hill" and *tnuyoo* (the prefix *tnu-* plus *yoo*) is "reed." Similarly, the Mixtec name of the Coastal town of Mechoacán, *ñuu tiyaca*, means "town of the fish"; *ñuu* is "town" and *tiyaca* is "fish," combining the animal prefix *ti-* and the word *yaca*.

Abbreviations may occur in Mixtec geographical substantives, which are sometimes shortened to their final syllable. That is, *yodzo* ("plain, valley") is occasionally abbreviated to *dzo* or *so*, and *yuta* ("river") to *ta* or *te*. In Schultze-Jena's vocabulary of Mixtec from the western Oaxaca and eastern Guerrero region of the Mixteca Baja, *yucu* ("hill") is at times shortened to *cu*, but this abbreviation does not appear to be prevalent in other sections of the Mixteca.[25] Another type of abbreviation that occurs in Mixtec is that words comprised of a consonant plus a vowel plus a glottal stop plus a repetition of the first vowel are often abbreviated to merely the initial consonant and vowel when they are placed in front of another word. For example, *sa'a* ("at the foot of") is shortened to *sa* in the place name *Sachio*, which means "at the foot of the temple platform" (*sa* from *sa'a* = "at the foot of"; *chio* or *chiyo* = "temple platform"). For the most part, however, Mixtec place names tend to use combinations of complete words rather than the abbreviated forms that are so typical of Nahuatl place names.

Another fairly common feature of Nahuatl place names is the use of diminutives. Two types of diminutives occur: *tzin*, which is a reverential and affectionate diminutive, and *ton*, a derogatory diminutive. Thus the place name Tulancingo means "at the small place of marsh grass," for

> *tul* from *tollin* = "marsh grass"
> *lan* = "place where something exists"
> *cin* from *tzin* = the reverential diminutive
> *go* from *co* = "in, at."

As can be seen in the sign of Tulancingo in Fig. 53b of this study, the *tzin* element is shown as the human buttocks and legs, because *tzintli* means "the lower part" in Nahuatl. Similarly, the Nahuatl name *Tilantongo* means "at the small black place," for

> *til* from *tlilli* = "black"
> *lan* = "place where something exists"
> *ton* = a derogatory diminutive
> *go* from *co* = "at, in."

The *ton* element is not represented in place signs by a specific pictorial motif as is its counterpart *tzin*.

In Mixtec place names diminutives are extremely rare and appear infrequently in names of towns located outside the Mixtec-speaking region. In the Reyes list of Mixtec place names, the Mixtec word for "small," *dzuchi*, occurs in only three of the 146 names on the list, and the

---

tion is published, along with an extensive commentary, in: Wigberto Jiménez Moreno and Salvador Mateos Higuera, *Códice de Yanhuitlán* (Mexico, 1940), plates I–XXIV. A smaller section of the Codex (four folios) is in AGN-Vínculos 272–10; it is published, along with a description of its contents, in: Heinrich Berlin, *Fragmentos desconocidos del Códice de Yanhuitlán y otras investigaciones mixtecas* (Mexico, 1947), plates A–G.

25 For example, Schultze-Jena (*Indiana*, III, 93) gives the Mixtec name of the town of Ometepec in southeastern Guerrero as *kuwui*, and the Mixtec name for the same town in the Reyes list is *yucuvui*. This name, as the town's Nahuatl name, *ometepec*, means "two hills"; *yucu* = "hill," and *uvui* = "two." In two place names from the same region that appear in the Villavicencio list (Appendix A–2), *yucu* is also abbreviated to *cu*: *cu chico* (the Mixtec name of Atlamajalcingo del Río) and *cu chiton* (the Mixtec name of Xalpatlahuaca).

three towns in question are located in the Nahuatl-speaking region of Central Mexico. In two cases, the name with *dzuchi* in the Reyes list follows another place name that is identical except that it lacks *dzuchi*. The first of these two groups is: Ixtapalapa (in the Distrito Federal) = *ñuu techiyo*; Ixtapaluca (in the State of Mexico) = *ñuu techiyo dzuchi*. The Mixtec name *ñuu techiyo* means "the town of the potsherds," for *ñuu* = "town," and *techiyo* = "potsherd" (*tiesto de cosa quebrada*; *casco de vasija*). Thus, in Mixtec the town of Ixtapalapa would be "the town of the potsherds," and Ixtapaluca would be "the small town of the potsherds."

The second group of two names with the Mixtec word *dzuchi* is: Chimalhuacan chalco (State of Mexico) = *ñuu yusa*; Chimalhuacan atenco (State of Mexico) = *ñuu yusa dzuchi*. As Jiménez Moreno has observed, *ñuu yusa* means "town of the shields," and therefore the second Chimalhuacan was known in Mixtec as "the small town of the shields."[26]

The third Mixtec place name in the Reyes list that includes the word *dzuchi* is that of the town of "Mitzquique," possibly present-day Mixcuic in the Distrito Federal. This town's Mixtec name is *saha tnudayn dzuchi*, which may mean "at the foot of the small *capulín* tree," for *saha* = "at the foot of," and *tnudayn*, probably *tnundaya* = "*capulín*" (a type of tree which resembles a cherry tree), and *dzuchi* = "small."

To my knowledge, these three names on the Reyes list that include the word *dzuchi* or "small" are the only Mixtec names of towns that have a diminutive. This is in contrast to Nahuatl place names in which diminutives are more common. In Codex Mendoza, which contains a corpus of 541 different Nahuatl place names, nineteen of these names include the reverential diminutive *tzin* and one includes the derogatory diminutive *ton*.

TOWN AND NON-TOWN GEOGRAPHICAL UNITS

In the Mixtec-speaking region prior to the Spanish conquest, the hereditary kingdoms included two levels of communities. The first of these was the major town or *cabecera*, and it was these that were governed by the native rulers or *caciques* whose genealogies are depicted in the Mixtec histories. In addition to the major towns, the kingdom often included several outlying villages that were subjects or dependencies of the major town and which are variously called *sujetos*, *estancias* or *ranchos* in Spanish.[27] The outlying subject towns were controlled for the *cacique* by a secondary class of nobility, who were known as *principales*.[28] *Caciques* were to marry only persons of their own ruling class and were not to marry

persons of the *principal* class.[29] Whether the *principales* inherited rights to control the outlying towns or were appointed anew by each generation of *caciques* is not known. In the Colonial period *principales* often claimed to be rulers of a subject town because their ancestors had ruled the same town, but it has not been ascertained whether this practice of inheriting control of subject towns was common in the pre-Conquest period.

It might be assumed that the place signs in the pre-Conquest history manuscripts that are associated with marriage pairs or single persons of nobility represent major towns or *cabeceras* rather than subject villages. But apparently this is not always the case, for some place signs of subject towns may be accompanied by figures who have calendrical and personal names as do the hereditary rulers or *caciques*. This is demonstrated by the post-Conquest Codex Muro, in which *principales* as well as *caciques* have both types of names. Many of the persons with personal and calendrical names in Muro are shown to be rulers of towns subject to Yanhuitlán, and thus they are of the *principal* rather than of the *cacique* class. It would seem, then, that the appearance of a place sign in connection with named nobility is no guarantee that the persons are of the ruling class and that the sign represents a *cabecera*, for the place sign may also represent a subject town controlled by the secondary nobility; and it is difficult to determine which geographical unit is depicted by any given place sign.

This problem also exists for place signs that are not associated with named personages and which may also represent subject towns, as can be seen in a comparison of two signs that appear in both the Codex of Yanhuitlán and in Codex Nuttall. One page of the post-Conquest Codex of Yanhuitlán contains a church with the Mixtec gloss *huey ñuhu Yucundaa*, or "the church of Teposcolula," and at the borders of this page are four place signs which Jiménez Moreno and Mateos Higuera believe to represent names of villages that were subject to the Mixteca Alta town of Teposcolula.[30] One of these four signs (Fig. 23a, left) is a double-peaked hill with a column and small dots suggesting sand between the two peaks. A second sign (Fig. 23a, right) shows a bird within a circle that is divided in half by a vertical line. As Robert Barlow has noted, these two signs of Teposcolula's subject villages also appear on page 69 of Codex Nuttall (Fig. 23b), as places which are either allies of or conquered by the

---

[26] Introduction to the 1962 edition of the Alvarado dictionary (*Vocabulario en lengua mixteca*), 90.

[27] The best description of the composition of the pre-Conquest Mixtec community is in Spores, *The Mixtec Kings and Their People*, 91–104.

[28] This type of political control as it was exercised by the Coastal Mixtec capital of Tututepec is described in documents quoted below, p. 86.

[29] This policy of class endogamy is stated emphatically in the group of 1580 *Relaciones Geográficas* from Juxtlahuaca and vicinity (*RMEH* II, 135–63). In the *Relación* of Juxtlahuaca (139): "... *el que era* cacique *se casava con* cacica *y el principal con* principala ...." Virtually the same statement is made in the accompanying *Relaciones* of Mixtepec (144), Ayusuchiquilazala (149), Jicayán de Tovar (153), Putla (158), and Zacatepec (161).

[30] *Códice de Yanhuitlán*, 65. Jiménez Moreno and Mateos Higuera translate the gloss *huey ñuhu Yucundaa* as "the great town of Teposcolula," for they believe *huey* to represent the Nahuatl word for "great" and *ñuhu* to mean "town." However, *huey* here is a dialect variation of Alvarado's *huahi*, meaning "house." *Ñuhu* means "sacred, holy"; and the combination *huahi ñuhu* (literally "sacred house") means "church." *Yucu ndaa* is the Mixtec name of Teposcolula.

eleventh-century ruler 8-Deer.[31] In Nuttall, a twin-peaked hill with a red-and-black column immediately follows the circle with a knobby outline which is divided into quarters and contains a black, long-billed bird. Thus, in the long sequences of place signs shown as visited or conquered by 8-Deer on the back of Nuttall and in Colombino and Becker I, the signs of subject towns would seem to be interspersed with signs of major town units.

A number of place signs in the Mixtec manuscripts represent ceremonial centers rather than towns or villages. Some signs are known to be ceremonial sites because the personage associated with the sign is a non-historical deity impersonator. Other place signs are conjectured to represent ceremonial sites because ceremonial activities are taking place on or in front of the sign, as for example a scene showing a ruler making an offering of incense or jewelry or performing a bloodletting ceremony.

Unfortunately, little is known about the place names of Mixtec ceremonial centers. For example, it is not certain whether a ceremonial site had the same Mixtec name as the major town near which it was located, or whether it had its own, distinct Mixtec name. As concerns the location of the ceremonial sites, Ronald Spores has summarized the known archaeological and documentary data and has stated that such sites were "most often situated on a mountain or hilltop, in a cave, at a spring, or in association with some unusual configuration," and that they were usually outside of, but adjacent to, the major town.[32]

It is possible, then, that a ceremonial site located near a town might have the same Mixtec name and place sign as the major town, and the place sign would be known to represent the town's ceremonial site because ceremonial activities are taking place on or near the sign. But it is equally possible that if the ceremonial site were located at some spectacular geographical feature—whether mountain, spring, or cave—the site might have its own place name. Or, if the site were important and not close to the major town, it might well have a distinct place name, much as do the town's outlying dependent villages. It is also possible that the most important ceremonial sites were autonomous and not dependencies of any one community kingdom. This would seem to be the case for two ceremonial sites whose place signs occur frequently in the Mixtec histories: the "Skull Place" associated with the female death deity 9-Grass, and the "Sun Place" associated with the male solar deity 1-Death.[33] Neither of these places is ever shown as being ruled by historical nobility, nor is either place sign shown as connected to a second place sign with historical personages, even though both

ceremonial sites are frequently visited by important rulers. It would appear that "Skull Place" and "Sun Place" were very prominent ceremonial sites to which pilgrimages were made, but that they were not necessarily subject to one town or allied with one specific dynasty of hereditary rulers.

Place signs may also represent names of places that are not inhabited, such as the sites of boundary markers, cultivated plots of land, and the like. These signs appear most frequently in the early Colonial maps of one town and its surrounding lands, such as the two Lienzos of Zacatepec (Figs. 85 and 122), which show the lands of the town of Zacatepec and include place signs of the town's dependencies, boundaries, and a number of uninhabited places within the boundaries.

One of the problems of place sign identification is that the four geographical substantives used for town names —ñuu, yucu, yodzo and yuta—are also utilized in names of places that are not towns. Thus, for example, any given place sign that has the hill motif representing yucu may depict the place name of a major town or cabecera, a dependency or subject village, a ceremonial center, or an uninhabited site such as the boundary of a town. There are apparently no pictorial signs incorporated into place signs to indicate the geographical unit of the place named by the sign, and for the most part the geographical unit can be determined only by the context of the place sign.

Place signs shown with marriage pairs of rulers are presumed to be inhabited places, either major towns ruled by caciques or possibly subject towns controlled by principales. Place signs that are consistently associated with non-historical personages or deity impersonators are thought to be ceremonial centers. In the early Colonial maps, a group of place signs arranged in an enclosing circle or rectangle around the sign of a town are considered to represent the names of the town's boundaries. But in many instances the context of place signs is not at all clear. This is particularly true of signs that are not associated with named persons, such as the numerous pages of place signs on the back of Nuttall that list places conquered or visited by 8-Deer. Many of these signs are not associated with named rulers, and some of them may be major towns, some may be dependencies, some may be ceremonial sites. (Although it may be conjectured that 8-Deer is not shown as conquering or visiting uninhabited places such as boundary sites, this is by no means certain.) Precisely which geographical unit is represented by most of the numerous places depicted on the back of Nuttall is not known.

Perhaps, when some of the signs have been identified in the various groups of place signs, it may be possible to identify other signs in the same group, if it can be assumed that each group of signs represents places in the same general location and that the conquest or pilgrimage route of 8-Deer may follow a pattern that is based on the proximity of places shown as conquered or visited in any one expedition. For example, the two place signs on page 69 of Nuttall that depict the names of two dependencies of

---

[31] Barlow, "Glifos toponímicos de los códices mixtecos," *Tlalocan*, Vol. II–3 (1947), 285–86. In Nuttall 69–70, the sequence of place signs containing the signs of Teposcolula's two subjects is not shown as conquered because the place signs are not pierced with an arrow; but in Colombino XVIII, 52–53, an analogous series of place signs is preceded by the warband motif.

[32] *The Mixtec Kings and Their People*, 96.

[33] The data on 1-Death in the Mixtec histories have been summarized by Caso, "El dios 1. Muerte," *Mitteilungen aus dem Museum für Völkerkunde und Vorgeschichte, Hamburg*, Vol. XXV (1959); the death deity 9-Grass is discussed above, p. 30.

Teposcolula occur within a sequence of eight place signs; and thus it might be conjectured that the other six signs in the group represent names of places that are also in the general region of Teposcolula. But this is merely a working hypothesis; so few of the many place signs on the back of Nuttall have been identified that it is impossible to determine whether any one group of signs shown as visited by 8-Deer represents names of places that are located near each other.

In addition to the geographical substantives *ñuu*, *yucu*, *yodzo*, and *yuta*, which may occur in any type of place name, whether that of a town or a smaller-than-town site, seventeen geographical substantives are frequently used in names of places that are not towns. These substantives and the signs that represent them are discussed below.

CHIYO AND ITNU

The two geographical substantives *chiyo* ("platform" or "foundation") and *itnu* ("slope") occasionally appear in names of towns, but they are equally or more common substantives in place names of geographical units smaller than towns. For this reason, *chiyo* and *itnu* are listed below in Chart 4, which sets forth the substantives usually found in smaller-than-town units, but they are singled out for discussion here, because the known signs which represent these two words present special problems.

Chiyo seems to be most frequently represented in place signs as a temple platform. Usually the platform is shown in profile (as in Figs. 80, 82b and 24c), often with a stairway indicated at one side; occasionally the platform is shown as front-facing (as in Fig. 82a), with the major stairway in the center of the sign. The notable exception to the general rule that *chiyo* is shown as a temple base is the sign for the important Mixteca Alta town of Teozacoalco (Fig. 28).[34] The Mixtec name of Teozacoalco is *chiyo ca'nu*, and the *chiyo* element is here represented by a frieze with multicolored geometric patterns—that is, the sign that usually represents the geographical substantive *ñuu* or "town." It is not known why the frieze is used instead of the temple platform in the Teozacoalco sign, nor can it as yet be ascertained whether this sign is the only one where the word *chiyo* is represented by the frieze motif.

Itnu, meaning "slope" or "hillock," seems to be illustrated by a variety of signs. For example, the post-Conquest Map No. 36 (Fig. 21) shows a town surrounded by signs of its boundaries, with each sign accompanied by a gloss of its Mixtec name;[35] and within this one map alone, several different motifs are used to depict the geographical substantive *itnu*. In two boundary signs where the gloss contains *itnu* as the geographical substantive, this word is represented by a hill with a slope on one side (Fig. 22 *a*, *b*). These two hills contrast with most of the hills in Map No. 36 that are accompanied by a gloss containing the word *yucu* ("hill"), because the latter are

usually bilaterally symmetrical (as in Fig. 11) rather than shown with a sloping side. The two signs in question, then, seem to be a straightforward rendering of *itnu*, or "slope." Another sign in Map No. 36 that is accompanied by a gloss containing *itnu* illustrates this substantive with a long hill formation that has a rounded peak on each side and a declivity in the center (Fig. 22c). The shape of this hill differs considerably from the hill with a sloping side, but it still presents the idea of a slope between two small hills.

However, three additional signs in Map No. 36 are also glossed with a name containing *itnu*, and in these three, *itnu* is expressed by a type of platform or frieze. In one instance the platform is merely an undecorated horizontal strip (Fig. 22d); in another instance, it is a frieze with geometric patterns usually associated with the word *ñuu* or "town" (Fig. 22e). In the third example (Fig. 22f), the platform encloses three horizontal bands of chevrons. In this case, the chevrons do not represent the warband motif, but the pattern of a straw mat or petate. According to the gloss below, this sign depicts the Mixtec name, *ytno caa yui*, or "the slope in the form of a petate," for *ytno (itnu)* = "slope"; *caa* = "to have the form or shape of"; and *yui (yuvui* in the Alvarado dictionary) = "petate or straw mat." In this last instance, the long rectangular shape of the sign is justified by the name of the slope—that is, a slope which has the shape of a petate. In the other two instances in which *itnu* is represented by a platform, the reasons for choosing this motif to depict the word "slope" are by no means clear. We see, then, that within a single map, the word *itnu* is shown as two variations on the sign for "hill" and as a rectangular platform or frieze.

In Codex Sánchez Solís, the word *itnu* appears in two different glosses that are connected with place signs, but these do little to clarify the situation. On page 20 of Sánchez Solís, *itnu* is represented by what appears to be a standard hill sign with no indication of a slope (Fig. 22g).[36] The *itnu* sign on page 31 of this codex (Fig. 22h) is shown as a stone rather than as a hill, although the stone motif would seem a more appropriate sign for *toto* ("rock") or *yuu* ("stone") than for *itnu*.[37]

Thus it would seem that there is no single sign for either *chiyo* or *itnu*. *Chiyo*, though usually a temple platform, is represented as a frieze in at least one instance; and *itnu* is variously shown as a hill with or without a slope, a platform with or without geometric decorations, and a stone.

GEOGRAPHICAL SUBSTANTIVES USED IN NAMES OF BOUNDARIES AND OTHER SMALLER-THAN-TOWN SITES

In addition to *chiyo* and *itnu*, fifteen other geographical substantives are most commonly used in place names of sites that are smaller than towns, and most frequently in names of a town's boundaries. These geographical sub-

---

[34] This place sign is discussed in more detail below, pp. 57–58.

[35] The glosses on Map No. 36 are translated and discussed in detail in Appendix E.

[36] This place sign in Sánchez Solís may be the sign of Chicahuaxtla, as is discussed below, pp. 150–51.

[37] Two possible identifications of this sign are suggested below, pp. 61–62.

stantives are listed in the left-hand column of Chart 4. The second column of this chart contains the meaning of the word when used as a geographical substantive, and the third column contains non-geographical meanings of the same word or of words that are homonymous except for variations in tone. The fourth and final column of the chart shows the pictorial sign that represents the geographical substantive, if the sign is known.

The principal source of our knowledge of the pictorial signs that represent these substantives is Map No. 36 (Fig. 21), in which each of the thirty-seven place signs that represent names of boundaries is accompanied by a gloss that sets forth the Mixtec place name shown in the sign. A second source of the signs that represent geographical substantives used in boundary names is the Lienzo of Jicayán (Figs. 143-59). This lienzo is an early Colonial map of the town of Jicayán and, in common with Map No. 36, shows the town encircled by place signs that represent the town's boundary sites, and some of these signs are accompanied by glosses in Mixtec.[38]

The geographical substantives for which signs are known are discussed briefly below. A number of the pictorial signs that represent geographical substantives have not as yet been surely identified, although the Mixtec word is known to be a substantive from Colonial-period land documents that set forth Mixtec names of boundary sites. At the present time, no pictorial sign is definitely known to represent the following geographical substantives: *itu* ("field"); *nduhua* ("gully, plain"); *nduta* ("water"); *siqui* ("hillock; section of a town"); *tayu* ("city, province"). It is very likely that the sign for *nduta*, or "water," is similar to, or a variation of, other pictorial signs that represent bodies of water (such as the *yuta* or "river" sign), but so far no specific sign is known to represent *nduta* when used in place names.

Cavua. In the Lienzo of Jicayán, the word *cavua*, which can mean "rock," "cave," or "ravine" is apparently depicted by the same type of "feather mat" motif that represents the word *yodzo*, or "field, plain." In this case, the feather-mat motif probably illustrates the "ravine" definition of *cavua*, because a ravine as a plain or valley may be a comparatively low stretch of ground surrounded by mountains or rocky cliffs. No pictorial sign has definitely been associated with the "rock" or "cave" definitions of *cavua*.

Chiyo. Discussed above, page 45.

Cuite. In Map No. 36 the sign for *cuite*, or "mound," is identical to the sign for *yucu*, or "hill."

Dzoco. A sign for *dzoco*, or "well, spring," probably occurs in the Lienzo of Jicayán. The sign in question consists of two motifs: (1) two vertical walls flanking a body of water (indicated by the curlicue waves on top)—a configuration that strongly suggests a cross-section view of a well or spring (*dzoco*), and (2) at the bottom of the sign, an L-shaped base with a loop—the pre-Conquest

sign for a cradle (also *dzoco* in Mixtec). None of the Mixtec glosses in the Lienzo of Jicayán sets forth the Mixtec place name illustrated in this particular sign, but it seems likely that the sign represents a spring or well, with the cradle motif (*dzoco*) used as a phonetic indicator to reinforce the idea that the enclosed body of water is a well or spring (*dzoco*). Concerning another possible sign for the substantive *dzoco*, see the discussion of *mini*, below.

Itnu. Discussed above, page 45.

Mini. In Map No. 36 the sign for *mini*, or "lake, hollow," may be a circle of water that appears to represent a lake as seen from above. The interior of the circle has wavy lines suggesting the rippling movement of water, and the enclosing border has the characteristic projections ending in circles which suggest the splashing, flowing quality of water. However, the gloss that accompanies this sign in Map No. 36, *mini dzoco cuiy* ("the lake of the spring of the tiger"), contains two substantives that refer to water, and thus it is possible that the circle of water represents a well or spring (*dzoco*) rather than a lake (*mini*).

Ndoyo. In the Lienzo of Jicayán the sign for *ndoyo* ("swamp, marsh, spring") is a U-shaped trough-like form with the interior border consisting of the small curlicues that represent the ripples of water. In its general shape this sign resembles the sign for *yuta* or "river"; but in the "river" sign the curlicues indicating ripples usually form the top border of the trough-like semicircle rather than being placed on the interior rim of the semicircle as is the case in the sign for *ndoyo*.

Toto. In Map No. 36 the pictorial sign for *toto* ("rock") is one of the traditional signs for a stone: a roughly sausage-shaped motif with one side filled in with black, plus two black stripes that run diagonally through the center of the motif to suggest the rough contour of the rock. At each end of the rock motif are projecting fleur-de-lis forms that further reinforce the idea of a rock as rough and craggy.

Yahui. The sign for *yahui* ("plaza, market") in Map No. 36 is a circle which encloses a group of footprints and thus suggests very succinctly the idea of a plaza or market as an enclosed place that is inhabited, at least temporarily, by many people.

Yuhua. The Mixtec word *yuhua* has three different meanings as a geographical substantive: (1) a wall, often a defensive wall of a city, (2) an enclosed space, and (3) a ballcourt. Although many crenelated enclosures and a number of brick walls appear in Mixtec manuscripts, no specific pictorial sign can yet be associated with the first meaning of *yuhua* as "wall." In the Lienzo of Jicayán the sign for *yuhua* meaning "enclosed space" is a simple line motif, roughly the shape of a crest, that encloses a falcon, the qualifying element of the place sign (Fig. 156, first place sign on the left). The native ballcourt, also *yuhua* in Mixtec, is always represented in the Mixtec histories as the H-shaped floor plan of the playing area of the court, the common plan of Middle American ballcourts from the

Classic period to the time of the Spanish conquest. The H-shaped section of the ballcourt is often divided into four sections which are painted in two or four different colors. At times the sections between the vertical projections of the H-shape contain a long rectangular frieze with geometric patterns similar to the sign for *ñuu* or "town"; these friezes suggest the vertical walls that enclose the playing area of the ballcourt.

Yuu. A common sign for *yuu* or "stone" appears in the Lienzo of Jicayán. This sign is a circular or ovoid shape

with a narrow border that also has the projections seen in "hill" signs to indicate the bumpiness or roughness of the surface. Often the interior of the stone sign contains a series of parallel diagonal lines that indicate the rough contours and striations of the stone. In Mixtec manuscripts where color is used, the diagonal stripes created by the lines are painted different colors.

A second sign for "stone" is seen in the Lienzo of Zacatepec, as for example in the second place sign from the top in the vertical line in Fig. 106—a sign that consists of a

CHART 4: Mixtec Words Most Frequently Used as Geographical Substantives in Names of Boundaries and of Smaller-Than-Town Geographical Units

Word	Meaning as Geographical Substantive	Mixtec Homonyms	Pictorial Sign
CAVUA (sometimes written *cahua*)	rock (*peña*) cave (*caverna*) ravine (*quebrada*)	gall, bile (*hiel*) to twist (*torcer*) to turn (*dar vueltas a*) to knead (*amasar*) to lie down (*reposar, acostarse*) to be frightened, as by thunder (*espantarse como de trueno*)	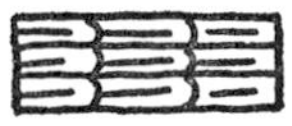 "ravine" (Lienzo of Jicayán: sign 9)
CHIYO	altar (*altar*) foundation, base (*cimiento*) house or place site (*sitio por asiento de casa o lugar*)	arm from shoulder to elbow (*brazo del hombro al codo*) to be cooked (*coserse*)	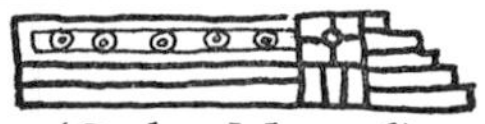 (Codex Muro 6)  (Codices Bodley, Selden; Map of Teozacoalco)
CUITE (written phonetically as *kʷíti*)	mound (*mogote*)	short (*breve; corta cosa, no larga*) narrow (*estrecho*) right, correct (*derecho*) justice (*justicia*) legitimate (*legítimo*) absolutely (*absolutamente*)	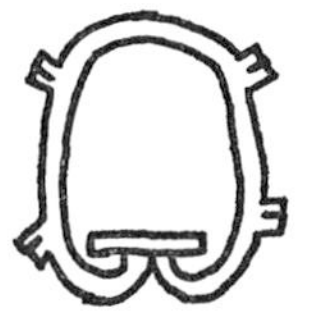 (Map No. 36: signs 5-left, 2-top)
DZOCO (See also in Chart V, "Modifiers of Geographical Substantives")	well, spring (*pozo, fuente pequeña*)	womb (*matriz*) afterbirth (*pares de mujer*) cradle (*cuna de niños*) cage or jail (*jaula*) hunger (*hambre*) shoulder (*hombro*) to offer (*ofrecer*) but, however (*pero, empero*)	 (Lienzo of Jicayán: sign 50)

CHART 4. *(cont.)*

Word	Meaning as Geographical Substantive	Mixtec Homonyms	Pictorial Sign
ITNU	slope (*ladera, repeche*) hillock (*loma*)	none	See Fig. 22
ITU	field, *milpa*	none	
MINI	lake (*lago*) lagoon (*laguna*) hollow (*hondura*)	none	(Map No. 36: sign 3-top)
NDOYO	swamp, marsh (*ciénaga*) spring (*manantial*)	damp, moist (*liento*) to soak, irrigate (*remojar, regar*) to be covered or hidden; secret (*cubrirse, ocultarse; secreto*) to be robbed (*ser robado*) to raise, climb (*levantar, subir*) to bear a load (*aguantarse con una carga*)	(Lienzo of Jicayán: sign 4)
NDUHUA	gulley (*cañada*) plain (*plan, valle*)	cobweb (*telaraña*) nobleman's foot (*pie del señor*) to dance, nobility only (*bailar, los señores*) to be cooked, heated, melted (*coserse, calentarse, fundirse*)	
NDUTA	water (*agua*)	juice of anything (*zumo de qualquier cosa*) broth (*cocina, el caldo*) to dissolve, evaporate (*deshacerse, evaporar*) to melt, as metals (*fundir, como metales*)	
SIQUI	hillock (*cuesta, altozano*) section of a town (*barrio del pueblo*)	border, corner, square (*borde, esquina, cuadro*) building block (*canto de canto o piedra*) fist (*puño*) corn husk (*camisa de mazorca de maiz*)	

	CHART 4. (cont.)		
Word	Meaning as Geographical Substantive	Mixtec Homonyms	Pictorial Sign
TAYU	city, town (ciudad, pueblo) palace (palacio) province (provincia)	seat, chair (asiento, silla) a pair (un par)	
TOTO	rock (peña)	rough, craggy (fragoso) many (muchos) degree of kinship (grado de parentesco) age of Indians who are 52 years old (edad de los indios de 52 años)	(Map No. 36: sign 5-bottom)
YAHUI	plaza market (mercado)	salary, price, gain, prize (salario, precio, logro, premio o galardón) expensive (caro)	(Map No. 36: sign 4-bottom)
YUHUA	wall, often a defensive wall (muro de ciudad; abarrada) enclosed space (espacio cerrado) ballcourt, ballgame (juego de pelota)	thread (hilo) to wind on a spool (devanar) snow, frost (nieve, hielo) common cress (mastuerzo)	"enclosed space" (Lienzo of Jicayán: sign 39) "ballcourt" (Codex Nuttall 1)
YUU	stone (piedra)	testicle (cojón) large hailstones (granizo grande) rocklike, solid (con características de piedra, sólido)	(Lienzo of Jicayán) (Lienzo of Zacatepec 1) (Map No. 36: sign 1-top)
YUVUI (sometimes written yuhui)	gully (arroyo, cañada) ravine between two hills (quebrada entre dos montes) estuary (estero)	grass mat (petate)	(Lienzo of Jicayán: sign 25) (Map No. 36: signs 2-left, 1-right)

temple platform, two stone signs, and a human face that is combined with a third stone motif. The sign for "stone" has two double volutes that are placed back to back so that an ovoid opening occurs in the center of the motif. This particular stone motif may appear singly, as in the place sign illustrated in Fig. 76*a*, or in groups of two or more, as seen in the place sign in the Lienzo of Zacatepec discussed above. In Map No. 36 the pictorial sign for *yuu* or "stone" is a stone motif that is very similar to the sign in the same map for *toto* or "rock." That is, the sign is somewhat sausage-shaped, half of it is black, and it terminates at each end with flower-like projections that suggest the "bumpiness" or irregular contour of the stones. The signs for *yuu* and *toto* in Map No. 36 resemble the sign for the Nahuatl word for "stone" (*tetl*) as seen in pictorial manuscripts from the region in and around the Valley of Mexico.

Yuvui. The geographical substantive *yuvui* can mean "gully," "ravine between two hills," and "estuary." In the Lienzo of Jicayán the pictorial sign for *yuvui* resembles the river sign in that it consists of a long rectangle of water with the curlicues that indicate waves forming the top border of the rectangle and with the projections that represent flowing water extending from the top and right side of the sign. This sign for *yuvui* lacks the trough-like enclosure that is typical of the river sign; a slab-like base is present in the sign, but the rectangle of water is not enclosed on both sides. This sign appears to illustrate the meaning of *yuvui* as "gully" or "small stream." In Map No. 36 two place signs depict the substantive *yuvui*, and both signs illustrate the translation of *yuvui* as "ravine between two hills." One of the signs shows a declivity between two hills of equal height. The other sign is less symmetrical: the flat base of the hill is flanked by a tall irregular hill on the left, and on the right by a shorter, scroll-like form that suggests a slope or stunted hill.

MODIFIERS OF GEOGRAPHICAL SUBSTANTIVES

In a number of Mixtec place names, the geographical substantive is preceded by a "modifier"—that is, a word that indicates more precisely the location of the place that is named. For example, in the Mixtec name *dzini yucu*, "at the top of the hill," the modifier *dzini* ("at the top of") tells us that the summit of the hill is the specific place referred to in this name. The modifiers most frequently used in Mixtec place names are listed in the left-hand column of Chart 5. The second column of the chart gives the meaning of the word as it is used in place names, and the third column lists the non-geographical meanings of the same word or of words that are homonymous except for variations in tone.

For the most part, these modifiers are known through written texts, principally Colonial land documents, rather than through their representation in place signs. The modifier that appears most frequently in place signs is *saha* ("at the foot of"), which is represented by a human foot. One example of a sign that depicts a place name with the word

saha is the place sign for San Andrés Sachio in the Codex of Yanhuitlán (Fig. 24*c*). *Sachio*, or "at the foot of the temple platform," is illustrated as a human foot placed on top of a temple platform, which in turn rests on a hill and frieze that do not depict any part of the town's name. A somewhat more baroque representation of *saha* is seen in the sign for the town of Chayucu ("at the foot of the hill") in the first Lienzo of Zacatepec (Fig. 101, lower-right corner): the hill sign is supported by two profile human feet, while two additional feet project from either side of the hill. If and when modifiers other than *saha* appear in a place sign, they are undoubtedly also represented as parts of the human body, because all the modifiers listed are homonymous with words that refer to a part of the human body, with the exception of *dzuma*, which can mean "tail of an animal" as well as "behind."

Another generalization that can be made concerning the modifiers is that they are most commonly used in names of boundaries rather than in names of towns. The principal exception to this generalization is, again, *saha* ("at the foot of"), which was discussed above in connection with the names of two towns: Sachio and Chayucu. In addition, the only modifier used in town names in the Reyes list of 146 towns is *saha*, which appears in three of the Mixtec names in this list.[39]

As concerns the use of modifiers in the names of boundaries, it is my impression that they are used fairly rarely in place names during the early Colonial period, but become increasingly frequent in place names of the late seventeenth and early eighteenth centuries. It seems as though in the sixteenth century a simple place name—as, say, "hill of the serpent"—was sufficient to identify a boundary, because everyone on both sides of the boundaries knew that this hill functioned as the dividing line between two towns. Later, after a century or so of land disputes, and perhaps as a result of the Spanish custom of marking the specific boundary site with a cross on a pile of stones, place names with modifiers become more common. The "hill of the serpent" is no longer sufficient; the name must now specify whether the location of the boundary is at the base of the hill, on the slope of the hill, or at its summit. A typical late-Colonial Mixtec boundary name is one of the boundaries listed for the Mixteca Alta town of San Pedro Cántaros in 1717, a name that consists of five words: *saha itnu yuhui ñuhu quede*.[40] This place name means "at the foot of the slope of the ravine of the clay." (*Saha* = "at the foot of"; *itnu* = "slope"; *yuhui* or *yuvui* = "ravine"; *ñuhu quede* = "clay"—or literally, "earth [to make] pottery," for *ñuhu* is "earth" and *quede* refers to various types of pottery.)

By way of contrast, in Map No. 36, which was presumably drawn in the sixteenth century, none of the thirty-

---

[39] *Saha yucu* ("at the foot of the hill") is one of two Mixtec names given by Reyes for Cuilapan in the Valley of Oaxaca. The Mixtec name of Piaztla in the State of Puebla is *saha ñuu quu* ("at the foot of the town of the incense burner"?), and the Mixtec name of the town of Mitzquique in the Distrito Federal is *saha tnundayn dzuchi* ("at the foot of the small *capulín* tree"?).

[40] AGN-Tierras, 1180–3, fol. 3/v, 8/v.

CHART 5: Modifiers of Geographical Substantives

Mixtec Word	Meaning in Place-Name Contexts	Mixtec Homonyms

CAHA	in back of, behind (*parte posterior*)	buttocks (*nalgas*)
		 cheap (*barato*)
		 palm tree (*palma*)
		    tîcaha = dates, nuts
		      (*datiles, nueces*)
		      and a type of
		      spider (*araña
		      otra*)
		      (*tî-* is an animal
		      or plant prefix)

CHISI	below, within, in (*abajo de, adentro, en*) on the slope of a hill (*ladera de cuesta*) = *chisi yucu* (*yucu* = hill)	stomach, abdomen (*vientre, barriga*) eve (*vigilia o víspera*)
DZEQUE sometimes written *siqui*, or phonetically as *síquî*	on top of (*encima de*) near (*acerca de*) behind (*detrás, espalda*)	head (*cabeza*) jewelry, adornment title, frontispiece of a book (*título*) personal name (*sobrenombre*) to joke; playful (*burlar; chistoso*) concerning (*tocante a*)

DZINI
 	
 sometimes written *sini*
	on top of, at the top of, at the summit of (*cima, cumbre*)	head (*cabeza*)
		 owner, chief (*dueño, jefe*)
		 personal name (*sobrenombre*)
		 age of Indians who are 52
		    years old (*edad de los
		    indios de 52 años*)
		 sacrificed captives
		    (*cautivos sacrificados
		    ante los ídolos*)
		 garland of flowers
		    (*guirnalda de flores*)
		 supper (*la cena*)

Mixtec Word	Meaning in Place-Name Contexts	Mixtec Homonyms
CHART 5. (cont.)		
DZOCO (See also in Chart 4.)	on the shoulder (or slope) of (a hill)	shoulder (hombro) womb (matriz) afterbirth (pares de mujer) cradle (cuna de niños) cage or jail (jaula) well, spring (pozo, fuente pequeña) hunger (hambre) to offer (ofrecer) but, however (pero, empero)
DZUMA (dzuʻma)	behind (atrás)	tail of an animal (cola de animal, rabo) afterward (después) tîdzuʻma = scorpion (alacrán) (tî- = animal prefix)
INI	in, inside of, within (en, adentro)	heart, life-giving spirit (corazón, espíritu lo que da vida) heat, hot (bochorno, caliente) to approach evening (atardecer)
NDAHA	toward, near (hacia un lugar)	hand; arm (mano; brazo) leaf; branch of a tree (hoja; rama) key (llave) rent, tribute (renta, tributo) hair ribbons used by women (cintas con que las indias se tranzan los cabellos) to satisfy, be filled (satifacer, hartar) to cure (sanar) to be stained (estar manchado) varnish used on wood sculpture (lustre, o barniz que se da a las imágenes)

	CHART 5. *(cont.)*	
Mixtec Word	*Meaning in Place-Name Contexts*	*Mixtec Homonyms*
SAHA often abbreviated to *sa-*	at the foot of, below *(al pie de, abajo)*	foot, on foot *(pie, en pie)* beginning *(comienzo)* earthenware pan or tub *(lebrillo)* strong, magnanimous, proud (of a person) *(fuerte, magnánimo, orgulloso)* to give, present *(dar, presentar)* to have an odor *(oler neutro)* to rot *(podrecerse)* to be blackened with frost, as trees *(quemarse los árboles con el hielo)* to be dyed, as textiles *(teñido ser)* for, in exchange for, on behalf of *(para, por)*
SATA	behind *(detrás de)* on the other side, beyond *(allende)*	back, shoulders *(espalda)* to empty, as a basket *(vaciar como chiquihuite)* to depopulate, make uninhabited *(despoblar)* to scatter, as grain or flowers *(derramar cosa de granos; esparzir o derramar flores)*
SITE	the lower part of	intestines *(tripas)* knee; elbow *(rodilla; codo)* foundation *(fundamento)* *(te-)site* = basket *(ençella, cesta, canasta)*
YUHU	at the edge of, bordering *(a la orilla, borde)*	mouth, mouthful *(boca, bocada)* swallow of something liquid *(trago de cosa líquida)* entrance *(entrada)* secret *(secreto)*

seven Mixtec names of boundaries has a modifier. Similarly, in the mid-sixteenth-century Lienzo of Jicayán, which has thirty-two glosses of Mixtec names of boundaries, only one place name contains a modifier.[41] In all probability, the comparative lack of modifiers in the place names of the early Colonial period is the reason why so few modifiers have been identified in place signs. By the time modifiers became a common feature of Mixtec names of boundaries, the native manuscript tradition—including the pre-Conquest type of place sign—had disappeared.

SUMMARY

Mixtec place names and the signs that represent these names are composed of two elements: a geographical substantive, followed by a qualifying element. The four geographical substantives most frequently used in Mixtec names of towns are: *ñuu* ("town, place where something exists"), *yucu* ("hill"), *yodzo* ("plain, valley"), and *yuta* ("river"). Two additional substantives, *chiyo* ("platform") and *itnu* ("slope"), occasionally appear in names of towns, but they are less common than the four substantives listed above.

The six substantives used in names of towns, as well as fifteen other substantives, are found in names of places that are not towns, such as outlying dependencies or subject villages, ceremonial sites, and uninhabited places such as boundaries. Because none of the place signs appears to contain a pictorial element that identifies the geographical unit of the place represented by the sign, the type of place shown in any given sign must be determined by its context.

A further complication is that the interpretation of geographical substantives in place signs is often difficult. The substantive *ñuu* ("town, place where something exists") is usually represented by a frieze with geometric patterns, and the substantive *yucu* ("hill") is usually represented by a bell-shaped hill motif, but these substantives are by no means mutually exclusive. In some signs, the two motifs appear to be interchangeable, as in the sign with a rib cage, which appears in Codex Nuttall with a hill (Fig. 20*a*) and in Codex Colombino with a frieze (Fig. 20*b*). In other place signs, both the frieze and hill motifs may be included in the sign even though the place name being depicted does not contain the words *ñuu* or *yucu*. For example, in the sign of San Andrés Andúa as it appears in the Codex of Yanhuitlán (Fig. 24*b*), the town's Mixtec name, *anduvua*, is represented by a human mouth (*a-*) and an arrow (*nduvua*), and the hill and frieze which support the sign seem to be superfluous and have no relation to the town's Mixtec name.

Nor are *ñuu* and *yucu* the only substantives which do not always function in a strictly "one sign the equivalent to one word" manner. The substantive *chiyo* ("temple base, foundation") is usually represented as a temple platform, with the notable exception of the place sign of

Teozacoalco, in which *chiyo* is depicted as the frieze with geometric patterns that is associated with the substantive *ñuu*. The substantive *itnu* ("slope") is also represented by more than one type of sign, as can be seen in Fig. 22, where signs accompanied by the gloss *itnu* depict this word by hills of three different shapes, by undecorated platforms or friezes with geometric patterns, and by a stone motif. Moreover, in Map No. 36, the sign for *cuite* or "mound" is identical to the sign for *yucu* or "hill"; and were it not for the identifying gloss in Mixtec, this sign would be thought to represent the word *yucu*.

Because of the occasional interchangeability of pictorial motifs that represent geographical substantives, it is not possible to look at any given place sign and with any great degree of certainty translate the pictorial substantive into an equivalent word in the Mixtec language. For if a literal translation were made of the place sign of San Andrés Andúa (Fig. 24*b*), the Mixtec name of this place would be *ñuu yucu anduvua*, translating the frieze as *ñuu*, the hill motif as *yucu*, the mouth as the prefix *a-*, and the arrow within the mouth as *nduvua*. But *ñuu yucu anduvua* is not recorded as the Mixtec name of any town either within or outside of the Mixteca, and the identification of this sign must be effected by means other than merely translating all of its pictorial motifs into words in the Mixtec language.

Because this place sign appears in the Codex of Yanhuitlán, it is assumed that it may be connected somehow with the Mixteca Alta region in and around the important town of Yanhuitlán, the town from which the manuscript comes. Furthermore, the sign of Andúa appears on a page of the Codex that contains twelve place signs, arranged in three rows with four signs in each row.[42] A hypothesis is formulated: the signs on this page represent towns that were formerly subjects of Yanhuitlán. This hypothesis seems to be confirmed by the three identifiable signs on this page which are discussed in this book: those of San Andrés Andúa, Santa María Suchixtlán (Fig. 82*a*), and San Andrés Sachio (Fig. 24*c*). All three of these towns were subjects of Yanhuitlán at the time of the Spanish conquest. Thus the sign of Andúa is identified not solely by a translation of every pictorial element shown in the sign, but by its context, for it is placed in a group of signs with a common characteristic—that is, these signs all appear to represent names of towns that were subjects of Yanhuitlán.

In the seventeenth and eighteenth centuries, modifiers of geographical substantives become a common feature of Mixtec place names. These modifiers describe more explicitly the location of the site that is named, such as "at the summit of (a hill)" or "at the base of (a slope)"; and they appear most frequently in names of boundary sites. With the exception of *saha* ("at the foot of"), the modifiers are rarely depicted in place signs, presumably because the use of modifiers in place names became common after the practice of pre-Conquest pictorial writing had died out.

---

[41] In this one place name, *chiti cuiñe,* or "the lower part of the tiger," the modifier is connected with a qualifying element rather than with a geographical substantive; and the name does not seem to be illustrated by any of the place signs in the Lienzo, as is discussed under "Sign 12" in Chapter VIII.

[42] Jiménez Moreno and Mateos Higuera, *Códice de Yanhuitlán,* Plate VII.

V

PLACE SIGNS THAT HAVE BEEN IDENTIFIED OR HYPOTHETICALLY IDENTIFIED

One of the best ways to understand the workings of Mixtec place signs and the problems involved in place-sign identification is to examine in detail the few signs that have thus far been identified. This chapter, therefore, will be devoted to an analysis of those place signs which are considered to be firmly identified, as well as those signs for which tentative or hypothetical identifications have been made.

In 1960, in the introduction to his commentary on Codex Bodley, Alfonso Caso listed the names of eight towns whose place signs had been identified: Tilantongo, Teozacoalco, Tlaxiaco, Texupan, Yanhuitlán, Coixtlahuaca, Amoltepec, and Cuquila.[1] I disagree with Caso's identification of the place sign of Tlaxiaco and shall offer an alternative hypothesis concerning this town's sign. In the case of the sign of Texupan, Caso postulated that this sign appears in Codex Sánchez Solís. As will be discussed below under the section entitled "Texupan and Acatlán," the sign in Sánchez Solís, although essentially the same as the Texupan sign, represents Acatlán in southern Puebla.

In my study of the glosses of Codex Colombino, I identified the signs of three Coastal towns: Tututepec, Santa María Acatepec, and Jicayán-Tulixtlahuaca.[2] The sign of Tulixtlahuaca is one of several place signs containing the marsh-grass motif, known as *tule* in Nahuatl. My interpretation of these signs differs considerably from that of Caso, who refers to most of the marsh-grass signs as "Tula," implying that they represent the important post-Classic Toltec capital northwest of Mexico City.

Throughout his commentaries on Codices Bodley and Selden, Caso makes hypotheses as to the identity of other place signs, such as those representing the towns of Apoala, Tequixtepec, Mitlatongo, Tecamachalco, Comaltepec, and Yucu Ita. In the case of both Apoala and Yucu Ita, Caso has given one name to two separate signs; one of the signs he identifies as Apoala probably represents the Coastal town of Juquila, and one of the signs he calls "Yucu Ita" may represent *chiyo yuhu*, or Santa María Suchixtlán in the Valley of Yanhuitlán in the Mixteca Alta. In the case of Tequixtepec, there are two different towns with this

name in the Mixteca, and I shall attempt to distinguish the two signs that represent the Mixtec names of the two Tequixtepecs. The signs of Mitlatongo, Tecamachalco, and Comaltepec will be discussed in order to demonstrate the difficulties incurred in relating Nahuatl names and Nahuatl pictorial place signs to the place signs in Mixtec manuscripts.

The approximate location of the towns discussed below is shown in Map 3.

TILANTONGO AND TEOZACOALCO

In his pioneering study of the Map of Teozacoalco, Alfonso Caso identified the signs of two important towns in the Mixteca Alta, Tilantongo and Teozacoalco. The Map was prepared to accompany the *Relación Geográfica* of Teozacoalco, which is dated January 21, 1580.[3] In addition to presenting a circular cartographic scheme of the lands belonging to Teozacoalco, this map contains three vertical rows of seated couples, who represent the genealogies of the ruling families of Tilantongo and Teozacoalco. The Teozacoalco dynasties are depicted in two of the three columns, one of which is within the map itself. The other column is placed outside the map at the left, but is connected to the cartographic circle by means of a road with footprints. The columns of seated figures are to be read from bottom to top, and below the first column at the left of the map is a Spanish gloss which states that the rulers of Teozacoalco originally came from Tilantongo.[4]

Tilantongo (17° 15′ N., 97° 17′ W.)

The derivation of the Teozacoalco rulers is illustrated in the Map of Teozacoalco by a line of footprints which connects the figures of these rulers with another vertical row of seated couples at the far left, which represents the dynasties of Tilantongo (Fig. 25). At the bottom of the latter column is the place sign of Tilantongo, a frieze containing a black-and-white stepped-fret pattern and a building with a band of stars across the top of its roof. We

---

[1] Caso, *Bodley*, 18.

[2] Smith, *Colombino*, 63–65, 69–73; 159–62, 166–69. The place sign of Tututepec is also discussed in Smith, "The Codex Colombino . . . ," *Tlalocan* Vol. IV–3, 277–79.

[3] Substantial portions of the text of the *Relación* are published in *RMEH* I, 174–76, and in Caso, "El Mapa de Teozacoalco," *Cuadernos Americanos*, Año VIII, No. 5 (1949), 177–79.

[4] "*Estos son los principales e señores que antiguamente salieron del pueblo de Tilanton para este de Teozacoalco, e los que de estos procedieron y hoy día son vivos, son don Felipe de Santiago y don Francisco de Mendoza, su hijo.*" (Caso, *ibid.*, 151.)

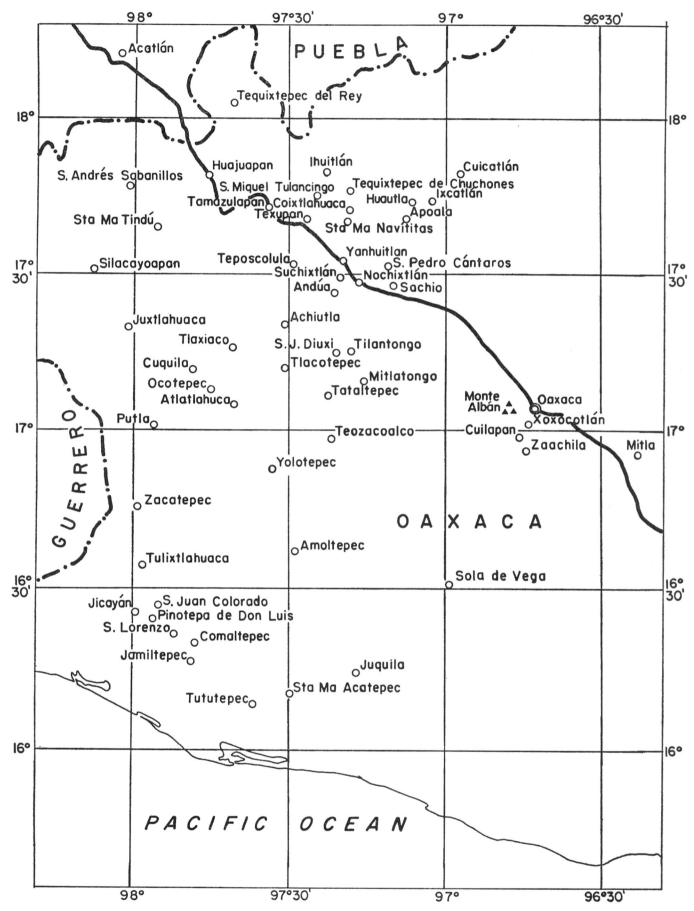

MAP 3.   The Mixteca, showing the location of the principal towns

learn from another source, the text of the *Relación Geográfica* of Tilantongo, that the full Mixtec name of Tilantongo is *ñotoo-huaidadehuj* (*ñuu tnoo huahi andehui* in the dialect of the Alvarado dictionary), which means "black town, house of the sky."[5] (*Ñuu* = "town"; *tnoo* = "black"; *huahi* = "house"; and *andehui* = "sky.") In many instances, the sign of Tilantongo represents only the first, or *ñuu tnoo*, section of Tilantongo's Mixtec name, and this sign is a frieze with black-and-white geometric patterns (Fig. 26 *a, c*). The frieze itself represents *ñuu* or "town"; and *tnoo* or "black" is represented by the use of black pyramidal frets in conjunction with white only, for the usual frieze in Mixtec place signs contains geometric patterns of several colors. In the place sign of Tilantongo in the Map of Teozacoalco (Fig. 26*d*), as well as in other more elaborate signs of this town (Fig. 26 *e, f*), the building placed above the black-and-white frieze has a band of stars across the roof, and this building with a "sky band" depicts the second section of Tilantongo's Mixtec name: *huahi andehui*, or "house of the sky."

Caso's identification of the rulers and place sign of Tilantongo was of the greatest importance in the interpretation of the Mixtec historical manuscripts, because all eight surviving manuscripts mention or describe in detail personages or events connected with Tilantongo. Substantial portions of the front of Bodley and the back of Vienna, as well as a small section of the Nuttall obverse, are devoted to recording the genealogies of Tilantongo. The hero 8-Deer "Tiger Claw," whose biography is told in detail in Colombino-Becker I and on the back of Nuttall, was the ruler of Tilantongo in the mid-eleventh century. Codices Selden, Becker II, and Sánchez Solís do not deal exclusively with Tilantongo-oriented events, but in all three manuscripts, intermarriage with nobility of Tilantongo is indicated. As Burgoa has testified, the ruling line of Tilantongo was the most prestigious of the Mixteca;[6] and undoubtedly one of the reasons the place sign of this town appears so frequently is that the rulers of other towns wished to demonstrate their affiliation with the Tilantongo dynasties.

But even a place sign as clearly identified as that of Tilantongo is not without problems, for in some instances, the sign appears without the distinctive black-and-white frieze.[7] For example, in Vienna VI-1 (Fig. 27*a*), Bodley 8-11 (Fig. 27*b*), and Sánchez Solís 6 and 15 (Fig. 27 *d, e*),[8] the identifying pictorial element of the Tilantongo sign is the sky symbols on the roof of the building accompanying the sign, reflecting only the second part of the town's name, *huahi andehui*, or "house of the sky." In Colombino XVII-44 (Fig. 27*c*) and XVIII-49, the frieze

connected with the place sign has been erased, so that it is not possible to determine whether the stepped frets were originally black and white; but the band of stars across the temple roof indicates that the signs in question represent Tilantongo. Moreover, these two place signs in Colombino appear in parallel passages of the same story on pages 53 and 68 of Nuttall, where the Tilantongo sign appears with a black-and-white frieze (Fig. 26 *c, f*).

In discussing the Tilantongo sign in Colombino XVIII-49, Caso states that the black bands on the red post and lintel of the building that is part of this sign represent the *tnoo* or "black" element of Tilantongo's name, *nuu tnoo*.[9] But this is clearly not the case, because the red-and-black post and lintel appear in buildings with many place signs that definitely do not represent Tilantongo.[10] And conversely, the red-and-black post and lintel do not invariably appear as a feature of buildings placed on the Tilantongo sign, as can be seen in Figs. 26 *d, f* and 27 *a, d, e*. The red-and-black post and lintel may identify a certain kind of building or a temple with a specific advocation, but this color combination does not seem to be associated with any one place sign, and the black bands on a red post and lintel do not represent the *tnoo* of Tilantongo's Mixtec name.

Teozacoalco (*17° 2′ N., 97° 15′ W.*)

At the bottom of the second column of seated couples in the Map of Teozacoalco is the place sign of Teozacoalco (Figs. 25, 28*e*). The motifs seen in this place sign are a small human figure bending a frieze with geometric decorations, a trefoil flower, and a building with two streams of blood and a cocoa bean on its roof.

The figure folding the frieze represents *chiyo canu*, the Mixtec name of Teozacoalco given in the 1593 Reyes list of Mixtec place names. *Chiyo ca'nu* means "large or great altar or foundation." *Chiyo* is given in the Alvarado dictionary as meaning "altar," "foundation" (*cimiento*), or "building site" (*sitio por asiento de casa o lugar*). In the case of this particular place sign, the geographical substantive *chiyo* appears to be represented with the same pictorial sign as *ñuu* ("town"): a frieze containing geometric decoration. *Ca'nu* means "large" or "great," but because these concepts are difficult to represent pictorially, a word that is homonymous except for differences in tone is depicted. *Ca'nu* also means "to break or cut,"[11] and the small figure who folds or "breaks" the frieze represents this meaning of *ca'nu* (as seen in Fig. 28 *c, e*). The use of homonyms to express ideas that are difficult to depict is what Gelb terms a logogram of "phonetic transfer" and

---

[5] *PNE* IV, 75.

[6] Burgoa, *Geográfica descripción*, I, 276: "... *el mayor señorío de estos mixtecas se conservó desde su antigüedad, hasta que les amaneció la luz del Evangelio en este pueblo de Tilantongo* ...."

[7] Caso, *Colombino*, 32, 34; 130, 132.

[8] In the three appearances of the Tilantongo place sign in Sánchez Solís (twice on page 6 and once on page 15), the sign is accompanied by a gloss giving the full Mixtec name of Tilantongo, *ñotnoo huey taatibi*, in the dialect of the annotator of the place signs in the manuscript.

[9] Caso, *Colombino*, 34, 132.

[10] For example, a place sign that may be described as "Loincloth River," which is shown as conquered by 8-Deer in Nuttall 75 and Becker I-2, includes a building with red-and-black post and lintel, and this place sign is clearly not Tilantongo. Also, in Selden, the temple accompanying the principal place sign of "Belching Mountain" occasionally has black bands on a red lintel (Selden 4–IV, 5–II and III, 6–I, 9–I, 12–II, and 14–III), and "Belching Mountain" is certainly not Tilantongo.

[11] The Dyk-Stoudt Mixtec vocabulary presents the differences in tone between the words for "large, great" and "to break, cut" in one dialect, that of San Miguel el Grande, Oaxaca. Here, *cá'nu* is given for "grande" and *ca'nù* for "quebrar, cortar, domar."

what is sometimes called "rebus writing."[12] Examples of phonetic transfer occur in many of the ancient Mediterranean languages and in Chinese. In Sumerian, for example, an arrow (*ti*) was used to express the word "life" (also *ti*).

A second place sign for Teozacoalco that appears in Codices Bodley and Selden, as well as in the Map of Teozacoalco, is a frieze accompanied by a trefoil flower (Fig. 28 *a, b, e*). The Mixtec name on which the "flower frieze" sign is based is not known. It does not seem to indicate a historical change in either the name or site of Teozacoalco, because in Bodley it occurs interchangeably with the "bent frieze" sign, and neither sign is restricted to a definite period of time and then replaced by the other.[13] In addition, as we have seen in the 1580 Map of Teozacoalco, the flower element appears together with the bent-frieze logogram, so that the Mixtec name on which the flower motif is based must have been known in the early Colonial period, even though it is not mentioned in the text of the *Relación Geográfica* of Teozacoalco.

Perhaps a Mixtec name given in the 1883 *Cuadros sinópticos* may provide a clue to the meaning of the flower motif. In the description of Teozacoalco it is stated that the site of the town is on a slope named *Yuhitaini*.[14] If this name is comprised of the three words *yuu ita ini*, then *yuu* would mean "stone"; *ita*, "flower"; and *ini* would specify the type of flower. But if the name is divided *yuhi ta ini*, *yuhi* could be a dialect variant of Alvarado's *yuvui*, meaning "ravine" (*quebrada entre dos montes*); *ta*, an abbreviation of *yuta* ("river"); and *ini* could mean "heart," "hot," or "within, inside of." A further investigation of the local place names in the immediate region of Teozacoalco may uncover a second Mixtec name of Teozacoalco, or clarify the name of the slope on which the town is located.

In one instance in Codex Bodley (Fig. 29*c*), Teozacoalco appears to be represented merely by the building with cocoa beans and a stream of blood, because the person shown making an offering there, ♂ 1-Lizard, is the son of a female ruler of Teozacoalco.[15] But this particular building is not usually a distinguishing sign of the town, for it appears in connection with place signs that are clearly not Teozacoalco. For example, in Bodley 22–I (Fig. 29*d*), these motifs occur in connection with a place sign described as "Hill of the Yellow Mask." In addition, a building whose interior contains bleeding cocoa beans appears periodically on the front, or ritual, side of Codex Vienna (Fig. 29 *a, b*).[16] Thus it would seem that a build-

ing with cocoa beans and blood, as the building with red-and-black post and lintel discussed above under the Tilantongo sign, cannot be connected exclusively with any one place sign and probably refers to a specific type of ritual performed at the building or is a temple associated with a specific cult.

TLAXIACO (17°15' N., 97°42' W.) AND TATALTEPEC (17°10' N., 97°22' W.)

Alfonso Caso has proposed that a frieze with a flame (Fig. 31) is the place sign of Tlaxiaco, an important town in the Mixteca Alta.[17] Caso bases this identification on a document in the Ramo de Tierras (Vol. 59–2) of the Archivo General de la Nación in Mexico City. This document is concerned with the inheritance of the town of Tlazultepec in the Mixteca Alta, and the written transcript of the litigation, dated 1597–1598, is accompanied by a pictorial manuscript drawn at the time of the litigation and called "The Genealogy of Tlazultepec" (Fig. 30).[18]

Caso believes that the place sign in the lower-left corner of the Tlazultepec Genealogy, a sign which consists of a flame within a hill, represents the Mixtec name of Tlaxiaco, which he says is *canutisi*. A careful reading of the written documents relating to the Tlazultepec litigation reveals that the hill with a flame is not the sign of Tlaxiaco, but of Santa María Tataltepec, a town about 20 miles southeast of Tlaxiaco. In addition, *canutisi* is not the Mixtec name of Tlaxiaco, but the name of an *estancia*, or dependency, of Tlaxiaco named San Agustín.

In the written documents that accompany the Tlazultepec Genealogy, one of the persons who claims the *cacicazgo*, or native rulership, of the town of Tlazultepec is Don Juan de Guzmán, the husband of the woman who rules Tataltepec. In the Tlazultepec Genealogy he is shown seated above the hill with a flame in the lower-left corner. Above his head is a gloss that sets forth his name, "do juº de goma." Above the head of the female figure seated opposite him is the name of the town she rules, "tlatlaltepe" (Tataltepec).

To support his case, Don Juan de Guzmán presents the last testament, in Mixtec, of his aunt, Doña María López, a former ruler of Tlazultepec. For the purposes of the 1597 litigation, a section of this will, which was dated April 25, 1571, is translated into Spanish.[19] In this section of the will María López states that her grandfather Don Pedro left Tataltepec and went to San Agustín, a dependency of Tlaxiaco. At San Agustín, whose Mixtec name is given as *ñutisi*, Don Pedro married Doña María,

---

[12] Gelb, *A Study of Writing*, 67, 101, 104.

[13] The "bent frieze" sign appears in Bodley 13–II, 15–III, 16–III, and 15–IV, and possibly in Selden 4–III. The "flower frieze" sign appears in Bodley 16–I, 18–V, 24–V, and 24–23–III, and in Selden 13–III. In Bodley one generation of rulers is associated with both signs: ♂ 2-Dog "Strand of Flint Blades" and ♀ 6-Reed "Feathered Serpent" or "Serpent Jewel" appear in connection with the "bent frieze" in Bodley 16–III and in connection with the "flower frieze" in Bodley 24–V.

[14] Manuel Martínez Gracida, "*Cuadros sinópticos*," n.p.

[15] Caso, *Bodley*, 43–44.

[16] In Vienna the building with bleeding cocoa bean always appears as one of a group of four buildings, and usually immediately precedes a

scene that depicts the lighting of the New Fire (Vienna 32d, 21, 19b, 18b, 14a, 12a, 11b, 10 and 5). Nowotny (*Archiv für Völkerkunde*, III, 195) conjectures that the four buildings may allude to the four directions of the sky or may be connected with the small houses used for fasting by Quetzalcoatl.

[17] Caso, *Bodley*, 18.

[18] For a general discussion of this pictorial manuscript and the documents that accompany it, see Spores, "The Genealogy of Tlazultepec," *Southwestern Journal of Anthropology*, Vol. XX–1 (1964), 15–31.

[19] AGN-Tierras, 59–2, fol. 46. The section of the Spanish translation of the will that is summarized below appears in Appendix B–1 of this book.

who was from this town. These statements are corroborated by the Tlazultepec Genealogy, for in the lower-central section of the drawing, Don Pedro and Doña María are shown seated on a platform which contains the inscription *s·no agustin tisin*, apparently a combination of "San Agustín" and the town's Mixtec name, *ñutisi*. Above the male figure seated on the left side of the platform is the notation "do pᵒe" (Don Pedro); above the female figure on the right is written "doña mᵃ" (Doña María). In addition, a line with footprints connects the figure of Don Pedro with the "flame hill" that is glossed "tlatlaltepe," indicating—as does the will—that Don Pedro came from Tataltepec to San Agustín *ñutisi*.

Thus we see that the "flame hill" sign cannot be the sign of Tlaxiaco, but is the sign of Tataltepec. Not only is this sign accompanied by the gloss "tlatlaltepe," but the relationship of personages to Tataltepec described in the written documents accompanying the Tlazultepec Genealogy is the same as their relationship to "flame hill" in the pictorial Genealogy. This identification is confirmed by the Mixtec name of Tataltepec, which is given in the 1593 Reyes list as *yucu quesi*. *Yucu* means "hill"; according to the Alvarado dictionary, *quesi* means "scorching heat" (*bochorno*), and the Dyk-Stoudt Mixtec vocabulary lists this word as meaning "fever" (*calentura*).[20] In addition, Alvarado gives *taa quesi* as one definition of "a fire giving off heat" (*escalentarse el fuego*); *taa* means "to beat" (*pegar*) and "to throw off" (*tirar*). Thus the flames in the place sign of Tataltepec represent the word for "scorching heat," and we have another case of an associative logogram, similar to the example discussed in Chapter III under "Road and Warpath," where the logogram of "road" is used to express the allied idea of "journey" or "comes from."

Such associative logograms were also common in the early Mediterranean languages. In Sumerian, the sign for sun not only meant "sun" but also "white" and "day"; the sign of the sun was also used to signify "day" in Egyptian hieroglyphic writing.[21]

Given that "flame hill" is the place sign of *yucu quesi*, or Santa María Tataltepec, is the "flame frieze" (Fig. 31) in the pre-Conquest manuscripts also the sign for Tataltepec? This is difficult to determine because, as was discussed in Chapter IV under the uses of the geographical substantives *ñuu* and *yucu*, the frieze for *ñuu* and the hill for *yucu* seem at times to be interchangeable, and at other times both motifs occur together in the same place sign. However, it is worth noting that in the Tlazultepec Genealogy the place sign of Tataltepec is represented with a hill only and without a frieze, although friezes occur in other place signs in this manuscript. Conversely, in the "flame frieze" sign as it appears in Codices Bodley and Selden, the flame motif occurs only with a frieze, and this

sign never includes a hill. Thus, unless it can be determined that an alternative Mixtec name of Tataltepec is *ñuu quesi*, or unless it can be established that the personages seated on the "flame frieze" in Bodley and Selden were the native rulers of Tataltepec, "flame frieze" cannot definitely be considered to be the sign of Tataltepec.

Nor is "flame frieze" the place sign of the town of Tlaxiaco, whose Mixtec name is usually given as *ndisi nuu*.[22] In the Alvarado dictionary *ndisi* means "wings," and also "visible" or "obvious." In the Dyk-Stoudt vocabulary, this word means "clear, openly," "wing," or "horizontal," depending on differences in tone.[23] *Nuu* has many meanings, also depending on variations in tone,[24] but the meaning that would be easiest to represent pictorially is "face." And in many dialects of Mixtec, *(ti)nuu* or *(te)nuu* means both "stars" and "eyes."[25] Thus the Mixtec name of Tlaxiaco might be translated literally as "visible face" or "visible eyes," or less literally as "clearly seen."[26] The Dyk vocabulary gives the phrase *tú ndisìn nuù-na* as "I cannot see." This phrase literally means "it is not clearly in front of me." *Tú* is the negative ("no" or "not"); *ndisìn* means "clearly"; *nuù* means "in front of" as well as "face"; *na* means "me."

Tlaxiaco is a notable example of a town whose Mixtec name is vastly different from its present-day Nahuatl name. The latter is represented in post-Conquest manuscripts of the Valley of Mexico as a ballcourt with raindrops (Fig. 32).[27] In his commentary on Codex Mendoza, Clark presents the following etymology of Tlaxiaco or "Tlachquiauco":

tlachtli = ballcourt
quiauitl = rain, ideograph for
quiauac = outside or away from
co = in

Thus the Nahuatl name means "place of the ballcourt outside of the town." As we can see by comparing this etymology with the etymology of *ndisi nuu* discussed

---

[20] *Quiji* in the dialect of San Miguel el Grande, where the *s* of Alvarado is *j*. Jiménez Moreno notes the meaning of *quesi* as "fever" in his discussion of the name of Tataltepec (1962 ed. of the Alvarado dictionary, 96), and further notes that the Nahuatl name Tlatlaltepec means "burned hill."

[21] Gelb, *A Study of Writing*, 99, 101.

[22] For example, in the Reyes 1593 list of town names, and in the Dyk-Stoudt vocabulary, where it appears as *ndijinu*, the equivalent of *ndisi nuu* in the dialect of San Miguel el Grande.

[23] *Ndijìn* = "claro, abiertamente; ala." *Ndìjin* = "horizontal." Again, the *j* of the San Miguel el Grande dialect is the equivalent of *s* in the Alvarado dictionary dialect. The final *n* on these words indicates nasalization of the final vowel.

[24] For example, in the Dyk-Stoudt vocabulary of the dialect of San Miguel el Grande:
nuu = "to descend, to become smaller; remnant, residue"
núu = "to be in a hurry; a short period of time"
nuù = "face; toward, in front of, in the place where something exists"
núú = "the first, the first time"; this word is also used to indicate a condition contrary to fact or a conditional mood.

[25] *Te-* or *ti-* is a prefix usually used for animals and some plants. Here, used as a prefix to *nuu*, which means "face," the implication probably is that the eyes are the animating feature of the face. In other dialects, such as that of San Miguel el Grande, the word for eyes is *nduchi*, homonymous with the word for "beans."

[26] Cf. the 1883 "Cuadros sinópticos" translation of Tlaxiaco's Mixtec name as "fine view" (*buenavista*), although here no attempt was made to analyze specifically the two words *ndisi nuu*.

[27] Telleriano Remensis, fol. 41/r; Codex Mendoza, fol. 45/r (place sign no. 532 of the Clark edition). Codex Telleriano Remensis is reproduced in: H. T. Hamy, ed., *Codex Telleriano-Remensis* (Paris, 1899).

above, the two names have nothing in common; nor does the Mixtec name contain the Mixtec word for "ball-court," which is *yuhua*.

Given a translation of *ndisi nuu* as "clearly seen" or "clearly visible," I believe that it is possible that the place sign usually described as "Observatory" (Fig. 33) may be the place sign of Tlaxiaco. This sign has been called "Observatory" because the crossed sticks on the platform of the building in this sign represent the astronomical device used by the Maya and Mexicans to observe the movement of stars, the planet Venus, and other celestial phenomena. The crossed sticks were fixed in a set place to record the position of a star or planet. Then, when the star or planet returned to this point a second time, the observer could calculate the time of its complete cycle. The "observatory" connotations of this place sign seem to be closely related to the meaning of *ndisi nuu* as "clearly seen," and the motif of the eye, (*ti*)*nuu* in Mixtec, may represent the *nuu* part of Tlaxiaco's Mixtec name. In one instance in Codex Bodley (Fig. 33*b*), a face is shown as emerging from the doorway of the building, and this motif may also represent *nuu* or "face."

In four appearances of the "Observatory" sign in Bodley, the eye motif rests on a pair of crossed legs (Fig. 33*a*).[28] The meaning of the crossed legs is not clear, although pictorially they seem to function in the same manner as the crossed sticks. In the section of the Reyes grammar which lists the parts of the human body,[29] the word for "legs" is *dzichi*, entirely different from the *ndisi* that appears in the name of Tlaxiaco. The basic Mixtec word for the verb "to cross the arms or feet" in the Alvarado dictionary is *dzama*, which also has nothing to do with Tlaxiaco's Mixtec name.

But I believe that the concept expressed in the "Observatory" sign resembles very closely the idiomatic translation of *ndisi nuu* as "clearly seen," and that the specific motif of an eye that is visible between two crossed sticks or above crossed legs reflects a literal translation of *ndisi nuu* as "visible eyes." This interpretation would seem to be confirmed by a sign that represents one of the personal names of a ruler who appears in Codex Muro. On page 2 of Muro, the principal male figure is accompanied by a calendrical name 8-Rabbit, and his personal name is shown as a sign with an eye inside of a flame motif which rests on a bowl-like base (Fig. 34).[30] Codex Muro is extensively annotated with glosses in Mixtec, and the gloss which sets forth this person's entire name is:

> *ñu na sayu*
> *ñuhu ndisi nuu.*

Ñu is a prefix used for nobility, and *na sayu* is the calen-

drical name 8-Rabbit. The remainder of the gloss refers to the personal name of 8-Rabbit. The word *ñuhu* means "flames" and thus describes the flame motif seen in the sign. The final two words of the gloss are *ndisi nuu*, or the same two words which comprise the Mixtec name of Tlaxiaco, and this section of the gloss is represented by the eye motif within the flame. This eye motif in Muro is identical to the eye seen between two sticks or placed on crossed legs in the "Observatory" sign, and thus it seems likely that "Observatory" is the sign of *ndisi nuu*, or Tlaxiaco.

Nonetheless, this hypothesis cannot as yet be corroborated by documentary evidence that the persons shown at "Observatory" were the native rulers of Tlaxiaco. In Codices Bodley and Selden, the birthdate of the last depicted ruler of "Observatory" is 1435,[31] so that we are probably missing at least two generations of rulers between this personage and the ruler of "Observatory" at the time of the Spanish conquest in the post–1520 period. What we lack, then, is a document which will bridge the gap of at least fifty years between Colonial-period Tlaxiaco and mid-fifteenth-century "Observatory."

TEXUPAN (17°15′ N., 97°17′ W.) AND ACATLÁN (18°12′ N., 98°5′ W.)

We know the place sign of the Mixteca Alta town of Texupan from two post-Conquest pictorial documents: the map accompanying the 1579 *Relación Geográfica* of Texupan (Fig. 37), and Codex Sierra (Fig. 36).[32] In both documents Texupan is represented as a hill containing a turquoise jewel. In the *Relación Geográfica* map and in one of the two appearances of the sign in Codex Sierra, a building is placed at the bottom of the hill. In both signs in Sierra, the base of the hill contains wavy lines to symbolize water. The "water" may be the equivalent of the stream that flows by the left of the hill in the *Relación Geográfica* map; or the water in combination with the hill may represent the Nahuatl concept of *altepetl* (*atl*, "water" plus *tepetl*, "hill"), which means "inhabited place." The written text of Codex Sierra, which deals with the expenditures of the town of Texupan from 1550 to 1564, is in Nahuatl, and the term *altepetl* is used throughout this text to mean "town."

The Mixtec name of Texupan is given as *ñuu ndaa* in the 1593 Reyes list and as *ñu ndaa* in the text of the 1579 *Relación Geográfica*. In the latter source, *ñu ndaa* is translated as "blue land."[33] *Ñuu* is the geographical substantive that means "town" or "place where something exists"; *ñu* is a short form of *ñu'u* meaning "land." In the Alvarado

---

[28] In Bodley 15–II the legs and crossed sticks appear together; in Bodley 27–II, 22–II, and 16–V, only the legs appear. In the remainder of the representations of the "Observatory" sign (Bodley 15–V, 20–II, 32–IV, 30–V, 23–III, 22–II, 21–III, 22–III; Selden 14–I, 17–IV), it is shown with the crossed sticks only.

[29] "Arte en lengua mixteca," 81–86.

[30] The entirety of page 2 of Codex Muro is illustrated in Glass, *Catálogo de la Colección de Códices*, plate 71.

[31] The ruler in question is ♂ 8-Grass "Tlaloc-Sun" who appears in Bodley 21, 22–III and 20–II, and in Selden 17–IV. Caso, *Bodley*, 48, 74, and *Selden*, 44; 91.

[32] *PNE* IV, 53; *Códice Sierra*, pp. 4, 15. An analysis of the pre- and post-Conquest elements of style in the *Relación Geográfica* map was made by Joyce Waddell DeBlois, "An Interpretation of the Map and Relación of Texupa in Oaxaca, Mexico, and an Analysis of the Style of the Map," unpublished M.A. thesis, Tulane University, April, 1963. The Map of Texupan is in the library of the Real Academia de la Historia in Madrid.

[33] *PNE* IV, 54–55.

dictionary, "blue" is *ndaa*.[34] In this particular place sign, then, a hill rather than a frieze is used to represent *ñuu* or *ñu*, and a turquoise jewel represents *ndaa* or "blue."

This place sign is very different from the sign of Texupan's Nahuatl name which appears in Codex Mendoza.[35] Here, "texopan" is represented by an ovoid patch of blue with a footprint above it (Fig. 35). Jiménez Moreno believes that the original Nahuatl name of the town was "texocpan," meaning "in or on the blue stone."[36] But in the Nahuatl sign, the blue stone or the color blue is not represented as a turquoise jewel as it is in the Mixtec sign for *ñuu ndaa*. In fact, the use of a turquoise jewel to represent *ndaa* or "blue" is unusual and, I believe, unique to the place sign of Texupan. In Mixtec pictorial manuscripts the turquoise jewel usually represents the Mixtec word *yusi*, which means "turquoise."[37]

A notable example of the turquoise-jewel motif as *yusi* occurs in the place sign of the important Mixteca Baja town of Acatlán, located in southern Puebla, on the Pan-American Highway between Puebla and Oaxaca. The place sign of Acatlán appears four times in Codex Sánchez Solís (Fig. 38), and in all four instances it is accompanied by a gloss containing two Mixtec names of Acatlán. The gloss accompanying the "turquoise hill" sign in Sánchez Solís is variously written: *yoco yoxi dixaa* or *yoco yoxi tixaha*, which in the dialect of the Alvarado dictionary would be *yucu yusi tisaha*. These Mixtec names are explained in the text of the *Relación Geográfica* of Acatlán, which is dated January 2, 1581.[38] This text contains an unusually detailed analysis of the place names of a single town, and because this analysis is indispensable to the identification of the Acatlán sign, it is quoted below in its entirety.

The said town of *Acatlan* in the Nahuatl language is named thus, "*Acatlan*," which means "Place of Reeds" in that language, because the Mexicans who first came to this town found near it a large canebreak, and for this reason, they gave it this name without preserving the name which the native inhabitants had given it in their Mixtec language, in which this town is called *Yucuyuxi*, which means "Hill of Precious Stones"; and also at the present time they call it in the Mixtec language *Yutta tixaa*, which means "water filled with ashes." The latter name was given because of a hill which is next to an arroyo which passes near the town, a hill named "Hill of Ashes." This name and that of the stream which passes near

the hill are combined [to produce] the said name of "water filled with ashes." They say that [the town] has other names, which as we have said earlier were in use before the Mexicans came here; these names are not remembered nor are the reasons for giving them, and thus they are not included here.[39]

This text is interesting not only for the specific information it provides concerning the Mixtec names of Acatlán, but as a statement that is undoubtedly applicable to Mixtec place names in general. We learn that the Nahuatl speakers who conquered much of the Mixtec-speaking region often gave the conquered town a new Nahuatl name whose meaning had nothing to do with the existing Mixtec name. We learn that a town may have more than one Mixtec name, that these names can change over a period of time, and that the former names may not be remembered. Indeed, in the 1593 Reyes list of Mixtec town names, published 12 years after the *Relación* of Acatlán was written, the only Mixtec name given for Acatlán is *Yuta tisaha*, the Mixtec name which apparently was current in 1581 and eventually supplanted the older name, *yucu yuxi*.

The Mixtec glosses in Codex Sánchez Solís that accompany the place sign of Acatlán contain both of the sixteenth-century names of the town. The first two words *yoco yoxi* (or *yucu yusi*) are of course the earlier name, and they mean "hill of the turquoise" or "hill of the precious stone." The second name, *tixaa* or *tixaha*, is the qualifying element of the later Mixtec name, *yuta tisaha*. *Yuta* means "river" or "arroyo with water"; *tisaha* means "soft, spongy," or "sterile" when referring to earth, which relates somewhat tenuously to the "filled with ashes" translation given in the 1581 *Relación* for the *tisaha* section of Acatlán's name.

It is noteworthy that the place sign of Acatlán in Sánchez Solís represents only *yucu yusi*, the earlier name of the town. In all four instances, this place sign consists of a hill (*yucu*) and a turquoise jewel (*yusi*), but contains no pictorial elements—such as a river and either ashes or soft earth—to represent the *yuta tisaha* name. This implies that the pictorial manuscript was painted *before* the *yuta tisaha* name became current (perhaps in the first half of the sixteenth century or earlier), whereas the glosses referring to place signs were written at a time when both names were known (the second half of the sixteenth century?).

The turquoise-jewel motif also occurs in the personal names of eight women and one man in Sánchez Solís (as, for example, in Fig. 6*f*),[40] and in all nine examples the section of the accompanying gloss that refers to the person's personal name contains the word *yusi*. In addition, the sign for *yusi* appears in a place sign in Sánchez Solís that is not Acatlán (Fig. 22*h*). This sign consists of a building which rests on a stone and to which is attached half of a turquoise jewel. The accompanying gloss reads:

---

[34] *Ndaa* has many other meanings, depending on tone. For example, in the dialect of San Miguel el Grande, as presented in the Dyk-Stoudt vocabulary and in Dyk's *Mixteco Texts*, *ndaà* means "truth, true," as well as a type of cactus fiber (*ixtle*); *ndáá* means "straight, unadulterated, correct, completely"; and *ndaa* means "to rise, ascend."

[35] Codex Mendoza, fol. 43/r (place sign no. 511 of the Clark edition).

[36] Introduction to the 1962 ed. of the Alvarado dictionary, 96. In his commentary on Codex Mendoza, James Cooper Clark gives another etymology of Texupan: *texotli* = blue color, ideograph for *texouia* = to put on blue color; and *pan* = on (represented by the footprint above the blue patch) and says that the name means "on the blue-painters" or "where they paint themselves blue."

[37] According to the Alvarado dictionary, *yusi* may also mean "small hailstones" (*granizo menudo*), "to lose a game or be defeated" (*perder en juego; vencido ser*), and "the nobleman grows" (*crecer el señor*).

[38] PNE V, 55–65. Unfortunately this *Relación* does not have an accompanying map.

[39] *Ibid.*, 58–59. The Spanish text of this quotation appears in Appendix B-2 of this book.

[40] On pages 6, 8, 12, 14, 16 (twice, one male and one female), 19, 23, 24.

ytno cuiy diyoxi; or, in the dialect of the Alvarado dictionary, *itnu cuii diyusi*, or *itnu cuii tiyusi*. *Itnu cuii* means "green slope" (*itnu* = "slope" and *cuii* = "green"), and this Mixtec name occurs in names of town boundaries,[41] but not to my knowledge in the name of any town within the Mixteca. The *diyusi* section of the Mixtec name may refer to at least two places in the Mixteca: the town of San Juan Diuxi in the Mixteca Alta, or San Andrés Sabanillos in the Mixteca Baja. In the 1579 *Relación* of Tilantongo, one of this town's subjects is listed as San Juan *Diyusi* (present-day Diuxi), and the Mixtec name *Diyusi* is translated as "mountain of the green stone."[42]

In a will from the Mixteca Baja town of Tonalá, written in Mixtec and dated 1643, one of the Mixtec names of a nearby town named "San Andrés Pueblo Viejo" is given as *tiyusi*.[43] The only San Andrés in the vicinity of Tonalá is a town which is today called San Andrés Sabanillos, located about 17°46′ N., 98°5′ W. In the dialect of the Sánchez Solís glosses, the *t* of the Alvarado dialect is often written *d*, and Alvarado's *nd* as *t*. Thus it is also possible that the *diyoxi* gloss on page 31 of Sánchez Solís refers to the Mixteca Baja town of *tiyusi*, or San Andrés (Sabanillos?); and considering that Sánchez Salís appears to have a Mixteca Baja orientation, it seems more likely that this sign represents the Mixteca Baja town.

We see, then, that the turquoise-jewel motif is used as a logogram for *yusi* ("turquoise") in Codex Sánchez Solís and as a logogram for *ndaa* ("the color blue") in the place sign of Texupan. This motif functions as both a primary logogram where the picture of a turquoise jewel means literally "turquoise jewel" and as an associative logogram where the jewel motif signifies one of its qualities, the color blue. This type of logogram with a dual meaning is also common in other languages, such as Chinese, in which the sign for tower not only means "tower" but also "high," one of the qualities of towers in general.[44] Because the place signs of both Texupan and Acatlán consist of a hill containing a turquoise jewel, the only way to distinguish the pictorial signs is by context. The sign must appear in a setting where it can be clearly identified, either by an accompanying text or by a document which states that the persons associated with the sign are the rulers of one or the other town.

YANHUITLÁN (17°32′ N., 97°21′ W.)

At the time of the Spanish conquest of Oaxaca, Yanhui-

tlán was one of the most important towns of the Mixteca Alta. It dominated a large, once fertile valley northwest of the city of Oaxaca, on the present-day Pan-American Highway between Puebla and Oaxaca. Today the principal surviving remnant of Yanhuitlán's former greatness is the large monastery built by the Dominican friars in the sixteenth century.[45]

The Place Sign in Bodley 19–III

A great many documents dealing with Yanhuitlán in the Colonial period have survived, and one document gives us the Mixtec names of the native rulers of Yanhuitlán at the time of the Spanish conquest.[46] According to testimony supporting a suit by Gabriel de Guzmán, ruler of Yanhuitlán in 1580, Guzmán was the grandson of a woman named *ca uaco*, who ruled Yanhuitlán and who married *na mahu*, a son of *xico* of Tilantongo. As Alfonso Caso has astutely pointed out, *ca uaco* is ♀ 1-Flower, *na mahu* is ♂ 8-Death, and *xico* is ♂ 10-Rain—the same three persons who are depicted on the final lines of the front of Codex Bodley.[47] The penultimate scene on the Bodley obverse shows the marriage of ♂ 8-Death "Tiger-Fire Serpent" and ♀ 1-Flower "Tiger Quechquemitl" (Fig. 40), and it is indicated that ♂ 8-Death is the son of ♂ 10-Rain "Tlaloc-Sun" of Tilantongo.

Thus the place sign on which ♂ 8-Death and ♀ 1-Flower are seated must be the sign of Yanhuitlán, and it should represent Yanhuitlán's Mixtec name, *yodzo cahi*.[48] As can be seen in Fig. 40, the Yanhuitlán sign in Bodley has the "feather mat" motif for *yodzo*, or "plain, valley." It is, however, more difficult to relate *cahi*, the qualifying element of Yanhuitlán's Mixtec name, with the pictorial sign in Bodley. In the sixteenth-century dictionary of Alvarado, the basic meanings of *cahi* are as follows:

> to take (*tomar*)
> to leave something (*quitar algo*)
> wide, as a mat or road (*ancha cosa como estera o camino*)
> many in number, crowd (*mucho en número, muchedumbre*)

---

[41] For example, one of the boundary signs in Map No. 36 (Fig. 22a) is glossed *itno cuii*. In an eighteenth-century document dealing with the region of Huajuapan in northern Oaxaca, *itnu cuii* is given as a boundary of Huajuapan (AGN-Tierras, 657–3, cuaderno 2, fol. 11/v, and cuaderno 3, fol. 32/v).

[42] *PNE* IV, 70–71. This town is located 17°13′ N., 97°18′ W., about three miles southwest of Tilantongo.

[43] AGN-Tierras, 657–2, fol. 46–47/v. In this will, "San Andrés Pueblo Viejo" is variously referred to as *tiyusi*, *ño cuchi tiyusi*, *tisiyu ñucuchi*, and *ñucuchi*. This will contains several Mixtec names for Mixteca Baja towns that are not included in the 1593 Reyes list. The Mixtec name of San Martín Zacatepec is given as *itnu yayu*, that of Santa Catarina (near Tonalá) as *saha yucu tachi*, and that of San Gerónimo (Silacayoapilla) as **yodzo ñoñoho** or *yodo ñuñuhu*.

[44] Gelb, *A Study of Writing*, 100.

[45] The monastery and its church are discussed in George Kubler, *Mexican Architecture of the Sixteenth Century*, 2 vols. (New Haven, 1948), *passim*. The official Mexican Government guidebook to the buildings is: José Gorbea Trueba, *Yanhuitlán* (Mexico, 1962) (Departamento de Monumentos Coloniales, Publicación 15). Line drawings of the monastery and church are included in Ross Parmenter, *Week in Yanhuitlán* (Albuquerque, 1965).

[46] AGN-Civil 516. Sections of this document and other Colonial documents relating to Yanhuitlán are contained in Jiménez Moreno and Mateos Higuera, *Códice de Yanhuitlán*, and in Spores, *The Mixtec Kings and Their People*.

[47] Caso, *Bodley*, 49–50, and "Los señores de Yanhuitlán," *ICA* XXXV, Vol. I (Mexico, 1964), 437–38. An English translation of the latter study appears in: John Paddock, ed., *Ancient Oaxaca* (Stanford, California, 1966), 313–35.

[48] The name *yodzo cahi* is given in the Reyes 1593 list and in numerous sixteenth-century documents relating to Yanhuitlán (e.g., AGN-Tierras 400–1). In the *Relación* of Tilantongo, the Mixtec name of Yanhuitlán is said to be *yoozo cai* (*PNE* IV, 72). The name is *yodzo quehe* in a barely visible gloss in the Codex of Yanhuitlán (*Códice de Yanhuitlán*, plate XX). *Yodzo cahi* will be used in this study because it is the most frequently cited name and because this version of the name is in the dialect of the Alvarado dictionary.

to spin (*hilar*)
cemetery (*cementerio*)

None of these meanings seems to have anything to do with the qualifying element of the Yanhuitlán sign in Fig. 40, which is the head of a bird whose beak terminates in arrows. The beak of a bird is *taya(te)* in Mixtec; the word for arrows is *nduvua*.

What the bird with arrow beak may represent is the Mixtec word *dzaa*. *Dzaa* not only means "bird," but it can also mean "point of something sharp" (*punta de cosa aguda*). If *dzaa* were the word represented in this pictorial sign, the arrowheads as sharp points (*dzaa*) would function as phonetic indicators to clarify that the bird motif represents the word *dzaa*, or "bird in general," rather than a specific type of bird.[49] But if *dzaa* were the qualifying element of this place sign, then the Mixtec name represented here would be *yodzo dzaa*, not *yodzo cahi*, the known Mixtec name of Yanhuitlán. If *yodzo dzaa* (or "bird plain") was at one time a name of Yanhuitlán, we have no record of it in the numerous Colonial documents relating to this town.

To my knowledge, the only place with a Mixtec name *yodzo dzaa* is a field within the town of Apoala that belonged to the native rulers of Yanhuitlán in the sixteenth century and which is included in two lists of the lands of the Yanhuitlán *cacicazgo*.[50] But it seems highly unlikely that the place sign in Bodley represents a mere field located in another town rather than the principal center of Yanhuitlán.

Another pictorial element in the Yanhuitlán sign is a human mouth placed at the top of the feather mat, between the marriage pair. The mouth motif has two different meanings in place signs. First, it may mean *yuhu*, or "mouth, at the edge of." Second, in the Valley of Yanhuitlán region, the mouth often represents the prefix *a-*, as in the signs of two towns in the vicinity of Yanhuitlán —Nochixtlán (Fig. 24*a*) and San Andrés Andúa (Fig. 24*b*)—in which the mouth depicts the *a-* element of *atoco* (the Mixtec name of Nochixtlán) and of *anduvua* (Andúa). But neither the word *yuhu* nor the prefix *a-* occurs in Yanhuitlán's Mixtec name.

Thus, in the case of the place sign of Yanhuitlán, we have a sign that must represent Yanhuitlán because the personages seated on the sign are clearly documented to have been the rulers of Yanhuitlán. But this sign cannot be correlated with the known Mixtec name of Yanhuitlán, *yodzo cahi*. Instead, the pictorial elements of the sign seem to represent a Mixtec name such as *yodzo dzaa* ("plain of the bird"), *yuhu yodzo dzaa* ("at the edge of the plain of the bird"), or *a-yodzo dzaa* ("at the plain of the bird"). Either Yanhuitlán had a second Mixtec name in addition

to *yodzo cahi*, or the Mixtec word *cahi*, the qualifying element of Yanhuitlán's name, has a meaning which is now lost, but which relates to the "bird with arrow beak" motif in the sign of Yanhuitlán. It seems to me more likely that Yanhuitlán had a second Mixtec name, much as Teozacoalco had a second name, now unknown, that is represented by a "flower frieze." It is this second name, possibly *yodzo dzaa*, that is represented by the place sign of Yanhuitlán in Bodley 19–III.

The Nahuatl Place Sign

Yanhuitlán provides another example of a Mixtec town whose Nahuatl name is not related in meaning to the town's Mixtec name. The Nahuatl name *yancuitlan* means "new place," and is represented in Codex Mendoza as a rectangle with two teeth attached at the bottom (Fig. 43*a*).[51] The rectangle is the logogram for *yancuic* or "new, recent," and the teeth (*tlantli*) represent "place" (also *tlantli*). In all probability, the Nahuatl name "new place" was a translation of the Mixtec name of one of the sections or *barrios* of Yanhuitlán, a barrio listed in the sixteenth-century documents as *ñuu saa*, or "new town."[52] (*Ñuu* = "town"; *saa* = "new.")

The Place Sign in Bodley 11–IV

Caso believes that another place sign that contains a bird with arrow-beak (Fig. 41) is also the sign of Yanhuitlán.[53] This place sign appears in Bodley 11–IV, as the town of ♂ 5-Eagle and ♀ 9-Serpent, the parents of ♀ 11-Serpent, who becomes the fourth wife of ♂ 8-Deer "Tiger Claw."[54]

But the geographical substantive of this place sign is not a feather-mat meaning *yodzo*, but a frieze which usually means *ñuu*. On the basis of the pictorial elements of this sign, it should represent the Mixtec name, *ñuu dzaa*, or "town of the birds." The frieze represents *ñuu*, and the bird's head represents *dzaa*, with the arrowheads functioning as a phonetic indicator because they represent "something with a sharp point" (also *dzaa* in Mixtec). According to the Reyes 1593 list of Mixtec town names, *ñuu dzaa* is the Mixtec name of Totomihuacan, a town in the State of Puebla, about seven miles south of the city of Puebla.[55] Whether the eleventh-century ruler 8-Deer would have married a woman from a town as far away as Totomihuacan is as yet difficult to determine. But I believe that *ñuu dzaa* is the most suitable Mixtec equivalent

---

[49] In the place sign of Tututepec (discussed below, pp. 67–68), the qualifying element "bird" (*dzaa*) is accompanied by a phonetic indicator, but in the Tututepec sign a beardless human chin (*dzaa*) is used instead of arrowheads.

[50] Both lists are in AGN-Tierras 400–1. A similar list, in AGN-Civil 516, includes the names of nine fields in the town of Apoala that belong to the native ruler of Yanhuitlán, but does not contain the name of *yodzo dzaa*.

[51] Codex Mendoza, fol. 43/r (place sign no. 513 of the Clark edition).

[52] *Ñusaa* is named as a barrio of Yanhuitlán in AGN-Civil 516, fol. 6 (1580) and in a list dated 1565 from the Archivo General de las Indias, Escribano 162. These two lists are published in Spores, *The Mixtec Kings and Their People*, 158–59, 194–96.

[53] "Los señores de Yanhuitlán," *ICA* XXXV, Vol. I (Mexico, 1964), 438.

[54] ♂ 5-Eagle and ♀ 9-Serpent, the rulers of the place in Bodley 11–IV, have no personal names and do not seem to appear in any other historical manuscript.

[55] The Nahuatl sign for Totomihuacan in Codex Xolotl (plate VI, A3 of the Dibble edition) is rather similar to the Mixtec sign in Bodley 19–III for Yanhuitlán. It consists of a bird combined with an arrow and reflects two of the Nahuatl components of the name: *toto* from *tototl* ("bird") and *mi* from *mitl* ("arrow"). A discussion of the possible relationship between the *totomitl* elements and the Otomí-speaking people is found in: Wigberto Jiménez Moreno, "Origen y significación del nombre 'Otomí,'" *RMEA* Vol. III–1 (1939), 62–68.

of the place sign in Bodley 11–IV, and that this sign may represent Totomihuacan rather than Yanhuitlán.

The "Cacaxtli Plain" Place Sign

Caso also believes that Yanhuitlán may be represented by a place sign which consists of the feather-mat or "plain" motif and a type of carrying device made of bound slats of wood and known in Nahuatl as a *cacaxtli* (Fig. 42).[56] His argument concerning this place sign is extremely complex, but the main points may be summarized as follows:

(1) A personage named ♂ 6-Water is shown as a ruler of "Cacaxtli Plain" in Bodley 24–III and Selden 13–I (Fig. 42), and he is also the last depicted descendant in a genealogical sequence in Nuttall 33–35 that sets forth the rulers of a place whose sign consists of a Bird River and Bent Hill with Tree and Flames (Fig. 39a). Thus the two place signs, "Cacaxtli Plain" and the large sign in Nuttall 33, seem to be related and may even represent the same town.

(2) The headdresses of most of the persons in the genealogical sequence in Nuttall 33–35 are the red-and-white headdresses that are characteristic of the deity known in Nahuatl as Xipe-Totec (Fig. 39 *b, c*). In the historical manuscripts these headdresses are worn only by persons who are connected with the place described as Bird River-Bent Hill with Tree (Nuttall 33–35, 61). On the wall of the recently discovered tomb at Zaachila, a town in the Valley of Oaxaca, are two sculptured figures who also wear this distinctive red-and-white headdress (Fig. 39 *d, e*).[57] One figure is accompanied by the calendrical name 5-Flower, and Caso believes this person to be the same as ♂ 5-Flower on page 33 of Nuttall (Fig. 39b). The second figure in the Zaachila tomb is accompanied by the calendrical name 9-Flower, and Caso thinks this figure to be the same as ♂ 9-Serpent in Nuttall 33 (Fig. 39c), notwithstanding the difference in the day signs of the two names. In addition, Caso postulates that the Zaachila tomb was constructed for the rulers of the nearby town of Cuilapan, formerly one of the principal centers of Mixtec-speaking people in the Valley of Oaxaca. He also believes that the rulers depicted in both Nuttall 33 and in the Zaachila tomb sculpture are the early Mixtec rulers of Cuilapan, and that the place sign in Nuttall 33 (Fig. 39a) represents Cuilapan.

(3) According to the sixteenth-century *Relaciones Geográficas*, the ruling families of Cuilapan intermarried with the ruling families of Yanhuitlán and also with the ruling family of Zaachila.[58] Caso feels that the known close connection of the Cuilapan and Yanhuitlán genealogies is paralleled in the close connection between the ruling families of the two place signs "Cacaxtli Plain" and "Bird River-Bent Hill with Tree." He thus suggests that either both of these place signs represent Cuilapan, or that the second place sign represents Cuilapan and the "Cacaxtli Plain" sign represents Yanhuitlán.

For several reasons, these arguments do not seem to cohere. First, even if the 5-Flower and 9-Flower of the Zaachila tomb are historical personages and the same persons as 5-Flower and 9-Serpent of Nuttall 33, there is no convincing reason to believe that the rulers buried in the Zaachila tomb are from Cuilapan or that the place sign on Nuttall 33 represents Cuilapan. Reyes gives two Mixtec names for Cuilapan: *yuta caha* and *saha yucu*. The meaning of these names is discussed in the 1581 *Relación Geográfica* of Cuilapan.[59] Here, the name *yuta caha* is called *yncha tica* (usually abbreviated to *yncha ca*); *yncha* means "river," and *tica* means "bell" (*cascabel*) or a type of date palm known in Nahuatl as *guacoyol*, or merely *coyol* (*Acrocomia mexicana*, Karw.). According to the Alvarado dictionary, *caa* means "bell" and *ticaha* means "date palm," and these are two different words, because the latter has a glottal stop between the two *a*'s, and the former does not. The *Relación Geográfica* of Cuilapan says that the town's Nahuatl name "cuyolapan" also means "place of the guacoyoles." The Nahuatl place sign of "cuyolapan" in Codex Mendoza depicts a bell within a river, and Clark gives the following etymology for this sign:

> *coyulli* = large bell, ideograph for
> *coyoli* = *Acrocomia mexicana*, Karw.
> *apantli* = canal, ideograph for
> *apan* = on the water

or, "on the water of the *coyoli*, a type of palm tree."[60] The *Relación* of Cuilapan also states that *saha yucu* was an earlier Mixtec name of Cuilapan, and that it means "at the foot of the hill." (*Saha* = "at the foot of"; *yucu* = "hill.") Unless the tree in the place sign in Nuttall 33 represents a guacoyol or date-palm, this place sign seems not to be related to the Mixtec names of Cuilapan that were known in the sixteenth century. Moreover, the tree motif in this sign is connected with the Bent Hill and is not the qualifying element of the River, as is the date-palm (*ticaha*) of Cuilapan's Mixtec name *yuta (ti)caha*.

A second objection to Caso's argument is that no specific relationship between the named personages in Nuttall 33–35 and known rulers of either Cuilapan or Yanhuitlán can be established. We know from sixteenth-century accounts that there was intermarriage between the rulers of

[56] *Bodley*, 49–50, and "Los señores de Yanhuitlán," *ICA* XXXV, Vol. I (Mexico, 1964), 438–48.

[57] The rich findings of the Zaachila tomb excavations are described briefly in Roberto Gallegos, "Zaachila: The First Season's Work," *Archaeology*, Vol. XVI–4 (1963), 226–33. Numerous photographs of the Zaachila tombs are included in Paddock, ed., *Ancient Oaxaca*, between pp. 306–29.

[58] The *Relación* of Cuilapan states that the rulers of Cuilapan intermarried at various times with rulers of Almoloyas, a subject of Yanhuitlán at the time of the Spanish conquest; that over three hundred years before the *Relación* was written (i.e., before 1280) many Mixtec-speaking people migrated to Cuilapan; and that one of the Mixtec noblemen of this

group married a noblewoman of the nearby Zapotec-speaking town of Zaachila (also called Teozapotlán) and received from his father-in-law the land on which the town of Cuilapan is located. (*Tlalocan*, Vol. II–1, 23) A similar story is told in the 1580 *Relación* of Teozapotlán, alias Zaachila (*PNE* IV, 190–91). Burgoa (*Geográfica descripción*, I, 395–97) also describes the Mixtec holdings in Cuilapan and in other communities surrounding the Zapotec center of Zaachila.

[59] *Tlalocan*, Vol. II–1, 22, 23.

[60] Codex Mendoza, fol. 44/r (place sign no. 521 of the Clark edition).

Cuilapan and Yanhuitlán, but these sources do not name the rulers involved. Thus it is impossible to identify the personages in the pictorial manuscripts as rulers of Cuilapan or Yanhuitlán.

In addition, we do not know the Mixtec word for the carrying device known in Nahuatl as a *cacaxtli*, which is the qualifying element of the sign "Cacaxtli Plain." Therefore it is not possible to determine whether this place sign represents *yodzo cahi* (Yanhuitlán) or the Mixtec name of some other town.

Caso's hypotheses concerning the place signs of Cuilapan and Yanhuitlán are provocative and intriguing, but they cannot as yet be substantiated. It is agreed that a town as important as Yanhuitlán is probably represented by a sign other than the "Bird with Arrow-Beak Plain" which appears only once in the historical manuscripts, on Bodley 19–III. But the alternative sign or signs for Yanhuitlán remain unidentified.

COIXTLAHUACA (17°42′ N., 97°18′ W.)

The place sign of the town of Coixtlahuaca in the Mixteca Alta is depicted in four published post-Conquest documents of the "Coixtlahuaca Group" of manuscripts: the Lienzo of Coixtlahuaca (and its copy, Codex Ixtlán), Codex Meixueiro, the Lienzo of Ihuitlán, and Lienzo Antonio de León.[61] The pictorial sign of the town also appears in a sketch-map drawn in connection with a 1590 land grant in the vicinity of Coixtlahuaca (AGN-Tierras 2729-5), and in a 1580 map from the neighboring town of Ixcatlán.

The Nahuatl name "coixtlahuaca" and the town's Mixtec name, *yodzo coo*, have the same meaning: "Serpent Plain." In the Mixtec name, *yodzo* means "plain, valley" and *coo* means "serpent."[62] Coixtlahuaca is today the center of the Chocho-speaking population of Oaxaca; and according to Martínez Gracida, the town's name in Chocho, *Inguinche*, also means "Serpent Plain."[63] (In = "plain"; *guinche* = "serpent.")

The Nahuatl Sign

The Nahuatl name *coayxtlahuacan* is represented in Codex Mendoza (Fig. 43b), and this place sign consists of a horizontal strip of land, a serpent, and two inverted eyes. Clark analyzes the Nahuatl name in this manner:

> *coatl* = snake
> *ixtlapal* = inverted; ideograph for
> *istlauatl* = a plain
> *can* = place,

or "place of the plain of the snakes."[64]

Lienzo of Coixtlahuaca (Codex Ixtlán) and Codex Meixueiro

The place sign for Coixtlahuaca in the Lienzo of Coixtlahuaca (Fig. 44a) and in Codex Meixueiro (Fig. 44b) is basically the same: a large feathered serpent. The serpent represents the *coo* section of the town's Mixtec name *yodzo coo*; and *yodzo*, which means "large feather" as well as "plain, valley," appears to be represented in these two manuscripts by the feathers of the serpent rather than by the traditional "feather mat" motif. As Alfonso Caso has suggested, the two subsidiary place signs with buildings that appear directly above the serpent probably represent sections or *barrios* of Coixtlahuaca, because in Lienzo Antonio de León these place signs are represented as separate from, but close to, the sign of Coixtlahuaca.[65]

Lienzo of Ihuitlán

In this manuscript the name of Coixtlahuaca is represented by a large horizontal rattlesnake with diamond patterns on its body, and the place sign is accompanied by the gloss "cuvayxtlavaca" (Fig. 45b). No element, such as feathers or a feather mat, is present to depict *yodzo*, the geographical substantive of the town's Mixtec name.

Above the large rattlesnake is a round rock formation suggesting a cave and containing the mummy bundle of ♂ 1-Lizard and a representation of the deity ♂ 9-Wind.[66] Placed on top of the rock is a platform covered with tiger hide, on which sit the personages who apparently founded the Coixtlahuaca dynasties, ♀ 4-Reed and ♂ 8-Wind. A vertical row of sixteen marriage pairs, beginning with this couple at the bottom, represents the rulers of this town.[67]

Lienzo Antonio de León

Coixtlahuaca is shown in this lienzo as two spotted, intertwined serpents with feathered tails (Fig. 45a). This configuration rests on an oval rock which contains two strands of rope and a human heart.[68] In this place sign, the feathered tails of the serpents probably relate to the Mixtec word *yodzo* meaning "plain" or "large feather."

The meaning of the rock sign below the serpents is not known, but it may be analogous to the rock with a building in Codex Meixueiro which is placed below the large central sign with a feathered serpent and which is connected to the sign by a vertical row of six male figures. The last five of these figures in Meixueiro have the same calendrical names as the male figures in the five couples placed above the Coixtlahuaca sign in Antonio de León: 1-Wind, 5-Flower, 3-Wind, 12-Serpent, and 5-Rabbit. The five marriage pairs above the Coixtlahuaca sign in Antonio de León are also the same as the first five couples of the Coixtlahuaca dynasties represented in the Lienzo of

[61] The manuscripts of the Coixtlahuaca Group are discussed in Appendix C.

[62] The name is *yodzo coo* in the Reyes 1593 list, and *yodo coo* (a dialect variation) in the nineteenth-century compilations of Martínez Gracida.

[63] *BSMGE* 1888, 310.

[64] Codex Mendoza, fol. 43/r (place sign no. 510 of the Clark edition). The interpretations of the "inverted eye" motif of this sign made by Clark and others are discussed in note 23, Chapter IV.

[65] "Los lienzos mixtecos de Ihuitlán y Antonio de León," *Homenaje a Pablo Martínez del Río* (Mexico, 1961), 268.

[66] As Caso has pointed out (*ibid.*, 242), 9-Wind is the calendrical name of the deity who resembles Quetzalcoatl of the Nahuatl-speaking peoples, but the deceased persons and deities in this lienzo have the attributes of the rain deity known in Nahuatl as Tlaloc.

[67] These genealogies are discussed in Caso's study of the lienzo (*ibid.*, 242-43).

[68] *Ibid.*, 268.

Ihuitlán, except for the name of the male figure in the initial couple, which Antonio de León lists as 1-Wind and Ihuitlán as 8-Wind.

AGN-Tierras 2729-5

The sign for Coixtlahuaca appears in the left-central section of this 1590 sketch-map as a pair of crossed serpents with feathered tails (Fig. 46).[69] Underneath the serpents is the gloss "couayxtlabaca"; above is a church which usually symbolizes "town" in Colonial-period maps. The Coixtlahuaca sign in this map most closely resembles the intertwined serpents of the sign in Lienzo Antonio de León, and again, the feathers of the serpents' tails may represent the Mixtec word *yodzo*, "large feather" or "plain, valley."

1580 Map of Ixcatlán

The one sign of Coixtlahuaca which does have a feather-mat motif for "plain" (*yodzo*) is the sign of this town in a 1580 land map from the neighboring town of Ixcatlán (Fig. 47).[70] Here, a serpent with a feathered tail is placed in front of the feather-mat motif, which serves as a platform for a church. An accompanying gloss identifies this structure as the church of Coixtlahuaca: "*esta es la yglesia de cuestlahuaca.*"

We see, then, that the basic element of the Coixtlahuaca sign as it appears in post-Conquest manuscripts from the Coixtlahuaca region is a serpent representing the *coo* section of *yodzo coo*, the town's Mixtec name. In all instances but one—the sign in the Lienzo of Ihuitlán—the serpent is represented with a plumed tail or plumed body, suggesting the *yodzo* section of the town's Mixtec name. With the exception of the sign of Coixtlahuaca in the 1580 Map of Ixcatlán, the serpent motif does not appear with a geographical substantive—such as a feather mat for *yodzo*—in any of the manuscripts discussed above. In Lienzo Antonio de León the rock on which the intertwined serpents rest appears to depict a second place name. In the Lienzo of Ihuitlán, the rock above the rattlesnake probably represents a cave or burial place not connected with the name of Coixtlahuaca.

The principal problem with the Coixtlahuaca sign is the relation of this sign as it is known in the post-Conquest manuscripts to pictorial signs with serpents in pre-Conquest manuscripts. The serpent motif appears in the pre-Conquest historical manuscripts accompanied by a river, a frieze, or a hill, but it is difficult to ascertain whether any of these signs refers to Coixtlahuaca.[71]

Alfonso Caso believes that the "Serpent River" that appears in Bodley 4-IV and 5-I and in Selden 1-II may be Coixtlahuaca,[72] but this sign does not correlate with the known representations of Coixtlahuaca. A river does not appear as a geographical substantive in any of the signs of Coixtlahuaca discussed above, nor does the word "river" (*yuta*) appear in Coixtlahuaca's Mixtec name. Caso also believes that a sign in Bodley 31-III with a frieze and a serpent with flint nose and tail is Coixtlahuaca.[73] The town represented by this sign was ruled in the late eleventh century by ♂ 4-Wind "Fire Serpent," who was also the ruler of an important, but as yet unidentified, place known as "Flint Frieze." But the flint blade seen in the nose and tail of the "Serpent Frieze" in Bodley 31-III does not occur with serpents in any of the known representations of Coixtlahuaca, and the post-Conquest manuscripts make no mention of 4-Wind as a former ruler of Coixtlahuaca.

A serpent with a feathered tail which appears twice in Becker I (pages 4 and 14) in connection with a building containing a *tule* plant may represent Coixtlahuaca, and this sign will be discussed below in the section entitled "Place Signs with the Marsh-Grass Motif." But in the case of the other signs with serpents, unless some connection can be established between the genealogies represented in the post-Conquest Coixtlahuaca group of manuscripts and personages seated on place signs with serpents in the pre-Conquest historical manuscripts, I do not believe that the Serpent Rivers, Serpent Friezes, and Serpent Hills in the latter group of manuscripts are place signs of Coixtlahuaca.

AMOLTEPEC AND CUQUILA

The place signs of Amoltepec and Cuquila present problems similar to those incurred with the sign of Coixtlahuaca. That is, the signs of both towns appear in a clearly identifiable context in post-Conquest documents, but they have yet to be identified in the pre-Conquest historical manuscripts.

Santiago Amoltepec (16°27' N., 97°29' W.)

The place sign of Amoltepec (Fig. 48) is the central sign in the post-Conquest map that accompanied the 1580 *Relación Geográfica* of Amoltepec.[74] The sign consists of a hill with *amole* plants and represents the town's Mixtec name, *yucu nama*.[75] *Yucu* means "hill" and *nama*

---

[69] This map is described in more detail in Appendix C.

[70] The Ixcatlán map is in the Bibliothèque Nationale in Paris (Fonds Mexicains No. 103) and has not been published. This map was apparently drawn in connection with a land dispute over a site named Axumulco, which is shown in the map to be within Ixcatlán's boundaries.

[71] A "Serpent River" appears in Bodley 4-IV and 8-I, in Selden 1-II, and as part of a large compound place sign in Nuttall 22. A "River with Serpent and Tree" is in Bodley 5-I; a "River with Two Intertwined Serpents" in Selden 11-IV; and a "Serpent Diving into a River" in Becker I-7. A frieze containing stars and with a serpent with flint nose and tail appears in Bodley 31-III. In Bodley 26-I and 25-I, there is a serpent accompanied by a frieze and a hill containing stars and circles. A "Hill with Serpent" is also a prominent place sign in two post-Conquest manuscripts, the Lienzo of Philadelphia and the Lienzo Córdova-Castellanos.

[72] Caso, *Bodley*, 29, 34, and *Selden*, 26; 73.

[73] Caso, *Bodley*, 62, and *Colombino*, 45; 143.

[74] The original Map of Amoltepec is in the Latin American Library of the University of Texas (García Icazbalceta Collection No. 1770). A small black-and-white photograph of the map was published in Robertson, "The *Relaciones Geográficas* of Mexico," 544, Fig. 3. A nineteenth-century copy of the map is in the Mapoteca of the Dirección de Geografía, Meteorología e Hidrología in Mexico City (Colección Orozco y Berra, No. 1193).

[75] *Yucu nama* is the name given for Amoltepec in the 1593 Reyes list and in the text of the Amoltepec *Relación Geográfica* (RMEH I-6, 177). The latter source translates *yucu nama* as "soap hill" (*serro de jabón*). A second town in the Mixteca with this Mixtec name is San Pedro Yucunama, near Teposcolula in the Mixteca Alta (17°34' N., 97°30' W.). The latter town has a pictorial genealogy that is unpublished, except for the place sign of Yucunama, which is reproduced in a drawing in Caso, *Selden*, 19. This sign consists of a platform supporting an amole plant which resembles the pre-Conquest motif for the human heart and which appears to be placed between two peaks.

means "soap," a product which was made from the roots of the amole plant. The Nahuatl term "amole" is a popular name that designates a number of soap-producing plants, many of which belong to the genus *Sapindus*.[76] The place sign of Amoltepec as it appears in the *Relación* map of the town seems to have no counterpart in any of the pre-Conquest codices.

Santa María Cuquila (17° 12' N., 97° 45' W.)

The place sign of the town of Cuquila in the Mixteca Alta appears in the post-Conquest Lienzo of Santo Tomás Ocotepec (Fig. 160, right side).[77] The sign consists of a tiger within a hill; at the summit of the hill is a frieze with a marriage pair, and written in the base of the hill is the name of the town, "cuquila." The Mixtec name of Cuquila is *ñuu cuiñe*, or "the town of the tiger."[78] (*Ñuu =* "town"; *cuiñe =* "tiger.") The *cuiñe* element of the name is represented by the tiger within the hill, and the *ñuu* element is apparently depicted by the frieze with geometric designs placed at the top of the hill. In this place sign, as in the sign of Texupan discussed above, the hill motif is present even though this motif has no counterpart (*yucu*) in the Mixtec name of the town.

Given that this sign in the Lienzo of Ocotepec represents *ñuu cuiñe*, or Cuquila, do any of the "tiger frieze" or "tiger hill" signs in the pre-Conquest histories also represent the name of this town? For example, the back of Nuttall shows several signs with tigers in connection with the biography of 8-Deer:

Tiger Hill   Nuttall 46a   Hill with Red Tiger (shown as conquered by 8-Deer)

            46b, 50b   Hill with Yellow Tiger (shown as conquered by 8-Deer in 46b)

            72d   Hill with Stone Pattern and Yellow Tiger (shown as conquered by 8-Deer)

Tiger Frieze   Nuttall 66a, 73a, 82c Frieze with Yellow Tiger (shown as conquered by 8-Deer in 73a)

A place sign consisting of a frieze with a tiger also appears in Bodley 14–V, as the hometown of ♀ 6-Wind "Bloody Feather Mat," who becomes the fifth and last wife of 8-Deer. If Cuquila's Mixtec name *ñuu cuiñe* were depicted in a strictly logographic manner—that is, one sign for one word—then it would be reasonable to assume that the "tiger frieze" signs in the Mixtec histories represent Cuquila. But the sign for Cuquila in the Lienzo of Ocotepec includes a hill as well as a frieze, and it is also

possible that the "tiger hill" signs in the pre-Conquest manuscripts refer to Cuquila. Thus the sign for Cuquila, as the sign for Amoltepec discussed above, is readily identifiable in one context, that of an early Colonial map, but it is difficult to determine with any assurance which other signs with a tiger motif are the sign of this town.

TUTUTEPEC (16° 10' N., 97° 38' W.)

The place sign of the Coastal town of Tututepec was first identified in Codex Colombino (Fig. 49a), where it appears with the following Mixtec gloss written across the roof of the building placed above the sign:

       *s*ⁿ *p*^o *yucu*
       dzaa aniñe
       don p^o *alvara*
          do

or "San Pedro Tututepec, the palace of Don Pedro Alvarado." *Yucu dzaa*, "hill of the bird," is given as the Mixtec name of Tututepec in the 1593 Reyes list and in all the other sources of Mixtec place names. *Aniñe* means "palace," and Pedro de Alvarado is the name of the native ruler of Tututepec from 1522 to about the mid-sixteenth century.[79]

In Colombino the eleventh-century ruler of Tilantongo, ♂ 8-Deer "Tiger Claw," is also shown as the ruler of Tututepec, the capital of the Coastal region of the Mixteca. In the representation of the Tututepec sign in Bodley 9–III (Fig. 49b), 8-Deer is also seated in front of Tututepec as its ruler. On the back of Nuttall, the Tututepec sign appears twice, on pages 45d and 50b (Fig. 49 c, d). On page 50b, 8-Deer is shown making an offering at Tututepec; on page 45 c–d, he is participating in a ballgame next to the Tututepec sign. In the latter sign, the ballcourt within the hill probably indicates that the ballgame took place at a site within the boundaries of Tututepec.

The basic sign of Tututepec is a hill and an eagle, with the hill representing the *yucu* section of Tututepec's name and the eagle standing for "bird" or *dzaa*. In the Tututepec sign as it appears in Bodley 9–III and Nuttall 50b, another pictorial element is added: a human face or chin enclosed by the beak of the eagle. The beardless human chin is *dzaa* in Mixtec,[80] and this element functions as a phonetic indicator to show that the bird in the sign is to be read as *dzaa* ("bird in general") rather than as *yaha*, the Mixtec word for "eagle." In the Colombino sign, the space enclosed by the eagle's beak has been completely erased; originally it too may have contained a human face or chin.

In Colombino, a second place sign is combined with the Tututepec sign. At the right side of the hill of this sign is a frieze with a knotted bunch of grass. This subsidiary sign probably represents the Coastal town of Juquila, and it is discussed below, in the section entitled "Apoala and Juquila" (pp. 75–76).

---

[76] The various plants which are called "amole" are listed and discussed in Manuel Urbina, "Notas acerca de los amoles mexicanos," appendix to *Anales del Museo Nacional*, Vol. VI–1 (1898), 1–12.

[77] The Lienzo of Ocotepec is in the municipal archive of Santo Tomás Ocotepec, a town about five miles south of Cuquila. A black-and-white photograph taken under ultra-violet light (on which Fig. 160 of this study is based) and a color photograph accompany the study of the lienzo by Alfonso Caso: "Mapa de Santo Tomás Ocotepeque, Oaxaca," *Summa anthropologica en homenaje a Roberto J. Weitlaner* (Mexico, 1966), 131–36. This lienzo is discussed in more detail in Chapter IX, below.

[78] *Ñuu cuiñe* is given as the Mixtec name of Cuquila in the 1593 Reyes list and in the nineteenth-century list of Martínez Gracida (*BSMGE* 1888, 316). In the Dyk-Stoudt vocabulary of the dialect of San Miguel el Grande, the name is given as *ñucuiñi*.

[79] Smith, "The Codex Colombino . . . ," *Tlalocan*, Vol. IV–3, 277–78.

[80] In the Alvarado dictionary *dzaa* is given as meaning "chin without beard" (*barba sin pelo*); and in the Reyes list of Mixtec names for parts of the body, *dzaa* means "*barba el lugar*" (i.e., "chin" as opposed to "beard").

The Nahuatl sign of Tututepec, as it appears in Codex Telleriano-Remensis (Fig. 50), is a straightforward rendering of the town's Nahuatl name, which means "in the hill of the bird." (*Tutu-* from *tototl*, "bird"; *-tepec*, a compound of *tepetl*, "hill," and the locative suffix *-c*, "in.") The bird in the Nahuatl sign is of an indeterminate species rather than an eagle, as in the Mixtec sign. Thus no phonetic indicator, such as the human chin in the Mixtec sign, is necessary to let the reader know that the bird represents the generic term "bird" rather than a particular type of bird.[81]

The identification of the Mixtec sign of Tututepec was important, because 8-Deer is now known to have ruled Tututepec, the principal town on the Coast, as well as Tilantongo, the most prestigious town of the Mixteca Alta. It thus seems very likely that, at least for a short period in the eleventh century, this ruler effected a temporary consolidation of the Mixtec-speaking people. But the sign of Tututepec as it has been described above appears only within the context of the 8-Deer biography. Does it appear elsewhere in the historical manuscripts, in relation to other periods of Mixtec history? At the present time, it is difficult to determine whether other representations of "Eagle Hill" or "Bird Hill" in the codices are the signs of Tututepec. None of these signs contains the human-chin element used as a phonetic indicator in at least two of the signs discussed above. Moreover, we do not know the complete genealogy of the pre-Conquest dynasties of Tututepec, so it is impossible to establish whether any of the "Eagle Hills" or "Bird Hills" in the pre-Conquest manuscripts are associated with known rulers of Tututepec.

ACATEPEC (16°11′ N., 97°33′ W.)

In Codex Bodley, one of 8-Deer's first activities after he is shown as seated on the Tututepec sign is the conquest of a place whose name is represented as "Hill of the Moon" (Fig. 51*a*). An analogous scene appears in Colombino XIII–37 (Fig. 51*b*), where either 8-Deer or his half-brother 12-Movement conquers "Hill of the Moon."[82] In Colombino, which presents the 8-Deer biography in much greater detail than does Bodley, the conquest of "Hill of the Moon" occurs almost eight pages after 8-Deer is shown as ruler of Tututepec on page V, 16–17 of Colombino. Also, the calendrical name of the ruler of "Hill of the Moon" is different in the Bodley and Colombino accounts; in Bodley he is named 3-Alligator, and in Colombino, 1-Movement.

At the right of line 36 of Colombino XII, in the scene immediately preceding the conquest of the Hill of the Moon, a person wearing the tiger skin usually worn by 8-Deer is shown visiting another person, now completely erased, who sits in front of a building. On the roof of the building is the gloss: [sⁿ] *ta m^a yucu yoo*, or "Santa María Acatepec." *Yucu yoò* is the Mixtec name of the Coastal town of Santa María Acatepec, whose boundary names are written on page XII of Colombino; and according to the citizens of Acatepec and Tututepec, with whom I spoke in 1964, *yucu yoò* means "hill of the moon." (*Yucu* = "hill"; *yoò* = "moon.") To my knowledge, Acatepec is the only town within the present-day Mixtec-speaking region with the Mixtec name *yucu yoò*.[83]

In all probability, then, the "Hill of the Moon" shown as conquered in Bodley 10–II and Colombino XIII–37 is Santa María Acatepec. Acatepec today is bounded on the west by Tututepec, and at the time of the Spanish conquest Acatepec was a subject of Tututepec. But in 1044, the date given for Acatepec's conquest in both Bodley and Colombino, the town may have been one of Tututepec's principal rivals on the Coast, and thus its conquest was necessary to consolidate 8-Deer's position as ruler of Tututepec.

If the conquest of Acatepec is shown on the reverse of Codex Nuttall, which narrates a biography of 8-Deer that is somewhat similar to that of Codex Colombino, this conquest is given rather less prominence in Nuttall than it is in either Colombino or Bodley. A sign which may represent Santa María Acatepec appears on page 48c of Nuttall; the sign in question consists of a hill (*yucu*) which contains a sign of the moon (*yoò*), and at the top of the hill are two *acate* or reed-like plants. *Acate* or "reed" is *tnu yoo* in Mixtec; *tnu* is a plant or tree prefix and an abbreviation of *yutnu*, meaning "wood." It is possible that this place sign is intended to be bilingual, with the hill and moon elements representing Acatepec's Mixtec name *yucu yoò*, and the hill and *acate* combination representing the town's Nahuatl name, which means "in the hill of the reeds or *acate* plants." (*Acatl* = "reed"; *tepec* = "in the hill.") It is also possible that the moon motif (*yoò*) is included in this sign as a phonetic indicator to specify that the plant motif is a reed (*tnu yoo*) rather than some other type of plant.

This place sign in Nuttall 48c is shown as conquered by 8-Deer in the year Six-Flint or 1044, the same date as is given for the conquest of Acatepec in Colombino and Bodley. However, the conquest of the Hill of the Moon

---

[81] Heinrich Berlin (*Fragmentos desconocidos*, 20) is not convinced that this sign in Telleriano-Remensis represents Tututepec, and he suggests that the bird in question may be a quail and that the sign may represent Sultepec or "quail hill." However, if the gloss below the sign is to be believed, it specifies that the "bird hill" represents "Tututepec, [a] province 80 leagues from Mexico City, near the Pacific Ocean" (*tototepec provincia ochenta leguas de mexico junta a la mar del sur*).

[82] In Colombino XIII–37, the day-sign of the calendrical name of the conqueror of "Hill of the Moon" is erased, and Caso (*Colombino*, 30; 128) believes this person to be 8-Deer's half-brother, 12-Movement "Bloody Tiger," because throughout Colombino 12-Movement is shown wearing the gold diadem worn by the person attacking "Hill of the Moon."

[83] Martínez Gracida ("*Cuadros sinópticos*"; and *BSMGE* 1888, 352) gives *yucu yoo* as the Mixtec name of another Coastal town, San Lorenzo (16°25′ N., 97°53′ W.), and he translates this *yucu yoo* as "hill of the moon." Bradomín (*Toponimia de Oaxaca*, 87) has the following comment on this translation of *yucu yoo*: "*Es muy poético, pero nada verídico, pues según la traducción de Prof. Hernández, significa: 'Cerro de bejucos,' de yóo, 'bejuco.'*" Without exception, the persons on the Coast with whom I spoke said that the Mixtec name of San Lorenzo is *yucu yo'o*, with a glottal stop between the two *o*'s, a feature which *yoò*, the word for "moon," lacks; and *yucu yo'o* was translated as "hill of *bejuco*" (a vine-like plant, often used as a rope) and "hill of the *mecate*" (a type of rope made from the maguey cactus and other plants).

and Acate in Nuttall is not isolated as a single, important event as is the case in Colombino and Bodley; rather, this sign is included in a series of 15 signs of places conquered by 8-Deer in 1044. Nor is the ruler of the Nuttall sign named or depicted as he is in the conquest of Acatepec in Colombino and Bodley.

A second sign that consists of a hill, the sign for the moon, and acate plants appears on page 72d of the Nuttall reverse, although in this instance the acate plants are lying horizontally across the top of the hill rather than being placed vertically near the top of the hill as in the sign on Nuttall 48c. This second hill-moon-acate sign is also represented as being conquered by 8-Deer, but in 1046, or two years later than the conquest of the similar sign in Nuttall 48c. It seems likely that both place signs in Nuttall are signs of Santa María Acatepec in the Coastal region of the Mixteca, though it is not known whether the horizontal placement of the plants in the sign on Nuttall 72d is linguistically significant and thus changes the name represented by the sign, or whether the placement was a variation chosen by the artist and has no linguistic significance.

Still another "Hill of the Moon" appears in Codex Selden, in a short but explicit sequence in the biography of ♀ 6-Monkey "Warband Quechquemitl." Here, however, "Hill of the Moon" is ruled by ♂ 6-Lizard "Hair-Bent Hill," who along with his ally ♂ 2-Alligator "Hair-Cacaxtli" of "Insect Hill" has the temerity to "speak stony words" or insult ♀ 6-Monkey (Fig. 52a). This event occurs in 1038, and in the same year ♀ 6-Monkey personally conquers these two towns. In the conquest scene the place signs of "Moon Hill" and "Insect Hill" are combined and shown as one sign (Fig. 52b), with the buttocks and legs of a human figure shown below the moon motif at the top of the hill. Two small groups of red flames are appended to the top of the sign, indicating that the place or places conquered were burned.

Is the "Hill of the Moon" that was subjugated by 6-Monkey in 1038 also the town of Santa María Acatepec which was conquered by 8-Deer in the 1040's? The "Hill of the Moon" sign in Selden 7–III has the same elements as the signs of Acatepec in Bodley and Colombino: a hill with the sign of the moon at its apex. The shape of the hill in Selden does not have the slope of the Acatepec sign in Bodley and Colombino, but this slope is lacking in the signs that may represent Acatepec in Nuttall 48c and 72d; and as can be seen in the different shapes of hills in the Tututepec sign (Fig. 49), the hill formation of a sign may vary from one manuscript to another.

However, I do not believe that the "Moon Hill" in Selden represents Santa María Acatepec. Rather, it seems to me more likely that the "Moon Hill" and "Insect Hill" conquered by 6-Monkey are located in the Valley of Oaxaca, in the vicinity of the present-day town of Santa Cruz Xoxocotlán and near the archaeological site of Monte Albán. In the eighteenth-century map of the town of Xoxocotlán (Fig. 162), the hills surrounding the town include pictorial signs representing the names of the hills; in addition, each hill is glossed with a Nahuatl and Mixtec name.[84] At the top of this map is a configuration showing ten hills located west of Xoxocotlán—that is, the hills which form the great mountaintop site of Monte Albán. On the right side of this configuration are two hills which may be analogous to the "Moon Hill" and "Insect Hill" represented in Selden 7–III and 8–I.

The first of these hills contains a plant, and within the hill is the Nahuatl gloss "acatepec" and the Mixtec gloss "yucu yoo." The plant motif and the Nahuatl gloss are in agreement because, as noted above, acatepec means "in the hill of the reed or acate plant." It is possible that the putto-like figure who stands on top of this hill is related to the "acatepec" gloss, because this figure holds a bow and arrow, and an arrow is used to depict the day-sign Reed, acatl in Nahuatl. However, the other human figures standing on the group of hills at the top of the map do not seem to illustrate the place name of the hill on which they are placed. Thus it is likely that the boy with bow and arrow is not intended to express the "acatl" of "acatepec," but is a warrior figure who appears cherubic because of the essentially European eighteenth-century style in which he is portrayed.

Many of the paired Mixtec and Nahuatl glosses on the Xoxocotlán map set forth the same place name in the two different languages, but this does not seem to be the case for the acatepec/yucu yoo glosses. Yucu yoo, as we have seen in the discussion of the Mixtec name of Acatepec on the Coast, can mean "hill of the moon." Probably the reason that yucu yoo is translated "acatepec" in the Xoxocotlán map—and perhaps the reason that the Nahuatl name "acatepec" was given to the Coastal town of that name—is because tnu yoo means "reed" in Mixtec. The tnu yoo combination is definitely used in place names, for in the Reyes list, the Mixtec name of the town of Acatepec in the Mixteca Baja is given as yucu tnu yoo, or "hill of the reed." But in the Xoxocotlán map, the tnu element does not occur in the Mixtec name of the "acatepec" hill. The Mixtec name of this hill is merely yucu yoo, which can be translated "hill of the moon."

This translation is confirmed by a map in AGN-Tierras 236–6 (Fig. 164) that shows the lands San Juan Chapultepec, Xoxocotlán's neighbor to the north. In the upper-left corner of the Chapultepec map, at the point where the lands of Chapultepec join those of Xoxocotlán is a site depicted in this map as a crescent moon and identified by glosses in Mixtec and Spanish as "hill of the moon." This site in the Chapultepec map is in roughly the same location as the acatepec/yucu yoo site in the Map of Xoxocotlán.

At the right of the hill of acatepec/yucu yoo in the Xoxocotlán map is a hill containing an insect. The Nahuatl gloss accompanying this hill is "saioltepec"; the Mixtec gloss is "tiyuqu." "Saioltepec" means "in the hill of the fly," a combination of zayollin, "fly (the insect)" and tepec, "in the hill"; the Mixtec gloss tiyuqu also means "fly."

[84] The Map of Xoxocotlán and its glosses are discussed in detail in Appendix F.

It may be mere coincidence that a "hill of the moon" and a hill with an insect occur together in the Xoxocotlán map, and that a "Moon Hill" and "Insect Hill" are closely associated in Codex Selden. But it is also possible that two allied towns formerly located on or near the "acatepec" and "saioltepec" hills in the Map of Xoxocotlán are represented separately as "Moon Hill" and "Insect Hill" in Selden 7–III and as together in the compound Moon and Insect sign in Selden 8–I. The human legs and buttocks attached to the moon in the compound sign (Fig. 52*b*) probably represent the Mixtec word *caha*, which means "buttocks" and when used as a modifier in place names means "at the base of, at the bottom of." What the compound sign may express is that the settlements located at the bottom of these two hills north of Xoxocotlán were destroyed by the conquering 6-Monkey.

I offer this interpretation of the "Moon Hill" and "Insect Hill" signs in Selden 7–III and 8–I merely as a tentative hypothesis. We cannot as yet identify the "Belching Mountain" sign that represents the principal town of the Selden genealogies and the town ruled by 6-Monkey, and thus it is difficult to determine the geographical context of the story told in Selden. In addition, it is not known whether the two hills north of Xoxocotlán were town sites in the eleventh century and whether they were destroyed around 1038.

PLACE SIGNS WITH THE MARSH-GRASS MOTIF: TULIXTLAHUACA OF JICAYÁN, MEXICO CITY, SAN MIGUEL TULANCINGO

A variety of marsh grasses known in Nahuatl as *tule* and in Mixtec as *co'yo* are the qualifying elements in a number of important place signs. The terms *tule* and *co'yo* are used to designate a great many sedge-like plants which grow near streams and in swampy places. Many of these plants are of the genus *Cyperus*,[85] but as in the case of the plant described as "amole" in Nahuatl, the plants called *tule* and *co'yo* are of several genera, and these two terms appear to mean merely "marsh grasses in general."

According to the Alvarado dictionary, the Mixtec word *cóyo* means "cattail" (*espadaña; typha latifolia*) and "sedge" (*juncia; cyperus*). In Martínez Gracida's study of Oaxacan flora and fauna, *coyo* is listed as meaning "cattail" (*typha latifolia*), and *coyo ita* as a type of sedge known as *cyperus thyrsiflorus*.[86] (*Ita* means "flower" or sometimes "grass.") In the vicinity of Jicayán in the Coastal region of the Mixteca, the name *co'yo* designates a marsh grass with purple spikelets (Fig. 56), possibly of the genus *pontederia* or *cyperus*.[87]

In the Mixtec pictorial manuscripts, the *co'yo* is always represented as a cattail-like plant (Figs. 55, 62–66). The leaves are green, yellow, or brown, and occasionally—as in Colombino XIII—the base of the plant is a reddish color. The cattail element itself is usually yellow.

The Tule in Nahuatl Signs

The Nahuatl place signs in early post-Conquest manuscripts painted in the Valley of Mexico, such as Codices Mendoza and Xolotl, the *tule* plant is shown as a group of sharp-pointed, rough-edged leaves, without inflorescence (Fig. 53). In early post-Conquest manuscripts from the present-day State of Puebla, such as the *Historia Tolteca-Chichimeca* (Fig. 54) and the 1581 *Relación Geográfica* map of Cholula (Fig. 57), the *tule* is a cattail-like plant, similar to the *co'yo* plant of Mixtec manuscripts.

The Nahuatl name *tullan* or *tollan* means not only "place of the marsh grass" but also implies that the town in question is a great site or center of population. In the text of the 1581 *Relación* of Cholula, it is said that *tollan* means "a congregation of many artists and craftsmen" and also signifies a thickly settled place because the tule plants or cattails grow close together in clumps.[88] Sahagún reports that *Tulla* means "place of fertility and abundance."[89] The great *tollan* of the early post-Classic period was the Toltec capital near present-day Tula, Hidalgo, a pre-Aztec site which flourished from the late tenth century until its overthrow in the late twelfth century. But the name *tollan* was also prefixed to the names of other great cities, such as the important center of Cholula, which is clearly labeled in the 1581 map as "Tollan Cholulan" (Fig. 57*b*). As we shall see in the discussion of place signs with the *tule* or *co'yo* motif in Mixtec manuscripts, there were undoubtedly several sites within the Mixteca that were considered to be *tollans* or "great centers."

Tulixtlahuaca of Jicayán (16° 35' N., 98° 3' W.)

In Codex Colombino, immediately after the conquest of Acatepec (XIII–37), 8-Deer presents the captive ruler of that town to a personage known as ♂ 4-Tiger "Face of Night."[90] As a result of this presentation, an important ceremony is performed, in which the septum of 8-Deer's nose is perforated, and he receives a nose ornament which signifies that he is a *tecuhtli* or "great lord." This ceremony is depicted in the upper-left corner of Colombino XIII (Fig. 55); and in Colombino, the place sign on which the nose-piercing takes place is a compound sign which represents the important Coastal town of San Pedro Jicayán and the town of Tulixtlahuaca, formerly a depen-

85 Plants of the genus *Cyperus* found in Mexico and Central America are listed and described in Paul C. Standley, "The *Cyperaceae* of Central America," *Publications of the Field Museum of Natural History, Botanical Series*, VIII (1930–32), 237–92.

86 Manuel Martínez Gracida, *Flora y fauna del Estado libre y soberano de Oaxaca* (Oaxaca, 1891). The *Cyperus thyrsiflorus* is listed in Standley (*ibid.*, 252) as *Cyperus hermaphroditus*.

87 A plant which appears to resemble the *co'yo* in Fig. 56 is illustrated in Francisco Hernández, "Historia natural de Nueva España," cap. LXXIV (*Obras completas*, II [Mexico, 1959], 392), where it is listed by the Nahuatl name *tliltollin*, or "black *tule*." The *tliltollin* is described by

Hernández as having leaves similar to those of the arum family and purple "flowers."

88 *RMEH* I, 159: "Tullam . . . *quiere dezir congregacion de muchos officiales esto dizen los indios antiguos y curiosos aunque no falta quien dize que* tullam *significa* multitud de gente congregada *en vno asimilitud del* Tule *que es la enea yerua* . . . ."

89 Prologue to Book VIII, Bernardino de Sahagún, *Historia de las cosas de Nueva España* (Miguel Acosta Saignes, ed., Mexico, 1946, II, 35): "*Tulla . . . quiere decir: lugar de fertilidad y abundancia* . . . ."

90 The calendrical name of 4-Tiger is completely erased in Colombino XIII, but is known from representations of the same scene in Bodley 9–II and Nuttall, 52 c–d (Caso, *Bodley*, 39, and *Colombino*, 30, 129).

dency of Jicayán.[91] Across the base of the roof of the building that accompanies this sign is the gloss:

aniñe s[ⁿ p]° *ñuusiquaha,*

or "the palace of San Pedro Jicayán." *Aniñe* means "palace"; *ñuusiquaha* is given in the 1593 Reyes list as the Mixtec name of Jicayán. A second line of writing is just barely visible in the red band that separates the palace roof from the lintel, but unfortunately this section of the gloss is not legible even in an ultra-violet photographic detail of the temple roof. The second line may originally have contained the Mixtec name of Tulixtlahuaca, which is *yoso co'yo,* usually shortened to *so co'yo.* This name, as the Nahuatl "tulixtlahuaca," means "plain of the marsh grass." (*Yoso* [the *yodzo* of Alvarado] = "plain, valley"; *co'yo* = "marsh grass."

In the compound place sign in Colombino XIII, the *yoso* or "plain" section of the Mixtec name is represented by the feather-mat motif which forms the base of the sign. On the right side of the feather-mat are three cattails, which represent the qualifying element *co'yo.*

The Sign of Jicayán (16°25' N., 97°57' W.)

Jicayán's Mixtec name, *ñuu sii qua'a,* may be translated in several ways. In Jicayán, I was told that *ñuu sii qua'a* means "the town of the red grandfather." (*Ñuu* = "town"; *sii* = "grandfather"; *qua'a* = "red.") But *ñuu sii qua'a* may be translated in another way, and it is this second translation which is represented in several place signs of Jicayán.

The town of Jicayán is located south of the town of Santa María Zacatepec, and in the sixteenth-century Lienzo of Zacatepec 1, which is oriented with east at the top, the sign of Jicayán can be identified by its position in the lower-right corner of the lienzo (Figs. 58*a,* 111). This sign consists of a frieze with stepped frets decorated with speech scrolls; the same sign also appears in the center, or genealogical, portion of the Lienzo of Zacatepec (Fig. 58*b*). Because of the use of the speech-scroll motif in this sign for Jicayán, it seems likely that another translation of the Mixtec name *ñuu sii qua'a* would be: "the town that says much." *Ñuu* = "town"; the Alvarado dictionary gives *sii* as one of the Mixtec words for "to say" (*dezir*); *qua'a,* depending on tone, may mean "much" or "many" instead of "red."[92] Thus the frieze with a multitude of speech

scrolls which represents the town of Jicayán in Lienzo of Zacatepec 1 is a logogram of a literal translation of *ñuu sii qua'a* as "the town that says much." Since speech scrolls not only represent the act of talking but also symbolize political authority or power, a less literal translation of *ñuu sii qua'a* might be "the town that has a great deal of power or authority."

Returning to the Tulixtlahuaca sign on page XIII of Codex Colombino (Fig. 55), we see that the frieze at the base of the large temple contains a row of speech scrolls. This frieze is appended to a frieze with geometric patterns that extends to the right behind the cattail motifs. The frieze with geometric patterns represents the *ñuu* section of Jicayán's name, and the frieze with speech scrolls represents the qualifying element *sii qua'a.*[93] Thus the large place sign in Colombino XIII combines the signs of Jicayán and its dependency Tulixtlahuaca, and in this manuscript 8-Deer's nose-piercing ceremony is shown as taking place at Tulixtlahuaca of Jicayán. In all likelihood, Tulixtlahuaca was one of the principal pre-Conquest ceremonial sites in the Coastal region of the Mixteca.

The "Cattail Frieze" in Codex Bodley

Codex Bodley also tells the story of 8-Deer's delivery of the captured ruler of Acatepec to 4-Tiger "Face of Night" and 8-Deer's subsequent receipt of a nose ornament (Fig. 61). In Bodley, however, the place where these events occur is represented as a cattail on a frieze rather than cattails on the feather-mat or "plain" motif as in the Tulixtlahuaca sign in Colombino XIII. Does the Cattail Frieze of Bodley represent an alternate name of Tulixtlahuaca, or does it represent another town whose Mixtec name includes the word *co'yo?*

The problem is further confused by the analogous scene in Codex Nuttall (Fig. 60), where the "cattail" element does not appear at all in connection with the nose-piercing ceremony. In Nuttall, this ceremony is shown as taking place merely on a platform draped with tiger hides; this platform is also present in the Colombino and Bodley versions of the scene, but it is not a meaningful part of the place sign. In Nuttall, it is possible that the depiction of the nose-piercing ceremony itself was sufficient to identify the town in question, for it may have been understood that these ceremonies took place in Tulixtlahuaca of Jicayán or in some other specific—but here unspecified—town. Perhaps, as in the case of many history or "current events" paintings of the nineteenth century, the locale in which an event is taking place is understood from the identity of the participants and from the activities in which they are engaged.

It is also very possible that, in both Bodley and Nuttall, 8-Deer's nose-piercing ceremony is represented as taking place at a ceremonial site other than Tulixtlahuaca. Codex Colombino is concerned with telling its story from the viewpoint of the Coast, and Tulixtlahuaca may have been the site where such ceremonies took place on the Coast. In

---

[91] Tulixtlahuaca is located about 11 miles north of Jicayán and was formerly within the town boundaries of Jicayán. In the sixteenth-century Lienzo of Jicayán, a small church denoting a town and accompanied by the gloss "tulistlauaca" is depicted within the circle of Jicayán's boundaries (Fig. 146, upper-left corner).

[92] As, for example, in the Dyk 1951 vocabulary, where in the dialect of San Miguel el Grande *cua'à* is "many, much" and *cuá'á* or *cuà'á* is "red." The possibility also exists that the *sii qua'a* section of Jicayán's Mixtec name refers to the calendrical name 10, 11, or 13 Deer. In the special calendrical vocabulary, *si* may be the numerical coefficients 10, 11, or 13; the day-sign Deer is usually written *quaa,* but in the glosses of a few manuscripts such as the Map of Xochitepec (Caso, "Mapa de Xochitepec," 464–65), it is written *quaha* (i.e., *qua'a*). To my knowledge, the place sign of Jicayán does not appear with the calendrical name 10, 11, or 13 Deer, although calendrical signs are used in place signs, such as that of Santa María Zacatepec in the first Lienzo of Zacatepec (discussed in Chapter VII).

[93] A place sign with speech scrolls in Nuttall 14, which may also represent the Mixtec name of San Pedro Jicayán, is discussed below, p. 74.

the Mixteca Alta and elsewhere, there may have been similar ceremonial sites whose signs contain the "cattail" element, and the Cattail Frieze in Bodley 9–II may represent such a site.

In Bodley the Cattail Frieze sign appears not only in connection with 8-Deer's nose-piercing ceremony, but also as a place that was ruled by heirs of 8-Deer and his fourth wife, ♀ 11-Serpent "Red Flower." The complex genealogical relationships of the rulers of Cattail Frieze in Codex Bodley are set forth in the accompanying chart, in which brackets enclose the names of couples who are seated on the place sign of Cattail Frieze.

In Bodley 11, IV–V, the maternal grandparents of ♀ 11-Serpent "Red Flower" are shown as the rulers of Cattail Frieze; in Bodley 12–V, ♂ 10-Movement "Flaming Eagle" and ♀ 2-Grass "Jewel-Copal," the children of ♂ 8-Deer and ♀ 11-Serpent, are carried to Cattail Frieze, where they make an offering at the Temple with Mound of Dots (Fig. 62a). The next scene in Bodley 12–V shows the marriage of ♂ 10-Movement and ♀ 2-Grass—that is, an example of brother-sister marriage, which is relatively rare in the Mixtec genealogies and occurs principally among the descendants of 8-Deer.[94] A daughter of ♂ 10-Movement and ♀ 2-Grass, ♀ 1-Flower "Parrot," marries ♂ 8-Deer "Feathered Serpent," ruler of Cattail Frieze and Steambath (Fig. 62 b, c). The short account of the genealogy of Cattail Frieze concludes in Bodley 14–II with the marriage of ♂ 1-Lizard "Serpent-Face of Night" and ♀ 9-Dog "Shining Jewel," who was the daughter of ♂ 5-Water "Stony Tiger" and ♀ 10-Reed "Jewel-Parrot" of Tilantongo. The mother of ♀ 9-Dog, ♀ 10-Reed, was the daughter of ♂ 8-Deer "Feathered Serpent" and ♀ 1-Flower "Parrot" mentioned above, who ruled at Cattail Frieze and Steambath. Thus both parents of ♀ 9-Dog are descendants of ♂ 8-Deer "Tiger Claw": her father is the grandson of 8-Deer and his second wife, ♀ 6-Eagle "Tiger-Cobweb," and her mother is the great-granddaughter of 8-Deer and his fourth wife, ♀ 11-Serpent "Red Flower."

Alfonso Caso, in his commentary on Codex Bodley, calls Cattail Frieze by the Nahuatl name "Tula,"[95] which I believe is misleading, because it implies that the place sign represents the important post-Classic site of Tula in the State of Hidalgo. The short genealogy of Cattail Frieze in Bodley is comprised of rulers of the eleventh and twelfth centuries, which is the period when Tula was flourishing; but none of the rulers of Cattail Frieze in Bodley appears to be connected with any of the known rulers of Tula in Hidalgo.

The Mixtec name of the town represented by Cattail Frieze should be *ñuu co'yo*, with the frieze representing *ñuu* or "town," and the cattail representing *co'yo*, or "marsh grass." Beginning as early as the sixteenth century and continuing up to the present time, *ñuu co'yo* is the Mixtec name of Mexico City. The 1593 Reyes list gives the Mixtec name of Mexico City-Tenochtitlan as *ñucòyo*;

and in the sixteenth-century Codex Sierra, the place sign for Mexico City is a frieze with cattails (Fig. 63), very similar to the Cattail Frieze in Bodley. But Mexico City-Tenochtitlan was not founded until the fourteenth century, and as we have mentioned, the genealogies of Cattail Frieze in Bodley are of the eleventh and twelfth centuries. The great centers near the Valley of Mexico were at that time Tula, whose Mixtec name we do not know and whose rulers do not seem analogous to the rulers of Cattail Frieze, and Cholula, which as we have seen was known as *tollan cholulan* in the sixteenth century.

At the site of Cholula, according to the 1581 *Relación* of the town, there occurred ceremonies which Nowotny and Caso have likened to the nose-piercing ceremonies performed at the place with a cattail motif in the Mixtec manuscripts.[96] The *Relación* of Cholula states that rulers of cities would come to Cholula to have the rights to their hereditary domains confirmed by the priests of this center; and the priests of Cholula would pierce their ears, nose, or lower lip, depending on the domain being confirmed.[97]

But the known Mixtec name of Cholula does not contain the word *co'yo* or "cattail"; instead, this name is *ñuu ndiyo*, which means "town of the steps."[98] Furthermore, it is questionable whether the rulers of important towns in the Mixteca would have had their sovereignty confirmed by nose-piercing rites at ceremonial centers as far away as Cholula or Tula, Hidalgo; and it is debatable whether the descendants of 8-Deer would have ruled either of these important sites. It seems equally possible that the Cattail Frieze in Bodley represents a town that was a local "tollan" *within* the Mixteca, and whose Mixtec name is now unknown but originally contained the word *co'yo*.

San Miguel Tulancingo (17° 42' N., 97° 25' W.)

The town of San Miguel Tulancingo in the Mixteca Alta is located about eight miles west of Coixtlahuaca and was formerly within the boundaries of Coixtlahuaca. The Mixtec name of Tulancingo is not recorded in any of the standard sources of Mixtec place names, but the town's place sign is readily identifiable in the cartographic context of the Lienzo of Coixtlahuaca and Codex Meixueiro. In both manuscripts the sign of Tulancingo consists of a temple platform with the cattail motif (Fig. 64). A similar sign of Tulancingo also appears in Lienzo Antonio de León (Fig. 66), where it is placed near the sign of Coixtlahuaca.

It is very possible that the Tulancingo sign also appears twice in Codex Becker I, on pages 4 and 14. On page 4 (Fig. 65a), a building with the cattail motif rests on the body of a serpent with a feathered tail. As was discussed above in the "Coixtlahuaca" section, the serpent with a feathered tail is the basic element in the place sign of Coixtlahuaca in several post-Conquest manuscripts (Figs. 44, 45a, 46–47). Thus the sign in Becker I is probably a

94 Dahlgren, *La mixteca*, 152–53.
95 Caso, *Bodley*, 38, 41–43, 61.
96 Nowotny, *Codices Becker I/II*, 16, 24; Caso, *Colombino*, 30–31; 129.
97 *RMEH* I, 161–62.
98 In the Alvarado dictionary, *ndiyo* means "step of a stair" (*grada, escalón*) and "to jump" (*saltar*).

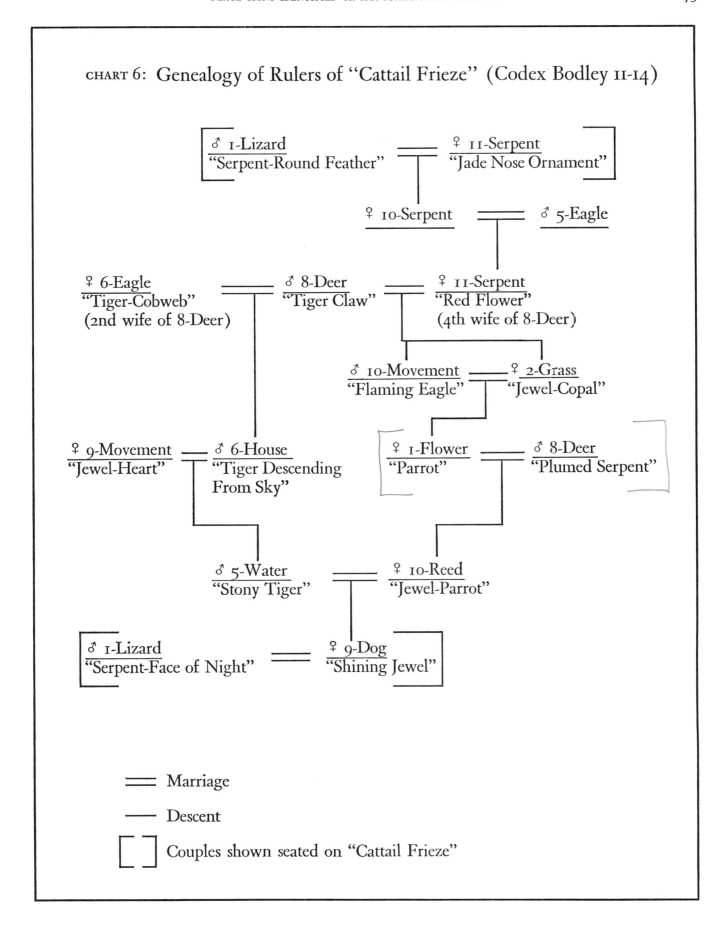

CHART 6: Genealogy of Rulers of "Cattail Frieze" (Codex Bodley 11-14)

♂ 1-Lizard "Serpent-Round Feather" — ♀ 11-Serpent "Jade Nose Ornament"

♀ 10-Serpent — ♂ 5-Eagle

♀ 6-Eagle "Tiger-Cobweb" (2nd wife of 8-Deer) — ♂ 8-Deer "Tiger Claw" — ♀ 11-Serpent "Red Flower" (4th wife of 8-Deer)

♂ 10-Movement "Flaming Eagle" — ♀ 2-Grass "Jewel-Copal"

♀ 9-Movement "Jewel-Heart" — ♂ 6-House "Tiger Descending From Sky"

♀ 1-Flower "Parrot" — ♂ 8-Deer "Plumed Serpent"

♂ 5-Water "Stony Tiger" — ♀ 10-Reed "Jewel-Parrot"

♂ 1-Lizard "Serpent-Face of Night" — ♀ 9-Dog "Shining Jewel"

═══ Marriage

─── Descent

⌐ ⌐ Couples shown seated on "Cattail Frieze"

compound sign, representing Tulancingo of Coixtlahuaca, much as the compound sign in Colombino XIII represents Tulixtlahuaca of Jicayán. On page 14 of Becker I (Fig. 65b), a temple again rests on a serpent with a plumed tail, and this serpent appears to have a cattail plant within its jaws, although the relationship between the serpent and the cattail is difficult to ascertain because part of the sign has been erased. This sign, too, would seem to represent Tulancingo of Coixtlahuaca.

The personage who is associated with the Serpent-Cattail sign in Becker I is ♂ 4-Tiger, the same person who is associated with 8-Deer's nose-piercing ceremony at Cattail Frieze in Bodley 9–II and at Tulixtlahuaca of Jicayán in Colombino XIII. This same 4-Tiger also performs a similar nose-piercing ceremony on ♂ 4-Wind "Fire Serpent" at Cattail Frieze in Bodley 34, II–I; and 4-Wind's nose-piercing is also depicted in Becker I–15 at the place sign whose determinants have been erased.

If 4-Tiger is an historical personage, how can he be the eleventh-century ruler of Tulancingo of Coixtlahuaca, as Becker I indicates, and the eleventh-century ruler of Tulixtlahuaca of Jicayán as is stated in Colombino? The obvious answer is that 4-Tiger is a non-historical personage or an impersonator of a deity named 4-Tiger. A careful study of the appearances of 4-Tiger in the historical manuscripts seems to confirm this hypothesis. First, in common with other deity figures such as the sun deity ♂ 1-Death and the death deity ♀ 9-Grass, 4-Tiger never appears as a partner in a marriage pair or as the parent or child of another person. This is especially evident in Codex Bodley where 4-Tiger performs a nose-piercing ceremony at Cattail Frieze, but does not appear as a functioning member of the short genealogy of Cattail Frieze in Bodley 11–14. Caso believes that a couple in Colombino XIX–54 who are united by the sign of a cradle are 4-Tiger and his wife 7?-Reed, and that this scene represents the marriage of these two individuals.[99] But the day sign of the man's calendrical name is almost completely obliterated, and it is difficult to ascertain whether or not it is Tiger. Moreover, neither the man or woman seems to have a personal name, which may indicate that they are both deity impersonators and that the scene represents a conference rather than a marriage.

In fact, 4-Tiger never appears with a personal name other than his face and body paint—usually black, but sometimes red-and-white stripes—which also is the trait of a deity impersonator. And finally, 4-Tiger appears, together with the lunar deity ♂ 2-Reed,[100] on page 14 of Codex Nuttall (Fig. 59), a page that is populated principally by deity figures. It seems very possible that the place sign on which 4-Tiger and 2-Reed stand in Nuttall 14 is a sign of San Pedro Jicayán. As was discussed above, Jicayán is represented in Lienzo of Zacatepec 1 and in Codex Colombino as a frieze with speech scrolls, and the

Mixtec name of Jicayán is ñuu sii qua'a, literally "the town that says much." The hill in Nuttall 14 contains nine volutes that appear to be speech scrolls. In addition, the volutes within the hill are all red, and one of the meanings of the qua'a element of Jicayán's name is "red."[101]

In all probability, the centers represented with the marsh-grass motif as "tollans" were the centers of the impersonators of 4-Tiger, and it seems likely that these deity impersonators played a political as well as a religious role. In Colombino, Becker I, and on the back of Nuttall, 4-Tiger is shown participating in the war expeditions of 8-Deer—much as the death deity ♀ 9-Grass is shown waging war in Bodley 4–III and Nuttall 20. Furthermore, in Bodley 33, III–II, at a time shortly after the death of 8-Deer, 4-Tiger has a dispute with 8-Deer's son-in-law and rival, 4-Wind "Fire Serpent"; and a reconciliation between 4-Tiger and 4-Wind is effected by the solar deity ♂ 1-Death.[102] The political power of 4-Tiger is most evident in the nose-piercing ceremonies, because he confirms the sovereignty of two of the most important personages in the Mixtec histories: 8-Deer "Tiger Claw" and 4-Wind "Fire Serpent." In all probability, 4-Tiger was the priest or deity impersonator in charge of such ceremonies, whether they were performed at Tulixtlahuaca of Jicayán, Tulancingo of Coixtlahuaca, or at a third ceremonial site represented by a Cattail Frieze in Codex Bodley.

To return briefly to the Cattail Frieze sign in Bodley, I believe that it is still a matter of conjecture as to which tollan this sign represents. The frieze with cattails seems similar to the platform with cattails of the Tulancingo signs in the manuscripts of the Coixtlahuaca group (Figs. 64, 66). But in the nose-piercing scene in Bodley 9–II, 4-Tiger is seated on a throne which contains the eyes and fangs of the rain deity Tlaloc, and these symbols may be analogous to the three "star eyes" that appear in the frieze accompanying the central building of Jicayán in the Lienzo of Jicayán (Fig. 147).

In addition, the events which lead up to the nose-piercing ceremony in Bodley seem to have a Coastal orientation. In the line of pictorial narrative immediately preceding the ceremony we see: 8-Deer as ruler of the Coastal capital of Tututepec (Bodley 9–III), and he is visited there by ambassadors from Cattail Frieze; above the sign of Cattail Frieze is the calendrical name of 4-Tiger, with speech scrolls issuing from the Tiger's mouth, as if an

99 Caso, Colombino, 35; 133.

100 As Caso (Selden, 23; 71) has observed, the Alvarado dictionary says that the calendrical name of the moon is caa huiyo, which can mean 2-Reed.

101 It is also interesting to note that a personage named ♂ 2-Reed appears in connection with one of the place signs of Jicayán in Lienzo of Zacatepec 1 (Fig. 58b). Here, he appears as a head only, wearing a chin ornament known as a bezote and with his hair drawn up into a triangle fastened at the top by a knot. He, and another head identified as ♂ 8-Eagle, are attached to a year sign on which rests the head of a dead person. The latter head, in turn, is connected to the figure of ♀ 12-Rabbit of Jicayán by what appears to be an umbilical cord with warpath chevrons. The connections of 12-Rabbit of Jicayán with the dead person on the year sign or with 2-Reed and 6-Eagle are not clear. Nor is it possible to say that the 2-Reed in Lienzo of Zacatepec 1 is the same person or deity as the 2-Reed in Nuttall 14, because the two figures do not share any common identifying characteristics other than the calendrical name 2-Reed.

102 Caso, Bodley, 61.

order were being given (Bodley 10–III). Next, 8-Deer conquers the Coastal town of Santa María Acatepec (Fig. 51a; Bodley 10–II); and finally, 8-Deer presents the captured ruler of Acatepec to 4-Tiger at Cattail Frieze and receives a nose ornament (Fig. 61; Bodley 9–II). Because of this Coastal context, the Cattail Frieze in Bodley may represent an alternate sign for Tulixtlahuaca of Jicayán, which may also have been known as *ñuu co'yo* ("marsh-grass town") in addition to its traditional name of *yoso co'yo* ("marsh-grass plain").

Several of the other Cattail Frieze signs in Bodley appear as components of compound place signs. In Bodley 12–V (Fig. 62a), the sign is connected with a building whose roof supports a neatly stacked pile of dots. In Bodley 13–V (Fig. 62b), Cattail Frieze is allied with "Steambath" and ruled by ♂ 8-Deer "Feathered Serpent" and ♀ 1-Flower "Parrot." In later passages (Bodley 13–IV and 13–14, III), when these rulers are named as parents of ♀ 10-Reed "Jewel-Parrot" and ♀ 2-Rain "Red Rhomboid," the compound sign consists of a steambath, a cacaxtli, plus a frieze with a cattail and a shining jewel (Fig. 62c). Because the context of a place sign is one of the most important factors in the identification of a sign, it may be necessary to determine the meaning of the other elements in these compound signs in order to ascertain which *tollan* or *tollans* are represented by the Cattail Frieze in Bodley.

APOALA AND JUQUILA

Alfonso Caso has postulated that two distinct signs represent the town of Apoala in the Mixteca Alta.[103] One of these signs consists of a River with a Hand Holding a Bunch of Feathers (Figs. 67, 68 a–c); the other is a Frieze with a Hand Holding Knotted Grass (Fig. 68 d–e). As we shall see in the discussion below, only the first of these signs is the sign of Apoala, and the second represents a different town, probably the Coastal town of Juquila.

Apoala (17° 42′ N., 97° 10′ W.)

In several Colonial sources on the Mixteca, the town of Santiago Apoala is stated to be the place of origin of the Mixtec rulers. In the first paragraph of the prologue of his Mixtec grammar, Fray Antonio de los Reyes says:

It was the common belief among the Mixtec-speaking natives that the origin and beginnings of their false gods and rulers were in Apoala, a town of the Mixteca, which is called in their language *yuta tnoho*, which means "river from which the rulers came," because the rulers are said to have split off from some trees which grew out of that river and which had special names. That town is also named *yuta tnuhu*, which means "river of the lineages," and this is the most appropriate name and the one which best fits it.[104]

In the list of Mixtec town names at the end of his grammar, Reyes gives *yuta tnoho* as Apoala's Mixtec name.

Caso first identified the River with Hand Holding Feathers as Apoala because of its context in the Mixtec historical manuscripts. The sign often appears near the beginning of the depiction of a dynastic line, signifying that it is the place of origin of the dynasty.[105] This identification is confirmed by an analysis of the Mixtec name *yuta tnoho*. *Yuta* means "river"; and one of the meanings of *tnoho* is "to pluck, as birds" (*pelar*), and this verb is represented by a hand holding the plucked feathers of a bird.[106]

Another motif which appears in connection with two of the signs of Apoala in Codex Nuttall is a bunch of knotted grass. In Nuttall 1 (Fig. 68c), the knotted grass and the hand-holding-feathers are placed within the same river sign; in Nuttall 36 (Fig. 68b), the two motifs appear in two separate river signs. The precise meaning of the knotted grass motif is not clear; but when it is shown held by a hand (Fig. 68 d–e), it probably represents a second meaning of *tnoho*, "to pull up by the roots" (*arrancar*).

Juquila (16° 12′ N., 97° 12′ W.)

The place sign illustrated in Fig. 68 d–e which combines the Hand Holding Grass with a frieze appears briefly in the historical manuscripts in connection with the ruler 8-Deer and his family. Caso believes that this sign is also Apoala, but it does not contain a river as the geographical substantive and thus does not depict the *yuta* section of Apoala's Mixtec name. I believe that the Frieze with Hand Holding Knotted Grass does not represent Apoala, but the Coastal town of Juquila.

Juquila is today within a Chatino-speaking rather than a Mixtec-speaking region, but the Mixtec name of Juquila is universally known throughout the Coast. This name, *ñuu sii to'o*, is usually translated by present-day Mixtec speakers as "town of the Virgin," because an important local shrine with a small cult image of the Virgin is lo-

---

103 Caso, "Lienzo of Yolotepec," *Memoria de el Colegio Nacional*, Vol. XIII–4 (1958), 44–45; *Bodley*, 39, 42, 52, 54–55; *Selden*, 27; 74.

104 Reyes, "Arte en lengua mixteca," i:
Vulgar opinion fue entre los naturales
Mixtecas, que el origen y principios de
sus falsos Dioses y señores, auia sido
en Apuala, pueblo desta Mixteca, que en
su lengua llaman yuta tnoho, *que es Rio,*
donde salieron los señores porque dezian

aver sido desgajados de unos Arboles que
salian de aquel Rio, los quales tenian
particulares nombres. Llaman tambien a
aquel pueblo, yuta tnuhu, *que es Rio de*
los linajes, y es el mas proprio nombre,
y el que mas le quadra.

Padre Burgoa (*Geográfica descripción*, I, 274, 369) also relates that the Mixtec rulers were reputed to have descended from trees at Apoala; and Gregorio García (*Origen de los indios*, 327–29) records a legend from Cuilapan, which states that the original Mixtec deities ♂ 1-Deer and ♀ 1-Deer built temples on a rock near Apoala.

105 As, for example, in Bodley 40–IV and 39–II, Selden 1–III, the lower-left corner of the Lienzo of Yolotepec (Fig. 67), and Nuttall 1, 18b, and 36. The sign of Apoala also appears throughout the front, or ritual, side of Vienna: pages 35b, 34d–33a, 26a, and possibly on 46b, where a figure in a river holds the feathered tail of a serpent.

106 In the Alvarado dictionary, *tnoho* also means "to extract, pull out by the roots" (*arrancar*), and a type of mistletoe with red berries or a type of dwarf oak (*marojo*). *Tnuhu*, the qualifying element of Apoala's alternate name *yuta tnuhu*, means "origin of a lineage" (*estirpe de linaje*; *çepa o tronco de linage*) and "embassy" (*embaxada*). According to the *Relación* of Juxtlahuaca (*RMEH* II, 141), *yucu tnuhu* is a medicinal plant called in Nahuatl *Tlacohuyltequizpatli*; *yucu* here means "shrub" or "bush."

cated at Juquila.[107] *Ñuu sii to'o*, however, literally means "town where the ruling grandfathers originated." *Ñuu* = "town"; *sii* = "grandfather"; *to'o* is the equivalent of the *tnoho* of Apoala's Mixtec name *yuta tnoho*, and Reyes translates *tnoho* as "where the rulers originated." A less literal translation of the combination *sii to'o* might be "ancestral ruler" or "hereditary nobility." The vocabulary appended to Dyk's *Mixteco Texts* lists *jito'ò* as meaning "master, owner." The *j* of the San Miguel el Grande dialect of *Mixteco Texts* is equivalent to *s* of the dialect of the Alvarado dictionary and Reyes grammar, so that in the latter dialect this word would be *sito'ò*. The Alvarado dictionary gives the word *stoho* as meaning "lord" (*señor*), and to my knowledge *stoho* is the only Mixtec word in the dictionary which contains the combination *st*. The word *stoho* undoubtedly is a contraction of *sii to'o*, and the phrase *sii to'o* originally meant "owner or master" in the sense of a hereditary ruler, much as the term *cacique* which now means "boss" originally referred to a hereditary native ruler.

The *ñuu* element of *ñuu sii to'o* is represented by the frieze of the sign in Fig. 68 *d–e*, and the *to'o* by the hand holding knotted grass, for as we have seen, *to'o* or *tnoho* may mean "to pull up by the roots." The *sii* element is not represented pictorially in this place sign, but this element may be included in the Mixtec name of Juquila to differentiate it from the name *ñuu to'o*, which on the Coast is used to designate the entire region of the Mixteca Alta. *Ñuu to'o* is translated by Mixtec speakers on the Coast as "the land where the Mixtecs of the Coast came from."

The identification of the Frieze with Hand Holding Knotted Grass as Juquila seems to be confirmed by the context in which this place sign appears in the historical manuscripts. In Bodley 9–III (Fig. 68*e*), 8-Deer visits the rulers of this place (♂ 1-Death "Serpent-Sun" and ♀ 11-Serpent "Flower-Feathers"), and in the very next scene we see 8-Deer seated as ruler on the place sign of Tututepec, the capital of the Coast. The hypothesis that the Frieze with Hand Holding Knotted Grass is also a Coastal town is substantiated by the large sign of Tututepec in Colombino V, 16–17 (Fig. 49*a*). This sign is a compound place sign and contains not only the place sign of Tututepec, but also a frieze with a bunch of knotted grass. The inclusion of this sign within the sign of Tututepec implies that the town in question was within the sphere of Tututepec, much as the compound sign of Jicayán-Tulixtlahuaca on Colombino XIII (Fig. 55) presents a central town (Jicayán) and its ceremonial site (Tulixtlahuaca).

The town of Juquila, today a Christian ceremonial site, may also have been an important ceremonial site in pre-Conquest times, as is indicated by its Mixtec name *ñuu sii to'o*, or "town of the hereditary nobility." Its importance is further demonstrated in Bodley 9–III by 8-Deer's courtesy call to the rulers of Juquila immediately before being enthroned at Tututepec, and in Bodley 14–13, IV, by the marriage of 8-Deer's son 6-House "Tiger Descending from the Sky" to 9-Flower "Jewel-Heart," a daughter of these same rulers of Juquila. The son 6-House is the offspring of 8-Deer who inherited the throne of Tilantongo, the most prestigious town in the Mixteca Alta, and this son's marriage to a daughter of the rulers of the Coastal town of Juquila may have been an attempt to continue the consolidation of the Coast and Alta regions that 8-Deer had effected by ruling both Tututepec on the Coast and Tilantongo in the Alta.

THE TWO TEQUIXTEPECS

Two towns in Oaxaca have the Nahuatl name "Tequixtepec," which means "conch-shell hill." (*Teccixtli* = "conch shell"; *tepetl* = "hill.") The Mixtec names of the two Tequixtepecs, however, are different; and in some instances, this difference is reflected in the place signs of the two towns.

Tequixtepec del Rey (18° 5′ N., 97° 43′ W.)
The town of San Pedro and San Pablo Tequixtepec is in the Mixteca Baja, near the Oaxaca-Puebla border, and the 1593 Reyes list calls this town "Tequitziztepec del Rey" because the Spanish Crown was *encomendero* of this Tequixtepec—that is, the Crown exacted tribute and services from the Indian population of the town during the Colonial period. According to the Reyes list, this town's Mixtec name is *yucu ndaa yee*. Jiménez Moreno translates this name as "hill of the pure or true shell."[108] (*Yucu* = "hill"; *ndaa* = "pure, true"; *yee* = "shell.") But the name *yucu ndaa yee* can also mean "hill of the straight (i.e., upright) shell" because *ndaa* also means "straight" as well as "pure, true";[109] and in the historical manuscripts the sign of Tequixtepec del Rey is a hill with an upright (vertically placed) conch shell.

This sign is clearly identified in Sánchez Solís 22 and 25 (Fig. 69) because it is accompanied by a gloss giving Tequixtepec's Mixtec name, which in the dialect of the Sánchez Solís annotator is: *yoco taa hyi*. In this dialect *o* is the equivalent of the *u* of the Alvarado dialect, and *t* is the equivalent of Alvarado's *nd*. The Mixtec word for "shell" is actually *yïï*, with the *ï* representing a high central unrounded vowel which does not exist in the Spanish language, and which is usually transcribed in the sixteenth-century sources on Mixtec as either an *e* or an *i*. In the transcription of Reyes and Alvarado, *yïï* is usually *yee*; in the transcription of the Sánchez Solís annotator, it is *hyi*. In the Alvarado dictionary, *yee* means not only "shell" (*caracol*), but "male" (*macho en cada especie*)

---

[107] On December 8, the day of the Immaculate Conception, many pilgrims come to Juquila to celebrate the feast day of the local cult image of the Virgin. The Virgin of Juquila is described briefly in José Antonio Gay, *Historia de Oaxaca*, 3rd ed., I–2 (Mexico, 1950), 212–15; and in Fray Esteban Arroyo, *Los dominicos, forjadores de la civilización oajaqueña, II: Los conventos* (Oaxaca, 1961), 327–29. Both authors cite a late-eighteenth-century account of the Virgin of Juquila: José Manuel Ruiz y Cervantes, *Memorias de la portentosa imagen de Nuestra Señora de Juquila* (Mexico, 1791).

[108] Introduction to the 1962 ed. of the Alvarado dictionary, 94.

[109] Concerning the various meanings of the word *ndaa*, see note 34 of this chapter.

and "to age" (*envejecerse*). The alternate translation of *yee* as "male" may account for the anthropomorphic and phallic quality of the shell motif.

Another "hill of the shell" sign occurs in Selden 15–I (Fig. 70), and Caso describes this sign as "Hill of the Snail with Feet (Teccixtepec?)."[110] This sign, too, probably represents Tequixtepec del Rey, because the shell motif is presented as upright and even has a pair of legs to make its upright quality more explicit.

Tequixtepec de Chuchones (17°47′ N., 97°18′ W.)

The second Tequixtepec is the Mixteca Alta town of San Miguel Tequixtepec, located about five miles north of Coixtlahuaca. In the Reyes list this town is called "Tequitziztepec de chuchones," because it is located in the Chocho-speaking region surrounding Coixtlahuaca. According to the Reyes list, the Mixtec name of this town is *yucu yee*, which—in common with the town's Nahuatl name—means "hill of the shell." (*Yucu* = "hill"; *yee* = "shell.")[111]

The place sign of Tequixtepec de Chuchones is known from several of the post-Conquest manuscripts of the Coixtlahuaca group. In the Lienzo of Coixtlahuaca and Codex Meixueiro, the Tequixtepec sign appears within the boundaries of Coixtlahuaca, and it consists of a hill and a shell placed horizontally (Fig. 71). A hill with horizontal shells also represents Tequixtepec de Chuchones in the Lienzo of Ihuitlán (Fig. 72), where the sign is clearly labeled with the gloss "tecçiztepec."

In the case of these two signs, the placement of the shell in a horizontal position is probably intended to differentiate this hill-with-shell sign from the hill-with-upright-shell which depicts the name of Tequixtepec del Rey. But the sign of Tequixtepec de Chuchones can also be represented by a hill with a vertical shell, for this is how the sign for the town is shown in Lienzo Antonio de León and in the unpublished Lienzo Seler II.[112] Thus it would seem that a hill with a shell that has no human characteristics is the sign of Tequixtepec de Chuchones, and the distinguishing characteristic of the place sign of Tequixtepec del Rey is an upright shell, often shown as standing on two feet, to depict the *ndaa* ("upright") section of *yucu ndaa yee*, the Mixtec name of Tequixtepec del Rey.

MITLATONGO (17°12′ N., 97°15′ W.)

Alfonso Caso has postulated that two signs in Codex Bod-

ley represent the town of Mitlatongo in the Mixteca Alta.[113] The first sign (Fig. 74) consists of a hill with a human skull, a crenelated wall, and a falling truncated human body. The second sign is a skull coupled with a frieze (Fig. 75–upper left).

Caso believes that these signs represent Mitlatongo because the first sign appears in Bodley 3–IV immediately following the birth of ♂ 1-Monkey "Tiger with Bird-Beak and Bee-Tail" (Fig. 74, *right*), and the 1579 *Relación* of Mitlatongo states that the first ruler of this town was named 1-Monkey.[114] But Bodley does not explicitly state that 1-Monkey ruled the town with the skull motif, and in the following line he appears to be the ruler of Serpent River, a town shown as ruled by his grandparents in Bodley 4–IV. The biography of 1-Monkey and his brother 9-Wind "Stone Skull" is told briefly in Bodley 3–IV, 3 and 4, V. Of the two brothers, 9-Wind is the elder; according to Bodley, he was born in the year Eight-Rabbit (843). The birth of 1-Monkey follows, but the date of his birth is not given. Then three place signs are depicted: the first is the Skull Hill described above; the second is a temple platform with a falling human figure, a cacaxtli, and an arrow; the third is a temple with a human leg, an owl, and braided grass or feathers. Then three personages present royal insignia to 9-Wind "Stone Skull." Behind 9-Wind sits his younger brother 1-Monkey, who is seated on a platform that is slightly higher than the platform on which 9-Wind is seated. This section of Bodley is difficult to read, because the paint has flaked at the fold between pages 3 and 4, but it appears that the platform on which 1-Monkey is seated (along with one other person, 1-Monkey's wife?) is connected with the sign of Serpent River. In the next scene we see 9-Wind "Stone Skull" and his wife seated on the place sign of Tilantongo, and they are the first rulers of the first dynasty of Tilantongo.

The implications of this sequence of events are, I believe, that 1-Monkey inherits Serpent River, which his father and grandparents had ruled, while the first-born 9-Wind receives royal insignia as the first known ruler of the important Mixteca Alta town of Tilantongo. Thus it seems likely that 1-Monkey ruled Serpent River, on which he is seated, and not the three places whose signs immediately follow the depiction of his birth. What these three signs in Bodley 3–IV may represent are the towns of the three persons who offer the royal insignia to 9-Wind in Bodley 3–V.

The second place sign which Caso suggested as a possible sign of Mitlatongo is a Skull Frieze which appears in Bodley 7, 8–V, 12–II, 14–IV, and 16, 17–V. The town represented by this place is extremely important in the Bodley version of the biography of 8-Deer. First, in Bodley 7, 8–V, 8-Deer's sister, 9-Monkey "Quetzal-Jewel," marries the ruler of Skull Frieze, a personage named 8-Alligator "Bloody Coyote." Second, this couple's daughter, 6-Eagle "Tiger Cobweb" becomes 8-Deer's second wife—

---

[110] Caso, *Selden*, 42; 89.

[111] *Yucu yee* appears as the Mixtec name of Tequixtepec de Chuchones in the original 1593 edition of the Reyes grammar; in the 1890 edition, the Mixtec name was erroneously printed as *yucu yu*, which would be "hill of the stone." A different etymology for Tequixtepec's Nahuatl name is suggested by Martínez Gracida (*BSMGE* 1888, 405), who translates "tequixtepec" as "salt-peter hill," from *tequequite* ("salt-peter") and *tepetl* ("hill"). He adds that the town's Mixtec name is *yucu ñuñi* and translates this name also as "hill of salt-peter." However, the Mixtec word *ñuñi* does not mean "salt-peter"; and, as will be seen in the discussion that follows, the place sign of Tequixtepec de Chuchones is not shown as a "hill of salt-peter" in any of the pictorial manuscripts.

[112] Concerning the sign of Tequixtepec in Lienzo Antonio de León, see Caso, "Los lienzos mixtecos de Ihuitlán y Antonio de León", *Homenaje a Pablo Martínez del Río* (Mexico, 1961), 270. Lienzo Seler II is discussed briefly in Appendix C, "The Coixtlahuaca Group of Documents."

[113] Caso, *Bodley*, 29, 38, 40, 42, 46.

[114] *PNE* IV, 78.

that is, she marries her mother's brother, or uncle.[115] Finally, in Bodley 14 (Fig. 75), 8-Deer attempts to conquer a place whose sign is a parrot on a tree in a river. Attached to the place sign are the calendrical and personal names of the second wife 6-Eagle "Tiger Cobweb," clearly indicating that 8-Deer is attempting to subjugate a place that belonged to his second wife. In the scene immediately following 8-Deer's attack, he is sacrificed at a place with a compound sign consisting of a frieze, a feather-mat plain with cactus plants, and a hill with an arm which holds a cacaxtli-frieze. Shown watching the interment of 8-Deer is his brother-in-law and father-in-law, 8-Alligator "Bloody Coyote," who is seated on Skull Frieze. The final appearance of Skull Frieze is on Bodley 17–V, where it is ruled by ♂ 13-Tiger "Warband Beard" in the late thirteenth and early fourteenth centuries, at least two hundred years after 8-Deer's sacrifice in 1063.

The Nahuatl sign of Mitlatongo is known from Codex Mendoza, where it appears as a skull combined with a mummy bundle (Fig. 73). The sign in Mendoza is glossed "mictlan," but it is known that this sign represents the Mixteca Alta town of Mitlatongo because the majority of places on this page are towns in the Mixteca Alta.[116] The Nahuatl name "mictlan" means "place of the dead"; mic- from micquetl ("dead person"), -tlan from tlantli ("place"). The -tongo suffix in the Nahuatl name "mitla-tongo" is a diminutive, and the name thus means "the little Mictlan." The diminutive suffix was probably added to the name of the Mixteca Alta "Mictlan" to distinguish this town from the "Mictlan" in the Valley of Oaxaca. The latter town is today called "Mitla," and adjacent to the present-day town is the important post-Classic archaeological site of the same name.

The Mixtec name of Mitlatongo is given as dzandaya in the 1593 Reyes list, and the 1579 Relación of Mitlatongo says that the town's Mixtec name is dzandaya, translated as "place of hell," and sandaya, "seat of hell."[117] The Mixtec name seems to be roughly equivalent in meaning to the Nahuatl "mictlan" or "place of the dead," and both the Nahuatl and Mixtec names imply that the town in question is an important burial site.

But the Mixteca Alta town of Mitlatongo undoubtedly was not the only important Mixtec burial site. The Reyes list says that dzandaya is also the Mixtec name of the Mixteca Alta town of San Miguel Huautla, located 17°45′ N., 97°8′ W.[118] In addition, Mitla in the Valley of Oaxaca was an important burial site, because large tombs were

constructed beneath the post-Classic structures. Unfortunately, the Mixtec name of Mitla is not known.

To return to the place signs with a skull motif in Codex Bodley, I do not believe that it is yet possible to identify with any assurance either the Skull Hill or the Skull Frieze as Mitlatongo. As in the case of signs with marsh grass which represent important ceremonial sites or tollans, the burial sites which may be signified by signs with skulls can only be identified by their context in the historical manuscripts, and these contexts are not yet known. It would be helpful, for example, to determine the identity of the place in Bodley 14–V, whose sign is a river with a parrot in a tree. As was mentioned above, the place belonged to 8-Deer's second wife, whose parents and brother ruled Skull Frieze, and 8-Deer's attempt to conquer this place immediately precedes his sacrifice. The Bodley narrative also indicates that 8-Deer may have been buried at Skull Frieze, or at least that ♂ 8-Alligator, the ruler of Skull Frieze, supervised his interment. Once the context of the events concerning 8-Deer's sacrifice is determined, it should then be possible to identify which dzandaya or mictlan is represented by Skull Frieze.

TECAMACHALCO (18°50′ N., 97°45′ W.)

Alfonso Caso has suggested that a sign whose qualifying element is a human jaw containing a stone motif may be the sign of Tecamachalco, a town in southern Puebla about 35 miles southeast of the city of Puebla.[119] A sign with these elements appears twice in Codex Bodley: in Bodley 8–III the jaw and stone are connected with a frieze (Fig. 76a), and in Bodley 7–V, they appear with a hill to which water is appended (Fig. 76b).

Caso's hypothesis that these place signs represent Tecamachalco is based on the etymology of the Nahuatl name "tecamachalco," which means "place of the stone jawbone." (Te- from tetl = "stone"; camachalli = "jawbone"; -co = "place.") In Codex Mendoza this Nahuatl name is depicted as a jaw placed within the sign for a stone (Fig. 77).

But the Mixtec name Tecamachalco appears to have nothing to do with stones or jaws. In the 1593 Reyes list, the town's Mixtec name is yucu tdu yaca, which is probably a misprint for yucu tnu yaca, because td is not a standard combination of consonants in Mixtec and tn is a very common combination in the dialect of the Reyes grammar. Yucu tnu yaca should probably be translated as "the hill of the stakes used for torture." Yucu means "hill," and in the Alvarado dictionary tnu yaca means "a stake which the Indians used for torture" (palo de tormento, que vsaban los Indios).[120]

As a working hypothesis, I believe it must be assumed that the place signs in the Mixtec pre-Conquest manuscripts represent Mixtec rather than Nahuatl names of places, especially in cases—such as that of Tecamachalco

---

[115] As Caso has noted (Bodley, 40), 8-Deer was the second husband of 6-House "Tiger Cobweb." In Bodley 12, I–II, her first marriage is with 13-Dog "Flower," ruler of "Hill of the Stone Eyes."

[116] Jiménez Moreno, Códice de Yanhuitlán, 10; Robert Barlow, The Extent of the Empire of the Culhua Mexica (Berkeley and Los Angeles, 1949), 115. The other signs on this page (fol. 43/r) of Codex Mendoza are of: Coixtlahuaca, Texupan, Tamazulapan, Yanhuitlán, Teposcolula, Nochixtlán, Xaltepec, Tamazola, Coaxomulco, and Cuicatlán.

[117] PNE IV, 72, 77. In the Alvarado dictionary, the principal word in the first definition of "hell" (infierno) is andaya.

[118] The 1580 Relación of Huautla (Ignacio Bernal, ed., "Relacion de Guautla," Tlalocan, Vol. IV–1 [1962], 3–7) does not include the town's Mixtec name, but translates the Nahuatl name as "hill of eagles."

[119] Caso, Bodley, 36–37.

[120] In the combination tnuyaca, tnu- is a prefix denoting wood. The word yaca alone means "granary, corncrib" (panera, troxe). Tiyaca means "fish" (ti- being an animal prefix), and ñuyaca means "dust" (ñu- being short for ñu'u, "earth").

—where the Mixtec name has a meaning that is very different from the meaning of the town's Nahuatl name. Thus the place signs in Bodley 8–III and 7–V probably do not represent Tecamachalco, but another, still unidentified town.

COMALTEPEC

In Codex Selden, a sign consisting of a hill which contains a large yellow disk (Fig. 79) appears four times: on pages 15–I, 16–I, 18–II, and 18–IV. Caso has tentatively identified this sign as Comaltepec,[121] because the sign closely resembles the Nahuatl sign of Comaltepec, which also is a hill with a large yellow disk (Fig. 78). The name "comaltepec" means "hill of the comal"; the comal, represented by the yellow disk, is a round clay griddle which is a common cooking utensil throughout Middle America. In the dialect of the Alvarado dictionary, the Mixtec word for "comal" is *siyo*.

It is very possible that the place sign in Selden is a "hill of the comal," but exactly which town does this sign represent? Comaltepec is a relatively common place name; within the State of Oaxaca, three towns have this name. Only one of these towns is within the Mixteca, the town of Santa Elena Comaltepec, in the Coastal region.[122] In the glosses on page XV–43 of Codex Colombino, the Mixtec name of this town is *yucu siyo*, or "hill of the comal." But apparently this is not the only Mixtec name of Santa Elena Comaltepec. On the Coast I was told that the inhabitants of Comaltepec call their town *yucu xiyo*, the equivalent of *yucu siyo* in the dialect of the Coast, but that outside of Comaltepec, the town's Mixtec name is *yucu tiyo*, which reportedly means "hill of the tiles" (*cerro de tejas*).

Whether the "hill of the comal" in Selden represents the Coastal town of Comaltepec is impossible to determine at this time. We do not know the point of view from which the story of Selden is told, because the "Belching Mountain" place sign ruled by the principal dynasties of the manuscript is still unidentified. Nor do we know the names of the rulers of Santa Elena Comaltepec, so that it cannot be ascertained whether the persons associated with the "comal hill" in Selden actually ruled Comaltepec on the Coast. In addition, at the time of the Spanish conquest, Comaltepec was a subject of the Coastal capital of Tututepec and thus may not have had an autonomous dynasty of native rulers.

FLOWER HILL OR "YUCU ITA"

In his commentary on Codex Bodley, Alfonso Caso suggests that two place signs represent the Mixtec name *yucu ita*, or "flower hill."[123] (*Yucu* = "hill"; *ita* = "flower.") One sign consists of a platform which supports a tree with white, four-petaled flowers (Fig. 80). The second sign is a hill with the trefoil type of flower usually found in the day-sign Flower (Fig. 81). But it is likely that these two signs represent two different places. The flower motifs of the two signs are not the same; and in one sign the motif which represents the geographical substantive is a platform, while in the other it is a hill.

A clue to the Mixtec name of the platform with white flowers is provided by two post-Conquest manuscripts from the vicinity of Yanhuitlán in the Mixteca Alta. In the Codex af Yanhuitlán, the list of place signs of Yanhuitlán's subjects includes a sign whose pictorial components are a platform and white four-petaled flowers (Fig. 82a). A platform with the same plant (Fig. 82b) appears three times in Codex Muro, a pictorial manuscript from San Pedro Cántaros, which is located about 12 miles southeast of Yanhuitlán. Codex Muro is extensively annotated with Mixtec glosses, and the couples who are seated above the platform with white flowers are said to be rulers of the town of *chiyo yuhu*. *Chiyo* means "platform, foundation"; the meaning of *yuhu* in a botanical context is not known, but it definitely refers to the plant on the temple platform. In several eighteenth-century land documents concerning disputed boundaries in the Yanhuitlán region, mention is made of a town named Santa María *chiyo yuhu*.[124] From the descriptions in the documents of this town's location, it is evident that Santa María *chiyo yuhu* is the present-day town of Santa María Suchixtlán, a town about two miles south of Yanhuitlán and formerly a subject of Yanhuitlán. The Nahuatl name "suchixtlan" means "flower place," a combination of *xochitl* ("flower") and *tlantli* ("place"). Thus the sign with white flowers in the Codex of Yanhuitlán and Codex Muro is the sign of Santa María Suchixtlán, and the analogous sign in Codex Bodley may also represent Suchixtlán (*chiyo yuhu*) rather than *yucu ita*, or "flower hill."

If the second sign—the hill with trefoil flowers—represents the Mixtec name *yucu ita*, it is still necessary to determine which town named *yucu ita* is referred to by the sign. *Yucu ita* is the Mixtec name of San Juan Xochitepec near Yanhuitlán in the Mixteca Alta, and it is also the former Mixtec name of Santa María Tindú, near Huajuapan in the Mixteca Baja. Assuming that the trefoil flower is *ita* ("flower in general") rather than *huaco* (the day-sign Flower in the special calendrical vocabulary) or the name of some specific type of flower, it is still not known which Flower Hill this sign represents.

SUMMARY

By way of summary, the signs of twenty-three Mixtec towns that I believe have been securely identified are listed below. In the left-hand column of this list is the present-day name of the town, with the town's Mixtec name and a translation of this name given in the second column. The third column contains a short description of the sign or signs that represent the Mixtec name, and the fourth column provides the figure number of this study where the sign or signs are illustrated.

---

[121] Caso, *Selden*, 42, 44, 45; 89, 91, 92.

[122] The other two Comaltepecs are in eastern Oaxaca: Santiago Comaltepec in the ex-district of Villa Alta and San Juan Comaltepec in the ex-district of Choapan. Both towns were well outside the sphere of Mixtec influence at the time of the Spanish conquest, and their Mixtec names are not known.

[123] Caso, *Bodley*, 31, 46, 48.

[124] AGN-Tierras, Vols. 985 and 400–1.

Town	Mixtec Name	Description of Place Sign(s)	Illustration (Fig. No.)
1. Tilantongo	*ñuu tnoo, huahi andehui* "black town, house of the sky"	(1) frieze with black-and-white geometric decorations (2) building with sky signs on the roof	26 27
2. Teozacoalco	*chiyo ca'nu* "large platform"	(1) frieze that is bent by a small human figure (2) frieze with trefoil flower	28 *c–e* 28 *a–b, e*
3. Tataltepec, Santa María	*yucu quesi* "hill of scorching heat"	hill with flame	30 (lower-left corner)
4. Texupan	*ñuu ndaa* "blue town"	hill with turquoise jewel	36–37
5. Acatlán	*yucu yusi* "hill of the turquoise jewel"	hill with turquoise jewel	38
6. Yanhuitlán	*yodzo cahi* "wide plain" ?	feather-mat plain with bird whose beak terminates in arrows (This sign is probably only one of at least two signs of Yanhuitlán, but other signs of this town have not yet been surely identified.)	40
7. Coixtlahuaca	*yodzo coo* "plain of the serpent"	(1) feathered serpent(s) (2) rattlesnake without feathers (3) feather-mat plain with feathered serpent	44, 45*a*, 46 45*b* 47
8. Amoltepec, Santiago	*yucu nama* "hill of the *amole* plant"	hill with plant	48
9. Cuquila, Santa María	*ñuu cuiñe* "tiger town"	hill with tiger	160 (right side)

Town	Mixtec Name	Descriptions of Place Sign(s)	Illustration (Fig. No.)
10. Tututepec	*yucu dzaa* "hill of the bird"	hill or stone with eagle whose beak contains a human chin	49
11. Acatepec, Santa María	*yucu yoò* "hill of the moon"	hill with sign of the moon	51
12. Jicayán, San Pedro	*ñuu sii qua'a* "the town that says much"	frieze with speech scrolls	55, 58
13. Tulixtlahuaca, San Pedro (subject of Jicayán)	*yodzo co'yo* "plain of the marsh grass"	feather-mat plain with cattails	55
14. Mexico City-Tenochtitlan	*ñuu co'yo* "town of the marsh grass"	frieze with cattails	63
15. Tulancingo, San Miguel (subject of Coixtlahuaca)	unknown	platform with cattails	64, 66
16. Apoala	*yuta tnoho* or *yuta tnuhu* "river of the lineages"	river with hand holding feathers or grass	67, 68 *a–c*
17. Juquila	*ñuu sii to'o* "town of the ancestral rulers"	frieze with hand holding feathers or grass	68 *d–e*; 49*a* (right side of hill)
18. Tequixtepec del Rey	*yucu ndaa yee* "hill of the upright shell"	hill with upright anthropomorphic shell	69, 70
19. Tequixtepec de Chuchones	*yucu yee* "hill of the shell"	hill with shell	71, 72
20. Suchixtlán Santa María (subject of Yanhuitlán)	*chiyo yuhu* "platform of the four-petaled white flower" ?	platform with four-petaled white flower	82
21. Nochixtlán	*atoco* "at the place of the *nopal* cactus"	human jaw with *nopal* cactus	24*a*
22. Andúa, San Andrés (subject of Yanhuitlán)	*anduvua* "at the place of the arrow"	human jaw with an arrow	24*b*

Town	Mixtec Name	Description of Place Sign(s)	Illustration (Fig. No.)
23. Sachio, San Andrés	*sa chiyo*	platform with human foot	24*c*
(subject of Yanhuitlán)	"at the foot of the platform"		

The detailed examination of the methods used to identify the signs of these twenty-three towns has served to demonstrate some of the specific as well as general problems involved in place-sign identification. The Mixtec name of a town may have a meaning that is completely different from the meaning of its present-day Nahuatl name. A town may have more than one Mixtec name, and therefore more than one place sign, as in the case of Teozacoalco where the Bent Frieze and the Flower Frieze are used interchangeably to represent this town. Or, as we have seen in the discussion of the place sign of Acatlán, one Mixtec name of a town may supersede an earlier Mixtec name; and if the first name is not recorded, it may be forgotten.

In addition, a town's Mixtec name may vary from one locality to another. For example, the Mixtec name of the Coastal town of Santa Elena Comaltepec that is used by the town's inhabitants is different from the Mixtec name by which Comaltepec is known in other towns on the Coast. Another example of regional variation of a given town's Mixtec name occurs in the Mixtec names of the Coastal communities of San Miguel Tetepelcingo and Santiago Tetepec. In some towns on the Coast the Mixtec name of Tetepelcingo is *yucu yuu* ("hill of the stone"), and the Mixtec name of Tetepec is *yucu yuu ca'nu* ("hill of the big stone"). In other towns of the same region, *yucu yuu* refers to Tetepec, and Tetepelcingo is known as *yucu yuta* ("hill of the river").[125]

Variations also occur in different pictorial signs of the same place name; and moreover, it is sometimes difficult to ascertain which elements of the pictorial sign are meaningful and express some portion of the town's name or location. For example, in the place sign of Santa María Acatepec in Codex Bodley (Fig. 51*a*), the town's Mixtec name *yucu yoò* ("hill of the moon") is portrayed by the sign of a hill containing a sign of the moon. But the hill also contains dark bands and a star-eye indicating night. It might be thought that the night symbolism is a reinforcement of the moon sign, but the dark bands and star-eye occur in other signs in Bodley (Figs. 74 and 75- upper right) where they are not connected with the moon. The meaning of these night symbols when they appear within a hill is not known, nor has it been ascertained whether they have any relationship to the name of the place that is depicted in the signs in which they appear.

In the analogous sign of Acatepec in Codex Colombino

(Fig. 51*b*), the hill is not decorated with black bands and a star, but with a motif consisting of a red spiral within a yellow circle with a scalloped outline. This motif appears in a number of hill signs in Colombino and Becker I,[126] and it occurs twice in connection with solar deities in these two manuscripts. In Colombino III–11 it is placed within a hill with a tree where 8-Deer pays homage to a person with a sun disk (Fig. 83*a*); in Becker I, 16, the spiral appears in a hill with a blackened top, and directly above this sign is a person descending from a sun disk (Fig. 83*b*). A clue to the meaning of the spiral motif is found in a place sign in the first Lienzo of Zacatepec (Fig. 105), where a church is placed on a platform consisting of two panels with this motif. It would seem likely from this context that the spiral indicates a sacred setting or ceremonial site. Perhaps the spiral, which is always red and yellow in Colombino and Becker I, is a stylized flame motif. According to the Alvarado dictionary, the Mixtec word for "fire" is *ñuhu*, and *ñuhu* can also mean "earth, ground" and "sacred, divine, holy." The star motifs discussed in the paragraph above may also indicate a ceremonial site; but until more of the signs which contain these motifs are identified, this is merely a tentative hypothesis.

Throughout this and the preceding chapter, it has been stressed that one of the most important factors in place-sign identification is context. Does the identification appear to fit the persons or events connected with the place sign? Is the identification demonstrable not only as a logogram of a known Mixtec name, but also as a coherent segment of the pictorial narrative of which it is a part? The story told in any one historical manuscript undoubtedly expresses the regional viewpoint of the town or towns whose rulers commissioned the painting of the manuscript. Thus, once the principal place signs of a manuscript are identified, it will be easier to identify the signs of towns with which the principal towns intermarry and wage war.

At the present time, however, too few firmly established identifications of place signs have been made to reveal a clearly defined context for most of the historical manuscripts. Codex Colombino appears to tell a Coastal version of the biography of 8-Deer, and Codex Sánchez Solís appears to be concerned with rulers of the northern Oaxaca-southern Puebla region. But the interpretation of these two manuscripts has been aided considerably by the Mixtec glosses that were written on them after the Spanish

---

[125] In the sixteenth-century glosses on page VIII-21 of Codex Colombino, a third version of Tetepelcingo's name is given as *yucu yuyuta*, apparently a combination of the two names *yucu yuu* and *yucu yuta*. The compound name is no longer used today.

[126] Colombino III–11, VI–14, VII–19 and 22, VIII–24, XIII–37, XIV–39 (twice), XVIII–52, XX–58, XXIV–64; Becker I, pages 13 (twice) and 16.

conquest. Three of the longest and most detailed historical manuscripts—Codices Nuttall, Bodley and Selden—have no accompanying texts in European script. Thus, to gain a better understanding of the Mixtec place sign, we must turn to post-Conquest manuscripts in which the pictorial signs can be related to the Mixtec names they represent.

One group of pictorial documents which provide a quantity of place signs in an identifiable context are the sixteenth-century maps of one town and its boundaries. For this reason, the examination of the early Colonial maps is worth while, not only for the information they contain on a specific town or region, but because they also present place signs in a cartographic relationship, where the signs can more easily be associated with the places whose names they represent.

The remainder of this book will be devoted to a discussion of early Colonial Mixtec maps, with a detailed analysis of the sixteenth-century maps of two towns on the Coast of Oaxaca: Santa María Zacatepec and San Pedro Jicayán. In order to place the maps of Zacatepec and Jicayán in a proper context, it is necessary first to discuss briefly the Coastal region, an important but comparatively little-known section of the Mixteca.

VI

THE COASTAL REGION OF THE MIXTECA

The maps to be discussed in Chapters VII and VIII are from the Coastal region of the Mixteca, a region that is in many respects different from the Mixteca Alta and Mixteca Baja. The most important difference is that at the time of the Spanish conquest, one town—the town of Tututepec—had gained control of most of the Coast and appears to have established a "tribute empire" similar to that of the Aztec rulers of Mexico City. Tututepec's consolidation of political power and tribute wealth was apparently unique in the Mixteca, for in the Alta and Baja there were several important towns, but no single town seems to have dominated either of these two regions.[1] The Coastal region, sometimes called "The Kingdom of Tututepec," was also unique in that it was the only region of the Mixteca that was never incorporated into the tribute kingdom of the Aztecs of Mexico City-Tenochtitlan, as were the Mixteca Baja and much of the Mixteca Alta.[2] Instead, Tututepec with its own tribute kingdom was an independent capital and may well have been competing with the Aztecs to gain domination over the Mixteca Alta.

Today, Tututepec is an unimposing village distributed among the rocks and crevices of a mesa about 15 miles north of the Pacific Ocean (Fig. 84a). But its former importance and the extent of its holdings in the sixteenth century are recorded in detail in several sources. Colonial land documents contain five different lists of towns on the Coast that were subject to Tututepec, and the Mixtec glosses on Codex Colombino deal almost exclusively with the names of the boundaries of Tututepec's subjects on the Coast.[3] The *Suma de Visitas*, a survey of towns in Mexico made about 1547-1550, describes eight towns as subjects of Tututepec:

San Agustín Chayucu
Santa Elena Comaltepec

Iztepec (probably present-day Ixtapa)
Pinoteca la Chica (present-day Pinotepa de Don Luis)
Quaquezpaltepec (present-day Huaxpaltepec)
Suchiopan (probably present-day Juchatengo)
12 *estancias* of Temaxcaltepec
Jamiltepec.[4]

These eight towns are included in Map 4 to provide a general idea of the extent of Tututepec's domain in the mid-sixteenth century.

Because many subject towns paid tribute to Tututepec, it was a wealthy town, and therefore the Spaniards subjugated it soon after they had completed the conquest of Mexico City-Tenochtitlan. Mexico City fell on August 13, 1521; Captain Pedro de Alvarado had conquered Tututepec by March 4, 1522.[5] Bernal Díaz states that Alvarado managed to obtain gold valued at 30,000 pesos from the native ruler of Tututepec before the latter died in prison in 1522 and that Alvarado obtained even more gold from this ruler's son and heir.[6]

As extensive as Tututepec's domain was at the time of the Conquest, it was probably even larger in pre-Conquest times. There is ample evidence that Tututepec had extended its empire—or at least attempted to extend it—beyond the Coastal region. No *Relación Geográfica* has been found for Tututepec itself, but the *Relaciones* of other towns often mention that they paid tribute to Tututepec or waged war against Tututepec. (The towns discussed below are also included in Map 4, to show their location relative to Tututepec.)

The Mixteca Alta towns of Mitlatongo and Tamazola claim they fought against Tututepec,[7] and the towns of Amoltepec and Peñoles, also in the Mixteca Alta, said that they were subjects of Tututepec.[8] Coatlán in the Zapotec-speaking region east of Tututepec fought contin-

---

[1] Concerning the Mixteca Alta, see Spores, *The Mixtec Kings and Their People*, 64–68.

[2] Heinrich Berlin, *Fragmentos desconocidos*, 17ff.; Claude Nigel Byam Davies, *Los señoríos independientes del Imperio Azteca* (Mexico, 1968), 181–213.

[3] These lists of Tututepec's subjects and the Colombino glosses are discussed in Smith, *Colombino*. The lists were prepared in connection with land and inheritance disputes, in which the native rulers of Tututepec were embroiled throughout the Colonial period. The lists of subject towns are included in two documents in the Archivo General de la Nación which deal exclusively with Tututepec litigation: Ramo de Tierras 29–1 (197 folios) and Ramo de Vínculos 272, 8–10 (91 folios). These documents and other sources on the Coastal region are discussed in Appendix D.

[4] *PNE* I, entry nos. 99, 100, 306, 456, 481, 491, 653, 809.

[5] Hernán Cortés, Third Letter to Charles V (Francis Augustus MacNutt, ed. and trans., *Fernando Cortes: his five letters of Relation to the Emperor Charles V*, II [Cleveland, 1908], 143).

[6] Bernal Díaz del Castillo, *Historia verdadera de la conquista de la Nueva España* (Mexico, 1944), II, 349. Cortés, Third Letter, (MacNutt, *Fernando Cortes* . . . , II, 143) says that Alvarado reported receiving gold worth 25,000 castellanos. Cortés had instructed the Spaniards to establish a settlement in Tututepec, but most of the Spanish population soon withdrew to the Valley of Oaxaca because of the relentlessly hot climate and the immense insect population on the Coast (Bernal Díaz del Castillo, *Historia verdadera*, 350–51).

[7] *PNE* IV, 79, 84.

[8] *RMEH* I, II.

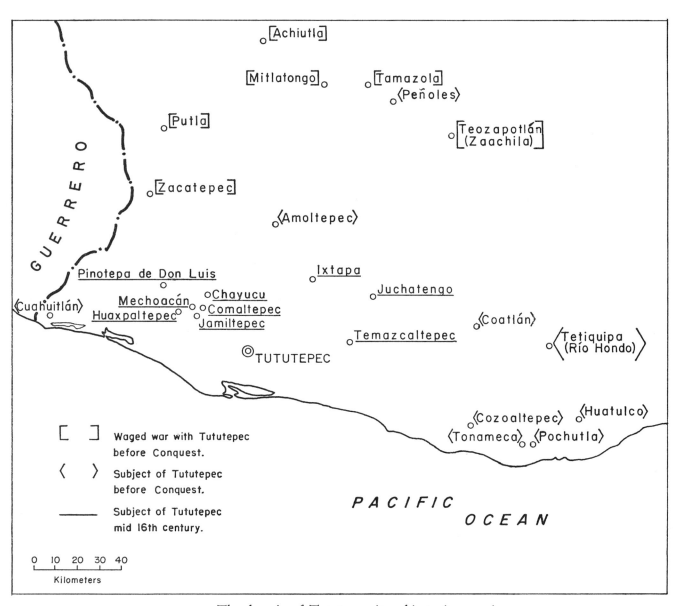

MAP 4. The domain of Tututepec: its subjects, its enemies

ual "battles of rebellion" against Tututepec,[9] and Herrera reports that the Zapotecs of Teozapotlán in the Valley of Oaxaca waged war with the ruler of Tututepec.[10] Padre Burgoa describes in detail an altercation between Tututepec and the Mixteca Alta town of Achiutla. Speaking of Achiutla, he says:

They have in front of this town a very high hill, with a peak which ascends loftily almost to the region of the clouds, and it is crowned with a very extensive brick wall more than a *stadium* high. And it is told in their paintings of a historical nature, that they retired here to defend themselves from their enemies, and because their rulers did not perform a certain obligation which they owed the king of Tututepec on the Coast. The obligation was to bring the produce of their town to a great fair which was held by order of that king on the plains of Putla, the beginning of the Coastal region, where

he would acquire whatever was necessary for his subjects; and because of the great victories [this king] had had in the surrounding territory, he imposed this obligation. [Putla] was from this town [Achiutla] a distance of more than 20 leagues of hilly and steep mountains and dense vegetation; the subjects of this ruler tried to excuse themselves and not comply with this obligation because it was a great hardship. When the people of Achiutla did not arrive, the king of Tututepec first sent ambassadors to threaten them. Then he sent valiant captains accompanied by a great number of people, which made it necessary for the citizens of Achiutla to climb to the impregnable castle with sufficient supplies, and enough easily rolled stones and rocks so that they could defend themselves from the assault by flinging the enemy off the mountain. The enemy arrived and besieged the mountain, and looked for a route by which to scale it and come within fighting distance; and the battle was so bloody that afterward they counted the dead of both sides, and more than 22,000 bodies were found.[11]

[9] PNE IV, 134: "Ellos tenían continuamente guerras con el cacique de Tututepeque, contra quien se habían rebelado y con muchos pueblos suyos."

[10] Historia general, VI, 329.

[11] Burgoa, Geográfica descripción, I, 352–53. The original Spanish text of this quotation appears in Appendix B–3.

On the Coast itself, Tututepec's pre-Conquest domain extended farther west and east than it did in the sixteenth century. The town of Cuahuitlán, west of Tututepec and near the present-day border between the States of Oaxaca and Guerrero, is reported to have been a subject of Tututepec; and the towns of Zacatepec and Putla in the northwest section of the Coast state that they waged war with Tututepec prior to the Spanish conquest.[12] Eastward, toward the Isthmus of Tehuantepec, the towns of Huatulco, Pochutla, Tonameca, Tetiquipa, and Cozoaltepec were tribute-paying subjects of Tututepec and helped Tututepec in its wars.[13] Tututepec's method of controlling subject towns through the rulers of these towns and through the subsidiary nobility or *principales* is described in the *Relación* of Tonameca:

... and the nature of [Tonameca's] government was that the rulers of Tututepec decide who would be governor in this town; and the person whom they name, who must be of this town's highest nobility, has to be obeyed before everyone else; and this governor placed in each section of this town noblemen (*principales*) who directed and governed the common people and collected the tribute, and this was the nature of their government; and they had to go to war, helping those of Tututepec, against those of Tehuantepec and other towns on this coast against whom they [the armies of Tututepec] waged war ....[14]

A similar story is told in the *Relación* of Pochutla:

... the rulers of Tututepec sent a person who stayed in the town to collect tribute and administer justice, and in addition to this person they named as governor of the town its highest noble, and this governor named others to help him and take charge of the town's precincts ... and before they were Tututepec's subjects, they waged war against Tututepec and having been defeated, they became the vassals of Tututepec.[15]

Tututepec may have exercised at least a nominal control over Santa María Zacatepec and San Pedro Jicayán, the two Coastal towns whose maps we shall examine. Both towns are located in the western section of the Coast: the present-day town of Zacatepec is in one of a series of valleys which extend northward to the Alta region below Tlaxiaco, and Jicayán occupies a ridge of hills northeast of Pinotepa Nacional. In the mid-sixteenth-century *Suma de Visitas*, neither Zacatepec nor Jicayán is said to be a subject of Tututepec,[16] although, as we have seen above, the *Suma de Visitas* describes eight Coastal towns as Tututepec's subjects. In addition, the 1580 *Relación* of Zacatepec claims that this town fought three times against warriors sent from the Aztec ruler Moctezuma and twice against Tututepec, but that the town was never captured.[17]

But the glosses of Codex Colombino, which list the Mixtec boundary names of Tututepec's subjects, include the boundaries of both Jicayán (pages XIII and XIV) and Zacatepec (page XX).[18] A list that was compiled in 1620 but which is stated to contain the names of Tututepec's subjects in the second quarter of the sixteenth century does not contain the name of Jicayán, but does include Zacatepec, listed only by its Mixtec name, *yucu satuta*.[19] The appearance of both Zacatepec and Jicayán in the Colombino glosses, dated 1541, would seem to indicate that at the time of the Spanish conquest, Tututepec claimed (unsuccessfully?) that both towns were its subjects; or it is possible that Jicayán and Zacatepec were allied to Tututepec by marriage.

The names of the native rulers of Jicayán in the early Colonial period are not known, and thus it is not possible to chart the native dynasties of this town and ascertain if Jicayán's rulers intermarried with those of Tututepec. In the case of Zacatepec, however, we have several Colonial documents relating to the town's native rulers, and it is clear from these documents that in the sixteenth century the rulers of Zacatepec not only intermarried with the nobility of Tututepec but also claimed to have descended from the Tututepec dynasties.

A seventeenth-century document in the Archivo General de la Nación includes the last will and testament of María de Alvarado, the native ruler of Zacatepec and Chayucu in the 1630's.[20] The genealogical information given in this document is presented in Chart 7, "Native Rulers of Zacatepec-Chayucu in the Early Seventeenth Century." In her will, dated July 19, 1638, María de Alvarado states that she is the daughter of Pedro de Alvarado and Juana de Rojas, and granddaughter of Pedro de Alvarado and Luisa de Mendoza, and that both her parents and grandparents were the rulers of Zacatepec and Chayucu. Elsewhere in this document it is said that the grandparents, Pedro de Alvarado I and Luisa de Mendoza, were first cousins and legitimate descendants of the "kings" of Tututepec.[21]

The information in this document is corroborated and supplemented by data on the native rulers of Zacatepec that is included in Manuel Martínez Gracida's unpublished manuscript on the kingdom of Tututepec.[22] These data are summarized in Chart 8, "Sixteenth-Century Native Rulers of Tututepec and Zacatepec-Chayucu." It is assumed that Martínez Gracida drew his data from Colonial documents which are now lost, because his information correlates fairly exactly with that given in extant documents on Tututepec and Zacatepec. It confirms, for example, the claim that the earliest generation mentioned in the seventeenth-century document cited above were first cousins of the rulers of Tututepec. According to the

---

[12] *PNE* IV, 158; *RMEH* II, 158, 161–62.

[13] *PNE* IV, 235, 238–39, 243–44, 248–49; *RMEH* II.

[14] *PNE* IV, 243–44. The original Spanish text of this quotation appears in Appendix B–4.

[15] *PNE* IV, 239. The original Spanish text of this quotation appears in Appendix B–4.

[16] *PNE* I, entry nos. 808 (Jicayán), 98 (Zacatepec).

[17] *RMEH* II, 161–62: "*Dizen estos naturales* [of Zacatepec] *que tuvieron guerra con los mexicanos enviados por* monteçuma *y que tuvieron recuentro con ellos tres vezes y dos vezes con los de* tututepeque, *y nunca los pudieron vençer* ...."

[18] Smith, *Colombino*, 64–65, 66–67; 160–62, 163, and "The Codex Colombino ...," *Tlalocan*, Vol. IV–3, 281–83.

[19] AGN-Tierras 29–1, fol. 41. Included in Smith, *Colombino*, 76; 172.

[20] AGN-Tierras, 1359–2, fol. 3–5.

[21] *Ibid.*, fol. 1.

[22] "La reseña histórica del reino de Tututepec" (1907). The known copies of this manuscript are discussed in Appendix D.

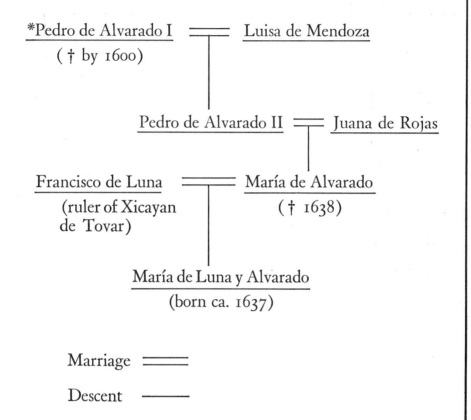

CHART 7: Native Rulers of Zacatepec-Chayucu
in the Early Seventeenth Century

(AGN-Tierras 1359–2)

*Pedro de Alvarado I ═══ Luisa de Mendoza
(† by 1600)

Pedro de Alvarado II ═══ Juana de Rojas

Francisco de Luna ═══ María de Alvarado
(ruler of Xicayan   († 1638)
de Tovar)

María de Luna y Alvarado
(born ca. 1637)

Marriage ═══

Descent ───

*This generation claims to be first cousins ("primos hermanos")
of the rulers of Tututepec.

Martínez Gracida manuscript, Pedro de Alvarado I of Zacatepec was the son of *Cuetzpalintzin*, who was baptized as Alonso de Castilla y Alvarado and who was ruler of Chayucu. *Cuetzpalintzin* was the second son of *Coaquitecuhtli* (or *Coaxintecuhtli*), the ruler of Tututepec who died in 1522, soon after the town's conquest by the Spaniards. This individual's first son, *Ixtac Quiautzin*, who was baptized as Pedro de Alvarado, inherited the domain of Tututepec.

According to Martínez Gracida, another marriage alliance between the rulers of Tututepec and those of Zacatepec-Chayucu occurs in 1581, when Melchor de Alvarado, heir to Tututepec, marries Isabel de Alvarado, daughter of *Cuetzpalintzin* or Alonso de Castilla. This is a case of

marriage between parallel cousins, for Isabel is Melchor's father's brother's daughter.[23]

What the Colonial documents discussed above do not define is the precise relationship between the two towns of Zacatepec and Chayucu. As we noted above, the 1547–1550 *Suma de Visitas* describes Chayucu—but not Zacatepec—as a subject of Tututepec. The 1580 *Relación* of Zacatepec makes no mention at all of Chayucu; it merely states that Zacatepec has six *estancias* or subject towns, but

[23] Dahlgren (*La mixteca*, 149–50) studied the instances of marriage by male personages with parallel and cross relatives in the pre-Conquest historical manuscripts, and she found five instances of marriage with parallel first-cousins and five instances of marriage with cross first-cousins, which seems to indicate that there is no preference for one or the other type of cousin marriage.

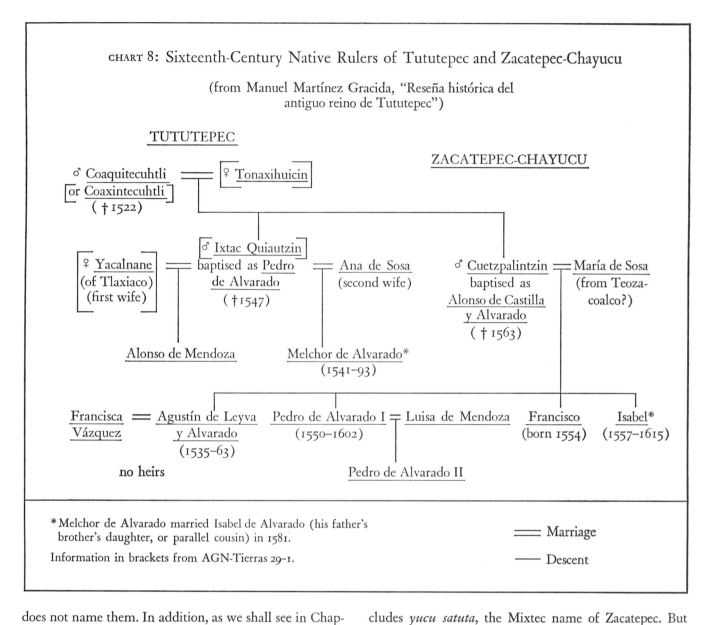

CHART 8: Sixteenth-Century Native Rulers of Tututepec and Zacatepec-Chayucu

(from Manuel Martínez Gracida, "Reseña histórica del
antiguo reino de Tututepec")

TUTUTEPEC

ZACATEPEC-CHAYUCU

♂ Coaquitecuhtli ═══ ♀ Tonaxihuicin
[or Coaxintecuhtli]
(† 1522)

♀ Yacalnane ═══ ♂ Ixtac Quiautzin
(of Tlaxiaco)   baptised as Pedro ═══ Ana de Sosa
(first wife)   de Alvarado   (second wife)
                       (†1547)

♂ Cuetzpalintzin ═══ María de Sosa
baptised as   (from Teoza-
Alonso de Castilla   coalco?)
y Alvarado
(† 1563)

Alonso de Mendoza   Melchor de Alvarado*
                        (1541–93)

Francisca ═══ Agustín de Leyva   Pedro de Alvarado I ═══ Luisa de Mendoza   Francisco   Isabel*
Vázquez   y Alvarado   (1550–1602)   (born 1554)   (1557–1615)
             (1535–63)

no heirs   Pedro de Alvarado II

*Melchor de Alvarado married Isabel de Alvarado (his father's
brother's daughter, or parallel cousin) in 1581.   ═══ Marriage

Information in brackets from AGN-Tierras 29-1.   ——— Descent

---

does not name them. In addition, as we shall see in Chapter VII, when Chayucu is represented in the sixteenth-century maps of Zacatepec, it is placed outside the boundaries of Zacatepec. It is possible that *Cuetzpalintzin*-Alonso de Castilla, who is the crucial link between the Tututepec and Zacatepec lineages, inherited either Chayucu or Zacatepec, or both towns, from his mother *Tonaxihuicin*, for the second son sometimes receives his mother's domain. But the town of origin of *Tonaxihuicin* is not known, nor is the date of her death given in any of the documents.

In this connection, it is interesting to note that the name of Chayucu appears in only one of the Colonial lists of Tututepec's subjects, a list made in 1620 that purports to include the names of the towns belonging to Pedro de Alvarado, *Cuetzpalintzin's* brother, who ruled Tututepec from 1522 to about 1547.[24] This is the same list that includes *yucu satuta*, the Mixtec name of Zacatepec. But neither town is given as a subject of Tututepec in any of the seventeenth- or eighteenth-century lists of Tututepec's subject towns. It would seem, then, that Zacatepec and Chayucu were part of the domain of Tututepec at the time of the Spanish conquest, but that they became separate entities about 1550. When the two towns were merged with Tututepec in the pre-Conquest period by marriage alliances or by conquest is difficult to decide, although, as has been noted, in the 1580 *Relación* of Zacatepec it is claimed that this town was never conquered by Tututepec. Perhaps Zacatepec preserved at least a vestige of autonomy in a region that was dominated by the tribute empire of Tututepec.

Having considered briefly the written documents that deal with the native rulers of Zacatepec in the early Colonial period, we shall turn now to the town's two important pictorial manuscripts, Lienzos of Zacatepec 1 and 2.

24 AGN-Tierras, 29–1, fol. 41. Included in Smith, *Colombino*, 76; 172.

VII

THE TWO LIENZOS OF ZACATEPEC

In the early Colonial period, two maps were drawn of the town of Santa María Zacatepec and its boundaries. These two maps are important as historical and cartographic documents of the same town drawn at two different periods in the sixteenth century. The earlier of the two (Figs. 85-111) will be called "Lienzo of Zacatepec 1" or merely "Zacatepec 1." The later manuscript will be referred to as "Lienzo of Zacatepec 2" or "Zacatepec 2."

The history of the two Lienzos is essentially the same up to the year 1900. They were in the municipal archive of Santa María Zacatepec until 1892, when the citizens of Zacatepec brought both maps to Mexico City as corroborating evidence in a land suit. In the following year, tracings were made of the two Lienzos. Each was copied on three large strips of tracing cloth, and the tracings of both manuscripts are dated March 29, 1893, and signed by Mauricio C. Castro (Figs. 112, 130a).[1] After the completion of the land suit in Mexico City, the citizens of Zacatepec returned to their town with the tracings of both Lienzos, and the originals were retained in Mexico City. The 1893 tracings are still today in the municipal archive of Zacatepec.

In 1900, Antonio Peñafiel published excellent photographs of Lienzo of Zacatepec 1, accompanied by a map of Zacatepec drawn in 1892 and a short text in Spanish and French.[2] In his text Peñafiel includes a brief account of the 1892 land suit and a description of Zacatepec 2, with a transcription and translation of the eight Nahuatl glosses written on the Lienzo (Fig. 123). But the second Lienzo is not illustrated in the 1900 publication.

In 1933, Zacatepec 1 was transferred from the archive of the Secretaría de Agricultura y Fomento to the Museo Nacional de Antropología, where it is today, catalogued as No. 35-63.[3] When this transfer was made, neither the second Lienzo of Zacatepec nor the written documents relating to the 1892 land suit could be located.

The location of the original Lienzo of Zacatepec 2 is still unknown, and all observations made about Zacatepec 2 in this study are based on the 1893 tracing (Figs. 122-30). As can be seen by a comparison of the 1893 copy of a section of Zacatepec 1 with the original from which it derives (Figs. 112, 111), the nineteenth-century tracings are reasonably accurate but pallid transcriptions of the original Lienzos. Thus all comments on the style of Zacatepec 2 are automatically to be qualified as "the style as perceivable in the 1893 copy."

The location of the Coastal towns mentioned in this and the following chapter is shown in Map 5, "The Coastal Region West of the Río Verde." The approximate area covered by the two Lienzos of Zacatepec is indicated on Map 6, which also shows the present-day municipal units of the western section of the Coast.

ZACATEPEC 1

The figures of Zacatepec 1 are drawn in a black, carbon-like ink on four vertical strips of cotton cloth which are sewn together. Each strip of cloth is about 325 centimeters long and 55 centimeters wide; the dimensions of the entire map are approximately 325 by 225 centimeters. The Lienzo seems to have been intended to be strictly a monochrome drawing, because it contains no vestiges of paint.

Across the center of the document are three large holes, and several smaller holes are in the lower third of the Lienzo. Although one place sign is completely obliterated and several others partially destroyed by these holes, the placement of the damage does not suggest intentional censorship of portions of the map. What seems more likely is that the document was chewed by rats or other animals while it was still in the local archive in Zacatepec.

Zacatepec 1 is both a cartographic and a genealogical-historical document. The boundaries of Santa María Zacatepec are defined by a large rectangle that encloses all but the top register of the Lienzo. Attached to the border of this rectangle are the signs of the names of boundary sites. In common with most of the sixteenth-century Mixtec maps of one town and its boundaries, the bases of all the boundary signs face inward. The orientation of the first

---

[1] The same legend is written on the tracings of both Zacatepec 1 and 2: "*Calca tomada de los originales en tela. Mexico, Marzo 29 de 1893*," followed by the signature of Mauricio C. Castro.

[2] Peñafiel, *LZ*. Peñafiel suggested that Zacatepec 1 be named "Códice Martínez Gracida" after the Oaxacan scholar, but this name has never been used, except parenthetically, in descriptions of the Lienzo. Brief descriptions of Zacatepec 1 are included in: Lehmann, *JSA* n.s., Vol. II (1905), 261-63; in José Alcina Franch, "Fuentes indígenas de Méjico" (*Revista de Indias*, Año XV, nos. 61-62, 1955), 494-95; and in Glass, *Catálogo de la Colección de Códices*, 115. The Glass catalog also contains a photograph (plate 66) of the entire Lienzo.

[3] This transfer is noted in: Agustín Villagra, "El Lienzo de Zacatepec: un nuevo lienzo que viene a enriquecer la colección de códices que existen en el Museo Nacional," *Boletín del Museo Nacional de Arqueología, Historia y Etnografía*, 5a. época, II (1933), 105-106.

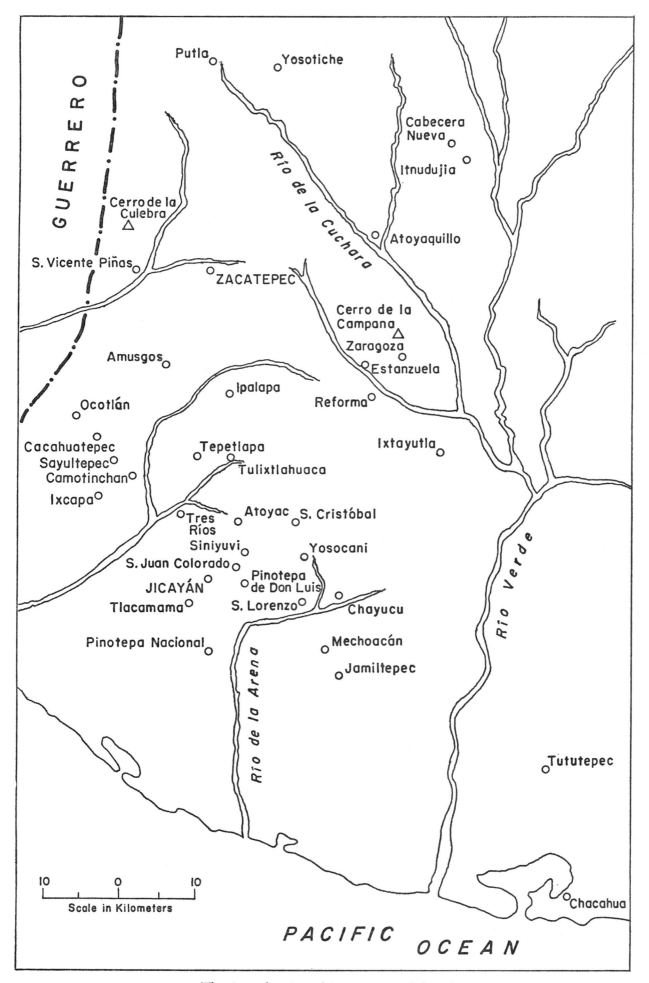

MAP 5.   The Coastal region of Oaxaca west of the Río Verde

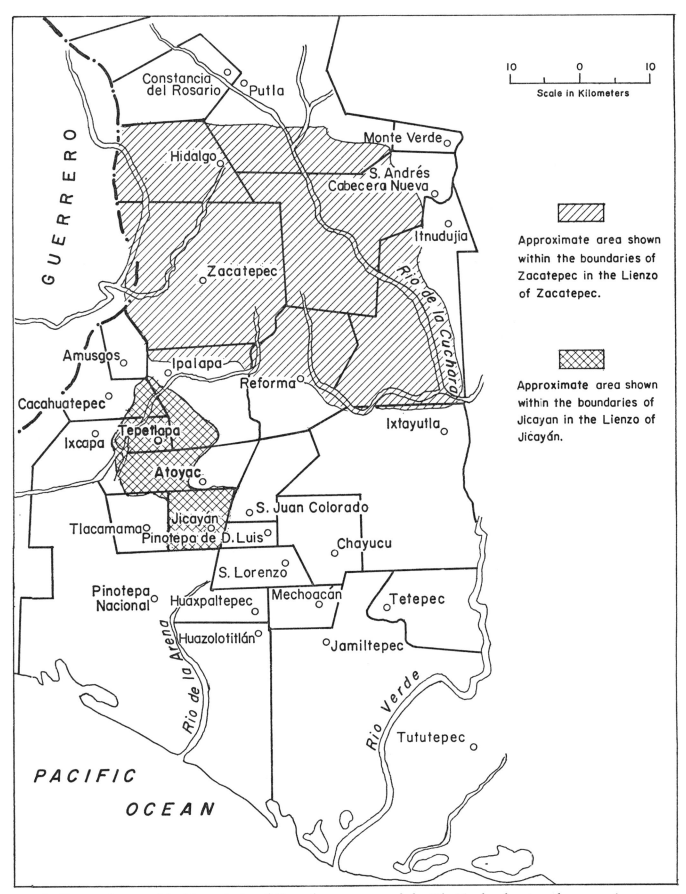

MAP 6. Present-day municipal boundaries of Coastal towns west of the Río Verde, showing the approximate areas covered by the Lienzos of Zacatepec and Jicayán. (After Jorge L. Tamayo, Carta general del Estado de Oaxaca, 1960)

Lienzo of Zacatepec is with approximate east at the top, and hence north at the left, west at the bottom, and south at the right.

The historical-genealogical narrative begins in the upper-left corner above the cartographic rectangle, extends across the top to the upper-right corner, and then continues within the rectangle, where it is organized in a rather rambling meander pattern. In addition to the principal narrative, which is connected by roads and warpaths, the large rectangle formed by the boundaries contains three types of place signs: (1) "non-cartographic signs" —that is, signs of towns which are actually located outside of Zacatepec's boundaries but which are placed *within* the rectangle of boundaries in the Lienzo, (2) the signs of Zacatepec's *estancias* or subjects, and (3) signs of uninhabited geographical features such as hills and rivers.

The non-cartographic signs are accompanied by a marriage pair, and an example of such a sign is the place sign of Jicayán as it appears within the boundaries of Zacatepec 1 (Figs. 58*b* and 103–104). This sign appears twice in Zacatepec 1: in a non-cartographic context within the boundaries of Zacatepec, and in a cartographic context outside the boundaries (Figs. 111, 58*a*), where it indicates the approximate location of Jicayán, south of Zacatepec.

The signs of Zacatepec's subjects are accompanied by a single personage, as for example the sign of San Vicente Piñas (Fig. 109), a town located west of Zacatepec. This sign consists of a hill and a butterfly, and thus expresses San Vicente's Mixtec name, which is reported by the officials of Zacatepec to be *yucu ticuvua,* or "hill of the butterfly." (*Yucu* = "hill"; *ticuvua* = "butterfly.")

The hill with a serpent (Fig. 109) at the left of the sign of San Vicente exemplifies the third type of place sign: an uninhabited geographical feature. This sign represents Cerro de la Culebra, a hill west of Zacatepec, whose Mixtec name is *yucu coò* or "hill of the snake." (*Yucu* = "hill"; *coò* = "snake.") The rivers which are represented in the Lienzo (Fig. 134) are also purely geographical features. For example, the large river which runs upward from the center of the left border and terminates in the right corner of the Lienzo is the Río de la Cuchara.

Characteristic of many of the place signs at the top of the Lienzo and within the rectangle of boundaries are the elaborate decorations on the friezes that support buildings and place signs. Two of the most frequently used decorations are a four-petaled flower and a diagonal configuration that is the sign for *ilhuitl* or "ceremonial day" in manuscripts from the Nahuatl-speaking region. In Zacatepec 1 these two designs appear separately (as in the platforms of buildings in Figs. 90, 91 and 104) or as alternating panels (Figs. 87, 94 and 109). The meaning of the various designs used in the friezes is unknown, and the use of so many different decorative motifs seems to be unique to the first Lienzo of Zacatepec. In other early Colonial Mixtec lienzos, friezes are usually shown as decorated with the standard pyramidal geometric patterns (as, for example, the Lienzo of Ocotepec [Fig. 160]).

Outside the rectangular frame on the left, bottom, and right sides of the first Lienzo of Zacatepec are the place signs of the towns which bounded Zacatepec on the north, west, and south, respectively. Unlike the boundary signs which all face inward, most of the signs which represent Zacatepec's neighbors face outward—that is, the base of these signs is placed toward the edge of the Lienzo rather than toward the interior of the map.

The figural style of Zacatepec 1 is closest to that of the Bodley-Selden-Becker II group of pre-Conquest historical manuscripts, although the human figures in Zacatepec do not have the distinctive "one-toed foot" of this group. But notwithstanding the pre-Conquest quality of the draftsmanship in Zacatepec, several European motifs clearly demonstrate that the Lienzo is post-Conquest. Obviously of European origin are the small churches which appear in connection with four place signs (Fig. 92, 105, 111). Peñafiel believed the map was drawn in the pre-Conquest period and that the churches were added after the Conquest, but this seems unlikely. As Lehmann has observed, the churches are not drawn in a style different from that of the rest of the Lienzo, and they are completely integrated into the composition of the place sign.[4] In one instance (Fig. 105), a platform is created specifically for the church.

Another European motif is a cross which is placed on the stone motif within one of the boundary signs (Fig. 107, 120*a*). In the Colonial period it was traditional to mark the boundaries between two towns with a cross set on a pile of stones or on a stone platform, a practice which is still continued today (Fig. 121).

The symbols of the moon seen throughout the Lienzo (Figs. 89, 96, 108) are also a European import. The crescent moon, particularly the crescent moon with a human face, probably derives from sixteenth-century European woodcuts and engravings, and in no way resembles the pre-Conquest sign for moon, as seen in the place sign of Santa María Acatepec (Fig. 51).

In addition, the frame line of the drawing in Zacatepec 1 is slightly less taut than that of the pre-Conquest manuscripts, and we see evidence of the post-Conquest trait which Robertson has characterized as "disintegrated frame line."[5] This is particularly noticeable in some of the standing figures (Fig. 102), where the entire leg is presented as a unit, rather than as a combination of two separable parts, as in the pre-Conquest manuscripts (Fig. 15*b*).

Essentially, however, the pictorial conventions of Zacatepec 1 are identical with the conventions of pre-Conquest manuscripts discussed in Chapter III. Dates, names of persons, marriage and conference, roads and warpaths, conquest, and place signs are for the most part represented in the pre-Conquest idiom. Because the Lienzo is a cartographic document, it may be thought that the bands of footprints which appear above and within the rectangle of the map represent roads in and near Zacatepec. But in Zacatepec 1 roads are used to express the genealogical

4 Lehmann, *JSA* n.s. Vol. II (1905), 262, note 2.
5 *Mexican Manuscript Painting,* 65–66.

sense of "going to" and "coming from" in a typically pre-Conquest manner.

On the basis of its style, the first Lienzo of Zacatepec can be dated about 1540 to 1560.[6] This would place it about contemporary with Codex Selden, whose latest date is 1556. The first Lienzo is assumed to be at least two decades earlier than the 1580 Map of Teozacoalco not only because its frame line is more taut than that of the Teozacoalco Map, but because of the format of its historical narrative. The composition of the principal narrative line in Zacatepec 1 resembles more closely the typical meander pattern of a pre-Conquest screenfold than does any other known post-Conquest pictorial document. By way of contrast, in the 1580 Map of Teozacoalco (Figs. 25, 132), the historical-genealogical material is arranged in vertical columns which are to be read from bottom to top—a format that appears only in post-Conquest manuscripts and which may have been imported from Europe.

ZACATEPEC 2

The 1893 tracing of Zacatepec 2 was executed in black ink on three large horizontal strips of white tracing cloth. As can be seen in Fig. 130a, there is some overlap of figures at the top and bottom edges of the adjoining strips, but when the three strips are perfectly joined, their entire dimensions are approximately 300 by 245 centimeters—the dimensions given by Peñafiel for the original Lienzo.[7] The tracing is in good condition, although slightly spotted with mildew (see Fig. 116b, for example). There is no color used in the 1893 tracing, and Peñafiel does not make any mention of color in his description of the original.[8]

Zacatepec 2 is essentially a redaction of some of the cartographic data presented in Zacatepec 1, but many of these data are expressed by European rather than by pre-Conquest conventions. The retention of pre-Conquest conventions is most evident in place signs, especially in the signs of the names of Zacatepec's boundaries that are placed around the border of Zacatepec 2. These boundary signs are, for the most part, fairly exact copies of the equivalent signs appended to the large rectangle in Zacatepec 1. Within the boundaries of Zacatepec 2, eight of the series of sharply delineated hills that encircle the center of the composition (Fig. 123) are named—both in the pre-Conquest manner of naming, for the eight hills are accompanied by pictorial qualifying elements that represent their names, and in a post-Conquest manner, because these hills are also accompanied by Nahuatl glosses with the names written in European script.

Zacatepec 2 omits virtually all of the material represented outside the large rectangle in Zacatepec 1. That is, the second Lienzo does not include the signs of the towns that bound Zacatepec, which appear along the left, bottom, and right borders of Zacatepec 1, nor does it include the register of genealogical-historical information found at the top of Zacatepec 1. In addition, Zacatepec 2 does not contain the extensive historical narrative that occupies the space within the rectangle of Zacatepec 1, but merely three isolated scenes with human figures (two of which are seen in Fig. 125 and one in Fig. 126). Nor are the brief historical notations in Zacatepec 2 exact copies of their counterparts in Zacatepec 1, but incorporate adaptations and amendments. The seated poses of the human figures as well as the place signs, friezes, and buildings in these scenes of Zacatepec 2 mirror the pre-Conquest style of Zacatepec 1, but none of the personages in Zacatepec 2 is accompanied by a typically pre-Conquest personal or calendrical name.

In one of the three scenes, it is possible to establish the identity of the person depicted by comparing the scene with analogous scenes in Zacatepec 1. Near the center of Zacatepec 2 (Fig. 126) is a building with an armed male human figure in a running pose; at the right of the building is a sign consisting of an eagle resting on the motif for stones. This scene derives from two distinct scenes in Zacatepec 1. The male human figure is copied from the figure of 3-Reed shown running along a warpath (Fig. 98). The building and place sign of "Eagle on Stones" are adapted from another scene (Fig. 103), which shows the same 3-Reed seated in front of this sign accompanied by his wife 9-Tiger. In Zacatepec 2 the frieze contains a stepped-terrace pattern rather than the stepped frets or roundels of the frieze in Zacatepec 1, and the second Lienzo omits the figure of 9-Tiger, but it is clear that the running male figure in this scene of Zacatepec 2 is 3-Reed.

The other two scenes with historical personages are less comparable to scenes in Zacatepec 1. One of the two scenes in Zacatepec 2 (Fig. 125) depicts a place sign consisting of a hill that terminates in a deer's head and also contains a human heart or flower motif. In front of this sign is a building with a male personage who is conferring with a marriage pair (the female figure on the left, the male figure in the center). The second scene in Zacatepec 2 (Figs. 125, 116b) shows a male personage seated in front of a building at the hill of Zacatepec, labeled "cacatepec." In Lienzo of Zacatepec 1 (Fig. 116a), the place sign of Zacatepec (the sign on the left) and the Hill of the Deer are united by a frieze containing a marriage pair; and it is the female figure, 13-Wind, who is seated at the Zacatepec end of the frieze. In Zacatepec 1, no conference between a marriage couple and a male figure is shown as taking place at Deer Hill, for this is the only appearance of that sign in the first Lienzo. Thus the conference scene at Deer Hill in Zacatepec 2 appears to have no analogy in Zacatepec 1; and it is also difficult to correlate the male figure in front of the hill of Zacatepec in the second Lienzo with any of the male personages in Zacatepec 1.

An interesting element in the Deer Hill sign in Zacatepec 2 is the trefoil motif placed within the hill. This motif does not occur in the Deer Hill sign in Zacatepec 1, and

---

[6] The year dates connected with historical events in the Lienzo are discussed below, pp. 116–19, but they are of no real help in determining when the Lienzo was drawn.

[7] LZ, 2. According to Peñafiel, the original Zacatepec 2 was composed of five pieces of cloth sewn together: four placed vertically and one horizontally. No indication of the seams of the original Lienzo appears in the 1893 tracing.

[8] Ibid.

whether the trefoil represents a flower or a human heart, it is a distinctly pre-Conquest motif. Another pre-Conquest sign that appears in Zacatepec 2 and has no analogy in Zacatepec 1 is the day-sign House utilized in the band around the atrium of the central church (Fig. 126) to suggest that the central square is surrounded by dwellings. In addition, in the upper-left corner of Zacatepec 2 there are several place signs of boundaries which do not have analogies with signs in Zacatepec 1: for example, the hill with a *cántaro* or water jar on the upper-left border, and the sign for a declivity containing the day-sign Water which appears on the top border (Fig. 124). Thus a number of purely pre-Conquest motifs in Zacatepec 2 are not copied from Zacatepec 1, which indicates that the pre-Conquest method of writing had not completely died out at the time Zacatepec 2 was drawn.

In contrast to Zacatepec 1 in which the area within the rectangle formed by the boundaries includes a relatively unified historical narrative, the analogous area of Zacatepec 2 presents a more detailed scheme of the geographical features within Zacatepec's boundaries. The comparison of Figs. 134 and 135, for example, shows clearly that the rivers and streams within the boundaries of Zacatepec are delineated in more detail in Zacatepec 2 than in Zacatepec 1.

It is in the cartographic notations of Zacatepec 2 that the influence of European pictorial conventions is most evident. The encircling hills, in common with the boundary signs, face the center of the manuscript; that is, they are all presented in elevation from the point of view of the town in the center. In contrast to the signs of boundary names, however, the enclosing ring of hills is depicted as a generalized landscape rather than as discrete signs that represent the names of specific hills.

This contrast is perhaps best seen in one of the hills on the right side of the Lienzo (Fig. 127), where a pre-Conquest place sign, labeled "pezutepec," is placed within the hill whose name it represents. The hill itself is essentially a landscape feature: it is part of the chain of hills south of Zacatepec; its outline is emphasized by a rudimentary attempt at shading; plants and bushes are placed on and within the hill, and these motifs do not represent the name of the hill, but merely indicate that foliage grows on the hill. The manner of representing the surrounding hills in the Lienzo resembles European woodcuts of the late fifteenth and early sixteenth century, as for example a frontispiece of a 1499 edition of Saint Bonaventure's *Instructione Novitiorum* (Fig. 131b), and clearly reflects imported rather than indigenous conventions. Conversely, the place sign within the hill is as much a label as the Nahuatl gloss written beneath it. Its intent is to represent the name of the hill, not the hill itself; and in the typical pre-Conquest manner, the interior of this hill sign contains no shading nor any elements, such as foliage, which are not meaningful in terms of the hill's name. The place sign is not a generalized portrait of a hill based on perception; it is a pictorial sign that reflects language rather than landscape.[9]

In Zacatepec 2, rivers are indicated by bands containing wavy lines. The use of wavy lines to indicate water is a convention common to sixteenth-century European prints and maps and to pre-Conquest manuscript painting. This convention is utilized for the smaller rivers or streams in Zacatepec 1 (Figs. 92, 96, 101, 108); but the larger rivers in this Lienzo are not merely bands with lines but also have the typical pre-Conquest motif for flowing water—bands with projections that terminate in concentric circles or circles that are represented as stars or eyes. In Zacatepec 2 this convention is seen only in a circular spring that is separated from the band of the river (Fig. 130c).

The larger rivers in Zacatepec 2 are populated with fish (Fig. 124), an occasional shellfish (Fig. 130b), and in one instance a quadruped which may be an otter or weasel (Fig. 128). In the pre-Conquest historical manuscripts fish and shellfish are at times shown within a river sign and have no apparent relationship to the place name represented by the sign, as in one of the place signs of Apoala in Codex Nuttall (Fig. 68b). But the method of depicting fish and shellfish in Zacatepec 2 is European rather than indigenous. For example, in pre-Conquest manuscripts the scales of fish are never delineated, as they are in European woodcuts and engravings of the late fifteenth and early sixteenth centuries (Fig. 131a).

The bands of footprints in Zacatepec 2 (Fig. 136) represent roads in the literal cartographic sense of a road. They no longer have the genealogical meaning of "going to" or "coming from" as is traditional in the pre-Conquest manuscripts and in Zacatepec 1. The use of footprints to symbolize roads and thoroughfares is extremely common in sixteenth-century Mexican maps; and in some Colonial maps, such as the 1579 *Relación* Map of Texupan (Fig. 37a), the bands which represent roads also contain the hoofprints of horses.

In the center of Zacatepec 2 (Fig. 126) is a church building placed at the east end of a square which has a cross in its center. The border of the square contains twenty-three representations of the pre-Conquest day-sign House, indicating that the central square is surrounded by dwellings; but no grid plan of the town is indicated as it is in the *Relación* Map of Texupan (Fig. 37a). Within the boundaries of Zacatepec are nine other small church buildings (Fig. 136), drawn in essentially the same manner as the central church and connected to the central town by roads. The buildings in the Lienzo are not intended to represent a specific church or chapel, but are used as a sign to indicate an inhabited place, much as a circle on contemporary road maps indicates a town. All of these buildings are portrayed as a front-facing brick façade with a single arched entrance, and they all have triangular straw roofs with a small cross at the top. The terraced layers of roof thatching are represented by saw-toothed projections, while the triangle drawn within this irregular

---

[9] The early post-Conquest conventions of cartography and landscape are discussed in Robertson, *Mexican Manuscript Painting*, 179–89, and "The Pinturas (Mapas) of the *Relaciones Geográficas*," to be published in *HMAI*, Vol. 12.

outline suggests the structure of the wooden rafters to which the straw thatching is attached.

The central church complex represents the present-day site of the town of Zacatepec, located about 16°45′ N., 97°59′ W. This site is a considerable distance from the town's former (or *pueblo viejo*) site, which was on or near a hill now called Cerro de la Campana ("Hill of the Bell"), some 15 miles east and slightly south of present-day Zacatepec, or approximately 16°40′ N., 97°47′ W.[10] It is the *pueblo viejo* site that is represented by the steep high peak labeled "cacatepec" near the top of the second Lienzo (Fig. 116b); the analogous sign of Zacatepec in the first Lienzo (Fig. 116a) also represents the town's earlier site. It is not known when the town of Zacatepec was moved from Cerro de la Campana to its present location, but the move was made before 1580, because in the *Relación* of Zacatepec written in that year, the description of the town's location indicates that the 1580 site is virtually the same as the present-day site. According to the 1580 *Relación*:

The town of Zacatepec is located on a slope of a small hill which is at the edge of a river which runs from east to west and which contains a great deal of water in the rainy season . . . from this town to the town of Amusgos there are four short leagues of steep and tortuous roads . . . [leaving] this town from the south.[11]

On most contemporary maps the present-day town of Zacatepec is slightly north of a river which runs from east to west (Fig. 137); in Zacatepec 2 this is the river at the right of the central church which runs toward the bottom (i.e., west) of the map. In addition, the distance from Zacatepec to Amusgos by road is approximately 15 miles, which is roughly equivalent to the distance of four leagues given in the 1580 *Relación*. As can be seen by comparing the drawing in Fig. 136 and a present-day map of the region (Fig. 137), the road which extends to the left and right of the central church in Zacatepec 2 also has a fairly similar pattern to the present-day road which runs north of Zacatepec to Putla and south-southwest of Zacatepec to Amusgos.

The nine subsidiary churches within the boundaries of Zacatepec 2 undoubtedly represent Zacatepec's dependencies, but the nine sites are not named either by pre-Conquest place signs or by glosses in European script. In the 1547–1550 *Suma de Visitas* Zacatepec is said to have twelve subjects; the 1580 *Relación* states that the town has

six subjects.[12] Neither source names the subject towns. The presence of nine churches in the second Lienzo might suggest that it was drawn between 1550 and 1580; but it is also possible that the six *estancias* referred to in the 1580 *Relación* are equivalent to the six churches closest to the central site of Zacatepec, excluding the three sites in the upper-left corner of the Lienzo (Fig. 124) which are outside a range of mountains that encloses the valley of Zacatepec on the East (the range represented at the bottom of the top third of the Lienzo). But because none of the names of Zacatepec's *estancias* is known, this is mere conjecture. The representation of the dependencies as small churches not identified by a pre-Conquest place sign is reminiscent of the 1580 *Relación* Map of Teozacoalco (Fig. 132), in which Teozacoalco's subjects are indicated not by place signs but by a small church roofed with a terraced fret that is topped by a cross.

The most distinctive feature of the second Lienzo of Zacatepec is the profusion of plants, animals, and birds that are scattered throughout the map. Birds are shown eating the berries of trees and shrubs (Fig. 126); a lizard perches on a flowering plant (Fig. 126, bottom); a toothy quadruped, perhaps a coyote or ocelot, lurks near the site of one of the subject towns (Fig. 130b). None of these flora or fauna appears to be linguistically or cartographically inspired; that is, these motifs do not seem to represent a place name or any distinctive landscape feature. This rather delightful assortment of wildlife is used merely as space-filling ornament, a frivolity that is rare in sixteenth-century Mixtec maps and completely foreign to a map of indigenous inspiration such as Zacatepec 1, in which only persons and places which can be given proper names are depicted, and the space separating these persons and places is left austerely blank.

Perhaps the only other sixteenth-century Mixtec map which approaches the lyrical qualities of Zacatepec 2 is the 1579 *Relación* Map of Texupan (Fig. 37a). In the Texupan map the interiors of the hills that surround the town are filled with plants and shrubs, many of which are placed at oblique angles so that they seem to be blown by the wind. Many of these hills are also peppered with light-colored dots, which heighten their two-dimensional tapestry-like quality. On the left side of the map the major river is flanked by tall grass and rushes which are appended to both sides of the band of water in the manner of a decorative fringe. Nonetheless, in the Texupan map the decorative elements are for the most part botanical and are used to define the landscape features. This map does not have the "earthly paradise" aura of Zacatepec 2, where the scatter pattern of animals, birds, and plants is

---

[10] The information that Cerro de la Campana, near the present-day town of Zaragoza, was the *pueblo viejo* site of Zacatepec was given to me by the town officials of Zacatepec. In 1892, when the two Lienzos were brought to Mexico City, the citizens of Zacatepec also described Cerro de la Campana as the former site of Zacatepec. (Peñafiel, *LZ*, 2: "Cerro de la Campana, donde estuvo situado Zacatepec.") A similar story is reported by Gutierre Tibón (*Pinotepa Nacional* [Mexico, 1962], 190), who was told in Zacatepec that the first location of the town was on a plain near the junction of the rivers of Atoyaquillo and Reforma.

[11] *RMEH* II, 159: "*Este pueblo de çacatepeque esta asentado en una loma de un çerro pequeño que está á orillas de un Rio que corre de oriente á puniente que en tiempo de aguas es muy caudaloso. . . . hay deste dho. pueblo al de los amusgos cuatro leguas pequeñas de caminos asperos y torçidos . . . á la vanda del Sur . . . .*"

[12] *PNE* I, entry no. 98; *RMEH* II, 162. The *Suma de Visitas* gives the tribute-paying population of Zacatepec as 550 and states that the tribute consisted of 30 pesos of gold and a load (*carga*) of honey every 80 days, plus an annual tribute of 115 pieces of clothing—skirts (*naguas*) and shirts (*camisas*)—and the labor of 34 Indians. The 1580 *Relación* says that the tribute-paying population at that time was 366. The *Relación* does not specify the amount or nature of the Colonial-period tribute, but it indicates that in the pre-Conquest period, the native ruler of Zacatepec received cloth, jewels, green stones, and labor (*RMEH* II, 160).

reminiscent of late-fifteenth- and early-sixteenth-century woodcuts of the Garden of Eden (Fig. 131c).

But the actual plants and animals in Zacatepec 2 are local products, and their random distribution throughout the map probably reflects the "scattered-attribute space" of the pre-Conquest manuscripts. "Scattered-attribute space," as defined by Robertson, is the even sifting of motifs on the page of a manuscript: "The large number of figures, forms, and signs seem to float on the picture plane held in place by a strong system of lines and frames."[13] In Zacatepec 2 the "lines and frames" are not the red guide-lines that set forth the pattern of reading in the pre-Conquest manuscripts, but cartographic elements such as rivers and roads.

The bushes and shrubs within the hills and especially in the lower third of Zacatepec 2 (Figs. 128–29) resemble the plant life in a map drawn in 1595 as supporting evidence in a land grant petition (Fig. 133).[14] The site of land for which the petition was written is located within the town of Cuquila in the Mixteca Alta; this town is represented by the church at the bottom of the map, with the neighboring towns of Chicahuaxtla and Mixtepec depicted by the two churches at the top of the map.[15] The 1595 Cuquila land-grant map still utilizes the pre-Conquest convention for flowing water in the river which flows near Cuquila, and the friezes supporting the roofs of the buildings contain fretwork patterns. Three of the hills in this map also retain the knobby outline used in pre-Conquest place signs to indicate the rough, stony surface of hills. This 1595 land-grant map, as well as the 1597 Tlazultepec Genealogy (Fig. 30), demonstrates that pre-Conquest pictorial conventions survived in some parts of the Mixteca into the last decade of the sixteenth century. Neither Cuquila, in whose archive the 1595 map was originally deposited, nor Tlazultepec were ever major centers of Spanish population; the same may be said of Santa María Zacatepec.[16]

Thus, notwithstanding the features which Zacatepec 2 shares with the 1580 Map of Teozacoalco and the 1579 Map of Texupan, it is possible that the second Lienzo was drawn as late as the 1590's. On the basis of its style, then, the second Lienzo of Zacatepec can be dated roughly 1580–1600. This would place it at least one generation, and possibly as many as two generations, later than the first Lienzo, which was tentatively dated 1540 to 1560.

THE PLACE SIGN OF ZACATEPEC

In Lienzo of Zacatepec 1, the place sign of Zacatepec (Fig. 116a) appears at the left side of a frieze within the top quarter of the large rectangle that delineates Zacatepec's boundaries. The compound sign, consisting of two hills attached by a line, is unusual because it is a bilingual sign, which represents Zacatepec's Mixtec and Nahuatl names.

The tall thin hill directly behind the seated figure of the woman named 13-Wind "Flowers-Feathers" represents the Mixtec name of Zacatepec: *yucu satuta* in the 1593 Reyes list, and *yucu chatuta* in the dialect of Zacatepec where the *s* of the Reyes dialect is *ch*. The Mixtec name means "the hill of Seven-Water." *Yucu* means "hill," and *satuta* is the date Seven-Water in the special Mixtec calendrical vocabulary. *Sa* is the calendrical numeral Seven, and *tuta* is the day-sign Water.[17] And within the tall thin hill in Zacatepec 1 is the pictorial sign for Seven-Water: seven dots and the day-sign Water.

The sign that represents Zacatepec's Mixtec name has several other pictorial elements in addition to the date Seven-Water. At the base of the hill is a front-facing "earth monster" mask, whose jaws enclose eleven "star-eyes." Appended to the slopes of the tall hill are four bald human heads, two on each side of the hill. At the summit of the hill is a Janus-head bird, probably an eagle, from which emerges what appears to be thick curls of smoke or a plant topped with a sign for a jewel. The meaning of these "extra" elements is unknown, and they seem to have no relation to Zacatepec's Mixtec name *yucu satuta*, when this name is translated as "Hill of Seven-Water."

In his unpublished study of the first Lienzo of Zacatepec, Alfonso Caso suggests that *yucu satuta* may be translated as "hill of the poisonous herb," because the Mixtec word *satu* can mean "poisonous herb."[18] It is possible that the twisted configuration at the top of the tall hill of Zacatepec is a plant and that it depicts the word *satu*, but the calendrical name Seven-Water seen within the hill seems to represent more completely the qualifying element *satuta*.

A second, smaller hill is attached to the tall hill by a thin line, and this second hill represents the Nahuatl name "zacatepec," or "zacate hill." *Zacate* is a generic term which refers to a great number of grass-like plants (Fig. 117) that are used principally as fodder for animals. In all probability, then, the second place sign, a hill with grass, depicts the Nahuatl name "zacatepec." The grass used in this sign is somewhat different from the pictorial sign for zacate used in Nahuatl signs, where the plant is represented in much the same manner as the grass which

---

[13] *Mexican Manuscript Painting*, 61.

[14] This map is in the Archivo General de la Nación, Ramo de Tierras, 876–1, fol. 122.

[15] The site of land, shown near the center of the map as a horizontal oval with the gloss *sitio de estancia*, was requested as a grazing site for sheep and goats (*estancia de ganado menor*) by the citizens of Cuquila (*ibid.*, fol. 111–21). According to the legends on the map, the site in question is one and one-half leagues from Cuquila (the church at the bottom of the map), almost three leagues from Chicahuaxtla (the church in the upper-left corner), and three leagues from Mixtepec (the church in the upper-right corner).

[16] Antonio de Alcedo in his 1786–1789 *Diccionario geográfico-histórico* (I, 716; V, 428) says that Cuquila has 76 families of Indians and that Zacatepec has 98 Indian families, but does not give a figure for the number of non-Indians in either town. Usually if a town has a substantial Spanish or non-Indian population, it is indicated in Alcedo—as, for example, in the entry for Pinotepa Nacional (IV, 224–25), whose population is given as 40 families of Spaniards, 74 families of mulattos, and 236 families of Indians.

[17] The calendrical vocabulary is apparently no longer known in Zacatepec, where the translation given to me for *yucu cha tuta* was "hill of his atole." In the everyday Mixtec vocabulary, *cha-* is the third person singular possessive pronoun ("his, her, its"), and *tuta* means "atole," a pap-like beverage made from corn flour boiled in water. In the Alvarado dictionary *tuta* also means "atole" and "pap" (*puchas*).

[18] "El Lienzo de Zacatepec," 11.

appears in one of the signs of Zacatepec's boundaries (Fig. 120a). But I believe that the grass-like plant on the hill attached to the sign of Zacatepec's Mixtec name also represents the zacate plant, and that the second sign representing the town's Nahuatl name is intended to identify beyond a doubt the name of the town whose lands and boundaries are delineated in the map.

In the second Lienzo of Zacatepec, only the sign of the Nahuatl name "zacatepec" is represented (Fig. 116b). The tall thin form of the hill in Zacatepec 2 is virtually identical in shape to the hill sign that represents the Mixtec name of Zacatepec in the first Lienzo. But the qualifying element at the top of the hill is clearly the zacate plant, and the hill is labeled with the Nahuatl name "cacatepec." As discussed earlier, the place sign of Zacatepec in both Lienzos do not represent the present-day site of Zacatepec, but the earlier or *pueblo viejo* site of the town, on the Cerro de la Campana near the present-day town of Zaragoza.

SIGNS OF TOWNS BORDERING ZACATEPEC

According to the 1547-1550 *Suma de Visitas*, the town of Zacatepec is bounded by Putla, Ayozinapa, and Amusgos.[19] The towns of Atoyac and Ixtayutla are also said to bound Zacatepec.[20] The signs of all these towns, with the possible exception of Ayozinapa, appear in Lienzo of Zacatepec 1. The sign of Ayozinapa may also have appeared in the Lienzo, but this town, which no longer exists, was located west of Zacatepec in the present-day state of Guerrero, and thus would have been at the bottom of the Lienzo, which is partially destroyed.[21]

The signs of towns which bounded Zacatepec are placed outside the rectangle of the boundaries on three sides of the Lienzo—left, bottom, and right. The sequence of signs placed at the top of the Lienzo depicts historical events at places which are assumed to have little or no cartographic relationship to the lands of Zacatepec. On the other three sides the place signs which face outward represent major town units or *cabeceras* which shared boundaries with Zacatepec. Three signs are placed outside the boundaries and face inward: a plain with a lizard and a platform with a bird on a drum, both on the left side of the Lienzo, and a hill with an eagle at the bottom of the Lienzo.[22] These signs represent outlying or subject towns rather than *cabeceras*.

The left side of the Lienzo corresponds approximately to the direction north, and this border contains the signs of Putla and Santiago Yosotiche, as well as a sign which may represent the town of Santa Cruz Itundujía. Owing to the frayed condition of the lower edge of the Lienzo, most of the signs of towns which bounded Zacatepec on the west have been at least partially destroyed, and the only sign from this section of the Lienzo which will be discussed is that of Amusgos, which appears inside the rectangle at the lower-right corner. The right side contains the signs of five towns south of Zacatepec. Reading from bottom to top, these signs represent the towns of: San Pedro Jicayán, Pinotepa de Don Luis, San Pedro Atoyac, San Agustín Chayucu, and Santiago Ixtayutla.

Putla

The place sign of Putla, a town which bounded Zacatepec on the north, appears at the left of the rectangle of boundaries (Fig. 113). This sign consists of a frieze with three axes and represents one of Putla's Mixtec names, *ñuu caa*, or "town of metal." *Ñuu* means "town" and is depicted by the frieze; *caa* means "metal" and is depicted by the axes, a standard logogram for "metal" in both Mixtec and Nahuatl place signs.

Putla also has a second Mixtec name not represented in the sign in Zacatepec 1: *ñuu ñuma*, or "town or place of smoke."[23] (*Ñuu* = "town, place where something exists"; *ñuma* = "smoke.") This second name is analogous to the Nahuatl name, "putla," which is derived from *pochtlan* or "place of smoke." According to the Reyes grammar, a very similar Mixtec name *ñu ñuma*, refers to the entire region around Putla: "And that entire mountain toward Putla which is the beginning of the Coast is called *ñuñuma*, because of the great deal of mist that is usually seen there, and because of the density of the mist, it looks like smoke, which is *ñuma* in Mixtec."[24] The *ñu* prefix of *ñuñuma* is an abbreviation of *ñuhu* or "land." Reyes goes on to say that the Coastal region itself was called by three other names:

The Coast, which begins at Putla, is called *ñundaa*, because the land there is flat, and *ñuñama*, which is land of the cornstalks, and *ñundeui* ["land of the sky"], because the land there more closely resembles the horizon, which they call *Sahaandevui*, which means "the foot of the sky."[25]

In Lienzo of Zacatepec 1, one of the personages associated with the place sign of Putla is mentioned in the 1580 *Relación* of Putla. According to the *Relación*:

---

19 *PNE* I, entry no. 98.

20 *PNE* I, entry nos. 304 (Atoyac, here called "Yzcatoyaque") and 305.

21 In the *Suma de Visitas* the towns of Amusgos and Putla are also said to be bounded by Ayozinapa (*PNE* I, entry nos. 32 and 452). The *Relación* of Tecuanapa, Guerrero, probably written about 1580, reports that Ayozinapa was about 20 leagues from the sea and four leagues from Xicayan de Tovar (J. Eric S. Thompson, ed., "The Relación de Tecuanapa, Guerrero," *Tlalocan*, Vol. V-1 [1965], 90). Dahlgren (*La mixteca*, Map IIIa) places the site of this town as northwest of Zacatepec and northeast of Xochixtlahuaca, Guerrero. Thompson (in the map accompanying the Relación of Tecuanapa) places Ayozinapa on the Río Ometepec about ten kilometers northeast of Tlacoachixtlahuaca, Guerrero.

22 Of these three signs, only the plain with the iguana (Santiago Yosotiche) will be discussed, because the identification of the other two signs is uncertain.

23 The name *ñuu ñuma* appears to be earlier than *ñuu caa*, although both names were current in the sixteenth century. In the Reyes 1593 list of town names, the entry for Putla reads: "*ñuu caa*, 1. *ñuuñuma*."

24 Reyes, "Arte en lengua mixteca," ii: ". . . *y toda aquella cordillera hasta Puctla que es el principio de la costa llamaron* ñuñuma, *por las muchas nieblas que alli se veen ordinariamente y por su espesura parecen humo, que en la lengua Mixteca se dize* ñuma."

25 *Ibid.*: "*A la cuesta del mar del sur, que se sigue a Puctla llamaron* ñundaa, *por ser tierra llana, y* ñunama *que es lo caña de Mahiz, y* ñundeui, *por que se parece mejor en aquella tierra el oriçonte que llaman* Sahaandevui, *que quiere dezir el pie del cielo.*" In the Alvarado dictionary only two of these names, *ñuundevui* and *ñuundaa*, are given for the Coast (*costa del mar del sur en esta tierra*).

Before the Spaniards came, this town of Putla had as ruler a cacique whose Mixtec name was *cusiviçu*, and they say that they did not recognize [as ruler] anyone else in all the land except this *cusiviçu* . . . . And when the cacique of this town who was named *cusiviçu* waged war with the Mexicans and with those of the province of Tututepec, they carried their *macanas* [a double-edged sword of obsidian blades] and shields and bows and arrows and their *ichcahuipiles*, which is quilted cotton armor.[26]

The Mixtec name *cusi viçu* is the personal name of ♂ 8-Lizard "Flints-Tiger," whose figure is attached to the place sign of Putla (Fig. 113). In this instance, the two words which make up 8-Lizard's personal name are in the special calendrical vocabulary used for day signs. *Cusi* is the day-sign Flint; *viçu* or *huidzo* is the day-sign Tiger.

This use of the calendrical vocabulary to express the elements of personal names is at variance with the glosses of personal names written on Codex Sánchez Solís, in which the normal Mixtec vocabulary is used for all personal names. For example, in the case of ♂ 5-House (Fig. 6e), whose personal name is "Tlaloc Flint," the "flint" portion of the personal name is glossed as *yuchi*, "flint blade" in everyday Mixtec, rather than *cusi*, the day-sign Flint. It is obvious that the calendrical vocabulary was not lost when Sánchez Solís was annotated, because all calendrical names of persons in the manuscript are given in this vocabulary. The use of calendrical vocabulary for personal names in the 1580 *Relación* of Putla may be a regional usage, or it may represent an older custom retained in the relatively isolated area around Putla, but which was lost in the more quickly acculturated Mixteca Baja by the time Sánchez Solís was annotated.

Attached to the figure of ♂ 8-Lizard "Flints-Tiger" is another personage, ♂ 10-House "Tlaloc Sun," who is not mentioned in the 1580 *Relación* and who does not appear as a historical figure in the pre-Conquest manuscripts. It is possible that 10-House is either the father or the son of 8-Lizard. He may also be an ally of 8-Lizard, either a ruler or warrior from a neighboring town or a deity impersonator.[27] And the situation of Putla as represented in Zacatepec 1 would seem to require an ally. For within the boundary rectangle and attached by a line to the figure of 10-House is another place sign of Putla,

here shown as a crenelated wall with axes. Issuing from the mouth of 10-House are two drawn-out speech scrolls, but whatever was said apparently had no effect, for the sign of Putla within the rectangle is shown as conquered. It is placed in the center of the warpath of ♂ 3-Reed, who is shown running toward the sign armed with shield and macana (Figs. 97–98); and the place sign itself is penetrated by an arrow, the traditional sign of conquest.

A column of smoke also rises from the crenelated wall; and while the smoke may represent Putla's alternate name, *ñuu ñuma*, or "place of smoke," it is more likely that it signifies that the town of Putla was burned and destroyed at the time of 3-Reed's attack. As is seen in the conquest of another town, Santa María Acatepec (Fig. 51a), a town may be shown as destroyed when small flames are appended to its place sign. I believe that the smoke in this sign of Putla has the same implications, because it is juxtaposed with the conquering arrow rather than with the axes which are this sign's qualifying element.

Santiago Yosotiche and Santa Cruz Itundujía(?)

Above the place sign of Putla on the left side of Zacatepec 1 is a sign consisting of an iguana on the feather-mat motif for valley or plain (Fig. 96). This sign represents Santiago Yosotiche, a town about five miles southeast of Putla. *Yoso* means "plain, valley," and *tiche* means "iguana."[28] The place sign of Yosotiche also includes a small church which indicates that the town may have been a ceremonial center. But it was not a major town unit or *cabecera*, and thus its place sign faces the interior of the Lienzo rather than the border, as does the sign which is placed directly above it.

The identity of the latter sign, a hill that contains large black drop-like forms, is less certain. This place sign may represent the town of Santa Cruz Itundujía, which according to the 1892 Huitrado map of Zacatepec (Fig. 139) bounded Zacatepec on the northeast and east. On this map the town of San Andrés is placed between Putla and Santa Cruz Itundujía. This town, whose full name is San Andrés Cabecera Nueva, did not exist in the sixteenth century, and its lands probably belonged to Putla, Zacatepec, Itundujía. Thus on the north side of Zacatepec, which is represented by the left side of Zacatepec 1, Putla and Itundujía were the principal towns that bounded Zacatepec.

The Mixtec name *itnu ndujia* is usually translated as "slope of foam" or "slope of *pozol*."[29] (*Pozol* is a stew made of hominy and some meat, usually pork.) *Itnu* means "slope"; in the Dyk-Stoudt vocabulary, *nduxià*, the equivalent of *ndujia* in the dialect of San Miguel el Grande, means "*posole*." Moreover, in this same vocabulary, *nduxian*, with nasalization of the final vowel, means "to vomit." None of these meanings of *ndujia* correlates exactly with a hill containing large drops, although *pozol* is liquid and "to vomit" implies falling liquid. The Mixtec word for "drop" (*gota*) is *yuyu*, which does not appear as

---

[26] *RMEH* II, 156, 158: "*este pueblo de puctla antes que los españoles viniesen tenian por señor a vn cacique que a llamavan en su lengua misteca* cusiviçu *y dicen no reconocieron de toda la tierra por señor sino á este* cusiviçu . . . . *Y quando el cacique deste pueblo que se llamava* cusiviçu *tenia guerra con los mexicanos y con los de la provincia de* tututepeque *llevaran su macanas y rodelas y arcos y flechas y sus* ichcahuypiles *que son unas armas estofades mantas y algodon.*"

[27] In the post-Conquest Selden Roll, there is a ♂ 10-House with a Tlaloc-like headdress of triangular points who appears with three other individuals wearing the same headdress and named ♂ 13-Lizard, ♂ 4-Monkey, and ♂ 9-Vulture. All four of these persons wear the black facial paint of priests and have no personal name other than the Tlaloc headdress. They always appear together: first as penitents making an offering at a temple of Quetzalcoatl, then in conference with a person named ♂ 2-Dog and subsequently defending a fortified hill, and finally lighting the Fire of the New Year. The 10-House in the Selden Roll, however, does not have a solar disk as part of his personal name, and thus it is not at all certain that the 10-House in Zacatepec 1 is related to this deity impersonator.

[28] *Titi* in the dialect of the Coast; *ti'ichi* in the dialect of San Miguel el Grande.

[29] Martínez Gracida, *BSMGE* 1888, 338.

part of the Mixtec name of any of the towns north of Zacatepec.

Another possible objection to designating the hill with drops as Itundujía is that this sign appears directly above the sign of Santiago Yosotiche, and Santa Cruz Itundujía is located about 16 miles southeast of Yosotiche. But in Zacatepec 1 the relationships between the towns which bound Zacatepec are relative, and the signs of towns are not located by any absolute scale of linear distances. In addition, the hill with drops is placed on the same level of the map as the River with Animal Hide on the right side of the map. The latter sign represents the town of Santiago Ixtayutla, and Ixtayutla is virtually on the same degree of longitude as Itundujía: about 97°40′ West of Greenwich. Thus the hill with drops appears in the general location where Itundujía should be.

I would say, then, that this place sign may represent Itundujía, but principally by default—because there does not seem to be any other town north or northeast of Zacatepec which can be represented by the hill with drops. But the correlation of the Mixtec name *itnu ndujia* with this pictorial sign is by no means clear or convincing.

Amusgos

The place sign of Amusgos, which bounds Zacatepec on the southwest, appears within the rectangle of boundaries in Zacatepec 1 (Figs. 111, 114). The inclusion of Amusgos within the rectangle apparently does not imply that the town was subject to Zacatepec; it was probably an expedient means of preserving the rectangular border of the map, because the signs of boundaries between Zacatepec and Amusgos are placed diagonally across the lower-right corner of the rectangle (Fig. 141). In the analogous section of Zacatepec 2 (Fig. 129), only the signs of the boundaries appear, and the sign of Amusgos is omitted, as are all the signs of towns that bounded Zacatepec. In addition, all of the Colonial sources list Amusgos as an autonomous *cabecera* and not as a subject of Zacatepec.

Amusgos is the center of a population which speaks a native language called "Amuzgo," a language that is different from Mixtec.[30] The present-day Amuzgo-speaking peoples are concentrated in a small area in southwestern Oaxaca and southeastern Guerrero (shown in Map 2). There are today Amuzgo speakers in Zacatepec; and according to the 1580 *Relación* of Zacatepec, there were Amuzgo speakers in Zacatepec in the sixteenth century.[31]

The place sign of Amusgos in Zacatepec 1 (Fig. 114) represents the town's present-day Mixtec name, which is *ñuu ñama*, usually translated as "town of the *totomoxtle*, or corn husk." This Mixtec name is very similar to *ñu-ñama*, or "land of the corn stalks," one of the names given

by Reyes for the region of the Coast.[32] According to the Alvarado dictionary, the word *ñama* may also mean "ball used in ballgames" (*bola para jugar a la pelota*) and "cocoon" (*capullo*). The qualifying element on the right side of the frieze of the Amusgos sign seems to combine these last two meanings of *ñama*, because it is circular and is divided by crossed lines as is the ball in the center of a ballcourt scene in Codex Bodley (Fig. 115), and because the small radiating lines around the ball suggest the downy quality of a cocoon. The *ñuu* element of the name *ñuu ñama* is of course depicted by the frieze itself.

The 1593 Reyes list of town names gives two different names for Amusgos, but does not include the name *ñuu ñama*. In Reyes, *yodzo taca* is listed as the Mixtec name of "Amusgos primeros," and *yodzo cosa* as "Amusgos segundos." Martínez Gracida translates *yodzo taca* as "plain of the *cuadrilla*, or section of a town," and *yodzo cosa* as "plain of the rabbit."[33] Gutierre Tibón reports that Santa María Amusgos is called *yodzo taca*, or "plain of the bird nest" and that San Pedro Amusgos is called *yodzo cosa* or "plain of the rabbit."[34]

Neither of these names seems to be represented in Lienzo of Zacatepec 1. In the name *yodzo taca, yodzo* means "plain," and *taca* can mean "bird nest." The translation of Martínez Gracida of *taca* as "section of a town (*cuadrilla*)" is probably related to the meaning of *taca* as "persons or animals grouped together." For example, in the Alvarado dictionary:

ee taca te	=	flock (*rebaño de ganado*)
	ee =	one, a
	te =	animal suffix
ee taca ticachi	=	herd of sheep (*hato de ovejas*)
	ee =	one, a
	ticachi =	sheep (literally, "cotton animal"; *ti-* = animal prefix, *cachi* = cotton)
ee taca quete	=	herd of animals (*manada de ganado*)
	ee =	one, a
	quete =	animal
dza taca ñuu	=	to populate a town (*poblar ciudad*)
	dza- =	causative verb prefix
	dzataca	also means "to glean, gather, scrape together" (*rebañar*)
	ñuu =	town

Also given as definitions of *taca* in the Alvarado dictionary are "chisel" (*escoplo*) and "magpie" (*pito ave*).

As mentioned above, both Martínez Gracida and Tibón translate *yodzo cosa*, the name given by Reyes for "Amusgos segundos," as "plain of the rabbit." If *cosa* means "rabbit," it must be a local term. Usually, in the normal Mixtec vocabulary, "rabbit" is *idzo*; in the calendrical vocab-

---

[30] The modern bibliography on the Amuzgo language and a summary of the theories concerning the relationship of Amuzgo to Mixtec and to the other Oaxacan languages are included in Jiménez Moreno's introduction to the 1962 edition of the Alvarado dictionary.

[31] *RMEH* II, 159: "*todos los naturales deste dicho pueblo hablan la lengua* misteca *y otra lengua que llaman* amusga *muy oscura y algunos la* mexicana." Today, the Amuzgo speakers in Zacatepec are concentrated in the barrios of El Rosario and Coyulito. Most of the Nahuatl speakers now live in the vicinity of La Culebra, west of Zacatepec.

[32] "Arte en lengua mixteca," ii; quoted above, note 25.

[33] "Reseña histórica del antiguo reino du Tututepec," p. 182 of the Van de Velde copy and p. 285 of the Castañeda Guzmán copy. The various copies of this manuscript are discussed in Appendix D.

[34] *Pinotepa Nacional*, 202.

ulary the day-sign Rabbit is *sayu*. On the Coast today, a Mixtec word is no longer used for "rabbit," which is called *cuneshu*, from *conejo*, the Spanish word for "rabbit." In fact, in the dialect of the Alvarado dictionary, *cosa* does not seem to be a word at all; and if the *cosa* of the name *yodzo cosa* is Mixtec, it may be in the special calendrical vocabulary and mean the day or calendrical name 1, 2, or 12 Eagle. (*Co* is the numerical prefix 1, 2, or 12; *sa* is the day-sign Eagle.)

Both Martínez Gracida and Tibón report that *yodzo cosa* is the name of San Pedro Amusgos. San Pedro is the saint's name of the present-day town of Amusgos, whose Mixtec name was invariably reported to me as *ñuu ñama*, Perhaps in the early Colonial period *ñuu ñama* referred to the entire Amuzgo-speaking region of the Coast, and then later became the name used to designate the town of Amusgos itself.

San Pedro Jicayán

The place signs of towns which are located south of Zacatepec begin in the lower-right corner of Zacatepec 1 with the sign of San Pedro Jicayán (Figs. 111, 58*a*), which is a frieze containing speech scrolls. This place sign is discussed in Chapter 5, under "Place Signs with the Marsh-Grass Motif," p. 71.

Pinotepa de Don Luis

Above the place sign of Jicayán (Fig. 111) is a sign which consists of the head and shoulders of a human figure who raises one hand to his mouth. This is the place sign of Pinotepa de Don Luis, which bounds Jicayán on the east.

The "Don Luis" in question is Don Luis de Castilla, a Spanish noble who came to Mexico in 1530 and who had succeeded Pedro de Alvarado as overlord or *encomendero* of the Tututepec region at least as early as 1542.[35] According to the 1547–1550 *Suma de Visitas*, Pinotepa de Don Luis was a subject of Tututepec.[36] The seventeenth-century documents on Tututepec's domain say that only one section (*barrio*) of Pinotepa de Don Luis, named *ñuñee*, belonged to Tututepec.[37] The adjectival clause "de Don Luis" continues to be added to the name of this Pinotepa to distinguish the town from the larger town of Pinotepa Nacional (Pinotepa del Rey in the Colonial period), located about nine miles southwest of Pinotepa de Don Luis. In the *Suma de Visitas*, Pinotepa de Don Luis is designated as "the little Pinotepa" (*Pinoteca la Chica*) and Pinotepa Nacional as "the big Pinotepa" (*Pinoteca la Grande*).[38]

The 1593 Reyes list gives *doyo yuhu* as the Mixtec name of "Pinotecpa," without specifying which Pinotepa the name designates. This Mixtec name is definitely that of Pinotepa de Don Luis, for the Mixtec name of Pinotepa Nacional is usually given as *ñuu yoco*.[39] *Doyo* or *ndoyo* has a number of meanings: damp or mist (*liento*); to be flooded (*aregarse*); wet, marshy land; something secret (*secreta cosa*); to be stolen; to lift (*levantar*).

It is this last meaning, "to lift or raise," which is depicted in the sign of Pinotepa de Don Luis in Zacatepec 1, and the verb is expressed by the hand raised to the mouth. The *yuhu* portion of the Mixtec name of Pinotepa de Don Luis means "mouth."

Today on the Coast, Pinotepa de Don Luis is no longer called *ndoyo yuhu*, but *ndoo yuhu*. According to the citizens of the town, *ndoo* means "to wash" and *yuhu* means "mouth."[40] What the change from *ndoyo* to *ndoo* may represent is merely a contraction, such as that which occurred when the place name "Saint Botolph's tun" became the name we know today as "Boston." But in the sixteenth century, when the Reyes list of Mixtec names was compiled and when Lienzo of Zacatepec 1 was drawn, the name of Pinotepa de Don Luis was *doyo yuhu*.[41]

Atoyac

Above the sign of Pinotepa de Don Luis is a sign that consists of a frieze within a river (Fig. 106, right border) and is the sign of San Pedro Atoyac, a town about five miles north of Jicayán. The present-day Mixtec name of Atoyac is *ñuu yuta* ("town of the river"), often shortened to *ñuta*.[42] The *ñuu* or "town" element is expressed by the frieze, and *yuta* or "river" by the river sign.

Chayucu

The sign above that of Atoyac is a hill to which four human feet are appended, two at the base of the hill as supports and two extending from either side of the hill (Fig. 101, lower-right corner). This sign represents the Mixtec name *chayucu* ("at the foot of the hill") and is the sign of San Agustín Chayucu, located ten miles southeast of Atoyac. *Cha-* is the abbreviated prefix form of *cha'a* ("foot, at the foot of"), equivalent to the *saha* of the Alvarado dictionary dialect; *yucu* means "hill."

The use of four feet to express the prefix *cha-* seems a

---

[35] Francisco A. de Icaza, *Conquistadores y pobladores de Nueva España*, II, No. 511 (Madrid, 1923); Berlin, *Fragmentos desconocidos*, 27. Also Tibón, *Pinotepa Nacional*, 246–47.

[36] *PNE* I, entry no. 456.

[37] These documents are included in Smith, *Colombino*, 76–77; 172–73.

[38] *PNE* I, entry nos. 456 and 454. At the time of the *Suma de Visitas*, Pinotepa de Don Luis was apparently larger than Pinotepa Nacional, for the former town is said to have 400 tribute-paying persons and the latter only 115. The *Suma* also reports that the arroyos of Pinotepa de Don Luis contained gold and that this town's tribute was 61 pesos of gold dust every 80 days. The tribute of Pinotepa Nacional was 17,000 cacaos every 80 days. The 1580 *Relación* of Cuahuitlán (*PNE* IV, 156–57) says that Pinotepa Nacional had at that time 100 tribute payers, but claims that before the

Conquest, Pinotepa had 100,000 men, and that the population was greatly reduced by a smallpox epidemic in 1534 and a measles epidemic in 1544. The estimate of 100,000 for the pre-Conquest population of the town seems rather high.

[39] AGN-Tierras 1875–3, fol. 98, and Mixtec speakers on the Coast. Today, the name of Pinotepa Nacional is usually contracted to *ñyoco*. An alternate Mixtec name for Pinotepa Nacional is given as *ñuu ndiví* in the Dyk-Stoudt Mixtec vocabulary.

[40] According to the Alvarado dictionary, *ndoo* can mean "something clean" (*limpia cosa*) and "clear, as water" (*clara, cosa no turbia*). *Quidza ndoo* means "to clean or purge" (*purgar, limpiar*); *quidza* is a causative, meaning "to make, do."

[41] The Mixtec name of Pinotepa de Don Luis is also written as *doyo yuhu* in the glosses of Codex Becker I; see above, p. 14.

[42] Martínez Gracida (*BSMGE* 1888, 298) gives the Mixtec name of Atoyac as *yuta cano* or "big river," and the list of Mixtec names of Coastal towns in Peñafiel (*LZ*, 3) says that Atoyac's Mixtec name is *ñuu ta cano* ("the town of the big river"), but these names are apparently not in current use today.

bit redundant, especially when this sign is compared with the sign of San Andrés Sachio (Fig. 24c), where the equivalent prefix sa- is depicted as only one profile human foot. But perhaps the scribe who drew Zacatepec 1 felt that if the hill appeared with only the two feet below the base, it might be construed to mean "hill that walks" rather than "at the foot of the hill," and so two extra feet were placed on the sides of the hill sign to make it more explicit.

As was discussed in Chapter VI, the Colonial documents of the late sixteenth and early seventeenth centuries report that the native rulers of Zacatepec also controlled the town of Chayucu. But in Zacatepec 1 the town of Chayucu appears as an autonomous unit, outside the boundaries of Zacatepec.

Ixtayutla

The last of the five signs on the right border of Zacatepec 1 consists of an animal hide within a river sign (Fig. 96) and represents the town of Santiago Ixtayutla, about 15 miles northeast of Chayucu. The Mixtec name of Ixtayutla is *yuta ñii*, which is usually translated as "river of salt." (*Yuta* = "river"; *ñii* = "salt.") But *ñii* can also mean "skin, leather, hide," and it is this meaning that is depicted in the sign of Ixtayutla in Zacatepec 1.[43]

SIGNS OF THE BOUNDARY MARKERS

In Zacatepec 1, fifty place signs representing the names of the town's boundaries surround the large rectangle delineating the lands of Zacatepec. Around the borders of the second Lienzo of Zacatepec are thirty-nine signs representing names of boundaries. The list below is a comparison of the boundary signs in the Lienzos; the figure numbers in parentheses indicate the illustration where each sign may be seen most clearly.

ZACATEPEC 1	ZACATEPEC 2
right border (top to bottom):	*right border (top to bottom):*
1. Plain; bird, torso of female figure (Fig. 96)	1. Plain; bird, torso of female figure (Fig. 125)
2. River with volute; rectangle with feet, ax surrounded by dots (Fig. 96) Cf. sign no. 50.	2. River with volute; rectangle with feet, ax (Fig. 125)
3. Hill; rabbit, moon (Fig. 96) Cf. sign no. 20.	3. Hill; rabbit, moon (Fig. 125)
4. Mound with flat top; head with hand pressing rattlesnake against it (Fig. 101)	4. Head with hand pressing rattlesnake against it (Fig. 125)
5. Declivity; frieze; mouth, small dots (Fig. 101)	5. Declivity; frieze; mound of small dots (Fig. 125)

[43] In the dialect of San Miguel el Grande, as recorded in the Dyk-Stoudt vocabulary, *ñii* means "hide" (*piel*) and "to be scraped or scratched" (*raerse, arañarse*); *ñii* means "salt," and *ñii* is "salty."

ZACATEPEC 1	ZACATEPEC 2
6. Animal skin on plant (Fig. 101)	6. Animal skin on plant (Fig. 125)
7. River with volute; small dots (Fig. 106)	7. River with volute; small dots, sign for stone (Fig. 127)
8. Platform; stones, head (Fig. 106)	8. Platform; stones, head (Fig. 127)
9. Hill; wing-like motif with reclining "S" (Fig. 106)	9. Hill; wing-like motif with reclining "S" (Fig. 127)
10. Platform; plain; coiled rattlesnake (Fig. 106)	10. Platform; plain; coiled rattlesnake (Figs. 127, 129)
11. Platform; bee, date 11-Wind (Fig. 106)	11. Platform; bee, date 11-Wind (Fig. 129)
12. River with volute; plant (Fig. 111)	12. River with volute; plant (Fig. 129)
13. Hill; building; quadruped (Fig. 111)	13. Hill; building; quadruped (Fig. 129)
lower border (right to left):	*lower border (right to left):*
14. Hill (Fig. 111)	14. Hill (Fig. 129)
15. Circular flowing water; tobacco leaves, eye with speech scrolls (Fig. 110)	15. Circular flowing water; tobacco leaves, eye with speech scrolls (Fig. 129)
16. River; fish or aquatic animal? (Fig. 110)	16. River; fish or aquatic animal? (Fig. 129)
17. Mound; water jar, mouth (Fig. 109)	Not in Zacatepec 2
18. River; sun, *zanate* bird, mouth (Fig. 109)	17. River; *zanate* bird (Fig. 128)
19. Declivity; seat or throne (Figs. 109–108)	Not in Zacatepec 2
20. Plateau; moon, rabbit (Fig. 108) Cf. sign no. 3	Not in Zacatepec 2
21. Plateau; water jar, rabbit (Fig. 108)	Not in Zacatepec 2
	left border (bottom to top):
22. Two rivers connected with line (Fig. 107)	18. Two rivers (Fig. 128)
23. Triple hill (Fig. 107)	19. Triple hill (Fig. 126)
left border (bottom to top):	
24. Hill on tripod bowl (Fig. 107)	Not in Zacatepec 2
25. Stone; cross, plant (Fig. 107)	20. Stone; cross, plant (Fig. 126)
26. Stone; seated human figure, *cacaxtli* (Fig. 102)	21. Stone; *cacaxtli*; day-sign House (Fig. 126)

ZACATEPEC 1	ZACATEPEC 2
27. Hill; flowing water with half of the day-sign Movement attached to the water spout; alligator head (Fig. 102)	Not in Zacatepec 2
28. Hill; eagle (Fig. 102)	22. Hill; eagle (Fig. 126)
29. Plain; butterfly (Fig.102)	Not in Zacatepec 2
30. Mound; human head, day-sign Vulture (Fig. 97)	23. Day-sign Vulture (Fig. 126)
31. Plain; frieze; hands pushing plain and frieze signs (Fig. 97)	24. Plain; frieze; hands pushing plain and frieze signs (Figs. 124, 126)
32. Platform (Fig. 97)	Not in Zacatepec 2
33. Declivity; frieze; wing-like motif with reclining "S" (Fig. 97)	25. Declivity; frieze; wing-like motif with reclining "S" (Fig. 124)
34. River; "Xolotl" figure (Fig. 92)	26. River; plant (Fig. 124)
35. Mound; mouth, turtle (Fig. 92)	Not in Zacatepec 2
36. Hill; bald head with insect on top, date or name 6-Deer (Fig. 92)	Not in Zacatepec 2
Not in Zacatepec 1	27. Hill; standing female figure (Fig. 124)
37. Rabbit surrounded by small dots, date 5-Flint (Fig. 92)	Not in Zacatepec 2
38. Hill; frieze; mouth (Figs. 87, 92)	Not in Zacatepec 2
Not in Zacatepec 1	28. Hill; water jar (Fig. 124)
top border (left to right):	
39. Bent hill; flowing water (Fig. 87)	29. Bent hill; flowing water (Fig. 124)
	top border (left to right):
Not in Zacatepec 1	30. Stone platform with cross (Fig. 124)
40. Hill; head with hatchets or mushrooms? (Fig. 88)	Not in Zacatepec 2
Not in Zacatepec 1	31. Bent hill; head of bird or animal? (not clear) (Fig. 124)
Not in Zacatepec 1	32. River; day-sign Water (Fig. 124)
41. River; hummingbird (Fig. 88)	33. River; hummingbird (Fig. 124)
42. Plain; three balls of down, cornhusks? (Fig. 88)	Not in Zacatepec 2

ZACATEPEC 1	ZACATEPEC 2
43. Plain; hill; knotted cloth or plant? (Fig. 89)	34. Plain; hill; knotted cloth or plant? (Fig. 124)
44. Ovoid stone (Fig. 89)	35. Ovoid stone (Fig. 124)
45. Platform; feet, rows of stakes (Fig. 89)	36. Platform; feet, rows of stakes (Fig. 124)
46. Plain; conch shell, plant (chile pepper?) (Fig. 90)	37. Plain; conch shell, plant (chile pepper?) (Fig. 124)
47. Plain; knotted grass (Fig. 90)	38. Plain; knotted grass (Fig. 125)
48. Plain; tree with day-sign Movement (Fig. 90)	39. Plain; tree with day-sign Movement (Fig. 125)
49. Hill with declivity; head, color black (Fig. 91)	Not in Zacatepec 2
50. River; rectangles, axes surrounded by volutes of small dots (Fig. 91). Cf. sign no. 2.	Not in Zacatepec 2

Of the thirty-nine signs in Zacatepec 2, twenty-nine are copies of signs in Zacatepec 1. Five additional signs (nos. 7, 17, 21, 23, and 26 of the Zacatepec 2 list above) have counterparts in Zacatepec 1, although the signs in Zacatepec 2 show minor variations. Another five of the Zacatepec 2 signs appear in the second Lienzo only and do not seem to repeat signs in Zacatepec 1. These five signs are all in the upper-left (northeast) corner of the Lienzo (nos. 27–28, 30–32 of the Zacatepec 2 list above).

The spacing and orientation of some of the boundary signs in Zacatepec 2 is also different from Zacatepec 1. As can be seen in the illustrations of the entirety of the two Lienzos (Figs. 85, 122), both maps show a sign on the left side with a plant on a circular rock which contains a cross. It is close to the bottom of Zacatepec 1; in Zacatepec 2 it is placed in the center of the left border. On the right side of the maps a similar but less drastic change is seen in the spacing of boundary signs in Zacatepec 2. The sign with a human head placed on the sign for stone, which occurs about one-third of the distance above the lower edge of the rectangle in Zacatepec 1, is placed in the center of the right border of Zacatepec 2. As a result, there is a greater concentration of boundary signs in the upper half of both the left and right borders of Zacatepec 2, in contrast to Zacatepec 1 where the boundary signs are for the most part evenly spaced along the rectangular outline.

In addition, several boundary signs which appear in the lower and upper borders of Zacatepec 1 are placed on the left border of Zacatepec 2. The sign of a bent hill with flowing water, the last sign at the left of the top border in Zacatepec 1 (Fig. 87), appears as the top sign in the left border of Zacatepec 2 (Fig. 124). The double-river and triple-hill signs which are placed on the left side of the lower border in Zacatepec 1 (Fig. 107) are the only two signs which occupy the lower half of the left border in Zacatepec 2 (Fig. 122). The sign consisting of a river with a *zanate* bird,[44] which occurs at the center of the lower border of Zacatepec 1, is placed at the far left of the lower border in Zacatepec 2.

What these changes in spacing and alignment of boundary signs in Zacatepec 2 probably represent are cartographic corrections of orientation and scale. As we have seen in the brief discussion above of the road and river patterns of Zacatepec 2, the second Lienzo is more clearly a "map," in the traditional sense of the term, than Zacatepec 1, because in the first Lienzo the space between boundary signs defines their general relationship but is not equivalent to actual linear distance between boundaries.

The differences between the two Lienzos in the spacing of boundary signs may also reflect the shift of the town site of Zacatepec. In the first Lienzo, the large bilingual sign of Zacatepec (Fig. 116a) in the center of the upper third of the Lienzo represents the earlier or *pueblo viejo* site of the town at Cerro de la Campana. Zacatepec 1 does not contain a sign to indicate the present location of the town; if such a sign were to appear, it would be placed in the general vicinity of the long warpath that extends across the bottom third of the Lienzo. But in the second Lienzo the central motif of a church, plaza, and dwellings (Fig. 126) represents the later site of Zacatepec, some 15 miles west and slightly north of Cerro de la Campana. This shift in town site from east to west is also reflected in the spacing of boundaries in Zacatepec 2, for the lower or western section of the second Lienzo is delineated in more detail, and the lower half of Zacatepec 2 is roughly equivalent to the lower quarter of Zacatepec 1.

Zacatepec-Amusgos Boundaries

In addition to the signs of boundaries which appear on the four sides of both Lienzos, a row of place signs placed diagonally across the lower-right corner of the two maps represents the boundaries between Zacatepec and Amusgos. Here, too, there are differences between the signs in Zacatepec 1 and those in Zacatepec 2, which are listed on pp. 106–109.

Lists of Zacatepec's Boundaries

Three documents set forth all the boundaries of Zacatepec. The first of these documents, dated December 1702, is in the Archivo General de la Nación in Mexico City, Ramo de Tierras, vol. 192–5.[45] The other two documents, both dated 1892, are included in Peñafiel's publication of Zacatepec 1. The first of these is a statement by the citizens of Zacatepec concerning their town's boundaries; the second is a map of Zacatepec and its boundaries drawn by José O. Huitrado. A fourth document, AGN-Tierras 191–3,

includes the boundaries between Zacatepec and Amusgos as reported in 1680; and a second map, which is dated 1893 and sets forth the lands claimed by Manuel Yglesias, shows the boundaries between this individual's holdings and the southwestern section of Zacatepec.

AGN-Tierras 192–5. The 1702 document concerns the rental of lands said to be within the boundaries of Zacatepec and includes the testimony of thirty witnesses about the town's boundaries. One of the most detailed accounts of the boundaries of Zacatepec is given by Pedro Hernández, described as a sixty-four-year-old Indian citizen of Santa María Ipalapa. Hernández describes first the boundary line on the north and west edges of Zacatepec as running from the Río de Santa Cruz north to the Hill of Santa Rosa, and west from the Río de Santa Cruz, where Zacatepec shares boundaries with Jicayán de Tovar, to the Río Zanate. The latter river serves as Zacatepec's boundary up to the point where the town begins to share boundaries with Amusgos. Concerning the remainder of Zacatepec's boundaries, he says:

All the rest of the lands which are within the boundaries of the town of Zacatepec [are those bounded by a line which] runs from the *Río de Santa Cruz*, to a slope named *La Mesa*, and from there to a hill called Hill of the Seven Pines (*Monte de los Siete Ocotes*), which is a boundary with the lands of the town of Atoyaquillo. And from there on a straight line to the Hill of the Large Ranch (*Cerro de la Estanzuela*), which bounds the lands of Ixtayutla. And from there on a straight line bounding the lands of the towns of San Cristóbal and Atoyac. And then [Zacatepec] bounds the lands of the town of Amusgos at a site called *Coscomamichi*. And from there to the Hill of Wax (*Cerro de la Cera*), and then to the Hill Possessed with a Devil (*Cerro Endemoniado*) which is also called the Hill That Frightens (*Cerro que Espanta*). And from there it descends on a straight line to the Stone of the Two Mouths (*Piedra de Dos Bocas*), alias [the Stone of] Two Drinking Vessels (*Dos Vasos*), and runs on a straight line to the Stone of the Face (*Piedra de la Cara*), which bounds Llanos de Merino, and from there to the Stony Hill (*Cerro Pedregoso*), and from there to the Hill of the Palmetto Tree (*Cerro de Palmito*); it descends to the river which comes from Jicayán de Tovar and runs on a straight line along this river, named Río Zanate, until it encounters the Río de Santa Cruz, which is the first boundary.[46]

The information on Zacatepec's boundaries given by Hernández and the twenty-nine other witnesses is compiled in Chart 9, "The Boundaries of Zacatepec in 1702."

1892 Testimony by the Citizens of Zacatepec. According to Peñafiel, on March 9, 1892, the citizens of Zacatepec made the following statement concerning their town's boundaries:

Our lands are delimited by the following points: beginning in the center of
—The Orchard of the Rock (*Huerta de Peña*), which belongs to the town of *Siniyuvi*, the boundary,
—*Fondicucuaa*,
next is

---

44 A bird of the Icteridae family (*Quiscalus macrourus*, Sw.), common to tropical regions of the Western Hemisphere.

45 This is the document described very briefly by Peñafiel (*LZ*, 2) as follows: "*En 9 de Diciembre de 1702, el Conde de la Moraleda, Caballero de la Orden de Santiago, Alcade Mayor y Teniente de Capitán General por Su Magestad en la Provincia de Jicayan, mandó levantar información de numerosos testigos para definir los derechos que reclamaban los habitantes de Zacatepec ya mencionados.*"

46 AGN-Tierras, 192–5, fol. 12–12/v. The original text of this document appears in Appendix B–5.

CHART 9: The Boundaries of Zacatepec in 1702

(AGN-Tierras 192–5)

1. Río de Santa Cruz

2. Cerro de Santa Rosa

3. La Mesa

4. Monte de los Siete Ocotes,   boundary with Atoyaquillo
   or Cerro(s) de Atoyaquillo

5. Cerro de la Estanzuela,   boundary with Ixtayutla
   or Cerro de Ixtayutla

6. Site named *coscomamichi*

7. Cerro de la Cera

8. Cerro Endemoniado,
   or Cerro que Espanta,
   or Cerro donde Espantan

9. Piedra de Dos Bocas,   — boundaries with Amusgos
   or Piedra de Dos Vasos

10. Piedra de la Cara*
    (*yuu nuu* in Mixtec)

11. Cerro Pedregoso

12. Cerro del Palmito

13. The river which comes from
    Jicayán de Tovar, which at
    this point is called Río Zanate

14. Río de Santa Cruz

---

*According to some witnesses, the stone in question appears to have a
face painted on it.

—The Hill of the "Cross of the Dead" (*Cruz de Muerto*) then
—San Andrés Viejo
—Rock of the Lion (*Peña de León*)
which is the boundary with the town of Palapa [Ipalapa], then going to
—The Stone "Two Mouths" (*Dos Bocas*), continuing to
—The Stone of the Face (*Piedra de la Cara*);
 Yunú in Mixtec,
continuing to
—The Hill Moniñan; in Mixtec, *Yucucuina,*
—Hill of the Little Doves (*Cerro de Palomitas*);
 in Mixtec, *Yucupatto*
—Hill of the Horse's Neck (*Cerro de Pescuezo de*
 Caballo); in Mixtec, *yucu sucu cuaye*
—The Large Rock of the Ladder (*Peñasco La Escalera*)
passing by the
—Rivers Zanate and Huajuco
continuing to
—The Hill of the Butterfly (*Cerro de Papalote*) where three boundaries join, that is: those of our town, the town of Cuziapa and the town of Suchixtlahuaca, where the above-mentioned rivers join in
—The Arroyo of Santa Cruz;
then on to a large hill named
—Green Hill (*Cerro Verde*),
which again marks the boundaries of three towns: Zacatepec, Suchixtlahuaca, and Huehuetona; then
—the stone named "Hand of the Lion" (*Mano de León*), which is the boundary with Huehuetona, and on to
—The Insect (*El Mosquillo*)
the boundary of Zacatepec, Huehuetona, and San Pedro Tlapa; then to
—the river of Jicayán [de Tovar],
a boundary between our town and San Pedro Tlapa; crossing the Río Jicayán, to
—The Hill of the *Otate* (a bamboo-like plant), a boundary of Tlapa and Zacatepec; continuing to
—The Hill of the "Old Hat" (*Sombrero Viejo*); to the boundaries of Zacateec, Jicayân [de Tovar], and Copala, continuing to
—The Hill of Cotemaca; in Mixtec, *yucha xuvua*, passing by
The Hill of Santa Rosa, boundary with Putla, descending to
—The Little Bird or Turkey (*La Totolita*),
a site called "Seven Pines" (*Siete Ocotes*), and continuing to Atoyaquillo and
—The Hill of the Bell (*Cerro de la Campana*) where Zacatepec was formerly located, then joining with Santiago [Ix]tayutla; next a site called
—Salty Water (*Agua Salada*); in Mixtec,
 Tiyacuiouva,
—Black Rock (*Peña Prieta*); in Mixtec,
 Cavua too,
—Rock of the Earthenware Jar (*Peña de Olla*), at the edge of the town of Mechoacan, Santa María Yosocani,
—The Large Rock of the Insect (*Peñasco del Mosquillo*) and finishing at the large rock called [in Mixtec]
—*Mini cuaa,*
completing the perimeter of our lands, which at this point are bounded by those of the town of San Pedro Siniyuvui already mentioned at the beginning of this account.[47]

1892 Huitrado Map. Peñafiel includes with his illustrations of Zacatepec 1 a relief map of Zacatepec drawn by the engineer José O. Huitrado (Fig. 139–40).[48] This map was probably initially sketched in August 1892, because the first line of script below the kilometer scale reports that the magnetic declination observed on August 12, 1892, was 8°27′ East. The map was completed the following month: in the lower-right corner is the date September 16, 1892, and Huitrado's signature.

As indicated in the second line of script below the kilometer scale in the original map, the boundaries set forth in the map are those which were designated by the citizens of Zacatepec.[49] But a comparison of the boundary names of the Huitrado map and the 1892 statement by the citizens of Zacatepec quoted above clearly shows that there is not a one-to-one correlation between the two descriptions of boundaries. Nor does either of the 1892 documents correlate exactly with the 1702 list of Zacatepec's boundaries. One major difference between the 1702 list and the 1892 map is that in 1702 the town of San Cristóbal, about twenty-three miles southeast of Zacatepec, is considered to bound Zacatepec, whereas in the Huitrado map this town is placed within the boundaries of Zacatepec (Fig. 140).

1893 Map of the Lands of Manuel Yglesias. In 1893 a map was drawn that sets forth the lands claimed by the individual land owner Manuel Yglesias (Fig. 138).[50] These lands are located south and west of Zacatepec and north and west of Jicayán, and include the towns of Amusgos, Ipalapa, Sayultepec, and Camotinchan.

Although this map and the 1892 Huitrado map are virtually contemporary, the two maps do not agree on the names of Zacatepec's boundaries on the southwest, shown at the top of the Yglesias map and in the lower-left corner of the Huitrado map. In the Huitrado map a hill named "Cerro Palo" is considered to be a boundary between Zacatepec and Amusgos, whereas in the Yglesias map this site is shown as within the lands of Yglesias. In the Huitrado map the boundary line between Zacatepec and Amusgos is shown as running through the plain named "Llanos de Merino," but in the Yglesias map this site, too, is within the lands of Yglesias. A third site named "Pescuezo de Caballo" appears in the Huitrado map as a boundary of Zacatepec with Amusgos and Cozoloapan, and in the Yglesias map this site is considered to belong to Domingo

---

[47] Peñafiel, *LZ*, 2.

[48] The Huitrado map illustrated in Figs. 139–40 is a simplified copy based on the Huitrado map as published in Peñafiel, *LZ*, and on a copy of the Huitrado map in the Dirección de Geografía, Meteorología e Hidrología, Mexico City (Colección General, no. 3580). For the sake of clarity, much of the relief detail in the original map is omitted in Figs. 139–40.

[49] "*La tinta carmín marca los linderos señalados por los del Pueblo de Zacatepec.*"

[50] The 1893 Yglesias Map illustrated in Fig. 138 is a simplified copy of a map on tracing paper in the Dirección de Geografía, Meteorología e Hidrología, Mexico City (Colección General no. 3663). The tracing was made and signed by Serafín Beristain and also signed by the engineer H. Espinosa; it measures 34 by 22½ inches. For the sake of clarity, much of the relief detail in the tracing is omitted in Fig. 138.

Ynfante, whose lands bound those of Manuel Yglesias on the north.

The two contradictory claims of boundary sites illustrated by these two contemporary maps are of course the type of disagreement which is the gist of land litigation; and it is very possible that a dispute over boundaries between the citizens of Zacatepec and Manuel Yglesias or another land owner may have been the reason the citizens of Zacatepec brought their lienzos to Mexico City in 1892. For the purposes of the present discussion, the boundaries of Zacatepec as delineated in the Huitrado map are considered to be of greater importance than those shown in the Yglesias map because, as noted above, the Huitrado map purports to set forth the boundaries that are claimed by the citizens of Zacatepec.

AGN-Tierras 191–3. This document is concerned with an early-eighteenth-century dispute between Amusgos and its neighbor to the southwest, San Juan Cacahuatepec. The town of Amusgos brings in various older documents to support its claims, and these documents include a review of the boundaries of Amusgos in 1680.[51] At that time the citizens of Zacatepec described their boundaries with Amusgos as follows:

The boundary of the lands [of Zacatepec] with Llanos de Medina [= Llanos de Merino?] is named *yuhu nuhu* which means "Stones of Eyes" (*piedras de ojos*) which is in the center of a hill named *yucu cuina* which means "Hill of Vision or Apparition" (*cerro de visión o fantasma*); then [the boundary line] descends to a stream named *nduhua tunyacua*, which means "Stream of the *Tlaxhipeguale* Tree" (*Cañada palo de Tlaxhipeguale*); and then goes across the Hill of Santa María, coming out at a site named *itnu socaa*, and concludes at a hill named *yucu ita*, which means "Hill of Roses" (*cerro de rosa*).[52]

Relationship between the Written Documents and the Two Lienzos

A careful comparison of the written lists of Zacatepec's boundaries and the two Lienzos of Zacatepec indicates that neither the lists nor the 1892 Huitrado map correlate exactly with the boundaries of the two sixteenth-century maps. There are, however, a few correlations, such as the Río Zanate which appears in the 1702 list and in the 1892 testimony. The sign for this river appears in both Lienzos: in Zacatepec 1 as a river with a zanate bird accompanied by a human mouth and the sign for the sun (Fig. 109), and in Zacatepec 2 merely as a river with a zanate bird (Fig. 128).

But for the most part, the lists and the 1892 map show little correlation with the Lienzos for the simple reason that the boundaries of Zacatepec in 1702 and 1892 were not the same as they were in the sixteenth century when the maps were drawn. During the Colonial period many towns lost a great deal of their land, either by sale, rental, or appropriation. In addition, many subject towns became separate towns or *cabeceras* and were thus no longer considered as part of the town of which they were formerly a subject.

In the case of Zacatepec, this is particularly evident in the region east of the town—the region represented by the upper section of the two Lienzos. As we have seen, the site named Cerro de la Campana was the former site of Zacatepec, and in both Lienzos the sign of this site is placed well within the rectangle of the boundaries. But in the 1892 testimony and in the 1892 Huitrado map, Cerro de la Campana is considered to be a boundary of Zacatepec rather than a site within the town's boundaries.

Similarly, the site called "Seven Pines" (*Siete Ocotes*), which is given as a boundary of Zacatepec in the 1702 and 1892 lists as well as in the 1892 map, is also within Zacatepec's boundaries in the first Lienzo of Zacatepec. In Zacatepec 1, this site is probably represented by two trees which appear at the left of the large stream of water that represents the Río de la Cuchara (Fig. 93, upper center). One of these trees has on its trunk a circular shield. According to the Alvarado dictionary, the Mixtec word for "shield" is *yusa*, and one of the Mixtec words for "pine" (*pino*) is *yutnu yusa* (*yutnu* meaning "tree"). The shield is used here to specify that this word for "pine" is intended rather than the alternate word given in Alvarado (*yutnu*) *ite*.

In the 1702 review of Zacatepec's boundaries, the hill of "Seven Pines" is said to be the boundary between Zacatepec and Atoyaquillo. The latter town is located near the Río de la Cuchara, and in the two Lienzos it is placed within the rectangle of Zacatepec's boundaries. In Zacatepec 1, the town of Atoyaquillo is represented either by the sign with a frieze, river, and a male figure with the two calendrical signs 5-Reed and 9-Wind (Fig. 89, lower left), or by the adjacent sign with a building in a river, or by both signs, because the two signs seem to be connected by lines to the year-sign Ten-Rabbit. In Zacatepec 2, the town of Atoyaquillo is probably represented by the small building in the upper-left corner, placed above the Río de la Cuchara, the large river with fish which runs diagonally across the top of the map (Fig. 124).

The Zacatepec-Amusgos Boundaries and the Town of Ipalapa

To demonstrate the difficulty of connecting the available written documents that describe Zacatepec's boundaries with specific place signs in the two Lienzos, we shall consider briefly the small group of signs that name the boundaries between Zacatepec and the town of Amusgos, which bounds Zacatepec on the southwest. Zacatepec 1 contains eight signs of boundaries between the two towns (Fig. 141), and Zacatepec 2 contains seven signs of boundaries with Amusgos (Figs. 127, 129). These signs in the

---

[51] AGN-Tierras, 191–3, fol. 55/v ff. This document also contains several intriguing references to a pictorial document belonging to the native rulers of Amusgos in the seventeenth century, and these are quoted and discussed in Appendix B–6.

[52] *Ibid.*, fol. 56: ". . . *el lindero con sus tierras con los llanos de medina se nombra Yuhunuhu que en Castilla se llama piedras de ojos que coresponde em medio un zerro nombrado Yucucuina que en Castilla quiere dezir zerro de Vision o pantasma que ba a caer al Cañada que llaman dûûa tuniacua que quiere desir en Castilla Cañada Palo de Tlaxhipeguale. Y ba subiendo por el zerro de Sta Maria a salir a un puesto que llaman Ytnu socaa y remata a un zerro que llaman yucuu itaa que en Castilla dise zerro de Rosa . . . .*"

two Lienzos are compared in Chart 10, "Boundaries Between Zacatepec and Amusgos in the Two Lienzos of Zacatepec." As we have seen, there are four documents which deal with the Zacatepec-Amusgos boundaries: three lists dated 1680, 1702, and 1892, and the 1892 Huitrado map. The names of boundaries set forth in these docu-ments are compared in Chart 11, "Boundaries Between Zacatepec and Amusgos in Post-Conquest Documents." How do the boundary signs of the two Lienzos correlate with the four lists of boundaries?

It seems very possible that the two human mouths in profile in Zacatepec 1 (Fig. 141) represent the *Piedra de*

CHART 10: Boundaries Between Zacatepec and Amusgos in the Two Lienzos of Zacatepec

Zacatepec 1 (Fig. 141)	*Zacatepec 2 (Figs. 127, 129)*
1. Hill; ladder	1. Hill; ladder (glossed "tlamamaltepec")
2. Hill; plant with *petate*-like leaves	Not in Zacatepec 2
Not in Zacatepec 1	2. River; post-and-lintel motif; shell
3. River with volute; plant	3. Post-and-lintel motif; plant inside
Not in Zacatepec 1	4. River; stone with cross; star-eye
4. Two mouths at side of river	Not in Zacatepec 2
5. River with volute; plant	5. River; post-and-lintel motif; plant on top
6. River with volute; plant with bell-shaped flowers	Not in Zacatepec 2
7. Stones; rectangle, copper ax surrounded by small dots (Cf. signs 2 and 50 of boundary signs appended to large rectangle)	Not in Zacatepec 2
Not in Zacatepec 1	6. Stone; two cylinders
8. Hill; head of deer	7. Hill; head of deer

CHART 11: Boundaries Between Zacatepec and Amusgos in Post-Conquest Documents

1680	1702	1892 Testimony	1892 Huitrado Map
	site named *coscomamichi*		
	Cerro de la Cera		
	Cerro Endemoniado, or Cerro que Espanta		
	Piedra de Dos Bocas, or Dos Vasos	Piedra Dos Bocas	Dos Bocas (boundary with Ipalapa)
Piedras de Ojos (*yuhu nuhu*)	Piedra de la Cara (*yuu nuu*)	Piedra de la Cara (*yunú*)	Piedra Cara
center of Cerro de Visión or Fantasma (*yucu cuina*)	Cerro Pedregoso	Cerro Moniñan (*yucu cuina*)	Cerro Palo
Cáñada Palo de Tlaxhipeguale (*nduhua tunyacua*)	Cerro del Palmito	Cerro de Palomitas (*yucu pattó*)	Cerro Palmito
Cerro de Santa María		Cerro de Pescuezo de Caballo (*yucu sucu cuaye*)	Pescuezo Caballo
itnu socaa		Peñasco La Escalera	
Cerro de Rosa (*yucu ita*)			

Dos Bocas ("stone of two mouths") given in the 1702 and 1892 lists as a boundary between Zacatepec and Amusgos, and in the 1892 Huitrado map as a boundary of Zacatepec and Ipalapa. This sign seems to be absent from Zacatepec 2.

In Zacatepec 2, the sign which consists of a stream containing a stone with a cross and a star-eye (Fig. 129) probably corresponds to the boundary whose Mixtec name is *yuu nuu*, translated in the 1680 list as *piedras de ojos*, or "stones of eyes." (*Yuu* = "stone"; *tinuu* = "star, eye.") In the remaining three lists, this boundary is called "stone of the face" (*piedra de la cara*), which is also *yuu nuu* in Mixtec, for *nuu* means "face."

The "Stream of the *Tlaxhipeguale* Tree," mentioned in the 1680 list, may be represented by one of three boundary signs in Zacatepec 1 which consist of a river with a volute accompanied by a plant (Fig. 141). It may also be represented in Zacatepec 2 by the stream which terminates beneath a post-and-lintel motif which has a plant on the lintel (Fig. 129). But since it is not known what kind of tree is designated by the Nahuatl word *Tlaxhipeguale* or by the Mixtec term *tunyacua*, it is difficult to connect the name of this boundary with a specific sign.

The last boundary sign between Zacatepec and Amusgos in both Lienzos is a hill which terminates in the head of a deer (Figs. 141, 129). This sign is the equivalent of

the site called "Hill of the Horse's Neck" (*Cerro de Pescuezo de Caballo*) which is included in the 1892 list and on the 1892 Huitrado map. The sign as it appears in the Lienzos should be read "Hill of the Deer's Neck," which in the Mixtec dialect of the Alvarado dictionary would be *yucu dzuq idzu*. (*Yucu* = "hill"; *dzuq* = "neck"; *idzu* = "deer.") In the Alvarado dictionary the word for "horse" is also given as *idzu*, and in some regions of the Mixteca, the Mixtec word for "deer" was applied to the horse because there was no word for "horse" in the pre-Conquest vocabulary. In the 1892 testimony the Mixtec name of "Hill of the Horse's Neck" is given as *yucu sucu cuaye*; in the town of Zacatepec, I was told that the Mixtec name of this site is *yucu sucu cuayu*.[53] The *cuayu* section of this name is undoubtedly an adaptation of *caballo*, the Spanish word for "horse." In all likelihood, the name of the site was *yucu sucu isu* in the sixteenth century, and it was first known as "hill of the deer's neck" and later as "hill of the horse's neck." Once the name "hill of the horse's neck" was firmly established, the *isu* or "deer" element was probably changed to *cuayu*, the Spanish loanword for "horse."

In the 1892 list, the entry immediately following *Cerro*

[53] *Yucu sucu cuayu* is still today a boundary of Zacatepec, with the town of San Antonio Ocotlán, located southwest of Amusgos and formerly a subject of Amusgos.

de Pescuezo de Caballo is *Peñasco La Escalera*, or "Large Stone of the Ladder." The latter entry may be out of order, for this description seems to refer to a hill with ladder that appears at the opposite end of the row of Zacatepec-Amusgos boundaries in both Zacatepec 1 (Fig. 141) and Zacatepec 2 (Fig. 127). In the second Lienzo the sign is accompanied by the Nahuatl gloss "tlamamaltepec," which Peñafiel translates as "ladder hill"; *tlamamal-* from *tlamamatlatl,* "ladder," and *-tepec* from *tepetl,* "hill."[54]

We see, then, that in the small sample of signs that represent the boundaries between Zacatepec and Amusgos, there is no one-to-one correlation between the signs of either Lienzo and the known lists of boundaries of Zacatepec with Amusgos. Some of these differences may be due to the fact that by the time the written documents were drawn up, the town of Santa María Ipalapa, east and slightly south of Amusgos, was an autonomous town unit or *cabecera* with lands that formerly belonged to Amusgos, San Pedro Jicayán, and Zacatepec. Ipalapa is not mentioned in the mid-sixteenth-century *Suma de Visitas* or in the other sixteenth-century documents, and at that time it was probably a subject of Amusgos.[55] The general location of Ipalapa in relation to Zacatepec and Amusgos is shown in the 1892 Huitrado map (Fig. 139), and one of the boundaries between Zacatepec and Ipalapa in this map —*Dos Bocas*—is considered to be a boundary between Zacatepec and Amusgos in the 1892 testimony and the 1702 list of Zacatepec's boundaries.

In the second Lienzo of Zacatepec the road which leads out of the central plaza of Zacatepec to the right splits before it reaches the row of signs that represent the Zacatepec-Amusgos boundaries. (Fig. 122). The branch of the road at the left, which runs past the sign which consists of a river containing a rock with a cross and a star-eye, is the road to Amusgos; the branch of the road at the right leads to Ipalapa. According to the officials of Zacatepec, the place where the road splits is called "Dos Caminos" ("two roads," or *uvi iti* in Mixtec), and this site marks the present-day boundary between Zacatepec and Ipalapa. This same site also appears in the upper-right corner of the 1893 map of the lands of Manuel Yglesias (Fig. 138), where it is called "Dos Caminos Nejapilla" and is considered to be a boundary between Zacatepec and the lands of Yglesias. The general extent of the present-day town of Ipalapa may be seen in Map 6, which shows the contemporary municipal units.

The Place Sign of Ipalapa in Zacatepec 1

Although Ipalapa was not a *cabecera* at the time of the Spanish conquest, it may well have been an important ceremonial site. The place sign of Ipalapa appears in the center of the lower section of Zacatepec 1 (Figs. 104–105), and the prominent element at the right side of the sign (Fig. 105) is a church on a platform decorated with the spiral motif which may denote ceremonial sites. The church and platform balance the pre-Conquest style of profile building on the left side of the place sign (Fig. 104), and in front of this building is seated a marriage pair: ♂ 11-Grass "Rattlesnake with Claws Surrounded by Sand" and ♀ 8-Rabbit "Hill with Vulture and Flowers."[56]

As was the case of the place sign of Zacatepec, the place sign of Ipalapa is a bilingual sign which depicts both the Mixtec and Nahuatl names of the town. The Mixtec name of Ipalapa is *ñuu tayu*, which means "town of the seat or throne." *Ñuu* means "town" and is expressed by the long frieze which forms the base of the entire sign, uniting the church on the right with the pre-Conquest building on the left. *Tayu* means "seat or throne" and is expressed by the high-backed seat of woven grass on which 11-Grass is seated.[57] It is interesting to note that 11-Grass is the only ruler in Zacatepec 1 who is seated on a throne of woven grass or *petate*. The rectangular grass mat does appear with ♀ 2 or 10-Dog, the ruler of Zacatepec's subject San Vicente Piñas (Fig. 109), but the only other occurrence of the "throne" motif outside of the compound Ipalapa sign is in a boundary sign on the lower border of the Lienzo (Fig. 108) where it appears within a declivity.

The sign which represents the Nahuatl name is attached to the right side of the frieze of the principal sign by a line (Fig. 105). This sign, slightly destroyed by a small hole in its center, consists of a river and a petate throne and depicts the name "ipalapa" or "throne river." (*Ipal-* from *icpalli*, "throne or seat"; *apa* from *apan*, "river.")

The Boundaries of Zacatepec and Codex Colombino

In my study of the glosses of Codex Colombino, I suggested that the glosses written on page XX of Colombino list the Mixtec names of Zacatepec's boundaries, because *yucu cha tuta*, the Mixtec name of Zacatepec, appears on this page.[58] In view of the large number of boundaries of Zacatepec shown in the two Lienzos, the names of Zacatepec's boundaries probably extend onto page XXI of Colombino. The names of the boundaries of San Pedro Jicayán, whose Lienzo contains fifty boundary signs accompanied by thirty-two Mixtec glosses, occupy two pages of Colombino (XIII and XIV); and it would seem likely that a transcription of the names of Zacatepec's boundaries would also fill more than one page of Colombino.

Unfortunately, pages XX and XXI of Codex Colombino have been so extensively erased that only illegible fragments of the glosses on these two pages are visible, even in ultra-violet photographs of the Codex. The glosses on these pages would have been extremely helpful to the interpretation of the two Lienzos of Zacatepec, not only because they list the Mixtec names of the boundaries of

---

54 *LZ*, 5.

55 In the 1629 will of Juan Rafael de Ávila, native ruler of Amusgos, part of his son's heritage is a group of tribute-paying subjects in both Amusgos and Ipalapa. (AGN-Tierras, 191–3, fol. 70/v: "*em manos de mi hijo dejo todos los mazeguales aqui en S^n Pedro Amusgos y Sta Maria Ypalapa . . . .*")

56 Neither of these personages appears in any other known Mixtec pictorial document.

57 In the Alvarado dictionary, *tayu* means not only "chair, seat" (*silla; asiento de indios*) but also "city, town, palace, province"; "a pair" (*un par; yunta de bueyes*); and "to rot" (*podrecerse*).

58 Smith, *Colombino*, 66–67; 163.

Zacatepec, but also because Colombino was annotated in 1541 and its glosses are thus closer in date to the two Lienzos than any other document that is known at the present time.

HISTORICAL PERSONS AND EVENTS IN ZACATEPEC 1

The principal historical narrative of Zacatepec 1 shows a series of scenes connected by roads and warpaths. This narrative begins in the upper-left corner of the Lienzo, above the rectangle of the boundaries; it proceeds across the top of the manuscript to the right border, then continues in a zig-zag pattern within the large rectangle.

Three generations of rulers appear in this narrative sequence: (1) ♂ 11-Tiger "Tlaloc-Smoking Frieze" and his wife ♀ 11-Monkey "Jeweled Heart"; (2) ♂ 8-Alligator "Tlaloc-Sun" and his wife ♀ 13-Wind "Flowers-Feathers"; (3) ♂ 3-Reed "Smoking Hair-Fire Flint" and his wife ♀ 9-Tiger "Butterfly-Beast." The various activities of these rulers are accompanied by dates, and a list of the events in the principal line of narrative with their respective year dates is on page 117. The correlation of these year dates with Christian year dates is discussed below, pages 116–19.

The First Generation: ♂ 11-Tiger and ♀ 11-Monkey
The first scene of the historical narrative (Figs. 87–88) shows ♂ 11-Tiger, the male ruler of the first generation, seated before ♂ 4-Wind "Fire Serpent" and his wife ♀ 10-Flower "Tlaloc-Cobweb." The couple 4-Wind and 10-Flower are the only assuredly historical personages in Zacatepec 1 who appear in any other known Mixtec pictorial manuscript.[59] The ruler 4-Wind plays an important role in Mixtec history in the late eleventh and early twelfth centuries and appears to have become one of the most powerful Mixtec rulers following the death of ♂ 8-Deer "Tiger Claw" in 1063. He was born in 1040 and was the son of ♂ 11-Wind "Bloody Tiger" and ♀ 6-Monkey "Warband Quechquemitl" of Belching Mountain, whose story is told in detail in Selden 6–8. The first wife of 4-Wind is the woman who accompanies him in the Lienzo of Zacatepec: 10-Flower "Tlaloc-Cobweb," a daughter of ♂ 8-Deer. According to Bodley 29–IV, 4-Wind and 10-Flower were married in 1072; this same manuscript (28–II) also reports that 4-Wind died in 1112.[60]

The principal town ruled by 4-Wind is represented by a place sign consisting of a frieze and flint blades, and he undoubtedly controlled other towns as well. In Codex Bodley, for example, he is shown as ruler of the compound sign which includes a frieze with two flint blades, a coiled serpent, a hoe, a thatched granary, and a sacred bundle (Fig. 118a). Neither the principal town represented by

the Flint Frieze nor the signs of any of the other towns ruled by 4-Wind have as yet been identified.

In Zacatepec 1, ♂ 4-Wind and ♀ 10-Flower are seated at Flint Frieze, and on the left side of the frieze is a building with an "observatory-eye" and a falling bird (Fig. 87). In the biography of 4-Wind as depicted on the back of Codex Bodley, this ruler makes a series of visits to several deity impersonators. On Bodley 30–IV he offers a bowl of chocolate to ♀ 9-Reed "Headdress of Intertwined Serpents" who is seated at a building containing the observatory-eye motif.[61] On Bodley 29–V, 4-Wind receives offerings from two deity impersonators named ♂ 6-Death at a building which is occupied by another deity impersonator named ♂ 10-Rain (Fig. 118b).[62] A falling bird appears at the rear of this building, and the building itself is attached to the sign of the town or towns ruled by 4-Wind: a frieze with two flint blades, a serpent, and a thatched granary with a hoe. It would seem likely, then, that the building in the first Lienzo of Zacatepec with the observatory-eye and the falling bird represents a ceremonial site or sites within the town whose sign is Flint Frieze.

The scene taking place at Flint Frieze (Fig. 88) shows 4-Wind spouting a group of speech scrolls at the silent 11-Tiger "Tlaloc-Smoking Frieze," the first male ruler of the three generations depicted in this Lienzo. In the same scene, 11-Tiger is shown to be the son of a woman named 10-Vulture "Tree with Human Head and Cloud of Dust" because of the umbilical cord which runs from the figure of this woman to the personal name ("Tlaloc-Smoking Frieze") of 11-Tiger. The figure of 10-Vulture is seated directly above that of 4-Wind, and these two individuals are connected by a line. Alfonso Caso believes that the line indicates that 10-Vulture is a wife of 4-Wind,[63] but this is by no means certain.

Connecting lines are used in Zacatepec 1 to illustrate several types of relationships. As we have seen in the discussion of the place sign of Putla (Fig. 113), the figure of ♂ 8-Lizard "Flints-Tiger," known to be the ruler of Putla, is connected by a line to another male figure, 10-House "Tlaloc-Sun," whose identity and relationship to 8-Lizard are unknown. Adjacent to the conference between ♂ 4-Wind and ♂ 11-Tiger (Figs. 88–89) is a row of four seated male figures (4-Serpent, 1-Reed, 5-Dog, and 10-Alligator) who are connected by a line to the Flint-Frieze place sign. All four of these persons are probably priests or deity impersonators because none of the four appears as a ruler of Flint Frieze in the pre-Conquest historical manuscripts. This line seems to be used here to indicate that they are to be read as a group and that they are all associated with, but not rulers of, the Flint Frieze on which one of the group (10-Alligator) is seated. Thus

---

[59] The biographical information on 4-Wind found in Bodley 11 and 34–28, Selden 8–I, Nuttall 83–84, Becker I (9–16), and Lienzo of Zacatepec 1 is compiled in Caso, "Vida y aventuras de 4. Viento 'Serpiente de Fuego,'" *Miscelánea de estudios dedicados al Dr. Fernando Ortiz* (Havana, 1955). In two of his commentaries (*Bodley*, 59; *Colombino*, 41; 139), Caso includes a genealogical chart of the complex interrelationships between 4-Wind and the family of 8-Deer.
[60] Caso, *Bodley*, 63, 65.

[61] The female deity 9-Reed "Headdress of Intertwined Serpents" appears five times on the front or ritual side of Codex Vienna: 46c, 33b, 28b, 7a and b.
[62] Personages named 6-Death and 10-Rain appear as priests on the front of Nuttall: 6-Death on pages 5a, 18b, 19a, and 10-Rain on pages 14, 15a, 17a and b, 19a, 20c, 21a, 22b.
[63] "Vida y aventuras de 4. Viento . . .," *Miscelánea de estudios dedicados al Dr. Fernanda Ortiz*, 298.

the connecting line appears to signify "connection in general" rather than a specific relationship, such as marriage or descent.

It is possible, then, that 10-Vulture may not have been a wife of 4-Wind but a sister or daughter or some more distant relation. And because neither 10-Vulture nor her son 11-Tiger appears in the other historical manuscripts, their precise relationship to 4-Wind is difficult to define.

The ruler 11-Tiger is mentioned in one non-pictorial document, the 1580 *Relación* of Zacatepec. According to the *Relación*:

Before the Spaniards came, this town of Zacatepec recognized as cacique and lord, a cacique whose name in Mixtec was *yyachihuyçu*, and they did not accord anything to any other cacique or lord except this *yyachihuyçu*, and to him they gave their tribute of cloth and jewels and green stones, and they cultivated his fields for him, and it was this lord who punished them and investigated the crimes which occurred among them.[64]

The Mixtec name *yyachihuyçu* means "the lord 11-Tiger." *Yya* is "lord, a member of the ruling class." *Chi* is the Coastal equivalent of *si* of the dialect of Alvarado's dictionary and may be 10, 11, or 13 in the special vocabulary used to designate the numerical coefficients of dates. *Huyçu* or *huidzo* means the day-sign Tiger in the special day-sign vocabulary. Unfortunately, the 1580 *Relación* does not specify how many years "before the Spaniards came" 11-Tiger was ruler of Zacatepec, nor does it mention the name of any other ruler of Zacatepec.

As Caso has suggested, the story told in the first Lienzo of Zacatepec indicates that 11-Tiger may have founded one of the dynasties of Zacatepec.[65] Following his conversation with 4-Wind, 11-Tiger journeys to four different places, whose signs appear along the top border of Zacatepec 1. The first sign (Fig. 89) consists of a hill with a bundle of wood and a crescent moon. The next place sign, Skull Frieze, is bypassed by 11-Tiger, because the band of footprints leads next to a place (Fig. 90) whose sign is a hill which contains fangs of the rain god Tlaloc and which is topped by the perforated stick used to light fires. The next stop on 11-Tiger's route (Figs. 90–91) is a double-peaked hill with a ravine in the center. The ravine is black and contains a human head; the interior of the hill contains a long-handled incense burner. Above this sign 11-Tiger is shown perched on a *volador* pole, as is a second male figure who is accompanied by two calendrical names: 7-Grass and 11-Deer.[66]

In the final scene at the top of the Lienzo (Fig. 91), 11-Tiger is seated at a place whose sign consists of a river

with the date 11-Wind and a building with an observatory-eye and warpath frieze. The ruler speaks to a group of nine male individuals, placed in two vertical rows, with six figures in the first row and three in the second row. Directly above 11-Tiger are two of the priests who were associated with Flint Frieze on the left side of the top border (Fig. 88, lower right): 4-Serpent who carries a torch, and 1-Reed who holds an incense burner. This scene probably represents an event which Caso has described as "the offering of the royal insignia," an event which takes place when an important personage is confirmed as ruler.

Caso first identified this ceremony in the 1580 Map of Teozacoalco, and two of the three representations of the event in the Teozacoalco Map appear in Fig. 25 of this study. Here, the "offerings" are performed by a group of seven male figures who are placed in a diagonal row at the right of the ruler whose rights are being confirmed. The offerings are placed in front of the first person in the row and consist of a bird, a bow with three jade beads, and a piece of cloth.[67] Near the head of the ruler who receives the offerings is a flaming torch, analogous to the torch carried by 4-Serpent in Zacatepec 1. The offering in Zacatepec 1 (Fig. 91) is held in the hand of 7-Movement, the person seated directly in front of 11-Tiger. This object may be an ear of corn, a jewel, or a conch shell, but it is difficult to identify because its distinctive features are not clear.

Seven of the nine individuals who participate in the offering to 11-Tiger are identified by calendrical names. It is interesting to note that some of these same calendrical names appear enclosed by the elongated oval at the right of the scene between 11-Tiger and 4-Wind (Fig. 88), and that some of the persons at the "offering" also appear within the rectangle of boundaries at place signs which probably represent subjects of Zacatepec.

As a working hypothesis it will be assumed that place signs within the boundaries which are occupied by a single person rather than a marriage pair represent Zacatepec's *estancias* or subjects. There appear to be thirteen such places in Zacatepec 1, and these are set forth in chart 12, "List of Place Signs that May Represent Subject Towns of Zacatepec." One place, a building with a bird and feathers (Fig. 96) appears twice, on opposite sides of a river; in both instances, the calendrical name of the person seated at this sign has been changed from 7-House to 7-Movement. This is most clearly seen in the sign on the left side of the river, where the day-sign Movement is written over the day-sign House.

In the 1547–1550 *Suma de Visitas* Zacatepec is said to have twelve subject towns, which is one less than the thirteen signs in the Lienzo. Perhaps at the time Zacatepec 1 was drawn, the subject town of San Vicente Piñas, represented as a Hill with Butterfly (Fig. 109), had a special status as a subject. In the Lienzo, the woman who rules this town is shown with a personal name ("Corncob-

---

[64] *RMEH* II, 160: "*Este pueblo de çacatepeque antes que los españoles viniesen Reconocian por Cacique y Señor á un cacique que llamaban en su lengua dellos yyachihuyçu y que no acudieron con ninguna cosa á otro ningun cacique ni Señor mas de á este yyachihuyçu y que á este acudian con sus tributos de mantas y joyas y piedras verdes y le labravan sus sementeras y que este señor era el que los castigava y averiguaba los delictos que entre ellos suscedian.*"

[65] "Vida y aventuras de 4. Viento . . . ," *Miscelánea de estudios dedicados al Dr. Fernando Ortiz*, 298.

[66] The presence of *volador* ceremonies in the Mixteca is discussed in Dahlgren, *La mixteca*, 279–85.

[67] Caso, "El Mapa de Teozacoalco," *Cuadernos Americanos*, Año VIII, No. 5 (1949), 160, 162.

CHART 12: Place Signs That May Represent
Subject Towns of Zacatepec

Place Sign	Person(s) or Calendrical Name(s) Connected with the Sign	Illustration (Fig. No.)
1. Frieze; water	5-Reed 9-Wind	89
2. Frieze; hill; mouth	8-Rabbit	92–93
3. Ravine; frieze; flowing water	5-Dog 7-Dog	93–94
4. Platform; head with serpent twined around neck	10-Vulture 2-Alligator	94
5. River; serpent	10-Reed 4-Movement	94–95
6. Platform; five dots, stone, face	6-Rabbit 2-Lizard	95
7. Platform; bird, plant, shell	male figure with no name	95
8. Platform; bird (parrot?), feathers	7-House, rewritten 7-Movement	96 (appears twice)
9. Platform; thorny plant	6-Flower	95–96
10. Platform; plant, shell	male figure with no name	100–101 (top)
11. Plain; hummingbird	7-Movement	107–108
12. Platform; building	10-Eagle	108
13. Hill; butterfly (S. Vicente Piñas)	♀ 2-Dog (formerly written ♀ 10-Dog); below place sign: 2-Dog 7-Vulture	109

Sun") as well as with her calendrical name 2-Dog,[68] whereas the persons connected with ten of the other twelve signs of subject towns have only calendrical names, and

[68] This woman's calendrical name was apparently first written as 10-Dog, expressed by the ten dots above the day-sign Dog which are now faint as if someone had attempted to erase them. The name 2-Dog is expressed by the two dots below the day-sign Dog; this calendrical name also appears below the place sign, attached to the name 7-Vulture.

the remaining two of the twelve persons have no names at all. If San Vicente Piñas is removed from the list of subject towns, then the remaining total of twelve signs is equal to the number of subjects reported in the *Suma de Visitas*.

It seems to be likely that the persons represented at the twelve or thirteen subject towns within the boundaries, as well as the persons represented at 11-Tiger's "offering of the royal insignia" (Fig. 91) and the persons indicated by calendrical name only at the meeting between 11-Tiger and 4-Wind (Fig. 88, within oval), are all *principales* or members of the secondary nobility who were controlled by the ruler of Zacatepec. The names of the persons or calendrical signs that appear in all three groups mentioned above are included in Chart 13, "List of Persons who may be *Principales* or Secondary Nobility." As can be seen from this list, only three individuals appear in all three situations: 6-Flower, 6-Rabbit, and 2-Lizard. In the case of 6-Rabbit and 2-Lizard, when the calendrical names of these two individuals appear within the elongated oval in the upper-left corner of the Lienzo (Fig. 88), they are attached by a line; and when the same two calendrical signs appear within the Lienzo, they are again attached by a line to one individual who is seated on a platform with five dots, a stone, and a face (Fig. 95). At the "offering," however, 6-Rabbit and 2-Lizard are represented as two distinct human figures (Fig. 91).

Five additional names of individuals in the elongated oval (4-Movement, 10-Reed, 10-Vulture, 2-Alligator, and 7-Dog) are names attached to persons at subject places but are not names of persons at the offering. Again, we see that two calendrical names, 4-Movement and 10-Reed, which are connected by a line when they appear in the oval are also connected to one figure at one place sign, Serpent River (Figs. 94–95). Similarly, the signs 10-Vulture and 2-Alligator are attached by a line within the oval and attached to one person at the sign within the Lienzo consisting of a platform and a human head with a snake coiled around its neck (Fig. 94).

Two other individuals—7-House and 7-Movement—appear at the "offering" and at subject towns within Zacatepec, but these calendrical names are not included within the elongated oval in the upper-left corner. Two individuals (11-Death and 4-Rain) are represented within the oval as calendrical names connected by a line but do not appear elsewhere in the Lienzo. Two additional persons (13-Grass and 7-Water) appear at the "offering" only. And seven persons or calendrical names (5-Reed, 9-Wind, 8-Rabbit, 5-Dog, 10-Eagle, ♀ 2 or 10-Dog, and 7-Vulture) are represented in connection with subject towns within the rectangle but do not appear in the oval or at the offering.

Returning now to the historical narrative along the top border of Zacatepec 1, the entire sequence of events, shown here as taking place outside the boundaries of Zacatepec, appears to represent a pilgrimage by 11-Tiger "Tlaloc-Smoking Frieze" prior to his becoming ruler of Zacatepec. First, as we have seen, he confers with 4-Wind (Fig. 88) and apparently receives orders or perhaps even receives the domain of Zacatepec from this ruler. Present at this ceremony are four priests who are attached by a line to Flint Frieze, the sign of the town ruled by 4-Wind. As we have noted, two of these priests, 4-Serpent and 1-Reed, re-appear at the "offering" ceremony in the roles of censer and torch-bearer (Fig. 91). Above the priest named 5-

Dog at the conference between 11-Tiger and 4-Wind is the elongated oval which contains the calendrical names of ten persons who are probably *principales* subject to 11-Tiger. Four other individuals also atend this conference: two persons named ♂ 2-Alligator and ♂ 8-House who are connected by a line and seated above a truncated feather-mat motif for "plain, valley," and above these two figures are ♂ 8-Flint "Falling Eagle" and ♂ 12-Flower "Composite Parrot and Hummingbird" (Fig. 88). Both of the latter individuals are accompanied by a *cacaxtli*, or carrying device made of slats of wood. Neither the status or function of these four persons is known; they do not appear elsewhere in Zacatepec 1, nor do they appear in other Mixtec pictorial manuscripts.

Attached to the figure of 11-Tiger in his conference with 4-Wind are several weapons: a bow and arrow, a macana, and a shield. These weapons are probably royal insignia received by 11-Tiger at the time of this conference and do not seem to indicate that 11-Tiger's subsequent journey is a journey of conquest. None of the place signs shown in connection with 11-Tiger is punctured by an arrow indicating that it is conquered, nor is this ruler ever shown on the warpath.

Following the "offering of the royal insignia" in the upper-right corner (Fig. 91), 11-Tiger enters the rectangle which represents the lands of Zacatepec. The Lienzo indicates two routes of entry. The first is depicted by a band of footprints which leads to a place sign (Fig. 95) that consists of a frieze accompanied by seven plants and a building with the observatory-eye motif. At this sign 11-Tiger is seated with his wife, 11-Monkey "Jeweled Heart." The second route to the interior of Zacatepec is indicated by footprints which follow the boundary line at the top of the rectangle (Figs. 90, 89, 88) to the boundary sign which is expressed by the feather-mat "plain" motif, three balls of down, and two ears of corn (Fig. 88). At this point the footprints end, and a line connects the boundary sign with the river below. At the right of the point where the connecting line meets the bank of the river is the sign of the Río Venado ("deer river"), a tributary of the Río de la Cuchara. According to the officials of Zacatepec, the Mixtec name of the Río Venado is *yuta sucu isu*, or "the river of the deer's neck." (*Yuta* = "river"; *sucu* = "neck"; *isu* = "deer.")

Returning to the place sign where ♂ 11-Tiger is seated with ♀ 11-Monkey (Fig. 95), it is noted that two calendrical names—7-Deer and 9-Movement—are connected to each other by a line and also attached to the observatory-eye motif placed on the platform of the building. These same two calendrical signs appear in connection with the four places on the top border which are visited by 11-Tiger (Figs. 89–91). As Karl Nowotny and Alfonso Caso have noted, these two calendrical names represent the names of two male deities who appear four times on the front, or ritual, side of Codex Vienna: pages 36d, 26b, 25b, and 4a.[69]

[69] Nowotny, "Erläuterungen zum Codex Vindobonensis (Vorderseite)," 180, 184, 190; Caso, "Representaciones de hongos en los códices,"

CHART 13: Persons Who May be
Principales or Secondary Nobility

Persons or Calendrical Names	Elongated Oval (Fig. 88)	"Offering" (Fig. 91)	Interior of Rectangle (Fig. No. below)
11-Death	X		
4-Rain	X		
6-Flower	X	X	95–96
6-Rabbit	X	X	95
2-Lizard	X	X	95
4-Movement	X		95
10-Reed	X		94
10-Vulture	X		94
2-Alligator	X		94
7-Dog	X		93
7-House		X	96 (appears twice; rewritten 7-Movement)
7-Movement		X	107
13-Grass		X	
7-Water		X	
5-Reed			88–89
9-Wind			89
8-Rabbit			92
5-Dog			93
10-Eagle			108
♀ 2 or 10 Dog			109
7-Vulture			109

These two deities always appear together, and 7-Deer wears the costume and helmet of a deer while 9-Movement wears the costume and headdress of an eagle. In Vienna 4a (Fig. 119), 7-Deer and 9-Movement both appear in front of place signs. In this scene, 7-Deer, who here wears a tiger helmet in addition to his deer helmet, brings a bag of copal incense to a building on a hill that has no apparent qualifying element. Below, 9-Movement stands before a building which contains the sign of the planet Venus and which is placed on a hill containing a plant. It seems very possible that the Venus sign within the building in Vienna 4a is the equivalent of the observatory-eye motif attached to the calendrical names 7-Deer and 9-Movement in two place signs of the 11-Tiger story in Zacatepec 1 (Figs. 91, 95).

Whether the plant motif within the hill in Vienna 4a is the same as the seven plants adjacent to the place sign in Zacatepec 1 (Fig. 95) is difficult to decide. Botanical motifs are very conventionalized in the Mixtec pictorial manuscripts, and the conventions for plants may vary from one manuscript to another. But the seven plants in Zacatepec 1 appear to be different from the plant in Vienna 4a.

Another possibility is that the sign with seven plants in Zacatepec 1 represents the site of *Siete Ocotes* ("seven pines"), discussed above under the boundary signs of Zacatepec. As we have seen, *Siete Ocotes* was a boundary of Zacatepec in the eighteenth and nineteenth centuries, but in the sixteenth century when Zacatepec 1 was drawn, this site was within Zacatepec's boundaries. Not only does the number of plants accompanying the sign in Zacatepec 1 total seven, but the foliage of these plants resembles the leaves of the two pine trees at the left of the Río de la Cuchara (Fig. 93). These two trees were identified as pines (*yusa* in Mixtec) because one of the trees has a pictorial phonetic indicator: a shield, also *yusa* in Mixtec. It is likely, then, that the sign in Zacatepec 1 which consists of a frieze accompanied by seven plants is the site of *Siete Ocotes*, which appears here in a non-cartographic context. The actual location of the site is indicated by the two pines at the left of the Río de la Cuchara (Fig. 93); the place sign of *Siete Ocotes* as it is occupied by ♂ 11-Tiger and ♀ 11-Monkey (Fig. 95) merely names this site as part of the historical narrative, and its placement here does not indicate its location within the lands of Zacatepec.

The presence of the calendrical names of the deities 7-Deer and 9-Movement at the latter sign of *Siete Ocotes* probably signifies that this place was a ceremonial site sacred to these deities. It is thus probable that the four sites shown as visited by 11-Tiger on the top of the Lienzo (Figs. 89-91) are also ceremonial sites because the calendrical names of these deities appear in connection with all four place signs. At the first three places these calendrical names are attached to a sacred bundle; at the fourth place,

the site of the "offering," the names are attached to the observatory-eye sign as they are below at *Siete Ocotes*.

The biography of 11-Tiger is principally concerned with the establishment of his authority as ruler of Zacatepec. His political authority derives from the great ruler 4-Wind "Fire Serpent," from whom 11-Tiger receives words in the first scene of the Lienzo (Fig. 88). This is followed by a pilgrimage to a series of four ceremonial sites.[70] At the last of these sites (Fig. 91), 11-Tiger receives an offering from a group of his nobles in the presence of the two priests 1-Reed and 4-Serpent who are from Flint Frieze, the town ruled by 4-Wind "Fire Serpent." Then 11-Tiger journeys to the ceremonial site of *Siete Ocotes*, within the boundaries of Zacatepec (Fig. 95), where he marries ♀ 11-Monkey "Jeweled Heart."

The Second Generation: ♂ 8-Alligator and ♀ 13-Wind
The second generation of Zacatepec's rulers consists of ♂ 8-Alligator "Tlaloc-Sun" and his wife ♀ 13-Wind "Flowers-Feathers." This generation appears only once in Zacatepec 1 (Fig. 116a), seated on a frieze which connects the bilingual place sign of Zacatepec on the left with a profile building and Deer Hill on the right.

A band of footprints connects this compound sign with the sign of *Siete Ocotes* (Fig. 95) occupied by ♂ 11-Tiger and ♀ 11-Monkey, the first generation of Zacatepec's rulers. This band of footprints leads to the right side of the frieze occupied by the second generation, which may serve to indicate that ♂ 8-Alligator who is placed on the right is the son of ♂ 11-Tiger and ♀ 11-Monkey.

The calendrical names of the deities 7-Deer and 9-Movement appear in connection with the building at the right of this place sign, which suggests that the building is a temple and that Deer Hill is a ceremonial site. On the left side of the place sign, the day-sign 9-Movement also occurs attached to the place sign of the Mixtec name of Zacatepec. This date may indicate the founding of the town of Zacatepec at the *pueblo viejo* site of Cerro de la Campana, and the day 9-Movement may be the founding date in honor of the deity 9-Movement.

The Third Generation: ♂ 3-Reed and ♀ 9-Tiger
The third generation consists of ♂ 3-Reed "Smoking Hair-Fire Flint" and his wife ♀ 9-Tiger "Butterfly-Beast," who appear for the first time at a sign with a frieze, twelve dots, a stone, and an upturned face (Figs. 94-95, 99-100). Again, a band of footprints connects this place with the sign of Zacatepec which is occupied by the preceding generation, ♂ 8-Alligator and ♀ 13-Wind; and because this band of footprints leads to ♂ 3-Reed's side of the frieze, it is assumed that he was the son of ♂ 8-Alligator and ♀ 13-Wind.

The marriage pair ♂ 3-Reed and ♀ 9-Tiger appear

Estudios de cultura nahuatl, IV (Mexico, 1963), 31. Caso also points out that these two deities are mentioned in the 1580 *Relación* of Acatlán in the Mixteca Baja (*PNE* V, 60) as principal deities of this town.

[70] This type of pilgrimage also appears in the pre-Conquest manuscripts when the life of a ruler is told in any detail. For example, in the biography of ♂ 4-Wind on the back of Bodley (32-V to 29-V), this ruler makes a series of visits to deity impersonators prior to his marriage to ♀ 10-Flower. In Codex Colombino, ♂ 8-Deer, wearing the black paint of a priest, makes a pilgrimage (pages IX-25 to X-27) prior to an important ballgame (page XI).

again at a place whose sign has been destroyed (Fig. 99), and this now-obliterated sign is connected to the Dots-Stone-Face sign by a band of footprints. The remaining appearances of the third generation in Zacatepec are connected by warpath bands. First 3-Reed attacks and conquers the place which has been identified as Putla (Figs. 98–97), then the warpath leads to a place designated as Eagle on Stones (Fig. 103), and finally to the Hill of Three-Reed (Figs. 105–106). Although neither of these last two place signs is pierced with an arrow, the traditional sign of conquest, both places are at the end of a warpath and are occupied by ♂ 3-Reed and ♀ 9-Tiger, and it is thus assumed that the two places were conquered by 3-Reed. With the exception of the sign of Putla, none of the place signs connected with 3-Reed and his wife can yet be identified.

The Dates Connected with the Principal Narrative Line

Sixteen year dates appear in connection with the principal narrative of the three generations discussed above, and these year-dates and the events to which they are attached are listed in Chart 14, "Sequence of Year Dates in Zacatepec 1." If the principal narrative line is continuous and the three generations in question consecutive, then the segment of history told in Zacatepec 1 spans 134 years from the first date Four-Flint at the conference between ♂ 4-Wind and ♂ 11-Tiger to the last date Eight-Rabbit, connected with the occupation of Hill of Three-Reed by ♂ 3-Reed and ♀ 9-Tiger.

As was mentioned, the only historical personages in Zacatepec 1 who appear in the extant group of Mixtec pictorial documents are the couple ♂ 4-Wind "Fire Serpent" and ♀ 10-Flower "Tlaloc-Cobweb," who are seated at the beginning of the sequence of the narrative. The ruler 4-Wind lived from 1040 to 1112, and thus the date Four-Flint associated with his conference with 11-Tiger should be analogous to the Christian year 1068, because according to Alfonso Caso's correlation of Mixtec dates with Christian year dates,[71] this is the only Four-Flint date that occurs within the lifetime of 4-Wind. Caso has also pointed out that the first date in Zacatepec 1—the year Four-Flint and the day One-Serpent—is exactly the same date on which 4-Wind is shown in Bodley 31–III (Fig. 118a) as the ruler of Flint Frieze.[72]

If the subsequent fifteen dates in the Lienzo represent an unbroken sequence of events and, again, if the three generations depicted in the principal line of narrative are consecutive generations, then the correlation of year dates in Zacatepec 1 with Christian year dates is represented by the first vertical column of dates in Chart 15, "Sequence of Year Dates in Zacatepec 1 and Seven Correlations with Christian Year Dates." In the correlation presented in this first column of dates, the events participated in by 11-Tiger, the ruler of the first generation, run from 1068 to 1092, or 24 years. The dates connected with the second

generation begin forty-four years later, in 1136; and the dates connected with the third generation begin in 1174, thirty-four years after 1140, the last date connected with the second generation. The dates attached to the third generation span a twenty-eight-year period, from an initial date of 1174 to the final date of 1202, the Eight-Rabbit year in which ♂ 3-Reed and ♀ 9-Tiger are shown seated on Hill of Three-Reed. The span of years shown for each generation does not exceed the plausible number of years of a normal lifetime; and the entire span of 134 years, from an initial date of 1068 to a final date of 1202, is also plausible for a span of three generations.

The only year date which offers any difficulty is the final date connected with the first generation. This date is attached to the appearance of ♂ 11-Tiger and ♀ 11-Monkey at *Siete Ocotes* (Fig. 95) and has been rewritten. The original year-sign, now smudged, appears to have been House, and the row of five numeral dots above appears to have been connected with this erased year-sign. The rewritten year-sign is Flint, and the two numeral dots at the left seem to be connected with the Flint sign. Thus it would appear that the year Five-House was changed to Two-Flint, the same date as the previous date in the sequence, which is associated with the journey of 11-Tiger (Figs. 91–90). The rewritten date Two-Flint makes more sense in terms of the historical sequence, because a date of Five-House is twenty-nine years later than the previous date Two-Flint, and it does not seem likely that so long a time span would separate 11-Tiger's journey and his appearance at *Siete Ocotes*. In addition, the date Five-House occurs fifty-three years after the initial date of 1068; and if the scene at *Siete Ocotes* represents the marriage of ♂ 11-Tiger and ♀ 11-Monkey, it does not seem likely that this event would have taken place fifty-three years after 11-Tiger had received his dynastic rights from 4-Wind.

What is curious about the sequence of dates in Zacatepec 1 is that if the 134-year span begins in 1068 and ends in 1202 (as indicated in the first column of dates in the accompanying chart), the final date of 1202 is more than three centuries earlier than the approximate date of 1540–60 when the Lienzo was drawn. It seems somewhat strange that the historical narrative would treat the 134 years from 1068 to 1202 but omit the span of over three hundred years that follows, because it is customary for sixteenth-century maps to present genealogical data on the generation which is alive at the time the map was prepared. In the 1580 Map of Teozacoalco, for example, the last rulers represented for the dynasties of both Tilantongo and Teozacoalco are those rulers who were alive in 1580.

At least three possible explanations may be offered for this apparent omission of three hundred years of Zacatepec's history. One explanation is that the three generations depicted in the Lienzo are not consecutive. That is, ♂ 11-Tiger of the first generation may have been a contemporary of ♂ 4-Wind, but the other two generations—those of ♂ 8-Alligator and ♂ 3-Reed—do not im-

---

[71] "Base para la sincronología mixteca y cristiana," chart following p. 66. All dates cited in this section are derived from this chart.
[72] "El Lienzo de Zacatepec," 6.

CHART 14: Sequence of Year Dates in Zacatepec 1

Event	Year Date	Number of Years from First Date	Number of Years from Previous Date	Illustration (Fig. No.)
1. Conference between ♂ 4-Wind and ♂ 11-Tiger	Four-Flint	0	0	88
2. ♂ 11-Tiger at hill with bundle of wood, moon	Five-House	1	1	89
3. ♂ 11-Tiger at hill with fire-lighting stick, fangs of Tlaloc	Nine-House	5	4	90
4. ♂ 11-Tiger at hill with incense burner, face in dark area between peaks	Two-Reed	11	6	91
5. ♂ 11-Tiger and ♂ 7-Grass/11-Deer as *voladores*	Three-Flint	12	1	90–91
6. ♂ 11-Tiger receives offering at River of 11-Wind, building with "observatory-eye"	Four-Rabbit	26	14	91
7. Journey of ♂ 11-Tiger	Two-Flint	24	–2	91–90
8. ♂ 11-Tiger and ♀ 11-Monkey at frieze with plants, building with "observatory-eye"	Two-Flint? (formerly Five-House?)	24 (53)	0 (29)	95
9. ♂ 8-Alligator and ♀ 13-Wind at Zacatepec and Deer Hill	Seven-Flint	68	44 (15)	94–95
10. Date attached to place sign of Zacatepec	Eleven-Flint	72	4	94
11. Road from Zacatepec to Dots-Stone-Face	Six-Rabbit	106	34	94
12. ♂ 3-Reed and ♀ 9-Tiger at Dots-Stone-Face	Six-Rabbit	106	0	94–95, 100
13. ♂ 3-Reed and ♀ 9-Tiger at place sign now destroyed	Eight?-Flint?	108	2	99
14. ♂ 3-Reed conquers Putla	Two-Flint	128	20	98–97
15. ♂ 3-Reed and ♀ 9-Tiger at Eagle on Stones	Five-Reed	131	3	103
16. ♂ 3-Reed and ♀ 9-Tiger at Hill of Three-Reed	Eight-Rabbit	134	3	105–106

mediately follow ♂ 11-Tiger's generation. In this event, only the dates that relate to 11-Tiger's generation would correlate with the year dates listed in the first column of the accompanying chart. The dates connected with 8-Alligator and 3-Reed might then correlate with any of the six lists of dates at the right of the first column.[73] How-

[73] If an eighth column were added to the accompanying chart of seven correlations, the 134-year period in the eighth column would begin in 1432 and end in 1566. But in this eighth column the date of the conquest of Putla would be 1560, and it does not seem likely that a native war of conquest would have been carried out at this late date. Thus the seventh column in the accompanying chart appears to be the latest possible group of correlation dates.

ever, because none of the historical personages except 4-Wind and his wife 10-Flower can be dated by comparison with other pictorial manuscripts, it is impossible to establish a known later date for the generations of 8-Alligator and 3-Reed. In addition, as we have noted, the three generations in Zacatepec 1 are connected by bands of footprints, which seem to indicate a father-son-grandson relationship, because footprints are used in the Lienzo in the pre-Conquest sense of "comes from"—i.e., "offspring of."

A second possibility is that the three generations repre-

CHART 15: Sequence of Year Dates in Zacatepec 1 and Seven Correlations With Christian Year Dates

Generation		I	II	III	IV	V	VI	VII
Generation 1	1. Four-Flint	1068	1120	1172	1224	1276	1328	1380
Generation 1	2. Five-House	1069	1121	1173	1225	1277	1329	1381
Generation 1	3. Nine-House	1073	1125	1177	1229	1281	1333	1385
Generation 1	4. Two-Reed	1079	1131	1183	1235	1287	1339	1391
Generation 1	5. Three-Flint	1080	1132	1184	1236	1288	1340	1392
Generation 1	6. Four-Rabbit	1094	1146	1198	1250	1302	1354	1406
Generation 1	7–8. Two-Flint	1092	1144	1196	1248	1300	1352	1404
Generation 1	8–bis. Five-House	1121	1173	1225	1277	1329	1381	1433
Generation 2	9. Seven-Flint	1136	1188	1240	1292	1344	1396	1448
Generation 2	10. Eleven-Flint	1140	1192	1244	1296	1348	1400	1452
Generation 3	11–12. Six-Rabbit	1174	1226	1278	1330	1382	1434	1486
Generation 3	13. Eight?-Flint?	1176	1228	1280	1332	1384	1436	1488
Generation 3	14. Two-Flint	1196	1248	1300	1352	1404	1456	1508
Generation 3	15. Five Reed	1199	1251	1303	1355	1407	1459	1511
Generation 3	16. Eight-Rabbit	1202	1254	1306	1358	1410	1462	1514

sented in Zacatepec 1 are the last three generations prior to the Spanish conquest and that ♂ 11-Tiger of the first generation is not actually a contemporary of ♂ 4-Wind "Fire Serpent" who lived from 1040 to 1112. In this case, 4-Wind and his wife 10-Flower would represent a generation in the remote past from whom 11-Tiger ultimately derived his authority;[74] and thus the line which connects 11-Tiger's mother 10-Vulture with 4-Wind may imply a connection through many generations of rulers who are not depicted in the Lienzo. If this were true, then the dates of the principal narrative in Zacatepec 1 would probably correlate with the seventh column in the chart, where the 134-year span runs from 1380 to 1514. A correlation of 1514 for the Eight-Rabbit year when ♂ 3-Reed and ♀ 9-Tiger are seated on the Hill of Three-Reed would indicate that either 3-Reed or one of his offspring was ruler of Zacatepec at the time of the Spanish conquest. But, again, because ♂ 4-Wind and ♀ 10-Flower are the only

[74] In Codex Bodley there are several examples of the juxtaposition of living persons with dead ancestors. In one instance (9–I; Caso, *Bodley*, 39) the eleventh-century ruler 8-Deer arrives on a warpath at a place with the calendrical names of the first rulers of the First Dynasty of Tilantongo, who ruled in the eighth century and thus could not have been contemporaries of 8-Deer. Elsewhere (Bodley 9-V) 8-Deer visits another couple who were rulers in the ninth century and, again, could not have been alive in the eleventh century. Concerning the latter visit, Caso (*Bodley*, 38) comments: "We have no evidence to show whether these visits were really made to the lords themselves or whether it is simply a question of offerings made to their memory."

datable personages in the Lienzo, it cannot be established whether other historical personages belong to a period at least three centuries later than the lifetime of this couple.

A third possibility is that the historical events depicted in Zacatepec 1 were copied from a pre-Conquest screenfold which is now lost and that this screenfold prototype dealt only with Zacatepec's history from 1068 to 1202. As was observed at the beginning of this chapter, the pattern of the principal narrative line of Zacatepec 1 is similar to the typical meander pattern of a pre-Conquest screenfold. It is possible that this pattern results from the adaptation of a screenfold pictorial narrative to the rectangular format of the map.

I believe, then, that the correlation of the year dates in Zacatepec 1 should be left an open question, pending the discovery of additional documents—either pictorial or written—which contain corroborative information on at least some of the numerous historical personages who populate the Lienzo. The fact that only ♂ 4-Wind and ♀ 10-Flower of Flint Frieze appear in the extant pre-Conquest historical manuscripts would seem to indicate that the Lienzo is a very local document, concerned primarily with events important only to the town of Zacatepec. But it would be extremely helpful to uncover other sources of information on ♂ 8-Alligator and ♂ 3-Reed, the rulers of the second and third generations represented in Zacatepec 1.

Non-Cartographic Place Signs

Five place signs, each of which is occupied by a marriage pair, appear within the large rectangle of Zacatepec 1 as unconnected with the principal narrative. In addition, none of the five seems to be a subject of Zacatepec.

Two of these signs have already been identified: the sign of San Pedro Jicayán (Figs. 58*b* and 103–104) occupied by ♂ 4-Deer "Sun-Death's Head" and ♀ 12-Rabbit "Fan-Observatory Eye," and the bilingual sign of Santa María Ipalapa (Figs. 104–105) occupied by ♂ 11-Grass "Rattlesnake with Claws Surrounded by Sand" and ♀ 8-Rabbit "Hill with Vulture and Flowers."[75] These two signs definitely appear in a historical rather than a cartographic context because both Jicayán and Ipalapa are located outside of Zacatepec's boundaries. As a working hypothesis, then, it will be assumed that the other three signs with marriage pairs also represent towns outside of Zacatepec's boundaries, although none of these signs can yet be identified.

The first of the three, consisting of a hill with the facial features of the rain god Tlaloc, appears twice within the large rectangle of Zacatepec 1. In one of these appearances (Figs. 92–93), we see that the rulers of this place are ♂ 3-Wind "Eagle-Ballcourt" and ♀ 7-Flint "Xolotl-Jewels." The second representation of the sign and its rulers (Fig. 100) is partially obliterated, but it is still possible to see the base of the hill which seems to be decorated with small fangs of Tlaloc. Also visible are the eagle costume of

♂ 3-Wind and the personal name of ♀ 7-Flint as well as the Flint sign of her calendrical name. The presence of ♀ 7-Flint is confirmed by a short two-line Mixtec gloss at the left of this sign:

> *iuhu nidisi*
> *nu sacusi*

which means "at the edge was visible 7-Flint." (*Yuhu* = "at the edge"; *ni*- is a past-tense prefix; *disi nu[u]* = "to be visible"; *sacusi* is 7-Flint in the special calendrical vocabulary, where *sa* is 7 and *cusi* is the day-sign Flint.)

The second of the three signs (Fig. 93) consists of the feather-mat "plain" motif and four motifs which are either clouds or folded blankets. This place sign is occupied by ♂ 7-Death "Serpent Supporting the Sky" and ♀ 7-Dog "Flower-Xolotl."

The third sign is a large Bent Hill (Figs. 99–100) with the marriage pair ♂ 11-Dog "Serpent Supporting the Sky" and ♀ 10-Alligator "Flower-Stone Figurine." A battle is taking place at Bent Hill, which is defended by a male figure with macana below the base of the hill (Fig. 100) and a female figure with macana who strides off the peak of the hill (Fig. 99). These two persons are presumably the same as the marriage pair seated at the base of the hill although neither of the defenders is identified by name. The attack on Bent Hill was perpetrated by four unnamed male individuals who are all shown as dead, indicating that their attack was unsuccessful. Three of the four are armed with shields or bow and arrow, and their eyes are represented as closed. The fourth attacker is unarmed, and a triangular incision in his chest indicates that he died by heart sacrifice. A small place sign, consisting of a hill and a bird, is attached to the year sign that indicates the date of the attack (Fig. 99), and this place sign may mean that Bent Hill was attacked by warriors from Tututepec ("bird hill").

Each of the five place signs discussed above is accompanied by a year date, but because it is uncertain how these signs fit into the principal narrative line, no attempt will be made here to correlate these dates with Christian year dates.

Group of Persons in a River

The only group of persons in Zacatepec 1 which has not been mentioned is a row of eight male figures who appear in the river at the upper-right corner of the rectangle of Zacatepec's boundaries (Fig. 91). These persons are identified by calendrical names only, and reading from left to right their names are: 6-Tiger, 7-Eagle, 11-Death, 4-Rain, 4-Movement, 4-Reed, 4-Serpent, and 4-Lizard. The precise role of this group is not known, but it seems likely that these persons are all deity impersonators. With the exception of 6-Tiger and 11-Death, persons with the same calendrical names as six of the eight individuals in the river appear on the front or ritual side of Codex Vienna.[76]

---

[75] The place sign of Jicayán is discussed above, p. 71; that of Ipalapa, p. 109.

[76] 7-Eagle: Vienna 50a, 37a, b.
4-Death: Vienna 36a, c, 13b, 12a.
4-Movement: Vienna 33b, 30, 24b, 20a.
4-Reed: Vienna 35a, 29d, 2a.
4-Serpent: Vienna 51b, 33a, 30a, 5a, 2a.
4-Lizard: Vienna 24a.

Moreover, the four persons on the right wear black facial paint, which is usually a characteristic of priests and deity impersonators.

SUMMARY

It has been stressed in the discussion of the genealogical data presented in the first Lienzo of Zacatepec that this manuscript is a very local document and that it is devoted primarily to three generations of Zacatepec's rulers, who do not appear in the pre-Conquest screenfolds. But it is precisely this local character—that is, the fact that the Lienzo is literally centered around the town of Zacatepec —which makes it valuable as a manuscript in which place signs can be identified. Many of the place signs in Zacatepec 1 are arranged in a cartographic context, and thus it is possible to identify the signs because of their location on the map. This is particularly true of the signs of towns that share boundaries with Zacatepec and which appear outside of the rectangular border that encloses Zacatepec's lands.

As a result of the analysis of the place signs in the Lienzo, ten new identifications of place signs of towns have been made, and these identifications augment considerably the list of the previously identified signs of 23 towns that appears at the end of Chapter V of this book. A summary list of the ten identified signs in Zacatepec 1 is given below. In the first column of this list is the present-day name of the town; in the second column is the town's Mixtec name and a translation of this name. The third column contains a short description of the sign that represents the Mixtec name, and the fourth column provides the figure number of this study where the sign is illustrated.

Town	Mixtec Name	Description of Place Sign	Illustration (Fig. No.)
1. Zacatepec, Santa María	*yucu satuta* "hill of the date or calendrical name Seven-Water"	hill with calendrical sign Seven-Water	116a
2. San Vicente, Piñas	*yucu ticuvua* "hill of the butterfly"	hill with butterfly	109
3. Ipalapa, Santa María	*ñuu tayu* "town of the seat or throne"	frieze with a straw (*petate*) throne	104–105
4. Putla	*ñuu caa* "metal town"	frieze with axes	113
5. Yosotiche, Santiago	*yoso tiche* "plain of the iguana"	feather-mat field with iguana	92
6. Amusgos, San Pedro	*ñuu ñama* "town of the corn husk, ball, or cocoon"	frieze with a ball with projections that resemble the fuzziness of a cocoon	114
7. Pinotepa de Don Luis	*doyo yuhu* "to raise [to] the mouth"	profile head and shoulders of human male who raises one hand to his mouth	111 (upper-right corner)
8. Atoyac, San Pedro	*ñuu yuta* "town of the river"	a river that contains a frieze	106 (right border)
9. Chayucu, San Agustín	*cha yucu* "at the foot of the hill"	hill with human feet	101 (lower-right corner)

Town	Mixtec Name	Description of Place Sign	Illustration (Fig. No.)
10. Ixtayutla, Santiago	*yuta ñii* "river of salt or of the animal hide"	river with animal hide	96 (right border)

Two of the largest and most important place signs in Zacatepec 1—those of Zacatepec (Fig. 116*a*) and Ipalapa (Figs. 104–105)—appear to be bilingual, with a sign of the Nahuatl name of the town attached by a connecting line to the sign of the town's Mixtec name. In the case of Zacatepec, a hill with plants that represents "zacatepec" or "hill of the *zacate* plant" is connected to the "Hill of Seven-Water" that depicts the town's Mixtec name. A sign consisting of a river and a throne that represents the Nahuatl name "ipalapa" or "throne river" is attached to the main sign of this town, which sets forth the Mixtec name "town of the throne."

VIII

THE LIENZO OF JICAYÁN

The town of San Pedro Jicayán (Fig. 84b) is today the most completely Mixtec town in the Coastal region. According to the 1950 census, 99.71 per cent of the town's 2,748 inhabitants are considered to be "indigenous"—that is, speakers of Mixtec; and of the total population, 1,166 persons, over 42 per cent, are monolingual and speak Mixtec only.[1]

Jicayán was probably an important pre-Conquest center, and indicative of the town's former importance is a large unexcavated mound about half a mile southeast of the present-day town on a hill called Cerro de la Iglesia, or "Hill of the Church," although there is now no church structure on the site. Jicayán was undoubtedly also an important town in the early Colonial period, although no written documents concerning its history in the sixteenth century have been located. The principal known early-Colonial document from Jicayán is a handsome pictographic map of the town (Figs. 143–59) that was probably drawn around 1550. This map, known as the Lienzo of Jicayán, is in the municipal archive of San Pedro Jicayán. The Lienzo includes none of the extensive genealogical information seen in the first Lienzo of Zacatepec nor none of the detailed cartographic and landscape features of Zacatepec 2. Its main intent is to set forth place names of sites that surround the town of Jicayán; and the building in the center that represents Jicayán (Figs. 146–47) is enclosed by an irregular circle of 52 place signs, many of which depict the names of the town's boundaries.

The Lienzo is made up of three long strips of woven cotton cloth which are sewn together; in its entirety it measures approximately six by four feet. There are many small holes in the Lienzo, and at the present time it is attached to a backing of white cloth. The pictorial signs and figures are drawn in a black, carbon-like ink; and in common with the two Lienzos of Zacatepec, there is no evidence of color in any of the figures.

At least two styles of drawing are seen in the Lienzo of Jicayán. The predominant style is essentially pre-Conquest in character and is seen in the place sign, personage, and date in the center of the Lienzo (Fig. 147), as well as in the 52 place signs that encircle the central configuration. But the Lienzo was undoubtedly drawn in the early Colonial period because this drawing style shows indications of the less taut line that is a characteristic of post-Conquest documents and which has been described by Donald Robertson as "disintegrated frame line."[2] This is particularly evident in architectural elements such as the building in the center (Fig. 147) and in a temple base and building in the lower-left corner (Fig. 152). Nonetheless, the pictorial conventions utilized in all the signs and figures drawn in this first style are pre-Conquest, and we see no European intrusions such as the churches, crosses, and crescent moons that appear in the first Lienzo of Zacatepec.

The second style of drawing in the Lienzo of Jicayán is characterized by a thinner, less bold line and a "sketchy" quality. The figures drawn in this style appear to be "footnotes" or addenda to the map and were probably either added to the Lienzo at a later date or were annotations added by a non-native artist soon after the map was drawn. This second style utilizes conventions which are essentially European, such as three small churches to indicate towns (Figs. 146, 149, 153), a cross on a stone platform (Figs. 146, 159), several palm trees as landscape (Figs. 146, 149), and a fish with scales within a river (Fig. 150).

As in the case of the two Lienzos of Zacatepec, all of the boundary signs face inward—that is, toward the central configuration that represents the town of Jicayán. If we consider the two borders which are parallel to the base of the Jicayán place sign to be the top and bottom of the Lienzo, then the map is oriented with northeast at the top, because a gloss indicating the direction of east ("Lebante") appears in the upper-right corner (Fig. 158).

In common with many other important towns of the

[1] These statistics are included in Chart 25 of: Comite de Estudio de la Cuenca del Río Balsas, *Estudios del Río Verde* (Mexico, Secretaría de Recursos Hidraúlicos, 1961), text volume. San Pedro Jicayán is not to be confused with Jicayán de Tovar, located within the present-day State of Guerrero, about 20 miles northeast of Tlacoachixtlahuaca, Guerrero.

The Reyes list of place names distinguishes between the two Jicayáns by designating San Pedro Jicayán as "Xicayan de P. nieto" and the other Jicayán as "Xicayan de tobar." "P. nieto" refers to Pedro Nieto, the Spanish overlord or *encomendero* of Jicayán, who shared the town with the Spanish crown. The "Tovar" of Jicayán de Tovar is also the name of one of the town's *encomenderos*, who shared the town with Francisco Guillen. Short descriptions of both towns are included in the *Relación* of Tecuanapa, Guerrero (edited by J. Eric S. Thompson, *Tlalocan*, Vol. V-1, 90, 92–93) and in the *Suma de Visitas* (*PNE* I, entry nos. 808 [San Pedro Jicayán] and 810 [Jicayán de Tovar]). Jicayán de Tovar is discussed in two *Relaciones Geográficas*: that of 1580 from the Juxtlahuaca region (*RMEH* II, 151–55) and that of 1582 from Jalapa in the State of Guerrero (*PNE* IV, 252ff.). San Pedro Jicayán is mentioned in the *Relación* of Cuahuitlán (*PNE* IV, 157).

[2] *Mexican Manuscript Painting*, 65–66.

Mixteca, Jicayán had a great deal more territory in the early Colonial period than it does today. According to the 1547–1550 *Suma de Visitas*, Jicayán was bounded by Tututepec, Tlacamama, los Amusgos, and *Taymeo* [Atoyac?].[3] The "Tututepec" in this list undoubtedly refers to one of Tututepec's subject towns, probably Pinotepa de Don Luis, which is listed as a subject of Tututepec in the *Suma*. Jicayán is also said to bound the towns of Amusgos, Atoyac, Chayucu, Pinotepa de Don Luis, and Tlacamama in the entries for these towns in the *Suma de Visitas*.[4] Three of the towns mentioned as bordering Jicayán in the *Suma de Visitas* are also referred to in glosses written on the Lienzo of Jicayán. The town of Pinotepa de Don Luis is cited in the legend *termino de pinote [pa de] D° luis* ("the boundary with Pinotepa de Don Luis"), which is written along the line that extends from the center of the Lienzo to the upper-right corner; beside the place sign at the end of this line is the gloss *pinotecpa* (Figs. 158–59). In the lower-right corner, the town of San Miguel Tlacamama, Jicayán's neighbor on the west, is represented by a church building and a palm tree (Fig. 149) which are also connected to the central configuration by a thick black line. Underneath the church building is the gloss *tlacamama—*. The boundary line with Amusgos, the town which formerly bounded Jicayán on the northwest, is indicated only by the gloss *termino de amosgo* ("the boundary with Amusgos") written between two boundary signs on the left border of the Lienzo (Fig. 153).

The approximate area shown as within the boundaries of Jicayán in the town's Lienzo is indicated on Map 6 (p. 91), which also sets forth the present-day municipal units in the Coastal region of Oaxaca west of the Río Verde. As can be seen in this map, the lands of Jicayán extended farther to the north than they do today. The town of San Antonio Tepetlapa, about 12 miles northwest of Jicayán and now a separate municipal unit, is shown in the Lienzo of Jicayán as a subject of Jicayán because it appears within the circle of boundary signs. This subject town is depicted as a small church drawn near the left border of the Lienzo (Fig. 153), and underneath the church is the legend "tepetlapa." Similarly, the town of San Pedro Tulixtlahuaca, about 11 miles north of Jicayán and now within the municipality of Tepetlapa, is shown in the Lienzo as a subject of Jicayán. Above and to the left of the central place sign (Fig. 146) is a small church, and underneath it is the gloss "tulistlauaca."[5] In the early Colonial period Jicayán also controlled much of the land within the present municipality of Atoyac.

THE CENTRAL CONFIGURATION

In the center of the Lienzo (Fig. 147) is a place sign which consists of a frieze that contains the characteristic pyramidal designs, as well as three "star-eyes" that are often associated with the rain deity Tlaloc. On the right side of the frieze is a profile building with the standard pre-Conquest post and lintel and a crenelated frieze of roundels above the lintel. In the center of the frieze is seated a male personage who wears a *xicolli*, the long shirt with tassels commonly worn by rulers in the pre-Conquest manuscripts. Attached to the head of the figure is his calendrical name: seven dots plus a day sign which is only partly visible because of a hole in the Lienzo, but which is probably the day-sign Grass because the skeletal jaw typical of this sign can still be seen. The figure of 7-Grass is not accompanied by a personal name. Underneath the platform of the building is a date: the year Ten-Rabbit and the day Nine-Serpent; and below this date is a gloss: *del pueblo de xicayan* ("of the town of Jicayán").

The Place Sign of Jicayán

The essential elements of the place sign of Jicayán as it appears in Zacatepec 1 (Fig. 58) and Codex Colombino (Fig. 55) are a frieze and speech scrolls. This sign expresses a translation of Jicayán's Mixtec name, *ñuu sii qua'a*, as "the town which says much." In addition, *ñuu sii qua'a* is sometimes translated as "the town of the red grandfather" and may also mean "the town of the calendrical date or name 10, 11, or 13 Deer." In the Alvarado dictionary *sii* can mean "grandfather" and "to say," and also "pearl" (*perla*; *aljofar*). It would seem that *sii* may also indicate something that is small, round, and hard, because Alvarado gives *ñuhu sii* as "pellet" (*bodoque*), and *ñuhu* means "earth, dirt." The basic meanings of *quaha* (*qua'a*) are "red (the color)"; "much, many, large"; "to give, lend"; "to go"; and "right" as in "right hand."

How, then, can the place sign in the center of the Lienzo of Jicayán—a frieze with three star-eyes—correlate with the Mixtec name *ñuu sii qua'a* or with the Mixtec signs of Jicayán in Zacatepec 1 and Colombino? First, it is difficult to find any point of comparison between the sign in the Lienzo of Jicayán and the signs of Jicayán in the other two manuscripts because in both Colombino and the first Lienzo of Zacatepec, the qualifying element of the signs is a quantity of speech scrolls, and the star-eye motif is not present. Second, none of the meanings of *ñuu sii qua'a* described above appears to relate to star-eyes. There is a remote possibility that "red grandfather" might have been a metaphor for the rain deity (who usually has star-eyes) or that "red pearl" might have been a metaphor for star-eyes, but both of these hypotheses seem unlikely.

Perhaps, as in the case of Teozacoalco, Jicayán had a second Mixtec name in addition to *ñuu sii qua'a*, and it is this second name that is depicted in the Lienzo of Jicayán. It is also possible that the place sign in the center of the Lienzo represents a ceremonial site within the boundaries of Jicayán rather than the town of Jicayán itself. In some place signs in which the star-eye motif appears, it does not function as a qualifying element but indicates a ceremonial or sacred location. But it does not seem likely that the sign of a ceremonial site would be placed in the center of a map of Jicayán's lands and the sign of Jicayán itself omitted. In addition, Tulixtlahuaca, a subject of

---

[3] *PNE* I, entry no. 808.

[4] *PNE* I, entry nos. 32, 98, 304, 456, 648.

[5] The Mixtec name of Tepetlapa is *ñuu toto*, "the town of the rock." *Ñuu* = "town"; *toto* = "rock, cliff" (*peña*). The Mixtec name and place sign of Tulixtlahuaca are discussed in detail above, pp. 70–71.

Jicayán, is shown in Colombino to be the important ceremonial site associated with Jicayán; and in the Lienzo of Jicayán, Tulixtlahuaca is merely represented by a church (Fig. 146, upper-left corner) and not by a pre-Conquest place sign.

Still another possibility is that the frieze and building in the center of the Lienzo are not a place sign at all but merely a configuration to show the presence of an important town. That is, this configuration is not the sign of Jicayán's Mixtec name, but a symbol of "important town," much as concentric circles are used in twentieth-century road maps to distinguish large or important towns from smaller places which are symbolized by a simple circle. In a number of early Colonial maps of one town enclosed by the place signs of its boundaries, the town in the center is not shown as a place sign but merely as a building, which is often accompanied by a gloss that identifies the name of the town. For example, in Map No. 36 (Fig. 21), the town or towns in the center are shown as a Christian church and as two post-and-lintel buildings which are accompanied by glosses in Mixtec but are not place signs. Also, in the first Lienzo of Zacatepec (Fig. 85), many of the place signs appear in connection with post-and-lintel buildings and friezes with a variety of elaborate geometric decorations, but neither the buildings nor the friezes depict part of the place names shown in the accompanying signs. In all probability, then, the building and frieze in the center of the Lienzo of Jicayán either represent a second name of Jicayán (a Mixtec name that is not *ñuu sii qua'a*), or they represent merely the general idea of an important town whose name appears only in the Spanish gloss under the frieze.

♂ 7-Grass

The personage ♂ 7-Grass, who is seated on the frieze in the center of the Lienzo, does not seem to be analogous to any of the historical personages with the same calendrical name in the pre-Conquest manuscripts, although he lacks a personal name which would identify him more securely.

In Codex Bodley 16–V a ♂ 7-Grass "Bloody Tiger" is shown as ruler of Monkey Frieze in the early fourteenth century and as husband of ♀ 4-Serpent "Crossed Legs-Jewels."[6] In Bodley 18–III, the calendrical and personal names of ♂ 7-Grass "Bloody Tiger" appear above Monkey Frieze, and he is here indicated to be the father of ♀ 2-Vulture "Jewel Ornament with Shining Flowers," who marries ♂ 2-Water "Fire Serpent-Torch" of Tilantongo.[7] In this passage, the name of 7-Grass' wife is ♀ 6-Rabbit "Sun-Quechquemitl," and she apparently was his second wife.

Another ♂ 7-Grass is depicted in the upper-right corner of page 28 of Codex Sánchez Solís. This personage wears a tiger costume and has a circle of black paint around his eye; his town of origin is not specified.

Two persons named 7-Grass appear in the group of 112

[6] Caso, *Bodley*, 46.
[7] *Ibid.*, 47.

deity impersonators and nobles shown in Nuttall 54–68 as convening with 8-Deer and his half-brother 12-Movement in the year 1045. One of the two, on Nuttall 60d, has as a personal name a vessel which consists of a tiger claw with a handle. The personal name of the second 7-Grass, who appears on Nuttall 54c, is a small figure of Tlaloc with speech scrolls, or a "talking Tlaloc" (Fig. 6d). The personal name of the latter 7-Grass includes the qualifying elements of the two possible place signs of Jicayán: the star-eye which is the prominent feature of the Tlaloc figure's face and which is also the principal element in the frieze in the center of the Lienzo of Jicayán, and the speech scrolls, which are the principal elements of the place sign of Jicayán in Codex Colombino and Lienzo of Zacatepec 1. Perhaps this personal name functions also as a place name, and the 7-Grass of Nuttall 54c was a ruler of Jicayán or an impersonator of one of this town's important deities. But this is merely a tentative hypothesis, because 7-Grass "Talking Tlaloc" cannot be identified in any other manuscript and because the 7-Grass in the Lienzo of Jicayán lacks a personal name.

Another personage who may be analogous to the 7-Grass in the Lienzo of Jicayán is the person named 7-Grass who is shown at the top of the first Lienzo of Zacatepec (Figs. 90–91) as a *volador* in the company of ♂ 11-Tiger, the first ruler of Zacatepec in Zacatepec 1. In this scene 11-Tiger appears with the black facial paint of a priest, and 7-Grass wears a headdress with triangular points that is often associated with the rain god Tlaloc. This 7-Grass has no personal name, but a second calendrical name or date, 11-Deer, is attached to the name 7-Grass (Fig. 90). In the calendrical vocabulary, 11-Deer would be *si quaa* or *si quaha*, and it is possible that this day-sign and numeral were added to the name of 7-Grass to indicate that he is from Jicayán (*ñuu sii qua'a* in Mixtec). But again, this is a tentative hypothesis, for the principal feature which the *volador* in Zacatepec 1 and the personage in the Lienzo of Jicayán have in common is the calendrical name 7-Grass, and on this evidence alone it cannot be determined that the two Lienzos refer to the same person.

The Year Date Ten-Rabbit (1542?)

Below the frieze with star-eyes is the year date Ten-Rabbit, with the day-sign Rabbit attached to a typically pre-Conquest "A–O" year sign. It is somewhat difficult to make an absolutely certain correlation of this date with a Christian year date because it is not known whether the personage 7-Grass was the ruler of Jicayán in the early Colonial period, whether he was the founder of one of the pre-Conquest dynasties, or whether he was a non-historical deity impersonator.

If, as a working hypothesis, we assume that 7-Grass was the ruler of Jicayán in the early Colonial period, then the date Ten-Rabbit may be 1490, 1542, or 1594. Furthermore, if it is assumed that the date Ten-Rabbit is roughly contemporary with the first drawing style seen in the Lienzo, then the year 1490 can be eliminated, because what is presumed to be the earliest style shows evidence of "disintegrated frame line"—that is, a style characteristic of the period following European contact, which cannot be earlier than the 1520's. And on the basis of the earliest style seen in the Lienzo, the date 1594 also seems unlikely. By 1590, both pre-Conquest style and iconography have become considerably diluted, as can be seen in three pictorial documents from the Mixteca which date from this decade: the 1590 sketch map of a land grant in the Coixtlahuaca region, a 1595 map of a site within the lands of Cuquila, and the 1597 Tlazultepec Genealogy.

On the sketch map from Coixtlahuaca (Fig. 46), the town sites are illustrated by small churches rather than by the typically pre-Conquest post-and-lintel building seen in the center of the Lienzo of Jicayán. In the Cuquila map (Fig. 133), the towns are also shown as churches with prominent bells, although the fretwork patterns of the large cornices between the church and belfry are strongly reminiscent of the friezes seen in pre-Conquest place signs. In the Lienzo of Jicayán, small churches are used to represent the three towns of Tlacamama (Fig. 149), Tulixtlahuaca (Fig. 146), and Tepetlapa (Fig. 153); but in all three instances, these churches are drawn in the second style seen in the Lienzo—that is, they were either drawn on the Lienzo at a later date, or executed by a European or more Europeanized artist than the draftsman responsible for the first style.

Another prominent European element in the Cuquila map is the great quantity of trees that appear within, on and around the hill motifs. The use of trees as landscape features rather than as part of a pictorial sign occurs in the Lienzo of Jicayán only in two isolated trees drawn in the second, presumably later, style: a palm tree near the town of Tlacamama (Fig. 149), and another smaller palm tree placed on the line which runs from the central configuration of Jicayán to the town of Tlacamama (Fig. 146, lower-right corner).

In the 1597 Tlazultepec Genealogy (Fig. 30), a number of pre-Conquest elements seen in the Lienzo of Jicayán are lacking, notably the year dates with an A–O year-sign, and calendrical names of persons with the twenty day-signs and dots. In addition, the place signs in the Tlazultepec Genealogy, although still pre-Conquest in format and iconography, are drawn in a very sketchy, non-native style. The hill motifs are delineated as mounds with wavy outlines and do not have the characteristic pre-Conquest border with rectangular projections or the volutes on both sides of the base of the hill—two features which occur in most of the hill signs in the Lienzo of Jicayán.

Moreover, if the Lienzo of Jicayán is compared with Lienzo of Zacatepec 1, which was tentatively dated 1540 to 1560, and with Lienzo of Zacatepec 2, which was tentatively dated 1580 to 1600, the Jicayán Lienzo most closely resembles the first Lienzo of Zacatepec in both style and iconography. The Lienzo of Jicayán has none of the elaborate landscape elements seen in the second Lienzo of Zacatepec, such as hills with hatchures indicating shading and with trees, nor does it have the extensive cartographic notations, such as the network of roads and streams, shown

in Zacatepec 2. Rather, the Lienzo of Jicayán, in common with the first Lienzo of Zacatepec, omits virtually all suggestion of landscape or of a Europeanized type of map. Both the Lienzo of Jicayán and Zacatepec 1 name rather than portray places; that is, all hills in these two maps depict the name of a place rather than the place itself. And both the Lienzo of Jicayán and Zacatepec 1 have pre-Conquest calendrical names and year dates with an A–O year-sign, two elements that are absent in the second Lienzo of Zacatepec.

Thus, if the date Ten-Rabbit in the center of the Lienzo of Jicayán is a date contemporary with the drawing of the Lienzo, it represents the year 1542. The "disintegrated frame line" seen in the drawing style indicates that it was done after the 1520's, and the central configuration and fifty-two signs that encircle the Lienzo show none of the strong intrusions of European style and iconography that are seen in Mixtec pictorial documents drawn as late as the 1590's.

THE MIXTEC GLOSSES

The Lienzo of Jicayán appears to have been annotated at least three different times with glosses in Mixtec. The only group of glosses that is now entirely legible are 32 place names written in black ink near the place signs that form an irregular circle around the border of the Lienzo (Fig. 144). Also in black ink are the legends under the three buildings in the center of the Lienzo ("del pueblo de xicayan," "tulistlauaca," and "tepetlapa"), the place names "pinotecpa" under the hill in the upper-right corner (Fig. 159) and "tlacamama" under the church in the lower-right corner (Fig. 149), as well as the phrases "termino de amosgo" on the left border (Fig. 153) and "termino de pinote [pa de] D° luis" accompanying the boundary line of the upper-right corner (Fig. 159), and the word "Lebante" in the upper-right corner (Fig. 158).

The Lienzo was also extensively annotated in a type of ink which turns brown owing to oxidation, and which for the sake of comparison will be called "brown ink." The only brown-ink gloss that is now completely legible is *duta ticaxi*, written at the right of a boundary sign which consists of a stone with flowing water (Fig. 153). Many other brown-ink glosses are still visible though not legible: for example, below the temple platform in the lower-left corner (Fig. 152), both below and above a black platform with a stone motif on the left border (Fig. 155), and below the initial "d" of the "del pueblo de xicayan" gloss in the center of the Lienzo (Fig. 147). Throughout the Lienzo there are evidences of glosses written in brown ink which are now merely small smears of brown (as, for example, in Figs. 151 and 157).[8]

A third group of Mixtec glosses was written on small rectangles of paper which were sewn onto the Lienzo near almost every boundary sign. Unfortunately these pieces of paper have been torn off, and all that remains of

---

[8] The location of the "brown ink" glosses is more easily seen in color photographs. The color transparencies which I consulted are available from the Archivo Fotográfico of the INAH, no. XLIX-5 (the entire Lienzo) and nos. XLIX-7 through XLIX-19 (13 details).

these glosses are a few shreds of paper still attached to the thread which originally tacked them to the Lienzo (Figs. 148, 153, 154). In one fragment of paper we can see the remnant of a Mixtec gloss (*Yoohi . . .* or *Yochi . . . ?*) written in what appears to be a nineteenth-century hand (Fig. 153). It is possible that these glosses were sewn on the Lienzo at a time when it was presented in court in connection with a land dispute, and it is regrettable that they have been removed, because the small rectangles of thread that remain on the Lienzo indicate that boundary signs which are not accompanied by a black-ink gloss were at one time glossed with one of the small pieces of paper.

RELATIONSHIP BETWEEN THE MIXTEC GLOSSES AND THE PICTORIAL SIGNS

Most of the Mixtec glosses written on the Lienzo of Jicayán in black ink appear to be written near a specific place sign, and thus it might be assumed that a gloss and the place sign it accompanies give the same Mixtec name of a site or boundary. But a careful analysis of the glosses and the pictorial signs shows that this is by no means the case. In fact, the Lienzo is an excellent example of a pictorial document to which a text has been added that is often difficult to correlate with the pictorial text it supposedly explicates.

It has been stressed in this study that one key to identifying place signs is the successful correlation of a pictorial sign and the Mixtec name represented by the sign. But the mere appearance of a pictorial sign in connection with a gloss in Mixtec is no guarantee that the two are necessarily equivalent. It was a standard practice in the early Colonial period to present a painted manuscript or pictographic map as evidence in land disputes; and many of these pictorial documents may well have been annotated by persons who could write Mixtec in European script but who had little or no idea of how to interpret the pictorial contents of the paintings or maps. Thus, the annotations in European script often have a haphazard or tangential relationship to the pictorial writing with which they are associated. This is precisely what seems to have happened in the Lienzo of Jicayán, and as a case in point, the relationship between the glosses and pictorial signs in the Lienzo will be discussed in detail below.

Each of the fifty-two signs that surrounds the central configuration is described briefly, and the description is followed by the figure number of this study where the sign is most clearly illustrated. If a gloss accompanies the sign, it is analyzed in connection with the sign near which it is written. In some cases, a gloss may refer to a pictorial sign in the Lienzo other than the one near which it is written, but these glosses, too, will be considered in the discussion of the sign they accompany rather than in connection with the sign to which they refer. For the sake of convenience, the pictorial signs have been numbered from 1 to 52 (Fig. 145), beginning in the upper-right corner of the Lienzo, below the black line with the legend "termino de pinote [pa de] Dº luis."

Sign 1

Description: Two streams of water which appear to be combined with a human hand motif, because both streams terminate in three fingers.

Fig. Nos.: 148, 159

Accompanying Gloss: *yuhui maa*

Translation: "the arroyo in the center"

Relationship of the Gloss to the Pictorial Sign:

In this case, the gloss apparently refers to the place sign with which it is associated. One of the meanings of *yuhui* is "arroyo," which is illustrated by the streams of water. *Maa* may mean "center, in the center of" and also indicates a movement from above to below. This word is represented by the inward and downward movement of the two streams. It is interesting to compare this place sign with a boundary sign in Map No. 36 (Fig. 22*d*), for the latter sign is accompanied by the gloss *itno nino maa*, a place name that also contains the word *maa. Itno* means "slope"; *nino* means "below." The *maa* element seems to be represented by the female figure with arms outstretched; her right hand appears to terminate in the round circles used to depict streams of water. This hand-and-water combination is similar to that seen in the *yuhui maa* sign in the Lienzo of Jicayán, where each of the two streams of water terminates in three fingers. It is not known why this combination of human hands and flowing water represents the Mixtec word *maa*.

Sign 2

Description: A stone with the head of a rabbit and one dot (possibly the date or calendrical name 1-Rabbit?)

Fig. Nos.: 148, 159

Accompanying Gloss: none

Comments:

If the combination of one dot and the rabbit motif is intended to represent the date or calendrical name 1-Rabbit, a translation of this pictorial sign into the Mixtec language would be: *yuu cosayu.* (*Yuu* means "stone"; *cosayu* or *casayu* is the calendrical name 1-Rabbit.)

Sign 3

Description: The head of an alligator combined with the figure of a dog or other quadruped.

Fig. No.: 148

Accompanying Gloss: none

Sign 4

Description: A semicircular enclosure with small curlicues indicating water on the interior rim; within the enclosure is the profile bust of a male human figure who points toward his mouth.

Fig. No.: 148

Accompanying Gloss: *yuu xaña*

Translation: "the stone which leaves or which makes noise"

Relationship of the Gloss to the Pictorial Sign:

This is a notable example of a difference between the place name shown in the pictorial sign and the name given in the gloss that accompanies it. The gloss, *yuu xaña,* is *yuu dzaña* in the dialect of the Alvarado dictionary. *Yuu* means "stone," and a stone is not part of the sign above the gloss. *Xaña*, or *dzaña*, means "to leave, let go," which is not represented by the figure who points to his mouth. The *xaña* section of the gloss might also be interpreted as *xañaa*, or *dzañaa*, which would mean "to make noise"; but this verb also is not depicted by the pointing human figure.

Actually, the sign in question does not seem to represent a boundary of Jicayán, but the neighboring town of Pinotepa de Don Luis. First, this sign resembles the sign of Pinotepa de Don Luis placed outside the rectangle of boundary signs in Lienzo of Zacatepec 1 (Fig. 111, upper-right corner), because one of the essential features of both signs is a profile bust of a male figure who lifts one hand to his mouth. Second, the Mixtec name of Pinotepa de Don Luis in the sixteenth century was *ndoyo yuhu*, which may be translated "the marsh of the mouth" or "to lift to the mouth." *Ndoyo*, depending on variations in tone, may mean "wet, marshy land" or "to lift, raise." The first of these definitions is represented by the semicircular enclosure which has on the inside border curlicues that depict water, and thus illustrates wet or marshy land. The second definition of *ndoyo* is shown by the lifted or raised hand of the human figure. This hand is lifted to, and points at, the figure's mouth, a gesture which not only reinforces the *ndoyo* section of the name, but literally points out the second section of the name: *yuhu*, or "mouth."

Sign 5

Description: A large stone placed in an upright position.
Fig. No.: 148
Accompanying Gloss: *cuiti yuqn̄*
Translation: the mound of the temple"
Relationship of the Gloss to the Pictorial Sign:

Cuiti means "mound"; and *yuqn̄* means "temple, church," as well as "row, furrow."[9] This place name undoubtedly refers to a site about half a mile southeast of Jicayán, located near the present-day road from Jicayán to Pinotepa de Don Luis. This site is known today as Cerro de la Iglesia, or "hill of the church," and it contains large unexcavated platforms that seem indicative of a ceremonial site. This mound is within the boundaries of Jicayán rather than being a boundary marker.

The relationship between the *cuiti yuqn̄* gloss and the upright stone with which it is associated seems to be non-existent. It is possible that the place sign with a stone represents the present-day boundary between Jicayán and Pinotepa de Don Luis, a site named *yuu ca'nu*, or "big stone" (illustrated in Fig. 121). But no element occurs in the sign to represent the *ca'nu* section of *yuu ca'nu*. As we have seen in the place sign of Teozacoalco (*chiyo ca'nu*), the word *ca'nu* ("large; to break") may be illus-

trated by a small human figure bending or "breaking" the frieze which represents the word *chiyo*.

The two essential pictorial elements in Sign 5 are "stone" and "upright," and it is possible that this sign represents a fairly common Spanish place name, *Piedra Parada*, or "upright stone." This place name would probably be *yuu ndaa* in Mixtec, for *ndaa* means "straight, upright." But Sign 5 seems to have little to do with the gloss *cuiti yuqn̄*, or "mound of the temple."

Sign 6

Description: A tree whose branches terminate in human hand motifs.
Fig. No.: 148
Accompanying Gloss: *yutnu yta yata*
Translation: "a type of tree known popularly as the *roble blanco* or *macuil* (*Tabebuia pentaphylla*)"
Relationship of the Gloss to the Pictorial Sign:

In this case, the gloss and pictorial sign seem to be in agreement. Martínez Gracida lists *yutnu yata* as the Mixtec name of the *roble blanco*,[10] and the Alvarado dictionary gives *yutnu yata* as one of two Mixtec names for "oak" in general (*roble*). The insertion of the word *yta* or *ita* (meaning "flower") between the two words *yutnu* and *yata* was probably made to distinguish this particular *yutnu yata*, which is a flowering tree, from other trees designated by the words *yutnu yata*—namely, the evergreen oak (*Quercus ilex*) which has no flowers, and a type of acacia which is more noted for its thorns than for its flowers.[11] The flowers of the *roble blanco* are usually a light pinkish purple, but it is the leaves of this tree that are represented in Sign 6. As the *pentaphylla* part of this plant's botanical name implies, the leaves grow in five leaflets, hence the Nahuatl name *macuil*, derived from *macuilli*, meaning "five." Paul C. Standley characterizes the leaves of the genus *Tabebuia* as "digitately five- or seven-foliate,"[12] and the "digital" quality is illustrated explicitly in Sign 6, where the leaves of the tree are represented as human hands with five fingers.

Sign 7

Description: A road containing three footprints; on top of the road is the head of a large lizard, probably an iguana.
Fig. No.: 148
Accompanying Gloss: none
Comments:

A pun is undoubtedly intended in this sign, for in some dialects of Mixtec the word for "road" and the word for "iguana" are homonymous except for variations in tone.

---

[9] The Mixtec word *yuqn̄* of this gloss is recorded in the Alvarado dictionary as *yuq*; in the Dyk-Stoudt Mixtec dictionary the comparable word is *yucùn*. The word is occasionally used as a geographical substantive in place names, as for example in one of the names associated with a boundary sign (10-top) in Map No. 36 (Fig. 21; discussed in Appendix E).

[10] *Flora y fauna del Estado libre y soberano de Oaxaca* (Oaxaca, 1891).

[11] The Alvarado dictionary lists *yutnu yata* as meaning "enzina," the Spanish name of the evergreen oak. In Jicayán I was told that *tun yata* (*tnu yata* in the Alvarado dictionary dialect) is the Mixtec name of the *Acacia hindsii* or "hat thorn acacia."

[12] *Trees and Shrubs of Mexico* (Washington, 1920–26 [Contributions from the United States Herbarium, vol. 23]), 1320. The leaves of the *macuil* tree are illustrated in a black-and-white drawing in Maximino Martínez, *Las plantas medicinales de México*, 4th ed. (Mexico, 1959), 450, and in a color drawing in Helen O'Gorman, *Mexican Flowering Trees and Plants* (Mexico, 1961), 41.

For example, in Jicayán and Pinotepa de Don Luis, the word for "road" is *iti*, and the word for "iguana" is *titi*, a combination of the animal prefix *ti-* and the word *iti*. In the Dyk-Stoudt dictionary for the dialect of San Miguel el Grande, *ichi* is listed as meaning "road," and *ti'ichí* as meaning "iguana." Thus the large lizard's head in Sign 7 serves as a phonetic indicator that reinforces the reading of the band of footprints as *iti* or *ichi*, as opposed to *yaya*, a second Mixtec word that means "road" or "street."

Sign 8

Description: A tree whose branches terminate in circular fruit.
Fig. Nos.: 148, 149
Accompanying Gloss: *yutnu yachi diqui*
Translation: "a type of *jícaro* or calabash tree"
Relationship of the Gloss to the Pictorial Sign:

Both the gloss and the sign above it refer to the same botanical motif: the *jícaro* or calabash tree. This tree is explicitly represented in Sign 8, because the four globular objects at the end of the tree's branches are the gourd-like fruit of this tree. In the gloss below, the two words *yutnu yachi* (*yutnu yasi* in the dialect of the Alvarado dictionary) mean "jícaro," a tree of the genus *Cresentia*. *Yutnu* is "tree," and *yachi*, or *yasi*, means "jícara," the fruit of this tree. The hard shell of this fruit is used throughout the Coast as a container, scoop, cup—or generally as an extension of the hand. On the Coast, as elsewhere in the Mixteca and in the Isthmus of Tehuantepec, women often wear the jícara on their head when it is not in use (Fig. 142).

The precise meaning of *diqui* or *ndiqui*, the final word in the gloss accompanying Sign 8, is difficult to ascertain. This word undoubtedly functions as an adjective describing the type of jícaro tree or the type of gourd produced by this tree. One of the meanings of *ndiqui* when it describes plants or trees is to signify that the plant in question has hard, pointed bristle-like projections.[13] For example, the Alvarado dictionary lists the phrase *ita ndeq[ue]* as the Mixtec term for the grass known in English as "darnel" and in Spanish as "zizaña" (*Lolium temulentum*). *Ita* here means "grass"; and *ndeq[ue]*, the equivalent of the *diqui* of the gloss under Sign 8, refers to this plant's lemma, which is a small pointed bristle. On the Coast, *iño ndiqui* is the Mixtec name of the plant known in English as "wild amaranth" and in Spanish as "bledo" (*Amaranthus blitum*). In this case, *iño* means "plant with thorns," and *ndiqui* indicates that the thorns are hard and bristly. But if such a translation is applicable to the word *diqui* in the gloss accompanying Sign 8, it is not indicated in the jícaro tree shown in this sign, for the tree has no bristly projections. Undoubtedly, there are in the Mixteca a variety of adjectives used to designate different types of jícaros, because they are an extremely common and useful tree.[14] A more extensive and penetrating study of Mixtec names of plants, shrubs, and trees will certainly uncover many more Mixtec names for specific varieties of plants, as well as the different regional Mixtec names used for plants in various sections of the Mixteca.

Sign 9

Description: A feather-mat field with a bird.
Fig. No.: 149
Accompanying Gloss: *cava yy tiñoo yucu*
Translation: "the sacred ravine of the wild chicken"
Relationship of the Gloss to the Pictorial Sign:

The gloss and the sign are probably related, although the identification of the bird shown in the sign is rather uncertain. The *cava* or *cahua* section of the gloss is represented by the feather-mat motif which in place signs of towns is usually associated with the Mixtec word *yodzo* ("plain, field"). Here the sense of *cahua* illustrated is probably "ravine" rather than its alternate meanings "rock" and "cave" because the feather-mat motif is indicative of a relatively flat region surrounded by elevated ground. The *yy* (or *ii*) section of the gloss means "sacred," perhaps signifying that the ravine in question is a sacred site. *Tiñoo* usually means "owl" or "chickens";[15] but the bird in the pictorial sign resembles neither an owl or a chicken, and it seems unlikely that a chicken would appear in an essentially pre-Conquest place sign because chickens were introduced into the New World by European colonists. A clue to the identity of the bird is provided by the final word of the gloss, *yucu*. When *yucu* is used as an adjective, it means "undomesticated, wild," and thus the entire phrase *tiñoo yucu* undoubtedly describes an undomesticated bird resembling a chicken that was native to the Mixteca prior to the Spanish conquest.[16]

Sign 10

Description: A tree or shrub with heart-shaped leaves.
Fig. No.: 149

word for "jícara," the following Mixtec phrases in which *yasi* is qualified by adjectives:

yasi tiyoo *yasi ndaha*	}	white and burnished jícara (*xicara blanca y bruñida*)
yasi coho *yasi coho cánu* *yasi tesiyo*	}	large jícara (*xicara grande*)
yasi ndaha *yasi cuisi* *yasi cuite*	}	a jícara to be carved (with decorative designs) (*xicara por labrar*)

There are undoubtedly many other qualifying adjectives that have not yet been recorded.

[15] In some dialects of Mixtec, such as that recorded in the Alvarado dictionary, *tiñoo* also means "stars."

[16] In the Nahuatl language as set forth in the Molina Nahuatl dictionary, the native word for "Spanish rooster" (*gallo de castilla*) is *vexolotl*—that is, the Nahuatl name for the native American turkey, known throughout Mexico today as the "guajolote." It is difficult to say whether the Mixtec word *tiñoo* similarly referred to the native turkey and was later used to refer to European-imported chickens, but this may have been the case. Unfortunately, the sixteenth-century Alvarado dictionary does not list a Mixtec word for the native turkey; and in the Mixteca today, the word for "native turkey" is *co'lo*, a loan word derived from the Nahuatl *guajolote*.

[13] When used as a noun, *ndiqui* (*ndeque* in the Alvarado dictionary, *ndíquí* in the dialect of San Miguel el Grande) may mean "horn of an animal, point, spike."

[14] The Alvarado dictionary lists, in addition to *yasi* as the basic Mixtec

Accompanying Gloss: *xicuvi duva*
Translation: "the herb that causes illness?"
Relationship of the Gloss to the Pictorial Sign:

Sign 10 and its gloss are probably related, for the word *duva* or *nduvua* in the gloss refers to the plant motif in the sign. *Nduvua* can mean "vegetable" or "herb" and is often used to refer to plants with pointed leaves or roots, probably because *nduvua* also means "arrow." The leaves of the plant in Sign 10 are cordate, or roughly heart-shaped, and relatively pointed at the end, and thus they depict the idea of *nduvua* as an herb with pointed leaves.

The translation of *xicuvi* is less certain. *Xi-* (*dzi-* in the dialect of the Alvarado dictionary) is a causative prefix used before verbs and denotes an action performed or caused to happen; this prefix can often be translated as "to make, cause to happen." *Cuhui* or *cuvui* is a verb which has a multitude of meanings, but the one which may be applicable here is "to be sick, to be in pain." Thus the entire phrase *xicuvi* or *dzicuhui* would be "to cause illness or pain." It is possible that the unidentified herb shown in Sign 10 and referred to as *duva* in the gloss is a plant which is poisonous and produces illness or pain.

Sign 11

Description: A tree or shrub with thorn-like projections.
Fig. No.: 144
Accompanying Gloss: *yuvi [yu?] tnu yñu yta*
Translation: "the arroyo of the flowering thorn tree"
Relationship of the Gloss to the Pictorial Sign:

The tree in the pictorial sign and the gloss beneath it are in agreement, although the specific type of tree referred to by both is not known. *Yuvi* or *yuvui* means "arroyo" or "ravine"; *[yu]tnu* means "tree"; *yñu* or *iñu* means "thorn"; and *yta* or *ita* means "flower," or when used as an adjective, "flowering." The pictorial sign shows a tree with thorny projections and thus illustrates the general type of tree described in the gloss.

The arroyo or ravine in question is not illustrated in the place sign itself, but it is no doubt an extension of the stream of water which is sketched lightly on the right side of the Lienzo and which runs from Sign 1 (*yuhui maa*) to the sign under discussion. Written inside this stream near the black line which extends from Jicayán to Tlacamama is the gloss *yuhui dita yutno* (Fig. 148), which may mean "the arroyo where there is an abundance of trees." *Yuhui* means "arroyo"; one of the meanings of *dita* or *ndita* is "to have an abundance of"; *yutno* or *yutnu* means "tree(s)."

Sign 12

Description: The lower half of a bird or animal.
Fig. No.: 144
Accompanying Gloss: *chiti cuiñe*
Translation: "the lower part of a tiger"
Relationship of the Gloss to the Pictorial Sign:

The upper section of the place sign has been obliterated because of a hole in the Lienzo, but it is still possible to distinguish the legs, feet, and tail of an animal or bird. The type of long rectangular tail seen in this sign seems to resemble closely the tail feathers of other birds drawn on the Lienzo, particularly those of a parrot-like bird within a curved rock (Fig. 154). Tails of animals are usually shown as narrow and rounded at the end rather than as a rectangular block. If, as seems most likely, Sign 12 represents a bird, then the gloss written underneath does not refer to this sign. *Chiti* (*site* in the dialect of the Alvarado dictionary) means "intestines," or when used in place names, it may mean "the lower part of." *Cuiñe* or *cuiñi*, when used as a noun, is usually translated as "tiger" and is a generic term that refers to various types of spotted or striped felines.[17] The animal in Sign 12 could not be a tiger, for not only does it have a tail that resembles the tail feathers of a bird, but it appears to have two legs, shown as one leg in profile, rather than being a quadruped, and it lacks the spots which are one of the principal characteristics of New World "tigers."

It would be tempting to assign the gloss *chiti cuiñe* to the next sign in the Lienzo, Sign 13 (Fig. 150), because this sign shows a quadruped with a stone motif placed in its middle, in the region of the animal's stomach or intestines (*chiti*). But this quadruped lacks not only the spots or stripes of a tiger; he also does not have a particularly feline appearance, and he does not have the usual furry chin found in most representations of tigers in Mixtec manuscripts. No other place sign in the Lienzo contains a feline or "tiger" motif, and thus the gloss *chiti cuiñe* does not seem to be represented by any pictorial sign in the Lienzo.

Sign 13

Description: A stone placed in a quadruped, possibly a rodent.[18]
Fig. No.: 150
Accompanying Gloss: *yuu coo*
Translation: "the stone of the serpent" or "the bowl-shaped stone"
Relationship of the Gloss to the Pictorial Sign:

The gloss *yuu coo* does not refer to Sign 13. *Yuu* means "stone," and the meaning of *coo* which is most easily represented by a pictorial sign is "serpent," which has nothing to do with the quadruped seen in the place sign. It is possible that the gloss *yuu coo* refers to one of two pictorial signs in the Lienzo. One of these is Sign 15, which consists of the head of a serpent whose neck has the form of a hatchet (Fig. 150). The serpent in Sign 15 is known to be a rattlesnake or viper, *coò cáá* in Mixtec, because the hatchet motif is the usual logogram for *caa* or "metal." *Coò cáá* literally means "serpent of metal," for *coò* means "serpent," and *cáá* means "of metal, metallic." The gloss *yuu coo* ("stone of the serpent") may refer to the serpent sign, although Sign 15 lacks a stone motif to depict the word *yuu*, and the gloss lacks the adjective *caa* that

[17] As a noun *cuiñe* can also mean "spot, stain. blemish, swelling, lump."

[18] The quadruped in Sign 13 seems very similar to two animal figures (one from Codex Laud 45 and one from Codex Fejérváry-Mayer 34) which Eduard Seler classifies as rodents of unknown species ("Die Tierbilder in den mexicanischen und den Maya-Handschriften," *Gesammelte Abhandlungen* . . . , Vol. 4, 522–23, Figs. 228, 229).

should modify *coo* and specify, as does the pictorial sign, that the serpent in question is a rattlesnake or viper.

A second possibility is that the gloss *yuu coo* should be *yuu co'o*, with a glottal stop between the two *o*'s, and that this gloss refers to Sign 16, a rounded stone with an opening at the top (Fig. 150). *Co'o*, when used as an adjective, means "in the form of a bowl" or "very open," and Sign 16 seems to represent very accurately a translation of *yuu co'o* as "a bowl-shaped stone" or "an open stone."

Sign 14

Description: A profile male figure whose hands appear to be manacled, as if he were a prisoner. He wears a *xicolli* and a loincloth; his head is bald; his face is decorated with a single vertical line of black facial paint; his knees are flexed in a running position.
Fig. No.: 150
Accompanying Gloss: none

Sign 15

Description: The head of a serpent whose neck has the form of a hatchet.
Fig. No.: 150
Accompanying Gloss: none
Comments:

It is possible that the gloss *yuu coo* written under Sign 13 refers to Sign 15, and this gloss is discussed above, under Sign 13.

Sign 16

Description: A hollow circular stone that is open at the top.
Fig. Nos.: 150, 151
Accompanying Gloss: *yuu chaā*
Translation: "the stone of the foot?"
Relationship of the Gloss to the Pictorial Sign:

As was discussed above under Sign 13, the gloss *yuu coo* written under Sign 13 may refer to Sign 16, because *yuu co'o* can be translated as "the bowl-shaped stone" or "the open stone."

In a similar fashion, the gloss associated with Sign 16 seems to be misplaced, and it probably refers to Sign 28, a human foot placed against a stone (Fig. 153). The gloss *yuu chaā* is probably *yuu cha'a*, with a glottal stop between the two *a*'s, and thus *yuu* would be translated as "stone," and *cha'a* (or *saha* in the dialect of the Alvarado dictionary) as "foot." The place sign which best illustrates this place name is Sign 28, which consists of a stone and a human leg with the foot pressed against the stone.

Sign 17

Description: Three streams of water which are shown as confluent.
Fig. Nos.: 150, 151
Accompanying Gloss: *yuta uni*
Translation: "three rivers"
Relationship of the Gloss to the Pictorial Sign:

The gloss and the place sign are in perfect agreement, for the sign represents three streams of water, and the gloss means "three rivers." (*Yuta* = "river"; *uni* =

"three.") The place represented by this sign is a site known as *Los Tres Ríos* ("the three rivers"), which is located about 10 miles northwest of Jicayán. This site is near the point where the *Río de la Hamaca* ("Hammock River") and the *Río Trapiche* ("Sugar Mill River") join to form the *Río Cortijos* ("River of the Farmhouses").

Sign 18

Description: A hill with a bird.
Fig. No.: 151
Accompanying Gloss: none

Sign 19

Description: A river with spouts of water and three trefoil-shaped flowers.
Fig. Nos.: 151, 152
Accompanying Gloss: *yuvua caa viyo*
Translation: "the wall or enclosure of 2-Reed, the moon deity"
Relationship of the Gloss to the Pictorial Sign:

This gloss does not refer to the sign under which it is written, nor does it appear to refer to any other sign in the Lienzo. *Yuvua* or *yuhua* means "wall, enclosure"; and *caa viyo* or *ca huiyo* is the calendrical name 2-Reed, which, according to the Alvarado dictionary, was the calendrical name of the moon in the pre-Conquest period.[19] Another possible translation of *yuvua caa viyo* would be "the wall which climbs up to the milpas or fields," for *caa* may mean "to climb, extend" and *viyo* or *huiyu* may mean "milpa, field." Neither of these two translations is illustrated by the river with flowers above the gloss, nor does this gloss appear to be related to another sign in the Lienzo.

Sign 20

Description: A profile platform whose rectangular base contains a pattern of squares and a stairway similar to the one seen in the front-facing platform of Sign 27 (Fig. 153).
Fig. Nos.: 151, 152
Accompanying Gloss: Underneath this sign is a vestige of a barely visible gloss in brown ink. A hole in the Lienzo has obliterated the beginning of the gloss; the final letters may be *tiyyo* or *tinyo*. However, the reading of this gloss is uncertain, and an analysis of it will not be attempted.

Sign 21

Description: A profile building that contains a plant with heart-shaped leaves.
Fig. No.: 152
Accompanying Gloss: none
Comments:

The plant in this place sign is similar to the plant in Sign 10 (Fig. 149), which is accompanied by the gloss *xicuvi duva*.

Sign 22

Description: A stone with two dots.

19 Caso, *Selden*, 23; 71.

Fig. Nos.: 151, 152
Accompanying Gloss: *yuu iño cuta*
Translation: "six round stones"
Relationship of the Gloss to the Pictorial Sign:

It seems very likely that this gloss does not refer to Sign 22, but to Sign 23, which is directly above Sign 22. Sign 23 consists of a stone which contains six small circles, and thus seems to illustrate the gloss *yuu iño cuta* when this phrase is translated as "six round stones." *Yuu* means "stone"; *iño* may mean "six," "thorns," or "snow, frost"; and *cuta* means "circular, round."

Sign 23

Description: A stone which contains six small dots.
Fig. No.: 152
Accompanying Gloss: *yucu yño*
Translation: "hill of thorns?"
Relationship of the Gloss to the Pictorial Sign:

As was noted above, the gloss written under Sign 22 refers to Sign 23. The gloss under Sign 23, *yucu yño*, may be translated in three ways: "six hills," "hill of thorns," or "snowy hill." None of these three translations seems to be illustrated by any of the signs in the Lienzo.

Sign 24

Description: A frieze with geometric patterns, a feather-mat field, and an eagle's head.
Fig. Nos.: 152, 153
Accompanying Gloss: *yucu yço*
Translation: "hill of the rabbit"
Relationship of the Gloss to the Pictorial Sign:

The gloss in no way corresponds to the sign above it, for the sign's qualifying element is a bird rather than a rabbit (*yço* or *idzo* in Mixtec). The only rabbit shown in the Lienzo is one in Sign 2 (Fig. 148), and this rabbit appears with a stone rather than a hill and thus probably does not represent the gloss *yucu yço*. The "hill of the rabbit" referred to in this gloss may be the same site as the *Cerro Conejo* (or "hill of the rabbit") shown in the lower-left corner of the 1893 map of the lands of Manuel Yglesias (Fig. 138), where this site functions as a boundary between Yglesias and the town of Ixcapa.

Sign 24 with a frieze, field motif, and eagle's head may be referred to by *cahua yachani*, the gloss written above Sign 42, or possibly by *duhua yoço ñoñami*, the gloss written above Sign 26.

Sign 25

Description: A river with spouts of water and a twisted vine with thorns.
Fig. Nos.: 152, 153
Accompanying Gloss: *yuvi yñu cuiy*
Translation: "arroyo of the green thorn"
Relationship of the Gloss to the Pictorial Sign:

In this case, the gloss relates to the place sign under which it is written. *Yuvi* or *yuvui* means "arroyo" and is represented by the cross-section of a river in the sign. *Yñu cuiy* or *iño cuii* is literally "green thorn," for *iño* means "thorn" and *cuii* means "green." The combination of the two words refers to a kind of thorny parasitic vine which is common around Jicayán, but whose botanical name was not ascertained. This plant is illustrated in the place sign by a twisted rope-like vine with prominent thorns on each side.

Sign 26

Description: A hill with the upper half of a profile male figure appended to the left side; one hand of this figure touches the summit of the hill.
Fig. Nos.: 152, 153
Accompanying Gloss: *duhua yoço ñoñami*
Translation: "the gully of the field where there are *camotes,* or sweet potatoes"
Relationship of the Gloss to the Pictorial Sign:

The gloss does not relate to the sign above which it is written, but it is possible that it may relate to one of two other signs in the Lienzo. *Duhua* or *nduhua* means "gulley, plain"; *yoço* or *yodzo* is "valley, field"; *ño* or *ñuu* is "place where something exists"; and *ñami* means "camote," an indigenous type of sweet potato. Given this translation, the gloss might refer to Sign 41 at the top of the Lienzo (Fig. 156). This sign consists of the feather-mat field which would represent *yoço* or *yodzo*, and a plant motif which may represent *ñami* or "camote." The lower section of the plant may depict the tubular sweet potato and a root, and the long, thin stem which projects from the top of the plant would be the tendril which is typical of the plant.

It is also faintly possible that this gloss may refer to the place sign directly to the left of the gloss, Sign 24, which consists of a frieze, a feather-mat field, and the head of an eagle. The usual Mixtec word for "eagle" is *yaha* or *ya'a*, but a variant phrase for "eagle" is given in the Dyk-Stoudt vocabulary as *yañá'mu*. The *ya* of this phrase is a shortened form of *ya'a* or "eagle," and the *ña'mu* of the dialect of San Miguel el Grande given in this vocabulary is equivalent to the *ñami* of the Alvarado dictionary and of the gloss on the Lienzo of Jicayán. But it is not known whether the word *ñami* alone, without the prefix *ya-*, can refer to an eagle or an eagle-like bird, nor is it known whether the term *ñami* was ever used on the Coast to refer to this type of bird. At the present time, the standard word for "eagle" in the Coastal region is *tasu*. This word is the equivalent of the *tadzu* of the Alvarado dictionary, where it is listed as referring to two types of birds: the eagle owl (*buharro*) and a bird of prey known in English as a kite and in Spanish as *milano*. Thus it seems more likely that the gloss *duhua yoço ñoñami* refers to the field with a sweet potato plant seen in Sign 41 at the top of the Lienzo.

Sign 27

Description: A frieze with geometric patterns, a front-facing platform with a central stairway, and a sign which resembles a pair of horns, but whose meaning is not known.
Fig. No.: 153
Accompanying Gloss: *yucu yoço quivi*
Translation: "the hill of the plain of the day"

Relationship of the Gloss to the Pictorial Sign:

Yucu is "hill"; *yoço* or *yodzo* is "plain, valley"; and *quivi* or *quevui* may mean "day."[20] This gloss does not refer to Sign 27, nor does it appear to refer to any of the other signs in the Lienzo.

Sign 28

Description: A stone with a human leg and foot appended on the left side.

Fig. No.: 153

Accompanying Gloss: *yua chacha huico*

Translation: "the enclosure of a type of falcon"

Relationship of the Gloss to the Pictorial Sign:

In the discussion of Sign 16 it was suggested that the gloss *yuu chaᾱ* written under that sign was depicted by Sign 28, because *yuu cha'a* means "the stone of the foot." Sign 28, a stone with a human leg, may represent a site named *Piedra Pie de Cacique* ("the stone of the foot of the native ruler") which appears in the lower-left corner of the 1893 map of the lands of Manuel Yglesias (Fig. 138) as a boundary between Yglesias and the town of Ixcapa.

The gloss *yua chacha huico*, written above and to the left of Sign 28, may well refer to another place sign in the Lienzo. *Yua* or *yuhua* means "enclosed place, wall, ballcourt." *Chacha* (*sasa* in the dialect of the Alvarado dictionary) means "falcon." *Huico* describes the type of falcon, perhaps referring to a crested falcon, because one of the meanings of *huico* is "crenelations, merlons" (*almenas*), and a crested falcon could be considered "a falcon with a crenelated head." Another meaning of *huico* is "cloud" or "mist," and it is also possible that the falcon in question is the same as a "falcon of the mist" described briefly by Sahagún in Book XI of the Florentine Codex. According to the description, the "mist falcon" (*ayauh-tlotli* in Nahuatl) is so named "because it hunts and strikes in the clouds."[21]

In all likelihood, the gloss *yua chacha huico* refers to Sign 39 (Fig. 156), which consists of an enclosure whose shape resembles that of a shield and a crested bird of prey that looks very much like a falcon.

Sign 29

Description: An upright stone with water in the interior and two streams of water that extend beyond the border at the top.

Fig. No.: 153

Accompanying Glosses: *crus xaño*; *duta ticaxi*

Translation: "the boundary cross; the water of the spoon"

Relationship of the Glosses to the Pictorial Sign:

The gloss *crus xaño* is written in black ink at the right of the prominent gloss *termino de amosgo* ("the boundary with Amusgos") that runs between Signs 28 and 29. This gloss undoubtedly refers to a wood or metal cross that marked the boundary line between Jicayán and Amusgos, for *cruz* is the Spanish word for "cross," and *xaño* is the

Mixtec word for "boundary." The cross described was probably similar to those seen in the two Lienzos of Zacatepec (Fig. 120) or to the present-day boundary marker between Jicayán and Pinotepa de Don Luis (Fig. 121).

Below the gloss *crus xaño* is a second gloss, *duta ticaxi*, written in brown ink. This gloss does not seem to be illustrated by Sign 29, for the sign includes no pictorial sign of a spoon (*ticaxi*, or *ticadzi* in the dialect of the Alvarado dictionary). Nor does "water of the spoon" appear to be represented by any other sign in the Lienzo.

Sign 30

Description: A feather-mat field with a profile head of the deity Xipe-Totec.

Fig. Nos.: 153, 154

Accompanying Gloss: *tnu ndica chaa quaa (xaño)*

Translation: "the fruit tree known as the *mamey* or red zapote (a boundary)"

Relationship of the Gloss to the Pictorial Sign:

This gloss is not illustrated by the sign above it, because the sign does not include a tree to represent the mamey tree (*Calocarpum sapota*) described in the gloss. The Mixtec name of the mamey in the dialect of the Coast is *tun dica cha'a*, which would be *tnu ndica saha* in the dialect of the Alvarado dictionary. The adjective *quaa* or *qua'a* which follows *tnu ndica chaa* in the gloss means "red." The addition of this word seems somewhat redundant because *tnu ndica cha'a* in itself refers to the red zapote; but occasionally on the Coast the generic term for the zapote tree is also considered to be *tnu ndica cha'a*, and the adjective *qua'a* was apparently added to the gloss to specify more clearly that the species of zapote referred to is the red zapote or mamey. This gloss appears to refer to none of the pictorial signs in the Lienzo because none of the plants in any of the place signs resembles the mamey tree with its large obovate leaves, nor does any of the fruit-bearing trees seen in the place signs have fruit resembling the mamey.

The head on the feather-mat field in Sign 30 represents the deity whose Nahuatl name is Xipe-Totec and whose Mixtec name may be *dzichi*.[22] Both the eye and mouth of this head are characteristic of priests and deity impersonators of Xipe-Totec who wear the dried skin of a sacrificial victim. The eye has no eyeball, and its shape is like the elongated slit seen in representations of Xipe-Totec in Codex Borgia and in other ritual manuscripts.[23] The mouth is open, and the jaw seems to have the flaccid boneless quality that is another feature associated with Xipe-Totec.

Sign 31

Description: A hill with a profile male figure, who is bald, has a black beard, and holds a staff or walking stick in his hand.

---

[20] *Quevui* can also mean "time; to be born; to leave; to enter."

[21] Dibble and Anderson (ed. and trans.), *Florentine Codex, Book XI: The Earthly Things* (Santa Fe, 1963), 44; Fig. 138.

[22] This Mixtec name for Xipe-Totec is discussed in Appendix E in connection with the Mixtec gloss written next to Sign 4-top of Map No. 36.

[23] As, for example, Codex Borgia 24 (lower-left corner). The characteristics of all of the representations of Xipe-Totec in the Borgia Group manuscripts are discussed and illustrated in: Bodo Spranz, *Göttergestalten in den mexikanischen Bilderhandschriften der Codex Borgia-Gruppe* (Wiesbaden, 1964), 291–301.

Fig. No.: 154
Accompanying Gloss: none

Sign 32

Description: A curved, upright rock with a bird.
Fig. No.: 154
Accompanying Gloss: none

Sign 33

Description: A hill with three feathers or balls of down.
Fig. No.: 154
Accompanying Gloss: none

Sign 34

Description: A bent hill with a stream of water on the left side; within the hill is a circle with markings that may represent a *petate* or grass mat.
Fig. No.: 154
Accompanying Gloss: *tnu yeye*

yoqua (xaño)

Translation: "the tree popularly known as *cucharillo* or *limoncillo* (a boundary)"
Relationship of the Gloss to the Pictorial Sign:

The gloss does not refer to the sign above it, because the initial prefix *tnu-* of the gloss indicates that *tnuyeye* is a type of tree. Several Mixtec names of trees contain the word *yeye*, but the tree that is probably indicated by the gloss is one known popularly in Spanish as *cucharillo* ("little spoon") or *limoncillo* ("little lemon tree"), a tree whose botanical name is *Trichilia havensis*.[24] The phrase *yoqua* in the second line of this gloss probably indicates that the tree or plant in question has yellow roots. *Yo* is a shortened form of *yo'o* or "root"; and *qua* or *quaan* means "yellow."

One of two signs on the Lienzo may illustrate the *tnu yeye* gloss. One possibility is Sign 35, immediately to the right of the place sign under which the gloss is written. sign 35 consists of a hill with a tree that could well represent the *cucharillo*, because the leaves of the tree in the sign are abruptly pinnate—that is, the leaflets are arranged along opposite sides of the branch with no leaf at the end of the branch—as are the leaves of the *cucharillo*.[25] The second sign which may represent the *tnu yeye* gloss is Sign 40 (Fig. 156), which is a hill with a tree very similar to that seen in Sign 35.

In all likelihood, one of these hill-with-tree signs represents the *tnu yeye* gloss, and the other represents the gloss *yucu tnu yaa*, written across the upper-left corner of the Lienzo (Fig. 155). *Yucu tnu yaa* may be translated as "the hill of the mulatto-wood tree," for *yucu* means "hill" and *tnu yaa* is the Mixtec name of a tree whose popular

name in Spanish is *palo de mulato* and whose botanical name is *Zanthozylum fagara*.[26] The *cucharillo* and the *palo de mulato* are by no means as similar as the two trees represented in Signs 35 and 40, for they are of different genera and have different types of fruit and flowers.[27] But in Signs 35 and 40 only the leaves of the trees are depicted, and the leaves of both the *cucharillo* and *palo de mulato* are pinnate, or arranged along opposite sides of the branch.[28] Thus one of these signs probably represents the *cucharillo* (*tnu yeye* in Mixtec), and the other represents the *palo de mulato* (*tnu yaa* in Mixtec), but it is difficult to distinguish which pictorial sign depicts which plant because it is impossible to distinguish between the two pictorial motifs of trees.

Sign 35

Description: A hill with a tree.
Fig. Nos.: 154, 155
Accompanying Gloss: none
Comments:

The tree in this sign resembles the tree in Sign 40 (Fig. 156). The gloss *tnu yeye yoqua* written under Sign 34 or the gloss *yucu tnu yaa* written under Sign 38 may refer to Sign 35; these glosses are discussed above, under Sign 34.

Sign 36

Description: A platform decorated with black squares and with a stone motif on top.
Fig. Nos.: 154, 155
Accompanying Gloss: none

Sign 37

Description: A hill with a plant that resembles a maguey cactus.
Fig. No.: 155
Accompanying Gloss: none

Sign 38

Description: A hill with a cocoon containing a caterpillar or worm.

---

24 The Dyk-Stoudt dictionary lists the phrase *tlyiyì* as referring to the mosquito (the insect) as well as to the *cucharillo* plant. Martínez Gracida (*Flora y fauna*) gives the phrase *yucu teyeye* as the Mixtec name for the "sweet palm tree" or *zoyate* (*Brahea dulcis*). In the Alvarado dictionary the phrase *yavui qchi tiyeye* is said to refer to "a small maguey cactus that grows among the rocks" (*maguei pequeño que nace en las peñas*); in this phrase *yavui* means "maguey cactus," *qchi* or *quachi* means "small," and the precise meaning of *tiyeye* is uncertain.

25 Standley, *Trees and Shrubs of Mexico*, 554.

26 The Alvarado dictionary lists *yutnu yaa* as the Mixtec name of both the oak tree (*roble*) and the white poplar tree (*álamo blanco*), but in Jicayán the term *tnu yaa* apparently refers only to the *palo de mulato*. The leaves of the *palo de mulato* are illustrated in a black-and-white drawing in Martínez, *Plantas medicinales*, 238.

27 A detailed description of the two plants is given in Standley, *Trees and Shrubs of Mexico*, 554 (*cucharillo*) and 533 (*palo de mulato*). The *cucharillo* is a member of the *Meliaceae* or Chinaberry Family, and the *palo de mulato* belongs to the *Rutaceae* or Rue Family.

28 According to Standley (*ibid.*), the leaves of the *cucharillo* occur in groups of three to nine leaflets which range in length from 3.5 to 15 centimeters and are abruptly pinnate. By way of contrast, the leaves of the *palo de mulato* occur in groups of 5 to 17 leaflets, which are 0.7 to 2.5 centimeters long and are odd-pinnate, which means that a leaflet occurs at the end of the branch or twig in addition to those on opposite sides of the branch. Thus the *palo de mulato* has smaller and, at times, fewer leaflets than the *cucharillo*, and it should have a leaflet at the end of the branch which the *cucharillo* lacks. But pictorial signs of plants in Mixtec manuscripts are extremely conventionalized, and differences in size, number, and arrangement of leaflets are often not delineated in detail, for the pictorial sign attempts merely to present a schematic idea of a tree or plant rather than a detailed botanical drawing. In Signs 35 and 40, the tree motifs are essentially the same, and both have branches with an average of eight pinnate leaves.

Fig. No.: 155
Accompanying Gloss: *yucu tnu yaa (xaño)*
Translation: "hill of the tree popularly known as the *palo de mulato* (a boundary)"
Relationship of the Gloss to the Pictorial Sign:

This gloss does not refer to Sign 38, but may refer to either Sign 35 (Figs. 154, 155) or to Sign 40 (Fig. 156). The gloss is discussed above, under Sign 34.

Sign 39

Description: A falcon within an enclosure whose shape resembles a shield.
Fig. No.: 156
Accompanying Gloss: none
Comments:

The gloss *yua chacha huico*, written above and to the left of Sign 28, refers to this pictorial sign. This gloss is discussed above, under Sign 28.

Sign 40

Description: A hill with a tree.
Fig. No.: 156
Accompanying Gloss: none
Comments:

The tree in this sign resembles the tree in Sign 35 (Figs. 154, 155). The gloss *tnu yeye yoqua* written under Sign 34 or the gloss *yucu tnu yaa* written under Sign 38 may refer to Sign 40; these glosses are discussed above, under Sign 34.

Sign 41

Description: A feather-mat field with a plant.
Fig. No.: 156
Accompanying Gloss: *yucu chichi ñuhu (xaño)*
Translation: "the hill where the fire or earth burns? (a boundary)"
Relationship of the Gloss to the Pictorial Sign:

The gloss does not refer to the place sign near which it is written, nor does it appear to refer to another sign in the Lienzo. *Yucu chichi ñuhu* may be translated in several ways; two possibilities are "the hill where the fire or earth burns," and "the hill which crosses the earth." *Yucu* is "hill"; *chichi* (*sisi* in the dialect of the Alvarado dictionary) may mean "to burn; to cross (as a river)"; and *ñuhu* can mean either "fire" or "earth." Neither of these translations seems to be illustrated by a place sign in the Lienzo.

As discussed above under Sign 26, the gloss *duhua yoço ñoñami* written above Sign 26 may refer to Sign 41.

Sign 42

Description: A square.
Fig. No.: 156
Accompanying Gloss: *cahua yachani (xaño)*
Translation: "the ravine of the nocturnal eagle?? (a boundary)"
Relationship of the Gloss to the Pictorial Sign:

The gloss does not refer to the sign above which it is written, but it is possible that it refers to Sign 24 in the lower-left corner of the Lienzo, a sign which consists of a frieze, a feather-mat field, and an eagle (Figs. 152, 153). *Cahua yachani* can be translated as "the ravine of a type

of eagle," for *cahua* means "ravine," and *ya* may be a shortened form of *ya'a*, meaning "eagle." The word *chani* (*sani* in the dialect of the Alvarado dictionary) is an adjective describing the type of eagle in question. The translation of *chani* is not certain, but it may be used here as meaning "dream" or "the dream spirit," with the implication that the eagle is being described as a nocturnal bird. The only eagle shown in the place signs of the Lienzo is that seen in Sign 24, where an eagle's head is placed on top of the feather-mat motif that sometimes illustrates the word *cahua* or "ravine" in the Lienzo of Jicayán. Thus it is possible that the gloss *cahua yachani*, tentatively translated as "the ravine of the nocturnal eagle," may refer to Sign 24.

Sign 43

Description: A deer's head.
Fig. No.: 156
Accompanying Gloss: *yucu nuni (xaño)*
Translation: "the hill of corn" or "the hill of a bundle of things tied together (a boundary)"
Relationship of the Gloss to the Pictorial Sign:

The gloss is not illustrated by the deer's head above it, for the Mixtec word for deer is *idzu* in the everyday vocabulary and *quaa* in the calendrical vocabulary.

It is possible that the gloss *yucu nuni* is illustrated by Sign 51, a large strand of rope which is placed outside of the row of place signs at the top of the Lienzo (Fig. 157). This strand of rope presents in a general way one of the meanings of *nuni*: "bundle of things tied together." But it is equally possible that the rope motif is the sign of the town of San Juan Colorado, Jicayán's neighbor to the northeast. The Mixtec name of San Juan Colorado is *yo qua'a*, or "the red rope." *Yo* is a shortened form of *yo'o*, meaning "rope," and *qua'a* means "red." No color is utilized in the Lienzo, so it is not possible to tell whether Sign 51 is supposed to be a red rope. In addition, the rope motif is not accompanied by a gloss indicating that it is the sign of San Juan Colorado, as are the church with the legend "tlacamama" (Fig. 149) and the hill with the legend "pinotecpa" (Figs. 158, 159). And there is no heavy black line that extends out from the central building to Sign 51, as do the black lines which connect the center of the Lienzo with the church of Tlacamama and the hill glossed "pinotecpa." Nor is there a gloss placed between the boundary signs to indicate the junction point between Jicayán and San Juan Colorado, as occurs on the left side of the Lienzo, where the legend "termino de amosgo" designates the boundary between Amusgos and Jicayán.

Again, I think an either-or situation is present with the gloss *yucu nuni*. Either this gloss is illustrated by the large rope in Sign 51; or Sign 51 is the place sign of the neighboring town of San Juan Colorado, and the gloss *yucu nuni*, meaning "hill of bundle of things tied together" or "hill of corn" (for *nuni* can also mean "corn"), does not refer to Sign 51 or to any other pictorial sign in the Lienzo. It is difficult to decide which of the two interpretations is correct on the basis of the rope motif alone. First, this motif illustrates neither the *qua'a* or "red" element of San Juan Colorado's Mixtec name nor the *yucu* or "hill" element of *yucu nuni*. Second, the Alvarado dictionary gives both the words *nuni* and *yoho* (*yo'o*) as Mixtec words meaning "a bundle of something tied up" (*manojo*). If the gloss *yucu nuni* is not illustrated by Sign 51, then it probably is not represented in the Lienzo because none of the other place signs appear to depict a "corn hill" or a "tied-bundle hill."

Sign 44

Description: A parrot's head.
Fig. No.: 157
Accompanying Gloss: *yucu guacote* (*xaño*)
Translation: "the hill of the parrot (a boundary)"
Relationship of the Gloss to the Pictorial Sign:

The gloss and the pictorial sign are in agreement, for *yucu* means "hill," and *guaco* or *huaco* means "parrot." In this gloss, the *te* element, which is usually used as a prefix denoting animals, appears as a suffix.

Sign 45

Description: A feather-mat field with a spear or arrow that is placed in an upright position on the field.
Fig. No.: 157
Accompanying Gloss: none

Sign 46

Description: The head of the "Xolotl" deity enclosed by an outline that has the shape of a ceramic vessel.
Fig. No.: 157
Accompanying Gloss: *yucu ndaye* (*xaño*)
Translation: "the craggy or inclined hill (a boundary)"
Relationship of the Gloss to the Pictorial Sign:

The gloss does not relate to the sign under which it is written, because the qualifying element *ndaye*, which may mean "craggy" (*áspero*) or "inclined" (*inclinado*), does not appear to refer to the "Xolotl" figure. It is possible that this gloss may refer to Sign 34 (Fig. 154), which includes a hill that is bent or "inclined."

Sign 47

Description: A tree with gourd-like fruit, and the sign for a stone placed in the trunk of the tree.
Fig. Nos.: 157, 159
Accompanying Gloss: *yutnu no cui achi* (*xaño*)
Translation: "a type of tree that bears sweet fruit (a boundary)"
Relationship of the Gloss to the Pictorial Sign:

The gloss is not related to this sign, for the jícaro tree in the pictorial sign is described by the gloss written under Sign 49, *tnu yachin ñee* (Fig. 157).

The gloss under Sign 47, *yutnu no cui achi*, refers to another type of tree which cannot as yet be identified. A literal translation of this gloss might be "the tree which has sweet or delicious [fruit]." *Yutnu* is "tree"; *no* or *nu* plus *cui* may be an abbreviation of *nucuhui*, "to have, wear," or *cui* may be an abbreviation of *cuihi*, "fruit." The final word *achi* is probably the equivalent of the *adzi* of the Alvarado dictionary and means "delicious, sweet, soft."

The word *achi* appears in the name of one plant that is common on the Coast, a leguminous plant of the genus *Crotalaria*, which is popularly known as *chipile* and whose Mixtec name is *yua achi* or *yua axi*, "delicious vegetable or herb." *Yua* or *yuvua* means "vegetable, herb," and *achi* or *axi* is "delicious." But the plant referred to in the gloss is a tree, because the Mixtec name begins with the word *yutnu* rather than *yuvua* ("vegetable"), which is the initial word in the Mixtec name of the *chipile*.

It is possible that the gloss *yutnu no cui achi* may refer to Sign 52, the place sign in the upper-right corner of the Lienzo which consists of a hill with a bean-bearing tree (Figs. 158, 159). The fruit which hangs from the branches of this tree has the appearance of a bean which is divided into circular sections. This fruit is presumably edible, and it is possible that the adjective *achi* or "delicious" might be applicable to this fruit, as it is to the bean-like fruit of the *chipile* (*yuvua achi*). But this is merely a tentative hypothesis, and one which cannot be confirmed or discarded until the identity of the tree referred to in the gloss *yutnu no cui achi* has been ascertained.

Sign 48

Description: A building inside of a rectangle which has curlicues representing water on the inside border.
Fig. Nos.: 158, 159
Accompanying Gloss: none

Sign 49

Description: A round stone with a small bird, possibly a hummingbird.
Fig. Nos.: 158, 159
Accompanying Gloss: *tnu yachin ñee* (*xaño*)
Translation: "a type of *jícaro* or calabash tree (a boundary)"
Relationship of the Gloss to the Pictorial Sign:

The gloss does not relate to the stone with a bird, because *tnu yachin* refers to the calabash or jícaro tree. In all likelihood, the gloss *tnu yachin ñee* describes Sign 47 (Fig. 157), which consists of a tree with gourd-like fruit that grows very close to the branches as do the gourds on the calabash or jícaro tree. As was discussed under Sign 8 where the gloss also refers to a type of jícaro tree, the phrase *yutnu yachi* or *tnu yachi* is the Mixtec name of this tree in the dialect of the Coast; the final *n* in the word *yachin* in the gloss under Sign 49 indicates nasalization of the final vowel. The adjective *ñee* that follows *tnu yachin* in this gloss refers to the specific type of calabash tree, and it is possible that *ñee* here means "solid, compact, firm."[29] This translation would seem to be reinforced by the stone motif which is placed in the tree trunk of Sign 47, for this stone motif may well indicate that the wood of this particular type of calabash is hard and solid ("stone-like").

---

29 *Ñee* can also mean "salt; skin, membrane, shell, drum." In phrases that refer to plants, *tnu ñee* means "otate," a generic term for several bamboo-like trees; and *ita ñee* refers to various plants with creepers.

Sign 50

Description: A cradle combined with an enclosure containing water.

Fig. Nos.: 158, 159

Accompanying Gloss: none

Comments:

The use of the cradle motif (*dzoco* in Mixtec) in connection with water indicates very clearly that this motif is also the sign for the geographical substantive *dzoco*, meaning "well, spring" (*pozo, fuente pequeña*).

Sign 51

Description: A strand of rope.

Fig. No.: 157

Accompanying Gloss: *yucu tnu ndacu chāha (xaño)*

Translation: "the hill of the tree popularly known as the *nanche* or pickle tree (a boundary)"

Relationship of the Gloss to the Pictorial Sign:

The gloss is not related to the place sign consisting of a strand of rope because, as was discussed under Sign 43, the rope motif either illustrates the gloss *yucu nuni* written under Sign 43 (Fig. 156), or it is the place sign of San Juan Colorado.

In the gloss under Sign 51, *yucu* is "hill," and *tnu ndacu chaha* (or *tnu ndacu saha* in the dialect of the Alvarado dictionary) is the Mixtec name of a fruit-bearing tree that is found in abundance in the Coastal region of Oaxaca. The popular name of this tree in Mexico is *nanche* from the Nahuatl *nantzin*, meaning "mother" or "old woman," because in pre-Conquest times the fruit of the tree was given to women in childbirth.[30] The botanical name of the *nanche* is *Byrsonima crassifolia*, and it is sometimes known in English as the "pickle tree." The "hill of the *nanche* tree" described in the gloss is apparently not illustrated by a pictorial sign in the Lienzo, for none of the trees in the place signs have either the oblong leaves of the *nanche* tree or the *nanche* fruit, which resembles a dark yellow cherry.

Sign 52

Description: A hill with a tree that has bean-like fruit.

Fig. Nos.: 158, 159

Accompanying Gloss: *pinotecpa*

Relationship of the Gloss to the Pictorial Sign:

Ostensibly the gloss identifies the place sign as the town of Pinotepa de Don Luis, Jicayán's neighbor to the southeast. In addition to the gloss *pinotecpa* which is written at the right of Sign 52, a black line runs from the central configuration to this place sign, and the line is accompanied by the legend: *termino de pinote [pa de] D° luis* ("the boundary with Pinotepa de Don Luis"). However, Sign 52 cannot represent the Mixtec name of Pinotepa de Don Luis, because this name, *doyo yuhu*, is illustrated by Sign 4, a semicircle of water that contains a human figure who points to his mouth (Fig. 148). Moreover, the name

doyo yuhu is not related to the known Mixtec names of trees with a bean-like fruit, and this type of tree is the principal motif of Sign 52.

In the discussion of the gloss *yutnu no cui achi*, written under Sign 47 (Fig. 157), it was tentatively suggested that this gloss might refer to the tree in Sign 52. It is also equally possible that the tree in Sign 52 represents one of several plants with bean-like fruit common in the Coastal region. Some of these bean-bearing plants are listed below; the popular name of the plant is given in the left-hand column; its botanical name appears in the center column; and in the right-hand column is the Mixtec name by which the plant is known in Jicayán.

Popular Name	Botanical Name	Mixtec Name in Jicayán
guaje	Leucaena esculenta	yua ndata[31]
tepeguaje	Lysiloma acapulcensis	tu ini
cacahuananche	Gliricidia sepium	tu nduti (= *tnu nduchi* in the dialect of the Alvarado dictionary)
cuajinicuil	Inga spuria	yakwa; diyakwa
cuapinole	Hymenea courbaril	tu lumbi
huamuchil	Pithecollobium dulce	tikwa'ndii

It seems likely, then, that if the tree in Sign 52 is not referred to by the gloss written under Sign 47, it represents one of the bean-bearing plants listed above and is not described by any of the glosses written on the Lienzo.

Summary of the Relationships between the Glosses and the Pictorial Signs

The complex relationships and non-relationships between the glosses and pictorial signs in the Lienzo of Jicayán are summarized in Chart 16. The first column of this chart lists the Mixtec glosses on the Lienzo, while the second column gives the number of the place sign that the gloss accompanies, and the third column provides the figure number of this study where the gloss and place sign are illustrated. If the gloss and the place sign are in agreement, an *X* is placed in the fourth column ("Relates to Accompanying Sign"). If the gloss refers to another sign in the Lienzo, the number of this sign is placed in the fifth column ("Relates to Another Sign in Lienzo"). If the gloss is not associated with any of the place signs in the Lienzo, then an *X* is placed in the sixth and final column of the chart ("Relates to No Sign in Lienzo").

As the chart indicates, only nine of the thirty-three glosses refer to the place signs near which they are written. Another thirteen glosses may refer to other signs in the Lienzo, but the relationship is often, at best, tenuous. At least eleven of the glosses—and possibly more than eleven —do not have any counterpart in the pictorial signs of the Lienzo. Thus the Lienzo of Jicayán seems to present

---

[30] Francisco Hernández, *Obras completas* (Mexico, 1959), III, 30. Line drawings showing the plant and its fruit appear in: Martínez, *Plantas medicinales*, 226, and in M. Walter Pesman, *Meet Flora Mexicana* (Globe, Arizona, 1962), 160.

[31] This Mixtec name for the guaje differs from names for this plant recorded in other sections of the Mixteca. In the dialect of San Miguel el Grande in the Dyk-Stoudt dictionary, the word for "guaje" is *tíya'à*, and in Tututepec I was told that this plant's Mixtec name is *kichi tundo'o*.

two different lists of sites that surround or bound the town of Jicayán. The first list consists of the 52 pictorial signs that are placed in an uneven circle around the Lienzo, and the second list is comprised of the 32 glosses in Mixtec plus the gloss *pinotecpa* which accompanies one of the 52 signs.

The reason there is only an occasional relationship between the Mixtec glosses and the place signs is a simple one. The place signs and the glosses are not contemporary, for the glosses were apparently written on the Lienzo when the names of Jicayán's boundaries were no longer the same as the boundary names expressed in the place signs. The place signs undoubtedly set forth the names of Jicayán's boundaries that were current at the time of the Spanish conquest, while most of the written glosses give different names of boundaries—those that were current in the early Colonial period and later. As will be seen in the discussion that follows, the Mixtec glosses on the Lienzo show a closer relationship to written land documents of the Colonial period—including a document as late as 1710 —than they do to the place signs around the border of the Lienzo.

RELATIONSHIP BETWEEN THE GLOSSES AND WRITTEN LAND DOCUMENTS

In addition to the glosses on the Lienzo of Jicayán, three other written land documents of the Colonial period are known that set forth Mixtec names of Jicayán's boundaries. One of these, the glosses on pages XIII and XIV of Codex Colombino, includes all of the town's boundaries; a second, a review of Jicayán's boundaries in 1710, includes all the boundaries with the exception of some of the sites where Jicayán shares boundaries with Pinotepa de Don Luis. The third document, dated 1680, lists the Mixtec names of the boundaries of Amusgos, Jicayán's neighbor to the north, and thus gives only the names of Jicayán's boundaries with Amusgos.

The Glosses on Codex Colombino

The written document with which the glosses on the Lienzo of Jicayán show the closest correlation is the group of Mixtec glosses on pages XIII and XIV of Codex Colombino. These glosses were supposedly added to Colombino in 1541, a date that is virtually contemporary with the year date 1542 represented in the center of the Lienzo.

A transcription of the glosses on pages XIII and XIV of Colombino appears in Chart 17, and the boundary glosses begin along the top of line 40 on page XIII with the phrase, *sañu ñuu siquaha,* or "the boundaries of San Pedro Jicayán." (*Sañu* means "boundaries"; *ñuu sii qua'a* is the Mixtec name of Jicayán.) The Mixtec names of boundaries begin with *yuhui maa* on the top of line 40 and continue across the top of line 39 on page XIV. The sequence then recommences on the bottom of line 40, page XIII; goes along the bottom of line 39, page XIV; then to the top of line 37, page XIII, and the top of line 38, page XIV.

A comparison of the black-ink glosses on the Lienzo of Jicayán and the legible glosses on pages XIII and XIV of Colombino appears in Chart 18.[32] As can be seen in this comparison, all of the visible glosses written on Colombino have counterparts in the glosses of the Lienzo of Jicayán. Ten of the thirty-two glosses of the Lienzo are not among the visible glosses on pages XIII–XIV of Colombino, but they may have been written in sections of these two pages where the glosses are no longer visible because of fading and erasure.

In the Colombino glosses, the Mixtec word *sicuhui* (page XIV–39, top) is modified by the phrase *sañu ñundusa,* or "the boundary with Tlacamama." *Sañu* means "boundary," and *ñundusa* (*ñuu nducha* in the dialect of the Coast) is the Mixtec name of Tlacamama, the town which borders Jicayán on the west.[33] Jicayán's relationship with Tlacamama is shown in the Lienzo of Jicayán by a thick black line which runs from the central configuration to a church that is outside of Jicayán's boundaries and is accompanied by the gloss "tlacamama" (Fig. 149). This line passes through the circle of boundary signs near Sign 10, under which is written the gloss *sicuvi duva,* the same place name as the *sicuhui* on Codex Colombino.

Another addendum in the glosses on Codex Colombino that is not present in the annotations on the Lienzo of Jicayán occurs in the last visible gloss on the top of line 38 of page XIV, where the gloss *yucu ñuni* is followed by the phrase *sañu yocuaha,* or "the boundary of San Juan Colorado." *Yoqua'a* ("the red rope") is the Mixtec name of San Juan Colorado, Jicayán's neighbor to the northeast. As was suggested above in the discussion of the gloss *yucu nuni* that is written near Sign 43 in the Lienzo of Jicayán, the rope at the top of the Lienzo outside the boundary signs may be the place sign of San Juan Colorado.

The 1710 Review of Jicayán's Boundaries

In 1710 the boundaries of Jicayán were reviewed, and at this time the Lienzo of Jicayán was produced as corroborating evidence of the names of these boundaries.[34] The review begins with the description of Jicayán's boundaries in the four cardinal directions. These are listed as:

---

[32] The relationship between the glosses on the Lienzo of Jicayán and those on pages XIII and XIV of Codex Colombino was first noted in Smith, "The Codex Colombino . . . ," *Tlalocan,* Vol. IV–3, 281–83. The transcription of the glosses in both manuscripts that is included in this study supersedes that of the earlier study. Owing to the ultra-violet photographs taken in 1964 by Prof. Arturo Romano of the Museo Nacional de Antropología, it has been possible to read more clearly some of the glosses on Colombino.

[33] The precise translation of the *nducha* section of Tlacamama's Mixtec name is uncertain. *Ñuu* means "town," and *nducha* may mean "to vomit; money, pledge; moulding (as a wooden moulding), sculptured." Martínez Gracida (*BSMGE* 1888, 408) gives the Mixtec name of Tlacamama as *ñu nducha* and translates this name as "land of the beans," which is not correct because the Mixtec word for "beans" in the dialect of the Coast is *nduti.*

[34] Archivo General del Departamento Agrario (Mexico City), Títulos, exp. 276.1/1069. In this document the officials of Jicayán state that their "*linderos se contienen en el mapa, de que hazemos demostración, para que en su vista se nos devuelva . . .*"; and three witnesses testify to the veracity of the map and state that Jicayán's boundaries are "*[como] se manifiesta en su Mapa por las figuras de ella . . . .*" The 1710 review was the result of a commission set up by a Royal Cedula of August 15, 1707, to make sure that the royal treasury was receiving its required tax on lands and land transactions.

Gloss	No. of Accompanying Sign	Illustration (Fig. No.)	Relates to Accompanying Sign	Relates to Another Sign in Lienzo (No. of sign given below)	Relates to No Sign in Lienzo
yuhui maa	1	148	X		
yuu xaña	4	148			X
cuiti yuqn̄	5	148			X
yutnu yta yata	6	148	X		
yutnu yachi diqui	8	148	X		
cava yy tiñoo yucu	9	149	X		
xicuvi duva	10	149	X		
yuvi [yu] tnu yñu yta	11	144	X		
chiti cuiñe	12	144			X
yuu coo	13	150		15 or 16?	
yuu chaā	16	150		28	
yuta uni	17	150	X		
yuvua caa viyo	19	151			X
yuu iño cuta	22	152		23	
yucu yño	23	152			X

CHART 16: Relationship Between Glosses and Place Signs in the Lienzo of Jicayán

Gloss	No. of Accompanying Sign	Illustration (Fig. No.)	Relates to Accompanying Sign	Relates to Another Sign in Lienzo (No. of sign given below)	Relates to No Sign in Lienzo
yucu yço	24	152			X
yuvi yñu cuiy	25	153	X		
duhua yoço ñoñami	26	153		41 or 24?	
yucu yoço quivi	27	153			X
yua chacha huico	28	153		39	
duta ticaxi	29	154			X
tnu ndica chaa quaa (xaño)	30	154			X
tnu yeye yoqua (xaño)	34	154		35 or 40	
yucu tnu yaa (xaño)	38	155		35 or 40	
yucu chichi ñuhu (xaño)	41	156			X
cahua yachani (xaño)	42	156		24?	
yucu nuni (xaño)	43	156		51?	
yucu guacote (xaño)	44	157	X		
yucu ndaye (xaño)	46	157		34?	
yutnu no cuiachi (xaño)	47	157		52?	
tnu yachin ñee (xaño)	49	158		47	
yucu tnu ndacu chāha (xaño)	51	157			X
pinotecpa	52	159		4	

CHART 16. (cont.)

CHART XVII. Transcription of the Glosses on Pages XIII and XIV of Codex Colombino

[XIII]

a[ni]ñe s[n p]o ñuusiquaha

[41]

sañu ñuu siquaha - yuhui maa

[40]

. . . .
. . . .
chiti cuiñe . . . .

yucu yso - yucu yoso quihui - tnundica ch . . . .   tnu yeye. . . .

yu. . . . .ca huico

[37]

[XIV]

[42]

. . . .

[yu]u saña - siqui tiyuqh - tnu ita yata - cahua tiño - sicuhui sañu ñundusa

. . . .
. . . . . .
. . .
. . . . .
. . .   [39]
. . . . . .   tnu yachi ndi. . .   . .   yucu . . . . . .
yuhu coo - yuu cha-a - yuhua cahuiyo - yuhu iñu cu. . . . .
                                                                                          . . . . .

[yu]cu tnu yaa - yucu chichi ñu[hu]. . - yucu ñun-i sañu yocuaha

yutnu nucuj. . . .

[38]

CHART 18: Comparison of Glosses on Lienzo of Jicayán and Codex Colombino XIII-XIV

Lienzo of Jicayán	Fig. No. of this book	Codex Colombino	Page and Line of Colombino
yuhui maa	148	yuhui maa	XIII–40, top
yuu xaña	148	. . . u saña	XIV–39, top
cuiti yuqn̄	148	siqui tiyuqh	XIV–39, top
yutnu yta yata	148	tnu ita yata	XIV–39, top
yutnu yachi diqui	148	tnu yachi ndi . . .	XIV–39, bottom
cava yy tiñoo yucu	149	cahua tiño	XIV–39, top
xicuvi duva	149	sicuhui (sañu ñundusa)	XIV–39, top
yuvi [yu] tnu yñu yta	144	erased or missing	
chiti cuiñe	144	chiti cuiñe	XIII–40, bottom
yuu coo	150	yuhu coo	XIV–39, bottom
yuu chaā	150	yuu cha-a	XIV–39, bottom
yuta uni	150	erased or missing	
yuvua caa viyo	151	yuhua cahuiyo	XIV–39, bottom
yuu iño cuta	152	yuhu iño cu . . .	XIV–39, bottom
yucu yño	152	erased or missing	
yucu yço	152	yucu yso	XIII–37, top
yuvi yñu cuiy	153	erased or missing	
duhua yoço ñoñami	153	erased or missing	
yucu yoço quivi	153	yucu yoso quihui	XIII–37, top
yua chacha huico	153	yucu . . . ca huico	XIII–37, center
crus xaño; duta ticaxi	154	erased or missing	
tnu ndica chaa quaa (xaño)	154	tnu ndica ch . . .	XIII–37, top
tnu yeye yoqua (xaño)	154	tnu yeye	XIII–37, top
yucu tnu yaa (xaño)	155	. . . cu tnu yaa	XIV–38, top
yucu chichi ñuhu (xaño)	156	yucu chi ñu . . .	XIV–38, top
cahua yachani (xaño)	156	erased or missing	
yucu nuni (xaño)	156	yucu ñuni (sañu yoquaha)	XIV–38, top
yucu guacote (xaño)	157	erased or missing	
yucu ndaye (xaño)	157	erased or missing	
yutnu no cuiachi (xaño)	157	yutnu nu cuj . . .	XIV–38, center
tnu yachin ñee (xaño)	158	erased or missing	
yucu tnu ndacu chāha (xaño)	157	erased or missing	

1. *To the East,* a tree named in Mixtec *ytntu yatze,* which means "the jícaro tree," where Jicayán shares a boundary with Pinotepa de Don Luis. (This boundary name is equivalent to the gloss *tnu yachin ñee* on the Lienzo of Jicayán, a gloss which is written near Sign 49 in the upper-right corner of the Lienzo [Fig. 158].)

2. *To the West,* a ravine named *yue ñu cuiy,* where Jicayán shares a boundary with Cacahuatepec. (This boundary name is equivalent to the gloss *yuvi yñu cuiy* on the Lienzo of Jicayán, a gloss which accompanies Sign 25 in the lower-left corner of the Lienzo [Fig. 153].)

3. *To the North,* a site with a mamey tree named *ytn dicaha,* where Jicayán shares a boundary with Amusgos. (This boundary name is equivalent to the gloss *tnu ndica chaa quaa* on the Lienzo of Jicayán, a gloss that is written near Sign 30 on the left side of the Lienzo [Fig. 154].)

4. *To to South,* a hill which is named *Quiti zucuu,* where Jicayán shares a boundary with Pinotepa de Don Luis. (This boundary name is equivalent to the gloss *cuiti yuqñ* on the Lienzo of Jicayán, a gloss that is written near Sign 5 on the right side of the Lienzo [Fig. 148].)

In addition to this statement concerning the boundary sites in the four cardinal directions, the 1710 review includes a visit to the sites of Jicayán's boundaries for the purpose of verifying their location and obtaining confirmation from the officials of the towns that bound Jicayán that the boundaries cited by Jicayán are correct. At this time the Mixtec names of all of Jicayán's boundaries are given, with the exception of those with Pinotepa de Don Luis; but the Mixtec names are not translated in the review of the sites.[35] The boundary names given in the 1710 review show a fairly close correlation with the glosses on the Lienzo of Jicayán, as can be seen in Chart 19. In the first column of this chart are listed the Mixtec names of Jicayán's boundaries as they appear in the 1710 review, and in the second column is the name of the town which is said to share this boundary with Jicayán in 1710. In the third column is the brief description of the boundary site given in the 1710 review, whether it is a hill, slope, river bank, and so forth. The fourth column lists the equivalent boundary name as it appears in the glosses of the Lienzo of Jicayán, and the final two columns provide the number of the place sign in the Lienzo near which the gloss is written and the figure number of this study which best illustrates the gloss.

Of the twenty-two names of boundaries given at the time of the 1710 review, all but two or possibly three are equivalent to Mixtec names of boundaries on the Lienzo of Jicayán. Conversely, of the thirty-two Mixtec glosses on the Lienzo, nineteen and possibly twenty have counterparts

in the 1710 list of Jicayán's boundaries. It is interesting to note that none of the glosses that are written near place signs on the outermost circle of the double row of place signs in the lower-left corner of the Lienzo (Figs. 151–52) is included in the 1710 list, although some of these Mixtec names are included in the glosses on Codex Colombino.[36] This would seem to indicate that the lands of Jicayán extended farther west (the direction in which the second row of place signs is located) when the glosses were written on the Lienzo and on Codex Colombino than they did at the time of the 1710 review of Jicayán's boundaries.

The relationship between the glosses on the Lienzo and the 1710 list is summarized in the drawing of the Lienzo on page 144; this drawing includes the numbers of the place signs on the Lienzo and the towns which bound Jicayán according to the 1710 review of boundaries. Three of the towns listed as bounding Jicayán in 1710 were formerly subjects of other towns: Ixcapa was formerly a subject of Tlacamama, Cacahuatepec was formerly a subject of Amusgos, and Sayultepec was still controlled by the native ruler of Amusgos in 1710. It is not known when Ixcapa and Cacahuatepec became independent towns, but it is likely that the place signs on the Lienzo represent Jicayán's boundaries before these towns became independent and that the Mixtec glosses on the Lienzo, in common with the 1710 review of boundaries, may represent the boundaries after these towns became independent, a time when some of Jicayán's boundaries may have been changed.[37]

These changes in boundary sites might account for some lack of correspondence between the Mixtec names depicted in the place signs on the Lienzo and those given in the glosses that were added later. Moreover, the fact that the town of Cacahuatepec was formerly a subject of Amusgos would account for the differences recorded in the Lienzo and in the 1710 review as to where Jicayán's lands bound those of Amusgos. In the Lienzo, the junction between Jicayán and Amusgos is indicated by a legend ("*termino de amosgo*") on the left side of the map between Signs 28 and 29 (Fig. 153). In the 1710 review of boundaries, the glosses on the left side of the map (those accompanying Signs 27, 30, and 34) are said to be the

---

[35] In the document that describes the 1710 review, the officials of Pinotepa de Don Luis are notified that their boundaries with Jicayán will be visited, but the visit itself is not recorded. Thus the only two boundaries between Jicayán and Pinotepa de Don Luis that are named are the two included in the description of Jicayán's boundaries at the cardinal points, discussed above. One of these two, *ytntu yatze,* appears to be the same as the name *yutnu yahinii* given below as a boundary between Jicayán and Atoyac, because both Mixtec names are analogous to the gloss *tnu yachi ñee* that accompanies Sign 49 on the Lienzo (Fig. 158). It is possible that the lands of Jicayán joined those of Atoyac as well as those of Pinotepa de Don Luis at this site.

[36] The glosses in the lower-left corner of the Lienzo that are not included in the 1710 list are: (1) *yuu chaā,* accompanying Sign 16 (Fig. 151); also in Colombino. (2) *yuu iñu cuta,* accompanying Sign 22 but probably related to Sign 23 above it (Fig. 152); also in Colombino. (3) *yucu yño,* accompanying Sign 23 (Fig. 152); not in Colombino. (4) *yucu yço,* accompanying Sign 24 (Fig. 152); also in Colombino. (5) *duhua yoço ñoñami,* accompanying Sign 26 (Fig. 153); not in Colombino. (6) *yua chacha huico,* accompanying Sign 28 (Fig. 153); also in Colombino.

[37] In a document dated 1625, Ixcapa is still considered to be a subject of Tlacamama (AGN-Tierras, 191–3, fol. 72). In the same document in the AGN, the native rulers of Cacahuatepec are named for three generations prior to the generation ruling in the mid-seventeenth century (as shown in a genealogical chart in Appendix D). At the time the *Suma de Visitas* was written, about 1447–50—or approximately the same time when the Lienzo of Jicayán was drawn—Ixcapa and Cacahuatepec were apparently still subject towns. In the *Suma* (*PNE* I, 31), Amusgos is said to be bounded by the towns of Ometepec (in Guerrero), Tlacamama, Xicayan, Zacatepec, and Ayocinapa (in Guerrero); and neither Ixcapa nor Cacahuatepec is mentioned as an autonomous town.

CHART 19: Comparison of Jicayán's Boundaries in 1710 and the Glosses on the Lienzo of Jicayán

Boundary in 1710 Review	Town which Shares Boundary with Jicayán	Description of Boundary Site in 1710 Review	Equivalent Boundary Name on Lienzo of Jicayán	Number of Accompanying Place Sign	Fig. No. of this book
yunu ini	Tlacamama	an extended slope (loma tendida)	yuvi tnu yñu yta	11	144
cahua tinuu ytixicauii	Tlacamama	a slope (ladera)	cava yy tiñoo yucu and xicuvi duva	9 and 10	149
yuta yuu itnu yata	Tlacamama	a slope (loma)	yutnu yta yata	6	148
xini yata yuvichi tiquini	Tlacamama	a slope (loma)	[same as?] yutnu yachi diqui	8	148
yutnu yahini	Atoyac	on a hill (sobre un cerro)	tnu yachin ñee	49	158
tnu noquichi	Atoyac	a hill (monte)	yutnu no cuiachi	47	157
yucu tudacu chaa	Atoyac	a hill (cerro)	yucu tnu ndacu chāha	51	157
quiti yosquieti	Atoyac	a tall hill (monte alto)	not on Lienzo		
yucu ndaie	Sayultepec (a subject of Amusgos)	on the bank of a river (a la orilla de un río)	yucu ndaye	46	157
yucu cuacu	Sayultepec (Amusgos)	a hill (monte)	yucu guacote	44	157
yucu nuñi	Sayultepec (Amusgos)	a high hill (monte alto)	yucu nuni	43	156
yucu chichi ñuu	Amusgos	a hill (monte)	yucu chichi ñuhu	41	156
yucu tnu yaa	Amusgos	a long slope (loma larga)	yucu tnu yaa	38	155
yucu yeye yoquo Camotinchan	Cacahuatepec	a ravine (cañada)	tnu yeye yoqua	34	154
yucu nda	Cacahuatepec	a small extended slope (lomita tendida)	not on Lienzo		
tnu dica haa quaa	Cacahuatepec	a slope (ladera)	tnu ndica chaa quaa	30	154
yucu yoso quihui	Cacahuatepec	a hill (monte)	yucu yoço quivi	27	153
yuhui inu cuii	Ixcapa	a ravine (cañada)	yuvi yñu cuii	25	153
yucu ca uiyo	Ixcapa	a hill (monte)	yuvua caa viyo	19	151
yuta unii	Ixcapa	on the bank of a site where three rivers join (a la orilla donde se juntan tres ríos)	yuta uni	17	151
yuu coo	Ixcapa	a hill (monte)	yuu coo	13	150
chite cuiñe	Ixcapa	an extended slope (loma tendida)	chiti cuiñe	12	144

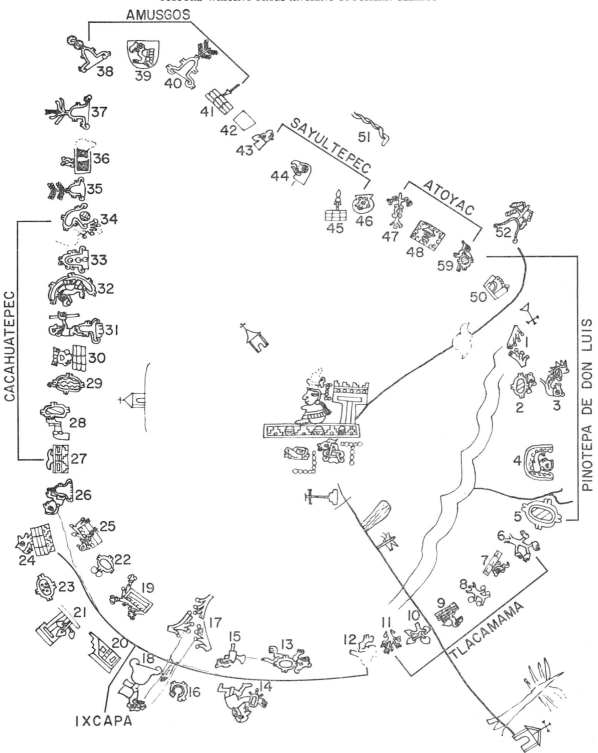

The Lienzo of Jicayán

boundaries between Jicayán and Cacahuatepec, while the glosses written near two signs at the top of the map (Signs 38 and 41) are given as the boundaries between Jicayán and Amusgos in 1710. But if Cacahuatepec were a subject of Amusgos when the Lienzo was drawn, then a boundary with Cacahuatepec would, in effect, be a boundary with Amusgos.

The Boundaries of Jicayán and Amusgos in 1680

A third written document that lists some of Jicayán's boundaries is a 1680 review of the boundaries of Amusgos,

the town which was Jicayán's neighbor to the north during the Colonial period.[38] In this document the Mixtec names of the five boundary sites between Amusgos and Jicayán, running from east to west, are given as follows:

> yagui titaa
> sucuu tixhihi
> yucu anunii
> yugui naa yucu chichi ñuhu
> dogua yoso ñamii.

The last three of these five names have counterparts in

[38] AGN-Tierras, 191–3, fol. 57.

the glosses on the Lienzo of Jicayán. The third boundary name, *yucu anunii*, is analogous to the gloss *yucu nuni*, written near Sign 43 on the Lienzo (Fig. 156). This place name also appears in the 1710 list of boundaries as a boundary between Jicayán and Sayultepec, a subject of Amusgos; and it is among the Mixtec names written on Codex Colombino, where it is said to be the boundary between Jicayán and San Juan Colorado.[39]

The last three words of the fourth name in the list, *yucu chichi ñuhu*, are the same as the gloss written under Sign 41 on the Lienzo of Jicayán (Fig. 156). The reason the phrase *yugui naa* precedes the name *yucu chichi ñuhu* is given in the 1710 review of Jicayán's boundaries. When the officials conducting the 1710 review reached the boundary site named *yucu chichi ñuhu*, Don Diego Santiago Ávila y Velasco, the native ruler of Amusgos, claimed that this site was not the boundary between his town and Jicayán, because the boundary was located below the hill named *yucu chichi ñuhu* in a ravine named *La Cañada Oscura* ("the dark ravine"), a site whose Mixtec name is *yugui naa*. Thus in the 1680 list of Amusgos' boundaries both Mixtec names are included, with the name of the site that Amusgos claims as the boundary followed by the name of the site that Jicayán claims as a boundary. The latter place name is also partly visible in the glosses on page XIV of Codex Colombino.

The last place name listed in 1680 as a boundary between Amusgos and Jicayán, *dogua yoso ñamii*, is the same as the Mixtec name *duhua yoço ñoñami* that is written near Sign 26 on the Lienzo of Jicayán (Fig. 153) but which may refer to Sign 41 at the top of the Lienzo (Fig. 156). This place name does not appear either in the glosses of Codex Colombino or in the 1710 list of Jicayán's boundaries.

The first two Mixtec names on the 1680 list do not appear in the glosses in the Lienzo of Jicayán and Codex Colombino, nor are they on the 1710 list of Jicayán's boundaries. In all likelihood, these two sites were claimed to be boundaries between Amusgos and Jicayán by the officials of Amusgos, but were not recognized as boundary sites by Jicayán. The first of the two Mixtec names may mean "the plaza or marketplace of the bananas," for *yagui* or *yahui* means "plaza, marketplace," and in the dialect of the Coast, *tita* means "banana." The second name, *sucuu tixhihi*, is probably *dzoco tidzihi* in the dialect of the Alvarado dictionary and can be translated as "the spring (or well) of the sparrow or of a blue bird that resembles the chachalaca." *Dzoco* means "spring, well"; in the Alvarado dictionary *tidzihi* is given as meaning "sparrow" (*gorrión*), and in the Dyk-Stoudt Mixtec dictionary, *xíhi*, the equivalent of the *dzihi* of the Alvarado vocabulary, refers to a blue bird similar to the chachalaca.

Summary of the Relationship Between the Glosses on the Lienzo of Jicayán and Written Land Documents

The Mixtec glosses on the Lienzo of Jicayán relate more

closely to the Mixtec names of Jicayán's boundaries written on Codex Colombino than they do to the pictorial place signs in the Lienzo. The probable reason for this is that both sets of glosses have a common written prototype, a list of Jicayán's boundaries that was prepared after the Lienzo was drawn and at a time when Jicayán's boundaries were no longer the same as the names set forth in the place signs on the Lienzo.

Because the glosses on Colombino are concluded with the date 1541, which appears on page XXIV of the Codex, these annotations are considered to be an early Colonial document, as opposed to the 1710 review of Jicayán's boundaries, which is a late Colonial document. But even as late as 1710, virtually all of the names listed in the early-eighteenth-century review of Jicayán's boundaries appear in the glosses on the Lienzo of Jicayán. The principal difference between the Colombino glosses and the Mixtec boundary names in the 1710 list is that a number of glosses in the lower-left corner of the Lienzo which are included in Colombino are absent in the 1710 list. This slight difference seems to indicate that Jicayán's boundaries had been amended again between the time when the Lienzo and Colombino were annotated and the early eighteenth century.

The 1680 list of boundaries between Jicayán and Amusgos presents five names of Jicayán's boundaries from the point of view of one of its neighbors, and some differences of opinion are apparent. The correlation between this list and the boundary names on the Lienzo of Jicayán is only 50 per cent—that is, of the five boundary names listed by Amusgos, only two and part of a third agree with any of the other lists of Mixtec names of Jicayán's boundaries.

PRESENT-DAY ORAL TRADITION CONCERNING THE LIENZO

If the Mixtec glosses on the Lienzo of Jicayán are from a written source, the pictorial signs may well reflect an oral tradition. That is, prior to the arrival of European writing, the names of the boundaries and other sites surrounding Jicayán were probably committed to memory much as the genealogies of nobility were memorized and formed an oral tradition for the Mixtec history manuscripts.

An oral tradition concerning the Lienzo still exists in Jicayán, but as might be expected, the stories concerning the pictorial map have more of a quality of a folktale than of well documented history. The following story of the Lienzo was told to the author by a prominent citizen of Jicayán in the spring of 1963.[40]

This town has a land title which is a rectangular piece of cloth made by an Indian woman from this town. And when this cloth was woven, the authorities of the town, and the police on order of the authorities, went to watch the woman who was responsible for weaving the cloth. And the woman

---

[39] The status of the town of San Juan Colorado in the early Colonial period is not clearly documented, but it may have been a subject of Atoyac.

[40] The original Spanish text of this story appears in Appendix B-7. The story was not told while the citizen of Jicayán was looking at the Lienzo, but from his memory of its contents. Other descriptions of sixteenth-century pictorial manuscripts are included in three eighteenth-century documents from the Zapotec-speaking region of Villa Alta in northeastern Oaxaca (Julio de la Fuente, "Documentos para la etnografía e historia zapotecas," *Anales del INAH*, Vol. III [Mexico, 1940], 185–97).

who made the cloth, made everything to the advantage of Jicayán. According to the drawings which she made, no rights were given to all the outlying towns that belonged to this town. Why? Because the authorities and the police were watching the progress of her work very carefully. Because if it happened that she should paint the figures on this map, or cloth, incorrectly, they would have taken away all of this woman's rights or would have ordered her to go home and would have punished her. And for this reason, everything on the map was made in favor of Jicayán, and that map was made by this town . . . it was an Indian woman of this town who made this map. Or, as it may be considered, the title of ownership of the communal lands of San Pedro Jicayán.

Interjected Question: When was the map made?

Narrator continues: I don't remember very well its date. . . . It seems as if it were made in 1805 or 1807. Between these years they made this map.

That woman made the figures or the "writing" on this map. Since formerly there was no one who knew writing in European script, it has no writing, but merely strange figures which more or less give one to understand the meaning of each neighboring town. As, for example, in the center of that map is the church, the church which still exists, and in front of the church is the former ruler of the town. And then comes . . . the town of Tlacamama is seen; the church is there; in the map is the church. There appears the little road from Tlacamama to Jicayán, from Jicayán to the Stone of the Sun,[41] from the Stone of the Sun to Pinotea de Don Luis. [On the map] is the Mixtec name of Pinotepa de Don Luis: *ndoo yu'u*. From Pinotepa de Don Luis to San Juan Colorado. Since formerly no one could write in European script because no one knew how, there is a picture of a rope; a red rope is seen. It is a strand of rope, but red, and it is on the map. And that means that here is San Juan Colorado, whose Mixtec name is *yoqua'a* or *yo'o qua'a*. And so on, mentioning successively each neighboring town, because formerly there was *no one* who knew how to write. The boundaries of the lands of Jicayán were:

Piedra Grande ["the big stone"][42]
Hondura del Toro ["the hollow of the bull"]
Las Palmas ["the palm trees"]
Soco tiyaca ("the spring of the fish")[43]
La Pastura ["the pasture"]
Yuta tita ("river of the bananas")[44]
up to *Cha tuta*, or Zacatepec[45]

to Amusgos, *ñuu ñama*[46]
San José *ñuu ti'yoo*[47]
Tres Ríos ["three rivers"] or *yuta uni*
Tulumbi tuni ("marked guapinoles")[48]
Yuta cu kixi ("arroyo of the pond")
Tu te itu ("hill or small slope of a plant known as 'the hard leaf' ")
Cava tiñuu ("rock of the royal turkeys")
Cha wa'vee ("ravine of the goats")
Yuta mini coò cáá ("arroyo of the hollow of the rattlesnake")

And from there, to La Piedra Grande ["the big stone"], which closes the circle of the boundaries. All of these towns formerly belonged to San Pedro Jicayán.

This legend, then, is the present-day oral tradition concerning the Lienzo of Jicayán. Probably the reason it is said that a woman was responsible for "making" the Lienzo is that today women are responsible for weaving cloth in the Coastal region. Although it is possible that the three large strips of cloth for the Lienzo were woven by a woman, it seems highly unlikely that a woman drew the figures on the Lienzo. The few documents and traditions that have survived concerning the scribes who drew pictorial manuscripts indicate that they were men.[49]

The description of the strict control of the contents of the map by municipal authorities and the statement that the map favored Jicayán at the expense of other towns have a certain common-sense truth. It seems highly likely that maps which set forth a town and its boundaries were supervised by the native ruler of the town; and the local bias seen in historical or genealogical manuscripts is also likely to be found in maps of one town. The date of 1805 to 1807 given for the drawing of the map is impossible, because no maps on cloth with clearly pre-Conquest style and iconography were made as late as the early nineteenth century, and because the map is documented as having been used as evidence in the 1710 review of Jicayán's boundaries. Either 1805–1807 was to this citizen of Jicayán synonymous with the general idea of "a long time ago," or perhaps the Lienzo was brought in as a corroborative document in a land suit that took place in the early nineteenth century.

The list of boundaries given at the end of the story supposedly sets forth the "old" boundaries of Jicayán, but it is actually a mixture of the present and past boundary sites of the town. Only two of the names on the list have counterparts in the glosses on the Lienzo: the site of Los Tres Ríos, represented by Sign 17 in the Lienzo where it is

---

[41] The site known as "Stone of the Sun" (*Piedra del Sol*) is virtually the same as the Cerro de la Iglesia or "Hill of the Church" which is about half a mile southeast of Jicayán on the road to Pinotepa de Don Luis. On the hill is a large unexcavated mound, and located at the base of this hill is a stone said to be "a stone of the sun," although the stone at present shows little evidence of carving.

[42] This site is the present-day boundary between Jicayán and Pinotepa de Don Luis (Fig. 121).

[43] The *soco tiyaca* mentioned here may be the same as the present-day village named Zocoteaca, which is located almost five miles east and somewhat north of Ipalapa and ten miles east and slightly south of Amusgos; this village is now a subject of Ipalapa.

[44] The location of *Yuta tita* is shown on the 1893 map of the lands of Manuel Yglesias (Fig. 138), where it appears directly west of Cerro Camalote, one of the boundaries of Yglesias's lands on the east.

[45] *Cha tuta* is an abbreviated form of the Mixtec name of Zacatepec, *yucu cha tuta* or *yucu sa tuta* ("the hill of the calendrical name or date 7-Water").

[46] *Ñuu ñama* ("the town of the corn husk, cocoon, or the ball used in the ballgame") is the present-day Mixtec name of Amusgos.

[47] The "San José" cited here may be the same place as the Cuadrilla San José that appears in the 1893 map of the lands of Manuel Yglesias (Fig. 138), where it is shown toward the bottom of the map, just above "Los Tres Ríos," the next site mentioned in this story as a boundary of Jicayán.

[48] The *guapinole* is a tree whose botanical name is *Hymenaea courbaril*; it is sometimes known as the "sausage tree" in English because its fruit has the general shape of a sausage. The resin of this tree is used for copal incense.

[49] Burgoa, *Palestra historial*, 210; Robertson, *Mexican Manuscript Painting*, 35–36 *et passim*.

accompanied by the gloss *yuta uni* ("three rivers"), and *cava tiñuu*, Sign 9 in the Lienzo and accompanied by the gloss *cava yy tiñoo yucu*. The naming of Zacatepec and Amusgos as neighbors of Jicayán is a description of the extent of the town's lands in the past, because as can be seen in Map 6 (p. 91), which shows the present-day municipal boundaries of towns on the Coast, Jicayán is now bounded on the north by Atoyac rather than by Amusgos or Zacatepec. But many of the names given in the list are Jicayán's boundaries at the present time, as for example the site named "Piedra Grande" or "big stone," which is the current boundary between Jicayán and Pinotepa de Don Luis. Moreover, two of the place names on the list include imported post-Conquest motifs: the bull in the "hollow of the bull," and the goat in "ravine of the goat."

SUMMARY

The Lienzo of Jicayán was probably drawn around the mid-sixteenth century because the drawing style of the central configuration and the fifty-two place signs that form an irregular circle around the border of the map shows close affinities with pre-Conquest manuscript style. The year date Ten-Rabbit below the central building is apparently equivalent to the year 1542.

The thirty-two Mixtec glosses which set forth the names of Jicayán's boundaries and which were added to the Lienzo later show only an occasional relationship to the pictorial place signs near which they are written. The reason the pictorial signs and the glosses are not equivalent is that the place signs represent the names of boundaries of Jicayán in the early sixteenth century, whereas the glosses set forth the names of the town's boundaries in the mid-sixteenth century or later, when the names of boundaries were no longer the same as those depicted by the place signs.

The Mixtec glosses on the Lienzo relate more closely to other written documents that list the names of the boundaries of Jicayán than they do to the pictorial signs in the Lienzo. The closest counterparts to the glosses on the Lienzo are the Mixtec names of the boundaries of Jicayán written on pages XIII and XIV of Codex Colombino; these annotations were supposedly added to the Codex in 1541. The Mixtec names of the boundaries of Jicayán as recorded in a 1710 survey of the town's boundaries also show a close correlation with the Mixtec glosses on the Lienzo, although the 1710 list lacks several of the Mixtec names written in the lower-left corner of the Lienzo—that is, sites that are west of Jicayán.

In summary, the Lienzo of Jicayán and the known written documents present three lists of the boundaries of Jicayán at three different times. The place signs on the Lienzo depict the names of the town's boundaries at the time of the Spanish conquest. The Mixtec glosses on the Lienzo and on pages XIII and XIV of Codex Colombino set forth the names of the boundaries in the mid-sixteenth century. The 1710 review of boundaries gives the Mixtec names of the boundaries as they existed at that time, and the principal difference between the lands of Jicayán as described in this list and in the mid-sixteenth-century lists is that by 1710, the town had lost lands on its western border.

IX

COMPARISON OF THE LIENZO OF JICAYÁN
WITH THREE OTHER MIXTEC MAPS

The Lienzo of Jicayán is only one of several Colonial maps which show one town and its boundaries and which are annotated with glosses in Mixtec. How is the Jicayán lienzo similar to these other maps, and how is it different? Is the lack of correspondence between the Mixtec glosses and the pictorial signs that is apparent in the Jicayán map typical of other maps with glosses, or is the Lienzo an exceptional case in this respect?

For the sake of comparison, three Colonial-period maps from three different regions of the Mixteca outside of the Coast will be discussed briefly: the Lienzo of Ocotepec from the Mixteca Alta, Map No. 36 from the Mixteca Baja, and the 1771 Map of Xoxocotlán from the Valley of Oaxaca. In common with the Lienzo of Jicayán, all three of these maps show the lands of a town surrounded by signs that represent the names of the town's boundaries, and all three are annotated with glosses that set forth the names of the boundaries.

LIENZO OF OCOTEPEC

The Lienzo of Ocotepec (Figs. 160–61) is a map of the lands of the town of Santo Tomás Ocotepec in the Mixteca Alta (17°9′ N., 97°47′ W.). The Lienzo is in the municipal archive of Ocotepec, and it measures approximately 1.04 meters high by 1.34 meters long. It was first published by Alfonso Caso in 1966, and accompanying Caso's interpretation of its pictorial content and glosses is an analysis by Irmgard Weitlaner Johnson of the technique used in weaving the Lienzo.[1]

On the basis of its style, the Lienzo of Ocotepec was probably drawn around 1580. In common with the 1580 Map of Teozacoalco (Fig. 132) and the second Lienzo of Zacatepec (Fig. 122), which was tentatively dated 1580–1600, the place signs of the boundaries are drawn in an

---

[1] Caso, "Mapa de Santo Tomás Ocotepeque, Oaxaca," *Summa anthropologica en homenaje a Roberto J. Weitlaner* (Mexico, 1966), 131–37; and Weitlaner Johnson, "Analisis textil del Lienzo de Ocotepec," *ibid.,* 139–44. Caso's study includes an ultra-violet photograph of the Lienzo by Walter Reuter, from which Fig. 160 of this book is derived, as well as a color reproduction. In contrast to the Lienzo of Jicayán and the two Lienzos of Zacatepec, which are black ink drawings with no color added, the landscape and many of the place signs in the Lienzo of Ocotepec are filled in with color. Green is used in the hills, blue in the streams of water, red in the church roofs, and yellow in the body of the ocelot in the place sign of Cuquila at the right side of the Lienzo. In addition, red, yellow, and blue are used to decorate the place signs around the border and the post-and-lintel building at the right of the central church. (Caso, *ibid.,* 132.)

essentially pre-Conquest style with some evidence of "disintegrated frame line," and the center of the Lienzo contains a European style of landscape, with towns represented as church buildings. In the Lienzo of Ocotepec the roads include hoofprints of horses as well as human footprints, a feature that is also seen on the 1580 Map of Teozacoalco and the 1579 Map of Texupan (Fig. 37). Moreover, the Ocotepec Lienzo shows fewer elements of European style and iconography than a 1595 map from the same region of the Mixteca Alta, a map that was drawn to show the location of a land grant within the town of Cuquila (Fig. 133). The latter map utilizes pre-Conquest conventions for the stream of water above the church of Cuquila, in the borders of the hills at the top of the map, and in the friezes with geometric decoration below the roofs of the churches; but the 1595 map contains no pre-Conquest place signs such as those seen around the borders of the Lienzo of Ocotepec, and the drawing style of this map is less sure than that of the Ocotepec Lienzo.

As a map, the Lienzo of Ocotepec is oriented with west at the top, and the approximate locations of the places shown within the Lienzo as well as the towns that border Ocotepec are indicated in Map 7. In the center of the Lienzo, the town of Ocotepec is depicted as a large church; written across the base of the church building is the legend "santo tomas ocotepeque." The place sign of Cuquila, the town which is Ocotepec's neighbor to the north, is drawn on the right side of the Lienzo. This sign consists of a hill with a tiger and represents Cuquila's Mixtec name *ñuu cuiñe* or "tiger town"; written on the base of the place sign is the name "cuquila." At the summit of the hill is a frieze on which are seated an unnamed marriage pair. This frieze is connected by a line with footprints to a pre-Conquest type of post-and-lintel building that is located between the church of Ocotepec and the place sign of Cuquila. This building is identified by a gloss as "san juan," and it probably represents the town of San Juan Mixtepec, almost eight miles northwest of Cuquila. This placement of Mixtepec within the boundaries of Ocotepec where it does not belong was undoubtedly done to give genealogical rather than cartographic information. Because the line of footprints connects the female figure seated on the place sign of Cuquila with the building that represents the town of San Juan Mixtepec, the implication may be that at the time the Lienzo was drawn, the native rulers of

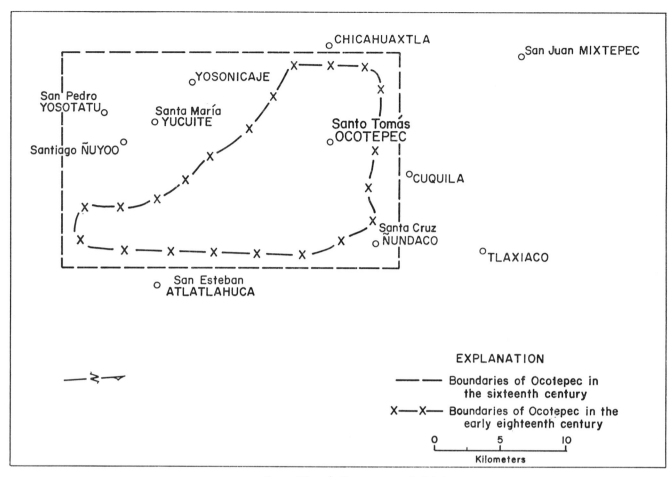

MAP 7. Santo Tomás Ocotepec and vicinity

Mixtepec were the offspring of, or related to, the rulers of Cuquila.

Connected to the large central church of Ocotepec by roads are five smaller churches that represent the towns that were subjects of Ocotepec in the sixteenth century. Across the base of each of these churches is written the saint's name of the town. In the lower-left corner is "santiago," or Santiago Ñuyoo, a town ten miles south of Ocotepec. Above Ñuyoo and near the left border of the Lienzo is "sn pedro," or San Pedro Yosotatu, about 12 miles south of Ocotepec. To the right of Yosotatu is "sta ma," or Santa María Yucuite, about eight miles south of Ocotepec. Above Yucuite and near the top border of the Lienzo is a church with a gloss that appears to be "santiago"; this church may represent the town of Yosonicaje, about six miles south and slightly west of Ocotepec and a town that is now a subject of Santa María Yucuite. Below and slightly to the right of the central church of Ocotepec is a church with the legend "santa cruz," which represents, as Caso has noted, the town of Santa Cruz Ñundaco, about five miles east and slightly north of Ocotepec.[2]

Around the border of the Lienzo are twenty-four place signs, all facing inward; most of these signs set forth the names of Ocotepec's boundaries at the time the map was drawn in the sixteenth century. Twenty-two of the twenty-four boundary signs are accompanied by glosses in

[2] Ibid., 133.

Nahuatl, but what appears to be a provincial type of Nahuatl.[3] In his study of the Lienzo, Alfonso Caso transcribes twenty of the twenty-two glosses; two are now completely illegible. He also translates fourteen of the Nahuatl glosses; and of these fourteen, nine relate directly to the pictorial sign which they accompany; the remaining five glosses possibly refer to the sign near which they are written, although the relationship is more tenuous.[4]

A second group of glosses consists of forty-one Mixtec place names, most of which are written on the hills of the

[3] Caso (ibid., 132) characterizes the Nahuatl written on the Lienzo as "bastante pobre." The Ocotepec Lienzo is but one of six Colonial-period maps from the Mixteca that are annotated in Nahuatl, which apparently was the *lingua franca* of Middle America at the time of the Spanish conquest. The glosses on the second Lienzo of Zacatepec are in Nahuatl (Fig. 123), as are some of the glosses accompanying place signs of boundaries in the unpublished Lienzo Seler II of the Coixtlahuaca group of manuscripts. The Map of Xochitepec, now in the National Museum of Copenhagen, shows the place sign of Xochitepec within a square formed by twenty-three place signs, all of which are glosses with a Nahuatl place name. Alfonso Caso, who published the map with a commentary on its contents, suggested that the "xochitepec" in question is San Juan Suchitepec, a town in the Mixteca Baja almost 15 miles northeast of Huajuapan de León ("El mapa de Xochitepec," *ICA* XXXII [Copenhagen, 1958], 458).

The Lienzo Córdova-Castellanos, which is presumably a map of San Esteban Atlatlahuca, Ocotepec's neighbor to the east, has thirty boundary signs accompanied by Nahuatl glosses. Concerning this Lienzo, see note 51, Chapter 2. The twenty boundary signs on the 1771 Map of Xoxocotlán (Figs. 162–63) are identified by glosses in both Nahuatl and Mixtec. These glosses are transcribed and translated in Appendix F.

[4] Caso, "Mapa de Santo Tomás Ocotepeque," *Summa anthropologica en homenaje a Roberto J. Weitlaner*, 133–35.

landscape within the boundary signs. Caso has transcribed these glosses and has suggested translations for thirteen of the glosses and a partial translation of sixteen others. He also notes that the Mixtec glosses are written in a hand and type of ink that are different from those of the Nahuatl glosses, but the same as a gloss *años 1701* ("the year 1701") that is placed below the central church of Ocotepec.[5] Moreover, the irregular circle formed by the Mixtec glosses (shown in Map 7) *excludes* the five churches which represent the towns that were formerly Ocotepec's dependencies. Thus, it might be reasonable to assume that the Mixtec glosses are boundary names added to the Lienzo in the early eighteenth century, and that by the time they were added, the territory of Ocotepec had shrunk and no longer included the five towns that were formerly its subjects.

This assumption is confirmed by a land document in the Archivo General de la Nación that contains a review of Ocotepec's boundaries made on March 10, 1726.[6] At the time of the 1726 review, thirty-four Mixtec names of boundaries of Ocotepec were recorded. In the comparative list in Chart 20, the Mixtec names in the left-hand column are the boundary names on the Lienzo of Ocotepec as transcribed by Alfonso Caso, beginning in the upper-right corner of the Lienzo and moving in a counter-clockwise direction. The second column lists the Mixtec names of Ocotepec's boundaries in 1726; in the third column is the name of the town which shared the listed boundary site with Ocotepec according to the 1726 land document. Twenty-seven of the Mixtec boundary names occur in both the Lienzo of Ocotepec and in the 1726 review of Ocotepec's boundaries, while fourteen names occur only in the Lienzo, and seven other names occur only in the 1726 document.

But perhaps the most significant information provided by the 1726 list of Ocotepec's boundaries is that by the eighteenth century Ocotepec shares boundaries with Santa María Yucuite, Santiago Ñuyoo, and Santa Cruz Ñundaco, three towns that were subjects of Ocotepec when the map was originally drawn in the second half of the sixteenth century. Thus the Mixtec glosses represent an "updating" or amendment of the Lienzo some 120 years after the Lienzo was drawn. This amendment was necessary because of a phenomenon that was common throughout the Mixteca during the Colonial period—the achievement of independent status by subject towns.

Colonial documents from the Mixteca are rich in case histories of subject towns attempting to establish their autonomy, and often the *principales* or secondary nobility who governed the subject towns claimed to be hereditary rulers with the same authority as the *caciques* or primary nobility of the *cabeceras* or major towns.[7] By the end of the Colonial period, the Mixtec community kingdoms had become fragmented, and consequently the territory of the

major towns was greatly reduced. This reduction of territory is vividly portrayed in the Lienzo of Ocotepec, which is in a sense two different maps. The first map consists of the place signs of names of Ocotepec's boundaries and the accompanying Nahuatl glosses which set forth the names of these boundaries in the second half of the sixteenth century. The second map consists of the Mixtec names of Ocotepec's boundaries that were added to the Lienzo in the early eighteenth century and which, as shown in Map 7, form an irregular circle that excludes the towns that were formerly subjects of Ocotepec. This second map is what might be termed a "written map"—that is, it is essentially a written document *per se*, for the Mixtec glosses are not associated with the place signs of boundaries but are inscribed on the landscape inside of the first map that is delineated by the boundary signs.[8]

Thus the eighteenth-century Mixtec glosses on the Lienzo of Ocotepec, in common with the Mixtec glosses on the Lienzo of Jicayán, are more closely related to Colonial land documents than to the place signs of the map on which they are written. In the case of both Lienzos, the reason the place signs and Mixtec glosses are not closely related is that the place signs present the towns' boundaries at one point in time, and the glosses set forth different names of boundaries at a later point in time.

The Place Sign of Chicahuaxtla

One of the twenty-four signs around the border of the Ocotepec Lienzo seems to represent the town of Chicahuaxtla, Ocotepec's neighbor to the west, rather than the name of a boundary. The sign in question is within the row of place signs at the top of the Lienzo, below and just to the left of the half-sun that indicates the direction "west." The place sign consists of an arch or loop inside of a hill, and standing on the loop is a profile male figure with the calendrical name 4-Flower. The gloss accompanying this sign reads: *tlamimilcu moha qui coyhua y tlatuani cicahuaztla*. Alfonso Caso translated this phrase as "4-Flower, the ruler of Chicahuaxtla, was overthrown . . ." and he observed that the two words *qui coyhua* are Mixtec and refer to the calendrical name 4-Flower, while the remainder of the gloss is Nahuatl.[9]

In the Reyes list of place names, the Mixtec name of Chicahuaxtla is *tnu tnono*; and *tnono*, the qualifying element of this name, also appears as the qualifying element in the place name *ytno tnono*, which is written near a place sign on page 20 of Codex Sánchez Solís (Fig. 22g). The sign in Sánchez Solís that illustrates the name *ytno tnono* consists of a hill with a semicircular arch or loop attached to the base of the hill—essentially the same elements that are seen in the place sign at the top of the Lienzo of Ocotepec. Thus, the hill with an arch or loop is probably the place sign of Chicahuaxtla. It is not at all clear how the arch or loop expresses the Mixtec word *tnono*, which

[5] *Ibid.*, 132, 134–36.

[6] AGN-Tierras, 876–1, fol. 20–22.

[7] Concerning another case of a subject town's attempt to establish its independence—the case of Tecomatlán, a former subject of Yanhuitlán—see Spores, *The Mixtec Kings and Their People*, 140.

[8] Eight of the Mixtec glosses at the bottom of the Lienzo are written beneath place signs, but the place names in these glosses are not the same as the place names depicted by the signs above the glosses.

[9] "Mapa de Santo Tomás Ocotepeque," *Summa anthropologica en homenaje a Roberto J. Weitlaner*, 134.

according to the Alvarado dictionary means "some, a group, a pair." It is possible that the loop is intended to suggest an enclosure that hypothetically would encompass a group, or that the loop as a yoke-shaped configuration is intended to suggest the joining of two persons, animals, or objects as a pair.

In contrast to the sign of Cuquila, Ocotepec's neighbor to the north, which is shown in the Lienzo of Ocotepec as larger than the boundary signs and does not face inward toward the church of Ocotepec, the sign of Chicahuaxtla is not differentiated from the signs of boundary names with which it appears. Were it not for the accompanying text that identifies the sign as Chicahuaxtla, the sign would be thought to represent the name of a boundary because it faces inward and is no more prominent than the boundary signs that appear on either side of it. A similar situation also occurs in the Lienzo of Jicayán in which the sign of Pinotepa de Don Luis, Jicayán's neighbor to the east, is placed among the signs of Jicayán boundaries (sign 4, Fig. 148). Thus while early Colonial Mixtec maps usually present place signs in a cartographic context which makes it easier to identify the signs, the context itself is at times unclear, for a place sign of a neighboring town is occasionally represented in the same manner as a sign for the name of a town's boundary.

MAP NO. 36

Map No. 36 (Fig. 21) is drawn in black ink on a piece of European paper measuring 85 by 87 centimeters. The patterns of crease-marks in the paper indicate that the map was at one time folded into twenty-four rectangles of unequal size. In all likelihood, it was folded to reduce its size so that it could be more conveniently included with legal-size documents. On the right side of the map is a missing section which may have become separated from the map because of the tearing of the creases in numerous unfoldings and refoldings, although the upper-left corner of the missing section does not correspond exactly with the creases.

The map has been in the Museo Nacional de Antropología in Mexico City (No. 35–36) since at least as early as 1907, and it was first published by Vladamiro Rosado Ojeda in 1945.[10] Rosado Ojeda's study includes a detailed description of the map's pictorial content and a transcription but not a translation of the Mixtec glosses written on the map. He suggests that the drawing was done in the sixteenth century, perhaps a few years after the Spanish conquest, because even though the place signs and the format have a pre-Conquest flavor, the drawing style exhibits the less taut line that is characteristic of early Colonial manuscripts.

In the center of Map No. 36 is a Christian church

flanked by two post-and-lintel buildings, each of which contains a marriage pair. Below the building on the left is an A–O year sign with the year Eight-Flint (1540 or 1592?) and the day Eight-Flower. Because part of the right side of the map is now missing, all that remains of a similar date below the building on the right is the lower half of an A–O year sign and the day-sign Grass. Below the central church is an A–O year sign with the year Six-House (1525 or 1577?) and the day Seven-Grass. At the right of this date is a seated male figure with the calendrical name 8-Death.

In the lower half of the map is a stream of water that runs parallel to the lower border and separates two horizontal rows of rectangles that represent plots of land. Each of the fourteen rectangles below the stream of water contains a profile male head. Around the border of the map are thirty-seven place signs which face inward and which presumably set forth the names of the boundaries of the town represented by the church in the center.

Each of the place signs on the border is accompanied by a Mixtec gloss that gives the same name as the pictorial sign. Glosses in Mixtec also appear in all of the fourteen plots of land below the river. In the eleven rectangles of land still visible above the river there appear two Spanish names: "do Jua" ["Don Juan"] and "doña macarita" ["Doña Margarita"], probably the names of the Indian rulers who owned these pieces of land.[11] In the center of the map, each of the five seated figures is accompanied by a short Mixtec gloss, as are each of the two buildings on either side of the central church. The Mixtec glosses on Map No. 36 are translated and discussed in detail in Appendix E. For the sake of brevity, only those glosses which shed some light on the provenience of the map will be considered below.

In common with the Lienzo of Ocotepec, the central town in Map No. 36 is depicted by a Colonial church rather than by a pre-Conquest place sign. Thus the only clue to the provenience of the manuscript is the written text in Mixtec. Probably the most significant Mixtec gloss is one written across the roof of the building at the right of the central church: *haey ñodi*. In the dialect of the Alvarado dictionary, this phrase would be *huahi ñuu dzai*, which means "the house of Huajuapan de León." *Huahi* means "house" and by extension "family" or "ruling line." In the Reyes list of Mixtec names of towns, *ñuu dzai* is given as the Mixtec name of Huajuapan de León, an important town in the Mixteca Baja and on present-day Pan-American Highway between Puebla and Oaxaca (17°48′ N., 97°47′ W.). The name of Huajuapan also occurs in a Mixtec gloss written in one of the plots of land at the bottom of the map. In the third rectangle from the left is a short text that includes the Spanish word *pleyto* or "litigation, lawsuit," and the Mixtec phrase *ñuhu ño diai*, or "the lands of Huajuapan de León." (*Ñuhu* is "land," and *ño*

---

[10] "Estudio del códice mixteco post-cortesiano Núm. 36," *Anales del INAH*, I (1945), 147–55. Included in John B. Glass, *Catálogo de la Colección de Códices* (p. 81 and plate 38), is a short description of the map and a black-and-white photograph that is somewhat clearer than the one published by Rosado Ojeda. According to the Glass catalog, the earliest known reference to Map No. 36 is the 1907 inventory of manuscripts in the Museo Nacional made by Eduard Seler.

[11] From left to right, the Spanish glosses written on the eleven fields above the river are: (1) *do Juan*, (2) *doña macarita*, (3–7) *do Jua*, (8–9) *doña macarita*, (10) *do Jua, doña macarita*, and (11) *do Jua*. It is possible that up to three more fields originally appeared above the river on the right side of the map in the section that is now missing.

CHART 20: Mixtec Names of the Boundaries of Ocotepec

Lienzo of Ocotepec	1726 Land Document	Town which Shares Boundary with Ocotepec
yuhui tisaha	yuhui tisaha	Chicahuaxtla
yucu yu	—	—
dute soco yuche	—	—
yoso ñucoiyo	yoso ñucôyo	Chicahuaxtla
tooto tiun	—	—
tuyu xauxa	—	—
yucu nuloa	—	—
yucu dzita	—	—
toto ñusaman	toto ñusama	Chicahuaxtla
yucu deso tayee	yucu ndoso tay	Chicahuaxtla
yuta soco yoyo	ndute soco yuyu	Chicahuaxtla
—	ndute soco niy	Chicahuaxtla
ytun namani	ytnu nama	Chicahuaxtla
—	ytno ita	Chicahuaxtla
—	yucu no cuica	Chicahuaxtla
duta sanis	—	—
yucu ite	—	—
yucu ñumin	—	—
—	yucu cuiti soho	Yucuite
—	nu manihi	Yucuite
cabau yeca	cahua yeca	Yucuite
yucu dzita tosua	ytno ndita tasu	Yucuite
yucu ñutee	yucu ñute	Ñuyoo
caba cuygis	cahua cuisi	Ñuyoo

CHART 20. (cont.)

Lienzo of Ocotepec	1726 Land Document	Town which Shares Boundary with Ocotepec
yucun tuncaa	yucu tnocaa	Ñuyoo
yubi diyoo	ytno ndoyoho	Ñuyoo
yucu coo	yucu coo	Ñuyoo
taa yuhuu	—	—
yoso nduyuu	yoso nduiu	Ñuyoo
yubi cuitimi	yuhui cuini	Atlatlahuca
cabaa ūnso ñun	cahua ndoso ñuhu	Atlatlahuca
caba nundo	cahua sundu	Atlatlahuca
ytun yahui	ytno yahui	Atlatlahuca
ytu ndacu yehe	ytno ndacu llehe	Atlatlahuca
caboia do(s)o ñaña	cahua ndoso ñaña	Ñundaco and Tlaxiaco
itu ndaso quicis	—	—
mini ndozo coo	—	—
ñu tuhui	—	—
ndun tich tiñuu	nduta sichi tiñum	Ñundaco and Tlaxiaco
cohua sitnuu	—	—
—	yucu ndoso ysu	Cuquila
—	nduhua teyu	Cuquila
yucu ñu nuj	yucu ñu suhui	Cuquila
ytun tabi yii	ytno tahui yti	Cuquila
nduhua ticuhuaa	nduhua ticuhua	Cuquila
cuitin nindee	yucu cuite binde	Cuquila
cachaa cua	cahua quaha	Cuquila
ycu tico ñuuii	yucu tico numi	Cuquila

diai is the Mixtec name of Huajuapan de León.) This gloss indicates that the rectangle of land in question belongs to Huajuapan and is under litigation.

The Mixtec gloss written above the post-and-lintel building at the left of the central church is probably also a place name. The gloss is *çoco xahuaco* (or *dzoco sahuaco* in the dialect of the Alvarado dictionary), which can be translated as "the spring or well of 7-Flower." (*Dzoco* means "spring, well," and *sahuaco* is the calendrical name 7-Flower.) Unfortunately, it is not known what town or place has the Mixtec name *dzoco sahuaco*. Another possible translation of this phrase is "the birthplace of 7-Flower," for *dzoco* can also mean "cradle" and by extension "birthplace." If this were the case, it is still unclear which person named 7-Flower is referred to by the gloss. None of the five seated persons on Map No. 36 is named 7-Flower, and there are so many persons—both male and female—in the Mixtec histories who are named 7-Flower that it is impossible to determine which specific person is named in the gloss on the map.

Because the Mixtec name of Huajuapan appears twice on Map No. 36—once in the building at the right of the central church and once at the bottom of the map in a field that is said to be the subject of a lawsuit—it seems likely that the map is from Huajuapan, or at least from the Mixteca Baja region. This hypothesis would appear to be substantiated by the dialect of the Mixtec glosses on the map, for these are written in a dialect of the Mixteca Baja. This dialect is closer to an unpublished Mixtec vocabulary compiled in 1800 by Josep Mariano Tupeus in the Baja region of southern Puebla than it is to the dialect of the Mixteca Alta recorded in the Alvarado dictionary and the Reyes grammar.[12]

Another indication that Map No. 36 is from the Mixteca Baja is the occasional relationship between the Mixtec names accompanying the place signs on the border of the map and eighteenth-century Mixtec names of boundaries of Huajuapan and of another town in the Baja region, Santa María Acaquizapan. Acaquizapan is located about 20 miles north and slightly east of Huajuapan, and it was probably a subject of nearby Tequixtepec in the early Colonial period. The glosses on Map No. 36 that seem to relate to names of boundaries of Huajuapan or Acaquizapan are listed in the left-hand column of Chart 21. In the second column is the number of the place sign in Map No. 36 which the gloss accompanies. (For the sake of consistency, the system of numbering the place signs is the same as that used by Rosado Ojeda in his 1945 study of the map: the signs on the left border are numbered 1 through 10 from bottom to top, those on the top are numbered 1 through 10 from left to right, those on the right border are numbered 1 through 6 from top to bottom, and those on the lower border are numbered 1 through 11 from right to left. Thus, for example, the sign with a band of

footprints on the left border is "9-left," the speckled mound on the right border is "3-right," and so forth.)

The third column of the chart gives the analogous Mixtec name as listed in eighteenth-century land documents, as well as a translation of the name if one is given in the document. In the fourth column are the names of the towns for which the site is a boundary, as well as the references to the documents in the Archivo General de la Nación from which the information is drawn. The locations of the towns mentioned in the accompanying chart are shown in Map 8.

In many respects, the incidental correlation between the Mixtec glosses on Map No. 36 and Mixtec names of boundaries in the Mixteca Baja creates more problems than it solves. First of all, the land documents in which the Mixtec boundary names occur are for the most part eighteenth-century documents, and therefore at least a century and possibly as many as two centuries later than Map No. 36. By the eighteenth century, the lands of Huajuapan and the other major towns of the Mixteca Baja were no longer the same as they were in the sixteenth century when the map was drawn, because these towns, as in the case of Santo Tomás Ocotepec, no longer controlled the lands belonging to their subject towns and because some of the lands had been granted to Spaniards as cattle-grazing ranches.[13] Consequently, many of the boundary sites named in the sixteenth-century map may no longer have been boundary sites in the eighteenth century.

Second, when plotted on a map (as in Map 8), the approximate locations of the sites whose Mixtec names appear both in the land documents and in Map No. 36 do not form a pattern that encloses any one town, as is common in maps that show a town surrounded by its boundaries. In Map 8, the line of dashes shows the hypothetical line connecting boundary sites named on the left side of Map No. 36 and in land documents; this line moves from east to north, and then to the southwest. The dotted line in Map 8 is a hypothetical line connecting boundary sites that are named in the top border of place signs on Map No. 36 and in land documents. If the boundary sites listed in the land documents are analogous to the Mixtec names on Map No. 36 as indicated in the accompanying chart, then it would be expected that the dotted line would run in a direction more or less at right angles to the line of dashes, much as the top border of place signs in Map No. 36 is placed at a right angle in relation to the row of signs on the left border. But such is certainly not the case, for the dotted line in Map 8 encircles the line of dashes, and in part runs in the same general direction.

A further complication is found in the one site at the bottom of Map No. 36 whose Mixtec name is analogous to that of a boundary site located to the west of the town of Popoltepec. It would be expected that this site would

---

[12] Tupeus, "Vocabulario, doctrina y oraciones," on microfilm at Yale University Library. The contents of the Tupeus manuscript are discussed in note 21, Chapter III. Appendix E includes a comparison of the dialect of the glosses written on Map No. 36 and the dialect of the Alvarado dictionary.

[13] In the case of Huajuapan, this loss of land is documented in a meticulously drawn map showing the boundaries to the south and east of Huajuapan in 1745 (AGN-Tierras, 657–3, fol. 82). In this map Huajuapan shares boundaries with Santa María Ayuu, a town that was probably a former subject of Huajuapan, and with a ranch belonging to a Spaniard named Leonardo Gil.

CHART 21: Mixtec Glosses on Map No. 36 and Boundaries in the Mixteca Baja

Gloss on Map No. 36	Sign Associated with Gloss	Mixtec Boundary Name from Land Documents	Towns which Share Boundary Site listed in Land Documents
yucu ño tica	1-left	yucu ndica	Tepalcatepec (belonging to Acaquizapan) and Nochixtlán (eighteenth century)
		"open or split hill"	AGN-Tierras, 779–1, fol. 57 AGN-Tierras, 649, 2a pte, fol. 92/v, 104/v AGN-Tierras, 1220–2, fol. 51/v
yucu ño cutu	3-left	yucu tnu cutu	Acaquizapan and Chazumba (1766)
		"hill of the copal tree"	AGN-Tierras, 649, 2a pte, fol. 36/v
no tayu cuixi	6-left	nuu tayuⁿ cuixiⁿ	San Juan Yolotepec and Santa Gertrudis Cozoltepec (1694)
		"the white chair or seat"	AGN-Tierras, 3489, penultimate expediente, fol. 8/v, 41
			Acaquizapan with Ixitlán, San José [Petlalcingo], and Totoltepec (1767)
			AGN-Tierras, 1220–2, fol. 19/v AGN-Tierras, 649, 2a pte, fol. 53, 102/v
		teyu cusi	Huajuapan with Miltepec, Ixitlán and Chila (1726) AGN-Tierras 657–3, fol. 31/v
yucu ñoo	7-left	yucu ñuuⁿ "hill of turtledoves"	Acaquizapan and cacique Juan Bautista Cortés de Velasco of Chila (1767) AGN-Tierras, 649, 2a pte, fol. 105
cuiti quaa	2-top	yucu tecua "hill of the bachelor"	Acaquizapan and Guadalupe, a barrio of Suchitepec (1767) AGN-Tierras, 649, 2a pte, fol. 105
yucu çichin	4-top	yucu dichi	site of Acaquizapan facing Zapoquila (1678) AGN-Tierras, 779–1, fol. 23/v
yucu niyiy	5-top	yucu nihi	boundary on west of Chichihualtepec (subject of Acaquizapan) (c. 1700) AGN-Tierras, 779–1, fol. 56/v
ytno cuiy	8-top	itno cuii	Huajuapan and Chila (eighteenth century) AGN-Tierras, 657–3, fol. 153/v Ibid., cuaderno 2, fol. 11/v Ibid., cuaderno 3, fol. 32/v
yuqo diqmi or yuqo diqnii	10-top	tiquimii	Huajuapan with Ixitlán and Chila (1745) AGN-Tierras, 657–3, fol. 153–153/v
yoço tayu	7-bottom	yodzo tayoⁿ	boundary on west of Popoltepec (subject of Acaquizapan) (c. 1700) AGN-Tierras, 779–1, fol. 56/v

be located opposite the dotted line that represents the hypothetical row of boundaries at the top of Map No. 36, and more or less at right angles to the line of dashes that represents the hypothetical row of boundaries on the left border of Map No. 36. But instead, this site is located between the two lines.

Thus, although the Mixtec glosses which accompany ten of the thirty-seven place signs in Map No. 36 seem to have counterparts in Mixtec names of boundaries from the Mixteca Baja as listed in eighteenth-century land documents, the boundary sites in the documents do not fall into the same rectangular pattern as do the place signs

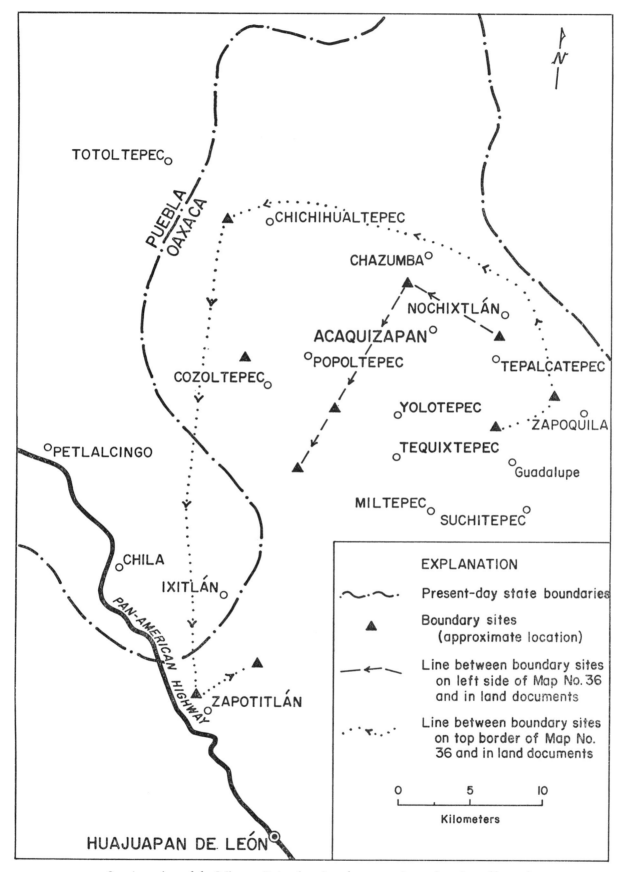

MAP 8.   A section of the Mixteca Baja, showing the approximate location of boundary sites mentioned in Map No. 36 and in eighteenth-century land documents

around the border of Map No. 36. Even if the eight glosses that are analogous to the eighteenth-century boundaries of Acaquizapan are considered separately, this group of boundaries does not form a pattern similar to that seen in Map No. 36.

One possibility is that if the two Mixtec glosses at the top of Map No. 36 that are listed in the eighteenth-century documents as boundaries of Huajuapan can be considered as a "group," then these two sites show roughly the same relationship in Map No. 36 as is described in a 1745 review of some of Huajuapan's boundaries. In this review, the site named *itno cuii*, the same Mixtec name written next to sign 8-top of Map No. 36, is described as being the boundary between Huajuapan and Chila, Huajuapan's neighbor to the northwest; and a site named *tiquimii*, analogous to the *diqmi* portion of the Mixtec name *yuqo diqmi* that is written next to sign 10-top of Map No. 36, is the boundary of Huajuapan with Chila and Ixitlán, Huajuapan's neighbor to the north. If these two names are the only two names that appear both on Map No. 36 and in the eighteenth-century documents, and also have the same spatial relationship when plotted on a map as they have in Map No. 36; then it is possible that Map No. 36 is a map of the lands of Huajuapan oriented with northwest at the top, and that the relationship between the Mixtec names of boundaries of Acaquizapan and the glosses on Map No. 36 is not significant.

Probably the only way to resolve the inconsistencies between Map No. 36 and the available eighteenth-century documents from the Mixteca Baja is to locate the written land documents that were prepared in connection with the litigation for which the map was drawn. The present location of these documents is unknown, but it seems evident that Map No. 36 was drawn specifically to be presented as evidence in a land dispute, because the Spanish word *pleyto* ("litigation, lawsuit") is written on two of the fields at the bottom of the map. In addition, *rúbricas* appear in four places on Map No. 36, which indicates that the map was signed by Spanish officials when it was presented as a document during a lawsuit.[14]

It is probably also significant that Map No. 36 is on European paper rather than on cloth as are the Lienzos of Jicayán and Ocotepec. Although it is not known how European paper was distributed in the Spanies colonies, of how available it was to native artists, it would seem that paper is used principally for maps that are drawn in connection with dealings with Europeans. All of the known maps from Oaxaca drawn to illustrate the written *Relaciones Geográficas* to be sent to Philip II of Spain are on European paper, even when they show strong elements of native style, as the 1580 Map of Teozacoalco.[15]

A number of drawings by native artists presented in connection with litigation and now bound with documents in the Archivo General de la Nación are also on European paper, as the maps drawn to accompany petitions for land grants in Cuquila (Fig. 133) and in the Coixtlahuaca region (Fig. 46), and the Tlazultepec Geneology (Fig. 30).

It is certainly possible that many of the pictorial documents on European paper, including Map No. 36, are based on older paintings on cloth.[16] Rosado Ojeda has compared Map No. 36 with the first Lienzo of Zacatepec,[17] and the Map does resemble this lienzo and the Lienzo of Ocotepec in that all three manuscripts present the place signs of boundaries facing inward and arranged in a rectangular format around the edges of the map. Map No. 36 may well have been a copy—at least in part—of a lienzo that is now lost, a copy made for a specific lawsuit over the two fields at the bottom of the map that contain the word *pleyto*. In connection with this litigation the Spanish officials may have provided the European paper for the map, and the native artist who drew Map No. 36 may have copied or adapted the pertinent information from the lienzo prototype.

More important than the fact that Map No. 36 is drawn on paper and the maps of Jicayán and Ocotepec are on cloth is the emphasis given in Map No. 36 to specific names of fields within the rectangle of boundaries. By way of contrast, in the Lienzos of Jicayán and Ocotepec the only named places within the boundary signs are subject towns and rivers or arroyos. This difference is one of function: the two lienzos were drawn to show the extent and boundaries of the lands of their respective communities, and Map No. 36 sets forth not only the region of a community but also shows in detail the lands within the community that were under litigation when the map was drawn. The Lienzos of Jicayán and Ocotepec are general land titles that could be produced whenever the communities had differences with neighboring towns over boundaries; Map No. 36 is a more specific document that illustrates a dispute over individual plots of land within the community.

Another significant way in which Map No. 36 differs from the Lienzos of Jicayán and Ocotepec is that in Map No. 36 the Mixtec glosses written near the place signs of the boundaries set forth the same name as the pictorial sign they accompany. In the Lienzo of Jicayán, the Mixtec glosses show only an occasional relationship to the place

---

[14] The location of the four *rúbricas* on Map No. 36 is as follows: (1) between the church in the center and the post-and-lintel building to the left of the church, (2) above the first field with the name "do Juan" at the left of the row of fields with Spanish names, (3) above the base of the second place sign from the right in the row of signs along the lower border (sign 2-bottom), and (4) above the base of the second place sign from the left in the same row of signs (sign 10-bottom).

[15] According to Donald Robertson ("The Pinturas of the *Relaciones*

Geográficas," to be published in *HMAI*, Vol. 12), the majority of the *Relación Geográfica* maps from the entire region of New Spain were drawn on European paper. Of the seventy-six extant maps, all but six are on European paper; five of the six exceptions are on *amatl*, a native paper made from fig-tree bark, and one is on parchment. Three of the *Relación Geográfica* maps that are now lost are described as being "lienzos," or painted on cloth. Elsewhere (*Mexican Manuscript Painting*, 112), Robertson observes: "European paper, rare and expensive in the Colony, identifies the artist as being closely associated with the Spanish part of Colonial society and strongly suggests a Spanish patron." In many cases it would seem that the patron was the Spanish-Colonial administrative or judicial system.

[16] The possibility of lost prototypes for the *Relación Geográfica* maps, such as the Map of Teozacoalco, is discussed in Robertson, "The Pinturas of the *Relaciones Geográficas*."

[17] "Estudio del códice mixteco post-cortesiano Núm. 36," 147.

signs, because they were added to the Lienzo at a later date, when the names of the boundaries were no longer the same as those shown in the place signs. In the Lienzo of Ocotepec, the Mixtec glosses are a revised list of boundary names added to the map in the eighteenth century and do not relate to the place signs of the former boundaries of the town. In Map No. 36 the correspondence between place signs and the Mixtec names written next to them indicates that the glosses and pictorial signs are contemporary—that is, the glosses were written on the map at the time it was drawn.

In summary, Map No. 36 is a map of a community and its boundaries, a community that is probably in the Mixteca Baja and possibly is Huajuapan de León. The map focuses on named plots of land within the community, two of which are described as being under litigation. Map No. 36 was probably drawn specifically to be presented as evidence during this litigation, and it may be based on an older map on cloth similar to the Lienzos of Jicayán and Ocotepec.

THE 1771 MAP OF XOXOCOTLÁN

The 1771 Map of Xoxocotlán (Figs. 162–63) is an excellent example of the persistence into the late Colonial period of the type of map that shows the community lands of a town enclosed by place signs of the town's boundaries. Xoxocotlán is located in the Valley of Oaxaca, about two miles southwest of the city of Oaxaca; the location of the town in relation to the neighboring towns is shown in Map 9. The 1771 map is painted in oil on canvas and is in the municipal archive of Xoxocotlán. The dimensions of the map are unknown.

In the center of the map the town of Xoxocotlán is represented by two buildings, both of which face the left side of the map. The largest of these is a twin-towered church that is identified as the church of Xoxocotlán by a short legend in Spanish ("La Yglesia de Xoxocotlan") written near the base of the church. The second building is a one-story civil structure with a tile roof and undoubtedly represents the *municipio* or town hall. This building is drawn in three-quarter view with still another viewpoint added on the right, so that three of the four sides of the building are shown: the brick side wall on the left, the main façade with its three arched entrances in the center, and the other side wall with a smaller entrance on the right. Two viewpoints are also evident in the church of Xoxocotlán: the façade and towers are seen from a front-facing viewpoint, and the roof between the towers is presented from a bird's-eye view.

The two buildings are situated in a valley that is shown in plan, or as if seen in an aerial photograph. Within this valley five streams of water are depicted by wide wavy lines painted horizontally across the valley floor, and the road between Oaxaca and Cuilapan is shown as a darker, narrower wavy line below the central church. At the edge of the valley, the viewpoint changes from plan to elevation, and the surrounding hills, especially those at the top and bottom of the map, are shown as large landscape con-

figurations, all of which face inward toward the town of Xoxocotlán.

The map is oriented with northwest at the top, and the group of hills at the top border represents the south elevation of the great archaeological site of Monte Albán, which was excavated in the 1930's and 1940's by Alfonso Caso and his colleagues.[18] The hills of Monte Albán in the Xoxocotlán map are populated by six human figures. Four persons stand on top of the hills: a woman who holds a macana, and three *putti*-like male figures, two of whom are armed with bows and arrows and the third with a macana and shield. Within the hill at the center is an oval cartouche of feathers that contains a seated male figure wearing the headdress of a bird. At the right of this oval is a second seated male figure with hands clasped in a gesture of reverence directed toward the figure inside of the oval. All of these human figures are unnamed and are drawn in a very Europeanized style, but it seems likely that they were ultimately derived from figures of named historical personages in an earlier manuscript, now lost, that was closer in style and iconography to pre-Conquest Mixtec painting.

A second landscape elevation at the bottom of the Xoxocotlán map represents the hills southeast of the town. At the base of the third hill from the right is a small church that faces the center of the map and is identified by a gloss as "S. Antonio," or San Antonio de la Cal, a town two miles east of Xoxocotlán. In the large hill at the left side of the landscape at the bottom is a second church, also facing inward. Above this church is the legend "San Agustin," which indicates that the church represents the town of San Agustín de las Juntas, located almost two miles east and south of Xoxocotlán. On the left side of the map are very low slopes that are the boundaries between Xoxocotlán and the town of Cuilapan to the southwest.

Twenty names of boundaries are given in the map: ten in the hills at the top, six in the hills at the bottom, and four in the slopes on the left side of the map. The names of boundaries are usually shown in three different ways: by a pictorial motif within the hill—a motif that depicts the qualifying element of the place name—and by two glosses that give the place name in the Mixtec and Nahuatl languages. In addition to the glosses that set forth the boundary names, four short texts in Mixtec and Spanish written above the bases of the hills at the bottom of the map identify specific sites that are located east and south

[18] Concerning the excavations of Monte Albán, see Caso, "Las exploraciones de Monte Albán, temporada 1931–1932," *Instituto Panamericano de Geografía e Historia, Publicación 7* (Mexico, 1932); *idem, 1934–1935, ibid., Publicación 18* (Mexico, 1935); and "Exploraciones en Oaxaca, quinta y sexta temporadas, 1936–1937," *ibid., Publicación 34* (Mexico, 1938); and Caso, Ignacio Bernal and Jorge R. Acosta, *La cerámica de Monte Albán* (Mexico, 1967). Caso's most spectacular discovery at Monte Albán was Tomb 7, which contained a Classic-period Zapotec burial and an intrusive post-Classic Mixtec burial. Associated with the latter burial was magnificent gold jewelry, as well as bones carved in low relief and in a style similar to the Mixtec history manuscripts. The finds in Tomb 7 have recently been handsomely published in Caso, *El tesoro de Monte Albán* (Mexico, 1969). The ceramic funerary urns typical of Classic-period Monte Albán and the Valley of Oaxaca have been studied by Caso and Bernal, *Urnas de Oaxaca* (Mexico, 1952).

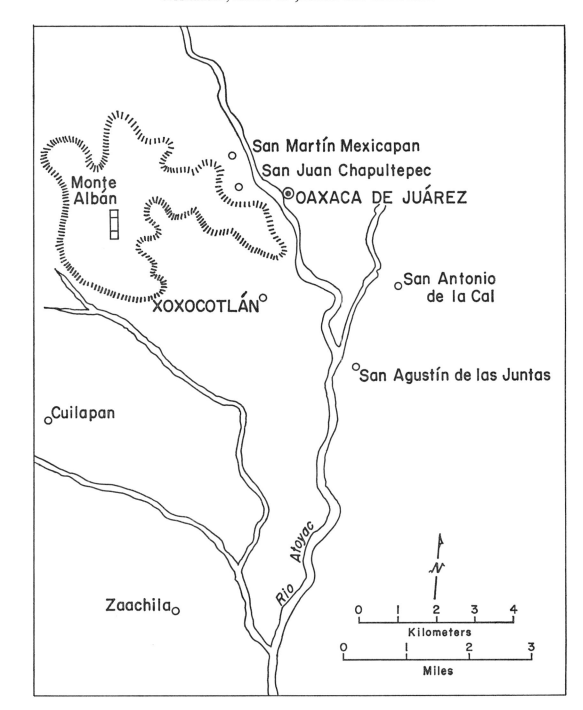

MAP 9. Xoxocotlán and vicinity
(After Cecil R. Welte, Mapa de las localidades del Valle de Oaxaca, 1965)

of Xoxocotlán. These four texts and the glosses of boundary names are translated and discussed in detail in Appendix F.

One of the reasons why the Xoxocotlán map and its glosses are important is that the map is one of the few documents from the Valley of Oaxaca that gives Mixtec names of the lands in this region, and most especially the Mixtec names of the hills that comprise the archaeological site of Monte Albán. For although Xoxocotlán, Cuilapan, and other towns in the Valley of Oaxaca had a considerable Mixtec-speaking population at the time of the Spanish conquest and throughout the Colonial period, there are

few, if any, native Mixtec speakers in the Valley at the present time, and thus the Mixtec names of places in this region are known only through historical documents such as the Map of Xoxocotlán.[19]

The style of the 1771 Map of Xoxocotlán, as might be expected from its late-eighteenth-century date, is more European than native. The hills at the top and bottom of

[19] Concerning the Mixtec-speaking population in the Valley of Oaxaca during the Colonial period, see John Paddock, "Mixtec Ethnohistory and Monte Albán V," in Paddock (ed.), *Ancient Oaxaca*, 367–85; and William B. Taylor, "The Valley of Oaxaca: A Study of Colonial Land Distribution" (unpublished doctoral dissertation, University of Michigan, 1969), 22ff.

the map are a generalized landscape rather than the stereotyped bell-shaped hills seen in pre-Conquest place signs. The hills in the map overlap, rather than being presented as discrete units, and they are accentuated with shading on the right side and with windswept tufts of grass along the top and sides. At the base of the hills are trees with feathery leaves that have been painted with rapid, somewhat impressionistic brush strokes, and shown among this foliage are bucolic scenes of grazing animals.

Unlike the late-sixteenth-century Lienzo of Zacatepec 2 (Fig. 122), in which the animals are arranged around the two-dimensional surface of the map in a pre-Conquest type of "scatter pattern," the animals in the Xoxocotlán map are integrated with the landscape in which they appear. Above and to the right of the central church, a goatherd and his dog accompany goats to a small stream of water, where one of the goats is shown as drinking. At the bottom of the map, a deer raises its head in an attempt to reach the lower branches of one of the trees, and a timid rabbit peers out from the juncture of two hills near the church of San Agustín de las Juntas. The human figures in the map are also closer to European than to pre-Conquest models, especially the three semi-nude male figures who stand on the hills at the top of the map and resemble rather static *putti* that might have been derived from European Baroque painting.

If the 1771 Map of Xoxocotlán is considered to be an archetype of a late Colonial community map and the Lienzo of Jicayán as an archetype of an early Colonial community map, then a comparison of the two manuscripts shows the differences between native maps that are comparatively pre-Conquest in style and those which show a greater degree of Europeanization. First of all, the materials used in the Lienzo of Jicayán are native: the figures are painted in a black, carbon-base ink on loosely woven cloth. The materials used in the 1771 map are imported: oil paint on closely woven canvas. A further contrast may be seen in the architecture in the center of the two maps: the town of Jicayán is shown as a post-and-lintel building on a frieze with geometric decoration, the type of structure common in the pre-Conquest Mixtec histories, while the architecture shown in the center of the 1771 Map of Xoxocotlán consists of a Christian church and a Spanish style of municipal building with European archways as entrances.

Probably the principal difference between the two maps is seen in their concept of what a map is and what it should look like. In the Lienzo of Jicayán, the building that represents the town of Jicayán is enclosed by the names of the town's boundaries shown as pictorial signs, which are in a sense just as much a written document as the glosses in the Mixtec language that were added to the map. Except for the churches and palm trees that were either drawn on the Lienzo later or by a different hand, there is nothing decorative or superfluous on the map; everything "says something" just as everything "says something" on a twentieth-century road map which names towns, rivers, and highways.

The 1771 Map of Xoxocotlán, on the other hand, contains much more descriptive and decorative detail that has nothing to do with the naming of places. This map is painted on a solid-colored ground that does, in essence, represent the ground, in contrast to the unpainted areas of cloth surrounding the place signs in the Jicayán map. Moreover, the configurations of hills at the top and bottom of the Xoxocotlán map are similar to the actual landscape elevations that can be observed from the town of Xoxocotlán, and this landscape serves to create a simulated physical environment. In fact, were the sections of the map with landscape folded along the bases of the hills so that they were vertical and at right angles to the section of the map that shows a plan of the valley, the map would resemble the interior of a rectangular container with the sides of this container showing a panoramic view of the landscape surrounding the central town. In addition to this creation of the geographical environment surrounding Xoxocotlán, the 1771 Map also contains decorative elements—such as the trees and animals—that create an atmosphere. The grazing cattle, goats, and deer suggest not only an idealized "peaceable kingdom" where human beings, animals, and plants live together in harmony, but also a prosperous, pleasant, and well-watered valley where no one has to eke out a living by tilling a small cornfield on the steep slope of a hill.

In summary, the 1771 Map of Xoxocotlán is perceptual and idealized; the Lienzo of Jicayán is conceptual, and the pictorial motifs in this map represent language rather than scenes.[20] But the 1771 Map of Xoxocotlán is not a totally Europeanized manuscript because within the landscape hills that represent the town's boundaries there occurs a strong recollection of pre-Conquest style in the signs that depict the qualifying elements of the name of each hill. Even though these signs of qualifying elements are for the most part painted in a European style, a number of motifs are strictly pre-Conquest in origin, such as the A–O year sign within the hill at the far left of the upper range of hills. Moreover, the placement of the pictorial motifs within the hills suggests that the landscape configurations may have been based on an earlier map in which the hills resembled more closely the rows of place signs seen around the borders, as is the case in the Lienzos of Jicayán and Ocotepec.

If the signs within the landscape in the 1771 Map of Xoxocotlán are reminiscent of boundary signs in earlier manuscripts, then what are the prototypes of the 1771 Map, and how does it relate to the other extant maps of this town? In addition to the 1771 Map, three other maps of Xoxocotlán are known. According to the Spanish texts on the 1771 Map, it is a copy of one of these other maps, a map dated 1718 which it resembles closely, and the 1718 map is, in turn, a copy of a lost map dated 1660. (A short description of the four known maps of Xoxocotlán and a

---

[20] A more detailed discussion of the general differences between maps that are closer to pre-Conquest style and those which more closely resemble European landscape is found in Donald Robertson, *Mexican Manuscript Painting*, 179–89, and in Robertson's study of the *Relación Geográfica* maps, to be published in Vol. 12 of the *HMAI*.

translation of the Spanish texts on the 1771 Map are included in Appendix F.) The lost 1660 map that is said to be the earliest prototype of the 1771 Map is also the earliest map of Xoxocotlán that has been described, and no reference has been found to a prototype for the 1660 map.

It is very possible that the 1660 map is the earliest map that shows the community lands of Xoxocotlán as such, and that the place signs on the 1660 map may have been drawn from other maps of the region. The reason for this is that during at least part of the Colonial period, Xoxocotlán was a subject of the native ruler of Cuilapan, the important, formerly Mixtec-speaking community four miles southwest of Xoxocotlán; and the lost 1660 map may well represent an attempt on the part of Xoxocotlán to establish its independence of the *cacique* of Cuilapan by mapping its own community lands.

According to the 1581 *Relación Geográfica* of Cuilapan, Xoxocotlán was a subject of Cuilapan in the sixteenth century, and according to a *Relación* of Cuilapan written about 1777–78, Xoxocotlán was still a subject of Cuilapan in the late eighteenth century.[21] However, Xoxocotlán apparently attempted to break away from Cuilapan as early as 1640, when the Spanish colonial government granted Xoxocotlán the right to elect its own municipal officials.[22] Moreover, even though the native ruler of Cuilapan in 1717 claimed that the citizens of Xoxocotlán were *terrasgueros* of Cuilapan—that is, essentially serfs who worked their community's lands in service of the native ruler of Cuilapan—these citizens of Xoxocotlán refused to serve the *cacique* of Cuilapan because they claimed that the land belonged to them.[23] Thus the maps of Xoxocotlán drawn in 1660, 1718, and 1771 show the community lands of a subject town that is attempting to achieve economic as well as political independence from the native ruler of Cuilapan.

The 1771 Map of Xoxocotlán, then, is the opposite side of the coin from the Lienzo of Ocotepec, which shows a *cabecera* that lost its subject towns between the late sixteenth century, when the Lienzo was drawn, and the early eighteenth century, when Mixtec glosses were added to the Lienzo. Xoxocotlán, on the other hand, was a subject town in the process of establishing its autonomy, and the 1771 Map shows the lands which Xoxocotlán claims as its own.

SUMMARY

Discussed briefly in this chapter were three Colonial Mixtec maps which, in common with the Lienzo of Jicayán, show the lands of one town surrounded by place signs of the names of its boundaries and which are annotated with glosses that set forth the boundary names. The Lienzo of Ocotepec, probably drawn about 1580, shows the town of

Ocotepec enclosed by a rectangle of twenty-four place signs, one of which represents the neighboring town of Chicahuaxtla, while the remaining twenty-three presumably represent the names of Ocotepec's boundaries. These twenty-four signs are accompanied by place names in Nahuatl which show a fairly close correlation with the pictorial signs they accompany and were probably written on the Lienzo at the time it was drawn. In the early eighteenth century, a "written map" consisting of boundary names in Mixtec was added to the Lienzo, and these Mixtec names delineate the reduced lands of Ocotepec after five former subject towns had achieved their independence of Ocotepec. The eighteenth-century Mixtec glosses do not relate to the pictorial place signs but show a close correlation with a written document dated 1726 that also sets forth the Mixtec names of Ocotepec's boundaries.

Map No. 36, which probably dates from the middle to the late sixteenth century, was prepared for a specific land suit over two plots of land shown in the lower half of the map. This manuscript may have been a copy of a lost lienzo. The town whose lands are delineated in Map No. 36 is probably in the Mixteca Baja, possibly the important Baja town of Huajuapan de León.

The 1771 Map of Xoxocotlán was based on a lost prototype dated 1660. The 1660 map, in turn, was presumably compiled from still earlier maps of this region—that is, maps in which the place signs and human figures were much closer to pre-Conquest traditions than those seen in the 1771 Map. In contrast to the Lienzo of Ocotepec, which illustrates a major town or *cabecera* that lost its subject towns, the 1771 Map of Xoxocotlán delineates the lands claimed by a subject town that was attempting to establish its autonomy.

In the case of Map No. 36 and the 1771 Map of Xoxocotlán, the Mixtec glosses of place signs show a close correlation to the pictorial signs which they accompany. The reason for this close correlation is that the glosses were written on the map at the same time it was drawn, and thus both picture and accompanying gloss present the same information.

The relationship between glosses and pictorial signs in the Lienzo of Jicayán is between the two extremes of close correlation and no correlation seen in the other three maps, because the glosses on the Lienzo of Jicayán show an occasional correlation with the pictorial signs. Again, the difference is one of time: in the Lienzo of Ocotepec a span of about 120 years separates the Nahuatl annotations which relate to the pictorial signs and the Mixtec annotations which do not relate to the pictorial signs. In the case of the Lienzo of Jicayán, an undetermined span of time occurred between the drawing of the Lienzo and its annotations. This span of time may have been as short as a few decades, for the pictorial place signs in the Lienzo of Jicayán probably represent the names of the town's boundaries at the time of the Spanish conquest (1520's) and the Mixtec glosses are virtually the same as the Mixtec names of the town's boundaries on Codex Colombino (accompanied by the date 1541).

---

21 Robert Barlow (ed.), "Dos Relaciones antiguas del pueblo de Cuilapa, Estado de Oaxaca," *Tlalocan*, Vol. II–1 (1945), 24, 26.

22 William B. Taylor, "The Valley of Oaxaca," 32 (table 3).

23 *Ibid.*, 65, 87. It is probably not coincidental that the 1718 Xoxocotlán map was painted in the year following the re-assertion by the *cacique* of Cuilapan of his control over the lands of Xoxocotlán.

X

STYLISTIC AND ICONOGRAPHIC CHARACTERISTICS
OF COLONIAL-PERIOD NATIVE MAPS FROM THE MIXTECA

In Chapters VII and VIII the two Lienzos of Zacatepec and the Lienzo of Jicayán were discussed as individual manuscripts. The two Lienzos of Zacatepec were compared as two maps of the same town drawn at two different periods in the sixteenth century, and it was possible to identify ten place signs in the first Lienzo of Zacatepec because these signs are arranged in a cartographic context. The Lienzo of Jicayán was considered as an example of a map of a town that shows place signs of the town's boundaries with these signs accompanied by glosses in Mixtec. The glosses show only an occasional relationship to the pictorial signs because the annotations are not contemporary with the drawing of the Lienzo and set forth later and different Mixtec boundary names. As was seen in Chapter IX, in which the Lienzo of Jicayán was compared with three other Colonial Mixtec maps with Mixtec glosses, the agreement between glosses and place signs is greatest when the glosses are written on the map at the time it is drawn.

To place the Lienzos of Zacatepec and Jicayán in a wider context of Colonial manuscript painting from the Mixteca, the stylistic and iconographic characteristics of these three Lienzos as well as eight other Colonial Mixtec manuscripts will be analyzed in this chapter. The stylistic and iconographic features to be discussed are listed in Chart 22. Across the top of the chart, the names of the eleven manuscripts to be considered are listed in what is judged to be chronological order, with the earliest at the left and the latest at the right. Some of the manuscripts are dated, and these dates appear with the name of the manuscript, along with the figure number of this study where the manuscript is illustrated. Those maps which are not dated have been placed within the framework of the dated manuscripts on the basis of an impressionistic evaluation of their over-all style. In the case of the Lienzo of Jicayán, in which two drawing styles are evident, the earlier style—that of the central configuration and the fifty-two boundary signs—is marked in the chart with an "X," and the later style is marked with an X in parentheses (X).

In the left-hand column of the chart are listed some of the important features found in Colonial-period manuscripts. These features have been grouped under the following general classifications: the general content and purpose of the manuscript, the type of material on which it was drawn or painted, the various ways of representing named places, the motifs on the interior of the map, the representation of human figures, the presence of such obviously imported features as a European crescent moon or sun motif, and the orientation of the map.[1]

GENERAL CONTENT OF MANUSCRIPTS

The eleven manuscripts under consideration contain five different types of information, and these are listed under section I of Chart 22. Three of the manuscripts contain more than one category of information. The first Lienzo of Zacatepec shows not only the lands of Zacatepec and its boundaries but also includes genealogical data. Map No. 36 is a map of a town and its boundaries and also emphasizes specific plots of land within the boundaries. Moreover, the rulers in the center of this map may have a genealogical relationship, although this relationship is not made explicit by lines with footprints that show the descent of one generation to another. The Map of Teozacoalco contains detailed genealogies of the ruling houses of Teozacoalco and Tilantongo as well as depicting the lands of Teozacoalco and the town's boundaries.

PURPOSE OF MANUSCRIPTS

The manuscripts under consideration served three general purposes or functions, and these are listed in section II of Chart 22. The function of the manuscript also seems to relate to the present location of the manuscript, for those that were painted for the community were retained by the community, while those painted for Spanish or Spanish-Colonial officials are now in museums, libraries, or archives.

Six of the eleven manuscripts listed in the chart functioned as community land titles throughout the Colonial period and into the nineteenth century; and of these six maps, three (the Lienzos of Jicayán and Ocotepec, as well as the 1771 Map of Xoxocotlán) are still in the municipal archive of the town whose lands they map. Two others (the Lienzos of Zacatepec 1 and 2) were in the town archive of Zacatepec until the late nineteenth century, when they were brought to Mexico City as supporting

---

[1] Some of these features, such as the treatment of the human figure, are based on Donald Robertson's list of the characteristics of graphic style in Colonial manuscripts that appears in "The Pinturas (Mapas) of the *Relaciones Geográficas*." Other features not in Robertson's list are included in my chart, which analyzes in more detail the iconography of early Colonial maps.

evidence for land litigation, and the town was given tracings of the two Lienzos in lieu of the originals. Map No. 36, the sixth map in this category, served a dual function as a community land title and as an illustration of a specific lawsuit over two plots of land within the community. This map originally accompanied written land documents, but it has become separated from these documents, whose present location is unknown, and the map alone is now in the manuscript collection of the Museo Nacional de Antropología in Mexico City.

Two of the manuscripts, the Maps of Texupan and Teozacoalco, were prepared in response to a request for a map in the 1577 questionnaire which was circulated in the New World by Philip II and which required each town to write a *Relación Geográfica*, or a long description of the resources, inhabitants, and general characteristics of the town. These two maps were sent to Spain along with the written *Relaciones* of their respective towns, and both are now in public repositories, as are all of the known *Relación Geográfica* maps.[2]

The remaining three manuscripts were drawn to illustrate either a single land grant or, as the Tlazultepec Genealogy, a specific lawsuit; and these three are now in the Archivo General de la Nación in Mexico City and bound with the written documents which they illustrate. Two additional features which these three manuscripts share is that they were drawn in the last decade of the sixteenth century and were commissioned by Indian patrons. The Coixtlahuaca land-grant map shows the location of a site petitioned for by the native ruler of Tonalá, a subject of Coixtlahuaca; the Cuquila land-grant map accompanies a similar petition by the natives of Cuquila; the Tlazultepec Genealogy was drawn for the native rulers of Ocotepec to support their claim to inherit the *cacicazgo* of Tlazultepec.

MATERIAL

The group of manuscripts under consideration was drawn or painted on three different materials: loosely woven native cloth (*lienzo*), European paper, and closely woven European canvas. The material on which a manuscript was drawn or painted appears to relate to its function, for those drawn or painted on cloth were maps for the community, while those manuscripts on European paper were drawn in connection with specific lawsuits or other dealings with Spaniards. The 1771 Map of Xoxocotlán is the only manuscript in this group that is painted on European canvas, and this material is more symptomatic of its late date than its function. Canvas is rarely used in sixteenth-century maps, probably because of its relative unavailability to non-European painters in the early Colonial period; but it is used for some of the community maps painted in the late seventeenth century and throughout the eighteenth century.

[2] *Ibid*. According to Robertson, all the known maps are in three collections: the Archivo de Indias in Seville, the Royal Academy of History in Madrid (whose collection includes the Texupan Map), and the Latin American Library of the University of Texas (whose collection includes the Map of Teozacoalco).

REPRESENTATION OF NAMED PLACES

Towns, whether major or subject towns, are shown in three ways in Colonial maps: as a place sign, as a pre-Conquest type of post-and-lintel building, or as a Christian church. In a number of instances, more than one of these motifs may be used to represent a town—as in the 1579 Texupan map, in which the name of the town of Texupan is shown as a place sign with a post-and-lintel building, or in the 1590 Coixtlahuaca land-grant map in which that town is shown as a place sign below a Christian church. In the 1580 Map of Teozacoalco, the town of Teozacoalco is shown in all three ways: in the rows of marriage pairs outside the map, Teozacoalco appears as a place sign with a post-and-lintel building (Fig. 25), and within the map of Teozacoalco's lands, the town is shown as a Christian church (Fig. 132).

Names of boundaries can also be shown in three ways: as place signs, as only the qualifying elements of place signs within landscape hills, and as glosses of place names in a native language. In Chart 22, glosses in the Mixtec language are indicated by an "M" and those in the Nahuatl language by an "N." It is interesting to note that names of boundaries appear as place signs or at least as qualifying elements of place signs in all of the maps that show boundary names, except for the "written map" on the Lienzo of Ocotepec where eighteenth-century Mixtec boundary names are written within the place signs of the town's sixteenth-century boundaries. That is, the names of boundaries often appear as place signs when the central town or subject towns on the map are shown as Christian churches, as is the case in Map No. 36, the second Lienzo of Zacatepec, the Lienzo of Ocotepec, and the 1771 Map of Xoxocotlán.

But even though the pre-Conquest type of place sign seems to persist longer in names of boundaries than names of towns, this probably does not mean that the pre-Conquest signs of towns had been forgotten before the end of the sixteenth century. Ample evidence to the contrary is seen in the 1580 Map of Teozacoalco and the 1590 Coixtlahuaca land-grant map, in which the major towns are shown both as a Christian church and as a place sign; in the 1579 Map of Texupan, where the town's place sign is shown in connection with a European grid plan of the town; and in the 1597 Tlazultepec Genealogy, where most of the towns are represented by place signs, albeit somewhat scruffily drawn place signs. It is possible that names of boundaries were shown as place signs more frequently than were names of towns because it was boundaries that were often under dispute, and if a map showed the boundaries as place signs, these boundary signs would appear to have greater antiquity and thus greater authenticity when a map was presented in a court of law.

Once the document was presented in litigation, then the explanatory glosses in European script were added to the manuscript so that the names of the boundaries were comprehensible to the Spanish-Colonial administrative and judicial officials. In the accompanying chart, the glosses in Mixtec or Nahuatl are classified in three ways: those that

CHART 22: Stylistic and Iconographic Features of Colonial-period Native Maps

	Lienzo of Jicayán (Figs. 143–144)	Lienzo of Zacatepec 1 (Fig. 85)	Map No. 36 (Fig. 21)	Lienzo of Zacatepec 2 (Fig. 122)	Map of Texupan, 1579 (Fig. 37)	Map of Teozacoalco, 1580 (Figs. 25, 132)	Lienzo of Ocotepec (Fig. 160)	Coixtlahuaca land-grant map, 1590 (Fig. 46)	Cuquila land-grant map, 1595 (Fig. 133)	Tlazultepec Genealogy, 1597 (Fig. 30)	1771 Map of Xoxocotlán (Fig. 162)
I. General Content of Manuscript											
A. The lands of the community and its boundaries	X	X	X	X		X	X				X
B. Specific plots of land within the community			X								
C. The plan and geographical situation of the community but not its boundaries					X						
D. Land grants of sites shown in relationship to several communities								X	X		
E. Genealogical relationships of ruling families		X	X?			X				X	
II. Purpose of Manuscript											
A. Community land title	X	X	X	X			X				X
B. *Relación Geográfica* map					X	X					
C. Illustration of written documents prepared for a land-grant petition or a specific lawsuit			X					X	X	X	
III. Material											
A. Cloth *(lienzo)*	X	X		X			X				
B. European paper			X		X	X		X	X	X	
C. European canvas											X
IV. Representation of Named Places											
A. Central or most important town(s)											
1. place sign	X?	X			X	X		X		X	
2. post-and-lintel building	X		X		X	X					
3. Christian church			X	X		X	X	X	X	X	X
B. Places (such as subject towns) within map other than the principal town											
1. place sign		X			X		X	X		X	
2. post-and-lintel building		X	X?				X				
3. Christian church	(X)	X		✗		X	X	X	X		X
C. Boundary names											
1. place signs	X	X	X	X		X	X				
2. qualifying elements of place signs within landscape hills				X							X
3. glosses in a native language											
a. relate to signs			M	N			N				M/N
b. show occasional relationship to signs	M										
c. show no relationship to signs							M				
D. Format of boundary signs											
1. irregular circle	X										
2. perfect circle						X					
3. rectangle		X	X	X			X				X

CHART 22. (cont.)

	Lienzo of Jicayán (Figs. 143–144)	Lienzo of Zacatepec 1 (Fig. 85)	Map No. 36 (Fig. 21)	Lienzo of Zacatepec 2 (Fig. 122)	Map of Texupan, 1579 (Fig. 37)	Map of Teozacoalco, 1580 (Figs. 25, 132)	Lienzo of Ocotepec (Fig. 160)	Coixtlahuaca land-grant map, 1590 (Fig. 46)	Cuquila land-grant map, 1595 (Fig. 133)	Tlazultepec Genealogy, 1597 (Fig. 30)	1771 Map of Xoxocotlán (Fig. 162)
V. Interior of Map (excluding towns and boundaries)											
A. Landscape and filling ornament											
1. absence of landscape and post-Conquest filling ornament	X	X	X					X		X	
2. hills as landscape but with hill-sign border					X				X		
3. shaded hills as landscape with no elements of pre-Conquest line				X		X	X				X
B. Water											
1. streams with wavy lines in interior and projections from sides		X	X			X	X		X		
2. streams with wavy lines in interior	(X)	X		X	X						
3. streams with fish	(X)			X	X	X					
4. streams with no wavy lines in interior	(X)										X
C. Roads											
1. none	X		X								
2. with human footprints				X				X	X		
3. with human footprints and horseshoe tracks						X	X	X			
4. line without footprints											X
5. footprints used to represent genealogical connection rather than road		X				X	X?			X	
VI. Human Figures											
A. Style											
1. more native than European	X	X					X			X	
2. mixed		X		X		X		X			
3. more European than native											X
B. Type of name											
1. personal name		X				X					
2. calendrical name	X	X	X			X					
3. nobility without pre-Conquest personal or calendrical name				X			X			X	X?
4. unnamed genre figures											X
VII. European crescent moon or sun motifs		X		X		X	X	X			
VIII. Orientation of Map											
A. E at top		X		X		X					
B. NE at top	X										
C. NW at top			X?								X
D. W at top								X	X	X	
E. SE at top					X						
F. none										X	

relate to the place signs of boundaries, those which show an occasional relationship to these signs, and those which show no relationship to the boundary signs.

It has been suggested that when the glosses relate to the boundary signs, then the glosses and the map are contemporary, as is the case with the Mixtec glosses on Map No. 36, the Nahuatl glosses on the Lienzos of Ocotepec and Zacatepec 2, and the bilingual glosses on the 1771 Map of Xoxocotlán. In the case of the Lienzo of Jicayán, where the glosses only occasionally agree with the place signs of boundaries, it seems apparent that the glosses were added to the map at some time after it was drawn when some of the boundaries were the same as those shown in the place signs and some were no-longer the same. The Mixtec glosses on the Lienzo of Ocotepec are a clear-cut and well-documented example of a "written map" added to an earlier map, for these glosses set forth the names of the town's boundaries as they were in the eighteenth century and do not relate to the place signs which depict the sixteenth-century names of boundaries.

Three different arrangements of the place signs of boundaries are seen in the manuscripts considered in Chart 22: an irregular circle, a perfect circle, and a rectangle. The irregular circle, seen in the Lienzo of Jicayán, shows the surrounding place signs in a generalized cartographic relationship to each other and to the central building of Jicayán; in other words, they are arranged more or less as they would appear if plotted on a map.[3] The rectangular and perfect-circle formats are "imposed" or arbitrary configurations, for the boundary sites themselves do not usually form the outline of a rectangle or a perfect circle when they are plotted on a map.

It is difficult to determine which of these three formats is closest to the pre-Conquest manner of representing a town and its boundaries, because no pre-Conquest maps of community lands have survived from the Mixtec-speaking or any other region of Middle America. The maps that are most closely related to pre-Conquest manuscripts in both style and iconography—the Lienzos of Jicayán and Zacatepec 1—utilize two different formats, and it is possible that both of these, the irregular circle and the rectangle, were current prior to the Conquest. It is my feeling that the perfect-circle format, seen in the 1580 Map of Teozacoalco, is a European import.

The typical medieval *mappa mundi* which shows the world as a perfect circle persisted well into the sixteenth century, and woodcuts of such maps may have been brought to the New World by Spanish friars.[4] In sixteenth-century Europe there were also radial maps of small

regions, which consisted of a perfect circle with one town in the center surrounded by the neighboring towns, and examples of these maps may well have reached the New World before the end of the sixteenth century.[5] Moreover, the perfect-circle format is not seen in maps from the Mixteca until it appears in two *Relación Geográfica* maps dated 1580 and drawn for Europeans; and it is clearly the least prevalent of map formats, for of the approximately eighteen Colonial maps from the Mixteca that show one town and its boundaries and have some vestige of native style, only three are drawn in the perfect-circle format.[6] The somewhat late and infrequent appearance of the arrangement of boundaries in a perfect circle seems to suggest that it was an imported rather than an indigenous format.

INTERIOR OF MAP

Section V of Chart 22 categorizes three elements (other than names of towns or boundaries) that are often found in the interior of Colonial maps. Under the category "Landscape and filling ornament," the manuscripts which lack landscape and other post-Conquest filling ornament are those which are closest to the pre-Conquest manuscript tradition. The presence of shaded hills that show no evidence of pre-Conquest line and which function as landscape is a European rather than a pre-Conquest trait; and the depiction of landscape hills with the typically pre-Conquest border that includes projections to suggest the roughness or bumpiness of the hill is considered to be a transition between the pre-Conquest type of place sign and European landscape.

Under the classification of "Water," the representation of water as a stream with wavy lines on the interior and with projections that terminate in circles or shells is considered to be pre-Conquest in style, whereas the method of representing water that is listed last—that is, streams with no decoration—is considered to be the most European in style. The second type of water listed, a stream with wavy lines on the interior but without the pre-Conquest type of

---

[3] The "irregular circle" format is also seen in the arrangement of the eighteenth-century Mixtec glosses on the Lienzo of Ocotepec.

[4] Two such circular maps, printed about 1500 as broadsheets from woodcuts, are discussed and illustrated by Leo Bagrow, "Rüst's and Sporer's World Maps," *Imago Mundi*, Vol. VII (1950), 32–36. As Robertson has observed (*Mexican Manuscript Painting*, 171, plate 64), one of the illustrations of Sahagún's Florentine Codex is a type of circular world map known as a "T–O" map. The circle (or "O") is divided into three sections by the "T" in the center, and the largest section within the circle represents the continent of Asia, with the two smaller sections representing Africa and Europe (Lloyd A. Brown, *The Story of Maps* [New York, 1949], 96).

[5] Probably the most famous radial map showing a town within a circle is a map of Nuremberg and its environs made in 1492 by the local cartographer Erhard Etzlaub (Herbert Krüger, "Erhard Etzlaub's *Romweg* Map and Its Dating in the Holy Year of 1500," *Imago Mundi*, Vol. VIII [1951], Fig. 1).

[6] In addition to the Teozacoalco map, the 1580 *Relación Geográfica* Map of Amoltepec consists of a perfect circle drawn on the map, with place signs of the boundaries on the edge of about two-thirds of the circle. The boundary signs are closed on the right side of the map by a river that runs from the bottom to the top of the circle at an oblique angle (Robertson, "The *Relaciones Geográficas* of Mexico," *ICA* XXXIII, Vol. II, 544, Fig. 3).

The third map from the Mixteca with a perfect-circle format is an eighteenth-century map of Sinaxtla in the Mixteca Alta. This map is bound with land documents in AGN-Tierras 308–1 (Jiménez Moreno and Mateos Higuera, *Códice de Yanhuitlán*, 4, Fig. 1).

In addition to these three maps, the known maps from the Mixteca that show one town and its boundaries are: Lienzo of Jicayán, Lienzos of Zacatepec 1 and 2, Map No. 36, Lienzo of Ocotepec, the 1718 and 1771 Maps of Xoxocotlán, Lienzo of Tamazulapan (Vischer III), Map of Xochitepec, Lienzo Córdova-Castellanos, 1870 Map of Ixcatlán, and four maps of the Coixtlahuaca group—Lienzo of Coixtlahuaca (Codex Ixtlán-Lienzo B), Codex Meixuiero-Lienzo A, Lienzo Seler II, and the Lienzo of Natívitas.

projections, may well be a simplification of streams with projections. The representation of flowing water as wavy lines is such a common convention in both pre-Conquest manuscript painting and European map-making that it cannot be labeled as either "completely native" or "completely European."

Four of the maps under consideration have streams of water with fish, the third category listed under "Water." Although fish do appear within signs for water in pre-Conquest manuscripts, the fish shown in all four maps are drawn in a European rather than a pre-Conquest style, for they resemble more closely the fish seen in European woodcuts of the late fifteenth century (Fig. 131a) than fish seen in pre-Conquest manuscripts (Fig. 68b). It is possible, then, that the representation of fish in streams of water in cartographic manuscripts may be a European rather than a native element.

The presentation of roads within a map to show the location and cartographic relationship of actual roads appears to be a phenomenon of Mixtec maps drawn in the second half of the sixteenth century, and one that is absent in the three maps that are thought to be the earliest in the group under consideration: the Lienzos of Jicayán and Zacatepec 1 and Map No. 36. No roads whatsoever appear in the Lienzo of Jicayán; and the roads within the first Lienzo of Zacatepec show genealogical relationships between marriage pairs, while those that connect the scenes at the top of the Lienzo show the pilgrimage route of one person to a series of places that are not arranged in a cartographic format. In Map No. 36, no roads are seen in the interior of the map, although one of the boundary signs on the left border contains a road because this sign represents a place named "hill of the road" (Fig. 11 and Fig. 21, sign 9-left).

In the group of manuscripts under consideration, the cartographic representation of roads within a map appears only in manuscripts that date from around 1580: the Lienzos of Ocotepec and Zacatepec 2, and the Maps of Texupan and Teozacoalco.

However, the absence of roads in the earlier maps does not necessarily mean that the cartographic representation of roads was not a feature of native maps earlier than the late sixteenth century. All of the maps listed in the accompanying chart are very local documents, and their purpose is to show community lands or a site of land situated among several contiguous communities rather than to show routes of travel as does a twentieth-century road map. But there were undoubtedly pre-Conquest counterparts, now lost, of the "road map" or map that shows routes from one region to another. Such a map is described by Hernán Cortés, who was given a lienzo in 1524 by the natives on the east coast of Mexico to show him the location of a town on the east coast of Honduras where Spanish settlers had been burning native villages. According to Cortés: ". . . they made me a drawing on cloth of the whole of it [i.e., of the territory between the present-day State of Tabasco in Mexico and eastern Honduras] by which I calculated I could go over the greater

part of it, especially as far as the place they indicated to me as the abode of those Spaniards."[7]

The appearance of roads as a cartographic element in the interior of community maps of the 1580's is probably related to the increasing interest in all kinds of cartographic details (roads, rivers, landscape hills) seen in these later maps. For example, the second Lienzo of Zacatepec shows not only the roads within the community, a feature that is absent in Zacatepec 1, but the later Lienzo also shows in more detail the rivers and arroyos within the community, as can be seen by comparing Figs. 134 and 135.

When roads do appear in a cartographic context in the maps, they are shown in one of two ways: as a band or line with human footprints only, and as a band containing both human footprints and the prints of horseshoes. The horseshoe motif is obviously an imported motif, but its appearance on roads in the Colonial-period maps seems to be a natural addition to the bands with footprints. The band with footprints is based on the observation of the tracks made on a traveled road, and once European horses arrived in the New World, the prints of horseshoes as well as human feet could be observed on roads. By the end of the Colonial period, both the footprint and the horseshoe motifs have disappeared, and, as can be seen in the 1771 Map of Xoxocotlán, roads are shown as merely a line, much as they are in twentieth-century road maps.

The pre-Conquest custom of using bands or lines with footprints to show the idea of "coming from" or "going to" in a genealogical sense continues into the Colonial period in manuscripts that present genealogical data, such as the 1580 Map of Teozacoalco and the 1597 Genealogy of Tlazultepec.

The only map of the group under consideration that shows an almost completely European approach to landscape, water, and roads is the late Colonial Map of Xoxocotlán, which was painted roughly two centuries later than the other manuscripts, all of which were drawn before the end of the sixteenth century. If the sixteenth-century manuscripts are considered as a group, then there is no clear-cut pattern of increasingly frequent European motifs toward the end of the sixteenth century, because two of the maps drawn in the 1590's (the Coixtlahuaca and Cuquila land-grant maps) show more evidence of native style than the maps drawn around 1580, such as the Lienzo of Ocotepec and the Maps of Texupan and Teozacoalco.

The Coixtlahuaca land-grant map has no landscape or other post-Conquest filling ornament, shows roads as a line with footprints but no horseshoe prints, and represents three of the five places shown on the map as place signs. In the 1595 Cuquila land-grant map, some of the landscape hills still resemble the pre-Conquest hill sign in that they are bell-shaped configurations with the small rectangular projections that indicate bumpiness and with no shading to give the hill a three-dimensional appearance. The water in this map is shown in a typically pre-

[7] Fernando Cortes: his five letters of Relation to the Emperor Charles V (Francis A. MacNutt ed., II (Cleveland, 1908), 232.

Conquest manner as a stream with projections terminating in shells, and the roads are lines with footprints and no horseshoe tracks.

By way of contrast, European landscape appears in all of the maps drawn around 1580. Moreover, the second Lienzo of Zacatepec and the *Relación Geográfica* Maps of Texupan and Teozacoalco have streams with fish; and in the Texupan and Teozacoalco maps, as well as in the Lienzo of Ocotepec, the roads are shown with horseshoe tracks as well as human footprints.

The fact that the manuscripts of the 1590's show comparatively fewer European elements than those of the 1580's demonstrates that the diffusion of European style in the Mixteca, as the diffusion of new art styles elsewhere in the world, is not a process as simple as systematically covering a previously painted building with a new, evenly applied coat of paint. New art styles diffuse unevenly in terms of both the geographical extent they cover and the amount of time necessary for them to be accepted and incorporated into the existing style. This is certainly nowhere more evident than in sixteenth-century Mixtec manuscript painting, where a fully developed art style that existed prior to the arrival of Europeans is gradually supplanted by a second, equally developed but imported, art style.

Another factor that may be involved in the differences between the manuscripts of the 1590's and those of the 1580's is the function the manuscript was intended to serve. All three of the manuscripts of the 1590's—the two land-grant maps and the Tlazultepec Genealogy—were prepared for a single and specific purpose: to accompany written documents that deal with either the allotment of one plot of land or a dispute over the inheritance of a *cacicazgo*.

All four of the maps that date from around 1580 show more evidence not only of European style but are in general more elaborate, perhaps in part because their function was more elaborate. Two of the four—the Lienzos of Ocotepec and Zacatepec 2—are maps of the lands of a community and were kept in the community archives throughout the Colonial period and utilized not merely for a specific land transaction but were general land titles that could be produced whenever there were questions concerning the community lands. The other two—the *Relación Geográfica* Maps of Texupan and Teozacoalco— were prepared to be sent to Spain and are, in a sense, public relations or "Chamber of Commerce" manuscripts. Thus it might be assumed that, as a matter of civic pride, these four maps are more elaborate and contain not only more European features but more detail in general than the three manuscripts of the 1590's, which were essentially "sketch" maps or genealogies prepared for a single litigation.

HUMAN FIGURES

In the accompanying chart the human figures seen in the eleven manuscripts under consideration are classified on the basis of their style as: more native than European,

more European than native, and "mixed."[8] The last term indicates that the style no longer has strong pre-Conquest elements but is not yet completely Europeanized; and one of the principal features of the "mixed" style, in addition to a noticeable degree of disintegrated frame line, is the handling of the human eye.

In pre-Conquest manuscripts, the eye is usually represented as an irregular semi-circle with a small circle attached to the inside of the upper border to represent the pupil of the eye (as in Fig. 5), and it almost seems as much a front-facing as a profile eye. A second form for the eye in pre-Conquest manuscripts is a concentric circle (as in Fig. 6c). In the "mixed" style the eye is often more triangular in shape or an arc within an angle that more truly suggests a profile eye or an eye surrounded by flesh, as in some of the human heads seen in the second Lienzo of Zacatepec (Fig. 130 c), in the Map of Teozacoalco (Fig. 132), and in the profile head on the place sign in the upper-right corner of the Coixtlahuaca land-grant map (Fig. 46). This last head has another feature seen in the "mixed" style, the representation of the eyebrow, which is often seen in "mixed" style manuscripts but is absent in native or pre-Conquest manuscripts.

Another variation on the representation of the human eye that is also considered a feature of the "mixed" style is an eye that is shown as a narrow horizontal oval with the pupil indicated by a black circle or band, either placed at the front of the oval as in the Map of Teozacoalco (Fig. 25) or in the center of the oval as in Map No. 36 (Figs. 21 and 22 b, d). In pre-Conquest manuscripts the small circle that represents the pupil of the eye is always white, never black or any other color, although at times the corner of the eye outside the pupil is filled in with color, usually red.

The "more European than native" style of representing human figures is very well exemplified by the figures who are standing on the hills at the top of the 1771 Map of Xoxocotlán. As can be seen in these figures, the human body is no longer represented as separable parts as is the case in pre-Conquest manuscripts. Rather, the figures are "unified," with each part of the body coordinated with the whole.[9] Also, the male figures in this map, who were probably intended to represent armed warriors in loincloths, appear more like the bland cherubs who witness scenes of Christian miracles in European painting; and the female figure, notwithstanding her nominally native costume, has the face and hair style of a Murillo Madonna.

Four manuscripts in the group of eleven are classified as having a figural style that is more native than European: the Lienzos of Jicayán, Zacatepec 1 and Ocotepec, and the Tlazultepec Genealogy. These four have been classified in this way not merely because the eyes of the figures in these manuscripts are presented in a style that

[8] These three classifications are adaptations of those proposed by Robertson ("The Pinturas of the *Relaciones Geográficas*"): native, European, and mixed. Because all of the eleven manuscripts under consideration show some degree of European style, the comparative terms "more native than European" and "more European than native" seem more appropriate classifications.

[9] *Ibid.*, and Robertson, *Mexican Manuscript Painting*, 17–19.

is native rather than "mixed," but because the line in which the figures are drawn shows less evidence of disintegrated frame line and because the general handling of the figure is closer to that seen in the pre-Conquest histories. Even in the late-sixteenth-century Tlazultepec Genealogy, where the line is anything but taut and sure, the human figures resemble more closely those seen in Codices Bodley and Selden than do the human figures of Map No. 36 and the 1580 Map of Teozacoalco. In the treatment of human figures, as in the handling of the interior of the map, some of the later manuscripts in the group under consideration are more native in style than those known to be earlier. For example, the human figures in the 1597 Tlazultepec Genealogy show less European influence than those in the 1580 Map of Teozacoalco, even though the place signs in the Teozacoalco map are much more native in style than those in the Tlazultepec manuscript. Again, we can see that the diffusion of European style is often uneven and incomplete, not only within the same general region of Mexico but within the same manuscript.

A second basis of classifying human figures is the method in which they are named. Two types of names are common in the pre-Conquest manuscripts—the personal name and the calendrical name—and these are found in manuscripts of the early Colonial period but apparently disappear before the end of the sixteenth century. As a general rule, the calendrical name seems to persist longer than the personal name in both pictorial and written manuscripts, but the 1580 Map of Teozacoalco is a notable exception to this rule. In this map, the nobility of the ruling lines of Teozacoalco and Tilantongo are shown with personal but not calendrical names, even though the subsidiary figures not shown as rulers of these two towns appear with both calendrical and personal names. In three of the manuscripts dating from about 1580 or later, persons of nobility are shown with neither a calendrical or personal name; and in one of these manuscripts, the Tlazultepec Genealogy, the figures are accompanied by glosses giving the Spanish name with which they were baptized (e.g., Don Gerónimo de Rojas) rather than a calendrical or personal name.

The category "unnamed genre figures," a feature that is the ultimate in Europeanization and unheard of in pre-Conquest manuscripts, is personified by the goatherd with his flocks seen in the 1771 Map of Xoxocotlán. It is very possible that the other human figures in this map—such as the male figure who wears a bird headdress and who is seated within an oval feathered cartouche at the top of the map, as well as the figures who are standing on the hills above this cartouche—are intended to represent specific historical personages, but none of them is named.

EUROPEAN CRESCENT MOON OR SUN MOTIFS

One very obvious European motif—in addition to Christian churches and roads with horseshoe tracks—that is found in early Colonial manuscripts is a crescent moon with a profile face. This motif appears in two place signs

in the first Lienzo of Zacatepec (Figs. 89, 96), a map whose only other blatantly European motifs are four Christian churches associated with place signs and a cross within one of the boundary signs. The crescent moon in one of the boundary signs in Zacatepec 1 also appears in Zacatepec 2 (Fig. 125).

A European sun motif on the border of a map to show its orientation appears in Colonial manuscripts at least as early as 1580, as in the Lienzo of Ocotepec and the Map of Teozacoalco, but this motif is absent in the earlier maps.

ORIENTATION OF MAPS

As can be seen in Chart 22, early Colonial maps are oriented with at least five different directions appearing at the top of the manuscript, and these five do not include the direction true north at the top, which emerged as the standard orientation in European maps. Of the eleven manuscripts, there are three with east at the top, three with west, one and possibly two with northwest, one with northeast, and one with southeast. The place signs in the Tlazultepec Genealogy are not arranged in the form of a map and thus have no cartographic orientation. It is not known how or why any of these directions was chosen to be placed at the top of a map.

GENERAL PURPOSE OF
EARLY COLONIAL MANUSCRIPTS

Over and above the specific function of the Colonial manuscripts discussed above, most of them were prepared for one general purpose: to protect the lands of the community and of the native nobility. Some of the manuscripts were drawn or painted for a specific lawsuit (as Map No. 36), and others were general community titles that could be produced at any time when lawsuits arose (as the Lienzo of Jicayán); but nearly all of the early-Colonial pictorial manuscripts under discussion represented an attempt to explain and to illustrate the extent of native land holdings to Colonial administrators. For whatever the system of justice might have been in the Mixteca prior to the Conquest, once the Spaniards arrived, the Mixtecs had to cope with a new and superimposed system of justice. This new system of justice was slow-moving and often conducted through interpreters; the litigation could go on for centuries, and its records filled folio after folio with writing in European script that was often incomprehensible to the native litigants.

One can sense in Colonial land documents an increasing weariness with litigation on the part of the native nobility and town officials. This is particularly evident in the litigation concerning the Coastal town of Tututepec, which is documented from 1554 into the eighteenth century.[10] In 1620, for example, a noblewoman named Isabel de Alvarado, who claimed to be the heir to the *cacicazgo* of Tututepec, withdrew her claim after consulting with the elders of the region, because she felt her claim might not stand up in court and she wanted "to free myself from

10 AGN-Tierras, 29–1; Vínculos 272, 8–10. The contents of these documents are outlined in Appendix D.

litigation and expenses, considering that the outcome of the litigation is doubtful."[11] Perhaps Isabel de Alvarado did not have a strong case for her claim to inherit the *cacicazgo* of Tututepec. She was, however, well aware that litigation was an expensive and time-consuming process and one that was not to be undertaken unless you had a reasonable chance of winning.

Another commentary on litigation occurs in the testimony of a witness in a 1717 suit over a section (*barrio*) of the Coastal town of Pinotepa de Don Luis that was disputed by Pinotepa and Tututepec. The witness states that he knows that the *barrio* in question was given to Lázaro de Salmerón, the native ruler of Pinotepa, by Melchor de Alvarado, the native ruler of Tututepec in the second half of the sixteenth century; but that after Salmerón initiated a lawsuit against Alvarado, the ruler of Tututepec took back the *barrio*, "saying that he did not want to give anything to someone who initiated lawsuits against him."[12]

The litigation from the Tututepec region also documents a notable conversion of a pre-Conquest pictorial manuscript into a Colonial type of written manuscript. In the early Colonial period, Codex Colombino, which deals principally with the conquests of 8-Deer and which apparently belonged to the native rulers of Tututepec in the sixteenth century, was annotated with Mixtec glosses that do not describe the pictorial content of the Codex but are essentially a written land document that lists the names of boundaries of Tututepec and its subject towns. For example, on pages XIII and XIV of Colombino, the pictorial narrative relates the story of the conquest of the Coastal town of Acatepec by 8-Deer and his half-brother, and the subsequent nose-piercing ceremony where 8-Deer becomes a *tecuhtli* or "great lord."

The Mixtec glosses on these two pages do not describe this conquest or ceremony, but set forth the boundaries of San Pedro Jicayán and show a very close correlation to the glosses on the Lienzo of Jicayán. The place signs of the boundaries named in the glosses do not appear in Colombino, and the glosses are just as much a "written map" added to an older document as the eighteenth-century Mixtec boundary names written on the Lienzo of Ocotepec. The use of the written map on Codex Colombino in actual litigation is well documented in the proceedings of a 1717 lawsuit, when the Codex was presented as corroborating evidence because it contained the names of boundaries of Tututepec's subject towns.[13]

The conversion of Codex Colombino into a Colonial land document was probably done after the native rulers of Tututepec, or their advisors, realized that the Spanish administrators could not understand the painted content of the manuscript and that many Colonial officials were doubtful of the validity of native pictorial documents. The suspicion of native paintings and maps is expressed in a communication written in 1676 to the Royal Auditor in Mexico City by Juan Martínez de Zorzano, who represented Pedro Martín, the administrator of land grants in the Coastal region of the Mixteca. Martínez de Zorzano claims:

... concerning the lands that belong to the Indians, they must be consistent with the law [and established by] legitimate titles and not by maps, because it is not easy to fabricate the titles, whereas the Indians prefer to introduce maps [in lawsuits], since by making a painting they will be able to initiate many lawsuits ... and in this event [the claims of] the Indians will be prejudicial not only to my client but to your Majesty in the lands which are part of and belong to the Royal Crown, because by producing a map fashioned in their way, they will establish themselves as owners and even usurpers of someone else's lands....[14]

But the Royal Auditor is not sympathetic to these suggestions, and his reply to Martínez de Zorzano leaves no doubt as to where the burden of proof lies:

... [the Indians] may have bought [the lands] or may have owned them since the days when they were pagans; and concerning these lands, all faith and confidence is given to their maps, because they are the legal instruments to which they are accustomed, and as such are admitted as titles by this Royal Court of Appeals; and in the event that they [the Indians] might wish to invent or falsify them [the maps] (which is not a legal presumption) by making new documents and by making additions, there remains the recourse of refuting them as false.[15]

The native rulers and town officials in the Mixteca continued to commission the type of maps and manuscripts "to which they were accustomed" well into the Colonial period. The earlier maps such as the Lienzo of Jicayán and the first Lienzo of Zacatepec are very close in style and iconography to pre-Conquest manuscript painting; and even though the native style was virtually replaced by European style around the end of the sixteenth century, a drawing such as the Tlazultepec Genealogy which contains human figures that strongly resemble those in the pre-Conquest manuscripts could still be produced as late as 1597. Moreover, combinations of European landscape and pre-Conquest place signs still appeared as late as the eighteenth century, as seen in the 1771 Map of Xoxocotlán.

In a number of the early Colonial native maps, such as the Lienzos of Jicayán and Ocotepec, Map No. 36 and the 1771 Map of Xoxocotlán, an attempt to bridge the gap between pre-Conquest picture-writing and European alphabetic writing in script is made in the annotations on these maps that are in a native language and in European script. Gradually, European script became more important, as can be seen in the 1597 Tlazultepec Genealogy, in which the written explanatory text occupies as much space as do the place signs and human figures. The new and

---

[11] AGN-Tierras, 29–1, fol. 46: "... *quitarme de pleytos y gastos considerando que el fin de los pleytos es dudoso....*"

[12] AGN-Vínculos, 272–8, fol. 35/v: "... *diciendo que no quería el dar nada a quien le ponía pleytos....*"

[13] Smith, *Colombino*, 77–78; 173–74.

[14] AGN-Tierras, 1877–6, fol. 15/v–16. The original Spanish text of this quotation is in Appendix B–8.

[15] *Ibid.*, fol. 17. The original Spanish text of this quotation is in Appendix B–8.

imported alphabetic writing in script eventually supplanted the pre-Conquest logographic system of writing, in part because it was the method of written communication used by the conquerors and administrators, and in part because it was more economical and efficient and could express a wider range of ideas.

The purpose of this book is to demonstrate the usefulness of early Colonial Mixtec maps in solving some of the problems connected with place signs in the Mixtec pre-Conquest historical manuscripts. Place signs are logographic representations of names of places, in which each significant pictorial element of the sign represents one or more words. Mixtec place signs usually have two components: a geographical substantive, such as "town," "hill," "river," or "plain," and a qualifying element, such as a bird, plant, animal, color, and so on.

One method of identifying place signs would be to translate the pictorial components of the sign into Mixtec and then attempt to find a town whose Mixtec name matches the name assigned to the pictorial sign. But this method has a number of serious drawbacks. First, because so few place signs have been identified, the range of pictorial vocabulary used in the qualifying elements is not known, and thus the elements may be equated with the wrong Mixtec words. For example, botanical motifs are common qualifying elements in place signs, but these motifs are often so conventionalized that it is difficult to identify the specific plant being represented and to ascertain its correct name in Mixtec.

Second, once a Mixtec name is given to a sign, it may still not be possible to correlate this assigned name with a specific town or site. An example of the difficulty of matching a pictorial place sign with the town it represents is provided by the sign of the place conquered by the ruler 8-Deer just prior to his sacrifice (Fig. 75, left side of the bottom line). This sign consists of a river (*yuta* in Mixtec), a parrot (*ti-huaco* in Mixtec), and a plant, which may represent the type of plant known as *huaco* in Mixtec.[1] Thus the Mixtec name of this place should be *yuta huaco* or *yuta (ti)huaco*, with the plant and the parrot acting as complementary phonetic indicators to specify that the qualifying element of the sign is *huaco*. But it cannot yet be determined what town, river, or site is represented by this sign because a site named *yuta huaco* in Mixtec is not known. It is necessary, then, to continue to extend our knowledge of the Mixtec names of places—not merely names of towns, but also of rivers, prominent hills, and boundary sites.

The two most productive sources of Mixtec place names are land documents of the Colonial period and the present-day Mixtec speakers in western Oaxaca. Land documents are particularly useful because they furnish data on historical geography, such as Mixtec names of sites which were formerly boundaries of towns but are no longer boundaries today. They also contain valuable information on the extent and composition of the major town units in the sixteenth century and often give Mixtec names of subject towns, fields, and other sites that belonged to the native rulers in the early Colonial period. But land documents usually cover only those towns or sites over which some dispute arose, and thus the study of historical documents must be supplemented by field work in the Mixteca itself.

Place-name field work is of necessity peripatetic because the citizens of one town will know in detail the names of the streams, landmarks, and other important geographical features within the immediate vicinity of their town, but may know little about a town 10 or 20 miles away. Nonetheless, one of the best methods of obtaining comprehensive and detailed information on Mixtec place names within a given region is to go to one or more towns in the region and ask.

The collection of Mixtec names of places will not, in itself, solve the problem of determining which site is represented by a specific place sign, for the same Mixtec name may refer to several different places. For example, *yuta ca'nu* ("big river") is the name of a number of sites in different sections of the Mixteca. According to the Reyes 1593 list of town names, *yuta canu* is the name of San Pedro Atoyac in the Mixteca Baja, about 20 miles west of Huajuapan. But *yuta canu* is also the name of a field belonging to the native ruler of Yanhuitlán in 1580,[2] the name of an orchard belonging to the native ruler of Teposcolula in 1566,[3] the name of a boundary between Nochixtlán and Amatlán,[4] the name of a river near the town of Tilló in the Valley of Yanhuitlán,[5] the name of a

---

[1] *Huaco* refers to several plants of the genus *Mikania*, whose popular name in Mexico is *guaco* (Mak, "Mixtec medical beliefs and practices," 147).

[2] AGN-Civil 516, fol. 6/v.

[3] AGN-Tierras 24–6, fol. 54.

[4] "Plano de la Villa de Nochixtlán," Mapoteca of the Dirección de Geografía, Meteorología e Hidrología, Colección General no. 3263. (Traced by Miguel Fuentes on July 5, 1907; date of original map not specified.)

[5] Martínez Gracida, "*Cuadros sinópticos*," n.p.

river near the town of San Juan Mixtepec,[6] and the name of the Río Santiago on the Coast. Thus if the name *yuta ca'nu* were given to a place sign, it would still be necessary to decide which *yuta ca'nu* the sign represents. The problem is somewhat similar to that faced by the United States Post Office when it received a letter addressed merely to "Three Rivers" with no designation of state, for there are towns named "Three Rivers" in Massachusetts, Michigan, Texas, New Mexico, and California.

One of the most important factors in identifying a place sign, then, is to establish the context in which the sign appears, and for this reason the study of post-Conquest maps is worthwhile because these documents present place signs in a cartographic context. In the case of the Lienzo of Zacatepec 1, it has been possible to identify the sign of Zacatepec itself, as well as the signs of nine nearby towns, because of the location of these signs on the map.

Another potential value of early Colonial maps is that they were often used as corroborating evidence in land disputes, and thus there is the possibility that the pictorial maps can be related to written documents that describe the places and place names depicted in the maps. In the case of the Lienzos of Zacatepec and Jicayán, no written documents that are exactly contemporary with these maps have been located, but such documents may yet be found in the archives of Mexico or Spain. In addition, some of the Colonial cartographic documents, such as Map No. 36 and the 1771 Map of Xoxocotlán, have been annotated with Mixtec glosses in connection with their use in land litigation. These glosses can be extremely helpful in place-sign identification, because they unite the pictorial sign with the words in the Mixtec language which it represents.

Ideally, then, place signs should be identified by an established context or accompanying text which indicates clearly the location or the name of the site which the sign represents. The analysis of other early Colonial Mixtec maps, as well as a study of the Mixtec glosses on Codices Sánchez Solís and Muro, should further our knowledge of both the vocabulary and syntax of Mixtec place signs. Moreover, place signs that are accompanied by glosses of the signs' Mixtec names are rich sources of the vocabulary of pictorial motifs that appear throughout Mixtec manuscripts. We have excellent early Colonial sources on the Mixtec language, notably the Alvarado dictionary and the Reyes grammar, and we have a corpus of important Mixtec pictorial manuscripts from both the pre-Conquest and early Colonial periods; but we have very few documents which unite specific pictorial motifs with the word they represent or with an explanatory text. For example, very few of the Mixtec names of deities are known, and there are no illustrated herbals from the Mixteca which show plants in connection with their Mixtec names.

Thus the relationships between the Mixtec pictorial signs and the words which they represent must be reconstructed piece by piece. The task is perhaps similar to reconstructing a great panoramic mosaic which has fallen off the wall, with all the tesserae scattered about the floor in little or no relationship to their original position. It is necessary, then, to attempt to reunite the fragmentary pictorial elements with their original background in such a way that the panorama is again visible and meaningful. In this slow process of reconstruction, place signs with glosses are crucial, because the qualifying elements of place signs comprise many different varieties of subject matter: deities, plants, animals, birds—in fact, any Mixtec word that can be represented by a pictorial sign.

The principal end of studying place signs as place signs is to enable us to interpret more completely the pre-Conquest historical manuscripts. The interpretation of the Mixtec histories without knowing the identity of the place signs is as difficult as it would be to interpret the Bayeux Tapestry without its Latin glosses. If no glosses were embroidered on the Tapestry, we would know only that a group of clean-shaven persons invaded by sea and defeated a group of people who wear mustaches. In the brief accompanying Latin text, the important persons and places in the Bayeux narrative are identified, and we learn that the Norman conquerors landed in Pevensey on the south coast of England and that the crucial battle with the English defenders took place at Hastings.

In the Mixtec histories, at least several hundred place signs appear which have not been identified, and thus we have no clear picture of where many of the ruling families lived, what towns they conquered, or how far their hegemony extended. In Colombino and on the back of Nuttall, the eleventh-century ruler 8-Deer "Tiger Claw" is shown as the conqueror of several long sequences of place signs. Does this indicate that the eleventh century was a period of expansion of the Mixtec-speaking people? Do these conquests represent wars that subjected many Mixtec towns to the rule of one family, or do they represent the Mixtec control of towns outside the Mixteca? These questions cannot be answered until many more signs of places conquered by 8-Deer have been identified.

Throughout this book it has been stressed that the pre-Conquest historical manuscripts are writing as well as painting, but where do they stand with respect to the history of writing? I. J. Gelb, one of the foremost historians of the development of writing, has characterized the Mixtec-Aztec system of pictorial writing as a "limited system," which utilizes logograms or "word signs" only for the writing of proper names.[7] This system may be contrasted with Chinese writing, which utilizes logograms to express all the words and concepts of the language.

It is an oversimplification to say that only names of persons and places are written logographically in the Mixtec system of writing. As we have seen in the discussion of "The Pictorial Conventions of the Mixtec Histories" in Chapter III, logograms are used to express words other than proper names. A chevron pattern is a logogram for the word "enemy," and probably by extension "hostile"; and when this sign appears as a road, it means "road to the enemy" or "warpath." Also, the pictorial sign for conquest, an arrow that penetrates a place sign, reflects

---

[6] *Ibid.*

[7] *A Study of Writing*, 51–59.

one of the Mixtec idioms for "conquest," which is "to put an arrow in the lands of another." However, many of the conventions in the Mixtec manuscripts—such as the basic conventions for marriage, birth, and death—appear to be strictly pictorial conventions and do not represent specific words in the Mixtec language, and Gelb's characterization of the Mixtec-Aztec system of writing as a "limited system" is accurate.

Notwithstanding the use of logograms in Mixtec manuscripts to represent words other than proper names, the writing system in the Mixtec histories exhibits a number of the features of what Gelb terms "forerunners of writing."

In the forerunners of writing, a picture or a series of pictures describes to the eye what the eye sees in a way parallel to that achieved by the picture which originated by the artistic-esthetic urge. All pictures, whether resulting from a communicative or an artistic-esthetic urge, generally convey meanings, ideas and only vaguely notions of linguistic value. In full systems of writing, signs do not directly express ideas or meanings but only words in the language. Or, to put it differently, they express ideas or meanings indirectly through the vehicle of words which in turn stand for ideas or meanings. Thus forerunners of writing are primary systems of communication, since they can achieve communication without the intervention of language, while full systems of writing are secondary systems of communication, since they achieve communication only by a process of linguistic transfer.[8]

In Mixtec writing the "pictorial" element is always present. With very few exceptions, names are attached to a human figure that represents in a stereotyped fashion the person named. The confrontation of a male and a female figure who share the same platform or place sign indicates that the two individuals are married, and this is a purely pictorial convention which appears to reflect no word or idiom in the Mixtec language. The individual figures which follow the marriage scene, shown either with or without an umbilical cord, are the offspring of the marriage; and again, this is a pictorial convention and not a reflection of language. The same may be said of the representation of death, which is expressed by showing the dead person in a seated position with his eyes closed or as a mummy bundle.

Even the logograms of Mixtec writing, such as the place signs which depict specific words in the language, are essentially relatively representational "pictures." Mixtec logograms are never as standardized or as abstract as, say, the logograms of Chinese or Hittite writing. In Hittite writing, a mountain peak of the type illustrated below is

used as the logogram for the word "city"; and a double-peaked mountain, as below, represents the word "land."

8 *Language*, XXXVIII-2, 210.

Although the idea of the tapering height of a mountain is present in these signs, they are essentially standardized forms, made up of a few easily drawn lines.

In Mixtec writing, the sign which usually represents the word *yucu* or "hill" is more elaborate. It is a large mound-like form, usually rounded at the top, and usually enclosed by a border with knobby projections, suggesting the rough or stony character of a hill. The base of the hill sign is often wider than the top, with volute-like extensions which enclose a fringe that forms the lower border of the sign (Figs. 20*a*, 29*d*, 51*b*). At times the fringe extends across the entire base of the hill, and the volutes on either side are omitted (Fig. 52). The fringe section of the sign is usually separated from the body of the hill by one or more thin bands. The hill sign may also assume a variety of shapes: It may be a simple mound (Fig. 52*a*), or have a slight slope (Fig. 79), or have an extended slope which serves as a platform for the ruler of the place (Fig. 51*a*).

In addition, the shape of the hill of the same place sign may vary from one manuscript to another. In the place sign of Tututepec as it appears in Codex Nuttall (Fig. 49 *c, d*), the hill element is a simple mound; in Codex Bodley (Fig. 49*b*), the hill is ovoid and more closely resembles a rock than a hill. In the large compound sign of Tututepec in Codex Colombino (Fig. 49*a*), the hill is a mound with a plateau-like extension. Thus we see that there is no standardized sign for "hill" such as the simple triangle filled with horizontal parallel lines used as a sign for "city" in Hittite writing. The hill sign in Mixtec manuscripts is still enough of a "picture" that it varies with the composition of a line or a page, or with the painting style of an individual artist or school of artists.

In general, then, Mixtec logograms are conventionalized signs that are not simplified and standardized to the same degree as the logograms of such "full writing systems" as Chinese or Hittite. But neither are Mixtec signs completely representational and based on perception. For example, the sign for "river" (Figs. 67, 68 *a, c*) is a cross-section of a river: a circular or rectangular area of blue with a frame on three sides that suggests the two banks and the bed of a river. The top of the river sign often has a white border with a series of small spirals to indicate ripples or waves. This schematic sign of a river is by no means as abstract as the Chinese sign for "river" as this word appears in place names:

Conversely, it is not intended to be a landscape portrayal of a specific river; it is a pictorial sign which expresses the Mixtec word *yuta*, or "river."

The Mixtec writing system is a "limited system" which utilizes logograms for names of places and persons, and for some verbs, as "to conquer" and "to go to war." But many of the narrative conventions utilized in the Mixtec histories are pictorial and without reference to language, and therefore the Mixtec writing cannot be considered a "full system" of writing, such as Chinese, in which the entire text of a narrative is expressed through logograms or "word signs."

In summary, this book has examined the general problems of place-sign interpretation and explored these problems in relation to specific signs which have been identified or tentatively identified. Many problems exist for which there is yet no solution, but several methods which will lead to the identification of more signs have been proposed. Three possible keys to the interpretation of Mixtec place signs are: (1) the collection of more Mixtec names of places, (2) the careful study of early Colonial maps in which place signs appear in a cartographic context, and (3) an analysis of place signs which are accompanied by glosses that include the Mixtec names represented by the signs.

APPENDIX A
Mixtec Names of Places

In the three lists of Mixtec place names below, the Nahuatl name, which is usually the name by which the town is known today, is given in the left-hand column, and the town's Mixtec name appears in the right-hand column. If the name in the left-hand column differs from the present-day name of the town, the latter name follows in brackets.

1. THE REYES LIST

The list below of Mixtec names compiled by Fray Antonio de los Reyes is from the original edition of *Arte en lengua mixteca* published in Mexico City in 1593 (pp. 66–68/v); the copy consulted is in the Latin American Library of the University of Texas at Austin. The place names with an asterisk (*) are analyzed and translated by Wigberto Jiménez Moreno in his introduction to the 1962 edition of Fray Francisco de Alvarado, *Vocabulario en lengua mixteca* (pp. 87–98).

Mixteca

Yanguitlan.	yodzocahi,
Chachuapa.	yutañani,
Cuyotepec.*	yucuñaña.
Tliltepec.*	yucutnoo.
Tepuzculula.*	yucundaa.
Tlachiaco.	disinuu,
Chicahuaztla.	tnutnono,
Cuiquila.	ñuu cuiñe,
Ocotepec.*	yucuite,
Cuixtlahuac.*	yodzocoo,
Tequiztiztepec de chuchones.	yucuyee,
Ychcatlan.	sidzaa,
Achiutla.	ñuundecu,
Malinaltepec.	yucuañe.
Tlatlaltepec.*	yucuquesi,
Atoyac.*	teyta.
Tlatzultepec.*	yucucuihi,
Chalcatongo.	ñuundaya,
Amoltepec.*	yucunama,
Yolotepec.	yucuñeni,
Atlatlauca. S. esteuan.*	ñuuquaha,
Apuala.	yutatnoho,
Quautla.	dzandaya,
Chicahuaztepec.	yucucadza.
Nuchiztlan.	atoco,
Quautlilla.*	yucundeq,
Etlantongo,*	yucunduchi.
Xaltepec.*	añute.
Tilantongo.*	ñuutnoo,
Mictlantongo.	dzandaya.

Patlaixtlahuac.*	yodzocono,
Texupa.*	ñuundaa,
Tzoyaltepec.*	añuu,
Tonaltepec.	yucundij,
Tamatzulapa.	tequevui,
Tuctla.	yucuyaa, ñuuhuiyu,
Teotzaqualco.*	chiyocanu.
Tzentzontepec.*	yucueetuvui,
Peñoles, y Elotepec.*	yucundedzi.
Mixtepec.*	yodzonuu huico,

Mixteca baxa

Tonala.*	ñuu niñe.
Atoyac.*	yutacanu,
Yhualtepec.	yucunicana,
Tlapanala.	ytnundahua,
Tzilacayoapa.*	ñuunduyu.
Tlapalcinco.	yutandaha,
Xustiahuac.*	yodzocuiya,
Tecomaxtlahuac.*	yodzoyaha,
Tlacotepec.	yucuquanuu.
Ycpactepec.*	yucunuuyuh.
Tetzoatlan.	nuusiya.
Huaxuapa.	ñuudzai.
Chila.	toavui.
Yxitlan.*	ñuusaha.
Cuyotepec.	ñuuñaña,
Miltepec.	daanduvua.
Camotlan.*	ñuundihi.
Xuchitepetongo.	ayuu.
Goaxolotitlan.	yuhuacuchi,
Tequiztiztepec del Rey.*	yucundaayee,
Chiyaçumba.	yodzoñuquende,
Guapanapa.	tnuhuito,
çapotitlan.	chiyoyadza,
Acatepec.*	yucutnuyoo,
Petlaltzingo.*	ñuuyuvui,
Acatlan.	yutatisaha.
Piaztla.	sahañuu quu,
Chiautla.	ñuuquende,
Tlapa.*	yutandáyu,
Alcuçauca:*	yutaquaa,

Costa

Puctla.*	ñuucaa, l. ñuuñuma.
çacatepec.	yucusatuta.
Amuscos primeros.	yodzotaca,
Los segundos,	yodzocosa,
Xicayan de P. nieto,	ñuusijquaha,
Xicayan de tobar,	nuudzavui,
Ometepec,*	yucuvui,

Yhualapa,	yutañeni,
Tututepec,*	yucudzaa,
Pinotecpa,	doyoyuhu,

Pueblos de la parte de Teutila

Cuicatlan,	yutayaq,
Quiyotepec,	ahehe,
Cuzcatlan,*	nuudzeque,
Huitzila,	ñuu naho,
Tepeutzila,	yucusanu,
Chinantla,	nama,

çapoteca

Guaxilotitlan,	ñuundodzo,
Etla,*	ñuunduchi,
Goaxacac,*	nuunduvua,
Cuilapa,	yutacaha, sahayucu,
Teozapotlan, [Zaachila]	tocuisi,
Tlalistaca,*	ñucuisi,
Teticpac.	miniyuu,
Ocotlan,*	ñundedzi,
Nixapa,*	yutanuyaa,
Xalapa,*	yutañute,
Tecoantepec,*	yutañaña.
çoçola,*	tuhu,
tamatzola,*	yahua.

Mexicano

Mexico,*	ñucòyo, tenuchtitlan,
Tlatelulco,	ñuutnusacu,
Tezcuco,	ñuutecucu,
Cuyocan,*	ñuuyuuñaña,
Xuchimilco,*	ñuunduhuaita.
Atzcapuçalco,*	ñuudzocoyoco,
Atlacubaya,*	ñuunduvuanàno,
Tepetlaoztoc,*	ñuutotoyuvui.
Ytztapalapa,	ñuutechiyo,
Ytztapaluca,	ñuutechiyodzuchi,
Chimalhuacan chalco.*	ñuuyusa,
Chimalhuacan atenco.	ñuuyusadzuchi.
Coatepec,*	ñuuyucucoo.
Tacuba, o tlacopa,	ñuundutayhua,
Toluca,	ñuuyondaye,
Mechuacan,*	ñuuteyaca,
Metztitlan.*	ñuuyoo,
Amaquemeca.*	ñuututu,
Tenango,*	ñuuyuhua,
Tlalmanalco,	ñuunicahatoñena.
Mitzquique,	sahatnudayndzuchi.
Ayutzinco.*	yuhunduta, yuuteyoo.
tepupula,	huahiyucu,
Tepapayeca,	ñuuyyondoho.
Tetela,	yutatnoo,
Tlatlapanala,	ñuudzinitáhui.
Goayapa,*	nononduta,
Ytzucan,*	dzitniyuchi.
Tepuztlan.*	ñuucaa.
Yautepec.	yucuyecu.
Coaxtepec.*	ñuunduta.
Coahunahuac,*	ñuunuuyutnu.
Cuitlahuac.*	ñuuyehui.
La Puebla.*	yutandeyoho.
Chulula.*	ñundiyo.
Tlaxcalla.*	ñuudzita.
Goaxotzinco.*	yutatnuñuu.
Acapetlahuac.	ñuuyuvuiyoo.

Tepeaca.*	dziñeyucu,
Tecoacan,*	yucutoñaña.
Tecamachalco.	yucutduyaca.
Acatzinco.*	yucutnuyoo.
Tlacotepec.	yucumañu.
Totomehuacan,*	ñuudzaa.
Tecali.*	huahiyuu,
Tepexic.*	cavua.
Guatinchan.*	huahiyaha.

2. THE VILLAVICENCIO LIST

The Mixtec names of towns listed below appear in a short Mixtec vocabulary in Fray Miguel de Villavicencio, "Arte, Prontuario, Vocabulario y Confesionario de lengua mixteca," fol. 59/v–60/v of the nineteenth-century copy by Francisco del Paso y Troncoso in the Archivo Histórico of the Museo Nacional de Antropología, Mexico City (Colección Antigua, no. 3–60 bis). The towns with an asterisk (*) are in the present-day State of Guerrero.

Atlamax^{co} [Atlamajalcingo]*	ñuchita
Atlamax^{co} [Atlamajalcingo] del Río*	cuchico
Collaqualco [Coyahualco]*	Taytecuan
La Costa (de la mixteca)	Andique
Guamuxtitlan [Huamuxtitlán]*	nutucha
Guaxaca [Oaxaca]	Ñundugua
Gueguetepeque [Huehuetepec]*	ñuucuuqhe
Iguala*	taxú
Yxcatiopan [Ixcateopan]*	ytu cuchi
México	ñucollo
Mixtecapan*	tazaguy
Puebla	llutandio, tanhdio
Quazoquitengo [Cuatzoquitengo]*	ñuquihi
Sollatlan [Zoyatlán]*	ytahño
Tepecocatlan*	quihun . . .
Tlacotla*	Nunducono
Tlapan*	tandalléé
Tlaquaca (Xalpatlahuaca)*	cuchiton
Tototepeque*	lloso nuni
Zacatipa*	tunhte

3. PLACES IN THE COASTAL REGION OF OAXACA

The Mixtec names listed below were collected by the author in the Coastal region of the Mixteca in 1963 and 1964. In the dialect of the Coast, *ch* is equivalent to the *s* of the Alvarado dictionary; and the fricative *x* is usually equivalent to the *dz*, or at times to the *s*, of Alvarado. The translations that are listed for some of the Mixtec place names are those that were provided by Mixtec speakers on the Coast.

Acatepec, Santa María	yucu yoò "hill of the moon"
Amusgos, San Pedro	ñuu ñama
Atoyac, San Pedro	ñuu yuta, ñuta
Cacahuatepec, San Juan	yucu xî'wa
Colorado, San Juan	yo kwa'a "the red rope"
Comaltepec, Santa Elena	yucu chiyo (in the town of Comaltepec)
	yucu tiyo (outside of Comaltepec)
Santa Cruz (near Tututepec)	yucu yaa
Huaxpaltepec, San Andrés	xini titi "the head of the iguana"

Huazolotitlán, Santa María Asunción	yuta yî'ndi, tye'ndî	Tataltepec de Valdés	ñuu kisi, ñuu kichi
Ipalapa, Santa María	ñuu tayu	Tepenistlahuaca, Santa Cruz	yucu yuu
Ixcapa, San Sebastián	ñuu chaa "new town"	Tepetlapa, San Antonio	ñuu toto
Ixtayutla, Santiago	yuta ñîî; chîkwî	Tetepec, Santiago	yucu yuu ca'nu (in Jicayán and Pinotepa de Don Luis)
Jamiltepec, Santiago	casa ndo'o		yucu yuu (in Jamiltepec)
Jicaltepec, Santa María Asunción	ñuu caan	Tetepelcingo, San Miguel	yucu yuta (in Jicayán and Jamiltepec)
Jicayán, San Pedro	ñuu xii kwa'a "town of the red grandfather"		yucu yuu (in Pinotepa de Don Luis)
Jicayán, San Juan	ñuu ndu'va	Tlacamama, San Miguel	ñuu nducha
Jocotepec, Santiago	yucu yî'î	Tututepec, San Pedro	yucu saa
Juquila, Santa Catalina	ñuu xii to'o, ñuu sto'o	Zacatepec, San Marcos	ñuu ita
San Lorenzo (near Pinotepa de Don Luis)	yucu yo'o	Zacatepec, Santa María	yucu cha tuta
		Río Verde	yuta tiyoo
Mechoacán, Santa Catalina	ñuu tiyaca	Lago Hermoso (south of Tututepec)	yucu ya'a
Panistlahuaca, San Miguel	so ta'yu, so cha'yu		
Pinotepa de Don Luis	ndoo yu'u	Río de la Arena	yuta atu, tatu
Pinotepa Nacional	ñuu yoco, ñyoco	Río Santiago	yuta ca'nu
Putla, Santa María	ñuu caa	Río de la Hamaca	yuta tundo'o

APPENDIX B
Spanish Documents that are Translated or Summarized in the Text

1. A paragraph from the last will and testament of María López, native ruler of Tlazultepec. The original will in the Mixtec language is dated April 25, 1571; this section was translated into Spanish in 1597. AGN-Tierras 59–2, fol. 46.

Iten, mando acerca del pueblo de Tlazultepec y su cacicazgo, que es mi voluntad de darlo y lo doy a don Juan de Guzmán y Velasco, y a doña Inés de Zárate, y les hago donación así del señorío como de las tierras, posesiones y bienes y todo lo demás anexo al dicho pueblo de Tlazultepec, a mí perteneciente, es mi voluntad que lo herede y haya el dicho don Juan de Guzmán, por cuanto mi abuelo procedió y salió de Tlatlaltepec y fue a San Agustín, estancia de Tlachiaco y allí se casó y de aquel pueblo de Sant Agustín de Tlachiaco que se llama en lengua mixteca Ñutisi, vino mi madre y se casó con don Tomás mi padre, los cuales dos vinieron a este pueblo de Tlazultepec, y heredaron legítimamente el dicho pueblo de Tlazultepec, y yo como hija y heredera de los dichos mis padres que heredé el dicho pueblo de Tlazultepec, lo doy a don Juan de Guzmán y Velasco, que es el pariente más cercano que yo tengo y debe heredar el dicho pueblo de Tlazultepec....

2. A discussion of the Mixtec names of Acatlán, Puebla. *PNE* V, 58–59.

El dicho pueblo de *Acatlan* en lengua *mexicana* se llama asi *Acatlan* que quiere dezir en la dicha lengua "Lugar de Cañas," porque los *mexicanos* que primero llegaron al dicho pueblo hallaron junta a el un cañaveral grande, y por eso le nonbraron asi sin curar el nonbre que los naturales le tenian puesto en su lengua *misteca*, en la qual nonbrauan al dicho pueblo *Yucuyuxi* que buelto en lengua castellana quiere dezir "Serro de piedras preciadas," y asi mismo le llaman el dia de oy en la dicha lengua *misteca Yutta tixaa* que buelta en lengua castellana quiere dezir "Agua ensenizada," el qual nonbre le pusieron por razon de vn çerro que esta junto a vn arroyo que pasa por el dicho pueblo que se llama "Serro de Seniza," el qual dicho nonbre y del agua que pasa junto a el se conpuso el dicho nonbre de agua ensenizada. Otros nonbres dizen que tiene, de los quales, y del que tenemos dicho en este capitulo que tenia antes que los *mexicanos* a el viniesen, no ay memoria ni se sabe la razon dellos, y por eso no se pone aqui.

3. A description of the pre-Conquest siege of Achiutla by Tututepec. Francisco de Burgoa, *Geográfica descripción*, I, 352–53.

... tienen enfrente de este pueblo [Achiutla] un cerro altísimo, con una punta que descuella soberbiamente, casi entre la región de las nubes, y corónase con una muy dilatado muralla de losas de más de un estado de alto, y cuentan de las pinturas de sus caracteres historiales, que se retiraban allí, para defenderse de sus enemigos, y que por no cumplir cierto vasallaje a que se obligaron al rey de Tututepeque en la costa del Sur, sus caciques, y el feudo era de acudir con los frutos de su pueblo a una gran feria, que se hacía por orden de aquel rey en los llanos de Puetla, principio de la costa de donde se adquiría lo necesario para sus vasallos, y por grandes victorias que había tenido de los comarcanos, les impuso esta obligación, era la travesía de este pueblo de más de veinte leguas de montuosa y áspera serranía, y de excesiva vegetación; trataron los sujetos de este señor, de excusarse, y no cumplir con este trato, por la molestia grande que recibían, a la primera vez que faltaron los envió a requerir con sus embajadores amenazándolos, a la segunda les envió valerosos capitanes, con inmensidad de gente que obligó a los del pueblo a subirse a aquel inexpugnable castillo, con bastimentos bastantes, y tanta multitud de galgas, y peñas rodadizas que pudiesen defenderse del asalto, despeñando al enemigo, llegó éste, y sitió el monte, y buscó camino para treparle, y llegar a las manos, y fue tan sangrienta la batalla, que se contaron después los muertos de una, y otra parte, y se hallaron más de veinte y dos mil cuerpos....

4. Two accounts of Tututepec's conquest and domination of other towns on the Coast of Oaxaca.

(a) The account of Tonameca. *PNE* IV, 243–44.

... que la manera de su govierno era que los Señores de *Tutepec* (sic) nombran en este pueblo quien auya de ser gouernador; y a este quellos nombrauan, que solia ser el mayor prinçipal deste pueblo, solian obedeçer sobre todos, y el tal gouernador ponya en cada barrio deste pueblo prinçipales que mandasen e gouernasen a los maçeguales y rrecogiesen los tributos, y esta era la manera de su gouernaçion; y solian yr a la guerra, ayudando a los de *Tututepec*, contra los de *Teguantepec* y otros pueblos desta costa contra quien trayan guerra....

(b) The account of Pochutla. *PNE* IV, 239.

. . . los Señores de *Tututepec* ymbiauan vna persona que asistiese en el pueblo a rrecoger los tributos y hazer justiçia, y demas desta persona nonbrauan por gouernador del pueblo al mas prinçipal señor del, para queste gouernase y rregiese el pueblo, y este gouernador nonbraua otros que le ayudasen y tuviesen cargo de los yndios de los barrios . . . y antes que ffuesen sujetos a *Tututepec* solian traer guerra con ellos y por averlos vençido vinyeron a ser sus vasallos.

5. The testimony of Pedro Hernández of Santa María Ipalapa concerning the boundaries of Santa María Zacatepec, December 1702. AGN-Tierras, 192–5, fol. 12–12/v.

. . . las tierras que caen en los terminos de Zacatepeque . . . [son] . . . desde el Rio de Sta Cruz hasta el cerro que llaman de Sta Rosa, que corre su derecera hacia el norte, y de alli hacia el Poniente, que llegan a lindar con tierras de Xicayan de Tovar hasta un Rio que sirve de lindero hasta llegar a tierras del Puº de Amusgos, a donde tiene por nombre dicho Rio, Rio de Zanate . . . . Todas las demas tierras que caen en los terminos del Puº de Zacatepec, Que corren desde el Rio de Sta Cruz, a la loma que llaman La Mesa, Y de alli corre hasta el monte que llaman de los siete ocotes que linda con tierras del Puº de Atoyaquillo. Y de alli va la derecera al Cerro de la Estanzuela que linda con tierras del Puº de Ystayutla. Y de alli corre la derecera, a linda[r] con tierras del Puº de San Cristobal, y del de Atoyaque, de esta Jurisdiccion. Y va corriendo a lindar con tierras del Pueº de Amusgos en un paraje que llaman *Coscomamichi*. Y de alli al Cerro de la Cera, y de alli al Cerro Endemoniado, por otro nombre que Espanta, Y de ay baja la derecera a la Piedra de Dos Bocas, alias Dos Vasos, y corre la derecera hasta la Piedra de la Cara, que linda con los Llanos de Merino, y de ay al Cerro Pedregoso, y de alli al de palmito, cae al Rio que viene de Xicayan de Tovar, Y va corriendo por dicho Rio nombrandole de Zanate, hasta topar el Rio de Santa Cruz, que es el primer lindero.

6. References to a pictorial manuscript belonging to the native rulers of Amusgos in the seventeenth century. AGN-Tierras 191–3.

Included in this document is the last will and testament of Juan Rafael de Ávila, dated 1629, in which this native ruler of Amusgos bequeaths to his son Pablo Ávila, "a painting of my genealogy and of my possessions." (Fol. 70/v: "una pintura de mi desendensia y de mi ventura.") In another section of the document, dated 1655, Pablo de Ávila describes his land holdings and declares that "these lands, hills and arroyos are mine legitimately as can be seen from my paintings and documents and from the information that has been presented to Your Worship by the oldest witnesses who could be found." (Fol. 78: ". . . estas tierras zerros y arroios son mias lixitimamente como paresera haser ante Vmd. con los testigos mas antiguos que se hallaron.") Several of the elderly witnesses who testify on behalf of Pablo de Ávila also men-

tion "a painting on old cloth which shows the ancestors of Pablo de Ávila." (Fol. 86: ". . . la pintura dello tiene em manta antigua de su desendencia del dicho D. Pablo de Ávila.") It seems questionable, however, whether this "painting" was actually presented in court during the mid-seventeenth-century litigation. Later in the proceedings, Pablo de Ávila states: ". . . I have a painting on cloth, which since it cannot be incorporated into the proceedings, I am not presenting; but because it demonstrates the possession that my ancestors obtained of the said towns and lands, I am prepared to show it if necessary in this court or in other higher courts . . . ." (Fol. 87–87/v: ". . . tengo pintura em manta que por no poder se Yncorporar en los autos no la presento de como por ella consta de la posesion que mis antepasados obtubieron de dichos pueblos y tierras de que estoy puesto a demonstrarla en caso necesario assi en este jusgado como en otros supremos . . . .") If such a painting on cloth did exist in the seventeenth century, its subsequent history is unrecorded, and its present location is unknown. It would be most interesting to discover a map of Amusgos, because this town is bounded by Zacatepec and Jicayán, the two towns whose Lienzos are under consideration in this study.

7. A story concerning the Lienzo of Jicayán told by Sebastián Santiago of Jicayán in April, 1963. With the exception of the few additions in brackets, the text below was transcribed verbatim from a tape recording of the narrative.

Esta población tiene un título que es una manta hecha de una mujer indígena de esta población. Y cuando esa manta lo tejieron, las autoridades del lugar y la policía a su mando subieron a presencia de esa mujer para que lo tejiera esa manta. Y esa mujer que le hizo esa manta, le hizo todo a favor de Jicayán. Según la figura que le hizo no le dió derecho a todas las agencias que pertenece a esta población. Por qué? Porque las autoridades y la policía estaban vigilando estrictamente según como va el trabajo de ella. Porque si daba lugar porque pinta de mal la figura que lleva este mapa, o manta, quitaban el derecho a esa mujer o mandaban a la casa y lo iban a castigar. Y por esa razón, más le hizo a favor a Jicayán para que tenga ese mapa, y ese mapa fué hecha de esta población—mujer indígena de esta población que hizo esa manta. O sea título de propiedad de terreno comunal de San Pedro Jicayán.

Interjected Question: Y cuándo fué hecho el mapa?

Narrator continues: Que cuya fecha no me recuerdo muy bien . . . . Que parece que en 1805 o 1807. Entre de estos años hicieron este mapa.

Esa mujer le hizo la figura o la letra en esa manta; pues como antes no había quien conocía la letra, no lleva ninguna letra, sino puras figuras extrañas que más o menos se da uno a entender la significación de cada pueblo vecino. Como, por ejemplo, aquí en el lugar, en medio de ese mapa, está la iglesia, la iglesia que existe todavía, y al frente de esa iglesia está el Señor Mandón. Y ya luego viene . . . se ve el pueblo de Tlacamama; allí está la iglesia;

en el mapa está la iglesia. Viene el caminito de Tlacamama a Jicayán, de Jicayán a la Piedra del Sol, de la Piedra del Sol a Pinotepa de Don Luis. Está su nombre [Pinotepa de Don Luis] en mixteco: *ndoo yu'u*. De Pinotepa de Don Luis a San Juan Colorado. Como antes no se podía escribir la letra que nadie no sabía, allí está forma de un mecate, [se] ve el mecate colorado. Es un pedazo de mecate, pero colorado, y está en este mapa. Y eso significa que aquí está San Juan Colorado, [cuyo nombre en mixteco es] *yo qua'a . . . yo'o qua'a*.

Así pues sucesivamente mencionando a cada pueblo vecino porque anteriormente no había *quien* escribía la letra. Los linderos del terreno de Jicayán [eran]:

piedra grande
hondura del toro
las palmas
soco tiyaca (pozo de pescado)
La Pastora
yuta tita (río de plátano)
[hasta] Zacatepec, *cha tuta* (hombre de calzón ancho)
de allí, hasta Amusgos, *ñuu ñama* (pueblo de llano huamil)
[a] San José *ñuu ti'yoo*
Yuta uni (Los Tres Ríos)
de allí, *tulumbi tuni* (guapinoles marcados)
de allí, *yuta ku kixi* (arroyo del charco)
de allí, *tu te itu* (cerro o lomita de hojas duras)
y de allí, *cava tiñuu* (peña de pavos reales)
cha wa'bee (barranca de los chivos)
yuta mini coò cáá (arroyo de la hondura de las culebras de cascabel)

y de allí cierran en los puntos cardenales con La Piedra Grande. Todos estos pueblos pertenecían a San Pedro Jicayán anteriormente.

8. A discussion concerning the veracity of native maps.

(a) A portion of a document dated August 27, 1676, addressed to the Royal Auditor from Juan Martínez de Zorzano, the lawyer of Pedro Martín, administrator of land grants in the Coastal region of the Mixteca. AGN-Tierras 1877–6, fol. 15/v–16.

. . . en las tierras que pertenecieron a los indios ha de ser solamente conforme a hordenansa, y Titulos Legitimos y no segun mapas, porque aquellos no ay fasilidad para fabricarlos, y en estas tienen los indios mucha para introducirlos pues con aser una pintura podran yntrodusir litigios . . . y en este caso no sola a mi pte sino a su Magd perjudicaran los indios en las tierras que conpone y pertenecen a su Rl Corona, pues con sacar un mapa formado a su modo se introduciran dueños y aun Vsurpadores de lo ageno . . . .

(b) A portion of the reply, dated September 13, 1676, by the Royal Auditor to Martínez de Zorzano. *Ibid.*, fol. 17.

. . . las [tierras] pueden haver comprado o pueden estar poseyendo desde su gentilidad; y en estas se da toda fe y credito a sus mapas, por ser los instrumentos a su usanza y estilo, y lo es de esta Rl. Auª. el admitirselos por titulos; y en caso q los quisiessen suponer o falsificar (que no es presumpcion legal) por nuevos y por añadidos; le queda el recurso a la parte de redargüirlos de falsos.

APPENDIX C

The Coixtlahuaca Group of Manuscripts

Lienzo of Coixtlahuaca 1-Codex Ixtlán-Lienzo B (*HMAI* Census No. 70)

Codex Meixueiro-Lienzo A (*HMAI* Census No. 195)

Lienzo of Ihuitlán (*HMAI* Census No. 157)

Lienzo Antonio de León (*HMAI* Census No. 8)

Lienzo Seler II-Lienzo of Coixtlahuaca 2 (*HMAI* Census No. 71)

Lienzo of Natívitas (*HMAI* Census No. 232)

Related Manuscripts:

Gómez de Orozco Fragment (*HMAI* Census No. 129)

Selden Roll (*HMAI* Census No. 284)

Codex Baranda (*HMAI* Census No. 24)

1590 Land-Grant Map, AGN-Tierras 2729-5

The Lienzos of San Miguel Tequixtepec 1 and 2 (*HMAI* Census Nos. 433 and 434)

The group of manuscripts from the region in and around the town of Coixtlahuaca are listed above, with the name or names of the manuscript followed by its number in the census of pictorial manuscripts in Volume 14 of the *Handbook of Middle American Indians*. The first six of these manuscripts were proposed as the nucleus of the Coixtlahuaca group by Ross Parmenter ("20th Century Adventures of a 16th Century Sheet: The Literature on the Mixtec Lienzo in the Royal Ontario Museum," *Boletín de estudios oaxaqueños*, no. 20 [1961], 2). Alfonso Caso has suggested that three additional manuscripts—Codex Baranda, the Gómez de Orozco Fragment, and the Selden Roll—may be related to the Coixtlahuaca group, for they contain mythological-origin scenes similar to those in Lienzo Antonio de León, an assuredly Coixtlahuaca-region manuscript. (Caso, "Comentario al Códice Baranda," *Miscelánea Paul Rivet, Octogenario Dictata*, I [Mexico, 1958], 375, 379–85, 389; and *Interpretación del Códice Gómez de Orozco* [Mexico, 1954], 10ff.) Still another manuscript that is related to the Coixtlahuaca group is a sketch map drawn in 1590 to illustrate a petition for a land grant north of Coixtlahuaca.

The Lienzo of Coixtlahuaca is in the Museo Nacional de Antropología in Mexico City (no. 35-113); black-and-white photographs of the Lienzo are published in John B. Glass, *Catálogo de la Colección de Códices* (Mexico, 1964, plates 123–24), along with a brief history and description of the manuscript (*ibid.*, 169–70). William Gates, an avid collector of Mexican documents in native languages and founder of the short-lived Maya Society, published a copy of this Lienzo as *Codex Ixtlán* (Baltimore, 1931; Maya Society Publication No. 3). Gates's copy was not drawn from the original Lienzo, but was a re-drawing of a photograph of a tracing made by the Mexican scholar Nicolás León after the original lienzo. Gates also published a copy of a second lienzo, which he called *Codex Meixueiro* (Baltimore, 1931; Maya Society Publication No. 4). This copy, too, was a re-drawing of a photograph of a León tracing of a lienzo which is now lost. The Nicolás León tracings of the two lienzos are now in the Latin American Library at Tulane University, where they are catalogued as "Lienzo A" (the prototype of Codex Meixueiro) and "Lienzo B" (the copy of the Lienzo of Coixtlahuaca and the prototype of Codex Ixtlán).

Gates's photographs of the León tracings and his drawings made after these photographs are now at Brigham Young University in Provo, Utah. The complex history of the two lienzos and the copies based on them is admirably sorted out by Ross Parmenter, "The Identification of Lienzo A: A Tracing in the Latin American Library of Tulane University," to be published in: Tulane University, Middle American Research Institute, *Philological and Documentary Studies*, Vol. II, No. 5 (1970).

Codex Meixueiro (Lienzo A) differs slightly from the Lienzo of Coixtlahuaca (Lienzo B-Codex Ixtlán). Both documents present a map of the region of Coixtlahuaca surrounded by place signs of the town's boundaries, but the orientation of the two maps differs by 90°—that is, the Lienzo of Coixtlahuaca is oriented with south or southeast at the top, and Codex Meixueiro with east or northeast at the top. In addition, the *dramatis personae* of the two manuscripts is somewhat different. Meixueiro, for example, contains a vertical row of genealogical figures below the central place sign of Coixtlahuaca, and these persons do not appear in the Lienzo of Coixtlahuaca.

The Lienzo of Ihuitlán is in the Brooklyn Museum (accession no. 42.160), and the Lienzo Antonio de León (also sometimes called "Codex Rickards" or "Lienzo of Tlapiltepec, Papalutla and Miltepec") is in the Royal Ontario Museum in Toronto (catalog no. 917.3). Both lienzos were published, with a study of their genealogical content, by Alfonso Caso, "Los lienzos mixtecos de Ihuitlán y Antonio de León," *Homenaje a Pablo Martínez del Río* (Mexico, 1961), 237-74. The complex acquisition and publication history of Lienzo Antonio de León is discussed by Ross Parmenter, "20th Century Adventures of a 16th Century Sheet," *passim.*

The Lienzo of Ihuitlán contains detailed genealogical data concerning the rulers of Santiago Ihuitlán, Coixtlahuaca, and an unidentified town whose sign is a hill with a stream of water. In addition, eighteen signs of other towns are shown, all accompanied by a gloss of the town's name in Nahuatl; many of these signs are shown with a single ruler, a marriage pair, or a short genealogy. This lienzo covers more territory outside the immediate Coixtlahuaca region than any other known Coixtlahuaca manuscript; included among the place signs are names of towns in the Mixteca Baja region of southern Puebla, as well as the sign of Tehuacán in southeastern Puebla.

Lienzo Antonio de León has in the upper-left section long genealogies of the rulers of two unidentified places, whose signs are described by Caso in his 1961 study as "Hill of the Points" and "Eagle-*Yucucuy* [green hill]-Ballcourt." A short genealogy of the rulers of Coixtlahuaca appears in the upper-center section. Scattered throughout the remainder of this lienzo are many place signs, most of which are accompanied by single figures, marriage pairs, or short genealogies.

The unpublished Lienzo Seler II or Lienzo of Coixtlahuaca 2 is in the Museum für Völkerkunde in Berlin, and this manuscript contains features that are also seen in Lienzo Antonio de León and in the Lienzo of Coixtlahuaca 1 and Codex Meixueiro. Seler II has a rectangular border with place signs of boundary names similar to that seen in Coixtlahuaca 1 and Meixueiro; and most of the place signs within the border of Seler II also occur in Coixtlahuaca 1 and Meixueiro. Thirty-four of the boundary signs in Seler II are accompanied by legible or barely legible glosses; these appear to be in three different languages: Nahuatl, Mixtec, and Choco. One important feature that Seler II shares with Lienzo Antonio de León is a large sign of a hill with two entwined serpents, a sign that is accompanied by a number of smaller place signs (16 in Seler II, 20 in Antonio de León). A similar entwined-serpent sign also appears in the Selden Roll and in Codex Baranda. Within the rectangle of boundaries of Seler II are five long rows of marriage pairs, as well as several shorter genealogies. In addition, single marriage pairs are associated with many of the place signs that appear both inside and outside the rectangle formed by the boundary signs.

The unpublished Lienzo of Natívitas is in the local archive of Santa María Natívitas, a town about five miles southwest of Coixtlahuaca. Photographs of a copy of the lienzo are in the Archivo Fotográfico of the INAH. This manuscript contains two vertical rows of marriage pairs within a rectangular border formed by the place signs of the town's boundaries, most of which are accompanied by glosses in Mixtec. One of the place signs in the lower border of the Lienzo is specified to be a boundary between Natívitas and Coixtlahuaca. The sign consists of a plat-form supporting a double-peaked hill; four flint blades are placed on the hill and one on the platform. The accompanying gloss reads: *ytnu yuhui yuchi, Daño yodo coo,* or "the slope of the ravine of flint blades, the boundary with Coixtlahuaca." (*Ytnu* = "slope"; *yuhui* = "ravine"; *yuchi* = "knife, flint blade"; *daño* = "boundary"; *yodo coo* is the Mixtec name of Coixtlahuaca.) Many of the persons in the genealogical section in the center of the Lienzo are identified by glosses that give their calendrical names in Mixtec; these have been analyzed by Barbro Dahlgren, *La mixteca* (Mexico, 1954), 366-70. A study of the entire lienzo is reportedly being prepared by Wigberto Jiménez Moreno and Barbro Dahlgren.

All of the six manuscripts discussed above are lienzos—that is, painted on cloth; even Codex Meixueiro, now known through a copy, had a lienzo prototype. All six utilize native pictorial conventions to express calendrical and place names, although these native conventions coexist with such early Colonial style characteristics as the less taut line described by Donald Robertson (*Mexican Manuscript Painting*, 65-66) as "disintegrated frame line" and such obvious iconographic intrusions as Christian churches. It is likely, then, that these six Lienzos were drawn around the middle of the sixteenth century, or certainly before the end of the sixteenth century when native style and iconography had for the most part disappeared.

The geographical information presented in the Coixtlahuaca group of manuscripts deserves a detailed study, because these manuscripts are teeming with place signs, most of which appear in a cartographic or quasi-cartographic context. In the Lienzo of Ihuitlán, the majority of the place signs represent the Nahuatl names of towns; the Lienzo of Coixtlahuaca, Codex Meixueiro, Lienzo Antonio de León, and Lienzo Seler II contain, as well, many signs that represent the names of smaller units such as *barrios, estancias,* and boundaries. A knowledge of the Chocho language would be extremely helpful, if not essential, in any such study. The few glosses written on Codex Ixtlán and the Lienzo Antonio de León, as well as a number of the glosses on Lienzo Seler II, appear to be in Chocho—the principal native language spoken in the Coixtlahuaca region today.

Three related manuscripts which may be from the Coixtlahuaca or an adjacent region are the Gómez de Orozco Fragment, the Selden Roll, and Codex Baranda. The Gómez de Orozco Fragment is an animal-hide screenfold of three "pages"; this manuscript contains a large mythological-origin scene consisting of a descent from the sky to the earth on one side of the screenfold, and one page of genealogical data on the other side. A photographic color facsimile of the fragment and a detailed commentary concerning its content and its relationship to other manuscripts appear in Caso's *Interpretación del Códice Gómez de Orozco.* The fragment was in the collection of Federico Gómez de Orozco of Mexico City when it was published by Caso in 1954, and Gómez de Orozco stated that the manuscript reportedly came from

Cuicatlán, which is the district that adjoins the district of Coixtlahuaca on the east (*ibid.*, 7–8).

The Selden Roll, a manuscript on native paper and now in the Bodleian Library at Oxford, contains an elaborate mythological-origin scene, followed by ceremonial scenes, such as the presentation of offerings at a temple, the lighting of the New Fire, and human sacrifice. A black-and-white photographic reproduction of the Roll, plus a color plate of one detail, appear in: Cottie A. Burland and Gerdt Kutscher, *The Selden Roll* (Berlin, 1955).

Codex Baranda, in the Museo Nacional de Antropología in Mexico City (no. 35–4), is a short (four-page) screenfold of animal hide, painted on one side only. The codex begins with a group of place signs which includes a hill with an entwined serpent and which is analogous to similar groups of place signs in Antonio de León, Seler II, and the Selden Roll. The remainder of the manuscript consists of two horizontal rows of thirteen marriage pairs each; between these two rows is depicted a short series of events, one of which shows a Spanish conquistador receiving two gold necklaces from two native nobles. Caso's "Comentario al Códice Baranda" includes both color and black-and-white photographs of the manuscript, as well as an interpretation of its contents. He suggests that though Baranda begins with a mythological-origin scene similar to that seen in the Selden Roll and Lienzo Antonio de León, the codex may well be from a region outside the Mixteca, because it lacks the typically Mixtec A–O year sign, and the year dates in the manuscript appear to have a Central Mexican rather than a Mixtec correlation with Christian dates (*ibid.*, 375–77, 388–89).

The 1590 Land-Grant Map, AGN-Tierras 2729–5 (Fig. 46), was drawn to indicate the location of a piece of land which was granted in 1590 by Viceroy Luis de Velasco to Francisco de Mendoza, who is described as being the native ruler of Santo Domingo Tonalá, a dependency of Coixtlahuaca in the sixteenth century. The piece of land in question is shown in the center of the right side of the map as a rectangular enclosure with a horse's head in the center; above the rectangle is the gloss *cabellería* (a term used to describe a tract of land that is approximately 33⅓ acres).

At the left of the rectangle is a small church with a legend underneath: *sancto domingo tepenene y tonalla.* The town of Tonalá (the *tonalla* of the gloss) apparently no longer exists, but it must originally have been located close to—and may even have been the same town as—present-day Santo Domingo Tepelmeme, which is about seven miles north of Coixtlahuaca. Below this church is a place sign with a double-peaked hill containing what appears to be a serpent or a worm or a strip of cloth. Below this sign is written *tepenene*; it is possible that this sign represents the *pueblo viejo* (or former site) of Santo Domingo Tepelmeme. A wavy line connects the church of Santo Domingo Tepelmeme and the rectangle of the land grant, and this line is accompanied by the legend

una legua, indicating that the two sites are one league apart.

At the left of the church of Tepelmeme is the church and the place sign of Coixtlahuaca: two crossed serpents with feathered tails. Below this configuration is the identifying gloss *couayxtlabaca*. The place sign of Coixtlahuaca and the church of Tepelmeme are connected by two footprints which are annotated *tres leguas*, indicating that the two towns are three leagues apart. Above the Tepelmeme church, and connected to it by a line of footprints, is another church labeled *coception*, which represents the present-day town of Concepción Buenavista, about nine miles northwest of Coixtlahuaca. In the upper-right corner of the map is a place sign consisting of a hill and a female head; underneath this sign is the gloss *monte de ndaga,* or "hill of . . . [?]." The meaning of the word *ndaga* in this gloss is unknown, and it may be a Chocho rather than a Mixtec word.

The cardinal directions are also written on the map: west at the top, indicated by a European sun motif and the gloss *oeste*; north at the right, indicated by an asterisk and the gloss *norte*; east at the bottom, with a sun motif and the gloss *este*; and south at the left, indicated by the gloss *sur*. In the lower-right corner of the map is the certification, *esta pintura ba çierta y lo firmo de mi nombre* ("this painting is correct, and I sign it with my name"), followed by the signature *Jhoan del Oro* (?).

The map is drawn in ink on a sheet of European paper; paint, apparently a type of water color, is applied to the serpents of the Coixtlahuaca sign, the hill sign of Tepelmeme, the sign of *monte de ndaga*, and the two sun motifs at the top and bottom of the map. A color photograph of this map is included as Photo 33 of Ronald Spores, "Cultural Continuity and Native Rule in the Mixteca Alta, 1500–1600," unpublished Ph.D. dissertation, Department of Anthropology, Harvard University, 1964; but the map is not illustrated in Spores' *The Mixtec Kings and Their People*, which is based on this dissertation.

In the spring of 1970, as the manuscript of this book was nearing completion, two hitherto unrevealed sixteenth-century lienzos in the municipal archive of San Miguel Tequixtepec (a town about five miles north of Coixtlahuaca) were brought to the attention of Mexican and United States scholars. They are the Lienzos of San Miguel Tequixtepec 1 and 2 (*HMAI* Census Nos. 433 and 434). Though they are Colonial documents, both are painted in native style. Each presents a long genealogy, with the first one containing cartographic material as well. The persons depicted in both lienzos will be described by Alfonso Caso in his forthcoming biographical dictionary of the nobility who appear in all of the Mixtec manuscripts (*Reyes y reinos de la Mixteca*). A study of the genealogical and cartographic content of the two lienzos is being prepared by Ross Parmenter, who—after nine years of angling to see them—had them shown to him by the village authorities on April 29, 1970.

In Chapter VI on the Coastal region, the only sources that were discussed were those which were concerned with the Coastal town of Zacatepec and its relationship with Tututepec, the capital of the Coast. The purpose of this appendix is to summarize the unpublished and recently published sources which deal with the Coastal region in general.

UNPUBLISHED SOURCES

The principal unpublished sources utilized in the preparation of this book were a manuscript on the kingdom of Tututepec by the Oaxaca scholar Manuel Martínez Gracida and a group of documents from the Archivo General de la Nación.

The Martínez Gracida Manuscript on Tututepec

Manuel Martínez Gracida was a prolific writer on the history and geography of the State of Oaxaca, and many of his studies have yet to be published. (A list of the works of Martínez Gracida, both published and unpublished, is given in: "Bibliografía de Don Manuel Martínez Gracida," *Boletín de la Biblioteca Nacional*, 2a. época, Vol. VI-4 [1955], 48–72.) Among the most important of his unpublished manuscripts is "La reseña histórica del antiguo reino de Tututepec," completed in Guadalajara on December 25, 1907.

Three copies of the manuscript have been located, but unfortunately the present location of the nineteen plates that originally accompanied the manuscript is unknown. A typewritten copy of 360 pages is in the collection of Lic. Luis Castañeda Guzmán of Oaxaca, and this copy is also in the microfilm archive of the Centro de Investigaciones Históricas in Mexico City (Série Oaxaca, Rollo 132). In addition, a carbon-copy typescript of 228 pages is in the Van de Velde Collection at the University of New Mexico, where it is catalogued as No. 4–42 of the Collection. Both of these copies contain essentially the same material, but the Castañeda Guzmán copy is on letter-size paper, while the Van de Velde copy is on legal-size paper and thus fills fewer pages. According to Heinrich Berlin (*Fragmentos desconocidos del Códice de Yanhuitlán* [Mexico, 1947], 13–14), a third copy of 228 pages is in the collection of Carlos Cortés Bermúdez of Tututepec.

The Martínez Gracida manuscript contains a summary of the Spanish conquest of the State of Oaxaca (pp. 1–59

of the Van de Velde copy) based for the most part on published sources, and a detailed discussion of the native rulers of Tututepec and its neighbors in the early Colonial period (pp. 60–183 of the Van de Velde copy) drawn principally from unpublished documents. Martínez Gracida had access to many documents whose present location is now unknown; some of these are summarized in his text, while others are reproduced in their entirety.

The manuscript also includes three appendices: the first presents geographical information on some of the important towns on the Coast, data that are similar to those in Martínez Gracida's "*Cuadros sinópticos*"; the second is a short essay on Negroes in Oaxaca; the third describes the nineteen missing illustrations. The first two of the nineteen plates were of a pictorial manuscript, sometimes called the "Códice de Tututepec" (*HMAI* Census no. 372); the present location of the original codex from which the two plates were taken is also unknown. Martínez Gracida's description of the Tututepec Codex as well as other short passages of his history of Tututepec are published in Berlin, *op. cit.*, 29–49 *passim*.

Documents From the Archivo General de la Nación *(AGN)*

This important national archive contains many documents that deal with the Coastal region. The listing below does not include all the documents in the AGN that relate to the Coast but only those that are pertinent to this book. All but one of the documents included in the list are from the *Ramo de Tierras*—that is, documents concerning disputes over lands. The one exception is from the *Ramo de Vínculos*, which contains documents dealing with entailed estates.

Tututepec

Two groups of documents are concerned with litigation relating to the native rulers of Tututepec from 1554 to 1717: *Ramo de Tierras*, vol. 29, expediente 1, and *Ramo de Vínculos*, vol. 272, expedientes 8–10.

Tierras 29-1 (197 folios). The longest of the two documents includes lawsuits from 1554 to 1710:

fol. 1–9/v (1554–70): Ana de Sosa, the widow of Pedro de Alvarado, the native ruler of Tututepec, lists the *estancias* or subjects that are under her domain and claims that several of these subjects do not recognize her authority and are not paying their tribute.

fol. 9/v–39/v (1558–88): Melchor de Alvarado, son of Pedro de Alvarado and Ana de Sosa, wins his claim to be heir to the *cacicazgo* of Tututepec. This claim is contested by his half-brother Alonso de Mendoza, who states that he is the older son and that Melchor cannot inherit because his mother, Ana de Sosa, is not a noblewoman (*señora*) but a member of the secondary nobility (*principala*). Melchor maintains that Alonso is the illegitimate son of Pedro de Alvarado and his first wife, *Yacalnane* of Tlaxiaco.

fol. 40–73/v (fol. 72–73 and a fol. numbered 153 are now bound between fol. 65–66): In 1620 Angel de Guzmán y Alvarado, son of Angel de Villafaña y Alvarado and grandson of Alonso de Mendoza (the half-brother of Melchor de Alvarado) claims and is awarded the *cacicazgo* of Tututepec. Isabel de Alvarado, the widow of Melchor de Alvarado, withdraws her claim to the *cacicazgo*, with the request that she be given the revenue of two lakes and a *cacao* orchard, all within the territory of Tututepec, for her support.

fol. 74–80/v (1648–50): Jacinto de Guzmán, the minor son of Angel de Guzmán y Alvarado and Gracia de Guzmán (*cacica* of Chicahuaxtla and Chicahuaxtepec) becomes the ruler of Tututepec following the death of his father.

fol. 81–110 (1654–83): Jacinto de Guzmán has died without heirs, and the *cacicazgo* of Tututepec is awarded to Francisco Pimentel y Guzmán, the native ruler of Yanhuitlán and Teposcolula in the Mixteca Alta. In the 30 years following 1654, attempts are made to usurp some of the lands of Tututepec because Francisco Pimentel y Guzmán lives in Teposcolula.

fol. 110/v–93 (1694–1710): In 1694, following the death of Francisco de Pimentel y Guzmán, his minor son Agustín Carlos Pimentel Guzmán y Alvarado becomes *cacique* of Tututepec. Fol. 112–193 contain a detailed delineation made in 1710 of the lands belonging to Tututepec and its subject towns.

fol. 194–97/v (1634, 1661–62): The final folios are concerned with the intrusion of livestock in the lands of Pinotepa del Rey.

Sections of the Tierras 29–1 document are quoted or summarized in Heinrich Berlin, *Fragmentos desconocidos del Códice de Yanhuitlán*, 29–45 *passim*. Charts showing the genealogy of the native rulers of Tututepec and based on information given in this document appear in *ibid.*, 42; Caso, *Colombino*, following p. 85; and Chapter VI of this book. Lists of lands belonging to Tututepec from this document are included in Smith, *Colombino*, 60–61, 65, 76; 157, 162, 172.

Vínculos 272, 8–10 (91 folios). The second document concerning Tututepec complements and supplements the first and includes litigation from 1554 to 1717:

expediente 8, fol. 12–24/v (fol. 1–11 lacking): a copy of documents dated 1554–74 relating to the dispute over the *cacicazgo* of Tututepec between Melchor de Alva-

rado and his half-brother Alonso de Mendoza. Cf. Tierras 29–1, fol. 9/v–39/v.

fol. 24/v–45/v: a copy of documents dated 1620 dealing with the establishment of the claim of Angel de Guzmán to the *cacicazgo* of Tututepec. Cf. Tierras 29–1, fol. 40–73/v.

expediente 9, fol. 1–14/v: In 1640 Angel de Guzmán claims for his son Jacinto de Guzmán lands owned by his deceased wife Gracia de Guzmán, *cacica* of Chicahuaxtla and Chicahuaxtepec. The son is awarded possession of the lands of Huaxintepec and Amatitlán within the town of Huazolotitlán on the Coast. Between fol. 9 and 10 is a sketch map of the region south of Tututepec, indicating an abundance of land for pasture near the Pacific Ocean east of the Río San Francisco.

fol. 15–16/v: In 1707 Agustín Carlos Pimentel y Guzmán, *cacique* of Teposcolula and Tututepec, claims the town of Chicahuaxtepec in the Mixteca Alta.

expediente 10, fol. 17–36/v (there is no break in the pagination between expedientes 9 and 10): In 1591 Melchor de Alvarado, the native ruler of Tututepec, petitions for and is granted a site for cattle grazing within the boundaries of Tututepec. The site is named Atlixco in Nahuatl and *ñunduta* in Mixtec. On fol. 35 is a sketch map showing the approximate location of the site.

fol. 37–50: In 1715–17 Agustín Carlos Pimentel de Guzmán y Alvarado, *cacique* of Tututepec, claims that Cristóbal García of Sola has usurped lands within the towns of Juchatengo and Ixtapa, which are subjects of Tututepec. Included in this section (fol. 44–48/v) are documents dated 1653–54 concerning the establishment of Francisco Pimentel y Guzmán, the father of Agustín Carlos, as *cacique* of Tututepec.

Following fol. 50 are four folios of drawings that are a section of the Codex of Yanhuitlán.

Excerpts of the written portion of this document have been published in Heinrich Berlin, *Fragmentos desconocidos del Códice de Yanhuitlán*, 43–44, 53 ff., and in Guillermo S. Fernández de Recas, *Cacicazgos y nobilario indígena de la Nueva España* (Mexico, 1961), 193–200. Berlin also published the four folios of the Codex of Yanhuitlán appended to the document (*op. cit.*, plates A–G); and lists of the subject towns of Tututepec given in this document are included in Smith, *Colombino*, 76–79; 172–75. A pictorial manuscript presented in 1717 at the time of the dispute between Tututepec and Sola and described on fol. 42/v–44 has been identified as Codex Colombino (Smith, *Tlalocan*, IV–3, 283–88).

Tlacamama-Pinotepa del Rey

Three documents in the *Ramo de Tierras* deal with the entanglements of the *cacicazgos* of the Coastal towns of Tlacamama and Pinotepa del Rey (present-day Pinotepa Nacional). The genealogical data in these documents are presented in Chart 23; the names of those persons who were considered to have been *caciques* or *cacicas* are in capital letters. As can be seen in the chart, the two *cacicazgos* were related by marriage in the sixteenth century, and much of the later litigation is concerned with attempts by the native ruler of one town to gain control over the other.

2729–1 (37 folios). This document contains litigation dated 1574–78 between Diego Mejía and Domingo Salmerón as to which is the native ruler of Tlacamama. Salmerón claims the *cacicazgo* because he is the husband of Ana, the second daughter of Don Diego, who was *cacique* of Tlacamama. Mejía is the son of a Spaniard named Melchor Mejía and Isabel, the first daughter of Don Diego of Tlacamama. Mejía wins his case on the basis of primogeniture—that is, his mother was the first daughter of the ruler of Tlacamama, and thus the *cacicazgo* passes to her offspring rather than to her sister Ana, the second daughter of Don Diego. One of the witnesses for Diego Mejía gives the Mixtec names of Mejía's great-grandparents (the parents of Don Diego), who were presumably the rulers of Tlacamama at the time of the Spanish conquest. The great-grandfather's name is *toca-quihuic,* or "the ruler 1, 2, or 12 Alligator." (*To-* is a shortened form of *toho* or "ruler"; *caquihuic* or *caquevui* is the calendrical name 1, 2, or 12 Alligator.) The name of the great-grandmother is *yya yta,* or "the noblewoman of the flowers." (*Yya* denotes a person of noble birth; *yta* or *ita* is "flower.") Neither of these persons seems to be represented in the known Mixtec pictorial manuscripts.

116–4 (26 folios). This document contains litigation dated 1675–77 dealing with a dispute over the *cacicazgo* of Pinotepa del Rey between Pedro Mejía, *cacique* of Tlacamama, and Joseph Salmerón and his sister María. In the course of the litigation, Pedro Mejía traces his genealogy back to his great-great-great-grandparents Don Diego and Doña María, native rulers of Tlacamama in the sixteenth century. Joseph and María Salmerón trace their genealogy back to their great-grandfather Domingo Salmerón. Joseph and María Salmerón are the illegitimate children of Francisco Salmerón, formerly *cacique* of Pinotepa, and Sebastiana Rodríguez; Francisco Salmerón, in turn, was the illegitimate son of Pedro Salmerón I and Angelina de Tapia. It is claimed in this document that there is no legal

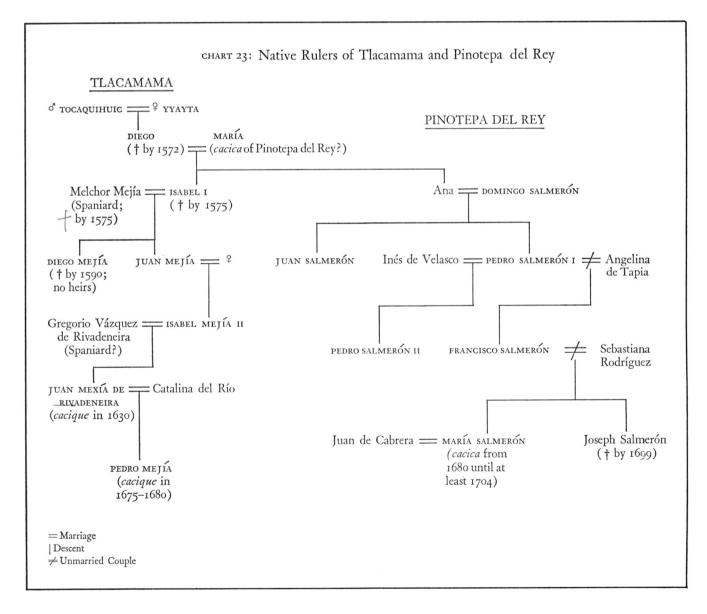

CHART 23: Native Rulers of Tlacamama and Pinotepa del Rey

precedent against the succession of illegitimate children to a *cacicazgo* and that if they are recognized by the town as *caciques*, then they are in effect the legitimate heirs (fol. 6/v–7). The Salmerón family introduces documents of the 1630's concerning an earlier phase of the same dispute, this time between Juan Mejía de Rivadeneira (the father of Pedro Mejía) and Pedro de Salmerón, which was settled in favor of Salmerón.

On November 26, 1676, the *cacicazgo* of Pinotepa del Rey is awarded to Pedro Mejía, and he takes possession of the sites belonging to the *cacicazgo*. At each of the sites in question a contradiction to Mejía's possession is voiced by María Salmerón. In addition, a petition is presented by the officials of Pinotepa requesting that María de Salmerón be awarded the *cacicazgo* and claiming that Pedro Mejía is a Spaniard and therefore anathema. (Fol. 24: ". . . y protestamos segir esta contradision asta gastar nuestras probecas y las nuestras muxeres y hijos y por el bien que reconosemos en nuestra cacica y lo mal que emos de pasar con un español pues saue Vmd. que los españoles son el cancer y las enfermedades y destruysion de los yndios . . .")

1875–3 (157 folios). In 1680 the decision made in the document discussed above (116–4) is reversed, and María de Salmerón is awarded the *cacicazgo* of Pinotepa del Rey and takes possession of the lands belonging to the *cacicazgo* (fol. 12–27).

Much of the remainder of the document is concerned with litigation dated 1699 to 1704 over sites within Pinotepa del Rey that were claimed both by the Mariscal de Castilla and by the *cacica* of Pinotepa, María Salmerón (fol.1–11, 28–132). According to María Salmerón, the sites in question have been rented to the Jesuits of the Colegio del Espíritu Santo of Puebla as grazing lands for sheep (*estancia para ganado menor*).

Also included is a petition dated 1578–79 made by Luis Pérez of Oaxaca for a grazing site for cattle (*estancia de ganado mayor*) within the town of Tlacamama (fol. 133–48); the petition is accompanied by a sketch map showing the location of the site (fol. 147). At the end of the document (fol. 149–57) is a petition dated 1780 submitted by Juan de Andrade of Pinotepa del Rey for permission to operate a sugar mill named Trapiche de Santa María del Rincón on lands rented from Agustín de Ovando.

Zacatepec

Two documents in the *Ramo de Tierras* deal with the native rulers of Zacatepec and their holdings in the seventeenth and early eighteenth centuries. The genealogical information presented in the first of these is discussed in Chapter VI, above; the lists of boundaries of Zacatepec in 1702 presented in the second document are discussed in Chapter VII.

1359–2 (17 folios). This document is concerned with various subjects relating to the *cacicazgo* of Zacatepec from 1600 to 1658:

> fol. 1–2 (1600): Luisa de Mendoza, widow of Pedro de Alvarado I, *cacique* of Zacatepec and Chayucu, requests a cornfield and a cotton field, as well as the personal service of an Indian man and woman, so that she can maintain her position as *cacica*.

> fol. 3–5 (1638): Last will and testament of María de Alvarado, granddaughter of Pedro de Alvarado I and wife of Francisco de Luna, *cacique* of Jicayán de Tovar. She leaves the *cacicazgo* of Zacatepec and Chayucu to her infant daughter María de Luna y Alvarado, to be administered by the child's father while the daughter is a minor.

> fol. 6–11 (1639): Following the death of María de Alvarado, testimony is given concerning the authenticity of the claims of her heirs to the *cacicazgo* of Zacatepec and Chayucu.

> fol. 12–17 (1648–58): Francisco Maldonado y Alvarado, *cacique* of Zacatepec and Chayucu following the death of Francisco de Luna, claims that Pedro García of Zacatepec is renting the lands of the *cacicazgo* to Spaniards for grazing sites and not paying the rent to the *cacique*.

192–5 (32 folios). In 1702, thirty witnesses give testimony in a dispute between the natives of Zacatepec and the Indian nobility as to whether a hacienda within the boundaries of Zacatepec and rented to the Jesuits of Puebla belongs to the community or to the *caciques*. Each witness also lists the names of the boundaries of Zacatepec. The two *caciques* against whom the suit is brought are Jacinto de Guzmán of Putla and Jacinto Maldonado y Alvarado of Tlapatzingo and Tonalá. Jacinto Maldonado's sister, Petrona Maldonado y Alvarado, is named as the *cocica* of San Agustín Chayucu, San Cristóbal, Santa María *nutíoo*, and Zacatepec.

Amusgos-Cacahuatepec

Tierras 191–3 (97 folios). In the early eighteenth century (1701–1706) a long-standing dispute between Amusgos and Cacahuatepec is revived: Diego de Santiago Ávila y Velasco, the native ruler of Amusgos and Ipalapa, claims to be the native ruler of Cacahuatepec as well; the *cacicazgo* of Cacahuatepec is also claimed by Francisco Bernardino Mejía, who is considered by the native ruler of Amusgos to be a *principal* or member of the secondary nobility. In the course of the litigation both men testify concerning their genealogy, and this information is summarized in Charts 24 and 25, in which the names of those persons considered to have been *caciques* are in capital letters. The document includes a review conducted in 1702 of the boundaries of Cacahuatepec with the neighboring towns of Jicayán, Ixcapa, Ometepec, and Xochistlahuaca (fol. 27–31/v), as well as the testimony of witnesses concerning these boundaries (fol. 16–22/v).

Both sides of the dispute present documents dated earlier than the eighteenth century to support their respective claims. Francisco Bernardino Mejía includes in the documents supporting his case three last wills and testaments of persons he claims are earlier rulers of Cacahuatepec: his great-uncle Diego Mejía y Mendoza (whose will is dated February 3, 1658), his great-aunt Francisca de Villafaña (whose will is dated August 5, 1677), and his

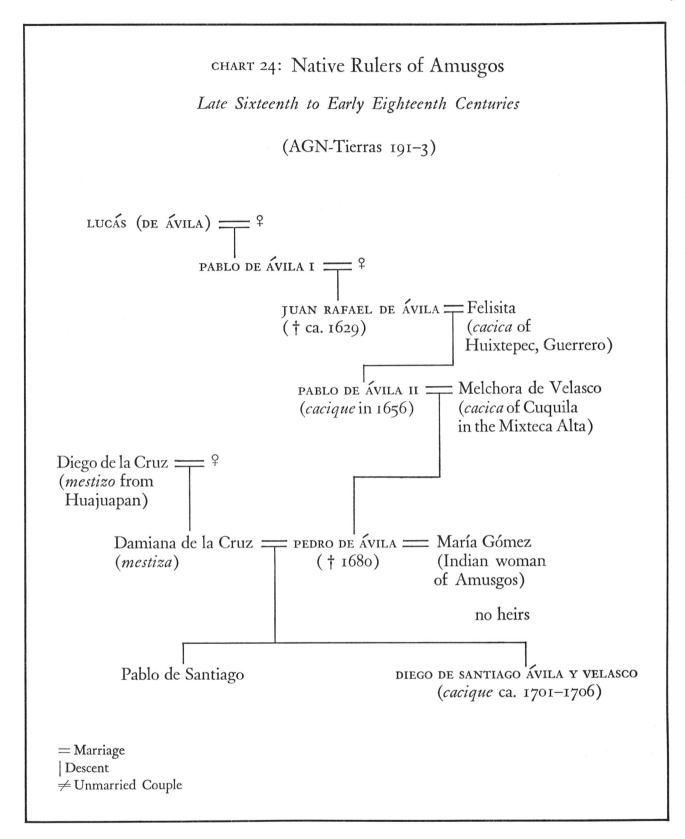

CHART 24: Native Rulers of Amusgos

Late Sixteenth to Early Eighteenth Centuries

(AGN-Tierras 191–3)

LUCÁS (DE ÁVILA) ══ ♀

PABLO DE ÁVILA I ══ ♀

JUAN RAFAEL DE ÁVILA ══ Felisita
(† ca. 1629)   (*cacica* of
                                 Huixtepec, Guerrero)

PABLO DE ÁVILA II ══ Melchora de Velasco
(*cacique* in 1656)   (*cacica* of Cuquila
                           in the Mixteca Alta)

Diego de la Cruz ══ ♀
(*mestizo* from
Huajuapan)

Damiana de la Cruz ══ PEDRO DE ÁVILA ══ María Gómez
(*mestiza*)   († 1680)   (Indian woman
                                              of Amusgos)

                                              no heirs

Pablo de Santiago   DIEGO DE SANTIAGO ÁVILA Y VELASCO
                                     (*cacique* ca. 1701–1706)

══ Marriage
│ Descent
≠ Unmarried Couple

father Luis Bernardino (whose will is dated December 6, 1692). The three original wills are in Nahuatl (fol. 6–11/v), accompanied by a translation into Spanish (fol. 13–15). Diego de Santiago Ávila y Velasco of Amusgos presents documents dated 1625 concerning the boundaries between Amusgos and Jicayán (fol. 72–75/v); the last will and testament of his great-grandfather Juan Rafael de Ávila, dated 1629 (fol. 70–72); and testimony dated 1680 concerning the *cacicazgo* of Amusgos and its lands, as well as a review made in that year of the boundaries of Amusgos with the neighboring towns of Zacatepec, Tlacamama, Jicayán and Cacahuatepec (fol. 40/v–59/v).

Also included are documents of the 1650's (fol. 62/v–70, 77–97) which deal with an earlier phase of the same dis-

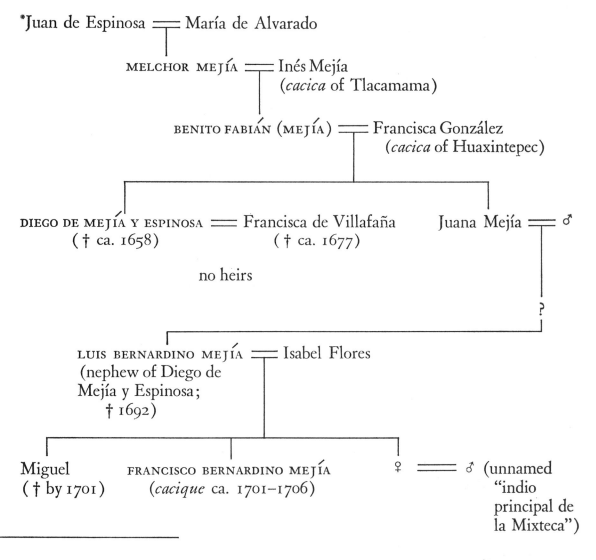

CHART 25: Native Rulers of Cacahuatepec

Late Sixteenth to Early Eighteenth Centuries

(AGN-Tierras 191–3)

= Marriage
| Descent
≠ Unmarried Couple

*This generation is never described as being the native rulers or *caciques* of Cacahua-tepec, although their son Melchor de Mejía is called the *cacique* of the town.

pute, this time between Pablo de Ávila II of Amusgos and Diego de Mejía y Espinosa of Cacahuatepec. Both men claim to be the native ruler of Cacahuatepec, and Ávila attempts to demonstrate that Mejía y Espinosa is an interloper who has no hereditary rights to Cacahuatepec. Nonetheless, on June 30, 1656, the *cacicazgo* of Cacahuatepec is awarded to Diego de Mejía y Espinosa.

The references made in this document to a pictorial manuscript on cloth that is described as having belonged to the native rulers of Amusgos in the seventeenth century are quoted and discussed in Appendix B–6 of this book.

Land-Grant Petitions

A common type of land document in the Coastal region, as well as in other regions of Mexico, is a petition for a grazing site for cattle and horses (*estancia de ganado mayor*). These sites were supposed to be located on lands that were unoccupied and uncultivated (*tierras baldías*). Of the eight documents from the *Ramo de Tierras* listed below, all but three (2777-7, 43-2, and 1877-6) are accompanied by sketch maps which show the location of the site in relation to the nearby towns. None of the five sketch maps bound with the land-grant documents listed here shows any indication of native style, as does a map accompanying a similar document from the Coixtlahuaca region (Fig. 46).

2776-7 (10 folios). In 1575-76 a grazing site for cattle and horses near the Pacific Ocean and within the towns of Pinotepa del Rey and Potutla is petitioned for, and awarded to, Martín Núñez, the son-in-law of conquistador Pedro Nieto. The officials of Pinotepa present a supporting petition—in Nahuatl. At the end of Núñez' petition it is stated that the written documents are not accompanied by a map showing the location of the site because there are no painters on the Coast ("La pintura que su Excelencia manda por su mandamiento no se envía atento que en esta costa no hay pintores . . ."). However, a map accompanies a petition from the same region dated three years later (Tierras 2737-29, listed below).

1875-2 (16 folios). In 1576 Alonso de Tarifa requests, and is granted, a site named Coatepec within the boundaries of Tututepec, to be used as a grazing site for cattle and horses.

2737-29 (19 folios). In 1578-79 a grazing site for cattle and horses within Tlacamama is petitioned for, and granted to, Lázaro Juárez.

3343-11 (10 folios). In 1579-80 a grazing site for cattle and horses within the boundaries of Pinotepa del Rey is petitioned for, and granted to, Pedro Bravo.

43-2 (8 folios). This document refers to the land grant made to Pedro Bravo in the document listed directly above. In 1579 the natives of Tlacamama object to the grant because the site in question is too close to the Río de Tlacamama where they have their fields.

2776-8 (20 folios). In 1580 Martín de Pedrosa petitions for a grazing site near the border between the towns of Pinotepa del Rey and Tlacamama. The officials of Tlaca-

mama object, because their fields are between the site in question and the Río de Tlacamama where the cattle will go for water. The objection is overruled, and the land is granted to Pedrosa.

2776-16 (13 folios). In 1580-81 a second grazing site for cattle within the boundaries of Pinotepa del Rey is petitioned for, and awarded to, Martín de Pedrosa.

1877-6 (22 folios). A dispute in 1676 between Pedro Martín of Puebla, the administrator of grants for grazing lands in the Coastal region ("provincia de Xicayan") and the Royal Auditor concerning the exact number and location of grazing sites in the Coastal region west of the Río Verde. The locations of thirteen of these sites are described in detail, and the descriptions include the Mixtec names of the sites. Objections are raised by Juan Martínez de Zorzano, Pedro Martín's lawyer, to the use of native maps in land litigation; these objections, plus the answer to them given by the Royal Auditor, are quoted in Appendix B–8.

RECENTLY PUBLISHED SOURCES

Most of the works on the Coast discussed briefly below were published in the present century. The published sources of the Colonial period are cited and analyzed in the books by Berlin and Byam Davies listed directly below.

History

A very useful summary of the history of Tututepec in the early Colonial period is found in Heinrich Berlin's *Fragmentos desconocidos del Códice de Yanhuitlán y otras investigaciones mixtecas* (Mexico, 1947). Berlin's study is divided into two sections. The first of these deals with the native rulers of Tututepec during the sixteenth century and quotes extensively from unpublished sources such as documents from the AGN and the Martínez Gracida manuscript on Tututepec. The second section describes the eight pages of the Codex of Yanhuitlán that are bound with documents relating to Tututepec in AGN-Vínculos 272 and are illustrated as Plates A through H of Berlin's study. The accompanying illustrations also include photographs of stone sculpture housed near the church of Tututepec (the stone figure illustrated in Fig. 3 is now in the Museo Nacional de Antropología in Mexico City), as well as line drawings of seven clay figures from the Tututepec region.

A second study which characterizes the holdings of Tututepec on the eve of the Spanish conquest is Claude Nigel Byam Davies' volume on those regions of Mexico that were independent of the Aztec Empire (*Los señoríos independientes del Imperio Azteca* [Mexico, 1968], 181-213). Byam Davies summarizes the material on Tututepec published in both the Colonial and modern periods and includes a map that shows the extent of Tututepec's tribute empire and the range of its military expeditions.

Archaeology

The first extensive archaeological survey of the Coastal region is being conducted at the present time by Professor Donald Brockington of the University of North Carolina. In the spring of 1969 he and his students surveyed the section of the Coast from Pochutla to the Río Verde, and in the spring of 1970 they worked in the sections west of the Río Verde to the Oaxaca-Guerrero border and east of Pochutla.

In the 126 sites examined, Brockington has found no pre-ceramic remains and little evidence of early pre-Classic ceramics. In the late pre-Classic and early Classic periods the Coast seems to have been relatively isolated from the great urban styles of Middle America, for there is little evidence of influence from the large Classic sites of Monte Albán and Teotihuacán. Ceramics of the late Classic period show an affinity with Maya style and may be related to contemporary ceramics of Tabasco on the Atlantic Coast. Brockington feels that the strong Maya influence in the late-Classic period substantiates the hypothesis made by Manuel Gamio in 1926 that the Coastal region of Oaxaca was one of the routes that linked the Maya region with Central Mexico. In the post-Classic period, the predominant ceramic types are two typically "Mixtec" wares: red-on-cream and fine polychrome, with the former being the most prevalent.

In connection with the current excavations, María Jorrín is preparing a master's thesis for the University of North Carolina on the group of thirty-four carved stone monuments found on the Coast. Miss Jorrín has isolated two different, apparently contemporary carving styles. The first of these is associated with stone monuments from Nopala and Chila, both near the Río Manialtepec, with Nopala being 27 miles northeast of Tututepec, and Chila about 19 miles south of Nopala and near the Pacific Coast. The second carving style is found in monuments from Río Grande, a town near the river of the same name and located about 17 miles southeast of Tututepec.

In excavations conducted in February and March, 1962, Donald Brockington concentrated on the site of Sipolite, near Puerto Angel, about 70 miles east of Tututepec and outside the Mixtec-speaking region (*The Archaeological Sequence from Sipolite, Oaxaca, Mexico,* published on microcards by The Society for American Archaeology and the University of Wisconsin Press [Madison, Wisconsin, 1966; Archives of Archaeology, No. 28]).

Brockington classified the ceramics from this site as belonging to three periods. Those of the earliest period seemed to share a common tradition with Monte Albán I and II ceramics of the Valley of Oaxaca, although the Coastal ceramics were not closely related to the contemporary styles from the Valley. The ceramics of the middle period from Sipolite were early Classic in style with many survivals from the late pre-Classic period; they showed greater influence from the Maya regions of Chiapas and Tabasco than from the Valley of Oaxaca. This affinity with the Maya region is also seen in the third period at Sipolite, where the ceramics of the late Classic and possibly early post-Classic are comparable to Tepeu 2 and 3 of the lowland Maya region. Brockington characterizes the ceramic development at Sipolite as "conserva-tive, long-lived and continuous" and suggests that this site may not have had close ties with other regions of Middle America because of its small population and comparative isolation.

In January and February of 1956, Gabriel de Cicco and Brockington made a brief survey of various sites on the Coast between Pinotepa Nacional and Pochutla (De Cicco and Brockington, *Reconocimiento arqueológico en el suroeste de Oaxaca* [Mexico, 1956]; and Brockington, "A Brief Report on an Archaeological Survey of the Oaxacan Coast," *Mesoamerican Notes,* Vol. V [Mexico, 1957], 98–104). A more detailed study of the late pre-Classic and early Classic site of Piedra Parada, located about three miles north of the airfield that serves the town of Jamiltepec, is presented in Brockington, "Piedra Parada: A Comparative Study of a Site in Jamiltepec, Oaxaca," unpublished M.A. thesis, University of the Americas, Mexico, D. F., 1957. A very brief consideration of Coastal archaeology by Román Piña Chán ("Algunos sitios arqueológicos de Oaxaca y Guerrero," *RMEA*, Vol. XVI [1960], 65–76) summarizes the material published by Brockington, discusses several sites not visited by Brockington, and includes illustrations of some of the stone sculpture found on the Coast. The platforms and stone sculpture found at one site near Pinotepa Nacional have been described briefly by Lorenzo Gamio ("Zona arqueológica Cola de Palma, Pinotepa Nacional, Oaxaca," *Boletín del INAH*, No. 28, 25–28 [Mexico, 1967]).

Prior to the excavations of the past fifteen years, the archaeology of the Coast was almost totally unknown. As noted above under "History," Berlin published in 1947 the stone sculpture in Tututepec and a few figurines from the Tututepec region. Antonio Peñafiel included drawings of two stone sculptures from the Coast in his *Monumentos del arte mexicano antiguo* (Berlin, 1890), plates 138 and 225. Peñafiel's plate 225 is a drawing of a female warrior from Santa Cruz Tututepec; this piece of sculpture is also illustrated as a photograph in Berlin, *Fragmentos desconocidos*, Figs. 1 and 2. Peñafiel's plate 138 is a drawing of an impressive Olmecoid monolith which now stands in front of the church in Jamiltepec; it is illustrated as a photograph in De Cicco and Brockington, *Reconocimiento arqueológico*, Figs. 4 and 5. Information on the provenience of the Jamiltepec monolith is given in T. Maler, "Notes sur la Basse Mixtèque," *Revue d'ethnologie,* II (1883), 159–60. When Maler visited the Coast, this monolith was not in Jamiltepec, but resting on its side, covered with dirt and vegetation, at a site named Los Herreros on the east or Tututepec side of the Río Verde.

Ethnology

The town of Jamiltepec is the subject of two recent studies: Thomas Stanford describes the contemporary music of this town ("Datos sobre la música y danzas de Jamiltepec, Oaxaca," *Anales del INAH*, Vol. XV [Mexico, 1962], 187–200), and Susana Drucker focuses on this town in her examination of the sociological factors connected with the abandonment of native costume in favor of European dress (*Cambio de indumentaria: La estructura social y el abandono de la vestimenta indigena en La Villa de Santiago Jamiltepec* [Mexico, 1963; Instituto Nacional Indigenista; Colección de Antropología Social, 3]).

The plants and foods which are believed by the various ethnic groups on the Coast to have medicinal properties are characterized by Lucille N. Kaplan and Lawrence Kaplan, "Medicinal Plant and Food Use as Related to Health and Disease in Coastal Oaxaca," in: Anthony F. C. Wallace, ed., *Men and Cultures: Selected Papers of the Fifth International Congress of Anthropological and Ethnological Sciences, Philadelphia, September 1–9, 1956* (Philadelphia, 1960), 452–58.

A more general book that is both helpful and interesting is Gutierre Tibón, *Pinotepa Nacional: mixtecos, negros, triques* (Mexico, 1962). Tibón describes his visits to Pinotepa Nacional, Tututepec, Jamiltepec, Zacatepec, and Putla, and he records many local legends and conversations with inhabitants of these towns.

A study that deals with a region of the Coast within the State of Guerrero and adjacent to the Mixtec-speaking region is Gonzalo Aguirre Beltrán's monograph on the town of Cuajinicuilapa (*Cuijla: esbozo etnográfico de un pueblo negro* [Mexico, 1956]), which is based on field research and on Colonial documents in the AGN.

Geography

The purple shellfish dye industry on the Coast, which has its center in Pinotepa de Don Luis, is discussed in two articles by Peter Gerhard: "Emperors' Dye of the Mixtecs," *Natural History*, Vol. LXXIII–1 (January 1964), 26–31; and "Shellfish Dye in America," *ICA* XXXV, Vol. III (Mexico, 1964), 184–85. The dye is used principally in the distinctive striped wrap-around skirts which are woven in Pinotepa de Don Luis. (Examples of these skirts are seen in Fig. 142 of this study.)

Other contemporary industries on the Coast have been examined by Professor Herbert M. Eder of California State College at Hayward: "Turtling in Coastal Oaxaca," *Pacific Discovery*, XXII–1 (January-February 1969), 10–15; and "Palms and Man in Coastal Oaxaca, Mexico," *Yearbook of the Association of Pacific Coast Geographers, 1969*, in press. Professor Eder is at present preparing a book on "The Changing Cultural Geography of Coastal Oaxaca."

A useful geographic and demographic survey of the Coastal region between the Río Ometepec and the Río Copalita was issued by the Mexican Government's Committee on the Río Balsas: Comite de Estudios de la Cuenca del Río Balsas, *Estudios del Río Verde* (Mexico, Secretaría de Recursos Hidraúlicos, 1961), 1 vol. text and 1 vol. atlas. This study contains a variety of information on the actual and potential economic resources of the Coast, with primary emphasis on the hydrological resources. The accompanying atlas contains thirty-two maps, which present data on the distribution of indigenous languages, density of indigenous population, transportation and communications, and so on.

APPENDIX E

The Mixtec Glosses on Map No. 36

Three groups of glosses in the Mixtec language appear on Map No. 36 (Fig. 21): those written near the persons and buildings in the center of the map, those written next to the place signs around the border of the map, and those written in the rectangular fields below the river in the lower half of the map. A translation will be suggested for all of these glosses in the discussion below. In some instances, my transcription of the glosses that accompany the place signs on the border of Map No. 36 is different from that published by Vladamiro Rosado Ojeda in his 1945 study of the map; and when this is the case, Rosado Ojeda's transcription is included along with my transcription. I am grateful to Señora Zita Basich de Canessi, curator of the Bodega de Códices at the Museo Nacional in Mexico City, for allowing me to study Map No. 36 in the summer of 1969.

GLOSSES IN THE CENTRAL SECTION

1. Building at right of church
   a. across roof of building: *haey ñodi* "the house of Huajuapan de León"
   b. accompanying male figure within building: *y[ia] coghi* "the nobleman 1, 2, or 3 Movement"
   c. accompanying female figure within building: *yia çiy nacuxi* "the noblewoman 8-Flint"
2. Building at left of church
   a. above roof of building: *çoco xahuaco* "the well or birthplace of 7-Flower"
   b. accompanying male figure within building: *yia caxa* "the nobleman 1, 2, or 12 Eagle"
   c. accompanying female figure within building: *yia goxayu* "the noblewoman 1, 2 or 3 Rabbit"
3. Accompanying figure of 8-Death below the central church:
   yia na maho
   cuiy daa niy
   "the nobleman 8-Death 'Tiger-[?]'"
   Yia or *yya* denotes a person of nobility, and *namaho* is the calendrical name 8-Death. The second line of this short text seems to set forth the personal name of 8-Death. The first word, *cuiy*, means "tiger" in the dialect of Mixtec written on Map No. 36. The meaning of the last two words, *daa niy*, is not certain. The only male ruler named 8-Death who is shown in the Mixtec histories as living about the time of the

Spanish conquest is 8-Death "Tiger-Fire Serpent" in Codex Bodley (Fig. 40), who is known from Colonial documents to be the ruler of Yanhuitlán in the Mixteca Alta during the early Colonial period. Should the Mixtec name *daa niy* in the gloss accompanying the figure of 8-Death in Map No. 36 mean "Fire Serpent," then the person on Map No. 36 would be the same as the person shown in Bodley.

GLOSSES ACCOMPANYING THE PLACE SIGNS AROUND THE BORDER

Each of the thirty-seven place signs arranged in a rectangle around the border of Map No. 36 is accompanied by a gloss of the same place name in Mixtec. (One possible exception to the general rule that the Mixtec glosses correspond to the place signs near which they are written occurs on the left side of the map, where the gloss written near the seventh sign from the bottom appears to refer to the eighth sign, and vice versa.)

The discussion of the place signs and glosses that follows will include a brief description of the pictorial sign, a transcription of the Mixtec gloss and the equivalent of the gloss in the dialect of the Alvarado dictionary, a suggested translation of the gloss, and comments when they are relevant. The signs are numbered and discussed in the same order as they were in Rosado Ojeda's 1945 study of the map: the signs on the left side are numbered from 1 to 10 from bottom to top, those on the top border from 1 to 10 from left to right, those on the right border from 1 to 6 from top to bottom, and those on the bottom border from 1 to 11 from right to left.

Left Border (bottom to top)

Sign 1-left
Description: a double hill that is split in the center
Mixtec gloss: *yucu ño tica*
Equivalent in the Alvarado dictionary dialect: *yucu ñu ndeca*
Translation: "the hill of the open or spread place"
   yucu = "hill"
   ñu- = a prefix indicating "place" or "land"
   ndeca = "to open (as the mouth, or a book), spread"

Sign 2-left
Description: a hill with two peaks and a ravine in the center; within the ravine is a plant

Mixtec gloss: *yuhui yaa çiy*
    (Rosado Ojeda: *yuqui yaa ciy*)
Equivalent in the Alvarado dictionary dialect: *yuvui yaha dzii*
Translation: "the ravine of the fibrous or withered chile pepper"
    yuvui = "ravine"
    yaha = "chile pepper"
    dzii = "fibrous; withered"

Sign 3-left

Description: a hill which contains a circle made up of small interlocking circles (a ball of copal incense?)
Mixtec gloss: *yucu ño cutu*
Equivalent in the Alvarado dictionary dialect: *yucu ñu cutu*
Translation: "the hill where there is copal incense"
    yucu = "hill"
    ñu- = a prefix that designates place, where something exists
    cutu = "copal incense"

Sign 4-left

Description: a hill with the head of an animal with large black spots or patches
Mixtec gloss: *yucu cama*
    (Rosado Ojeda: *yucu ama*)
Translation: "the hill of [the animal with] patches [a type of dog?]"
    yucu = "hill"
    cama = "patch"
Comments: The word *cama* is undoubtedly a term used locally in the Mixteca Baja, but not elsewhere in the Mixteca, to refer to an animal with spots, perhaps a type of dog. In the Tupeus dictionary from southern Puebla, the term *cama* means "patch," a meaning not given for *cama* in the Alvarado dictionary from the Mixteca Alta.

Sign 5-left

Description: a hill that contains a tree or plant
Mixtec gloss: *cuiti tno yaa*
    (Rosado Ojeda: *cuti tno yaa*)
Equivalent in the Alvarado dictionary dialect: *cuiti tnu yaa*
Translation: "the mound of the oak tree or of the palo de mulato"
    cuiti = "mound"
    tnu yaa = "oak tree" (*roble*) and also a tree known popularly as "palo de mulato" (*Zanthoxylum fagara*)

Sign 6-left

Description: a terraced pyramidal structure with a horizontal black band near the base
Mixtec gloss: *no tayu cuixi*
    (Rosado Ojeda: *ito tayu cuxi*)
Equivalent in the Alvarado dictionary dialect: *nuu tayu cuisi*
Translation: "in front of or at the white altar"
    nuu = "in front of, at"
    tayu = "altar"
    cuisi = "white"

Sign 7-left

Description: a hill that contains a pattern resembling a turtle shell
Mixtec gloss: *yucu ñoo*
Equivalent in the Alvarado dictionary dialect: *yucu ñuhu*
Translation: "the mountain," "the hill of earth"; or "the hill of the turtledove"
Comments: It seems very likely that the gloss *yucu ñoo* refers to sign 8-left, a hill with a bird, and that the gloss on sign 8-left—*yucu yqui* or "hill of the turtle-shell"—refers to this sign, which is a hill with a turtle-shell pattern. In the Alvarado dictionary, the word *ñuhu* appears as part of the Mixtec names of several types of birds: the turtledove is given as *caa ñuhu cuiya*, the partridge and quail as *caa ñuhu*, and the vulture as *teyoco ñuhu*. The principal reason that the turtledove is given in the translation above is that in one of the eighteenth-century documents listed in the chart on p. 155, the Mixtec name *yucu ñuun*, a boundary between the Mixteca Baja towns of Chila and Acaquizapan and perhaps analogous to the *yucu ñoo* gloss on Map No. 36, is translated as "hill of the turtledoves."

    A second possibility is that the gloss *yucu ñoo* does refer to sign 7-left, because this Mixtec place name can also mean "mountain" or literally "hill of earth," and the irregular patterns within the hill might represent patches of earth. However, if this were the case, there would still remain the problem of the Mixtec gloss accompanying sign 3-left, which does not appear to relate at all to that sign, but does relate to sign 7-left.

Sign 8-left

Description: a hill with a bird
Mixtec gloss: *yucu yqui*
    (Rosado Ojeda: *yucu yhni*)
Equivalent in the Alvarado dictionary dialect: *yucu yeque*
Translation: "hill of the turtleshell"
    yucu = "hill"
    yeque = "turtleshell, bone"
Comments: As was discussed above under sign 7-left, the gloss *yucu yqui* probably refers to that sign; and the gloss that accompanies sign 7-left (*yucu ñoo* or "hill of the turtledove") refers to sign 8-left.

Sign 9-left

Description: a hill with a vertical band of footprints to represent a road
Mixtec gloss: *yucu ychin*
Equivalent in the Alvarado dictionary dialect: *yucu ichi*
Translation: "the hill of the road"
    yucu = "hill"
    ichi = "road"

Sign 10-left

Description: a hill with an animal ear appended to each side of the hill sign

Mixtec gloss: *tutno ñañan*

Equivalent in the Alvarado dictionary dialect: *tutnu ñaña*

Translation: "the ears of the cat"

  tutnu = "ears"

  ñaña = "cat"

Comments: *Ñaña* is a word that seems to be used to designate various types of carnivorous quadrupeds. In the Alvarado dictionary, it is given as the word for "cat" (*gato*) and "male fox" (*raposo*). In the Coastal region, I was told in Tututepec that *ñaña* referred to the pine marten (*marta*) and in Jamiltepec it was said to be the word for "puma" (*león*).

  This place sign in Map No. 36 seems to be the same as a place sign on page 18 of Codex Sánchez Solís. The latter sign consists of a hill with an ocelot head at the top and with a large ocelot ear projecting from the right side of the hill; the sign is accompanied by the gloss *tutno ñaña*. The place shown in Sánchez Solís seems to be a town rather than merely a boundary site because it appears with a named marriage pair, presumably the rulers of the place. The present-day name of the town whose Mixtec name is *tutnu ñaña* is not known, although this town may well be in the Mixteca Baja, because the pages that follow the appearance of this sign in the Codex, pages 20–25, are concerned with the rulers of two towns in the Mixteca Baja: Acatlán (whose sign appears on pages 20, 23, and 24) and Tequixtepec del Rey (whose sign appears on pages 22 and 25).

Top Border (left to right)

Sign 1-top

Description: a stone with a quadruped (probably a rat)

Mixtec gloss: *yuu tata yyn* or *yuu tuta yyn*

  (Rosado Ojeda: *yucu tata yyu*)

Translation: "the stone of the rat?"

  yuu = "stone"

  tata yyn or *tuta yyn* = *titni* = "rat"

Comments: The interpretation of this gloss is based in part on the representation of the animal in the pictorial sign, for the animal has the basic characteristics of rats seen in place signs from the Nahuatl-speaking region: a long, thin tail and a stippled head and body. (As, for example, in the sign for the Nahuatl name *Quimichtepec* or "rat hill," illustrated in Antonio Peñafiel, *Nombres geográficos de México*, pl. XXIII.)

  In the Tupeus dictionary from the Mixteca Baja, the word for "rat" is given as *titni*, somewhat different from *tneñe*, the word for "rat" in the Alvarado dictionary from the Mixteca Alta. The phrase *tata yyn* or *tuta yyn* in the gloss accompanying the sign in Map No. 36 may either be a somewhat flamboyant adaptation of the word *titni* or may be an alternate phrase meaning "rat." A third possibility is that the *tata* section of the gloss refers to the stone rather than to the animal, for the phrase *yuu tata* means "mirror" or "glassy stone." However, the stone in the place sign seems to be represented as merely a plain stone, with no indication of any glassy or mirror-like qualities.

Sign 2-top

Description: a hill with a profile male head inside the hill near the top

Mixtec gloss: *cuiti quaa*

Translation: "the mound of the bachelor or of the blind man"

  cuiti = "mound"

  quaa = *tay quaa* = "bachelor; blind man" (*tay* = "man")

Sign 3-top

Description: a circle of water enclosing a tiger

Mixtec gloss: *mini çoco cuiy*

  (Rosado Ojeda: *nico çoniy*)

Equivalent in the Alvarado dictionary dialect: *mini dzoco cuiñe*

Translation: "the hollow of the spring of the tiger"

  mini = "hollow"

  dzoco = "spring, well"

  cuiñe = "tiger"

Comments: In the Tupeus dictionary the Mixtec word for "tiger" is listed as *cuy*, and this would seem to be the usual word for "tiger" in the Mixteca Baja, rather than the *cuiñe* of the Alvarado dictionary dialect.

Sign 4-top

Description: a hill with a cactus plant on the right side and the head of a deity (Xipe-Totec?) on top

Mixtec gloss: *yucu çichin*

Equivalent in the Alvarado dictionary dialect: *yucu dzichi*

Translation: "the hill of the pitahaya cactus, and of the deity Xipe-Totec?"

  yucu = "hill"

  dzichi = "pitahaya" (a type of fruit-bearing cactus); and possibly also the deity Xipe-Totec

Comments: The only Mixtec name of a deity that is known with any assurance is that of the rain god: *dzavui* in Mixtec (the equivalent of *Tlaloc* in Nahuatl). But it seems possible that the head in sign 4-left represents the deity known in Nahuatl as Xipe-Totec, because the feature that differentiates this head from the two heads of rain deities in place signs on the right border of Map No. 36 (signs 2-right and 4-right) is a triangular projection just below the nose of the deity. This projection seems to be a schematized rendering of a prominent and projecting flint-blade nosepiece that is often worn by Xipe-Totec in representations of this deity in the manuscripts of the Borgia Group. (See Bodo Spranz, *Göttergestalten in den mexikanischen Bilderhandschriften der Codex Borgia-Gruppe* [Wiesbaden, 1964], 293, 296.) Other deities shown in the Borgia group manuscripts may occasionally wear a flint-blade or triangular nosepiece, as, for example, some of the representations of Tezcatlipoca (*ibid.*, 158), Tlahuizcalpantecuhtli (*ibid.*, 208–209), and a deity described by Spranz as "the god with the flint-blade bundle" (*ibid.*, 366–67); but the projecting flint-blade nosepiece appears most frequently with the deity Xipe-Totec. Thus the Mixtec word *dzichi*, which means "pitahaya," the cactus shown at the right of the hill in sign 4-left, may also refer to the deity Xipe-Totec, whose head appears at the top of the hill in this sign.

Sign 5-top

Description: a hill with a profile male figure who has an arrow or spear in his left hand

Mixtec gloss: *yucu niyiy*

Equivalent in the Alvarado dictionary dialect: *yucu nihi*

Translation: "the strong or fortified hill"

    yucu = "hill"

    nihi = "strong, secure" (*i.e.*, "fortified")

Sign 6-top

Description: a hill with a plant or flower appended to each side

Mixtec gloss: *yucu tutno*

Equivalent in the Alvarado dictionary dialect: *yucu tutnu*

Translation: "the hill of the ear"

    yucu = "hill"

    tutnu = "ear"

Comments: It is not entirely clear how the gloss "the hill of the ear" relates to the flower or plant on either side of the hill in the place sign. The Mixtec word *tutnu* usually means "ear" or "firewood." The two-word phrase *tutnu quedze* means "handle of a pot," with *quedze* meaning "pot"; and the two-word phrase *ñuma tutnu* means "thick or dense smoke," with *ñuma* meaning "smoke." In the context of this place sign, it is possible that *yucu tutnu* means "eared hill" in the sense that two clusters of vegetation grow on either side of the hill near the summit and thus give the hill an "eared" appearance, or that *tutnu* means "dense" in the sense that the hill is dense with foliage and vegetation, for *yucu* not only means "hill" but also "shrub" and "grass."

Sign 7-top

Description: a hill with a slope on the left side, and at the base of the hill is seated a profile male figure wearing a woven cloth garment.

Mixtec gloss: *ytno xiyo doo*

Equivalent in the Alvarado dictionary dialect: *itnu dziyo dzoo*

Translation: "the slope of the weft of the woven garment"

    itnu = "slope"

    dziyo = "weft of a textile"

    dzoo = "woven garment"

Sign 8-top

Description: a hill with a slope on the left side

Mixtec gloss: *ytno cuiy*

Equivalent in the Alvarado dictionary dialect: *itnu cuii*

Translation: "the green slope"

    itnu = "slope"

    cuii = "green"

Sign 9-top

Description: a platform with the bust of a profile male figure from whose mouth is emitted a volute resembling a speech scroll

Mixtec gloss: *noho tayoco*

    (Rosado Ojeda: *noho tayoo*)

Equivalent in the Alvarado dictionary dialect: *ñuhu tay yoco*

Translation: "the land of the man of vapor or of the exhaling man"

    ñuhu = "land"

    tay = "man"

    yoco = "vapor, exhalation"

Sign 10-top

Description: a temple whose interior contains a stairway that runs from the platform to the lintel of the building; on the left side of the temple is a checkerboard pattern

Mixtec gloss: *yugo diqmi*

    (Rosado Ojeda: *yugo diquii*)

Equivalent in the Alvarado dictionary dialect: *yuq[ue] tiquemi*

Translation: "the temple [devoted to] the planet Venus as the morning star"

    yuq[ue] = "temple"

    ti- = prefix denoting thing, animal, plant

    quemi = "Venus as the morning star"

Comments: The transcription of the gloss by Rosado Ojeda—*yugo diquii*—can be translated as "the temple of the grill or grate," which would seem to relate more closely to the rectangular checkerboard attached to the temple in this sign than does the gloss *yugo diqmi* or "temple of the planet Venus." *Diquii*, or *ndeque* in the dialect of the Alvarado dictionary, can mean "grill" or "grate" or any type of openwork in a rectangular pattern. For example, *ndeque ñono* means "the mesh of a net" (*ojo de red*). *Ñono* means "net," and *ndeque* refers to the rectangular openwork pattern—*i.e.*, the mesh.

    The general form of the rectangular pattern in the place sign is similar to a black-and-white checkerboard motif that appears in place signs and buildings in pre-Conquest Mixtec manuscripts, as for example in Vienna 21, where there is a hill with a checkerboard summit and a building with the same black-and-white checkerboard pattern in the interior. But the checkerboard pattern in the pre-Conquest manuscripts seems to be a solid rather than an openwork construction and resembles more closely a mosaic wall or an actual wooden checkerboard than grillwork. Moreover, the sign in Map No. 36 lacks the distinctive alternation of black and white squares seen in the place signs in pre-Conquest manuscripts.

Right Border (top to bottom)

Sign 1-right

Description: a declivity between a hill and a somewhat stunted slope; within the declivity is a bird

Mixtec gloss: *yuhui tiñoho taxa*
Equivalent in the Alvarado dictionary dialect: *yuvui tiñoo ndasa*
Translation: "the ravine of the pheasant"
　　yuvui = "ravine"
　　tiñoo ndasa = "pheasant"

Sign 2-right
Description: a hill with the head of the rain deity at the summit
Mixtec gloss: *yucu çahui*
Equivalent in the Alvarado dictionary dialect: *yucu dzavui*
Translation: "the hill of the rain deity"
　　yucu = "hill"
　　dzavui = "the rain deity" (*Tlaloc* in Nahuatl)

Sign 3-right
Description: a mound filled with dots
Mixtec gloss: *ditighic*
Equivalent in the Alvarado dictionary dialect: *dzi teque-que*
Translation: "the speckled substance"
　　dzi- = a prefix denoting substance, condition, color
　　tequeque = "speckle, spot"
Comments: It is not clear precisely what type of "speckled substance" is referred to by the gloss and illustrated in the sign that it accompanies, but it is possible that the phrase refers to a type of earth or stone found at this boundary site. In Nahuatl place signs, for example, the white magnesium soil known as *tizatl* is shown as black dots against a white background (as in the signs for the towns of *Tizatepec* and *Tizayocan*, illustrated in Antonio Peñafiel, *Nombres geográficos de México*, Pl. XXIX).

Sign 4-right
Description: a hill with the head of a rain deity at the summit
Mixtec gloss: *çahui çini quaā*
　　(Rosado Ojeda: *çahui çini qua*)
Equivalent in the Alvarado dictionary dialect: *dzavui dzini quaha* or *quaa*
Translation: "the rain deity with the red (or yellow) head"
　　dzavui = "the rain deity" (*Tlaloc* in Nahuatl)
　　dzini = "head"
　　quaha = "red"
　　quaa[n] = "yellow"

Sign 5-right
Description: a platform decorated with the patterns of a straw mat
Mixtec gloss: *ytno caa yui*
Equivalent in the Alvarado dictionary dialect: *itnu caa yuvui*
Translation: "the slope that has the form of a straw mat"
　　itnu = "slope"
　　caa = "to have the form of"
　　yuvui = "*petate* or straw mat"

Sign 6-right
Description: a hill with a bird
Mixtec gloss: *yucu cucu*
　　(Rosado Ojeda: *yucu caca*)
Translation: "the hill of the turtledove"
　　yucu = "hill"
　　cucu = "turtledove"
Comments: The word *cucu* is undoubtedly a loan word, derived from the phrase *kukukurukuku*, which emulates the cooing sound made by turtledoves. The word may have entered the Mixtec vocabulary during the Colonial period, because in the sixteenth-century Alvarado dictionary the two phrases for "turtledove" (*tórtola*) are *diyuu* and *caa ñuhu cuiya*. These Mixtec phrases seem to have been used concurrently with the loan word *cucu*, because a shortened form of the second phrase (*ñuhu*) appears in the gloss written next to sign 7-left and apparently refers to the bird in sign 8-left. At the present time, the word *cucu* and other variants of the phrase *kukukurukuku* seem to be very common throughout the Mixteca. The Dyk-Stoudt dictionary lists the word *cúcu* as meaning "turtledove," and throughout the Coastal region of the Mixteca I was told that the "Mixtec" word for "turtledove" was *kukuru*.

Bottom Border (right to left)

Sign 1-bottom
Description: a hill with a profile head of a serpent
Mixtec gloss: *yucu cogo xaa*
Equivalent in the Alvarado dictionary dialect: *yucu coo saha*
Translation: "the hill of a type of serpent"
　　yucu = "hill"
　　coo saha = "a type of serpent" ("culebra otra" in the Alvarado dictionary)

Sign 2-bottom
Description: a twin-peaked slope with a plant that has two black-and-white rectangles appended to the stem; the base of the slope and the tops of the two peaks are also black
Mixtec gloss: *ytno mino yagi*
　　(Rosado Ojeda: *ytno nino yagi*)
Equivalent in the Alvarado dictionary dialect: *itnu minu yavui*
Translation: "the slope of the dark *epazote*"
　　itnu = "slope"
　　minu = "epazote," an aromatic herb (*Chemopodium ambrosioides* L.)
　　yavui = "dark"
Comments: The adjective "dark" seems to be represented by the use of black in the base and peaks of the slope and in the flags that project from the stalk of the plant.

Sign 3-bottom
Description: a hill with a plant on the left side
Mixtec gloss: *yucu yoo*
　　(Rosado Ojeda: *yucu yca*)
Translation: "the hill of the reed"

yucu = "hill"
(tnu)yoo = "reed"

Sign 4-bottom
Description: a circle with footprints that represents a plaza or marketplace; in the center of the circle is a head of an animal
Mixtec gloss: *yahniyy*
Equivalent in the Alvarado dictionary dialect: *yahui yehe*
Translation: "the plaza or marketplace of the wolf"
   yahui = "plaza, marketplace"
   (ti)yehe = "wolf"

Sign 5-bottom
Description: the sign for a rock and an eagle
Mixtec gloss: *dodo yaa*
Equivalent in the Alvarado dictionary dialect: *toto yaha*
Translation: "the rock of the eagle"
   toto = "rock"
   yaha = "eagle"

Sign 6-bottom
Description: a frieze with geometric decoration and three stalks with flint blades
Mixtec gloss: *ytno diyuchi*
   (Rosado Ojeda: *ytno diyudi*)
Equivalent in the Alvarado dictionary dialect: *itnu dziyuchi*
Translation: "the slope of the husks of ground grain"
   itnu = "slope"
   dziyuchi = "husks of ground grain"
Comments: The word *yuchi* alone when used as an adjective can mean "pulverized"; when used as a noun, it means "knife" or "flint blade," and this meaning of *yuchi* is illustrated by the flint blades that are appended to the stalks.

Sign 7-bottom
Description: the feather-mat motif that represents a field, and leaves that resemble those of the maguey cactus
Mixtec gloss: *yoço tayu*
Equivalent in the Alvarado dictionary dialect: *yodzo ndaa yu[vui]*
Translation: "the plain of *ixtle* (a fiber made from the leaves of maguey cactus)"
   yodzo = "plain"
   ndaa = "*ixtle*, plant fiber"
   yuvui = "maguey cactus"

Sign 8-bottom
Description: a platform with a black interior and a person (or deity?) who wears a hat with a triangular peak and has one hand extended
Mixtec gloss: *çahi ndiy*
   (Rosado Ojeda: *çahi nidy*)
Equivalent in the Alvarado dictionary dialect: *dzahi ndihi*
Translation: "the black ring"
   dzahi = "ring"
   ndihi = "black"
Comments: The part of the body of the figure in this sign that is emphasized is the extended hand, and on this hand are circles that resemble finger rings. The idea of "black" appears to be represented by the black rectangle within the platform on which the figure stands.

Sign 9-bottom
Description: a platform with a female figure
Mixtec gloss: *doço tiyatna*
Equivalent in the Alvarado dictionary dialect: *ndodzo tiyatna*
Translation: "the golden-colored statue or royal wet nurse"
   ndodzo = "statue; royal wet nurse"
   ti- = prefix denoting thing, animal, plant
   yatna = "golden in color"
Comments: According to the Dyk-Stoudt vocabulary, *ndosò* (the equivalent of the *ndodzo* of the Alvarado dictionary dialect) can mean "idol, a stone which has the form of a man or some other being; the figure of a false deity"; and *ndoso* can mean "breasts" or "divided in half." This last definition seems to be expressed in the place sign by the horizontal line drawn across the platform, a line which does in effect divide the platform in half. In the section of the Reyes Mixtec grammar that lists the vocabulary used to refer to persons of nobility ("Arte en lengua mixteca," Ch. XXV, 74–81), one of the phrases listed for a wet nurse, if she is a *principala* or a member of the secondary nobility, is *dodzo yya*, or literally, "royal breasts."

Sign 10-bottom
Description: a hill from which flowering plants are growing
Mixtec gloss: *yucu tay*
Equivalent in the Alvarado dictionary dialect: *yucu ndai*
Translation: "hill where [plants] are planted"
   yucu = "hill"
   ndai = "to be planted"

Sign 11-bottom
Description: a platform with a female figure; the woman's hands are extended, and the fingers on her right hand appear to terminate in circles similar to those that are appended to signs for flowing water
Mixtec gloss: *ytno nino maa*
Translation: "the slope above or below the center"
   ytno = "slope"
   nino = "above, below"
   maa = "center, in the middle"
Comments: For reasons that are not clear, the word *maa* seems to be illustrated by a human hand combined with a sign associated with water. A similar place sign occurs in the Lienzo of Jicayán (sign 1, Fig. 148), where two streams of water are combined with human fingers. The sign in the Jicayán Lienzo is accompanied by the Mixtec gloss *yuhui maa*. (*Yuhui* means "arroyo, gully.")

NAMES OF FIELDS

Tentative translations of the Mixtec names of the fourteen

fields at the bottom of Map No. 36 are presented below, with the fields numbered 1 to 14 from left to right. The names of the fields are rather more difficult to translate than those of the boundary signs because the Mixtec names of the fields are not represented by pictorial signs. For if the glosses are helpful in interpreting the place signs of the boundary names, the reverse is also true. Every Mixtec word usually has at least two or three different meanings, and the pictorial sign usually narrows down the number of possible meanings to one, or at most two. Thus the translations suggested below are hypothetical, and in many cases, only one of several possible translations of the Mixtec place names. In the word-by-word translations of the glosses, the word as it appears in Map No. 36 is followed in parentheses by the equivalent of the word in the dialect of the Alvarado dictionary.

Field 1
ditnaha "where [the lands] meet or join"
    di- (*dzi-*) = a prefix denoting condition, substance
    tnaha = "to be joined"

Field 2
yuhu coho "at the edge of the circle [hollow?]"
    yuhu = "at the edge of"
    coho = "circular, cup-shaped"

Field 3
pleyto ñuhu ñodiai "[under] litigation, the lands of Huajuapan de León"
    pleyto = "litigation, lawsuit"
    ñuhu = "land"
    ñodiai (*ñuu dzai*) = the Mixtec name of Huajuapan de León

Field 4
ñoño quidi "the lands of clay or chalk"
    ño (*ñuhu*) = "land"
    ñoquidi (*ñuhu quedze*) = "clay, chalk"

Field 5
pleyto ñoho huixi yoo "[under] litigation, the land of the reed leaves"
    pleyto = "litigation, lawsuit"
    ñoho (*ñuhu*) = "land"
    huixi (*huisi*) = "leaves"
    (*tnu*)*yoo* = "reed"

Field 6
ñoho co xayo "the lands [belonging to a person named] 1, 2, or 3 Rabbit"
    ñoho (*ñuhu*) = "land"
    coxayo = "1, 2, or 3 Rabbit (the calendrical name)"
It seems likely that the person named 1, 2, or 3 Rabbit to whom this field belongs is the woman seated within the building at the left of the central church, because this figure is accompanied by the gloss *yia goxayo* (*i.e.*, "the noblewoman 1, 2, or 3 Rabbit").

Field 7
ñoho yago "the lands of a type of small maguey cactus that grows among rocks"

    ñoho (*ñuhu*) = "land"
    yago (*yacu*) = the type of cactus described above

Field 8
ñoho xiçaa "the land which is heated up or dried by the sun"
    ñoho (*ñuhu*) = "land"
    xi- (*si-*) = a prefix denoting action
    çaa (*dzaa*) = "to be heated up, dried in the sun"
According to the Reyes list of place names, *sidzaa* is also the Mixtec name of Santa María Ixcatlán, a town about 40 miles east of Huajuapan de León.

Field 9
ñoho ñotnoho "the land of the town of the lineages or family" or "the land of the deceased lineages or family"
    ñoho (*ñuhu*) = "land"
    ño- (*ñu-*) = a prefix that can refer to a town or to a deceased person
    tnoho = "lineage, family"

Field 10
ño tua "flat land" or "land of the gully"
    ño (*ñu*) = "land"
    tua (*nduhua*) = "valley, gully"

Field 11
yoço quey "the wide field"
    yoço (*yodzo*) = "field"
    quey (*cahi*) = "wide"
Yodzo cahi is also the Mixtec name of the important town of Yanhuitlán in the Mixteca Alta.

Field 12
ytu aniyn "the field of the palace [*i.e.*, of the native nobility or *cacicazgo*]"
    itu = "field"
    aniyn (*aniñe*) = "palace"

Field 13
ytu aniy "the field of the palace" (same as Field 12)

Field 14
ñoho ñocoho "the lands of the town of the plate or cup"
    ñoho (*ñuhu*) = "land"
    ño (*ñu*) = "town"
    coho = "plate, cup"
Of the fourteen fields, at least one belongs to a town: Field 3, which belongs to Huajuapan. Two other fields (12 and 13) belong to the "palace"—that is, to the native nobility. Still another field (6) belongs to a specific noblewoman, the *cacica* named 1, 2, or 3 Rabbit who is seated in the building at the left of the central church. The ownership of the remaining ten fields is unknown.

COMPARISON OF THE DIALECT OF THE GLOSSES ON MAP NO. 36 AND THE DIALECT OF THE ALVARADO DICTIONARY

The dialect of the glosses on Map No. 36 is a dialect of the Mixteca Baja that is different from the dialect recorded in the principal sixteenth-century source of Mixtec vocabulary, the dictionary of Fray Francisco de Alvarado, who was vicar of the Dominican monastery of Tamazulapan in the Mixteca Alta. In the dialect of the Map No. 36 glosses, the letter *o* when it appears after *n, ñ,* or *tn* is equivalent to the *u* of the Alvarado dictionary, and this use of *o* is seen in the glosses accompanying Signs 1-left, 3-left, 5-left, 6-left, 7-left, 10-left, 6-top, 7-top, 8-top, 9-top, 5-right, 2-bottom (twice), 6-bottom, 11-bottom, and Fields 3, 4, 5, 6, 7, 8, 9, 10 and 14. The *c* with a cedilla (*ç*) in the glosses on Map No. 36 is the equivalent of the *dz* of the Alvarado dictionary, as is seen in the glosses accompanying Signs 2-left, 3-top, 4-top, 2-right, 4-right (twice), 7-bottom, 8-bottom and Fields 8 and 11. As a general rule, the *x* in the Map No. 36 glosses is the equivalent of the *s* of the Alvarado dictionary, as can be seen in the glosses accompanying

Signs 6-left, 1-right, 1-bottom and 9-bottom. The one exception to this rule occurs in Sign 7-top, where *x* is the equivalent of the *dz* of the Alvarado dictionary. The letter *t* in the glosses on Map No. 36 is not only the same as the *t* of the Alvarado dictionary but is also equivalent to the *nd* of that dictionary, as in the glosses accompanying Signs 1-left, 1-right, 7-bottom, 10-bottom and Field 10. The *d* of the Map No. 36 glosses is the equivalent of three different sounds recorded in the Alvarado dictionary: *dz, t,* and *nd*. The *d* of Map No. 36 equals the *dz* of the dictionary in the glosses accompanying Signs 7-top, 3-right, 6-bottom and Fields 1, 3, and 4; it is equivalent to Alvarado's *t* in Signs 10-top and 5-bottom (twice), and to *nd* in Sign 9-bottom.

APPENDIX F

The Four Maps of Xoxocotlán and the Texts and Glosses on the 1771 Map

The 1771 Map of Xoxocotlán discussed briefly in this study as an example of a late Colonial map of one town enclosed by the place signs of its boundaries is one of four extant maps of this town. A short description of each of the four maps is as follows:

1. *1718 Map.* Water color on European paper. 58 x 42.5 cm. Present location: Dirección de Geografía, Meteorología e Hidrología (Tacubaya, Mexico, D. F.), Orozco y Berra Collection, No. 1176.

2. *1771 Map.* Oil on canvas. Dimensions unknown. Present location: municipal archive of Xoxocotlán. This map is a copy of the 1718 map. This version of the Xoxocotlán map was published as an illustration to a popular one-page article on Oaxaca ("Oaxaca histórica y tradicional," *México al Día,* June 15, 1932, p. 12), where it is described as an "old map of the city of Oaxaca." A photographic negative of the map is in the Archivo Fotográfico of the INAH, negative No. XII–3.

3. *1686 Map.* Oil on canvas. 87.5 x 76 cm. Present location: AGN-Tierras 129-4. At the bottom of this map are two short texts which state that it was copied faithfully from another map (now apparently lost) on October 25, 1686.

4. *1879 Map.* Water color (?) on European paper. Dimensions unknown. Present location: municipal archive of Xoxocotlán (?). This map is a copy of the 1686 map. A photographic negative of the map is in the Archivo Fotográfico of the INAH, negative No. XII–2.

The four maps of Xoxocotlán are essentially two different presentations of the town's lands, and both presentations may well be derived from a common prototype that is now lost. The 1718 and the 1771 copy of it show the extent of the community lands of Xoxocotlán, with the church of the town near the center of the map. In both the 1718 and 1771 maps the names of the town's boundaries are set forth around the border of the map by pictorial signs accompanied by place names in both Mixtec and Nahuatl.

In the 1686 and 1879 maps, the main concern is not the community of Xoxocotlán and its boundaries but specific lands located south of Xoxocotlán. In these two maps the church of the town of Xoxocotlán is shown on the right side of the maps, and on the left side is a long rectangle enclosed by a black line that demarcates the land under dispute. The 1686 map has only ten places labeled with Mixtec glosses, nine of which also appear in the 1879 copy; and in all cases the glosses are within or near the rectangle of disputed land on the left side of the map. The configuration of hills which appears at the top of the 1718 and 1771 maps and which represents the archaeological site of Monte Albán is drawn in a more schematized fashion in the top-center and upper-right corner of the 1686 and 1879 maps; but in the latter maps, these hills are not labeled with glosses and only four hills are accompanied by pictorial motifs that indicate they are place signs, as contrasted with the ten hills with pictorial signs at the top of the 1718 and 1771 maps. Thus the 1686 map and the 1718 map have two distinct focuses: the earlier map delineates specific lands south of Xoxocotlán, whereas the 1718 map is concerned with setting forth the boundaries of the entire municipality.

For the purposes of the present discussion, only the 1771 map and its glosses will be considered in detail, with occasional references to the 1718 map of which it is a copy. The four maps deserve a separate and more detailed study as a group of maps from one town; and ideally, all four should be published in color, because color is an important factor in the 1686 and 1718 maps, which are the two that I have examined personally.

TEXTS AND GLOSSES ON THE 1771 MAP

Three types of texts or glosses appear on the 1771 Map of Xoxocotlán: (1) "certifying" texts that attest to the veracity of the map, and which are in Spanish only; (2) short bilingual (Spanish/Mixtec) texts written within the town's boundaries and which refer, for the most part, to non-boundary sites; and (3) the bilingual (Nahuatl/Mixtec) glosses that set forth the names of Xoxocotlán's boundaries. All the writing on the 1771 map appears to be in the same hand, presumably that of Gabriel Josef Martínez, the royal scribe from the city of Oaxaca whose signature is appended to the text that is dated 1771 and written within the horizontal oval at the bottom of the map.

Certifying Texts

Three certifying texts appear on the 1771 map, and two of these are copies or paraphrases of certifying statements that appeared on earlier maps of Xoxocotlán. At the right of the central church ("Text II" in Fig. 163) is a three-line passage which states that evidence was obtained from the map by order of the judge and at the request of the citizens [of Xoxocotlán] in the city of Oaxaca on September 29, 1718, and this statement is followed by the name of Joseph de Araujo, the royal and public scribe.[1] This short text is a greatly abbreviated version of the certifying text written on the reverse of the 1718 map, a text that is signed by Joseph de Araujo as scribe.

Above and to the left of the central church in the 1771 map is a seven-line text ("Text I" in Fig. 163) to the effect that the citizens of Xoxocotlán presented "this painting" to Don Francisco de Lagunas Portocarrero, the *alcalde mayor* of the Cuatro Villas of the Marquesado del Valle, in the city of Oaxaca on December 4, 1660; that the demarcation of the lands on the painting was approved by the citizens of Xoxocotlán on December 14 and 15 of the same year; and that the original map was returned to them. The statement is followed by the names of the Judge, Antonio Gómez Pinar; the *alcalde mayor*, Francisco de Lagunas; and a witness, Feliciano de Laguna.[2] This text on the 1771 map is virtually an exact copy of a text that also appears on the reverse of the 1718 map, where it is quoted within the certifying statement made by scribe Joseph de Araujo. According to the latter text, the 1718 map is a faithful copy of a map of Xoxocotlán on which appeared the text dated 1660. The present location of the map presented in 1660 is unknown, but it was presumably similar to the 1718 map which is certified as being a faithful copy of the earlier map and thus also similar to the 1771 map which is a copy of the 1718 copy.

The third certifying text on the 1771 map is contemporary with the map itself and is placed within a cartouche at the bottom of the map ("Text III" in Fig. 163). The six-line statement on the part of the royal scribe Gabriel Josef Martínez testifies that the 1771 map is a faithful copy of the "original"—and in this case the original is apparently the 1718 map, because the text invokes the names of both Joseph Araujo (scribe at the time the 1718 map was painted) and Francisco de Lagunas (*alcalde mayor* of the Cuatro Villas in 1660 when the prototype of the 1718 map was presented). The 1771 copy was made at the order of the *alcalde mayor* of Oaxaca, Joaquín Ramírez, and the Marqués del Valle, the Duke of Terranova y Monteleón; and it was presented and signed by the scribe Martínez on March 8, 1771.[3]

---

[1] The Spanish text on the map is as follows: *Sacose Testim^to de este Mapa de mandata de Jues/ y Pedim^to de los Natt^s en Oaxaca a beinte nuebe/ de Septiembre de mill Setezientos y Dies y ocho años/ Joseph de Arauxo (rúbrica)/ Escr^o Pu^o y Re^l.*

[2] The Spanish text on the map is as follows: *En la Villa de Oaxaca del marquesado en quatro de Diciembre de mil y/ seisientos y Sesenta años ante mi Don Franc^o de Lagunas Portocarrero/ Alcalde Mayor de este Marquesado presentaron esta pintura los naturales/ del Pueblo de Xoxocotlan Y en catorce Y quince de este mes la aprobaron y/ la demarcacion de las tierras con Ynformacion que se les Entrego Original/ Y para que conste de su pedimento di el presente dho dia honce* ["quince" in the text on the reverse of the 1718 map] *por ante de mi como/ Juez Receptor y testigos de mi Jusgado. Antt^o Gomez Pinar (rúbrica)/ Franc^o de Lagunas (rúbrica) Feliciano de Laguna.*

Short Geographical Texts within the Boundaries

Above the base of the configuration of hills at the bottom of the 1771 map are four brief texts that designate specific sites in the region east of the town of Xoxocotlán. These texts are bilingual, in Spanish and Mixtec, and they do not appear on the 1718 map. It is possible that these short texts were copied from a written land document; and in the case of the Mixtec half of the texts, there seem to be a number of errors, made either by a copyist who did not know the language or by an accurate copyist who was faithfully replicating errors found in the document copied.

The first of these texts ("A" in Fig. 163) states that Xoxocotlán shares a boundary on the east with San Antonio de la Cal.

Spanish: [*un?*] *lindero de S. Ant^o por donde sale el Sol* "[a] boundary with San Antonio to the East (literally, where the sun rises)"

Mixtec: [*t*]*naha Dzaño S. Ant^o noo caña n*[*e?*]*hi canchi* "boundaries are joined with San Antonio to the East" *tnaha* = "to be joined" *dzaño, dzañu* = "boundary" *noo caña n*[*e*]*hicanchi* (*nuu cana ndicandii* in the Alvarado dictionary dialect) = "the direction East (where the sun rises)"

The second text indicates the junction of two rivers and is written near the spot where two wavy lines representing water come together ("Text B" in Fig. 163).

Spanish: *Junta de los dos Rios de la Laguna* "junction of the two rivers of the lake"

Mixtec: *nontnatnatan Yucha mini* "where the rivers of the lake are joined" *nontnatnatan Yucha* (*nu tnaha tnaha yuta* of the Alvarado dictionary dialect) = "where rivers are joined" *mini* = "lake"

The third brief text is written below the church that represents San Agustín de las Juntas ("C" in Fig. 163) and merely describes a "black mound."

Spanish: *mogote prieto* "black mound"

Mixtec: *cuiti* [*yu*]*hui t*[*a?*]*yee* "the mound of the gully of the bruise" *cuiti* = "mound" *yuhui, yuvui* = "gully, ravine, estuary" *tayee = teyee* = "bruise, bump on the head (*chichón*)"

The "black mound" referred to in this text may be either the dark hill above which the gloss is written or the large hill behind the church of San Agustín, the hill which contains the Nahuatl gloss *Tlite, tepeque* or "black hill."

---

[3] The Spanish text on the map is as follows: *Gabriel Josef Martinez Escrivano del Rey Nuestro Señor Vesino de la Ciudad de Antequera Certifico para Verdadero testimonio/ que el precente Mapa es copiado segun y Como se manifesta del Original que te*[*ne*]*mos Los Alcaldes Comun y Naturales del Pueblo de/ Santa Cruz Xoxocotlan el que se halla autorisao a lo que . . . de Don Josef Araujo Escrivano Real y de Don Franc^o Lagunas/ Alcalde mallor que fue de esta Jurisd^n de mandato del Señor Don Joachin Ramires de Arellano Alcalde mallor por solici/tud y al Exm^o Señor Duque de Terranoba y Monteleon Marquez del Valle de estas quatro Villas se rrenobo y di la precente en la/ Villa de Oaxaca a 8 de Marzo de 1771./ Fe verdad. Gabriel Josef Martines (rúbrica).*

On the 1718 map, the Mixtec gloss *yuhui tayee*—probably the equivalent of the *cuiti [yu]hui t[a?]yee* on the 1771 map—is written below the Nahuatl gloss *Tlitltepeque* on this hill, suggesting that it is the Mixtec equivalent of the Nahuatl gloss *Tlitltepeque* or "black hill."

But it is not clear precisely how the Mixtec phrase *yuhui tayee* relates to either the "black hill" of the 1718 map or to the "black mound" (*mogote prieto*) of the 1771 map. The usual words for "black" in Mixtec are *tnoo, ndayu,* and *ndihi.* One possibility is that *tayee* is a transcription of *ndayu* written in a different dialect; but this does not seem likely because in another gloss accompanying one of the boundary signs on the 1771 map (Sign 20 on the left border) the word *ndayu* is written as *nchayu.* A second possibility is that *tayee* is intended to be *teyee,* which can mean "bruise, bump on the head (*chichón*)," according to the Alvarado dictionary. The implication might be that the ravine (*yuvui* or *yuhui*) has a bruised (*i.e.,* darkened or blackened) color.

The fourth brief text on the 1771 map is written under a tree on the left side of the map ("D" in Fig. 163) and describes a water hole.

> Spanish: *ojo de Aguacero/ nopal* "the water hole of the nopal cactus"
> Mixtec: *ñoo dzahui* "water hole"
> *ñoo* = "place where something exists"
> *dzahui* = "rain water"

The Mixtec text apparently omits the "nopal cactus" (*huinda* in Mixtec) qualifying element that appears in the Spanish place name.

The Glosses Accompanying the Boundary Signs

Around the border of the 1771 map are twenty names of the boundaries of the town of Xoxocotlán. In the case of most of these boundaries the name is indicated in three ways: a pictorial sign, a gloss of the Nahuatl name of the place, and a gloss of the Mixtec name of the place. In a few cases only one of these three types of "naming" may be evident, usually a gloss in Mixtec. For the purpose of the discussion of the glosses, the boundary signs have been numbered from 1 to 20, beginning in the upper-left corner of the map and moving clockwise; the location of the glosses accompanying the twenty boundary signs is shown in Fig. 163. The consideration of each sign will include a description of the pictorial sign, a transcription and translation of the Nahuatl gloss that accompanies the sign, a transcription and word-by-word translation of the Mixtec gloss that accompanies the sign, and comments, when these are relevant.

Van de Velde Transcription and Translation of the Mixtec Boundary Glosses. In the Van de Velde Collection at the University of New Mexico are unpublished notes on the 1771 Map of Xoxocotlán made by Paul Van de Velde, a Belgian citizen who lived in Mexico in the 1920's and 1930's. Van de Velde and his wife edited the short-lived *Mexican Magazine* (1925–28); and from 1931 to 1937, he owned the Zavaleta gold and silver mine at the edge of the Valley of Oaxaca. He was also interested in the archaeology and ethnology of Oaxaca, and his papers at the University of New Mexico include many pages of typescript of information on Oaxacan topics. Among these are a transcription and translation of thirteen of the twenty Mixtec glosses on the 1771 Map, made by Van de Velde at an unspecified date and presumably from the original map in the municipal archive of Xoxocotlán.[4] In these notes, Van de Velde considers only the ten Mixtec glosses on the hills at the top of the map (those accompanying Signs 1–10 of this study) and the three that are visible at the left side of the map (those accompanying Signs 17, 19, and 20 of this study); he neither transcribed nor translated any of the glosses that appear in the range of hills at the bottom of the map (Signs 11–16 of this study). In the case of seven of the thirteen Mixtec glosses studied by Van de Velde (those accompanying Signs 1 through 5, as well as 19 and 20), his transcription and translation are different from mine. In these instances, I have included the Van de Velde transcription and translation in the "comments" following my own translation of the gloss.

Sign 1

Description: a hill with the Mixtec A-O year sign

Nahuatl gloss: *Mecatepeque* "*mecate* or rope hill"

Mixtec gloss: *yucu yoho* "the hill of the *mecate* or rope"
> *yucu* = "hill"
> *yoho* = "*mecate* or rope"

Comments:

The description of the A–O year sign as a "rope" seems to indicate that the "O" section of the sign is a rope that binds a sun ray, represented by the "A" section of the year sign.

Paul Van de Velde transcribes the Mixtec gloss *yucu so Ica,* which he translates as "the hill where benediction is given to all." (*Yucu* = "hill"; *so* = "where"; *I* = "benediction"; *ca* = "all.")

Sign 2

Description: a hill with two horizontal bars with nine dots across the top of the bars. Toward the summit of the hill is a small male figure, wearing a loincloth and carrying a shield in his left hand and the native weapon known as a *macana* in his right hand; this figure is not part of the place sign.

Nahuatl gloss: *Chalchiu,tepetl* "the hill of the jadeite jewel"

Mixtec gloss (1771 map): *yucu yu dziñoho* "hill of the precious or valuable stone"
> *yucu* = "hill"

---

[4] Van de Velde's notes on the 1771 map are located in three different places in the University of New Mexico collection. The largest group of notes is in Volume III (pp. 397–407) of a group of bound volumes of typescript notes on miscellaneous subjects related to the State of Oaxaca; included in these notes are a word-by-word translation of the thirteen Mixtec glosses into Spanish and typescript copies of documents concerning Xoxocotlán, probably from the town's archive. In Volume VI of the bound volumes of typescript (pp. 781, 784) is a typed one-page list of the Mixtec boundary names with a translation of each into English, as well as a copy of the page of the magazine *México al Día* (June 15, 1932) where the 1771 Map was published. Finally, in a box (numbered 4–25) of miscellaneous papers is another word-by-word translation of the thirteen Mixtec glosses into Spanish.

yu[*u*] = "stone"

dziñoho (*dziñuhu* of the Alvarado dictionary dialect) = "money," and by extension, "precious, valuable"

Mixtec gloss (1718 map): *yucu yusi dzeñoho* "the hill of the precious or valuable turquoise"

yusi = "turquoise"

(The first and last words of this place name have the same meanings as those given in the translation of the gloss on the 1771 map.)

Comments:

It is possible that the slight difference between the gloss on the 1771 map and that on the 1718 map may be due to a copyist's error. That is, the scribe who wrote the glosses on the 1771 map and was presumably copying the glosses on the 1718 map may well have abbreviated the *yusi* section of the gloss on the 1718 map to the *yu* that appears on the 1771 map.

The pictorial sign within the hill is not the usual sign for jadeite or turquoise jewel, which is usually a circle that represents the jewel itself, as in the place sign of Acatlán (Fig. 38). In the case of the sign in the Map of Xoxocotlán, what may be shown within the hill is a jeweled ornament, such as a necklace or bracelet.

Van de Velde transcribes this gloss as *yucu yu aziñoho*, which he translates as "hill of the stone which is given to the town." (*Yucu* = "hill"; *yu* = "stone"; *azi* = "to give"; *ñoho* = "town.") He also states that the present-day name of this hill is "La Mesa."

Sign 3

Description: a hill containing an ocelot. At the summit of the hill is a *teponaztle*, a horizontal tubular drum, with two drumsticks shown above it. On the left slope of the hill is a woman dressed in native costume and carrying a *macana* in her right hand. The woman does not appear to be part of the place sign.

Nahuatl gloss: *Oselotepeque* "ocelot hill"

Mixtec gloss: *yucu quii tocuisi* "the hill of the *teponaztle* of Zaachila?"

yucu = "hill"

quii (*q*[*ue*]*hu* of the Alvarado dictionary dialect) = "teponaztle"

tocuisi = the Mixtec name of the town of Zaachila

Comments:

This place sign is bilingual, with the ocelot inside the hill representing the Nahuatl *oselotepeque* and the *teponaztle* at the summit of the hill representing the Mixtec name *yucu quii*. It is not known why the drum is associated with the important town of Zaachila, which is located about five miles south and slightly west of Xoxocotlán. The implication may be that this particular hill was a ceremonial site not only for Zaachila, but for the Valley of Oaxaca region as a whole. *Tocuisi* is the Mixtec name of Zaachila, and *tocuisi ñuhu* is the Mixtec phrase that designates the entire Valley of Oaxaca region. *Tocuisi ñuhu* may mean "the sacred white dominion." (*To* is a shortened form of *toho*, "nobleman," and by extension the domain of a nobleman; *cuisi* means "white," and *ñuhu*

means "sacred.") Arana and Swadesh (*Los elementos del mixteco antiguo*, 76) suggest that *tocuisi ñuhu* may mean "sacred flat or level domain" (*señorío-llano-sagrado*), because *cuisi* can also mean "flat, level, as a plain."

Van de Velde transcribes the Mixtec gloss accompanying this place sign as *yucu quii 4 ocaño*, and he proposes two translations of this phrase: "the green hill of the 4 mounds" and "the green hill of the 4 Tiger (captains)."

Sign 4

Description: Within the hill is an oval cartouche with a feathered border, and inside the cartouche is a male figure wearing a bird headdress and seated on a throne. At the right of the cartouche is a second male figure, seated with clasped hands, probably in a pose of reverence toward the person in the cartouche. Placed on top of the hill is what appears to be a doorway, with a lintel supported by two volutes. On the left slope of the hill stands a male figure wearing a loincloth and holding a bow in his left hand and an arrow in his right; this figure is not part of the place sign.

Nahuatl gloss: *Teutli,tepeque* "hill of the nobleman or ruler"

Mixtec gloss (1771 map): *yucua niyyo doo ñomana* "the hill where was now (or was now seated) the purified one who is sleepy??"

yucu = "hill"

a = indicates completed action

ni- = past-tense prefix

yyo = "is, is seated"

[*n*]*doo* = "clean, purified"

ñomana (*ñumana*) = "sleepiness, sleepy"

Mixtec gloss (1718 map): *yucu dini yodzo ñomana* "the hill of the feathered head that is sleepy??"

yucu = "hill"

dini (*dzini*) = "head"

yodzo = "large feather"

ñomana (*ñumana*) = "sleepiness, sleepy"

Comments:

Because of its prominent size and its central location in the range of hills that comprise the site of Monte Albán, this sign is undoubtedly the most important place sign in the Map of Xoxocotlán. And the Mixtec gloss that accompanies it is also the most difficult to translate so that it makes any sense. The Mixtec gloss is by no means the equivalent of the Nahuatl gloss *Teutlitepeque*, which means "hill of the nobleman or ruler," for the Mixtec words for "nobleman" are *stoho* or *yya*, and neither of these words is part of the Mixtec gloss on either the 1771 or 1718 maps.

The difference between the Mixtec gloss on the 1718 map, *yucu dini yodzo ñomana*, and that on the 1771 map, *yucua niyyo doo ñomana*, may be the result of a misunderstanding or error on the part of the scribe who copied the glosses from the 1718 map. In terms of the pictorial sign, the phrase *dini yodzo* or "feathered head" in the 1718 gloss seems more appropriate—because the seated figure in the sign wears a feathered headdress—than the phrase *a niyyo doo* in the 1771 gloss which was tentatively translated as "there was now—or there was seated—a purified [person]."

Moreover, Paul Van de Velde's notes on the Map of Xoxocotlán include a typescript copy of a document dated March 16, 1718, that sets forth the names of Xoxocotlán's boundaries; and according to this document, between a boundary named Quetzaltepec (shown in the Xoxocotlán map as directly to the right of Sign 4) and a boundary whose Mixtec name is *yucu cui* (probably equivalent to the *yucu quii* written on Sign 3 at the left of the sign under discussion) is a boundary where there is a doorway to an ancient building. In the Map of Xoxocotlán this doorway is shown at the top of the hill in Sign 4, where a lintel is supported by two volute-like posts. According to a parenthetical note on this boundary in the Van de Velde typescript, a note apparently made by Van de Velde, the present-day name of the site is "the stone of the metate," which would be *yuu yodzo* in Mixtec and includes the word *yodzo* found in the gloss associated with Sign 4 in the 1718 map. Perhaps the *yo doo* section of the gloss on the 1771 map is an inaccurate copy of the *yodzo* seen in the 1718 gloss; and the uncertainty of the scribe who wrote the gloss on the 1771 map is evident in the erasure and rewriting seen in the final two *o*'s of the *doo* element of the gloss.

The Mixtec phrase *ñomana* (*ñumana* in the dialect of the Alvarado dictionary) appears at the end of the gloss accompanying Sign 4 on both the 1718 and 1771 maps, and to my knowledge the principal, if not the only, meaning of this phrase is "sleepiness, drowsiness." Precisely what the phrase means in the context of the gloss on the Xoxocotlán maps is not clear. It is possible, perhaps, that the "sleepiness" is a rather oblique reference to an entombed nobleman and to Monte Albán as a royal necropolis. According to Burgoa (*Geográfica descripción*, II, 120), the Zapotec name for Mitla, another notable necropolis in the Valley of Oaxaca, is *Lio baa*, which means "resting place," and it might be implied that those who receive, or deserve, rest are those who are sleepy or drowsy. But the connection does seem a bit tenuous.

Van de Velde transcribes the Mixtec gloss accompanying Sign 4 as *Yucu ani Iyo 13 ocoñaña*, which he translates "the hill where there is [the temple of] our god 13 Ocoñaña, or 'Twenty Tigers' (the name of a prince)." (*Yucu* = "hill"; *a* = "where"; *ni* = "he" [is?]; *I* = "god"; *yo* = "our"; *oco* = "20"; *ñaña* = "tiger.") It is difficult to see why Van de Velde reads the last section of the gloss as "13 ocoñaña," although it is possible that he found this phrase in some written documents in the town archive of Xoxocotlán. Wilfredo C. Cruz, in an essay on the name of Monte Albán (*Oaxaca recóndita*, Mexico, 1946, 159–60) says that according to written documents in the town of Xoxocotlán, the Mixtec name of the hills of Monte Albán is *yucu-oco-ñaña*, or "the hill of twenty tigers." Cruz also states that the same documents give the Spanish name of Monte Albán as "hill of the tiger," which

may be a reference to the hill illustrated by Sign 3, which is a hill with an ocelot and is accompanied by the Nahuatl gloss *Oselotepeque*, "ocelot or tiger hill."

The Mixtec phrase *oco ñaña* or "20 Tigers" is the personal name of at least two rulers shown in the Map of Teozacoalco and in the pre-Conquest historical manuscripts. The first of these, ♂ 2-Rain, whom Caso calls Ocoñaña I, lived from 971 to 992 and was the last ruler of the first dynasty of Tilantongo (Caso, "Mapa de Teozacoalco," 160–65; *Bodley*, 31–32; "Explicación del reverso del Codex Vindobonensis," 23–25). He appears in Bodley 5, II-I and 6-I, Selden 6-II, Nuttall 24b, Vienna V, 2 and 1, and the Map of Teozacoalco. In the story of his short life as told in Codex Bodley, he committed suicide at a place that is described as "River of the Tree and the Serpent" and ascended to the sky as the planet Venus. The second Ocoñaña, ♂ 5-Reed, was born in 1345 of parents who ruled Tilantongo, and he became the fourth ruler of the third dynasty of Teozacoalco (Caso, *Bodley*, 47; "Explicación del reverso del Codex Vindobonensis," 42–43; "Mapa de Teozacoalco," 176). He appears in Bodley 17-IV, Nuttall 32b, Vienna XIII-3, and the Map of Teozacoalco. The usual method of presenting the personal name "Ocoñaña" is a tiger helmet or costume enclosed by 20 dots—as, for example, the figure of 2-Rain in the Map of Teozacoalco (Fig. 36, second figure from the bottom in the column of figures on the left). But no such figure appears in the 1771 Map of Xoxocotlán; the seated person in Sign 4 wears a bird helmet rather than a tiger helmet, and the ocelot in Sign 3 is not enclosed by 20 dots. In addition, the phrase *oco ñaña* does not occur in any of the Mixtec glosses written on the configuration of hills representing the site of Monte Albán, and thus it is difficult to determine how the document referred to by Wilfredo Cruz relates to the known maps of Xoxocotlán. One possibility is that an alternate Mixtec name for Sign 3, "ocelot hill" in Nahuatl, might have been *yucu oco ñaña*, rather than the present Mixtec gloss *yucu quii . . .*, which refers to the drum at the summit of the hill.

Sign 5

Description: a hill with a deer placed near the base of the hill. The deer does not appear to be part of the place sign.

Nahuatl gloss: *Quetzatepeque* "*quetzal*-bird or *quetzal*-feather hill"

Mixtec gloss (1771 map): *yucu yodzo cucha* "the hill of the circular feather"

   yucu = "hill"

   yodzo = "feather"

   cucha (*cuta* in the Alvarado dictionary dialect) = "round, circular"

Mixtec gloss (1718 map): *yucu yodzo cudia* "the hill of the feathers of the royal thrush?"

   cudi = (*te*)*cundi* of the Alvarado dictionary = "thrush" (*tordo* in Spanish)

   -ia, -ya = a suffix denoting nobility, royalty (The first two words of this gloss are translated in the same way as in the gloss on the 1771 map.)

Comments:

Because the hill on which these glosses are written contains no pictorial element that is described by the gloss, it seems very possible that the glosses refer to the oval cartouche of feathers that encloses the seated personage in Sign 4. The two-line gloss, *quetzatepeque/yucu yodzo cucha*, is written just to the right of the feathered oval border, and certainly the Mixtec gloss on the 1771 map, "the hill of the circular feathers," would appear to refer to the "circle of feathers" at the left of the gloss.

The Mixtec name of the *quetzal* bird (a trogon whose Latin name is *Pharomacrus mocinno*) is given as *ndodzo* in a gloss written on Codex Muro.[5] Thus it is unlikely that the term *cudia* or *(te)cundi ya* in the Mixtec gloss on the 1718 map refers to the *quetzal* bird. This phrase seems to mean literally "royal thrush," and the thrush or *Turdidae* family, no matter how royal, is a rather drab group of birds when compared to the *quetzal*, whose long green tail feathers were highly prized in pre-Conquest times.

Van de Velde transcribes the Mixtec gloss on the 1771 map as *yucu yoo iticha*, which he translates as the "hill of the moon of the divine bird." (*Yucu* = "hill"; *yoo* = "moon"; *i* = "divine"; *tichá* = "bird.")

Sign 6

Description: a hill with a plant. On the summit of the hill is a male figure wearing a loincloth and carrying a bow and arrow; this figure is not part of the place sign.

Nahuatl gloss: *Acatepeque* "reed hill"
Mixtec gloss: *yucu yoo* "hill of the moon"
    yucu = "hill"
    yoo = "moon"

Comments:

In the case of this hill, the Nahuatl and Mixtec names appear to be different, for in Mixtec the word for "reed" or *acatl* is *tnu yoo*, with the word *yoo* prefixed by *tnu*, the shortened form of *yutnu* ("tree, wood") used to designate trees and plants. The word *yoo* alone usually means "moon, month." However, the place sign only depicts the Nahuatl name "reed hill" and does not include any pictorial elements representing the *yoo* or "moon" of the Mixtec name.

A similar problem encountered with a Coastal town whose Nahuatl name is Acatepec and whose Mixtec name is *yucu yoò* or "hill of the moon" is discussed in Chapter V (pp. 68–70), where it was suggested that the *Acatepec-yucu yoo* sign in the Xoxocotlán map and the *Saioltepec-tiyuqu* at the right (Sign 7) may be the same as a compound place sign in Codex Selden 7-III and 8-I.

Comparison with the Map of San Juan Chapultepec. The *yucu yoo* or "hill of the moon" of the Xoxocotlán map is probably the same place shown in the upper-left corner

of a map of San Juan Chapultepec (Fig. 164), Xoxocotlán's neighbor on the east and north. The map of Chapultepec is in AGN-Tierras 236-6 and has been published by Genaro V. Vásquez (*Para la historia del terruño*, Mexico, 1931, 22–bis). The map shows the lands of Chapultepec, which are described by short texts in Mixtec and Spanish; it also depicts as profile heads the native rulers of the various sections of Chapultepec, with the Spanish names of these personages written near the profile heads. In the upper-right corner of the map, the longest bilingual text is a certifying statement by Don Diego Cortés, who was the native ruler of Chapultepec and of the *barrio* of Santa Ana; Cortés' Mixtec name is given as *dhahui yuchi*, probably the personal name "Tlaloc-Flint Blade."

This certifying text states that the map was made and presented in 1523, and the map is bound in the AGN-Tierras volume with an extremely waterlogged Mixtec text that sets forth Don Diego Cortés' title to his holdings and is also dated 1523. The AGN volume also contains a Spanish translation of the Mixtec text made in 1696, and this translation was published by Vásquez (*ibid.*, 23–25). Luis Ceballos of the Archivo General de la Nación mentioned in conversation that he felt that the water-stained 1523 Mixtec text had been artificially aged, and this may also be true of the Chapultepec map. It is difficult to believe that the map was drawn as early as 1523, just a few years after the Spanish conquest of Oaxaca, because it contains no vestige of native iconography, or of the sure, taut pre-Conquest drawing style. The map may have had a 1523 prototype, now unknown, but it seems likely that the drawing now in the AGN may well have been done as late as 1696, the year in which the Spanish translation was made of Diego Cortés' title claim.

For the purposes of the present book, I wish to discuss only the glosses on the left side of the Chapultepec map, because these glosses set forth San Juan Chapultepec's boundaries on the south with Xoxocotlán. In the lower-left corner is a bilingual text in Mixtec and Spanish to the effect that Chapultepec shares a boundary named "the stone box or container" with Xoxocotlán.

    Mixtec: *saha to ñyu nitan dsaño noo yoo* "the box of stone where [Chapultepec] joined boundaries with Xoxocotlán"
        sahato = *satnu* of the Alvarado dictionary = "box, container"
        ñyu = *yuu* = "stone"
        ni- = past-tense prefix
        tan = *tnaha* = "to be joined"
        dsaño = *dzañu* = "boundary"
        noo yoo = the Mixtec name of Xoxocotlán
    Spanish: *llaman en la lengua misteca* = *xathuni yuâ La caxa de piedra linda la moxonera de Xoxocotlan* "The marker which marks the boundary with the lands of Xoxocotlán is called in the Mixtec language *xathuni yuâ* [*satnu yuu*], 'the box of stone.' "

The names of boundaries written on the 1771 Map of Xoxocotlán do not appear to include a boundary named *satnu yuu* or "the stone box." It may be that this site was

---

[5] The personal name of the noblewoman 2-Flower on page 6 of Codex Muro is a turquoise jewel with a *quetzal* bird; the Mixtec gloss describing this ersonal name is *yusi tedza dodzo*. *Yusi* means "turquoise jewel"; *tedza(a)* means "bird"; and thus *(n)dodzo* specifies that the bird is a *quetzal*. The Alvarado dictionary does not include a Mixtec word for *quetzal*, nor is a Mixtec name for this bird known by any of the present-day Mixtecs with whom I have spoken.

a disputed site—that is, one that was claimed by the natives of San Juan Chapultepec to be a boundary between their town and Xoxocotlán, but not acknowledged as a boundary by Xoxocotlán.

On the map of San Juan Chapultepec, a second boundary between Chapultepec and Xoxocotlán is described in a bilingual gloss written in the upper half of the left border of the map. The first line of the two-line Mixtec gloss at the edge is partly obliterated and difficult to read, but the second line reads:

> . . . *yucu tica nitan dzaño noyoo* "the hill of the grasshopper, where [Chapultepec] joined boundaries with Xoxocotlán"
> *yucu* = "hill"
> *tica* = "grasshopper"
> *ni-* = past-tense prefix
> *tan* = *tnaha* = "to be joined"
> *dzaño* = "boundary"
> *no yoo* = the Mixtec name of Xoxocotlán

The Spanish text written beneath the Mixtec inscription contains essentially the same information:

> *Biene corriendo assia el monte que llaman Yucu tica, quiere decir el monte o Mogote de Chapulin linda la moxonera de xoxocotlan.*
> "[The boundary line] continues toward the hill named *yucu tica*, [which] means 'the hill or mound of the grasshopper,' the site [where Chapultepec] joins boundaries with Xoxocotlán."

At the right of the Spanish gloss is a sketchy picture of a grasshopper. This "hill of the grasshopper" is also shown on the 1771 Map of Xoxocotlán. Sign 8, the second hill to the right of the *Acatepec/yucu yoo* hill under discussion, contains the figure of a grasshopper, as well as the Mixtec gloss *yucu tica* and the Nahuatl gloss *Chapultepeque*, which also means "grasshopper hill."

Above the description of the "grasshopper hill" boundary in the map of San Juan Chapultepec is a crescent moon which encloses a profile human head. This sign is accompanied by the Mixtec gloss *yucu yoo* and the Spanish gloss *monte de Luna*, both of which mean "hill of the moon." This "hill of the moon" is undoubtedly the same place as the *Acatepec/yucu yoo* on the 1771 Map of Xoxocotlán, because in the Chapultepec map, west is at the top, and thus the "hill of the moon" is shown as being roughly west of the "hill of the grasshopper," much as it is on the 1771 Xoxocotlán map, where the top of the map is west-northwest.

In the written documents bound with the Chapultepec map in AGN-Tierras 236–6, the boundary between San Juan Chapultepec and San Martín Mexicapan, Chapultepec's neighbor to the northwest, is described as being the slope of a hill variously known as "the hill of the moon" (in a 1692 Spanish translation of the will of the native nobleman Diego Cortés, translated from a Mixtec original dated 1565; fol. 33) and as "acatepeque" (in a clarification of boundaries between Chapultepec and Mexicapan dated August 22, 1709; fol. 26).

Sign 7

Description: a hill with a winged insect
Nahuatl gloss: *Saioltepeque* "fly (insect) hill"
Mixtec gloss: *tiyuqu* "fly (the insect)"
Comments:

In the 1718 Map of Xoxocotlán the Mixtec gloss is *tiyuqh nduchi*, and the precise meaning of *nduchi* as it is used here to modify *tiyuqh* or "fly" is not clear, but the added word probably designates the species of fly shown in the sign. *Nduchi* usually means "beans," and it may mean here that the fly in question is a type common in bean fields. According to Van de Velde, this hill is today called *Cerro Mozcón*, "the hill of the large fly," and on this hill is a configuration of stone that very much resembles a fly.

Sign 8

Description: a hill with a grasshopper
Nahuatl gloss: *Chapul [tepeque]* "grasshopper hill"
Mixtec gloss: *yucu tica* "the hill of the grasshopper"
> *yucu* = "hill"
> *tica* = "grasshopper"
Comments:

As was discussed above in the comments on Sign 6, this "hill of the grasshopper" is a boundary between Xoxocotlán and its neighbor to the north and northeast, San Juan Chapultepec. Although the Nahuatl name, "chapultepec," of the neighboring town is the same as that of this boundary sign, the Mixtec name of San Juan Chapultepec is *yuta ita* or "river of flowers" (AGN-Tierras, 236–6, *passim*).

Sign 9

Description: an owl within a hill
Nahuatl gloss: *Teculutlan* "owl place"
Mixtec gloss: *cahua tinumi* "ravine, rock, or cave of the owl"
> *cahua* = "ravine, rock, cave"
> *tiñumi* = "owl"
Comments:

In a land document concerning San Juan Chapultepec, supposedly dated 1523, this site is considered a boundary between Chapultepec and Xoxocotlán (AGN-Tierras, 236–6, fol. 9). But it is not included as a boundary of Chapultepec in the sketch map of this town (Fig. 164), also supposedly dated 1523.

Sign 10

Description: unsure, because this section of the map is damaged
Nahuatl gloss: *Tepetoco*
Mixtec gloss: *yucu mini* "hill of the hollow"
> *yucu* = "hill"
> *mini* = "hollow, lake"

Sign 11

Description: a hill that apparently has no pictorial sign to illustrate the place name's qualifying element.
Nahuatl gloss: *Mexicatepeque* "hill of the Mexicans"
Mixtec gloss: *yucu sami noo* "hill of the Mexicans"
> *yucu* = "hill"

sami noo or *nuu* = "Mexican"

Comments:

The Alvarado dictionary lists four Mixtec phrases under the entry "mexicano"—that is, a Nahuatl speaker from in or around the Valley of Mexico. These are:

tay sami nuu
tay ñuu dzuma
tai yecoo
tay ñuu coyo.

The common word in these four phrases, *tay* or *tai*, means "man." The remainder of the first phrase, *sami nuu*, means "to burn the face or the surface" (*sami* = "to burn"; *nuu* = "surface"), and thus by this definition the Mexicans are those who burn the face or the surface [of the earth?]. The second phrase refers to the Mexicans as "the men of the town or place of the tail" (*ñuu* = "town, place"; *dzuma* = "tail of an animal"). Whether this name refers to the inhabitants of a specific place whose Mixtec name is *ñuu dzuma* or "Tail Town" is not known; no such town is included in the Reyes list of Mixtec names of towns in the Mexican region. In the third phrase, the precise meaning of *yecoo* is uncertain. One possibility is that the *ye-* is a shortened form of *yehe*, which when it appears as *ye-* generally means "is," "has," "is dressed as"; and *coo* may mean "serpent." Thus the phrase *tai yecoo* might mean "the man who is serpent-like." The last phrase, *tay ñuu coyo*, means "a man of Mexico City-Tenochtitlan," for *ñuu coyo* (literally "the town of the cattails") is the Mixtec name of Mexico City-Tenochtitlan.

Sign 12

Description: a hill with a rectangular block

Nahuatl gloss: *Tlapatoya*

Mixtec gloss: *noo yuu catni* "near, on or toward the square stone"
  noo (*nuu* in the Alvarado dictionary dialect) = "near, on, toward"
  yuu = "stone"
  catni = "square"

Comments:

Catni is not the most common word for "square" or "squared," which is usually *siqui* or *nduq* in Mixtec; but the Alvarado dictionary gives *yutnu catni* ("wood in squares") as the definition for "chessboard," and the square shape of the object in the hill seems to indicate that *yuu catni* should be translated as "square or squared stone."

Sign 13

Description: an oval lake at the top of a hill

Nahuatl gloss: *Tepechalco* "in the lake of the hill"

Mixtec gloss (1718 map): *yucu mini* "the hill of the lake"

Comments:

The Mixtec gloss in the 1771 map is merely *yuhu*, "mouth, at the edge of," perhaps a copyist's error or interpolation. The *yucu mini* gloss on the earlier version of the map appears to relate more closely to the pictorial sign of a hill with a lake and to the Nahuatl gloss *Tepechalco*.

Sign 14

Description: a double hill which apparently has no pictorial qualifying element

Nahuatl gloss: none

Mixtec gloss: *yucu saqui* "the hill that sets the boundaries"
  yucu = "hill"
  saqui = *saq* of the Alvarado dictionary = "to set boundaries"

Sign 15

Description: a hill with no pictorial qualifying element

Nahuatl gloss: none

Mixtec gloss: *itno cuchi* "the slope of the hillock"
  itno = "slope"
  cuchi = "hillock"

Sign 16

Description: a hill with no apparent pictorial qualifying element

Nahuatl gloss: *Tlite, tepeque* "black hill"

Mixtec gloss (1771 map): none

Mixtec gloss (1718 map): *yuvui tayee* "the dark (bruise-colored) ravine?"
  yuvui = "ravine"
  tayee = *teyee* = "bump, bruise"

Comments:

As was discussed above, in the section of this appendix entitled "Short Geographical Texts within the Boundaries," the *yuvui tayee* written on Sign 16 in the 1718 map seems to be equivalent to the *cuiti [yu]hui t[a]yee* written under the church of San Agustín in the 1771 map ("Text D" in Fig. 163).

Sign 17

Description: a low hill with two serpents

Nahuatl gloss (most legible in the 1718 map): *Qiechcua-tepetl* "rattlesnake hill"

Mixtec gloss: *cuiti coo caa* "mound of the rattlesnake"
  cuiti = "mound"
  coo caa = "rattlesnake" (literally, "serpent of metal";
    coo = "serpent"; *caa* = "metal")

Comments:

The *Qiech* section of the Nahuatl gloss is undoubtedly a somewhat inaccurate rendering of *Cuech*, a Nahuatl word that refers to a non-poisonous type of rattlesnake described in Francisco Hernández, "Historia natural de Nueva España," tratado tercero, cap. xvii (*Obras completas*, III [Mexico, 1959], 372).

Sign 18

Description: a circular dish within a low hill

Nahuatl gloss (1771 map): none

Nahuatl gloss (1718 map): *Tepecaxetl* "the cooking pan (*cajete*) of the hill"

Mixtec gloss (1771 map): none

Mixtec gloss (1718 map): *yuu saha* "the stone of the ceramic cooking dish"
  yuu = "stone"
  saha = "ceramic cooking dish (*lebrillo*)"

Comments:

In the 1771 map, only the pictorial sign is shown;

neither the Nahuatl nor the Mixtec gloss was copied from the 1718 map.

Sign 19
Description: a deer lying down
Nahuatl gloss: *Masatepeque* "deer hill"
Mixtec gloss: *no nicaa ydzu* "where there was a deer"
    no = "where"
    ni– = past-tense prefix
    caa = "to be, to be present"
    ydzu = "deer"
Comments:
    Van de Velde transcribes this gloss as *nu nica izu*, which

he translates as "where the deer fell." (*Nu* = "where"; *ni* = "the"; *ca* = "fell"; *izu* or *azu* = "deer.")

Sign 20
Description: a body of water with a dark border
Nahuatl gloss: *Soquitlan* "mud place"
Mixtec gloss: *noo nchayu* "where there is mud"
    noo = "where"
    nchayu (*ndayu* of the Alvarado dictionary dialect) = "mud"
Comments:
    Van de Velde translates *noo chayuu* as "stone face or place." (*No* = "face"; *cha* = "place"; *yu* = "stone.")

BIBLIOGRAPHY

Part I: Selected Books and Articles

Adelhofer, Otto. *Codex Vindobonensis Mexicanus I*. Graz, Austria, 1963.

Alcedo, Antonio de. *Diccionario geográfico-histórico de las Indias Occidentales o América*. 5 vols. Madrid, 1786–89.

Alcina Franch, José. "Fuentes indígenas de Méjico: ensayo de sistematización bibliográfica," *Revista de Indias*, Año XV, Nos. 61–62 (1955), 420–521.

Alvarado, Francisco de. See Jiménez Moreno, Wigberto.

Arana Osnaya, Evangelina. "El idioma de los señores de Tepozcolula," *Anales del INAH*, Vol. XIII, 1960 (1961), 217–30.

———, and Mauricio Swadesh. *Los elementos del mixteco antiguo*. Mexico, 1965.

Barlow, Robert H., ed. "Dos Relaciones antiguas del pueblo de Cuilapa, Estado de Oaxaca," *Tlalocan*, Vol. II–1 (1945), 18–28.

———. *The Extent of the Empire of the Culhua Mexica*. Berkeley and Los Angeles, 1949. (Ibero-Americana, 28)

———. "Glifos toponímicos de los códices mixtecos," *Tlalocan*, Vol. II–3 (1947), 285–86.

———, and Byron McAfee. *Diccionario de elementos fonéticos en escritura jeroglífica: Códice Mendocino*. Mexico, 1949.

Berlin, Heinrich. *Fragmentos desconocidos del Códice de Yanhuitlán y otras investigaciones mixtecas*. Mexico, 1947.

Bernal, Ignacio, ed. "Relación de Guautla," *Tlalocan*, Vol. IV–1 (1962), 3–16.

Borah, Woodrow, and S. F. Cook. *The Population of Central Mexico in 1548: An Analysis of the Suma de visitas de pueblos*. Berkeley and Los Angeles, 1960. (Ibero-Americana, 43)

Bradomín, José María. *Toponimia de Oaxaca (crítica etimológica)*. Mexico, 1955.

Brand, Donald D. "Place-Name Problems in Mexico as Illustrated by Necotlán," *Papers of the Michigan Academy of Science, Arts and Letters*, Vol. XXXIV (1948), 241–52.

Burgoa, Francisco de. *Geográfica descripción*, 2 vols. Mexico, 1934. (Publicaciones del Archivo General de la Nación, Vols. XXV–XXVI)

———. *Palestra historial*. Mexico, 1934. (Publicaciones del Archivo General de la Nación, Vol. XXIV)

Burland, Cottie A. *Codex Egerton 2895*. Graz, Austria, 1965.

———. "Some errata in the published edition of Codex Nuttall," *Boletín del Centro de Investigaciones Antropológicas de México*, Vol. II–1 (1957), 11–13.

———, and Gerdt Kutscher. *The Selden Roll*. Berlin, 1955.

Byam Davies, Claude Nigel. *Los señoríos independientes del Imperio Azteca*. Mexico, 1968. (Instituto Nacional de Antropología e Historia, Série Historia, Vol. XIX)

Caso, Alfonso. "Base para la sincronología mixteca y cristiana," *Memoria de el Colegio Nacional*, Vol. VI–6 (1951), 49–66.

———. "El calendario mixteco," *Historia mexicana*, Vol. V–20 (1956), 481–97.

———. "Calendario y escritura en Xochicalco," *RMEA*, Vol. XVIII (1962), 49–79.

———. "Comentario al Códice Baranda," *Miscelánea Paul Rivet, Octogenario Dicata* (Mexico, 1958), Vol. I, 373–93.

———. "El dios 1. Muerte," *Mitteilungen aus dem Museum für Völkerkunde und Vorgeschichte, Hamburg*, Vol. XXV (1959), 40–43.

———. *Las estelas zapotecas*. Mexico, 1928.

———. "Explicación del reverso del Codex Vindobonensis," *Memoria de el Colegio Nacional*, Vol. V–5 (1950), 9–46.

———. "The Historical Value of the Mixtec Codices," *Boletín de estudios oaxaqueños*, No. 16 (1960), 1–7.

———. *Interpretación del Códice Colombino/Interpretation of the Codex Colombino*. Mexico, 1966.

———. *Interpretación del Códice Gómez de Orozco*. Mexico, 1954.

———. *Interpretación del Códice Selden 3135 (A.2)/Interpretation of the Codex Selden 3135 (A.2)*. Mexico, 1964.

———. *Interpretation of the Codex Bodley 2858*. Mexico, 1960.

———. "El Lienzo de Filadelfia," *Homenaje a Fernando Márquez-Miranda* (Madrid–Seville, 1964), 135–44.

———. "El Lienzo de Yolotepec," *Memoria de el Colegio Nacional*, Vol. XIII–4 (1958), 41–55.

———. "El Lienzo de Zacatepec." Unpublished manuscript, 25 typescript pp.

———. "Los lienzos mixtecos de Ihuitlán y Antonio de León," *Homenaje a Pablo Martínez del Río* (Mexico, 1961), 237–74.

———. "Mapa de Santo Tomás Ocotepeque, Oaxaca," *Summa anthropologica en homenaje a Roberto J. Weitlaner* (Mexico, 1966), 131–37.

———. "El Mapa de Teozacoalco," *Cuadernos Americanos*, Año VIII, No. 5 (1949), 145–81.

———. "El Mapa de Xochitepec," *ICA* XXXII (Copenhagen, 1958), 458–66.

———. "Mixtec Writing and Calendar," *HMAI*, Vol. III, part II (Austin, Texas, 1965), 948–61.

———. "Representaciones de hongos en los códices," *Estudios de Cultura Nahuatl*, Vol. IV (1963), 27–36.

———. "Los señores de Yanhuitlán," *ICA* XXXV (Mexico, 1964), Vol. I, 437–48.

————. "La vida y aventuras de 4. Viento 'Serpiente de Fuego,'" *Miscelánea de estudios dedicados al Dr. Fernando Ortiz* (Havana, 1955), 291–98.

Clark, James Cooper, ed. and trans. *Codex Mendoza: The Mexican Manuscript Known as the Collection of Mendoza and Preserved in the Bodleian Library, Oxford,* 3 vols. London, 1938.

————. *The Story of "Eight Deer" in Codex Colombino.* London, 1912.

Cline, Howard F. "The *Relaciones Geográficas* of the Spanish Indies, 1577–1586," *Hispanic American Historical Review,* Vol. XLIV (1964), 341–74.

Cortés, Hernán. *Fernando Cortes: his five letters of Relation to the Emperor Charles V,* ed. and trans. by Francis Augustus MacNutt, 2 vols. Cleveland, 1908.

Dahlgren de Jordan, Barbro. *La mixteca: su cultura e historia prehispánicas.* Mexico, 1954.

Dark, Philip, and Joyce Plesters. "The Palimpsests of Codex Selden: Recent attempts to reveal the covered pictographs," *ICA* XXXIII (San José de Costa Rica, 1959), Vol. II, 530–39.

Dávila Garibi, José Ignacio. *Toponimias nahuas.* Mexico, 1942. (Instituto Panamericano de Geografía e Historia, Publicación 63)

DeBlois, Joyce Waddell. "An Interpretation of the Map and Relación of Texupa in Oaxaca, Mexico, and an Analysis of the Style of the Map." Unpublished M.A. thesis, Tulane University, April, 1963.

Díaz del Castillo, Bernal. *Historia verdadera de la conquista de la Nueva España,* ed. by Joaquín Ramírez Cabañas, 3 vols. Mexico, 1944.

Dyk, Anne. *Mixteco Texts.* Norman, Oklahoma, 1959. (Summer Institute of Linguistics, Linguistics Series, 3)

————, and Betty Stoudt. *Vocabulario mixteco de San Miguel el Grande.* Mexico, 1965. (Instituto Lingüístico de Verano, Vocabularios Indígenas, 12)

Fuente, Julio de la. "Documentos para la etnografía e historia zapotecas," *Anales del INAH,* Vol. III, 1947–48 (1949), 175–97.

Gallegos, Roberto. "Zaachila: The First Season's Work," *Archaeology,* Vol. XVI–4 (1963), 226–33.

García, Gregorio. *Origen de los indios de el Nuevo Mundo e Indias Occidentales,* 2nd ed., Madrid, 1729.

García Granados, Rafael. "Estudios comparativo de los signos cronográficos en los códices prehispánicos de Méjico," *ICA* XXVII (Mexico, 1942), Vol. I, 419–69.

————. "Observaciones sobre los códices pre-hispánicos de México y reparo que estas sugieren acerca de su clasificación," *El México Antiguo,* Vol. V, 1–2 (1940), 41–47.

García Payón, José. "El símbolo del año en el México antiguo," *El México Antiguo,* Vol. IV, 7–8 (1939), 241–53.

Gelb, I. J. "Review of Marcel Cohen, *La grande invention de l'écriture et son évolution,*" *Language,* Vol. XXXVIII–2 (1962), 207–11.

————. *A Study of Writing,* rev. ed., Chicago, 1963.

Gerhard, Peter. "Emperors' Dye of the Mixtecs," *Natural History,* Vol. LXXIII–1 (1964), 26–31.

Glass, John B. *Catálogo de la Colección de Códices.* Mexico, 1964.

————. "The Pictorial Manuscripts of Middle America," to be pubished in *HMAI,* Vol. 14.

Hernández, Francisco. *Obras completas,* 3 vols. Mexico, 1959.

Herrera, Antonio de. *Historia general de los hechos de los castellanos en las islas y tierra firme del Mar Océano,* Vol. VI. Madrid, 1947.

Icaza, Francisco A. de. *Conquistadores y pobladores de Nueva España,* 2 vols. Madrid, 1923.

Jiménez Moreno, Wigberto, ed. *Vocabulario en lengua mixteca por Fray Francisco de Alvarado.* Mexico, 1962.

————, and Salvador Mateos Higuera. *Códice de Yanhuitlán.* Mexico, 1940.

Kubler, George. *The Art and Architecture of Ancient America.* Baltimore, 1962.

Lehmann, Walter. "Les peintures mixteco-zapotèques et quelques documents apparentés," *JSA,* n.s., Vol. II–2 (1905), 241–80.

Long, Richard C. E. "The Zouche Codex," *Journal of the Royal Anthropological Institute of Great Britain and Ireland,* Vol. LVI (1926), 239–58.

López, Hector F. *Diccionario geográfico, histórico, biográfico y lingüístico del Estado de Guerrero.* Mexico, 1942.

Lyell, J. P. R. *Early Book Illustration in Spain.* London, 1926.

Mak, Cornelia. "Mixtec medical beliefs and practices," *América Indígena,* Vol. XIX–2 (1959), 125–50.

Martínez, Maximino. *Catálogo de nombres vulgares y científicos de plantas mexicanas.* Mexico, 1937.

————. *Las plantas medicinales de México,* 4th ed. Mexico, 1959.

Martínez Gracida, Manuel. "Catálogo etimológico de los nombres de los pueblos, haciendas y ranchos del Estado de Oaxaca," *BSMGE,* 4a. época, I, 5–6 (1888), 285–438.

————. *Colección de "Cuadros sinópticos" de los pueblos, haciendas y ranchos del Estado libre y soberano de Oaxaca.* Oaxaca, 1883.

————. *Flora y fauna del Estado libre y soberano de Oaxaca.* Oaxaca, 1891.

————. "Reseña histórica del antiguo reino de Tututepec." Unpublished manuscript, 1907.

Mexico. Secretaría de Recursos Hidráulicos. Comite de Estudios de la Cuenca del Río Balsas. *Estudios del Río Verde,* 1 vol. text and 1 vol. atlas. Mexico, 1961.

Molina, Alonso de. *Vocabulario en lengua castellana y mexicana.* Madrid, 1944. (Colección de Incunables Americanos, Vol. IV)

Nicholson, H. B. "The Significance of the 'Looped Cord' Year Symbol in Pre-Hispanic Mexico: An Hypothesis," *Estudios de Cultura Nahuatl,* Vol. VI (1966), 135–48.

Nowotny, Karl A. *Codices Becker I/II.* Graz, Austria, 1961.

————. "Erläuterungen zum Codex Vindobonensis (Vorderseite)," *Archiv für Völkerkunde,* Vol. III (1948), 156–200.

————. "Die Hieroglyphen des Codex Mendoza: Der Bau einer mittelamerikanischen Wortschrift," *Mitteilungen aus dem Museum für Völkerkunde und Vorgeschichte, Hamburg,* Vol. XXV (1959), 97–113.

Nuttall, Zelia. *Codex Nuttall, Facsimile of an ancient Mexican codex belonging to Lord Zouche of Harynworth, England.* Cambridge, Massachusetts, 1902.

O'Gorman, Helen. *Mexican Flowering Trees and Plants.* Mexico, 1961.

Paddock, John, ed. *Ancient Oaxaca: Discoveries in Mexican Archaeology and History.* Stanford, Calif., 1966.

Parmenter, Ross. "Break-Through on the 'Lienzo de Filadelfia,'" *Expedition,* Vol. VIII–2 (1966), 14–22.

————. "The Identification of Lienzo A: A Tracing in the Latin American Library of Tulane University," to be published in: Tulane University, Middle American Research

Institute, *Philological and Documentary Studies*, Vol. II–5 (1970).

———. "20th Century Adventures of a 16th Century Sheet: The Literature on the Mixtec Lienzo in the Royal Ontario Museum," *Boletín de estudios oaxaqueños,* No. 20 (1961).

Paso y Troncoso, Francisco del, ed. *Papeles de Nueva España,* segunda série, Geográfica y Estadística, Vols. I, IV, and V. Madrid, 1905.

Peña, M. T. de la. *Problemas sociales y económicos de las Mixtecas.* Mexico, 1950. (Memorias del Instituto Nacional Indigenista, Vol. II, Núm. 1)

Peñafiel, Antonio. *Códice Mixteco. Lienzo de Zacatepec.* Mexico, 1900.

———. "El códice mixteco precortesiano Javier Córdova y un antiguo plano de San Andrés Cholula," *Revista histórica mexicana,* Vol. I (1907), 75–80.

———. *Nombres geográficos de México.* Mexico, 1885.

———. *Nomenclatura geográfica de México.* Mexico, 1897.

Pesman, M. Walter. *Meet Flora Mexicana.* Globe, Arizona, 1962.

Pike, Kenneth L. *Tone Languages.* Ann Arbor, 1948. (University of Michigan Publications, Linguistics, Vol. IV)

———. "Tone Puns in Mixteco," *International Journal of American Linguistics,* Vol. XI (1945), 129–39.

Raymond, Joseph. "The Indian Mind in Mexican Toponyms," *América Indígena,* Vol. XII–3 (1952), 205–16.

Revista mexicana de estudios históricos, Vols. I and II. Mexico, 1927–28.

Reyes, Antonio de los. "Arte en lengua mixteca," *Actes de la Société Philologique,* Vol. XVIII, 1888 (Paris, 1890).

Robertson, Donald. "Los manuscritos religiosos mixtecos," *ICA* XXXV (Mexico, 1964), Vol. I, 425–35.

———. *Mexican Manuscript Painting of the Early Colonial Period: The Metropolitan Schools.* New Haven, 1959.

———. "The Pinturas (Mapas) of the *Relaciones Geográficas,*" to be published in *HMAI,* Vol. 12.

———. "The *Relaciones Geográficas* of Mexico," *ICA* XXXIII (San José de Costa Rica, 1959), Vol. II, 540–47.

———. "Review of *Codices Becker I/II,*" *American Antiquity,* Vol. XXVII–2 (1962), 254–55.

Rosado Ojeda, Vladamiro. "Estudio del códice mixteco postcortesano Núm. 36," *Anales del INAH,* Vol. I (1945), 147–55.

Saussure, Henri. *Le Manuscrit du Cacique.* Geneva, 1892.

Seler, Eduard. *Gesammelte Abhandlungen zur amerikanischen Sprach- und Alterthumskunde,* 5 vols. Berlin, 1902–23.

Smith, Mary Elizabeth. "The Codex Colombino: A Document of the South Coast of Oaxaca," *Tlalocan,* Vol. IV–3 (1963), 276–88.

———. *Las glosas del Códice Colombino/The Glosses of Codex Colombino.* Bound with: Caso, Alfonso, *Interpretación del Códice Colombino/Interpretation of the Codex Colombino.* Mexico, 1966.

Spinden, Herbert J. "Indian Manuscripts of Southern Mexico," *Annual Report of the Smithsonian Institution, 1933* (Washington, 1935), 429–51.

Spores, Ronald. "The Genealogy of Tlazultepec: A Sixteenth Century Mixtec Manuscript," *Southwestern Journal of Anthropology,* Vol. XX–1 (1964), 15–31.

———. *The Mixtec Kings and Their People.* Norman, Oklahoma, 1967.

Spranz, Bodo. *Göttergestalten in den mexikanischen Bilder-handschriften der Codex Borgia-Gruppe: eine ikonographische Untersuchung.* Wiesbaden, 1964. (Acta Humboldtiana, Series Geographica et Ethnographica, 4)

Standley, Paul C. *Trees and Shrubs of Mexico.* Washington, 1920–26. (Contributions from the United States National Herbarium, Vol. 23)

Stenton, Sir Frank *et al. The Bayeux Tapestry: A Comprehensive Survey,* 2nd ed. London, 1965.

Taylor, William B. "The Valley of Oaxaca: A Study of Colonial Land Distribution." Unpublished doctoral dissertation, University of Michigan, 1969.

Thompson, J. Eric S., ed. "The Relación of Tecuanapa, Guerrero," *Tlalocan,* Vol. V–1 (1965), 85–96.

Tibón, Gutierre. *Pinotepa Nacional: mixtecos, negros, triques.* Mexico, 1962.

Troike, Nancy P. "Observations on Some Material Aspects of the Codex Colombino," to be published in *Tlalocan,* Vol. VI–3.

———. "Observations on the Physical Form of the Codex Becker I," to be published in *Archiv für Völkerkunde,* Vol. XXIII.

———. "The Provenience of the Mixtec Codices Nuttall and Colombino-Becker," paper presented at the 68th Annual Meeting of the American Anthropological Association, held in New Orleans, November 20–23, 1969.

———. "The Structure of the Codex Colombino-Becker," to be published in *Anales del INAH,* época 7, Vol. II, No. 50.

———. "A Study of Some Stylistic Elements in the Codex Colombino-Becker," to be published in *ICA* XXXVIII (Stuttgart, 1970).

Tupeus, Josep Mariano. "Vocabulario, doctrina y oraciones [en lengua mixteca]." Unpublished manuscript on microfilm at Yale University Library.

Vásquez, Genaro V. *Para la historia del terruño.* Mexico, 1931.

Villagra, Agustín. "El Lienzo de Zacatepec: un nuevo lienzo que viene a enriquecer la colección de códices que existen en el Museo Nacional," *Boletín del Museo Nacional de Arqueología, Historia y Etnografía,* 5a. época, Vol. II (1933), 105–106.

Villavicencio, Miguel de. "Arte, Prontuario, Vocabulario y Confesionario de la lengua mixteca." Nineteenth-century copy by Francisco del Paso y Troncoso, Museo Nacional de Antropología, Mexico City, Archivo Histórico, Colección Antigua, No. 3–60 bis.

Weitlaner Johnson, Irmgard. "Análisis textil del Lienzo de Ocotepec," *Summa anthropologica en homenaje a Roberto J. Weitlaner* (Mexico, 1966), 139–44.

Part II: Reproductions

This section lists the most useful and accessible reproductions of most of the published pictorial manuscripts mentioned in the text and describes briefly the type of reproduction. Accompanying the name of the manuscript and its present location is the manuscript's number in the census of Mexican pictorial manuscripts to be published in Volume 14 of the *Handbook of Middle American Indians* (*HMAI*). The *HMAI* census includes all the pictorial manuscripts from Middle America except the *Relación Geográfica* maps, which are treated in a study by Donald Robertson to appear in Volume 12 of the *HMAI*.

AMOLTEPEC, 1580 *Relación Geográfica* Map of. Austin, University of Texas Latin American Library, García Icazbalceta Collection, No. 1770.

Robertson, Donald. "The *Relaciones Geográficas* of Mexico," *ICA* XXXIII (San José de Costa Rica, 1959), Vol. II, 544, Fig. 3.
Black-and-white photograph.

ANTONIO DE LEÓN, Lenzo. Toronto, Royal Ontaro Museum, Catalog No. 917.3. (*HMAI* Census No. 8)
Caso, Alfonso. "Los lienzos mixtecos de Ihuitlán y Antonio de León," *Homenaje a Pablo Martínez del Río* (Mexico, 1961), 237–74.
Black-and-white photographs.
Rickards, Constantine George. "Notes on the 'Codex Rickards,'" *JSA* n.s. Vol. X (1913), 47–57.
Drawings of isolated motifs.

BADIANUS HERBAL. Rome, Vatican Library, Codex Barberini, Latin 241. (*HMAI* Census No. 85)
Cruz, Martín de la. *Libellus de medicinalibus indorum herbis. Manuscrito azteca de 1552. Versión española con estudios y comentarios por diversos autores.* Mexico, 1964.
Photographic color facsimile.
Emmart, Emily Walcott. *The Badianus Manuscript (Codex Barberini, Latin 241), Vatican Library. An Aztec Herbal of 1552.* Baltimore, 1940.
Color photographs of a copy.

BARANDA, Codex. Mexico City, Museo Nacional de Antropología, No. 35–4. (*HMAI* Census No. 24)
Caso, Alfonso. "Comentario al Códice Baranda," *Miscelánea Paul Rivet, Octogenario Dicata*, Vol. I (Mexico, 1958), 373–93.
Color and black-and-white photographs.

BECKER I and II, Codices. Vienna, Museum für Völkerkunde, Inv. Nr. 60306 and 60307. (*HMAI* Census Nos. 27, 28)
Nowotny, Karl A. *Codices Becker I/II.* Graz, Austria, 1961.
Photographic color facsmiles.

BODLEY, Codex. Oxford, Bodleian Library, Ms. Mex. d.l. (*HMAI* Census No. 31)
Caso, Alfonso. *Interpretation of the Codex Bodley 2858.* Mexico, 1960.
Photographic color facsimile.

BORGIA, Codex. Rome, Vatican Library. (*HMAI* Census No. 33)
Seler, Eduard. *Comentarios al Códice Borgia*, 3 vols. Mexico, 1963.
Vol. III contains color photographs of the Codex; vols. I and II, a Spanish translation of the 1904–1909 Seler commentary, cited below.
———. *Codex Borgia. Eine altmexikanische Bilderschrift der Bibliothek der Congregatio de Propaganda Fide*, 3 vols. Berlin, 1904–1909.
This edition contans monochrome line drawings of the manuscript.

COIXTLAHUACA, Lienzo of. Mexico City, Museo Nacional de Antropología, No. 35–113. (*HMAI* Census No. 70)
Glass, John B. *Catálogo de la Colección de Códices* (Mexico, 1964), plates 123–24.
Two black-and-white photographs, one of the entire Lienzo and one detail.
Codex Ixtlán. Baltimore, 1931. (Maya Society Publication No. 3)
Re-drawing of photographs of a tracing of the Lienzo of Coixtlahuaca.

COLOMBINO, Codex. Mexico City, Museo Nacional de Antropología, No. 35–30. (*HMAI* Census No. 72)

Caso, Alfonso. *Interpretación del Códice Colombino/Interpretation of the Codex Colombino.* Smith, Mary Elizabeth. *Las glosas del Códice Colombino/The Glosses of Codex Colombino.* Mexico, 1966.
Photographic color facsimile.

CÓRDOVA-CASTELLANOS, Lienzo. Present location of original unknown. (*HMAI* Census No. 77)
Peñafiel, Antonio. *Ciudades coloniales y capitales de la República Mexicana*, vol. V: *Las cinco ciudades coloniales de Puebla* (Mexico, 1914), plates 24–32.
Drawings of lost original.
Codex Abraham Castellanos. Baltimore, 1931. (Maya Society Publication No. 5)
Re-drawing of photographs of a tracing of lost original.

COSPI, Codex. Bologna, University Library. (*HMAI* Census No. 79)
Nowotny, Karl A. *Codex Cospi. Calendario Messicano 4093 Biblioteca Universitaria Bologna.* Graz, Austria, 1968.
Photographic color facsimile.

CRUZ, MARTÍN DE LA. *Libellus de medicinalibus indorum herbis.* See BADIANUS HERBAL.

FEJÉRVÁRY-MAYER, Codex. Liverpool, Free Public Museum, 12014/M. (*HMAI* Census No. 118)
Seler, Eduard. *Codex Fejérváry-Mayer: An old Mexican Picture Manuscript in the Liverpool Free Public Museum, 12014/M, Published at the Expense of His Excellency the Duke of Loubat*, trans. by A. H. Keane. Berlin and London, 1901–1902.
Monochrome line drawings.

FERNÁNDEZ LEAL, Codex. Berkeley, University of California, Bancroft Library. (*HMAI* Census No. 119)
Tompkins, John Barr. "Codex Fernández Leal," *The Pacific Art Review*, II (1942), 39–59.
Black-and-white photographs.

FLORENTINE CODEX. Florence, Laurentian Library. (*HMAI* Census No. 274)
Dibble, Charles E. and Arthur J. O. Anderson, ed. and trans. *Florentine Codex: General History of the Things of New Spain [by] Fray Bernardino de Sahagún*, 12 vols. Santa Fe, 1950–70. (Monographs of the School of American Research, No. 14, parts II–XIII)
Black-and-white photographs of a lithographic copy.

GÓMEZ DE OROZCO, Codex. Mexico City, Gómez de Orozco Collection. (*HMAI* Census No. 129)
Caso, Alfonso. *Interpretación del Códice Gómez de Orozco.* Mexico, 1954.
Photographic color facsimile.

HISTORIA TOLTECA-CHICHIMECA. Paris, Bibliothèque Nationale, Fonds Mexicains, Nos. 46–58. (*HMAI* Census No. 359)
Berlin, Heinrich and Silvia Rendón, ed. and trans. *Historia Tolteca-Chichimeca, Anales de Quauhtinchan.* Mexico, 1947. (Fuentes para la historia de México, 1)
Black-and-white drawings.

IHUITLÁN, Lienzo of. Brooklyn, Brooklyn Museum, Accession No. 42.160. (*HMAI* Census No. 157)
Caso, Alfonso. "Los lienzos mixtecos de Ihuitlán y Antonio de Léon," *Homenaje a Pablo Martínez del Río* (Mexico, 1961), 237–74.
Black-and-white photographs.

IXTLÁN, Codex. See COIXTLAHUACA, Lienzo of.

Laud, Codex. Oxford, Bodleian Library, Ms. Laud Misc. 678. (*HMAI* Census No. 185)

Burland, Cottie A. *Codex Laud*. Graz, Austria, 1966.

Photographic color facsimile.

Meixueiro, Codex. Present location of original unknown. (*HMAI* Census No. 195)

Codex Meixueiro. Baltimore, 1931. (Maya Society Publication No. 4)

Re-drawing of photographs of a tracing of lost original.

Mendoza, Codex. Oxford, Bodleian Library, Ms. Arch. Seld. A.1. (*HMAI* Census No. 196)

Clark, James Cooper, ed. and trans. *Codex Mendoza: The Mexican Manuscript Known as the Collection of Mendoza and Preserved in the Bodleian Library, Oxford*, 3 vols. London, 1938.

Photographic color facsimile.

Muro, Codex. Mexico City, Museo Nacional de Antropología, No. 35–68. (*HMAI* Census No. 228)

Glass, John B. *Catálogo de la Colección de Códices* (Mexico, 1964), plate 71.

Black-and-white photograph of page 2 only.

Nuttall, Codex. London, British Museum, Add. Mss. 39671. (*HMAI* Census No. 240)

Nuttall, Zelia. *Codex Nuttall, Facsimile of an ancient Mexican codex belonging to Lord Zouche of Harynworth, England*. Cambridge, Massachusetts, 1902.

Color facsimile of a copy.

Ocotepec, Lienzo of. Santo Tomás Ocotepec, Oaxaca, Municipal Archive. (*HMAI* Census No. 242)

Caso, Alfonso. "Mapa de Santo Tomás Ocotepeque, Oaxaca," *Summa anthropologica en homenaje a Roberto J. Weitlaner* (Mexico, 1966), 131–37.

A color photograph and a black-and-white photograph taken in ultra-violet light.

Philadelphia, Lienzo of. Philadelphia, University of Pennsylvania Museum. (*HMAI* Census No. 251)

Caso, Alfonso. "El Lienzo de Filadelfia," *Homenaje a Fernando Márquez-Miranda* (Madrid-Seville, 1964), 135–44.

Black-and-white photograph.

Parmenter, Ross. "Break-Through on the 'Lienzo de Filadelfia,'" *Expedition,* Vol. VIII–2 (1966), 14–22.

Black-and-white photograph.

Porfirio Díaz, Codex. Mexico City, Museo Nacional de Antropología, No. 35–50. (*HMAI* Census No. 255)

Chavero, Alfredo, ed. *Antigüedades mexicanas (Homenaje a Cristóbal Colón), publicadas por la Junta Colombina de México en el cuarto centenario del descubrimiento de América*, vol. II (Mexico, 1892), plates A*–V*, A'–V'.

Colored lithographs.

Glass, John B. *Catálogo de la Colección de Códices* (Mexico, 1964), plates 51–52.

Two black-and-white photographs of details.

Sánchez Solís, Codex. London, British Museum, Egerton Ms. 2895. (*HMAI* Census No. 279)

Burland, Cottie A. *Codex Egerton 2895*. Graz, Austria, 1965.

Photographic color facsimile.

Selden, Codex. Oxford, Bodleian Library, Ms. Arch. Seld. A.2. (*HMAI* Census No. 283)

Caso, Alfonso. *Interpretación del Códice Selden 3135 (A.2)/Interpretation of the Codex Selden 3135 (A.2)*. Mexico, 1964.

Photographic color facsimile.

Selden Roll. Oxford, Bodleian Library, Ms. Arch. Seld. A.72(3). (*HMAI* Census No. 284)

Burland, Cottie A. and Gerdt Kutscher. *The Selden Roll*. Berlin, 1955.

Black-and-white photographic facsimile and one detail in color.

Sierra, Codex. Puebla, Academia de Bellas Artes. (*HMAI* Census No. 289)

León, Nicolás. *Códice Sierra*. Mexico, 1933.

Color facsimile of a copy.

Telleriano-remensis, Codex. Paris, Bibliothèque Nationale, Fonds Mexicains, No. 385. (*HMAI* Census No. 308)

Hamy, H. T., ed. *Codex Telleriano-Remensis: Manuscrit mexicain du cabinet de Ch.-M. LeTellier, archevêque de Reims à la Bibliothèque Nationale (MS. mexicain no. 385)*. Paris, 1899.

Colored lithographs.

Teozacoalco, 1580 *Relación Geográfica* Map of. Austin, University of Texas Latin American Library, García Icazbalceta Collection, No. 1770.

Caso, Alfonso. "El Mapa de Teozacoalco," *Cuadernos Americanos*, Año VIII, No. 5 (1949), 145–81.

Color photograph of entirety, as well as one black-and-white photograph and two drawings of details, of the nineteenth-century copy of the Teozacoalco Map in the Dirección de Geografía, Meteorología e Hidrología, Mexico City (Colección Orozco y Berra, No. 1186).

Benítez, Fernando. *Los indios de México* (Mexico, 1967), following p. 320.

Color photograph of entirety of original map.

Texupan, 1579 *Relación Geográfica* Map of. Madrid, Library of the Real Academia de la Historia.

Paso y Troncoso, Francisco del, ed. *Papeles de Nueva España*, 2a. sér., vol. IV (Madrid, 1905), 53.

Black-and-white photograph.

36, Map No. Mexico City, Museo Nacional de Antropología, No. 35–36. (*HMAI* Census No. 215)

Rosado Ojeda, Vladamiro. "Estudio del códice mixteco post-cortesiano Núm. 36," *Anales del INAH*, Vol. I (1945), 147–55.

Black-and-white photograph.

Tlazultepec, Genealogy of. Mexico City, AGN-Tierras, 59–2. (*HMAI* Census No. 355)

Spores, Ronald. "The Genealogy of Tlazultepec: A Sixteenth Century Mixtec Manuscript," *Southwestern Journal of Anthropology*, Vol. XX–1 (1964), 15–31.

Tracing.

Vienna, Codex. Vienna, Nationalbibliothek, Mexicanus 1. (*HMAI* Census No. 395)

Adelhofer, Otto. *Codex Vindobonensis Mexicanus I*. Graz, Austria, 1963.

Photographic color facsimile.

Caso, Alfonso. "Explicación del reverso del Codex Vindobonensis," *Memoria de el Colegio Nacional*, Vol. V–5 (1950), 9–46.

Black-and-white photographs of reverse.

Xochitepec, Map of. Copenhagen, National Museum, Ms. No. EE 6.1. (*HMAI* Census No. 409)

Caso, Alfonso. "El Mapa de Xochitepec," *ICA* XXXII (Copenhagen, 1958), 458–66.

Black-and-white photograph.

Xolotl, Codex. Paris, Bibliothèque Nationale, Fonds Mexicains, Nos. 1–10. (*HMAI* Census No. 412)

Dibble, Charles E. *Códice Xolotl*. Mexico, 1951.
Black-and-white photographs.

YANHUITLÁN, Codex of. Puebla, Academia de Bellas Artes; Mexico City, AGN-Vínculos, 272–10. (*HMAI* Census No. 415)

Jiménez Moreno, Wigberto and Salvador Mateos Higuera. *Códice de Yanhuitlán*. Mexico, 1940.
Black-and-white photographs of the major section of the Codex in Puebla.

Berlin, Heinrich. *Fragmentos desconocidos del Códice de Yanhuitlán y otras investigaciones mixtecas*. Mexico, 1947.
Black-and-white photographs of fragments of the Codex in AGN-Vínculos, 272–10.

YOLOTEPEC, Lienzo of. New York, American Museum of Natural History, Accession No. 30–9533. (*HMAI* Census No. 419)

Caso, Alfonso. "El Lienzo de Yolotepec," *Memoria de el Colegio Nacional*, Vol. XIII–4 (1958), 41–55.
Black-and-white photographs.

ZACATEPEC 1, Lienzo of. Mexico City, Museo Nacional de Antropología, No. 35–63. (*HMAI* Census No. 422)

Peñafiel, Antonio. *Códice Mixteco. Lienzo de Zacatepec*. Mexico, 1900.
Black-and-white photographs of entirety and 25 details. (Fig. 85 of this study is after Peñafiel's photograph of the entirety; Figs. 87–111 are after the photographs of the 25 details.)

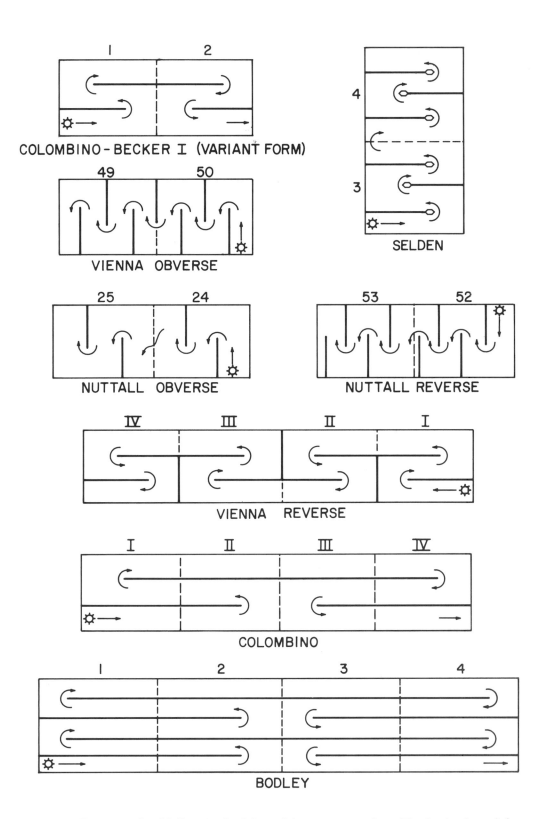

FIG. 1. Patterns of guidelines in the Mixtec history manuscripts. The beginning of the sequence of reading in each example is indicated by an asterisk (*). The accompanying numbers are the page numbers of the original manuscript from which the example is taken.

FIG. 2.   Cartoon from *Punch* (January 12, 1966, p. 54).

a

b

FIG. 3. Scenes from the Bayeux Tapestry, former Bishop's Palace, Bayeux, France. (From *The Bayeux Tapestry*, edited by Sir Frank Stenton, published by Phaidon Press, London and New York.)

(*a*) Norman soldiers capture Dol on the Norman coast, as their opponent flees by sliding down a rope.

(*b*) After the Battle of Hastings, Norman soldiers pursue the defeated English soldiers.

219

FIG. 4.   The "A–O" year sign.

(a) Eight-House. Nuttall 30a.
(b) Nine-Flint. Nuttall 39.
(c) Four-House. Selden 6–II.
(d) Eight-House. Bodley 37–II.

(e) Five-House. Bodley 7–IV.
(f) Seven-Flint. Colombino V–17.
(g) Eleven-House. Becker I, 8.

FIG. 5.   Personages from the Mixtec history manuscripts.

(a) ♀ 5-Water "Xolotl-Jewel." Selden 14–IV.
(b) ♀ 2-Vulture "Jeweled Feather Staff." Nuttall 12.
(c) ♂ 11-Water "Smoking Ballcourt." Selden 1–I.

γ yagnmaoçahui yuchi

yyacycaçuaayuṡitiçayi

a

b

c

d

e

f

FIG. 6. Personages from the Mixtec history manuscripts.

    (*a*) ♀ 6-Monkey, here shown with two personal names:
        "Serpent Quechquemitl" (attached by a line) and "Warband Quechque-
        mitl," which she wears. Selden 8–III.

    (*b*) ♂ 5-Rain "Smoking Mountain." Nuttall 56b.

    (*c*) ♂ 5-Rain "Smoking Mountain." Becker I, 6.

    (*d*) ♂ 7-Grass "Talking Tlaloc." Nuttall 54c.

    (*e*) ♂ 5-House "Tlaloc Flint." Sánchez Solís 23.

    (*f*) ♀ 2-Deer "Parrot Jewel." Sánchez Solís 23.

221

a

b

c

d

FIG. 7. Marriage scenes.

(a) ♀ 9-Eagle "Garland of Cocoa Flowers" and ♂ 5-Alligator "Tlaloc Sun." Nuttall 42 a–b.

(b) ♂ 8-Deer "Tiger Claw" and ♀ 13-Serpent "Flowered Serpent." Nuttall 26c.

(c) ♂ 3-Death "Gray Eagle" and ♀ 3-Serpent "Garland of Cocoa Flowers." Selden 15–III.

(d) ♂ 11-Wind "Bloody Tiger" and ♀ 6-Monkey "Serpent Quechquemitl." Selden 7–I.

FIG. 8. Marriage scene showing the parents of one of the marriage pair as calendrical and personal names only. The marriage of ♀ 13-Flower "Jade-Quetzal" to ♂ 4-Alligator "Serpent-Smoking Copal," the son of ♂ 8-Deer "Tiger Claw" and ♀ 13-Serpent "Flowered Serpent." Bodley 30–III.

a

b

c

d

FIG. 9. Representations of birth.

   (*a*) ♂ 4-Wind "Fire Serpent." Bodley 34–III.
   (*b*) ♂ 4-Wind "Fire Serpent." Selden 8–IV.
   (*c*) ♀ 4-Death "Jewel" gives birth to ♂ 13-Dog "Eagle-Venus Sign." Nuttall 27c.
   (*d*) ♀ 3-Flint "Feathered Serpent" gives birth to ♀ 3-Flint "Flint Quechque-mitl." Nuttall 16a.

223

a   b   c

FIG. 10.   "Toothless" personages.
      (a) The priest ♂ 10-Lizard. Selden 2–I.
      (b) A mythological "old couple": ♀ 10-Flower and ♂ 1-Flower. Nuttall 36.
      (c) "Old Woman Hill." Vienna 40c.

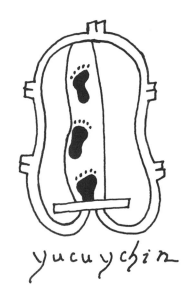

yucuychin

FIG. 11.   "Hill of the Road." Map No. 36, sign 9-left.

a   b

FIG. 12.   The place sign *yucu ñu ycu*.
      (a) Sánchez Solís 29.   (b) Sánchez Solís 31.

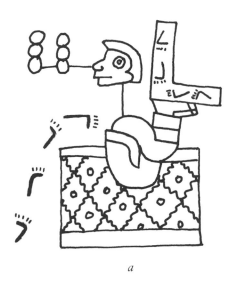

FIG. 13. Escape scenes.
    (*a*)   ♀ 6-Monkey dives into a rectangular patch of earth. Selden 6–III.
    (*b*)   ♂ 4-Wind dives into a Tlaloc mouth with flames. Bodley 33, III–II.

FIG. 14.   Representations of dead personages.
    (*a*)   ♂ 3-Monkey and ♂ 4-House. Bodley 3–III.
    (*b*)   ♂ 8-Deer "Tiger Claw." Vienna IX–2.
    (*c*)   ♀ 7-Water "Sun Feathers" and ♂ 1-Monkey "Tlaloc-Sun." Selden 17–I.
    (*d*)   ♀ 4-House and ♂ 2-Dog. Bodley 35–I.

225

a

b

FIG. 15. Scenes showing prisoners of war.

(*a*) ♂ 6-Lizard "Hair-Bent Hill" as a prisoner (*right*) and as a sacrificial victim (*left*). Selden 8–II.

(*b*) ♂ 8-Deer "Tiger Claw" captures ♂ 4-Wind "Fire Serpent." Nuttall 83 a–b.

a

b

FIG. 16. Sacrifice scenes.

    (*a*) ♂ 10-Dog "Copal-Eagle" is sacrificed in gladiatorial combat. Nuttall 83 c–d.

    (*b*) ♂ 6-House "Strand of Flint Blades" dies by arrow sacrifice. Nuttall 83d–84a.

FIG. 17. The sacrifice of ♂ 12-Movement at "Steambath." Nuttall 81a.

a   b   c   d

FIG. 18. Examples of speech scrolls.
  (a) Bodley 28–III.
  (b) Nuttall 4b.
  (c) Selden 1–III.
  (d) Bodley 2–V.

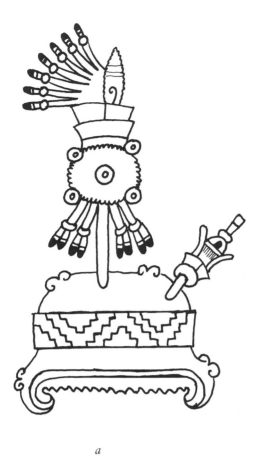

a

b

FIG. 19.   Place signs with a Venus-staff motif.
(*a*) Nuttall 47d.
(*b*) Colombino VIII–21.

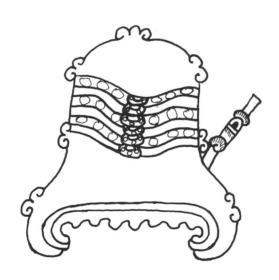

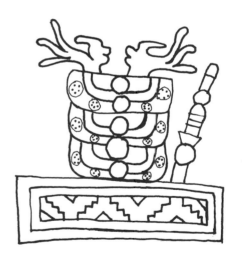

a

b

FIG. 20.   Place signs with a rib-cage motif.
(*a*) Nuttall 46d.
(*b*) Colombino VII–23.

FIG. 21. Map No. 36. Museo Nacional de Antropología, Mexico City, No. 35–36.
(Photograph courtesy of Instituto Nacional de Antropología e Historia)

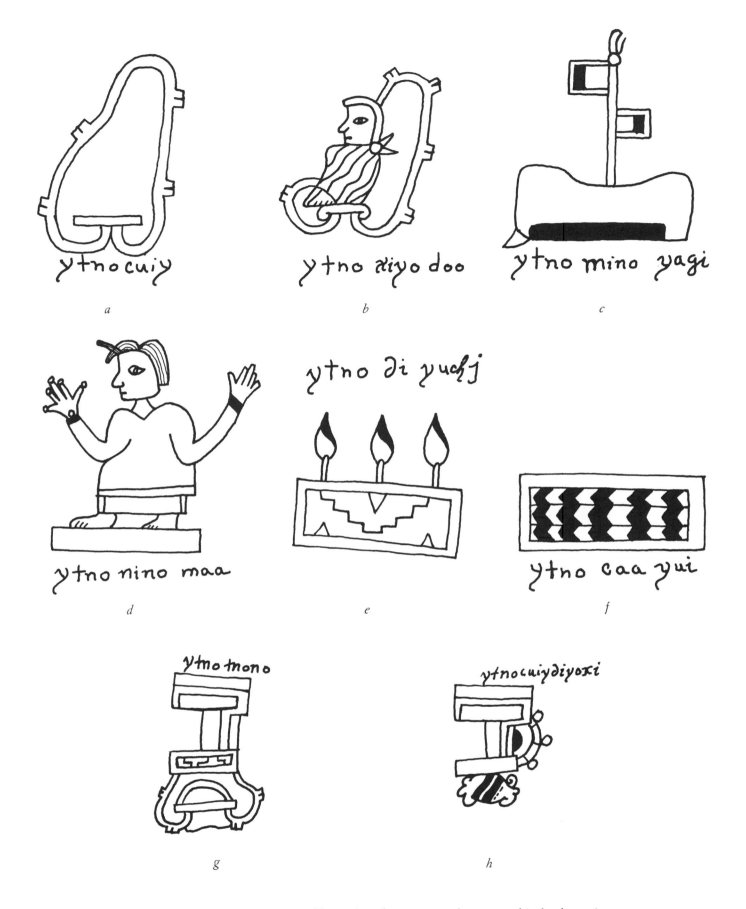

y t n o c u i y

a

y t n o ꝺ i y o d o o

b

y t n o m i n o   y a g i

c

y t n o   ꝺ i   y u ꝯ j

y t n o n i n o   m a a

d

e

y t n o   c a a   y u i

f

y t n o t n o n o

g

y t n o c u i y ꝺ i y o x i

h

FIG. 22. Place signs accompanied by a gloss that contains the geographical substantive
itnu ("slope").

(*a*) Sign with gloss **ytno cuiy**. Map No. 36, 8-top.

(*b*) Sign with gloss **ytno xiyo doo**. Map No. 36, 7-top.

(*c*) Sign with gloss **ytno mino yagi**. Map No. 36, 2-bottom.

(*d*) Sign with gloss **ytno nino maa**. Map No. 36, 11-bottom.

(*e*) Sign with gloss **ytno diyuchi**. Map No. 36, 6-bottom.

(*f*) Sign with gloss **ytno caa yui**. Map No. 36, 5-right.

(*g*) Sign with gloss **ytno tnono**. The place sign of Chicahuaxtla (?). Sánchez Solís 20.

(*h*) Sign with gloss **ytno cuiy diyoxi**. The place sign of San Juan Diuxi or San Andrés Sabanillos (?). Sánchez Solís 31.

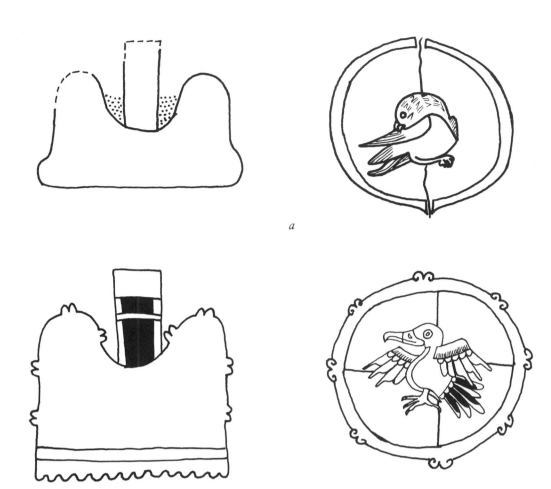

a

b

FIG. 23.   Place signs of two subjects of Teposcolula.

    (*a*) Codex of Yanhuitlán, plate XVIII.
    (*b*) Nuttall 69 c–d.

a   b   c

FIG. 24.   Place signs of towns in the Valley of Yanhuitlán as shown in the Codex of
          Yanhuitlán.

    (*a*) Nochixtlán, plate VI–1.
    (*b*) San Andrés Andúa, plate VII–12.
    (*c*) San Andrés Sachio, plate VII–10.

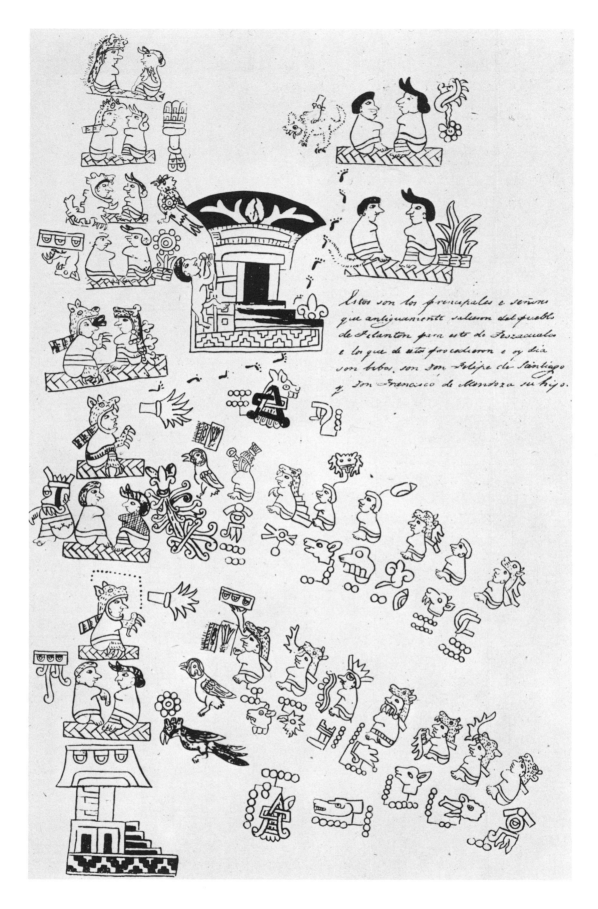

Estos son los principales e señores
que antiguamente salieron del pueblo
de Itlanton para este de Teozacualco
e los que de estos procedieron e oy dia
son bibos, son don Felipe de Santiago
y don Francisco de Mendoza su hijo.

FIG. 25.   1580 *Relación Geográfica* Map of Teozacoalco: detail, lower-left corner. (After
Caso, "El Mapa de Teozacoalco," 158)

FIG. 26.   The place sign of Tilantongo, with black-and-white frieze.

(*a*) Bodley 9–I.   (*d*) Map of Teozacoalco.
(*b*) Selden 5–IV.   (*e*) Nuttall 42a.
(*c*) Nuttall 53d.   (*f*) Nuttall 68b.

a   *b*   *c*

ñotmo hneytaati8i

ñotno hueytaefidi

d   *e*

FIG. 27.   The place sign of Tilantongo, without black-and-white frieze.

     (*a*)   Vienna VI–1.   (*d*)   Sánchez Solís 6.
     (*b*)   Bodley 8–II.   (*e*)   Sánchez Solís 15.
     (*c*)   Colombino XVII–44.

FIG. 28.   The place sign of Teozacoalco.
    (*a*) Selden 13–III.   (*d*) Bodley 15–III.
    (*b*) Bodley 18–V.   (*e*) Map of Teozacoalco.
    (*c*) Bodley 13–II.

FIG. 29.   Temples with blood and cocoa beans.

    (*a*) Vienna 32d.   (*c*) Bodley 13–I.
    (*b*) Vienna 18b.   (*d*) Bodley 22–I.

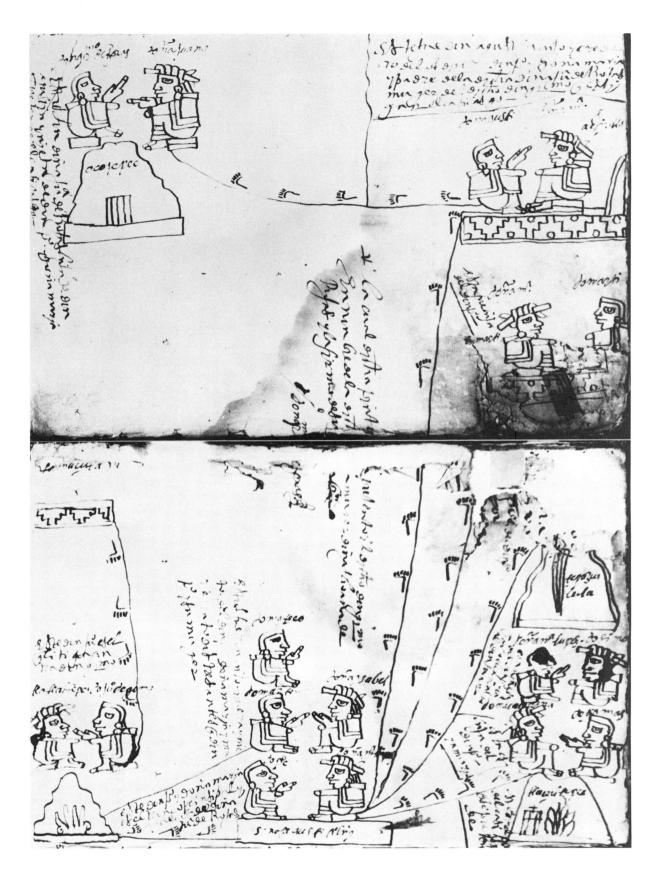

FIG. 30. The Genealogy of Tlazultepec. AGN-Tierras, 59–2.

237

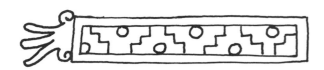

FIG. 31. "Flame Frieze." Bodley 23–III.

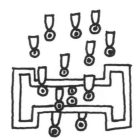

FIG. 32. The place sign of "tlachquiauco" (Tlaxiaco).
Telleriano-Remensis, fol. 41.

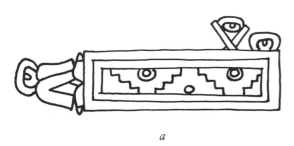

a

b

c

FIG. 33. "Observatory" Place (Tlaxiaco?).
(*a*) Bodley 15–II.
(*b*) Bodley 32–IV.
(*c*) Selden 14–I.

FIG. 34. A sign accompanied by the
Mixtec gloss *ñuhu ndisi nuu*.
Codex Muro 2.

a

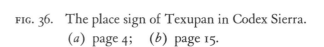

b

FIG. 36. The place sign of Texupan in Codex Sierra.
(*a*) page 4; (*b*) page 15.

texopan

FIG. 35. The place sign of Texupan.
Codex Mendoza, fol. 43/r.

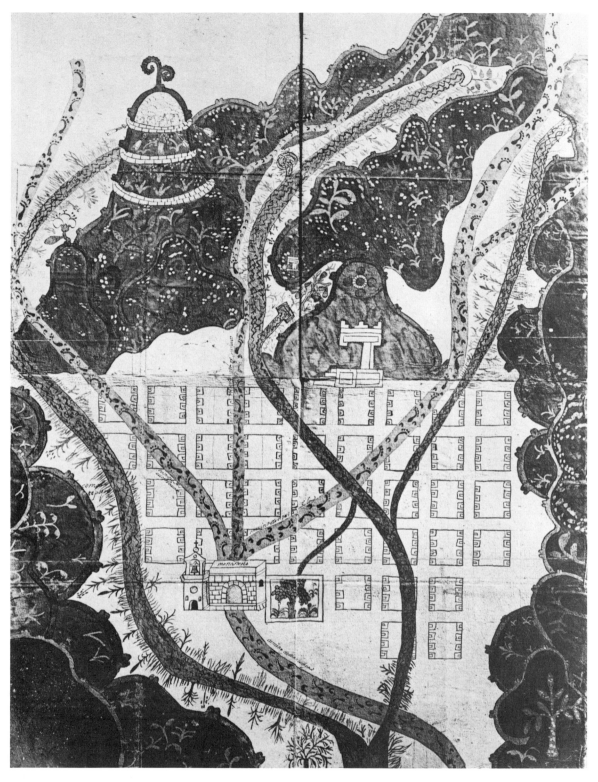

a

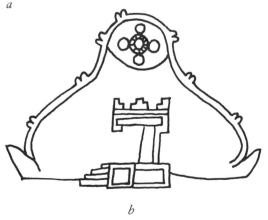

b

FIG. 37. 1579 *Relación Geográfica* Map
of Texupan. (After *PNE* IV, 53)

(*a*) The entire map.
(*b*) Detail, place sign of Texupan.

yocoyoxindixaa

a

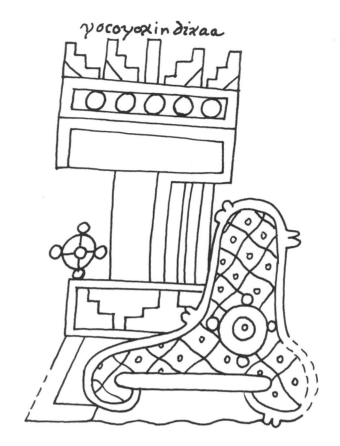

yocoyoxindixaa

b

FIG. 38.   The place sign of Acatlán in Codex Sánchez Solís.
(*a*) page 16;   (*b*) page 20;
(*c*) page 23;   (*d*) page 24.

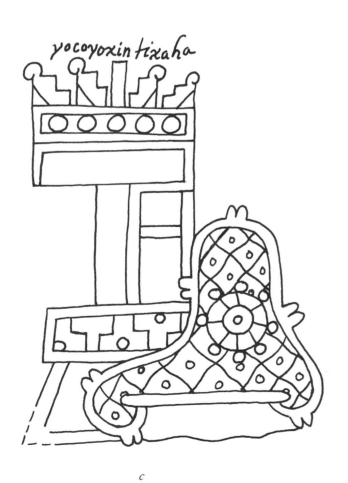

yocoyoxintixaha

c

yocoyoxidixaa

d

a

b

FIG. 39.   Persons wearing the headdress of Xipe-Totec.

(*a*)   ♂ 7-Rain at "Bird River-Bent Hill with Tree and Flames." Nuttall 33.

(*b*)   ♂ 5-Flower. Nuttall 33.

(*c*)   ♂ 9-Serpent. Nuttall 33.

(*d*)   ♂ 9-Flower. Sculpture, Tomb 1, Zaachila, Oaxaca.

(*e*)   ♂ 5-Flower. Sculpture, Tomb 1, Zaachila, Oaxaca.

c   *d*   *e*

FIG. 40. The rulers of Yanhuitlán at the time of the Spanish conquest: ♂ 8-Death "Tiger-Fire Serpent" (*na mahu*) and ♀ 1-Flower "Tiger-Quechquemitl" (*ca uaco*). Bodley 19–III.

FIG. 41. "Bird with Arrow-Beak Frieze" (Totomihuacan?). Bodley 11–IV.

a

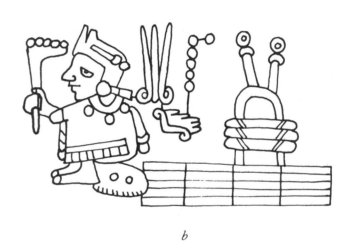

b

FIG. 42. "*Cacaxtli* Plain."
(*a*) Bodley 24–III.　　(*b*) Selden 13–I.

a

b

FIG. 43. Nahuatl place signs from Codex Mendoza, fol. 43/r.
(*a*) Yanhuitlán;　(*b*) Coixtlahuaca.

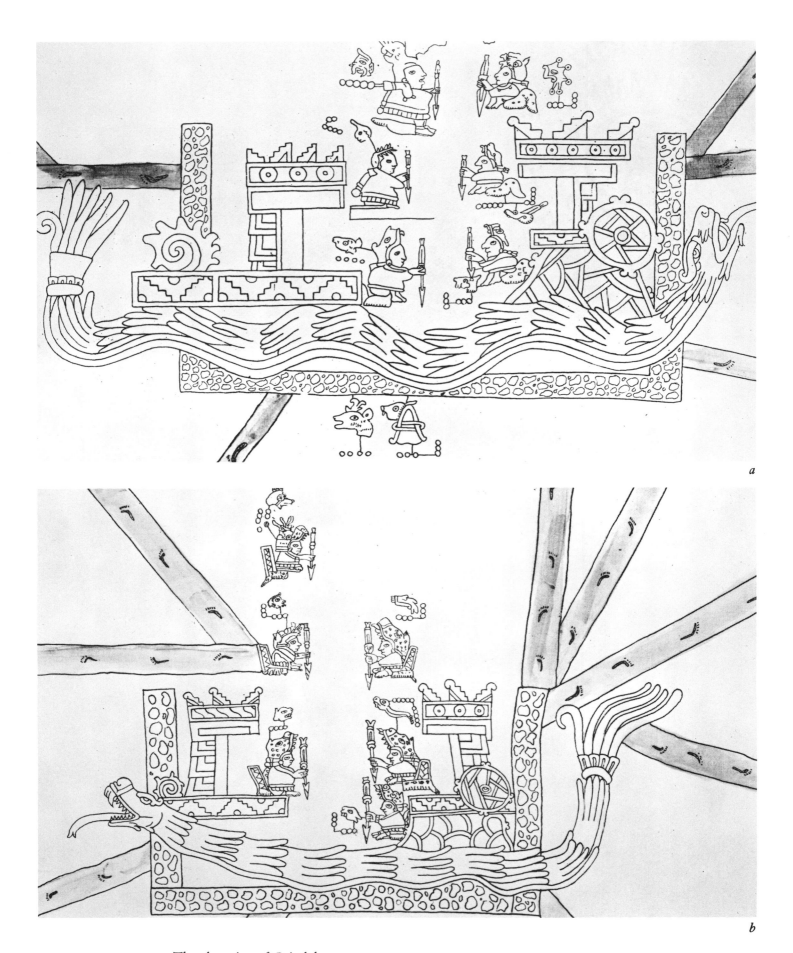

FIG. 44.   The place sign of Coixtlahuaca.

(*a*) Codex Ixtlán (a copy of the Lienzo of Coixtlahuaca).   (*b*) Codex Meixueiro.

a

b

FIG. 45.   The place sign of Coixtlahuaca.
   (*a*) Lienzo Antonio de León. (After Rickards, *JSA*, n.s., X, 52)
   (*b*) Lienzo of Ihuitlán. (Photograph courtesy of The Brooklyn Museum)

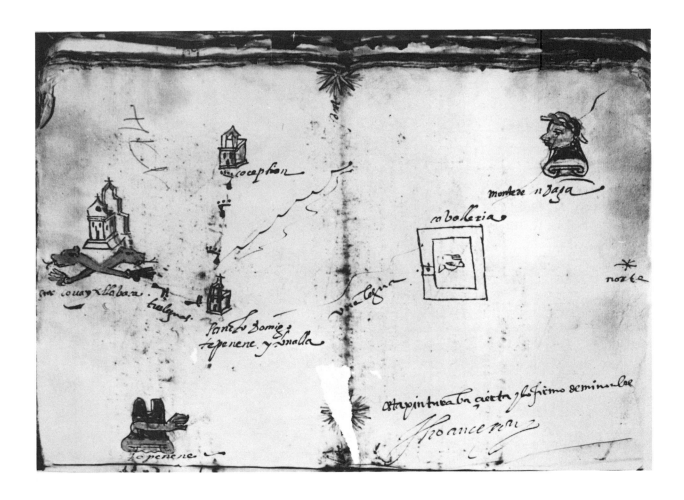

FIG. 46. 1590 sketch-map illustrating a land grant in the Coixtlahuaca region. AGN-Tierras, 2729–5.

FIG. 47. The place sign of Coixtlahuaca. 1580 Map of Ixcatlán.

FIG. 48. The place sign of Santiago Amoltepec. 1580 *Relación Geográfica* Map of Amoltepec.

a

b   *c*   *d*

FIG. 49.   The place sign of Tututepec.
(*a*) Colombino V, 16–17.   (*c*) Nuttall 45d.
(*b*) Bodley 9–III.   (*d*) Nuttall 50b.

1513

En este x ño de ocho casas y d 1513
su Jeptaron los mexicanos a toto
tepec provincia ochenta leguas
de mexico Junto a lamar del sur

FIG. 50.   The place sign of Tututepec. Telleriano-Remensis, fol. 43/r.

FIG. 51.   The place sign of Santa María Acatepec.

(a)   The town is conquered by ♂ 8-Deer "Tiger Claw," who captures Aca-
       tepec's ruler ♂ 3-Alligator. The destruction of the town is indicated by
       a small flame on the left side of the hill. Bodley 10–II.

(b)   The town is conquered by ♂ 12-Movement (?), who captures Acatepec's
       ruler ♂ 1-Movement. Colombino XIII–37.

FIG. 52.   "Hill of the Moon" and "Insect Hill."

(a)   As two separate place signs. The rulers of these places, ♂ 6-Lizard "Hair-
       Bent Hill" and ♂ 2-Alligator "Hair-Cacaxtli," are shown speaking
       "stony" or insulting words because flint blades are attached to their
       speech scrolls. Selden 7–III.

(b)   As a compound place sign, with the moon and insect motifs incorporated
       into one hill sign. The destruction of the two places represented by this
       sign is indicated by two small flames appended to the top of the hill.
       Selden 8–I.

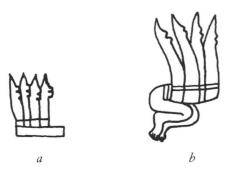

FIG. 53. Place signs with tule-grass in Codex Mendoza.
   (*a*) Tollan, fol. 8/r.
   (*b*) Tulancingo, fol. 30/r.

FIG. 54. The place sign of Tula. Historia Tolteca-Chichimeca.

FIG. 55. 8-Deer's nose-piercing ceremony at Tulixtlahuaca of Jicayán. Colombino XIII, 40–41.

a

b

FIG. 56. The *co'yo* plant.

       (*a*) In an arroyo near San Pedro Jicayán.

       (*b*) Leaves and spikelets.

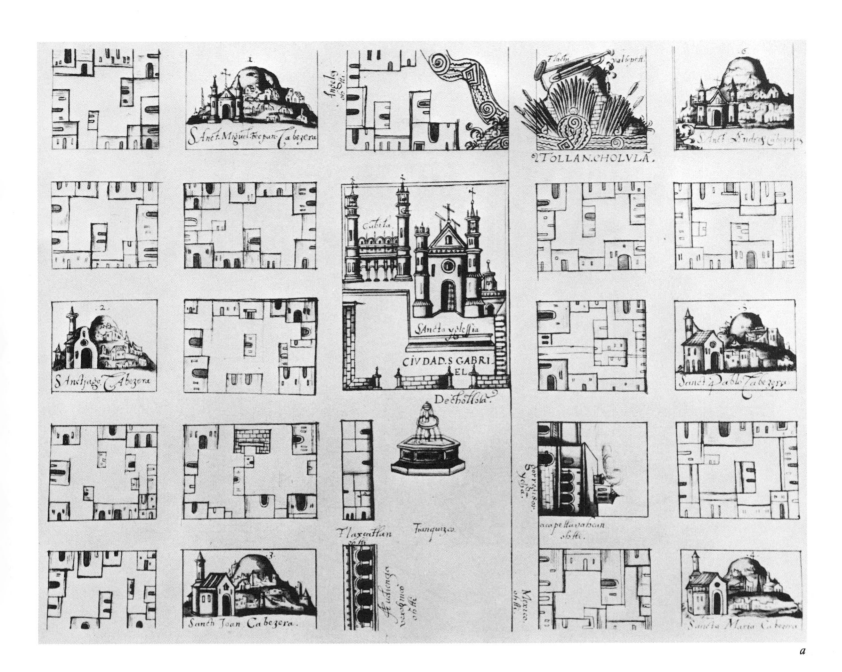

FIG. 57. 1581 *Relación Geográfica* Map of Cholula, Puebla; 1892 copy by Rafael Aguirre, Museo Nacional de Antropología, Mexico City, No. 35–23. (Photograph courtesy of Instituto Nacional de Antropología e Historia)

(*a*) The entire map.

(*b*) Detail, place sign of Cholula.

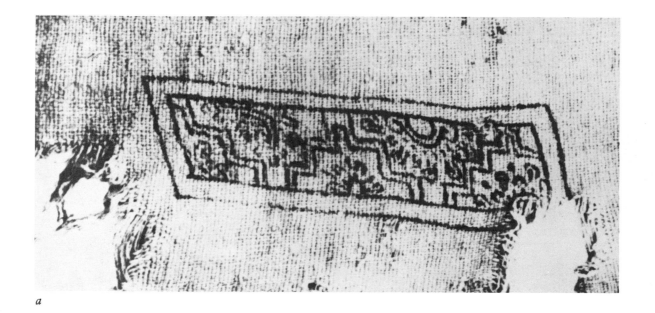

a

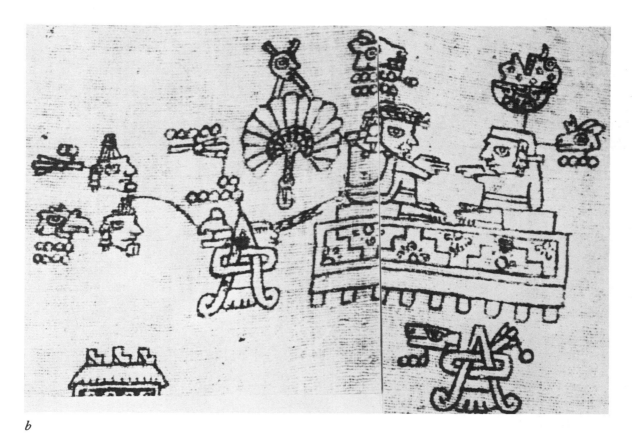

b

FIG. 58.   The place sign of San Pedro Jicayán. Lienzo of Zacatepec 1.
(*a*) Outside the boundaries of Zacatepec (detail of Fig. 111 of this volume).
(*b*) Inside the boundaries of Zacatepec (detail of Figs. 103–104 of this volume).

252

FIG. 59. The place sign of San Pedro
Jicayán (?). Nuttall 14.

FIG. 60. 8-Deer's nose-piercing ceremony in Nuttall (52 c–d).

FIG. 61. 8-Deer's nose-piercing ceremony in Bodley (9–II). (*Right to left*:) ♂ 8-Deer
speaks "stony" words as he delivers the prisoner ♂ 3-Alligator (holding flag)
to ♂ 4-Tiger at Cattail Frieze; the nose-piercing ceremony follows at the left.

a

b

c

FIG. 62.   Place signs with Cattail Frieze in Codex Bodley.

    (*a*) ♀ 2-Grass "Jewel-Copal" and ♂ 10-Movement "Flaming Eagle" make an offering at Cattail Frieze and Temple with Mound of Dots. Page 12–V.

    (*b*) ♀ 1-Flower "Parrot" and ♂ 8-Deer "Feathered Serpent" at Cattail Frieze and Steambath. Page 13–V.

    (*c*) The names of ♀ 1-Flower "Parrot" and ♂ 8-Deer "Feathered Serpent" at Steambath, Cacaxtli, and Frieze with Cattail and Shining Jewel. Page 13–IV.

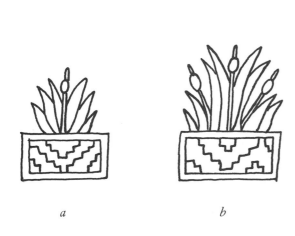

a   b

FIG. 63.   The place sign of Mexico City in Codex Sierra.
(*a*) page 34;   (*b*)   page 38.

FIG. 64.   The place sign of San Miguel Tulancingo. Codex
Ixtlán (a copy of the Lienzo of Coixtlahuaca).

a   b

FIG. 65.   The place sign of San Miguel Tulancingo (?).
(*a*) Becker I, 4.   (*b*) Becker I, 14.

255

a

FIG. 66. The place sign of San Miguel Tulancingo. Lienzo Antonio de León.
(After Rickards, *JSA*, n.s., X, 56)

b

FIG. 67. The place sign of Apoala. Lienzo of Yolotepec: detail, lower-left corner, where
the sign is shown at the beginning of a series of events. (Photograph courtesy
of American Museum of Natural History)

a   *b*

c   *d*

e

FIG. 68. Place signs with a Human Hand Holding Feathers or Grass.

(*a*) The sign of Apoala. Bodley 39–II.

(*b*) The sign of Apoala. Nuttall 36.

(*c*) The sign of Apoala. Nuttall 1.

(*d*) The sign of Juquila. Bodley 13–IV.

(*e*) The sign of Juquila, where ♂ 1-Death "Serpent-Sun" and ♀ 11-Ser-
pent "Flower-Feathers" are visited by ♂ 8-Deer "Tiger Claw." Bodley
9–III.

257

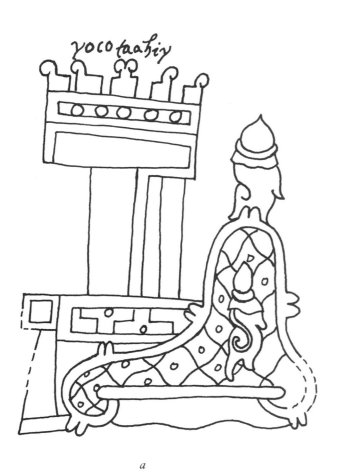

yocotaahiy

yocutaahyi

a   *b*

FIG. 69.   The place sign of Tequixtepec del Rey in Codex Sánchez Solís.
(*a*) page 22;   (*b*) page 25.

FIG. 70.   The place sign of Tequixtepec del Rey. Selden 15–I.

FIG. 71.   The place sign of Tequixtepec de Chuchones.
Codex Ixtlán (a copy of the Lienzo
of Coixtlahuaca).

FIG. 72. The place sign of Tequixtepec de Chuchones. Lienzo of Ihuitlán. (Photograph courtesy of The Brooklyn Museum)

FIG. 73. The place sign
of Mitlatongo.
Codex Mendoza,
fol. 43/r.

FIG. 74. Hill with Skull, Crenelated Wall, and Falling Dead Body. At right: the birth
of ♂ 1-Monkey "Tiger with Bird Beak and Bee Tail." Bodley 3–IV.

FIG. 75. The sacrifice and interment of 8-Deer. Bodley 14, V–IV. *Lower band, left to right*: On the day One-Grass in the year Twelve-Reed (1063), 8-Deer, armed with bow and arrow, attacks River with Parrot in Tree. This place belongs to 8-Deer's second wife ♀ 6-Eagle "Tiger Cobweb," whose calendrical and personal names are attached to the place sign. (The "tiger" element of the personal name is abbreviated to a tiger's ear.) 8-Deer is sacrificed by ♂ 9-Wind and ♂ 10-Tiger.

Top band, right to left: The sacrifice takes place at a site represented by a compound place sign which consists of a frieze, a feather-mat with cactus plants, and a hill with an arm holding a frieze and a cacaxtli. On the day Twelve-House in the same year Twelve-Reed, 8-Deer is entombed, and his burial is supervised by ♂ 8-Alligator "Bloody Coyote" of Skull Frieze.

FIG. 76. Place signs with jaw that contains a stone motif.
    (*a*) Bodley 8–III.
    (*b*) Bodley 7–V.

FIG. 77. The place sign of Tecamachalco.
    Codex Mendoza, fol. 42/r.

FIG. 78. The place sign of Comaltepec.
    Codex Mendoza, fol. 16/v.

FIG. 79. Hill with comal.
    (*a*) Selden 18–II.   (*b*) Selden 18–IV.

FIG. 80. Platform with white, four-petaled
    flowers. Bodley 6–II.

FIG. 81. Hill with trefoil flowers. Bodley 16–V.

a   b

FIG. 82. The place sign of Santa María Suchixtlán (*chiyo yuhu*).
(*a*) Codex of Yanhuitlán, plate VII–6.
(*b*) Codex Muro 6.

a

FIG. 83. Place signs with the "spiral" motif.
(*a*) Colombino III–11.
(*b*) Becker I, 16.

b

a

b

FIG. 84. Towns in the Coastal Region of the Mixteca.

(*a*) San Pedro Tututepec: the central plaza.
(*b*) San Pedro Jicayán: a section of the town west of the central plaza.

FIG. 85. Lienzo of Zacatepec 1. Museo Nacional de Antropología, Mexico City, No. 35–63. (*LZ*, "Vista de Conjunto")

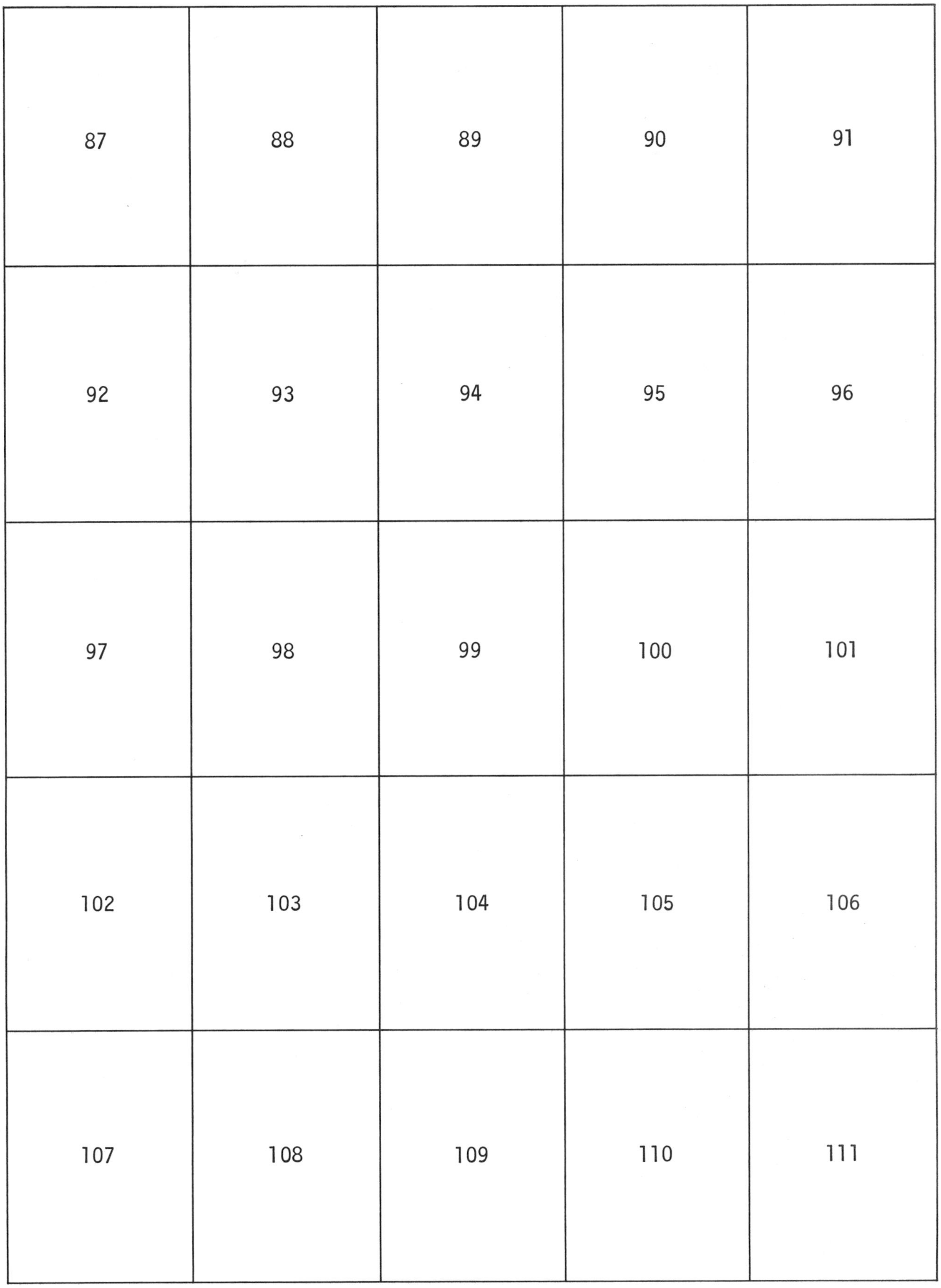

87	88	89	90	91
92	93	94	95	96
97	98	99	100	101
102	103	104	105	106
107	108	109	110	111

FIG. 86. Lienzo of Zacatepec 1: diagram showing the sections of the Lienzo illustrated in the photographs of details (Figs. 87–111 of this study).

FIG. 87. Lienzo of Zacatepec 1, detail (*LZ*, plate I).

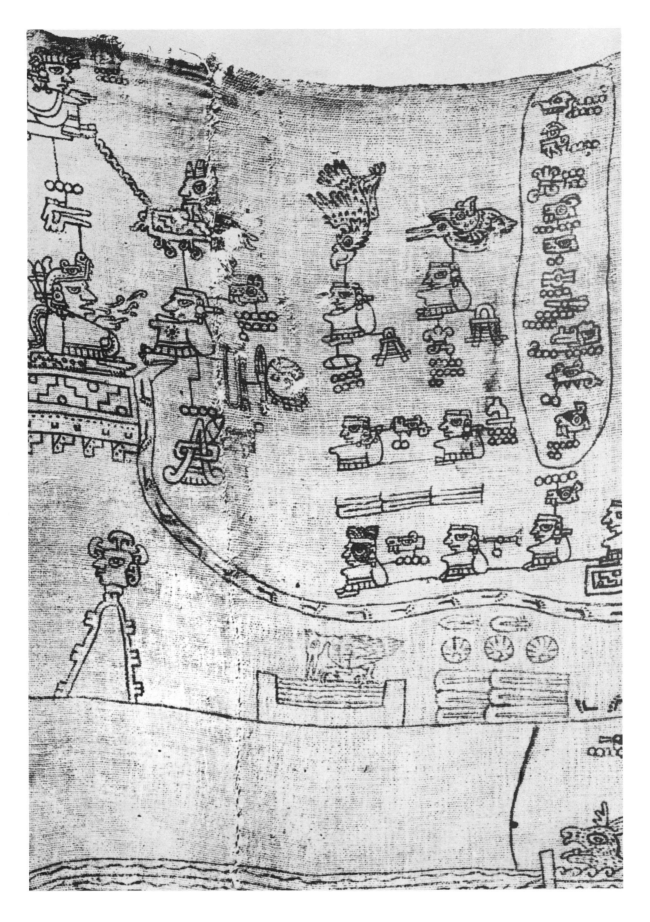

FIG. 88. Lienzo of Zacatepec 1, detail (*LZ*, plate II).

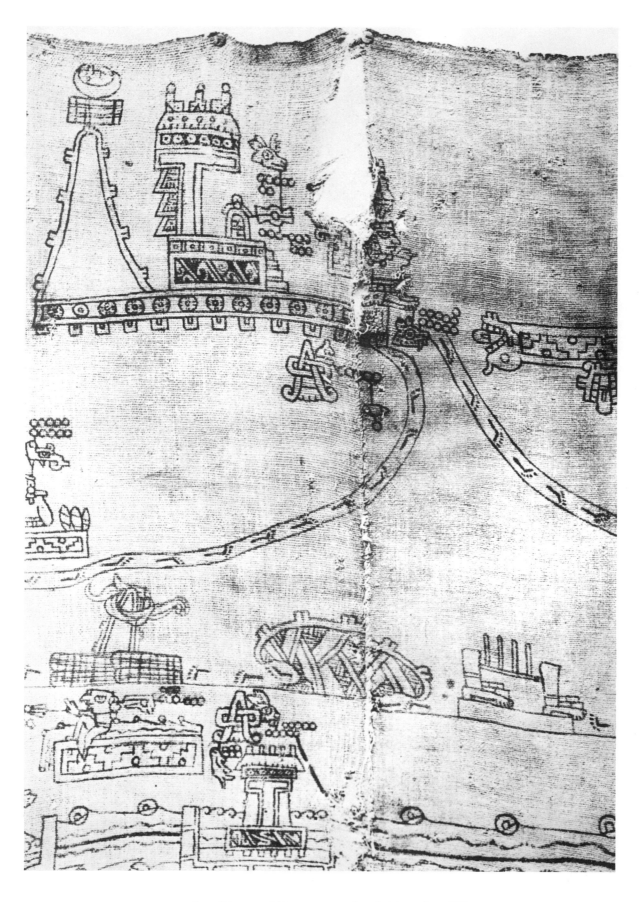

FIG. 89. Lienzo of Zacatepec 1, detail (*LZ*, plate III).

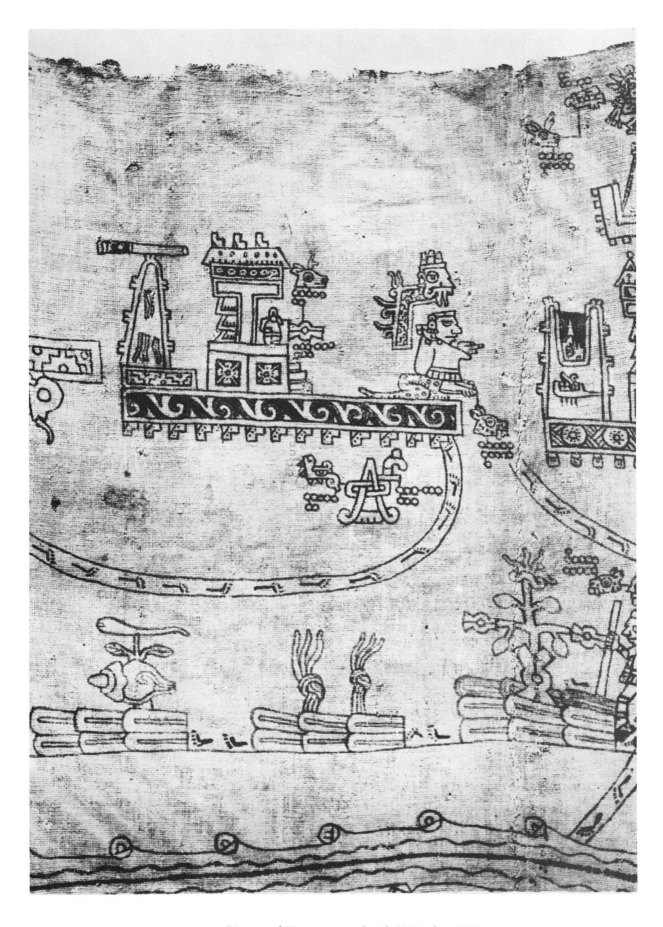

FIG. 90. Lienzo of Zacatepec 1, detail (*LZ*, plate IV).

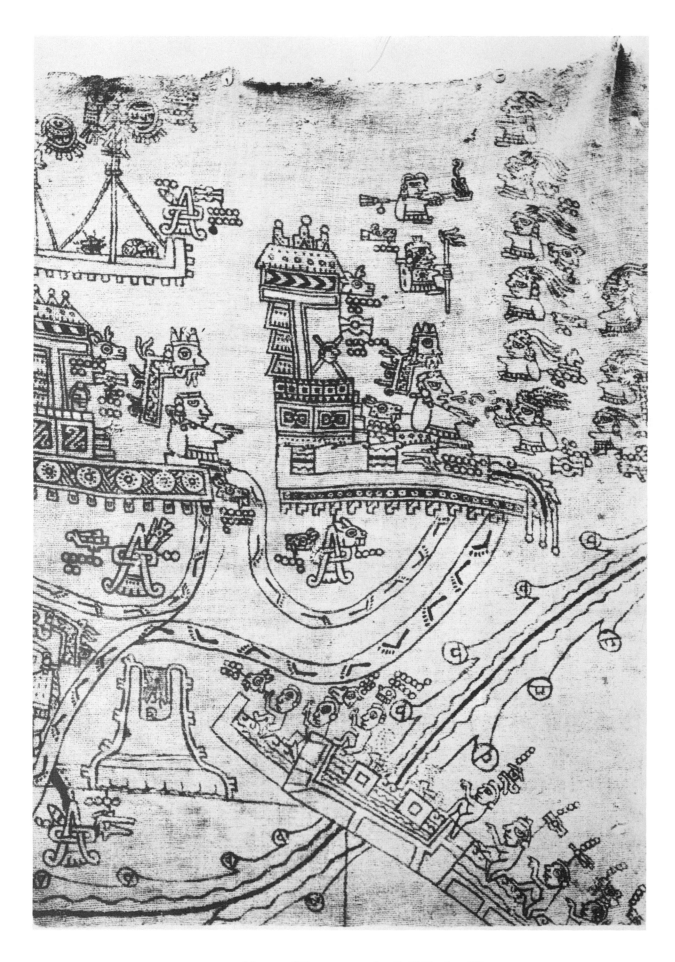

FIG. 91. Lienzo of Zacatepec 1, detail (*LZ*, plate V).

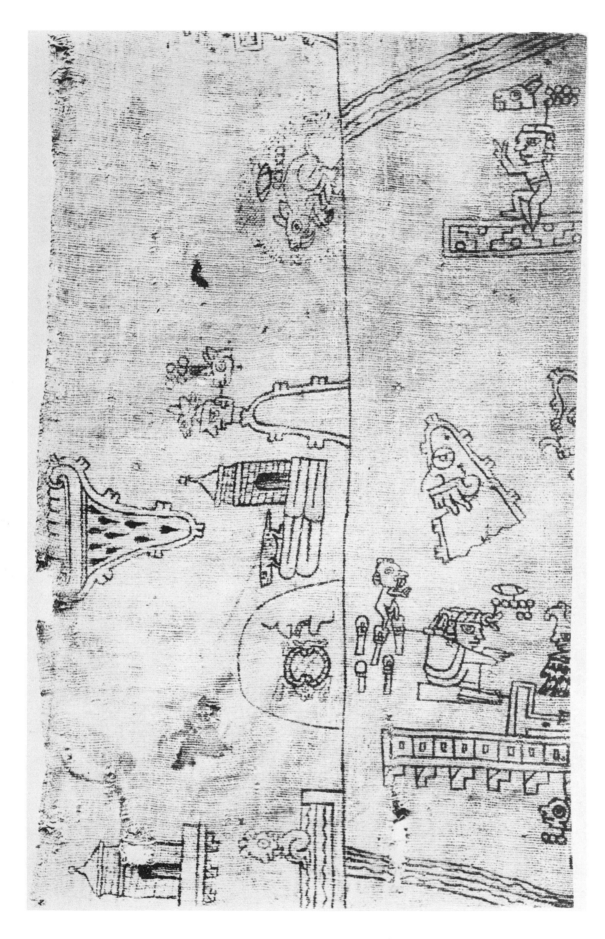

FIG. 92. Lienzo of Zacatepec 1, detail (*LZ*, plate VI).

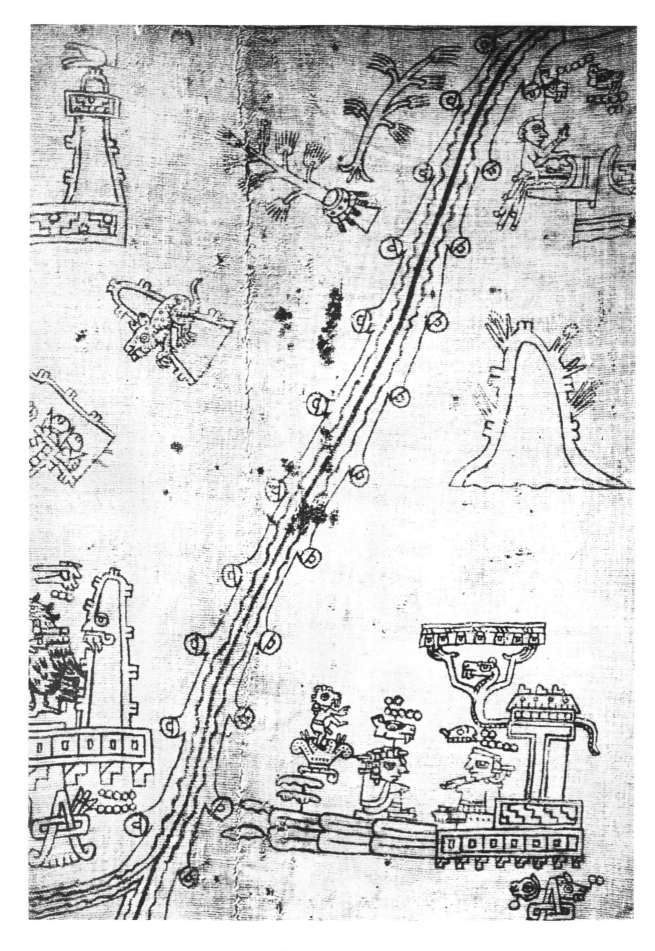

FIG. 93. Lienzo of Zacatepec 1, detail (*LZ*, plate VII).

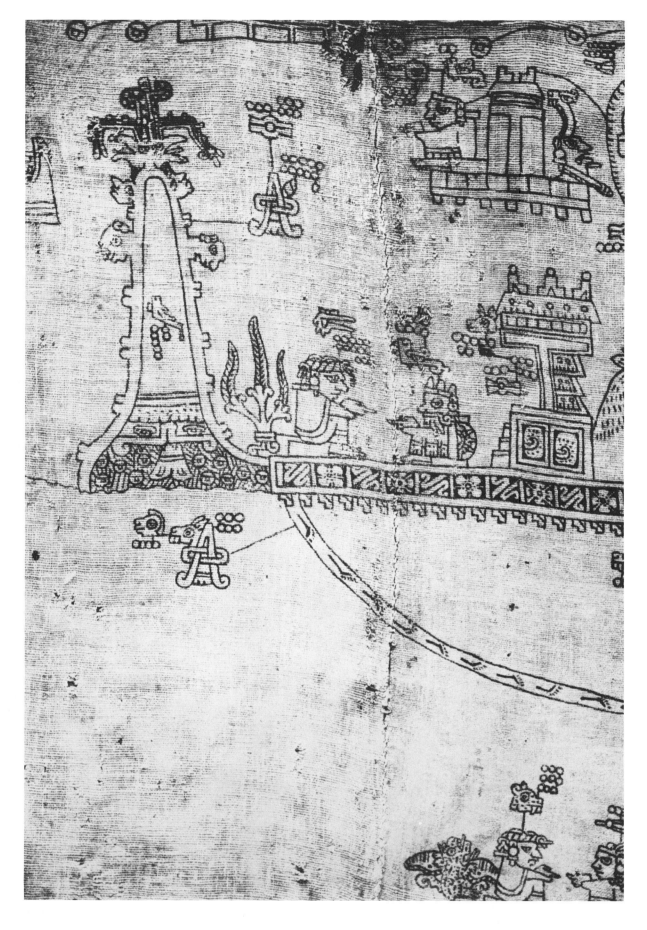

FIG. 94.   Lienzo of Zacatepec 1, detail (*LZ*, plate VIII).

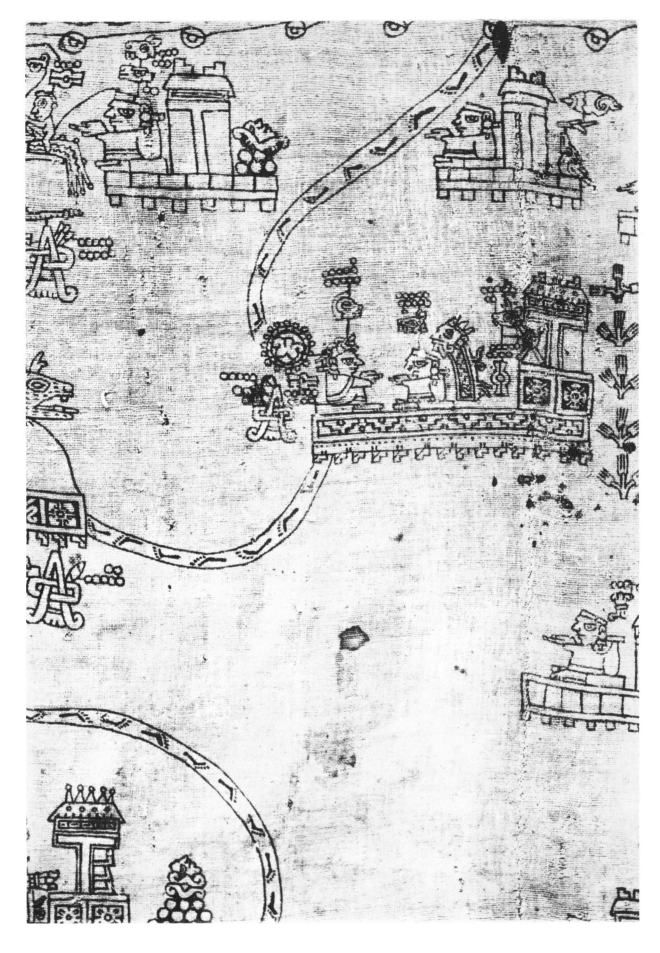

FIG. 95. Lienzo of Zacatepec 1, detail (*LZ*, plate IX).

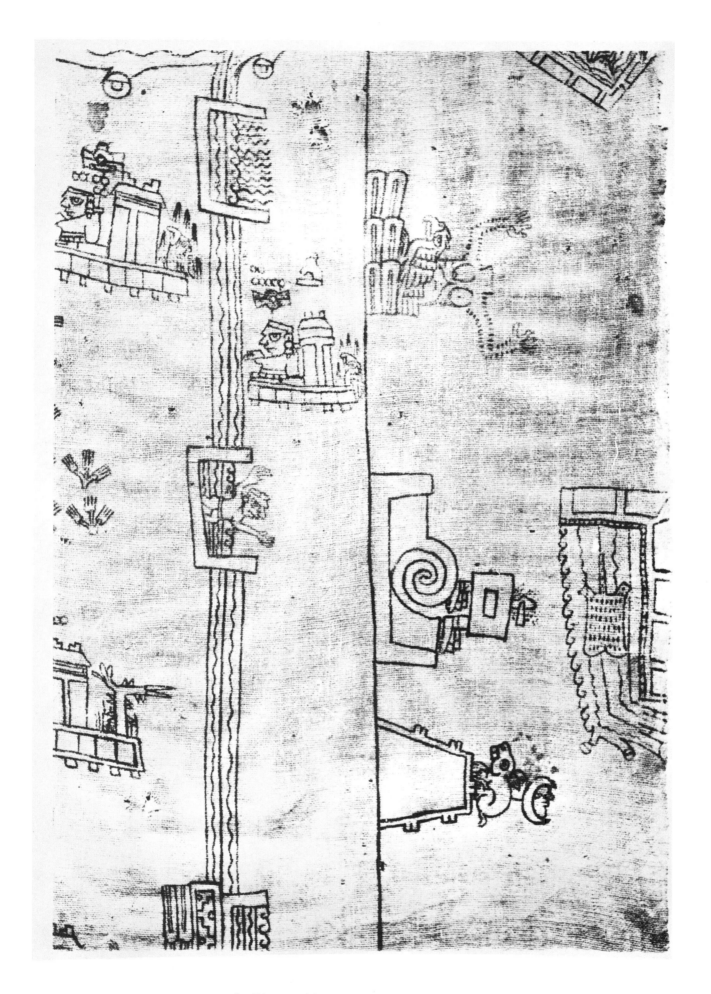

FIG. 96. Lienzo of Zacatepec 1, detail (*LZ*, plate X).

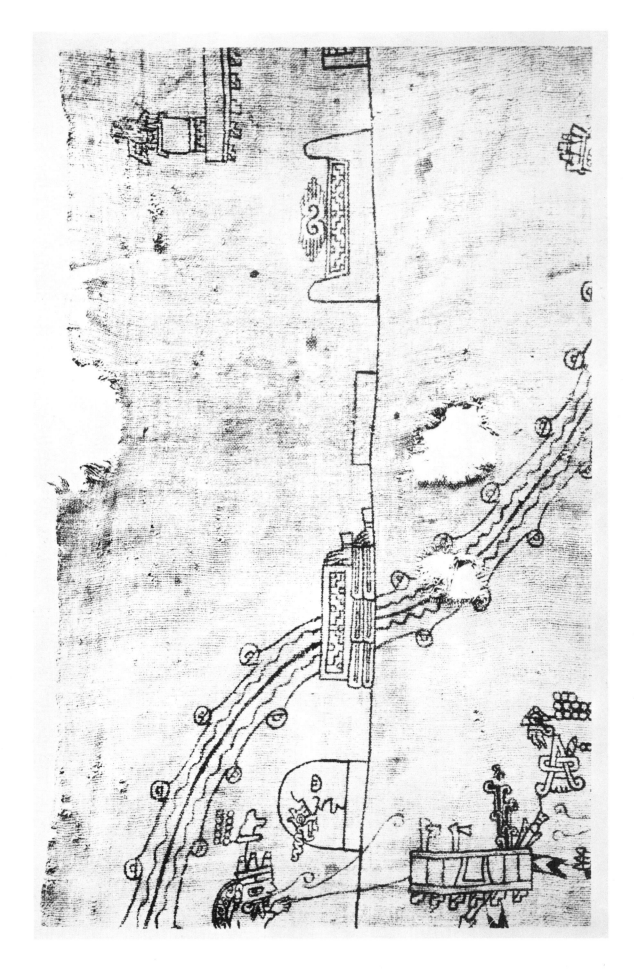

FIG. 97. Lienzo of Zacatepec 1, detail (*LZ*, plate XI).

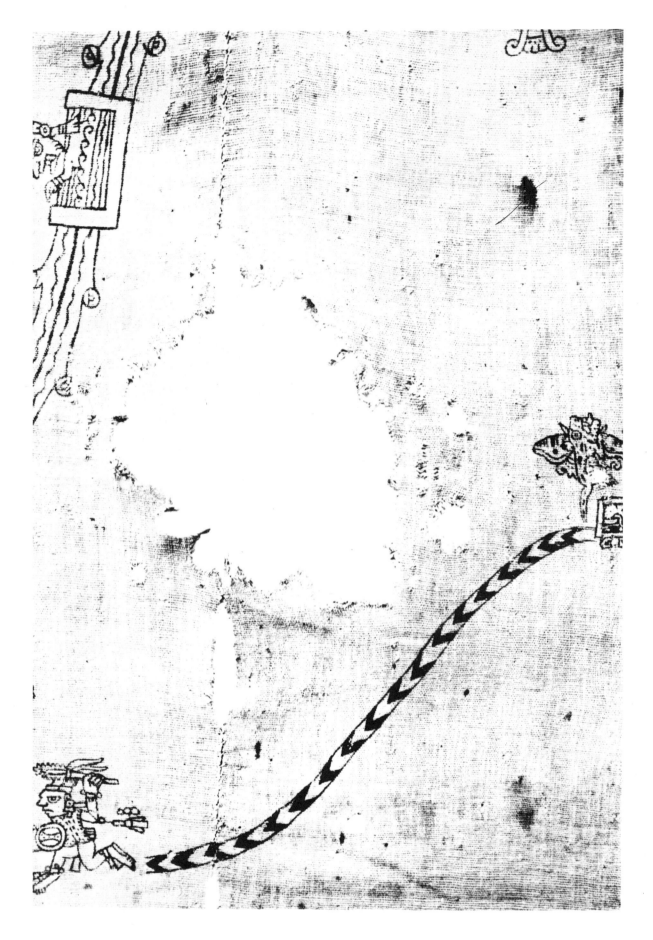

FIG. 98. Lienzo of Zacatepec 1, detail (*LZ*, plate XII).

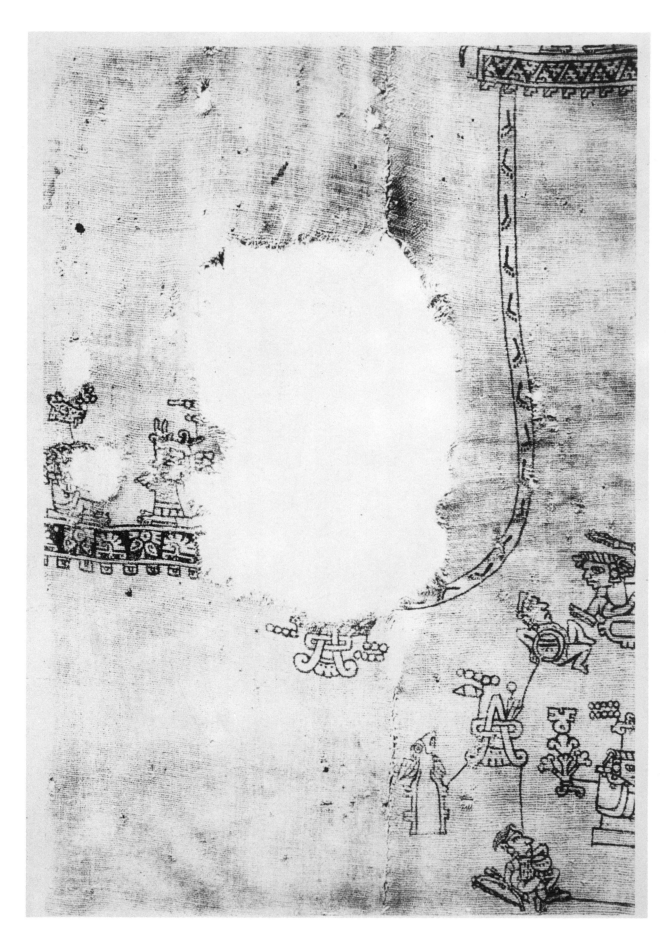

FIG. 99. Lienzo of Zacatepec 1, detail (*LZ*, plate XIII).

278

FIG. 100. Lienzo of Zacatepec 1, detail (*LZ*, plate XIV).

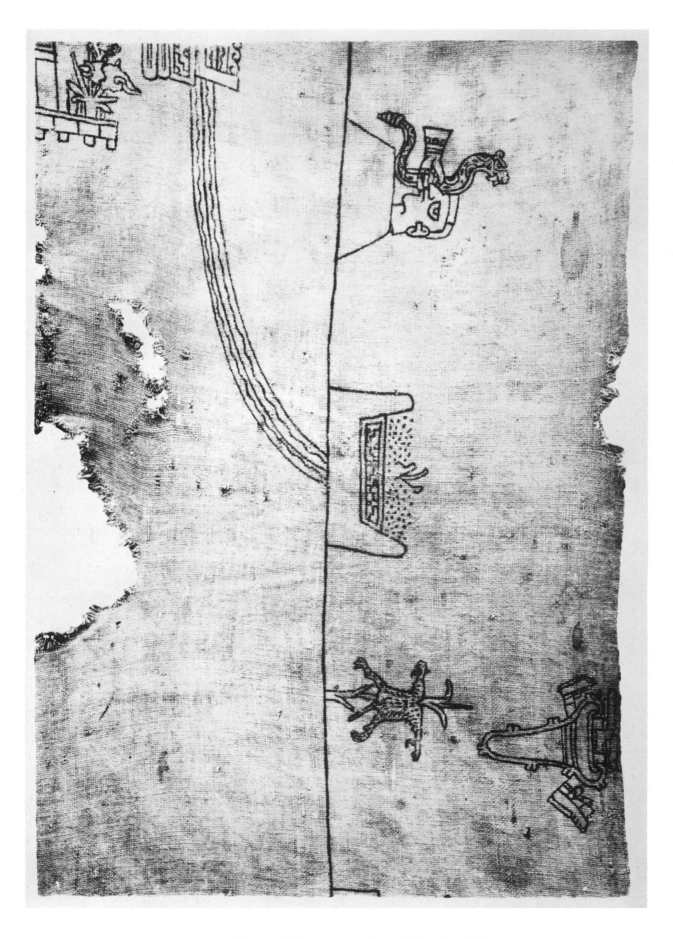

FIG. 101. Lienzo of Zacatepec 1, detail (*LZ*, plate XV).

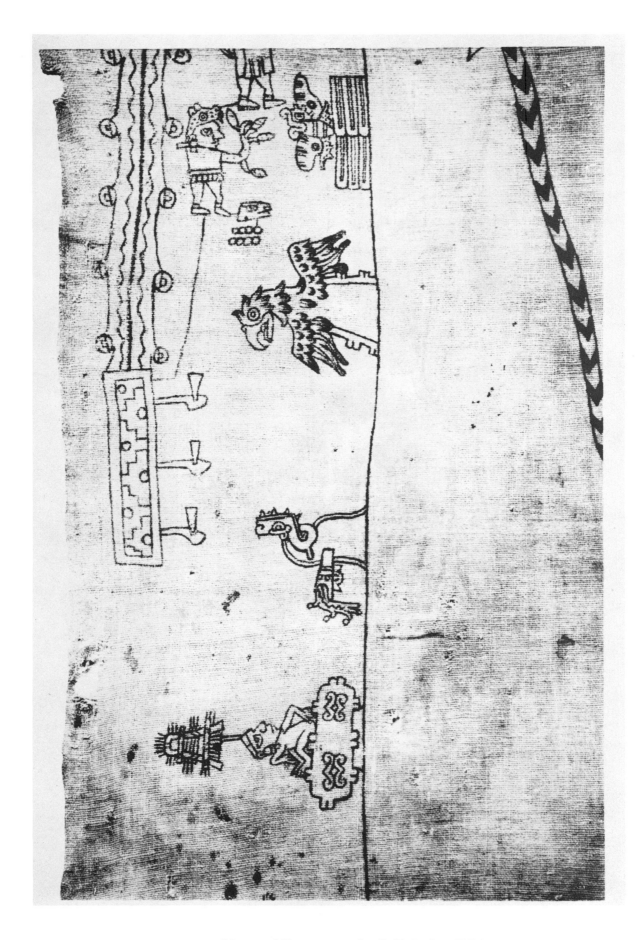

FIG. 102. Lienzo of Zacatepec 1, detail (*LZ*, plate XVI).

FIG. 103.   Lienzo of Zacatepec 1, detail (*LZ*, plate XVII).

282

FIG. 104. Lienzo of Zacatepec 1, detail (*LZ*, plate XVIII).

FIG. 105.   Lienzo of Zacatepec 1, detail (*LZ*, plate XIX).

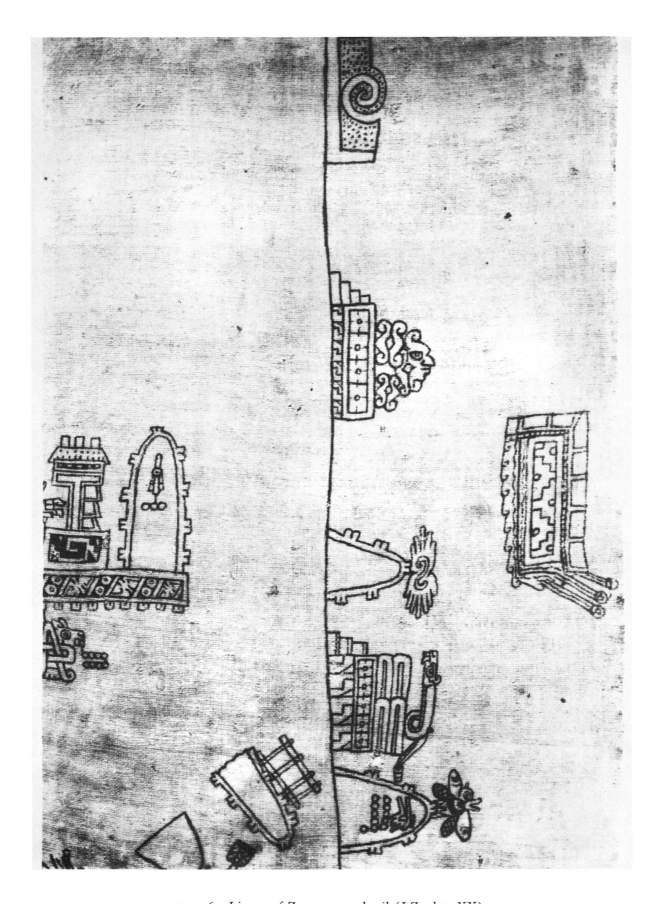

FIG. 106. Lienzo of Zacatepec 1, detail (*LZ*, plate XX).

FIG. 107. Lienzo of Zacatepec 1, detail (*LZ*, plate XXI).

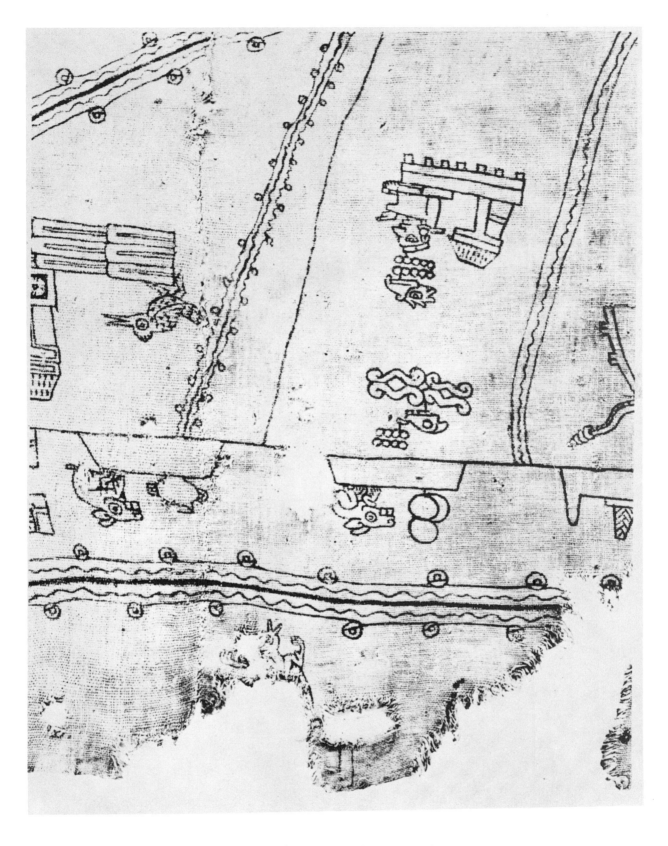

FIG. 108. Lienzo of Zacatepec 1, detail (*LZ*, plate XXII).

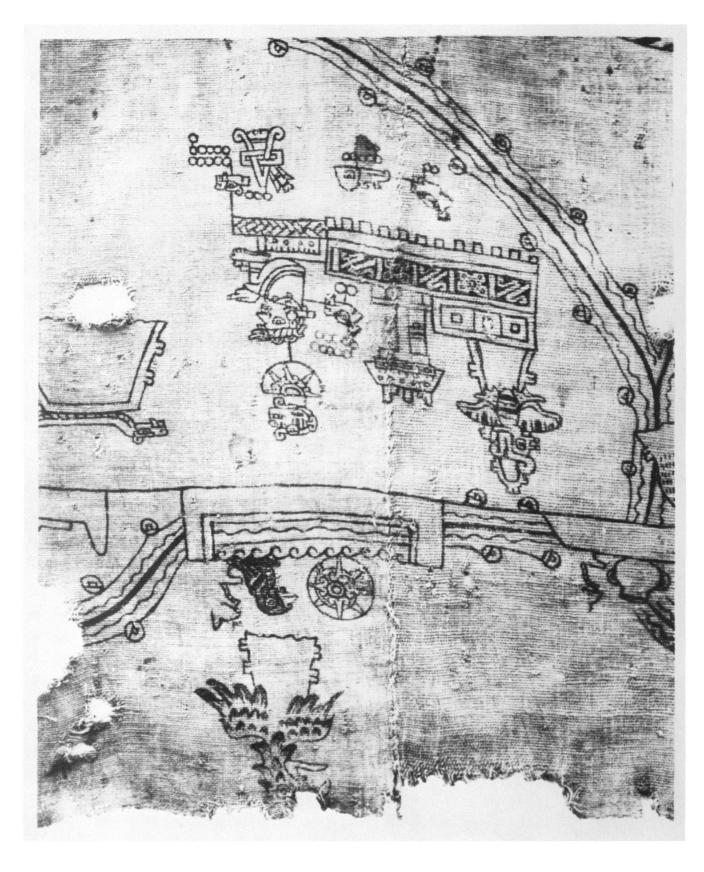

FIG. 109.   Lienzo of Zacatepec 1, detail (*LZ*, plate XXIII).

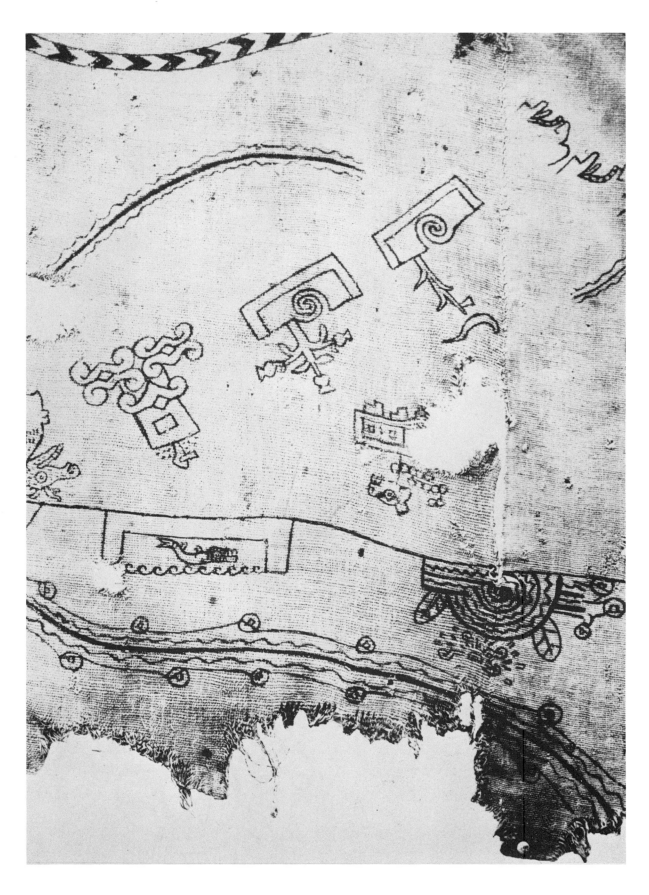

FIG. 110. Lienzo of Zacatepec 1, detail (*LZ*, plate XXIV).

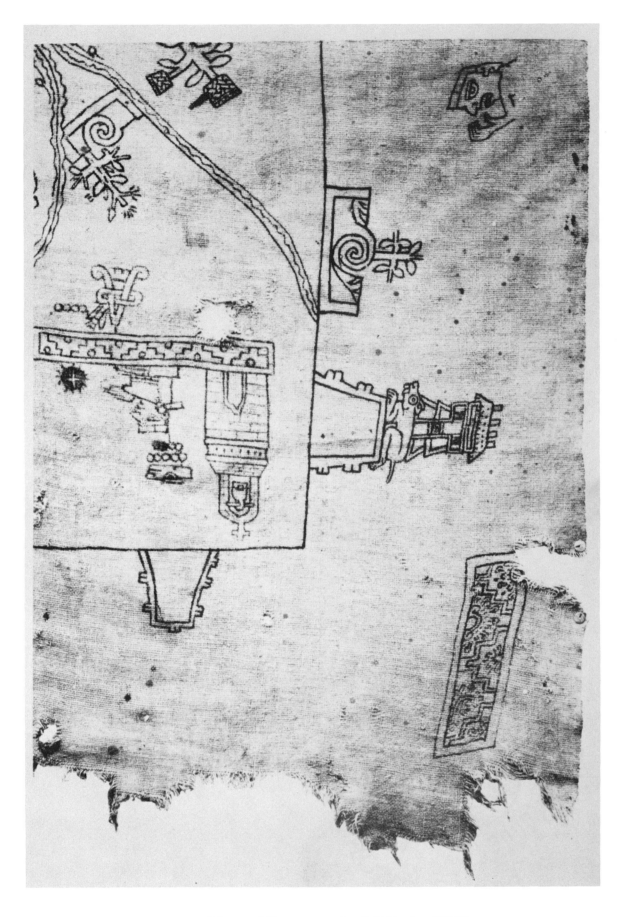

FIG. 111. Lienzo of Zacatepec 1, detail (*LZ*, plate XXV).

FIG. 112. Lienzo of Zacatepec 1, 1893 copy: detail, lower-right corner.

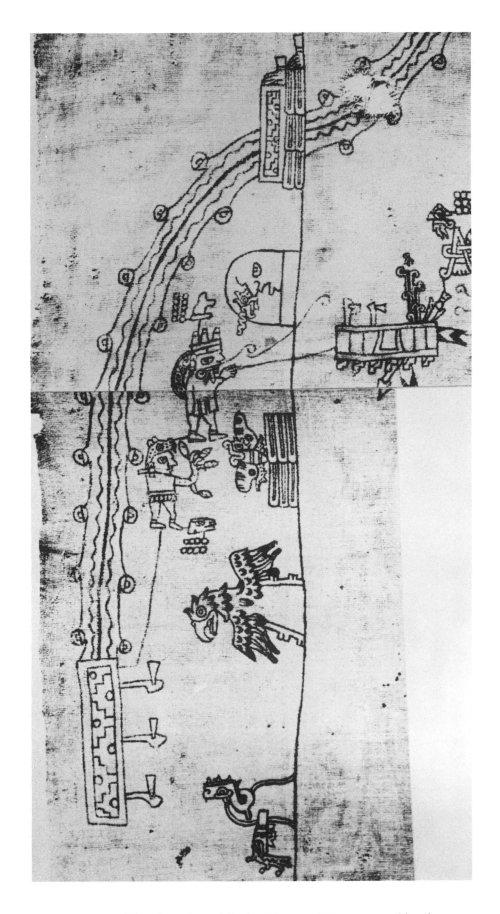

FIG. 113. The place sign of Putla. Lienzo of Zacatepec 1 (details of Figs. 97, 102).

FIG. 114.   The place sign of Amusgos. Lienzo of Zacatepec 1 (detail of Fig. 111).

FIG. 115.   Ballcourt scene: a game between ♂ 1-Movement "Death Mask" and ♂ 8-Deer "Tiger Claw." Bodley 10–IV.

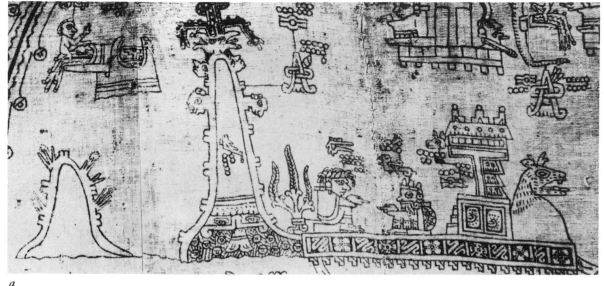

a

b

FIG. 116.   The place sign of Zacatepec.
(*a*) Lienzo of Zacatepec 1 (details, Figs. 93–95).
(*b*) Lienzo of Zacatepec 2, 1893 copy (close-up, top center).

FIG. 117. The *zacate* plant.

a

b

FIG. 118. Place sign of the town or towns ruled by ♂ 4-Wind "Fire Serpent."
(*a*) Bodley 31–III.   (*b*) Bodley 29–V.

295

FIG. 119. The deities ♂ 7-Deer and ♂ 9-Movement. Vienna 4a.

a   b

FIG. 120.   Place signs that include a cross as a boundary marker.

(a) Lienzo of Zacatepec 1. (For context of sign, see Fig. 107).

(b) Lienzo of Zacatepec 2, 1893 copy. (For context of sign, see Fig. 124).

a   b

FIG. 121.   The site *yuu ca'nu* ("the big stone"), present-day boundary between San
Pedro Jicayán and Pinotepa de Don Luis.

(a) "The big stone" with its boundary cross.

(b) Close-up of boundary cross.

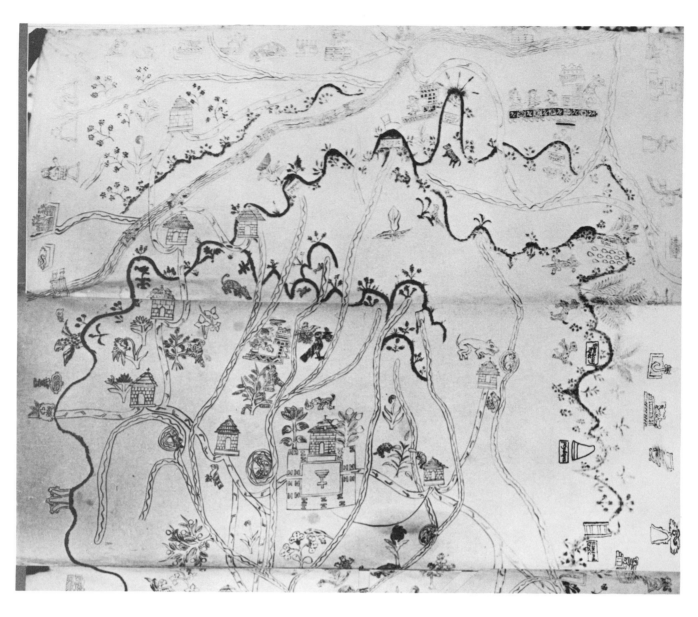

FIG. 122.   Lienzo of Zacatepec 2, 1893 copy. Municipal archive, Santa María Zacatepec.
(Photographs courtesy of Instituto Nacional de Antropología e Historia)

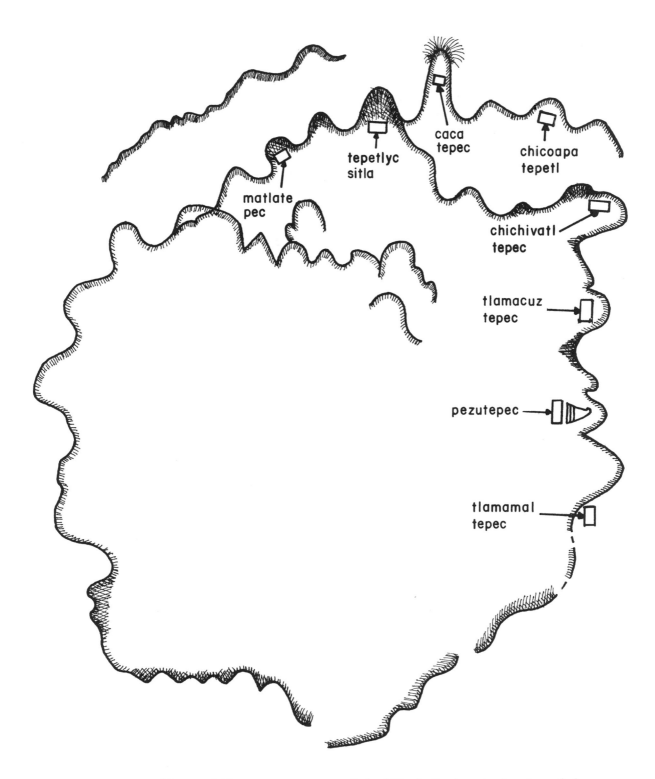

FIG. 123. Lienzo of Zacatepec 2: pattern of the hills, indicating the location of the eight Nahuatl glosses.

FIG. 124. Lienzo of Zacatepec 2, 1893 copy: detail, top left. (Photograph courtesy of Instituto Nacional de Antropología e Historia)

FIG. 125. Lienzo of Zacatepec 2, 1893 copy: detail, top right. (Photograph courtesy of Instituto Nacional de Antropología e Historia)

FIG. 126. Lienzo of Zacatepec 2, 1893 copy: detail, center left. (Photograph courtesy of Instituto Nacional de Antropología e Historia)

FIG. 127. Lienzo of Zacatepec 2, 1893 copy: detail, center right. (Photograph courtesy of Instituto Nacional de Antropología e Historia)

303

FIG. 128. Lienzo of Zacatepec 2, 1893 copy: detail, bottom left. (Photograph courtesy of Instituto Nacional de Antropología e Historia)

FIG. 129. Lienzo of Zacatepec 2, 1893 copy: detail, bottom right. (Photograph courtesy of Instituto Nacional de Antropología e Historia)

a

b

c

FIG. 130. Lienzo of Zacatepec 2, 1893 copy, details:

    (*a*) Center right, showing juncture of two sections of the tracing and the signature of Mauricio C. Castro.

    (*b*) Center right, showing architecture and animals.

    (*c*) Bottom center, showing architecture and pool of water with a marriage pair.

a

b

c

FIG. 131. European woodcuts of the late fifteenth and early sixteenth centuries.

    (*a*) The creation of the birds and fishes. Hartmann Schedel, *Liber chroni-*
       carum, Nuremberg, Anton Koberger, 1493.

    (*b*) Frontispiece of Saint Bonaventure's *Instructione Novitiorum,* Mon-
       serrat, J. Luschner, 1499.

    (*c*) The Garden of Eden. Bergomensis, *Suma de todas las crónicas del*
       mundo, Valencia, Jorge Castilla, 1510.

(*b–c* after Lyell, *Early Book Illustration in Spain,* figs. 77, 87)

307

FIG. 132. 1580 *Relación Geográfica* Map of Teozacoalco: detail, upper-left corner. (After Caso, "El Mapa de Teozacoalco," between 174–75)

FIG. 133. 1595 map accompanying a land-grant petition for a site in the town of Cuquila. AGN-Tierras, 876–1, fol. 122.

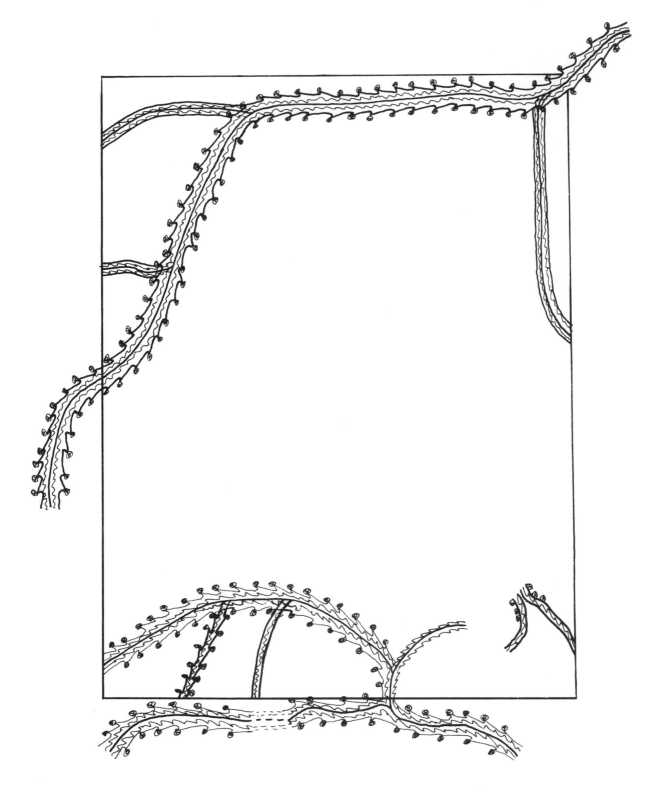

FIG. 134. Lienzo of Zacatepec 1: pattern of the rivers.

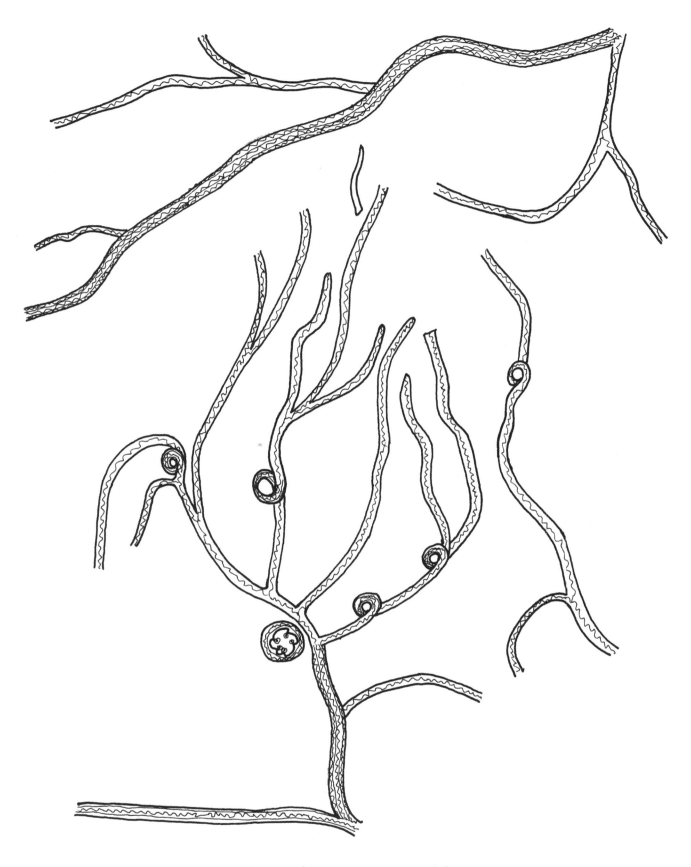

FIG. 135.   Lienzo of Zacatepec 2: pattern of the rivers.

FIG. 136. Lienzo of Zacatepec 2: patterns of the rivers, roads and hills.

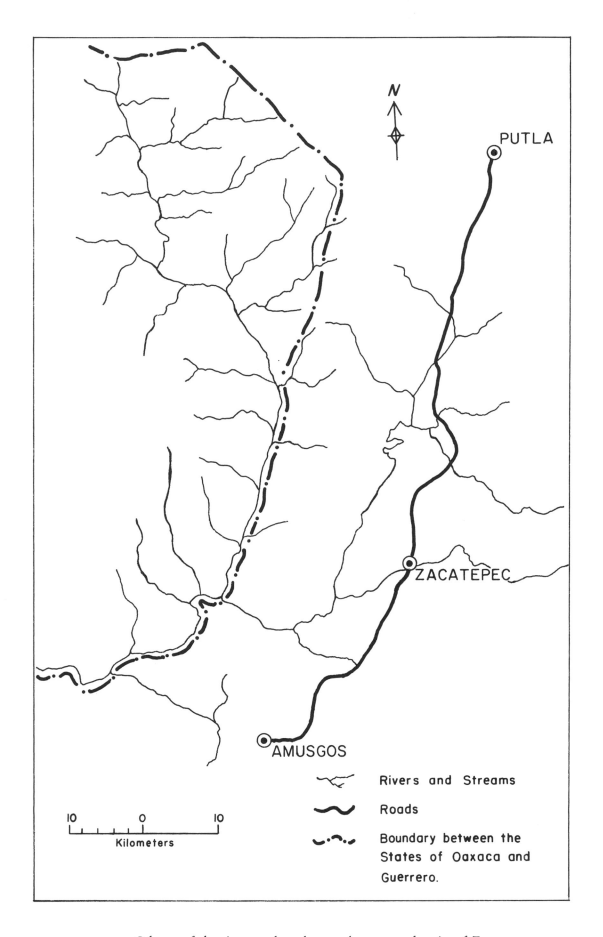

FIG. 137. Scheme of the rivers and roads near the present-day site of Zacatepec.

Rivers and Streams

Roads

Boundary between the States of Oaxaca and Guerrero.

313

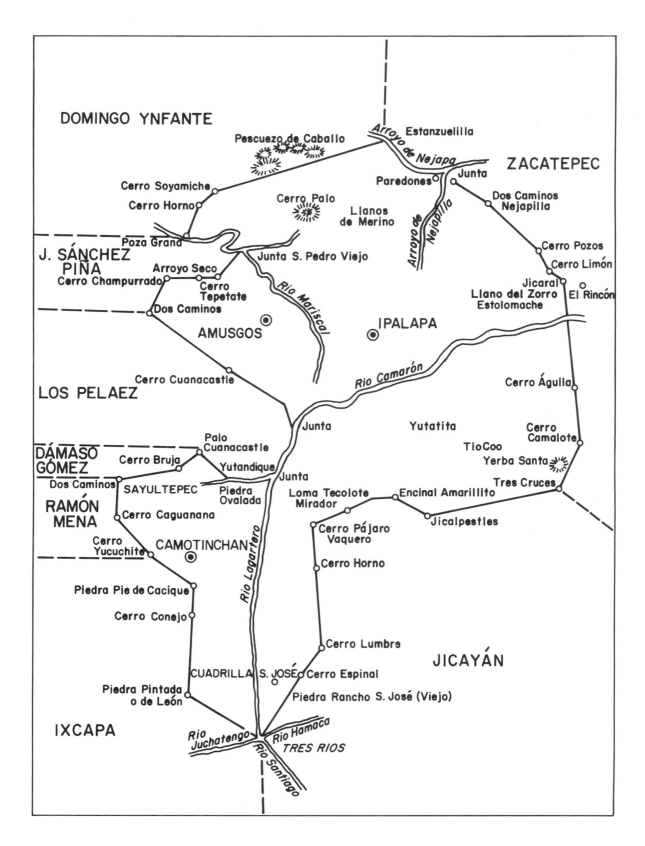

FIG. 138. 1893 map of the lands of Manuel Yglesias. (After a tracing in the Mapoteca of the Dirección de Geografía, Meteorología e Hidrología, Colección General, No. 3663)

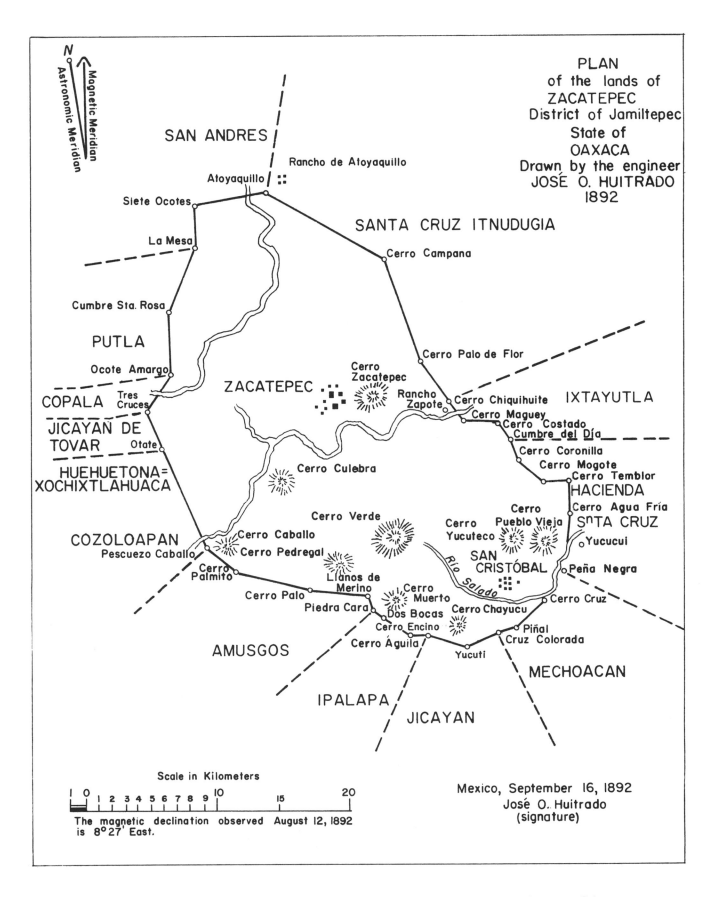

N

SAN ANDRES

Rancho de Atoyaquillo

Atoyaquillo

Siete Ocotes

La Mesa

SANTA CRUZ ITNUDUGIA

Cerro Campana

PUTLA

Cumbre Sta. Rosa

Ocote Amargo

Cerro Palo de Flor

ZACATEPEC

Cerro
Zacatepec

Rancho
Zapote

Cerro Chiquihuite

IXTAYUTLA

COPALA   Tres
          Cruces

Cerro Maguey
Cerro Costado
Cumbre del Día

JICAYAN DE
TOVAR   Otate

Cerro Coronilla
Cerro Mogote
Cerro Temblor

HUEHUETONA=
XOCHIXTLAHUACA

Cerro Culebra

HACIENDA
Cerro Agua Fría

Cerro Verde

Cerro
Pueblo Vieja

SᴺTA CRUZ

COZOLOAPAN

Cerro Caballo

Cerro
Yucuteco

Yucucui

Pescuezo Caballo

Cerro Pedregal

Cerro
Palmito

Llanos de
Merino

SAN
CRISTÓBAL

Peña Negra

Río Salado

Cerro Palo

Cerro
Muerto

Cerro Cruz

Piedra Cara

Dos Bocas

Cerro Chayucu

Cerro Encino

Piñal
Cruz Colorada

AMUSGOS

Cerro Águila

Yucuti

MECHOACAN

IPALAPA

JICAYAN

Scale in Kilometers

0 1 2 3 4 5 6 7 8 9 10   15   20

The magnetic declination observed August 12, 1892
is 8°27' East.

PLAN
of the lands of
ZACATEPEC
District of Jamiltepec
State of
OAXACA
Drawn by the engineer
JOSÉ O. HUITRADO
1892

Mexico, September 16, 1892
José O. Huitrado
(signature)

FIG. 139. 1892 map of the lands of Zacatepec by José O. Huitrado. (After Peñafiel, *LZ*, and a tracing of the map in the Mapoteca of the Dirección de Geografía, Meteorología e Hidrología, Colección General, No. 3580)

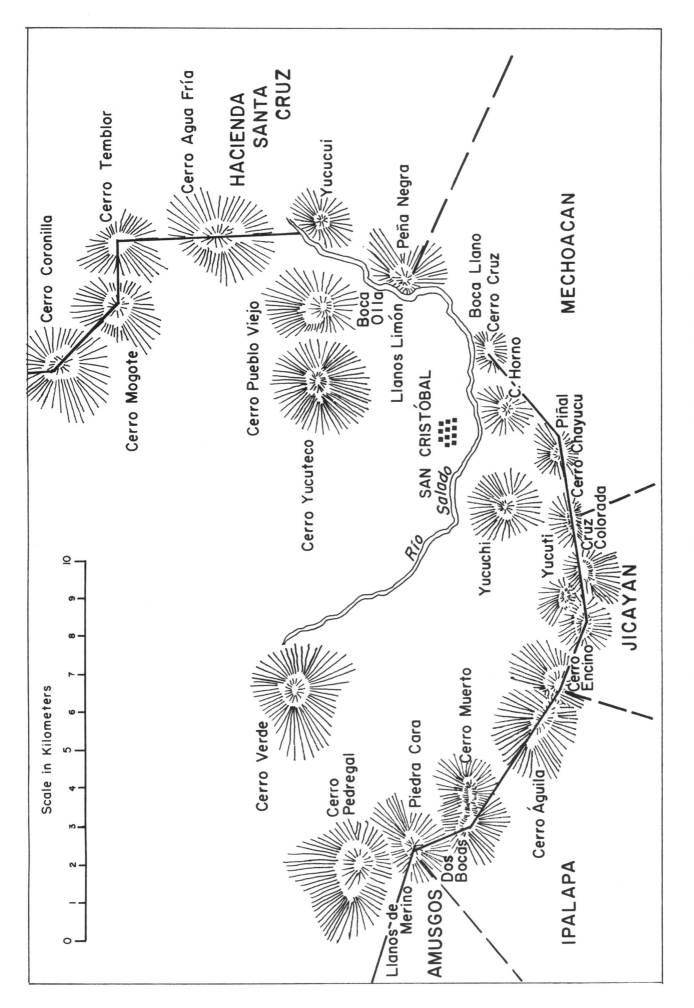

FIG. 140.   1892 map of the lands of Zacatepec by José O. Huitrado: detail, lower-right corner.

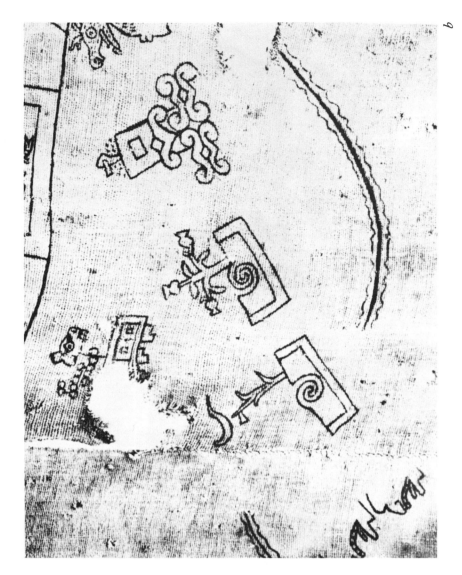

FIG. 141. Place signs of the names of boundaries between Zacatepec and Amusgos. Lienzo of Zacatepec 1 (details of Figs. 106, 111, and 110).

_b_

_a_

317

FIG. 142. Market scene in Pinotepa Nacional.

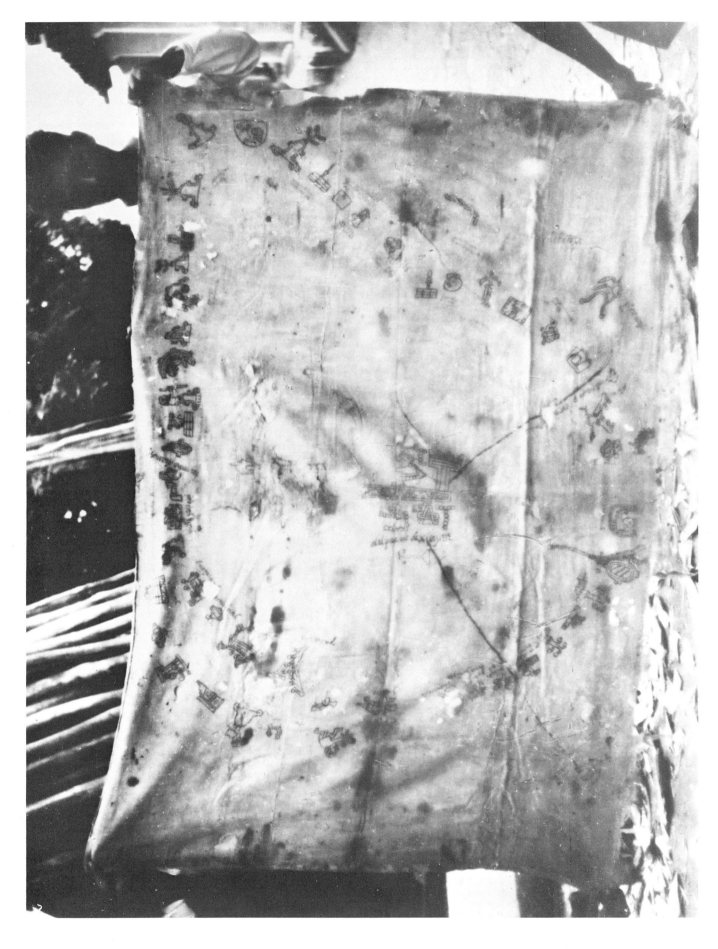

FIG. 143. Lienzo of Jicayán. Municipal archive, San Pedro Jicayán.

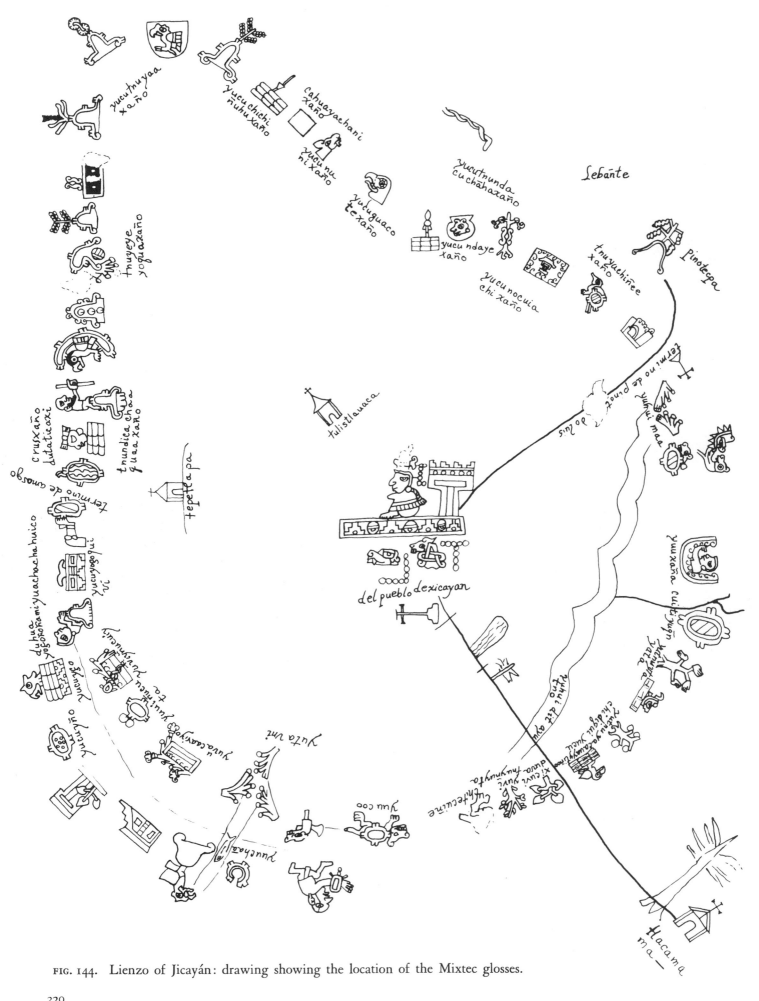

FIG. 144. Lienzo of Jicayán: drawing showing the location of the Mixtec glosses.

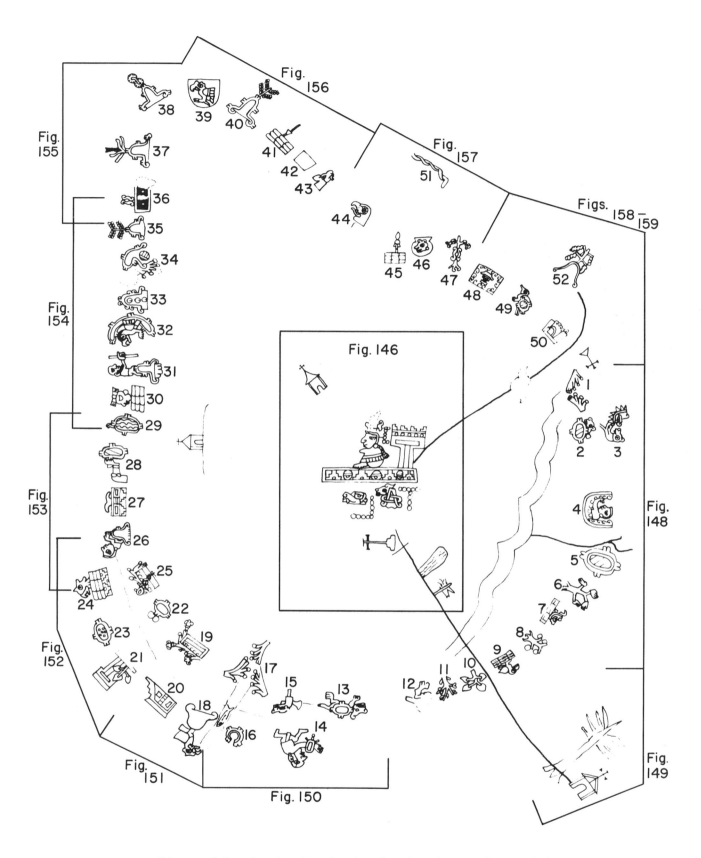

FIG. 145. Lienzo of Jicayán: drawing showing the place-sign numbers and the sections of the Lienzo illustrated in the photographs of details (Figs. 146–59 of this study).

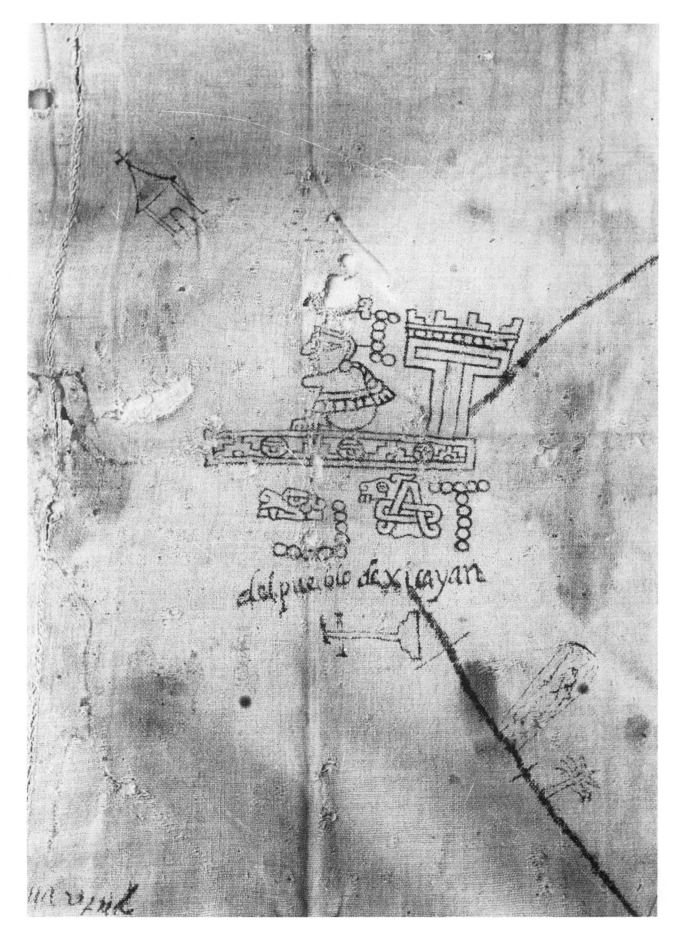

FIG. 146. Lienzo of Jicayán: detail, center section.

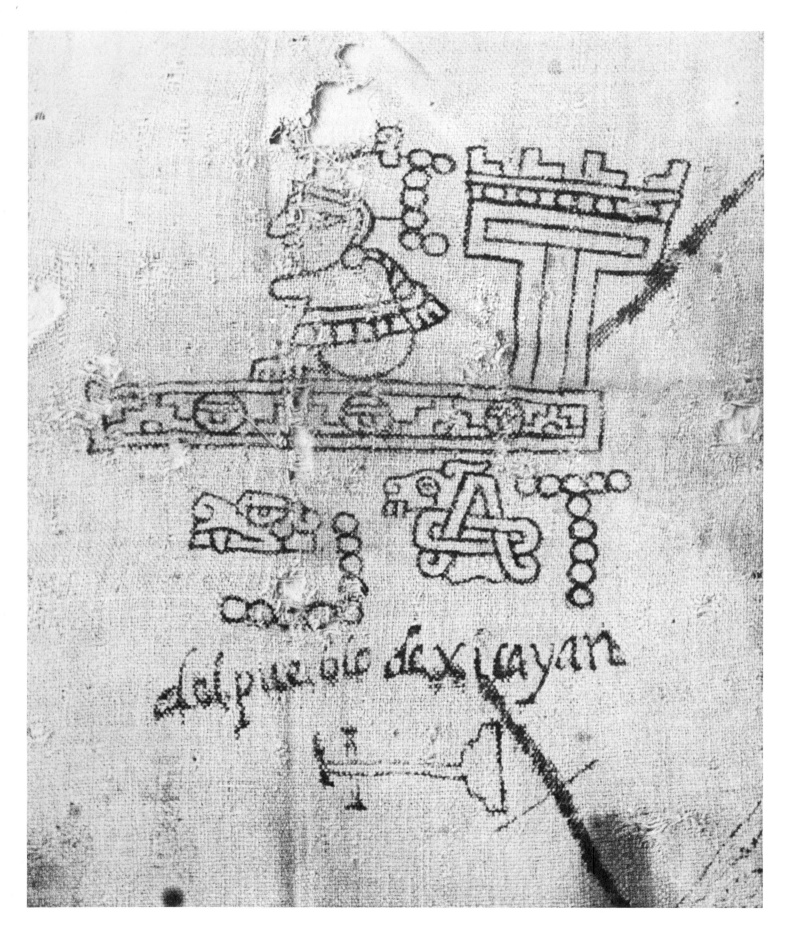

FIG. 147. Lienzo of Jicayán: detail, the central configuration.

FIG. 148. Lienzo of Jicayán: detail, upper-right corner (signs 1–8).

324

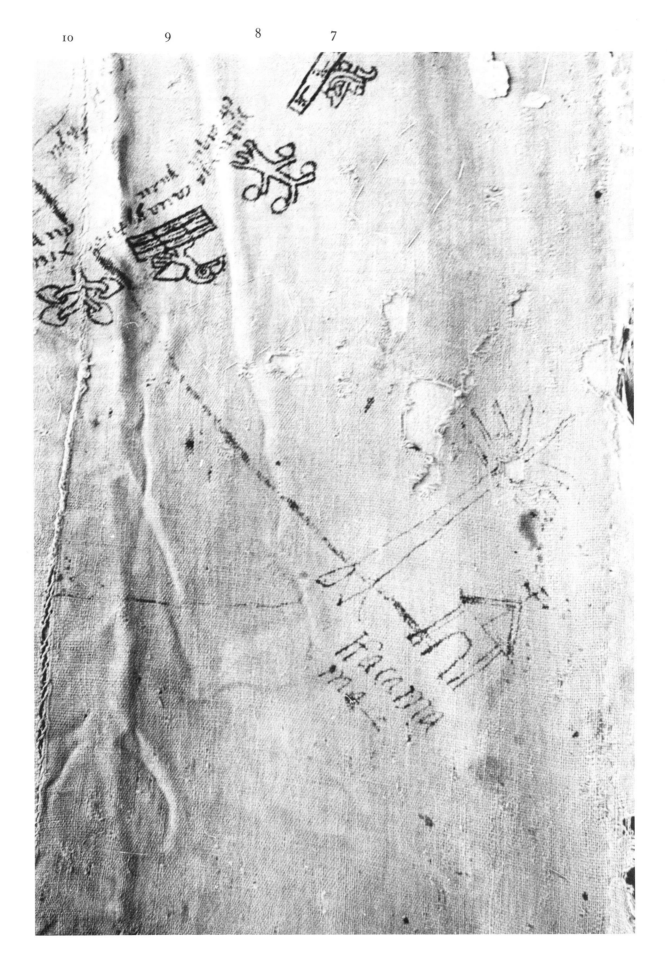

FIG. 149. Lienzo of Jicayán: detail, lower-right corner (signs 7–10).

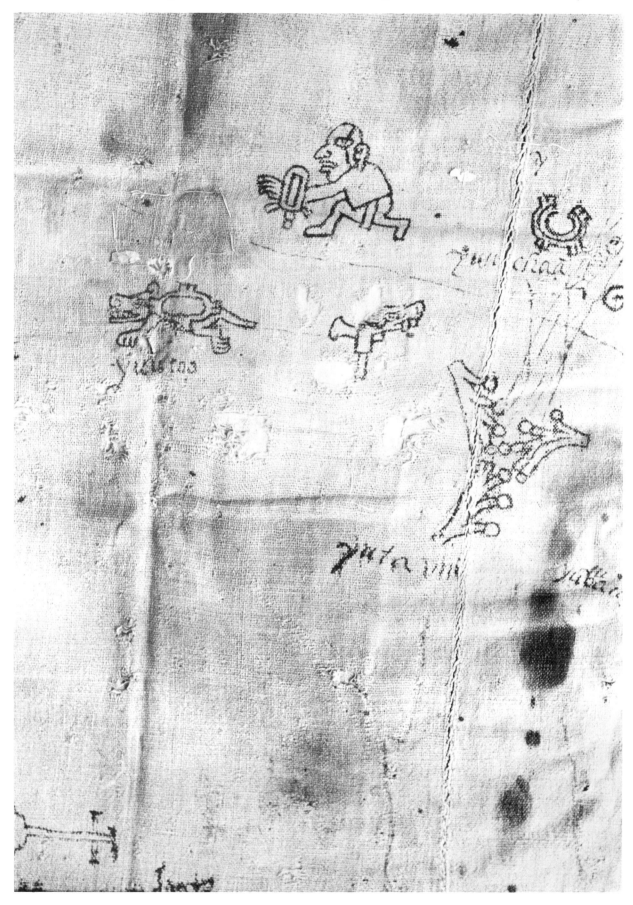

FIG. 150. Lienzo of Jicayán: detail, lower border (signs 13–17).

FIG. 151. Lienzo of Jicayán: detail, lower-left corner (signs 16–20, 22, 25).

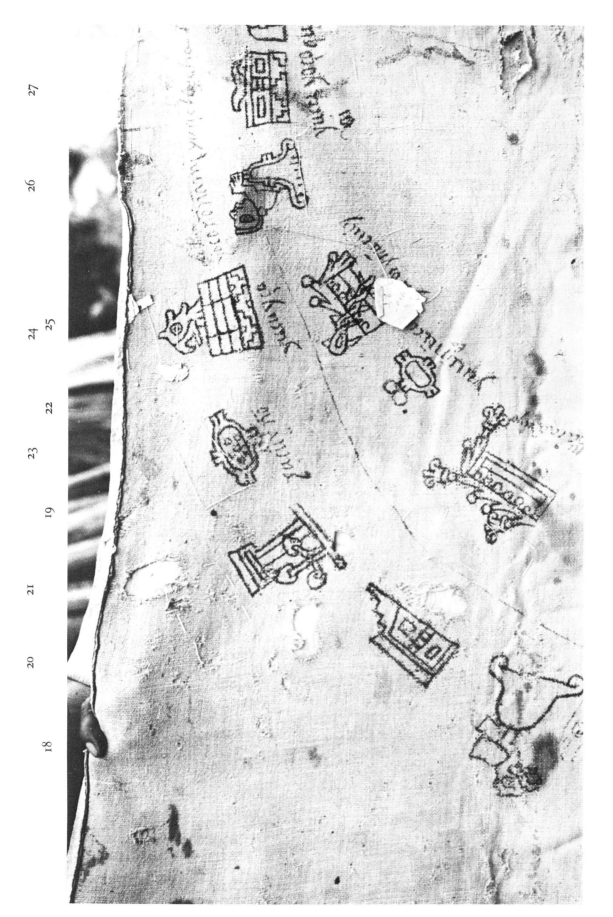

FIG. 152. Lienzo of Jicayán: detail, lower-left corner (signs 18–27).

FIG. 153. Lienzo of Jicayán: detail, left border (signs 22, 24–31).

329

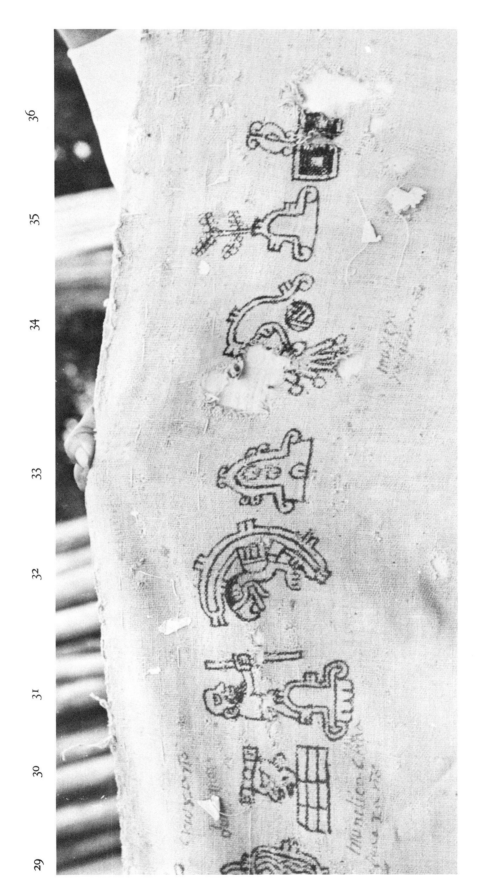

FIG. 154. Lienzo of Jicayán: detail, left border (signs 29–36).

FIG. 155. Lienzo of Jicayán: detail, upper-left corner (signs 35–38).

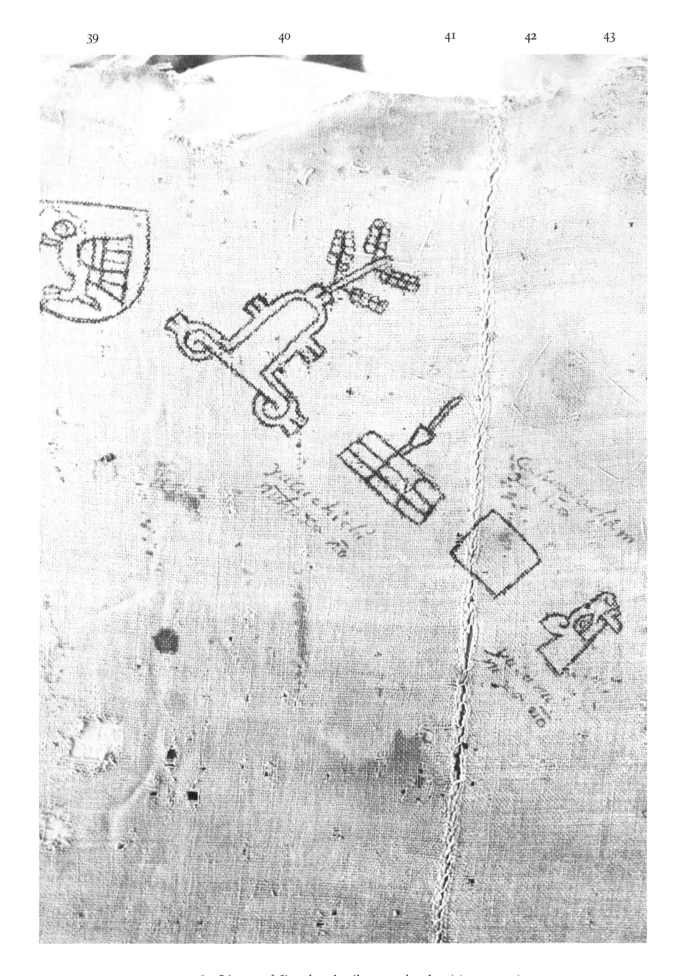

FIG. 156. Lienzo of Jicayán: detail, upper border (signs 39–43).

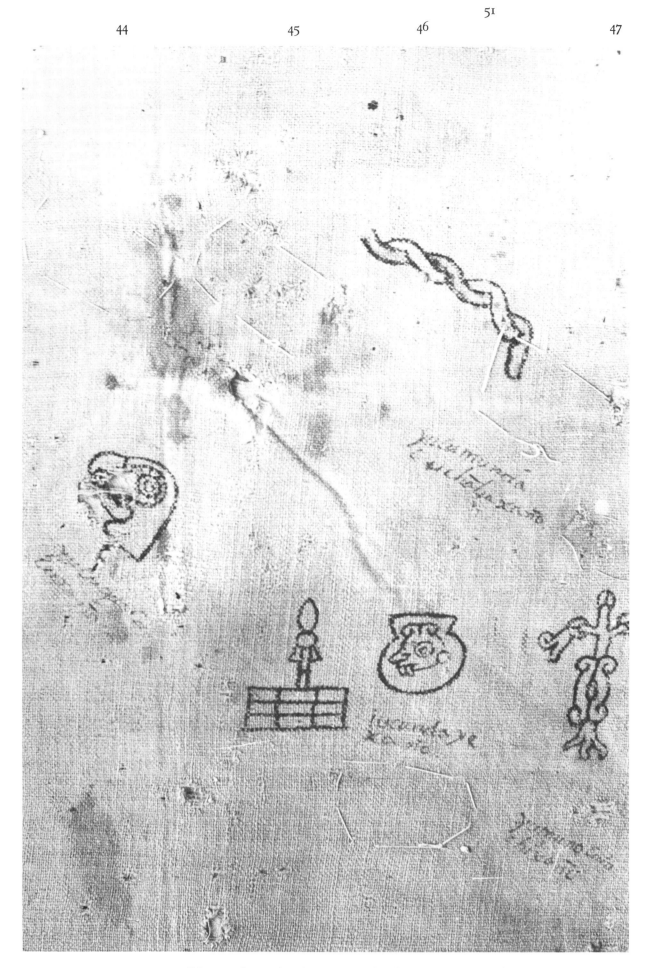

FIG. 157. Lienzo of Jicayán: detail, upper border (signs 44–47, 51).

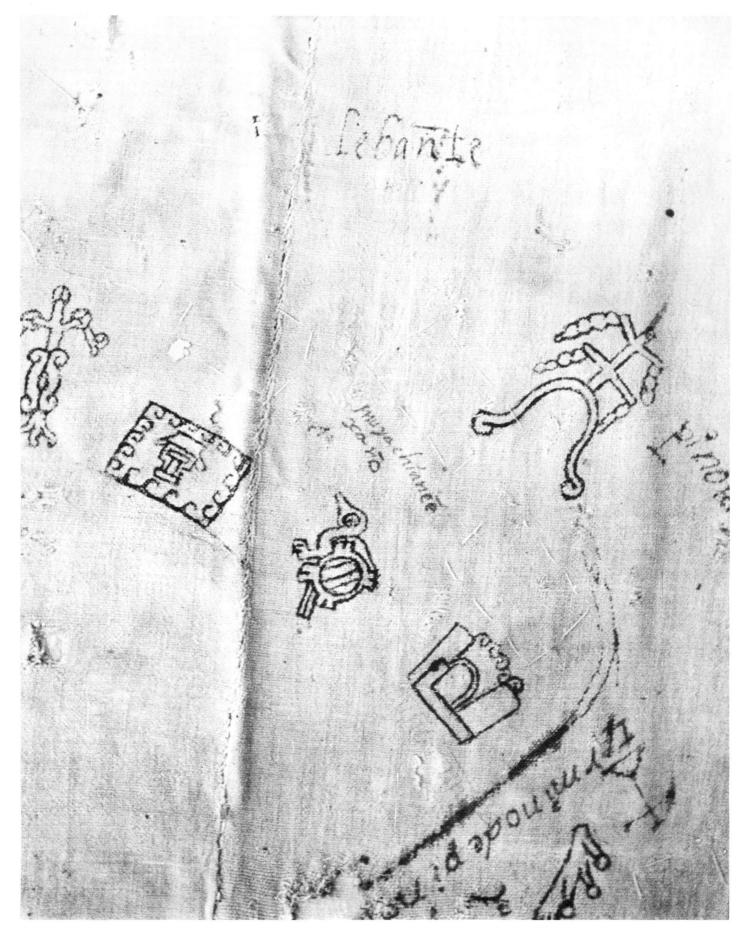

FIG. 158. Lienzo of Jicayán: detail, upper-right corner (signs 47–50, 52).

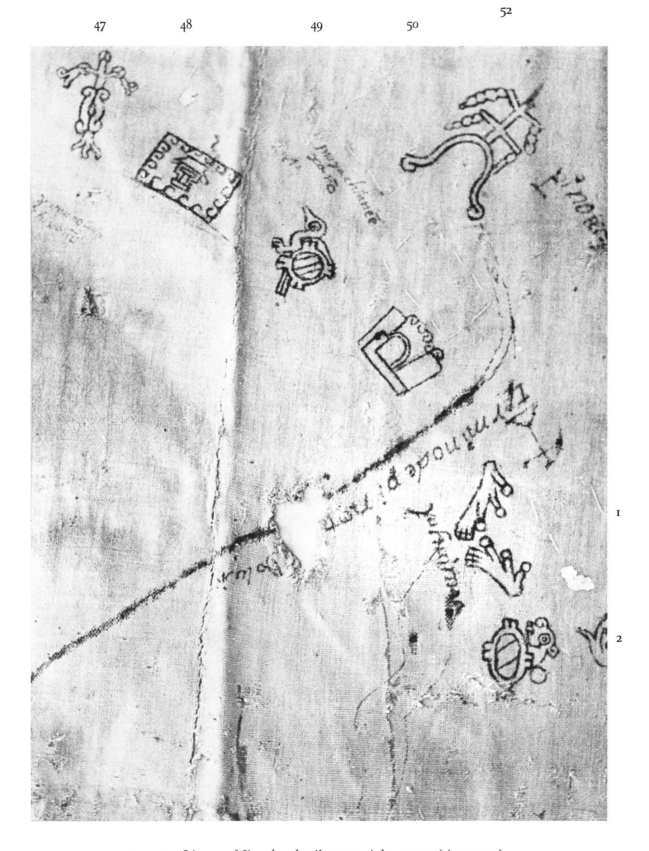

FIG. 159.   Lienzo of Jicayán: detail, upper-right corner (signs 47–2).

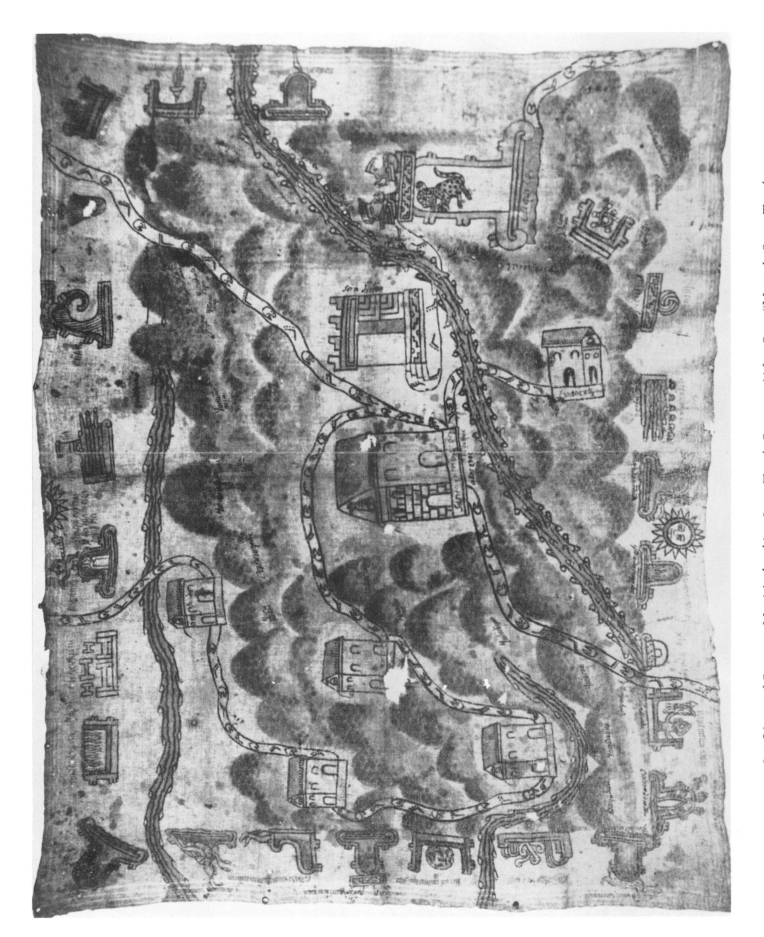

FIG. 160. Lienzo of Ocotepec. Municipal archive, Santo Tomás Ocotepec. (After Caso, "Mapa de Santo Tomás Ocotepeque, Oaxaca," fig. 3; photograph in ultraviolet light by Walter Reuter)

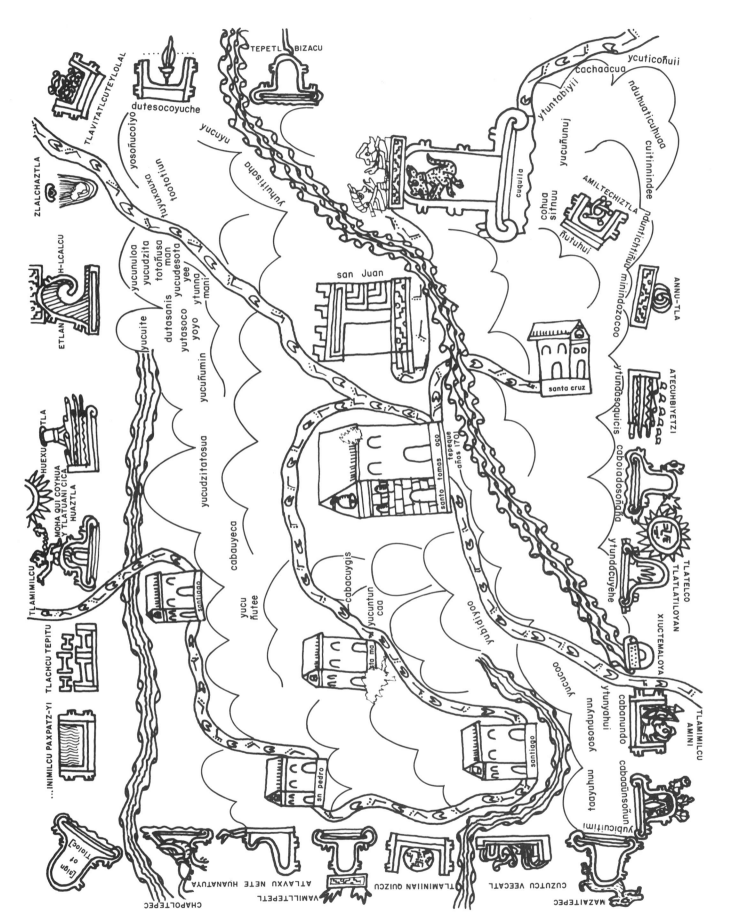

FIG. 161. Lienzo of Ocotepec: drawing showing location of glosses. The Nahuatl glosses are in capital letters and the Mixtec glosses in lower-case letters.

337

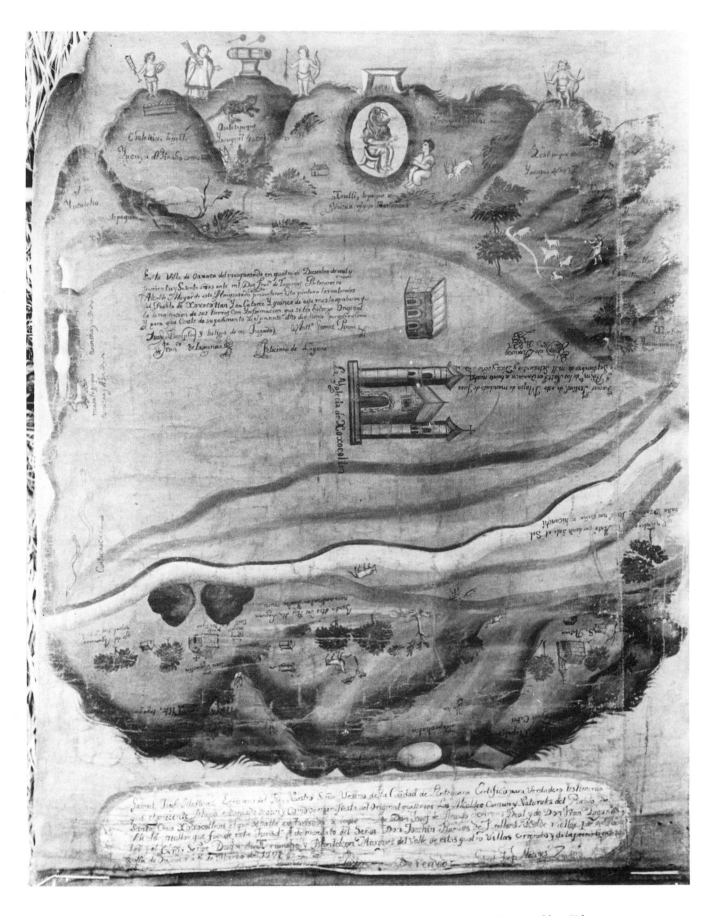

FIG. 162. 1771 Map of Xoxocotlán. Municipal archive, Santa Cruz Xoxocotlán. (Photograph courtesy of Archivo Fotográfico, Instituto Nacional de Antropología e Historia)

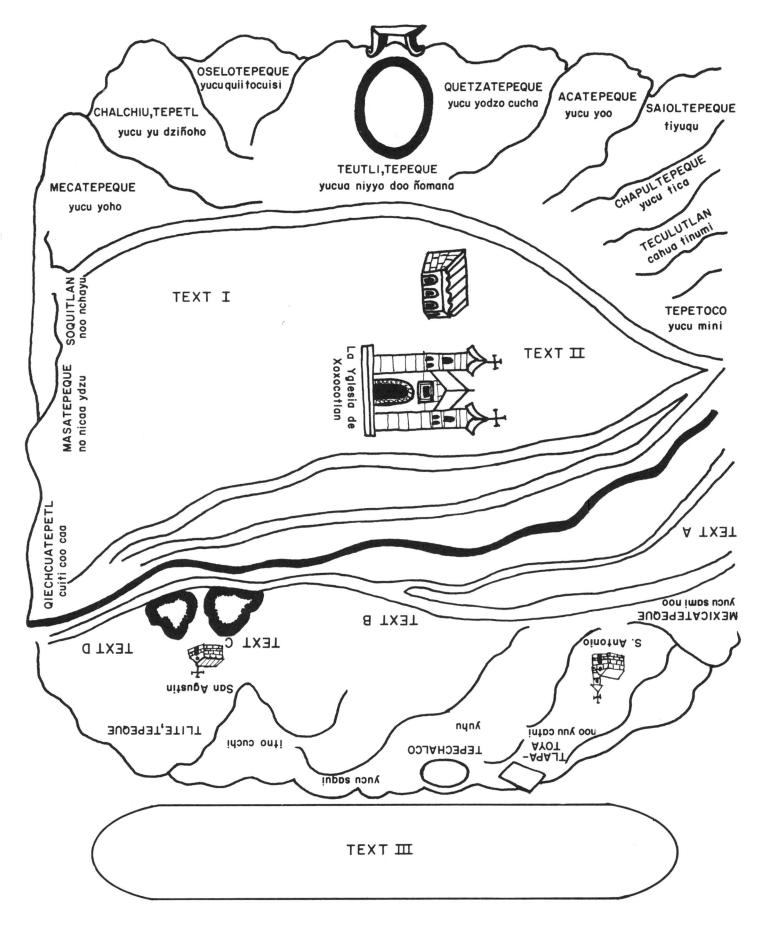

OSELOTEPEQUE
yucu quii tocuisi

CHALCHIU,TEPETL
yucu yu dziñoho

MECATEPEQUE
yucu yoho

QUETZATEPEQUE
yucu yodzo cucha

ACATEPEQUE
yucu yoo

SAIOLTEPEQUE
tiyuqu

TEUTLI,TEPEQUE
yucua niyyo doo ñomana

CHAPULTEPEQUE
yucu tica

TECULUTLAN
cahua tinumi

SOQUITLAN
noo nchayu

TEXT I

TEPETOCO
yucu mini

MASATEPEQUE
no nicaa ydzu

La Yglesia de
Xoxocotlan

TEXT II

QIECHCUATEPETL
cuiti coo caa

TEXT A

TEXT D   TEXT C

TEXT B

MEXICATEPEQUE
yucu sami noo

San Agustin

S. Antonio

TLITE,TEPEQUE

itno cuchi

TEPECHALCO

yuhu

TLAPA-
TOYA
noo yuu catni

yucu saqui

TEXT III

FIG. 163. 1771 Map of Xoxocotlán: schematic drawing showing location of glosses.
The Nahuatl glosses are in capital letters and the Mixtec glosses in lower-
case letters.

339

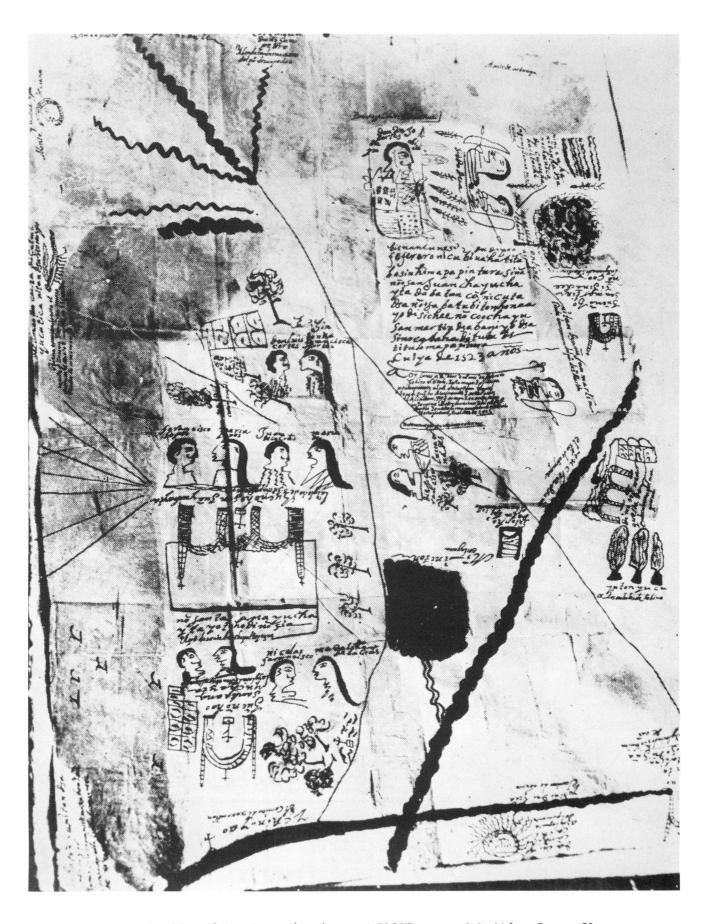

FIG. 164. Map of San Juan Chapultepec. AGN-Tierras, 236–6. (After Genaro V. Vásquez, *Para la historia del terruño*, 22-bis)

INDEX

INDEX OF PERSONS IN THE MIXTEC HISTORY MANUSCRIPTS

Persons in the Mixtec history manuscripts mentioned in this book are listed below by their calendrical names. The twenty day signs appear in alphabetical order (from Alligator through Wind). Under each day sign the calendrical names are given in numerical order (1–13) with the names of males first and those of females second. The names of those persons who appear in Lienzo of Zacatepec 1 only are followed by a Z in parentheses (Z).

ALLIGATOR

Males
2-Alligator "Hair-Cacaxtli": 34, 69, Fig. 52*a*
2-Alligator (Z) 112, 113, 114, Figs. 88, 94
3-Alligator: 68, Figs. 51*a*, 61
4-Alligator "Serpent-Burning Copal": 31, 32, Fig. 8
5-Alligator "Tlaloc-Sun": 28, 31, 34n., Fig. 7*a*
8-Alligator "Bloody Coyote": 77–78, Fig. 75
8-Alligator "Tlaloc-Sun" (Z): 110, 115, 116–17, 119, Figs. 94, 116*a*
10-Alligator (Z): 110, Figs. 88–89

Females
10-Alligator "Flower-Stone Figurine" (Z): 119, Figs. 99–100

DEATH

Males
1-Death (solar deity): 30, 33n., 44, 74
1-Death "Serpent-Sun": 29, 32, 76, Fig. 68 *d, e*
3-Death "Gray Eagle": 29, Fig. 7*c*
6-Death: 110 & n.
7-Death "Serpent Supporting the Sun" (Z): 119, Fig. 93
8-Death "Tiger-Fire Serpent": 62, Fig. 40
8-Death "Tiger-?": 194
11-Death (Z): 113, 114, Fig. 88
11-Death (Z): 119, Fig. 91

Females
4-Death "Jewel": Fig. 9*c*

DEER

Males
1-Deer: 75n.
4-Deer "Sun-Death's Head" (Z): 119, Fig. 58*b*, 104
7-Deer (deity): 113, 115, Fig. 119
8-Deer "Feathered Serpent": 72, 75, Fig. 62 *b, c*
8-Deer "Tiger Claw": 9, 10, 11, 12, 13, 15, 21, 27, 29, 30, 32 & n., 63, 72, 82, 110, 115n., 118n., 124, Figs. 7*b*, 8, 14*b*, 115; as ruler of Tilantongo, 10, 57, 67, 68, 76; nose-piercing ceremony of, 16, 70–72, 74–75, Fig. 55, 60–61; conquests and journeys of, 21, 34, 36–37, 40n., 44–45, 67, 68–69, 78, 173, Figs. 15*b*, 51*a*, 68*e*; birth of, 31; as ruler of Tututepec, 67–68, 76; sacrifice of, 78, 172, Fig. 75
11-Deer (Z): 111, 124, Figs. 90–91

Females
1 Deer: 75n.
2-Deer "Parrot Jewel": Fig. 6*f*

DOG

Males
2-Dog: Fig. 14*d*
5-Dog (Z): 110, 112, 113, Fig. 88
5-Dog (Z): 113, Fig. 93
7-Dog (Z): 112, 113, 114, Figs. 88, 93
10-Dog "Copal-Eagle": 34n., Fig. 16*a*
11-Dog "Serpent Supporting the Sky" (Z): 119, Fig. 100
13-Dog "Eagle-Venus Sign": Fig. 9*c*

Females
2- or 10-Dog "Corncob-Sun" (Z): 109, 111–12, 113, Fig. 109
7-Dog "Flower-Xolotl" (Z): 119, Fig. 93
9-Dog "Shining Jewel": 72

EAGLE

Males
5-Eagle: 63, Fig. 41
7-Eagle (Z): 119, Fig. 91
8-Eagle (Z): 74n., Fig. 103
10-Eagle "Stone Tiger": 32n.
10-Eagle (Z): 112, 113, 114, Fig. 108

Females
6-Eagle "Tiger-Cobweb" (wife of 8-Deer): 72, 77–78, Fig. 75
9-Eagle "Garland of Cocoa Flowers": 31, Fig. 7*a*

FLINT

Males
8-Flint "Falling Eagle" (Z): 113, Fig. 88

Females
3-Flint "Feathered Serpent": Fig. 9*d*
3-Flint "Flint Quechquemitl": Fig. 9*d*
7-Flint "Xolotl-Jewels" (Z): 119, Figs. 92, 100
8-Flint: 194

FLOWER

Males
1-Flower: Fig. 10*b*
4-Flower: 150
5-Flower: 64, Fig. 39 *b, e*
5-Flower: 65
6-Flower (Z): 112, 113, 114, Figs. 88, 91, 95–96
9-Flower "Copal Ball with Arrow": 31
9-Flower: 64, Fig. 39*d*
12-Flower "Composite Parrot and Hummingbird" (Z): 113, Fig. 88

Females
1-Flower "Tiger Quechquemitl": 62, Fig. 40
1-Flower "Parrot": 72, 75, Fig. 62 *b, c*
9-Flower "Jewel-Heart": 76
10-Flower "Tlaloc-Cobweb": 110, 116, 117–19, Fig. 87
10-Flower: Fig. 10*b*
13-Flower "Jade Quetzal": 31, 32, Fig. 8

GENERAL INDEX